american economic history

*A COMPREHENSIVE REVISION OF
THE EARLIER WORK
BY HAROLD UNDERWOOD FAULKNER*

HARPER & ROW, PUBLISHERS

american economic history

HARRY N. SCHEIBER
Professor of History
University of California, San Diego

HAROLD G. VATTER
Professor of Economics
Portland State University

HAROLD UNDERWOOD FAULKNER
Late Professor of History
Smith College

NEW YORK, HAGERSTOWN, SAN FRANCISCO, LONDON

HC
103
.F3
1976

Sponsoring Editor: John Greenman
Project Editor: Richard T. Viggiano
Designer: Michel Craig
Production Supervisor: Kewal K. Sharma
Photo Researcher: Myra Schachne
Compositor: The Clarinda Company
Printer and Binder: Halliday Lithograph Corporation
Art Studio: J & R Technical Services Inc.
Photo credits for part opening photographs: Part 1, Granger; Part 2, Granger; Part 3, Wide
World; Part 4, Wide World.
Cover photo: Bettmann

AMERICAN ECONOMIC HISTORY, Ninth Edition

Library of Congress Cataloging in Publication Data

Faulkner, Harold Underwood, 1890–1968.
  American economic history.

  Includes Index.
  1. United States—Economic conditions. I. Scheiber, Harry N. II. Vatter, Harold G.
III. Title.
HC103.F3 1976   330.9'73   76-16126   ISBN 0-06-042001-4

*To the memory of Louis Morton and
to our colleagues in Reed Hall.*
HNS

To Robert Brady and Leo Rogin.
HGV

contents

This book provides the student of American history and the student of contemporary economics with a case study in modern economic development. We hope that it will offer insight, from the economic historian's vantage point, into one of the most urgent issues of modern life: the achievement of material betterment and the need for intelligent solution of problems generated by a process of economic change that over the last 300 years has transformed the human condition.

American Economic History is in most respects a new book, but it is also in part a revision of portions of the long-standard textbook by the late Harold U. Faulkner. We have retained much of Prof. Faulkner's text (from the eighth edition) covering the period from World War I to the New Deal era of the 1930s. Some of Faulkner's text has also been retained for the colonial period. But half of the material on the colonial era, and most of the text on the period from the American Revolution to 1918, are entirely new, being the contribution of Harry N. Scheiber.

The modern era of development, from the late New Deal to the present, has been treated in different terms from Faulkner's text. This new book incorporates what is perhaps the fullest analysis of post-World War II economic change available in any modern textbook, this section being the contribution of Harold G. Vatter.

Our decision to undertake the large task of new analysis and writing, instead of merely editing and updating the original Faulkner text, was made partly in response to vital changes in the discipline of economic history, changes described in the Introduction. Still, we have retained some of the classic features of Faulkner's textbook, especially the provision of full data for the student to make informed, critical judgments on the interpretations given here and also in other scholars' writings (now increasingly available in anthologies and paperback books). We have sought as well to retain a sound balance between strictly economic analysis, informed by theory, and the important institutional aspects of American economic development. We have not subordinated the type of questions that theory-oriented texts so often push into the background: the content of government policy and law, the development of corporate business and other capitalist institutions, the motives that impelled imperialist expansion, the human dimensions of income distribution and poverty, and the impact of economic change on the environment. Instead, we have placed such issues in the foreground.

Moreover, this book provides a full analysis of accelerating economic change in the twentieth century to the mid-1970s. Not only modern economic growth but also its attendant problems—the income gap between rich and poor nations, the performance of the mixed economy, and the failures and successes of economic management in the post-Keynesian era—all have cast in new light the historic performance of American economic institutions and the behavior of market forces. This book seeks to treat such issues fully in the perspective of the society's earlier economic history as well as in the light of contemporary experience.

We are grateful to the editorial staff of Harper & Row for their aid in the undertaking of this work. Thanks are due especially to John Greenman, sponsoring editor, whose informed concern and guidance have been indispensable; to Claire Rubin, the house editor in charge of this study over several years; and to Richard Viggiano, who supervised its production. Our agent, Gerard McCauley, was also a source of invaluable advice in planning the work.

Professors Morton Rothstein of the University of Wisconsin and Hugh G. J. Aitken of Amherst College read portions of the manuscript, and their painstaking critiques were much appreciated. (The eighth edition of Faulkner's work, portions of which are retained here, also benefited from the criticisms of Professor Clarence Danhof.) We must also acknowledge the stimulus and pleasure of teaching economic history over many years to the excellent students in Dartmouth College; the University of California, San Diego; Carleton College; and Portland State University. Not least, we are grateful for the help, patience, and support of our families.

Harry N. Scheiber
Harold G. Vatter

american economic history

introduction: the study of economic history and American economic development

Economic history, as a field of study, is concerned mainly with the way societies have functioned in the quest for material survival and betterment, and the way they have coped with the problems of economic growth and decline. The study of economic change in times past can enrich and broaden our understanding of the possibilities of the human condition. On the one hand, individual nations and cultures have held a vast variety of values and have expressed widely varying attitudes toward problems of economic change. The study of American economic history is, for the most part, the study of a heterogeneous people that shared a widely held faith in the desirability of economic expansion; but by no means have all peoples and nations throughout history reflected the same sort of faith. On the other hand, even when we concentrate on the record of American economic development, much can be learned of the way social structures and mechanisms different from those prevailing today have accommodated the processes of economic change. Successive changes in technology, expansions of the resource base, shifts in population size and distribution, and other causal factors have worked to produce successive transformations in the American economic system. By seeking to understand these transformations and the reasons for their occurrence at the time they appeared and the form they took, the economic historian addresses himself or herself to probably the most useful and fascinating task of the discipline: the explanation of the way our society has produced the economic order in which we find ourselves today.

Sixty years ago one of the founders of the discipline in the United States, Guy Stevens Callendar, asserted that the proper subject of the economic historian "ought to be the wealth of nations." The practitioner of the discipline, Callendar said,

> ought to make clear what factors have determined the ability of each nation to produce wealth at any particular time and what ones have influenced its distribution; he [or she] should also reveal the forces which have acted to change economic conditions from time to time, producing economic progress or economic decline; and . . . must know in detail how individuals and communities have made a living and what circumstances have affected their ability to do so.[1]

This is a comprehensive mandate to the economic historian, and it is a mandate hard to improve upon. Nonetheless, since Callendar's time research and writing in the field of economic history, together with approaches to the teaching of the discipline, have undergone important shifts in emphasis and style. This textbook, like any such effort to bring together the knowledge of a major discipline, derives a great deal from the work of many scholars, representing the manifold emphases and techniques that have come into prominence over the course of more than seventy-five years. Hence it is important to recognize the rich diversity of the discipline as it has developed over time.

[1]Guy S. Callendar, "The Position of the American Historian," *American Historical Review,* 19 (1913):88.

THE DEVELOPMENT OF ECONOMIC HISTORY

Around 1900 economic history was mainly a branch of "political economy," a field of study that evolved into modern economics, but which then incorporated a concern with both the processes of historical economic change and matters of "correct" public economic policy. In the United States at the beginning of the twentieth century, economic history was also a major field of interest within the broader discipline of political history. Many historians (as opposed to political economists) wrote on economic subjects that were concerned with the relationship of political, constitutional, and legal development to the processes of economic change.

Theories of capitalist development

By the 1930s, the study and writing of American economic history were greatly influenced by the work of a school of German economists and sociologists who, in the tradition of Karl Marx, had developed theories of the stages of capitalist development. Many scholars thus became absorbed with the interpretation of American development in terms of the way "precapitalist" forms had given way to mercantile capitalism in an era (including the colonial period and the first decades of the nineteenth century) when merchants held the levers of economic power in the American business system, and the way mercantile capitalism had given way in turn to "industrial capitalism," which then yielded to "finance capitalism" at the end of the nineteenth century.

Business cycles

In the 1930s the great worldwide depression prompted many economists to do research on the causes of business cycles, the patterns of expansion and contraction that had characterized modern capitalism. Aided by new techniques in the field of statistics, these economists produced a large volume of detailed studies of American business-cycle history, in both national and world economic perspective. Some business-cycle theorists stressed internal sources of expansion and decline, such as the process of capital investment or the relationship of immigration and labor-force change to aggregate demand; others stressed forces external to the economic institutions of the society, especially the impact of technology or of entrepreneurial activity. (A few went so far as to try to relate business cycles to sunspots and the tides!) Whatever their differences in interpreta-

tion, the business-cycle students bequeathed a legacy of valuable empirical data—information about the conditions that prevailed in the economy during business cycles, historically considered—which continue to be expanded and built upon today, for purposes both of elaborating or testing economic theories and of assessing the history of the economy more broadly.

Entrepreneurial studies

Meanwhile, beginning in the Depression era of the 1930s and flourishing in the post-1945 period, "entrepreneurial studies" were further enriching the emerging discipline of economic history. This type of analysis, undertaken by sociologists and economists as well as by historians, and later by social psychologists also, focused upon the business leader and business organization. Efforts were made to classify entrepreneurial functions—the ways in which leaders of business firms created organizations, introduced new products, shaped markets, and managed both "creative" (or "innovative") and "imitative" applications of new knowledge—and related efforts were made to generalize about the behavior of business or entrepreneurial types. This mode of analysis, pioneered by Joseph Schumpeter, made innovation the center of attention in the study of economic history. It was closely related to business-cycle studies in the sense that *entrepreneurship* was defined as the creative process of forging new economic relationships; and the process of creative innovation, spawning imitative responses but also *destroying* older technologies, organizations, and markets as part of that process, was of fundamental importance to explaining why economies underwent surges of growth and then periods of slackness and consolidation, as well as periods of temporary decline or stagnation. Entrepreneurial history thus became an important common meeting ground for historians, economists, and other social scientists.

Historians also derived both data and useful theory from research in the history of science and technology, economic geography, urban sociology, the study of rural institutions, and work in other disciplines in which some scholars, at least, used historical evidence and techniques in connection with their own main work. The cumulative impact of these developments was to increase the interest of economic historians in the rigorous application and testing of social theory and economic theory.

Economic growth

In the 1950s and 1960s—as the income and production gaps between developed and "underdeveloped" or "less developed" economies became the central policy issue of that era—concern on the part of economists with "economic growth" and "economic development" further intensified the cross-fertilization between economics and economic history. Increasingly American economic history was conceptualized and studied with a view toward deriving practical information as to how economies could achieve economic growth. Not that the American case was a useful model for all countries or societies. On the contrary, there were unique elements of the American situation that could hardly be considered comparable to conditions elsewhere, in particular the incredibly rich and diverse natural resources that were available on the North American continent. Also peculiar to the American case were the ideology and social and political structures that prevailed throughout the history of the United States. Too often economic historians steeped in the theory of economic development tended to take such factors as given rather than as part of the explanation of economic change in the United States.

The new economic history

Current scholarship in economic history continues to be diverse in methodology and substantive concerns. One important movement of the last decade and a half is what is generally called "the New Economic History." This style of analysis stresses quantification: both the reconstruction of historical statistics for such indices of output as gross national product and the creation of "plausible" statistics (based upon speculation, founded in assumptions whose reasonableness can be scrutinized by their careful specification) describing phenomena for which few concrete data are available. The New Economic History also stresses the building and use of explicit models in the study of history. Advocates of the New Economic History in its extreme form, at least for a while, also engaged in speculative study of "hypothetical history": the way economic change might have occurred if one or another variable had been different in historical fact. One study that attracted much scholarly attention sought to describe in considerable detail, replete with statistical computations about developments that were purely imagined, the way American economic development would have gone forward *if* the railroad had *not* been introduced in the

nineteenth century. This sort of analytic construct can do violence to the complexity of historical change, especially if the "counterfactual" assumptions are applied to long-term change. In recent years, however, even some of the founders of the so-called New Economic History have rediscovered the importance of institutional factors and of ideology. Meanwhile, the best of the quantitative history has been absorbed into the mainstream of the discipline—for example, Robert Gallman's pioneering research on quantification of gross national product and national income in the nineteenth century is universally respected—and undoubtedly all economic historians have benefited from the new concern with careful specification of assumptions and premises.

Legal-economic history

Another important school or movement in economic history is the style of scholarship often termed "legal-economic history." This mode of institutionalist research has explored the impact of the constitutional system and the legal environment upon the shaping of economic institutions. Legal rules, social values, ideology, and social structure are not readily quantified. Moreover, they tend to be controversial subjects, involving normative preferences. For both these reasons, the new economic historians tended to neglect them, usually taking law and values as given, directing attention instead to market factors (the forces of supply and demand). The scholars who work in the mode of legal-economic history insist that law, ideology, and social structure tend to shape and define the institutions within which and through which market forces operate. They have directed their scholarly labors to enrichment of our understanding of these ingredients of decision making and their institutional consequences. They have thus provided us with important new perspectives on the inputs and outputs of legal process: factors such as commonly held social values; the capacity of government at various periods in American history to articulate and settle conflicts over the allocation of resources; the role of the courts and legislatures in giving certain forms of enterprise priority over other (competing) forms, often frustrating what would have been the allocation had market forces operated without hindrance or government intervention; and the effects of private contract arrangements on the market. Other students' research on the way government has functioned—the role of administrative agencies, the financing of major public projects, the interplay of government and the private sector—has complemented the work of the legal-economic historians.

Economic power and organization

Finally, in recent years there has been an upsurge in economic historians' research on the long-neglected problem of economic power and organization. This research makes its focus the impact of institutional arrangements—such as the giant modern corporation, or the formal links between government and major business interests, or the functioning of regulatory agencies—upon the distribution of power and upon economic welfare. Some of the most interesting scholarly literature in this vein has been the work of critics of the American business system. They include both critics of the left, who believe that private values and goals have overwhelmed the public interest, and critics of the right, who believe that the aggregation of private power in giant business firms, labor unions, and farm organizations has resulted in unfortunate distortion of the market and consequent losses of both efficiency and integrity in the economic system. Whether their bias is toward stronger collectivism or toward greater individualism, these social critics have stressed in their historical studies the fact that both economic growth and the particular form that modern capitalism takes have exacted important social costs: the diversion of wealth and consequent power into the hands of a favored few, the exploitation of workers and the middle class, pollution of the environment, the creation of rising scarcities, and some staggering problems of resource depletion.

In the pages that follow, we present a history of the American economy that incorporates some of the best of recent research in these various modes. We have tried to provide enough in the way of both divergent perspectives and substantive information about the developing economy to convey the intellectual challenge that is involved in the interpretation of the past. We have not attempted to achieve a "scientific" ideal by omitting from our analysis all value judgments and preferences. For we believe that any study of society must necessarily involve critical analysis, and a mode of analysis that is stripped of its critical elements is more likely to be sterile than scientific.

BIBLIOGRAPHIC NOTE

Gottfried Haberler, *Prosperity and Depression,* 4th ed. (Cambridge: Harvard University Press, 1958) provides a summary and analysis of business-cycle theories. The classic work is Joseph Schumpeter, *Business Cycles* (New York: McGraw-Hill, 1939). See also Wesley C. Mitchell, *Business Cycles and Their Causes* (Berkeley: University of California Press, 1941), and a superbly edited modern collection, *Business Fluctuations, Growth, and Economic Stabilization,* ed. John J. Clark and Morris Cohen (New York: Random House, 1963).

The best studies of cycles are Rendigs Fels, *American Business Cycles, 1865–1897* (Chapel Hill: University of North Carolina Press, 1959); Robert Aaron Gordon, *Economic Instability and Growth: The American Record* (New York: Harper & Row, 1974); Walter B. Smith and Arthur H. Cole, *Fluctuations in American Business, 1790–1860* (Cambridge: Harvard University Press, 1935); J. R. T. Hughes and Nathan Rosenberg, "The United States Business Cycle Before 1860," *Economic History Review,* 2nd ser., 15 (1963); and the important paper, stressing long swings, by Moses Abramovitz, in U.S. Congress, Joint Economic Committee, *Employment, Growth, and Price Levels,* Hearings, pt. 2 (86th Cong., 1st Sess. [Washington, D.C.: U.S. Government Printing Office, 1959]). For background on stage theories, a useful introduction is provided by George Rogers Taylor, "Stage Theories of Economic History," in *Approaches to American Economic History,* ed. Taylor and Lucius F. Ellsworth (Charlottesville: University Press of Virginia, 1971).

Hugh G. J. Aitken, "The Entrepreneurial Approach to Economic History," in *Approaches to American Economic History,* ed. Taylor and Ellsworth; John E. Sawyer, "Entrepreneurial Studies: Perspectives and Directions, 1948–1958," *Business History Review,* 32 (1958); and a statement of entrepreneurial theory in Joseph Schumpeter, "The Creative Response in Economic History," *Journal of Economic History,* 7 (1947) provide basic analysis of the entrepreneurial approach to the discipline. An effort at synthesis in this mode is Thomas C. Cochran, *Business in American Life: A History* (New York: McGraw-Hill, 1972).

A study that attracted much attention in the

1960s and that attempted to generalize about similarities and differences that marked individual nations' industrialization records was Walt W. Rostow, *The Stages of Economic Growth: A Non-Communist Manifesto* (Cambridge: The University Press, 1960). Rostow sought to define the conditions that produced a takeoff into self-sustaining growth, and he argued that there was basic discontinuity in the American record, with the takeoff occurring in the period 1843–1860. Although Rostow's thesis has been subjected to devastating attacks by other scholars, the issue of the extent to which growth really was discontinuous remains a vexed and unsettled one among students of American economic history.

An appreciative overview of the New Economic History is Albert Fishlow and Robert W. Fogel, "Quantitative Economic History," *Journal of Economic History,* 31 (1971). Systematic criticism is offered in Fritz Redlich, "'New' and Traditional Approaches to Economic History and Their Interdependence," *Journal of Economic History* 25 (1965) and Harry N. Scheiber, "On the New Economic History—and Its Limitations," *Agricultural History,* 41 (1967). Robert W. Fogel, *Railroads and American Economic Growth: Essays in Econometric History* (Baltimore: Johns Hopkins University Press, 1964) presented the argument concerning a world without railroads—a study in counterfactual history.

Robert Gallman, "The Pace and Pattern of American Economic Growth," in Lance E. Davis et al., *American Economic Growth: An Economist's History of the United States* (New York: Harper & Row, 1972), summarizes Gallman's monumental research. A work that presents concisely some of the major findings of the "new" economic history is Douglass C. North, *Growth and Welfare in the American Past: A New Economic History* (Englewood Cliffs, N.J.: Prentice-Hall, 1964); and a more comprehensive, less polemical summary analysis is provided by Albert W. Niemi, Jr., *U.S.*

Economic History: A Survey of the Major Issues (Skokie, Ill.: Rand McNally, 1975).

For analysis of the public sector, see Harry N. Scheiber, "Government and the Economy: Studies of the 'Commonwealth' Policy in Nineteenth-Century America," *Journal of Interdisciplinary History,* 3 (1971); Scheiber, "At the Borderland of Law and Economic History: The Contributions of Willard Hurst," *American Historical Review,* 75 (1970); Carter Goodrich, "Internal Improvements Reconsidered," *Journal of Economic History,* 30 (1970); and James H. Soltow's broad-ranging and especially useful study, "American Institutional Studies: Present Knowledge and Past Trends," *Journal of Economic History,* 31 (1971). The classic interpretive work is Willard Hurst, *Law and the Conditions of Freedom in the Nineteenth-Century United States* (Evanston: Northwestern University Press, 1956).

The best studies that present a critique from the left are Paul A. Baran and Paul M. Sweezy, *Monopoly Capital: An Essay on the American Economic and Social Order* (New York: Modern Reader Paperbacks, 1966), and the more recent book by Douglas F. Dowd, *The Twisted Dream: Capitalist Development in the United States Since 1776* (Cambridge: Winthrop, 1974). See also the striking essays in Robert L. Heilbroner, *Between Capitalism and Socialism* (New York: Random House [Vintage Books], 1970). The best introduction to the historical critique from the right is the collection of essays in Murray N. Rothbard and Ronald Radosh, *A New History of Leviathan: Essays on the Rise of the American Corporate State* (New York: Dutton, 1972), especially Rothbard's own contributions. See also the study of the late-nineteenth-century economy by Louis M. Hacker. *The World of Andrew Carnegie, 1865–1901* (Philadelphia: Lippincott, 1968).

See, finally, the summary views of growth and social costs provided in Stuart Bruchey, *Growth of the Modern American Economy* (New York: Dodd, Mead, 1975).

chapter *1*
the modernity of
American economic history

The economic history of the present-day United States is largely a history of growth and development in the "modern" — as opposed to the "premodern" — epoch. World economic history since the early 1700s is set apart from the premodern epoch before that time by the phenomena of (1) sustained population increase and (2) sustained long-term increase in per capita production. About the year A.D. 1000, total world population was perhaps 275 million. By the middle of the eighteenth century, world population had risen only to an estimated 711 million persons. Within a century's time, by 1850, population had grown to approximately 1.1 billion. By 1960 it was over 3 billion. This demographic growth was closely related to economic growth (sustained increases in real production on a per capita basis), which in England dates from the early or middle eighteenth century, and which spread to Europe generally and also to the English colonies in North America. As shown in Table 1–1, North America experienced rapid population growth when Europe did. And indeed, in both economic and demographic terms, North America was an extension of Europe's economy and peoples, drawing in addition millions of slaves from Africa even while the native American Indian population outside Mexico was being heavily depleted.

Whereas other regions of the world did not begin the process of industrialization and did not achieve economic growth (or, in most cases, even sharp rises in population) until a later time, from the colonial era onward the American economy has been part of the most dynamic segment of the world economy. Within seventy-five years after the beginnings of English settlement in the New World — that is, by the last quarter of the seventeenth century — the British North American colonies were expanding their production rapidly in response to (and as part of) the dramatic rise in world trade that is known as the Commercial Revolution.

By the early eighteenth century, per capita production in America was rising, slowly at first and then, at mid-century, probably with gathering speed. Statistical data of any reliability are difficult to come by, and our knowledge of the growth phenomenon in this early period is extremely limited. Nonetheless, it seems likely that in the period from 1790 to 1840, per capita output in America was probably rising at an average rate of about 0.5 percent annually. Between 1825 and 1835, American economic growth seems to have accelerated significantly; and from 1840 to the end of the nineteenth century per capita growth of national product was sustained at an average rate of about 1.4 to 1.7 percent annually.[1] A process of industrialization was under way. Manufacturing development, successive innovations in transportation, and other basic changes in the economy contributed to this process. By 1890 the United States was the world's leading industrial nation. It was also attracting immigrants from Europe and other areas of the world: The United States, with its open-immigration policy, was the chief receiving nation for tens of millions who left Europe from 1880 to 1914. In the

[1]A work that postulates a higher growth rate for 1790–1840 is Paul David, "The Growth of Real Product in the United States Before 1840," *Journal of Economic History,* 27 (1967). Raymond Goldsmith has estimated the rate of growth from 1760 to 1839 at about 0.6 percent (U.S. Congress, Joint Economic Committee, *Employment, Growth, and Price Levels,* pp. 267–279). The data for 1839–1899 derive from Goldsmith, ibid., and the work of Robert Gallman on output and gross national product, summarized by him in Davis et al., *American Economic Growth* (New York: Harper & Row, 1972).

TABLE 1–1. ESTIMATES OF WORLD POPULATION BY REGIONS, 1650–1968

		INDUSTRIALIZED REGIONS				DEVELOPING REGIONS			
YEAR OR PERIOD	WORLD TOTAL	TOTAL	EUROPE AND USSR	NORTHERN AMERICA	OCEANIA	TOTAL	ASIA	LATIN AMERICA	AFRICA
A. ESTIMATED POPULATION (Millions)									
1968	3483	934	693	222	18.5	2549	1946	267	336
1960	3008	857	640	200	16.5	2151	1685	211	255
1950	2509	756	576	267	13.0	1753	1384	162	207
1940	2249	730	573	146	11.3	1519	1212	131	176
1930	2015	671	532	135	10.4	1338	1072	109	157
1920	1811	613	487	117	8.8	1198	966	91	141
1900	1590	510	423	81	6	1079	886	63	130
1850	1131	302	274	26	2	829	698	33	98
1800	912	200	192	6	2	712	596	21	95
1750	711	147	144	1	2	564	456	10	98
1650	507	106	103	1	2	402	292	10	100
B. IMPLIED AVERAGE ANNUAL RATES OF GROWTH (Percent)									
1950–1960	1.83%	1.26%	1.06%	1.82%	2.41%	2.07%	1.99%	2.68%	2.11%
1940–1950	1.10	0.35	0.05	1.35	1.41	1.44	1.34	2.15	1.64
1930–1940	1.11	0.85	0.75	0.79	0.83	1.28	1.24	1.86	1.15
1920–1930	1.07	0.91	0.89	1.44	1.68	1.11	1.05	1.82	1.08
1900–1920	0.65	0.92	0.71	1.86	1.93	0.52	0.43	1.86	0.41
1850–1900	0.68	1.05	0.87	2.30	2.22	0.53	0.48	1.30	0.57
1800–1850	0.43	0.83	0.71	2.98	0.00	0.31	0.32	0.91	0.06
1750–1800	0.50	0.62	0.58	3.65	0.00	0.47	0.54	1.50	−0.06
1650–1750	0.34	0.33	0.34	0.00	0.00	0.34	0.45	0.00	−0.02

Source: United Nations demographic data.

twentieth century, the pattern of sustained growth was continued. From 1929 to 1955, American *net national product* (NNP, the value of all goods and services produced in the economy less the value of capital goods depreciation) was about three times what it was in the late nineteenth century (1869–1888). In constant dollars (that is, when adjustments are made to take changing price levels into account), per capita production rose more than two and a half times between 1920 and 1970, despite the effects of the Great Depression of the 1930s. By 1970 American average income per capita had reached $4274, as compared with $2660 in all the other "developed" nations (nations that, like the United States, had achieved a pattern of sustained economic growth), and only $210 in the "underdeveloped" nations.[2]

Hence a major analytic problem before the student of American economic history is the explanation of this country's remarkable growth and relative prosperity. That is not to say, however, that we are dealing with a success story lacking in any elements of failure or without pe-riods of economic decline or stagnation. Until the Civil War (1861–1865), productivity and rising output gains were achieved by the enslavement of several million black people. Poverty has never been absent from American society. In 1929 one individual in three lived at the poverty line or below, and in 1970 one in eight was still in that condition. Moreover, the very changes in technology that made possible enormous gains in *productivity* (the efficiency with which capital, human labor, and natural resources are combined to generate output) were also sources of hardship and misery for many of the workers in the fields, on the assembly lines, in the forests, and under the earth in mines.

Mass society

As mass-production techniques took hold, the problems of mass society were emerging: giant cities with intractable social dislocations and a host of menacing if not dehumanizing structures; enormous pressure on natural resources that were subject to depletion and exhaustion; and the tensions and stresses of highly disciplined work. Not least, there was a buildup of discontent among economic and ethnic groups that began to lose faith in the possibility of sharing fully in the prosperity of what became popularly known as the "affluent society."

[2]The 1970 income data are in United Nations, *Yearbook of National Accounts Statistics, 1971,* vol. 3 (U.N., 1973). The production data are Simon Kuznets' as given in Stuart Bruchey, *Growth of the Modern American Economy* (New York: Dodd, Mead, 1975), p. 116.

TABLE 1–2.   U.S. GROSS NATIONAL PRODUCT (BILLIONS OF DOLLARS) AND PER CAPITA GNP (DOLLARS) 1839–1970

PANEL A

YEAR OR DECADE	GNP, CURRENT PRICES[1]	GNP, 1860 PRICES[1]
1839	$ 1.54	$ 1.62
1844	1.80	1.97
1849	2.32	2.43
1854	3.53	3.37
1859	4.17	4.10
1869–1878	7.87	6.40
1879–1888	11.20	10.60
1889–1898	13.20	14.40
1899–1908	22.40	21.80

PANEL B

YEAR OR PERIOD	GNP, CURRENT PRICES	GNP, 1929 PRICES	PER CAPITA, 1929 PRICES (DOLLARS)
1889–1893	$ 13.5	$ 27.3	$ 424
1902–1906	24.2	46.8	569
1912–1916	40.3	62.5	632
1917–1921	75.6	71.9	683
1929	104.4	104.4	857
1933	56.0	74.2	590
1940	100.6	121.0	916
1950	284.6	187.1	1,233

PANEL C

YEAR	GNP, CURRENT PRICES	GNP, 1958 PRICES	PER CAPITA, 1958 PRICES (DOLLARS)
1940	$ 99.7	$227.2	$1,721
1950	284.8	355.3	2,342
1960	503.7	487.7	2,699
1970	974.1	720.0	3,515

Sources: Panel A, Robert Gallman data, in National Bureau of Economic Research, *Output, Employment, and Productivity in the United States After 1800*, vol. 30 of *Studies in Income and Wealth* (New York: Columbia University Press, 1966), Table A–1, p. 26. Panel B, U.S. Department of Commerce, Bureau of the Census, *Historical Statistics of the United States, Colonial Times to 1957* (Washington, D.C.: U.S. Government Printing Office, 1960), p. 139. Panel C, *Economic Report of the President*, January 1972 (Washington, D.C.: U.S. Government Printing Office, 1972), pp. 195–196 (GNP data), 213 (population data). Data in Panel A, copyright 1966, by the National Bureau of Economic Research. Reproduced by permission.

[1]Excludes value added by home manufactures, certain farm improvements, and changes in inventories.

Nor has the long-term march of material growth been without its darker chapters. It is one of the great paradoxes of the American record that the acceleration of growth in the late nineteenth century was achieved despite prolonged economic depressions in the 1870s and 1890s. The continuing growth of the present century, moreover, has taken place despite two world wars and a ten-year depression of unprecedented severity in the 1930s, in addition to crises of shorter duration in other periods, including the dual crisis of inflation and unemployment following the end of American involvement in the Vietnam war. Crises such as these must also come within the purview of any effort to analyze the American record.

Expansion and contraction

All business-type economies have grown in a pattern of alternating waves of expansion and contraction in prices, output, and employment. The most common pattern, which became established through many generations, was the ordinary business cycle of eight to eleven years'

Figure 1–1.   American Business Activity Since 1790. This graph gives a picture of American business activity from January 1, 1790, until the end of 1974. The dark line represents the changes in wholesale commodity prices. (Source: Various data by the late General Leonard P. Ayres and the Cleveland Trust Company. Used with the permission of the Cleveland Trust Company.)

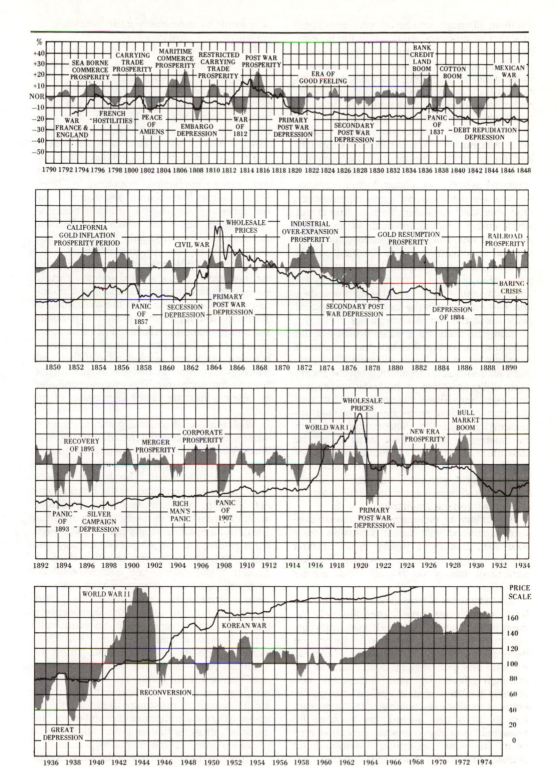

duration, although economists have also found so-called long waves, especially in the influential construction industry, of about twenty years' duration. It appears that operating in both types of economic fluctuation was the propensity of businessmen to make overly optimistic investment commitments in times of prosperity. Such optimism carried expansion into a boom with increasing speculative components that sooner or later led to excess capacity and the recognition that new purchases should be cut. The typical result was a downturn in economic activity which soon became cumulative and was reinforced by a growing pessimism that intensified the contraction in output and employment. This pattern recurred again and again, but not with strict periodicity. It meant that full employment, which obtained only in the late phase of expansion, was the exception rather than the rule. Long-term growth in the gross national product nevertheless proceeded, and was expressed in the fact that each cyclical peak was higher than the one before.

Everyone liked the prosperity phase of the economic cycle, but the fact that investment decisions lay in the hands of myriad businessmen, all desirous of capitalizing on the boom, assured the repetition of the same overexpansion each time. When the contraction hit, people often panicked at the thought of their impending losses, and the business community in the nineteenth century thus came to call the downturns "panics," an inadequate term referring to only a short phase of the total cycle. Yet the term stuck, because it expressed so clearly the feelings of financial and mercantile interests within the business community.

A number of expansions and contractions were connected with war. It is notable, however, that, contrary to popular belief, wartime was not always a period of prosperity. This was particularly true of the War of 1812 and the Civil War.

The character of peacetime cyclical fluctuations changed over time. During the early national period, commerce, and particularly foreign commerce, was the center of the process that generated the cycle. There was little industry, and the predominant agricultural sector, although affected by price fluctuations, was strongly insulated against cyclical changes by virtue of its substantial volume of home production for home use. Indeed, on the farm the household and the enterprise aspects of economic life were inextricably intertwined. Of course, later in the nineteenth century, agriculture became ever more commercialized, and

as a result became much more intimately involved in the cyclical process.

By the end of the first quarter of the nineteenth century the character of the cycle began to change. The domestic economy now came to determine the pattern of expansion and contraction. For example, during the era of canal building, from the mid-1820s to the early 1850s, canal construction proceeded, along with the rate of public land sales, in massive waves that generated the famous expansion peak in the mid-1830s and the consequent long and severe contraction troughing in 1843. Some analysts have found long waves in this era, others emphasize the ordinary business-cycle pattern, but in any case it was clear that domestic factors, particularly in transport and land acquisition, were now overriding.

After the Civil War the character of the cycle became increasingly identified with the onrushing industrialization, railroadization, and urbanization of the economy. With the wellsprings of prosperity and depression centered in the manufacturing, railroad, and residential construction sectors, it was fluctuations in fixed investment—business plant and equipment together with housing—that now shaped the overall fluctuations in the economy. This process continued to operate into the Great Depression of the 1930s.

With the use of massive government intervention characterizing the mixed economy after World War II, the forces in the private business sector making for cyclical instability became very much dampened. The federal government was now committed by the Employment Act of 1946, however reluctantly it adhered to that commitment in peacetime, to maintain maximum employment and purchasing power. Furthermore, a large public employment sector, together with the countercyclical influence of the income tax, also insulated the economy against extremes. There were no severe depressions, only "recessions," from World War II to the mid-1970s. The recessions that did occur were often governmentally induced. And general prices—the bellwether, along with profits, of cyclical instability in the historical past—rarely fell very much when total business sales contracted. Aggregate consumption exhibited a new tenacity in resisting the influences of investment declines, and the power of large corporations and unions to "administer" prices further reinforced the tendency of general prices to maintain a high floor.

Thus the record of cyclical fluctuations mirrors in a multitude of ways the great structural and institutional changes that have accompanied the long-run evolution of the U.S. economy. When the fluctuations were severe, they often elicited strong social and political responses from the groups of people directly affected. And in due time the people determined that they would no longer tolerate such a defect in the performance of the economic system.

THE MECHANISMS OF GROWTH AND DEVELOPMENT

The history of any economy, modern or premodern, is in great part the history of society's satisfaction of wants. The measure of a national economy's output most commonly used is gross national product (GNP), the sum value of goods and services to which market transactions have attached a value in money prices. (Net national product, as noted earlier, subtracts from GNP the value of depreciation of capital goods; that is, the goods that themselves are the means of production, such as machinery.) Neither GNP nor NNP takes account of nonmarketplace work and production; for example, the value of child care in private homes. And activities to which no value in money prices is attached, ranging from students' volunteer work with the poor or the coaching of Little League baseball to voluntary religious activities, are left out altogether.

The supply of goods and services depends upon the main "factors of production": labor, capital goods, and natural resources. The ratio of these inputs to consequent output is a measure of what we call *productivity,* or *efficiency;* and, necessarily, for a society to achieve economic growth, sustained productivity gains must be attained. Let us consider first each of the factors of production that determine the supply of economic goods and services in an economy.

Labor

A nation can increase its output by changes in the absolute number of workers employed. Thus, with a technology of constant (unchanging) efficiency, and with an increase in resource inputs proportional to the increase in number of workers, the GNP will rise—but "growth" will not be attained, since *per capita* product will remain constant. In American economic development, rising labor-force levels have accounted for a significant element of rising GNP. Growth of population in the colonial period and the early nineteenth century was largely the result of high rates of natural increase: people married young, and they tended to have large families. Gradual decline in the death rate also contributed to growth of popula-

tion, as advances in medicine and public health extended the average life span and reduced infant mortality.

An important consideration in the impact of labor force on growth is the *participation rate,* the proportion of total able-bodied persons willing and able to find work. Another consideration is the *quality* of the labor force. The word "quality" is impersonal and has a clinical tone to it, but it represents issues of the greatest humane as well as economic importance: the degree of workers' education and special skills, the health and physical vigor of labor, and the adaptability of the labor force to work needs and opportunities. In this respect, the American labor force—despite persistent elements of poverty, despite the plight of minority ethnic groups, and the like—has ranked high among those of the world's nations since the colonial period, although the United States does not by any means stand first in public health among the industrialized modern nations of today. Since the mid-1840s, the size and character of the American labor force have been much influenced also by the effects of immigration.

Land and other natural resources

To a certain extent, it makes sense to think of land and other natural resources—the soil, water, vegetation, fauna, minerals, climate, and terrain that a nation's economy controls by dint of its political jurisdiction—as gifts of nature. And to an extent, it makes sense to think of these resources as fixed; of course they are not static, since soil can erode, a river can change its course, and so on, but they are fixed in the ecological design within which they were placed by the earth's natural evolution. For purposes of understanding the economy or the processes of economic change over time, however, a society's natural resources need to be defined in the context of human wants and abilities. Thus the value of a resource—say, coal—to a society depends upon that society's knowledge (or technology relative to the extraction and uses of the resource); it depends upon the accessibility of the resource and the cost of exploiting it; and it depends upon the related obstacles that must be overcome in order to achieve the exploitation of that resource. A prominent economic geographer has written that

> nature offers freely only an infinitesimal fraction of her treasure; she not only withholds the rest, but seems to place innumerable, and, in many cases, well-nigh insurmountable obstacles [such as locational and topographical obstacles, or the problems that arise from pollution and resource loss associated with resource extraction] in the way of resource-seeking and resource-creating MAN.
>   . . . To be sure, coal is found in nature. But coal readily accessible and available for human use is rare indeed. Without the aid of power-driven machinery, human inventions, and man-made contraptions, mankind long ago would have run out of coal. Coal occurs in nature, to be sure, but not coke, or sulfate of ammonia, tar, dyes, aspirin, nylon. All the elements are found in nature . . . [but] there are billions of compounds which can be built up, by commutation and permutation, out of the . . . elements.[3]

In other words, the volume of a society's usable resources is a function of technology. Uranium is today a highly valuable resource, but a century ago a society possessing uranium deposits would have regarded them as economically worthless.

Historically, the United States has been a resource-rich country. That is to say, it acquired abundant land and other resources relative to population and relative to our knowledge of means to extract, transport, process, and consume those resources; how to use rivers and lakes for transport (and later for power production); and how to maximize production of commodities particularly suited to the resource endowments (including climate) of the various regions of the country. Moreover, the policies of American government—national, state, and local government—have been conducive to rapid exploitation of available natural resources by private interests for purposes of economic production. Finally, the institutions of the society and the social values that support those institutions have given a high priority to application of resources for current production:

> Much of American history can be regarded as the story of the dynamic release of energy under the favoring auspices of political and economic freedom. It is only in the past [eighty-five] years or less that Americans have witnessed the antithetical philosophy of social control of the environment with centralized planning and a network of regulatory checks. . . .
> Historically a people of plenty, we [have been] reluctant to practice prudential restraint or to think in terms of possible future scarcity.[4]

It has been the popular belief in the United States, historically, "that it was common sense, and it was good, to use law to multiply the productive power of the economy."[5] Hence the content of property, contract, and other branches of law was shaped so as to reduce costs of access to resources. The American society was restless, impatient, materialistic. In consequence, resources were attacked ruthlessly rather than conserved. As the economy grew, however, new technology expanded the possibilities of productive use of the remaining natural resources.

Capital goods

Capital goods are defined as a society's "stock of *produced or manmade means of production,* consisting of such items as buildings, factories, machinery, tools, equipment and inventories of goods in stock."[6] The word "capital" is also used to denote money and other forms of financial assets, but when it is used to describe a factor of production it refers to goods used to produce other goods. The process of creating new capital goods—of adding to the stock of such goods—is *capital formation;* it is accomplished through *investment,* or the allocation (through saving) of a portion of what an economy produces for the purpose of expanding the economy's capacity for future production. Among the major types of capital investment in America's colonial period were the transformation of undeveloped land into productive farms through clearing, fencing, con-

---

[3]Erich W. Zimmermann, *World Resources and Industries,* rev. ed. (New York: Harper & Row, 1951), p. 9.

[4]Arthur Ekirch, *Man and Nature in America* (New York: Columbia University Press, 1964), pp. 7–8.

[5]Willard Hurst, *Law and Economic Growth: The Legal History of the Lumber Industry in Wisconsin, 1836–1915* (Cambridge, Mass.: Harvard University Press, 1964), p. 172.

[6]Richard T. Gill, *Economic Development: Past and Present,* 2nd ed. (Englewood Cliffs, N.J.: Prentice-Hall, 1967), p. 10.

struction of buildings, and the like, and the construction of shipping and related commercial facilities. In the early nineteenth century, both of these types of capital formation continued to be important. But by the 1820s there was new investment as well in factory construction, industrial machinery, and improved transport facilities (roads, canals, and bridges). Beginning in the mid-1840s, railroad construction became a leading component of capital formation and continued to be so after the Civil War (1861–1865), by which time investment for manufacturing and mining purposes was growing rapidly. Construction in the major industrial cities, the creation of electrical power producing facilities, and other areas of capital investment, such as housing, followed.

Typically, the facilities built through the capital-formation process incorporate new technology and thus reduce the inputs of labor or resources necessary to produce a given volume of goods. Hence real capital investment is a process by which the productivity (or efficiency) of the economy is increased, and it is a crucial source of economic growth. Both government and the private sector have contributed to capital formation in American economic development, and the United States has sustained high rates of capital investment for long periods of time.[7] Moreover, domestic savings—channeled into capital formation through financial intermediaries such as banks and the securities markets—have been supplemented by foreign investment in the United States. Thus, from colonial times to the early twentieth century, European investment funds helped to finance American expansion and imported capital goods supplemented domestic capital formation.

Table 1–3 indicates the relative contributions of factor inputs and productivity change in the pattern of U.S. growth. The table illustrates two major features of the growth record since 1840: (1) that the growth rate of net national product (the value of all goods and services less depreciation of capital stock) has slowed in the twentieth century from the 1840–1900 rate; (2) that accelerated productivity gains (repre-

senting new technologies, more efficient forms of organization and management, economies of scale, and so on) have accounted for over 44 percent of growth from 1900 to 1960, as compared to 17.3 percent of growth from 1840 to 1900.[8]

A recent study of American growth concludes that national income rose at a rate of 3.3 percent annually during the period 1929–1969. Fully 46 percent of this growth is accounted for, according to economist Edward F. Denison, by "advances in knowledge" and other qualitative factors such as improved resource allocation and economies of scale. They have served, in formal economic terms, to produce a shift in the production function: they have increased the efficiency, in other words, of each unit of labor, capital, and natural-resource input. Absolute increases in those inputs (that is, quantitative factors: rising numbers of workers and total time devoted to work, rising inputs of resources, and net additions to the stock of capital goods) account for the remaining 54 percent of 1929–1969 growth.[9]

Demand and distribution

The other main issues that will concern us in this book have to do with the structure of demand in the economy, the distribution of income, and the welfare of the people. Per capita average figures on income and output tell us whether economic growth is occurring, and examination of supply factors indicates the process by which the economy engages in production. But demand and distribution provide the necessary focus for understanding how the benefits of growth are distributed in the society, what the social costs of material growth have been and on whom they fell, and similar questions.

In studying the American economy of the eighteenth century and the early nineteenth century, we will find that foreign demand for American products and shipping services made major contributions to the general pattern of growth. As industrialization went forward in the U.S. economy during the nineteenth century, a labor-force shift into nonfarm employment (with concomitant urbanization) established the basis for a mass consumer market in the domestic economy. Meanwhile, regional speciali-

---

[7]Thus the value of capital stock rose at 5.4 percent annually from 1840 to 1900. Whereas some 15 percent of GNP was reinvested for capital-formation purposes in the 1840s and 1850s, the ratio increased steadily thereafter and amounted to a phenomenally high 24 percent in the 1870s and 28 percent in the 1880s. See pp. 164–166 of this book and Gallman, "Pace and Pattern," in Davis et al., *American Economic Growth*, p. 35.

[8]Ibid., pp. 35–39.

[9]Edward F. Denison, *Accounting for United States Economic Growth, 1929–1969* (Washington, D.C.: Brookings Institution, 1974), p. 127.

TABLE 1–3. CONTRIBUTIONS OF FACTOR INPUTS AND PRODUCTIVITY TO THE GROWTH OF NET NATIONAL PRODUCT, 1840–1960

	1840–1960	1840–1900	1900–1960
Panel 1: Average Annual Rates of Growth			
Labor force	1.52%	1.88%	1.12%
Land supply	.21	.38	.08
Capital stock	.81	1.03	.60
Productivity	1.02	.69	1.32
Totals (growth of NNP)	3.56%	3.98%	3.12%
Panel 2: Percentage Distributions (Panel 1 data in percentage terms)			
Contributions of:			
Labor force	42.7%	47.2%	34.8%
Land supply	5.9	9.6	2.5
Capital stock	22.8	25.9	18.6
Productivity	28.6	17.3	44.1
Totals	100.0%	100.0%	100.0%

Source: Lance E. Davis et al., *American Economic Growth: An Economist's History of the United States* (New York: Harper & Row, 1972), Table 2.12, p. 39; based on data from Edward C. Budd, "Factor Shares, 1850–1910," in National Bureau of Economic Research, *Trends in the American Economy in the Nineteenth Century*, vol. 24 of *Studies in Income and Wealth* (Princeton: Princeton University Press, 1960), p. 382, and Edward F. Denison, *The Sources of Economic Growth in the United States* (New York: Committee for Economic Development, 1962), p. 30. Original data from Budd, Copyright 1960, National Bureau of Economic Research. Used by permission. Original data from Denison, Copyright 1962, Committee for Economic Development. Used by permission.

zation—of the South in staples agriculture, of the Northeast in manufacturing, and of the West in foodstuffs and other primary products and also in manufacturing to a rising degree—increased overall efficiency in the economy. Income distribution was highly uneven. Over the long run, rising productivity permitted gains in the real income of most workers in the labor force. But poverty remained a persistent problem (as it does today), and recurrent instabilities in the form of depression and "recession" conditions imposed enormous hardships on large portions of the population. Moreover, rising average incomes have been accompanied by only limited changes in the distribution of wealth and income. Thus in 1860, it has been estimated, the top 5 percent of families, by income level, held more than half the private wealth (53 percent); the top 10 percent held nearly three-quarters of the wealth.[10] By 1929 there had been some diminution in the degree to which the highest income groups were taking a highly disproportionate share of total private income, as shown in Table 1–4. But from that time, at the onset of the Great Depression, through the years of the Second World War and after, despite major changes in the structure of the economy and large gains in output and average real earnings of workers, there was only a small degree of income redistribution.

The role of government

Some of the major twentieth-century trends that we will be considering in this book are these: First, there has been a major shift in the role of government in the nation's economic life. The trend toward increased governmental activity—both for regulation of private-sector interests and for purposes of providing needed public services—began early in the century, leveling off in the boom period of the 1920s. But since the New Deal programs of 1933 went into effect, there has been sweeping change in the role of government. The increase in comprehensive regulation during the 1930s was swift and had transforming effects. Agriculture became largely a "managed sector," with government rather than the market forces of supply and demand becoming the major determining factor in setting prices and allocating resources. Transport and communications fell into much the same category; banks and the securities markets, the chief financial intermediaries in the economy, came under intensive regulation. And the federal government undertook a major role

[10]Robert E. Gallman, "Trends in the Size Distribution of Wealth in the Nineteenth Century: Some Speculations," in *Six Papers on the Size Distribution of Wealth and Income*, ed. Lee Soltow (National Bureau of Economic Research, *Studies in Income and Wealth*, vol. 33, New York: Columbia University Press, 1969). Also Gavin Wright, " 'Economic Democracy' and the Concentration of Agricultural Wealth in the Cotton South, 1850–1860," *Agricultural History*, 44 (1970):63–85; Lee Soltow, "Economic Inequality in the United States in the Period from 1790 to 1860," *Journal of Economic History*, 31 (1971): 822–839.

TABLE 1–4. PERCENTAGE OF INCOME RECEIVED BY U.S. FAMILIES AND INDIVIDUALS, 1929–1968

FAMILIES AND INDIVIDUALS BY INCOME RANK	1929[1]	1935[1]	1941[1]	1947[2]	1957[2]	1962[2]	1968[2]
Total[3]	100%	100%	100%	100%	100%	100%	100%
Lowest fifth	13	4	4	4	4	3	4
Second fifth		9	10	11	11	11	11
Middle fifth	14	14	15	17	18	17	17
Fourth fifth	19	21	22	24	25	25	·25
Highest fifth	54	52	49	46	43	44	44
Top 5%	30%	27%	24%	19%	17%	17%	15%

Source: U.S. Department of Commerce, Bureau of the Census, *Historical Statistics of the United States, Colonial Times to 1957* (Washington, D.C.: U.S. Government Printing Office, 1960), p. 166; Herman P. Miller, *Income Distribution in the United States* (Washington, D.C.: U.S. Government Printing Office, 1966), p. 21; and previously unpublished Bureau of the Census data for 1968, cited in Herman P. Miller, *Rich Man, Poor Man* (New York: Crowell, 1971), p. 50.

[1]Distribution of personal income received.
[2]Money income received.
[3]Sums may not equal totals because of rounding.

in providing work and income for the unemployed, as well as providing for welfare through social security and other programs.

Second, the vast rise in cost and sweep of the new programs pushed up government's share of GNP from the 2–5 percent level of the nineteenth century to the level of about 20–25 percent—a development given additional impetus and permanence by the Second World War and the "defense economy" of the post-1945 period. Government's military programs came to support a major new industry, aerospace, as well as other areas of production.

Third, and most important, the higher level of expenditures by the central government established the conditions for modern fiscal policy by which, since the 1930s, deficit spending has become a vehicle for counteracting recessionary business cycles. Moreover, the magnitude of expenditures and revenues has meant that government's taxation policies gained the potential for major redistributive effects—a potential not by any means fully realized in fact.

Finally, the greatly increased role of government has had major effects on the structure and functioning of the modern business system, dominated by large-scale corporate interests, and upon labor, both through policies that have accommodated worker organization in labor unions since 1933 and through such measures as minimum-wage laws and unemployment insurance.

Patterns of change

Another major trend of the twentieth century has been the shift in the nature of demand, with consumer goods playing an increasingly important part in the net flow of private goods to the market. Also, there has been continuing technological change, creating new products (both capital and consumer goods), successive changes in sources of energy, new information and management systems, and—not least important—rising pressure on the stock of depletable natural resources.[11] These modern domestic trends have been complemented by shifts as well in the international context of U.S. growth. The two world wars have left the United States with significant economic advantages in the structure of competition within the international economy. But the pattern of change in the world economy since the late 1950s (when nearly full recovery from the war had been attained by other industrial nations) has also put new pressures on the American economy. In the 1970s, these pressures have reached crisis proportions with respect to inflation, maintenance of the dollar in world trade relationships, reliance upon imported energy resources, and the like. All of these pressures were intensified by the protracted war in Vietnam and by the maintenance of American military power on a global scale, for good or for ill, since World War II.

[11]For the basic trends since 1945, see Chapters 25–28, and Harold G. Vatter, *The U.S. Economy in the 1950s* (New York: Norton, 1963). On the way very recent economic growth has put pressure on resources, see the insightful study by Barry Commoner, "The Environmental Costs of Economic Growth," in *Energy, Economic Growth, and the Environment,* ed. Sam Schurr (Baltimore: Johns Hopkins University Press, 1972), reprinted with other useful readings on population pressure, the costs of growth, and future prospects in *America and the Future of Man,* ed. Jane L. Scheiber (Del Mar, Calif.: CRM Books, 1973).

SELECTED READINGS

NOTE: Here and in subsequent chapters' selected readings, the asterisk(*) denotes a work issued in a paperback edition.

Studies of the discipline
Aitken, Hugh G. J., "On the Present State of Economic History," *Canadian Journal of Economics and Political Science,* XXVI (1960).

*Andreano, Ralph L., ed., *The New Economic History: Recent Papers on Methodology* (New York: Wiley, 1970).

*Baughman, James P., "New Directions in American Economic and Business History," *American History: Retrospect and Prospect,* G. A. Billias and G. N. Grob, eds. (New York: Free Press, 1971).

Cochran, Thomas C., "Economic History, Old and New," *American Historical Review,* LXXIV (1969).

Galambos, Louis, "Business History and the Theory of the Growth of the Firm," *Explorations in Economic History,* IV (1966).

Journal of Economic History, two issues that contain numerous excellent articles on the literature of the field: XIX (March 1959), and XXXI (March 1971).

McClelland, Peter D., *Causal Explanation and Model Building in History, Economics, and the New Economic History* (Ithaca: Cornell University Press, 1975).

*Taylor, George Rogers, and Ellsworth, L. F., eds., *Approaches to American Economic History* (Charlottesville: University Press of Virginia, 1971).

Bibliographic aids
American Economic Association, *Index of Economic Journals, 1886–1959* (Homewood: Irwin, 1961–1962).

American Historical Association, *Writings in American History* (annual vols., Washington, 1902–), with cumulative index to 1940.

Daniells, Lorna M., *Studies in Enterprise* (Boston: Harvard Business School, 1957). A bibliography of business and entrepreneurial history.

*David, Henry et al., eds., *Economic History of the United States* (New York: Holt, Rinehart and Winston, 1945–). Eight volumes published to 1975; each contains a full analytical bibliography.

Freidel, Frank, *Harvard Guide to American History,* 2nd ed. (Cambridge: Harvard University Press, 1975).

*Kirkland, Edward C., *American Economic History Since 1860,* Goldentree Bibliographies in American History, edited by Arthur S. Link (New York: Harcourt Brace Jovanovich, 1971).

Lovett, Robert W., *American Economic and Business History: A Guide to Information Sources* (Detroit: Gale Research, 1971).

*Taylor, George Rogers, *American Economic History Before 1860,* Goldentree Bibliographies (New York: Harcourt Brace Jovanovich, 1969).

Historical statistics on the American economy
*Denison, Edward F., *Accounting for U.S. Economic Growth, 1929–1969* (Washington: Brookings Institution, 1974). Analysis and statistical series.

National Bureau of Economic Research. [Sponsors and publishers of numerous important statistical works.] The following are especially pertinent collections of essays in quantitative history: *Output, Employment, and Productivity in the U.S. After 1800* (Conference on Income and Wealth, Studies, XXX, New York: Columbia University Press, 1966); and *Trends in the American Economy in the 19th Century* (Conference on Income and Wealth, Studies, XXIV, Princeton: Princeton University Press, 1960).

U.S. Congress, Joint Economic Committee, 86th Congress, 1st Session., *Hearings: Employment, Growth and Price Levels* (Washington: U.S. Government Printing Office, 1959).

U.S. Department of Commerce, Bureau of the Census., *Historical Statistics of the United States, Colonial Times to 1957* (Washington: U.S. Government Printing Office, 1960), and *Continuation to 1962 and Revisions* (Washington: U.S. Government Printing Office, 1965).

*———, *Long Term Economic Growth, 1860–1970* (Washington: U.S. Government Printing Office, 1973).

the colonial age

part 1

THE RISE OF MERCHANT CAPITALISM

The discovery of America was brought about by a train of circumstances extending back through centuries of European history and culminating at the end of the fifteenth century. Intellectual, political, and, above all, economic factors contributed to make this a turning point in world history. The fifteenth century and the beginning of the sixteenth marked the height of the Renaissance, a period of inquiry and dissatisfaction with the old order. In political life the modern state was being erected on the ruins of feudalism; with the national state came a cessation of the private warfare of the Middle Ages, greater protection to travelers and merchants, and fewer tolls. More settled conditions encouraged the extension of trade and commerce, and the revived economic life led naturally to exploration and discovery. Exploration was aided by the compass and astrolabe, by that time in general use, and by the improvement in charts and maps. The news of scientific and commercial progress was disseminated by means of the printing press, invented about the middle of the fifteenth century.

Although all of these influences contributed to the great era of European expansion, particular emphasis should be placed upon the development of merchant capitalism, which transformed feudalism into a capitalist economy and gave a tremendous impetus to colonization and the development of overseas trade. Despite the condemnation of the church, moneylending continued throughout the late Middle Ages. Great private bankers, like the Medici of Florence and the Fuggers of Augsburg, accumulated surpluses as merchants and then turned to moneylending. By the end of the fifteenth century Flemish speculators were operating an exchange at Antwerp where commodities and the shares of joint-stock companies were bought and sold. These merchant princes and bankers helped to finance the struggle of kings against their feudal lords and contributed much to the eventual establishment of the great national states. Above all, this capital accumulation contributed to the development of medieval industry and commerce, which formed the immediate background for the discovery of America.

As feudal society gave way to national monarchical states, a new impetus was given to the expansion of trade and the development of merchant capitalism. Internally conditions became more stabilized, to the benefit of trade and industry. In need of money to strengthen their position within their realms and their military power, the new monarchs encouraged industry and granted trading monopolies to groups of "adventurers" willing to risk their fortunes in foreign commerce. The new merchant and trading class was encouraged at the expense of the old nobility. At the same time the Protestant revolt weakened the prestige of the Catholic church, which had frowned on interest taking and excessive profit making and had emphasized the doctrine of the "just price," with ultimate reward in the world to come.[1] In many ways the foundations were being laid for a great expansion.

TRADE WITH THE EAST

As for the immediate impetus to the discovery of America, no factor was more important than the desire on the part of Europeans to find a quicker and cheaper route to the East. From the dawn of commerce Europe had been dependent upon Asia for most of its luxuries and many of its necessities. The importance of spices in the Middle Ages is difficult to appreciate today, when meat is kept fresh by cold storage or curing; but the monotonous diet and coarse food of those times made spices and condiments so desirable that they were frequently sent as gifts of honor from one sovereign to another. Pepper from the Malabar coast of India was a staple import during the Middle Ages and was used by all who could afford it. Cloves, cinnamon, nutmeg from the Moluccas, and sugar from Arabia and Persia were more expensive and less commonly used, but still in great demand. Apothecaries obtained many of their drugs from Asia, among them rhubarb, balsam, gums, aloes, cubebs, and camphor. The precious stones that adorned the persons of the upper classes in Europe came almost exclusively from the East.

Trade with the East, however, was not confined to such luxuries as spices, drugs, and precious stones. An important class of wares that served manufacturing industries — dyestuffs — found its source there. Indigo was a chief staple of Bagdad, and brazilwood, producing a red dye, came from India. Alum, considered indispensable for fixing colors in dyeing and one of the most desirable products of the Levant trade, was procured mainly in Asia Minor. Manufactured products, superior in workmanship, material, and design to anything known in Europe, came also from the East: glass and cutlery from Damascus, Samarkand, and Bagdad; porcelain from China; a great variety of cottons and silks from India, China, Persia, and Asia Minor. Persian rugs, cashmere shawls, taffeta silk, damask linen, and japanned ware all testify to the Eastern nomenclature and origin of the most sought-after textiles, rugs, tapestries, and household luxuries.

In return for these products, Europe could offer only woolen fabrics and such metals and minerals as arsenic, antimony, quicksilver, tin, copper, and lead. Although these products were much valued in the East, their weight and bulk made transportation on the long overland routes an arduous and unrewarding task. Gold and silver, on the other hand, found such ready acceptance that they were well worth the trouble of transporting them. This movement of the precious metals from Europe to Asia was made possible by the fact that the monetary system of Europe in the Middle Ages was not highly developed. The continued movement of gold and silver to Asia, however, undoubtedly caused a scarcity of these metals in Europe, which was not relieved until the opening of mines in Mexico and Peru.

While trade with the Near and the Far East was a leading factor in the economic life of the Middle Ages, Europeans knew little of Asia or the ways to get there. Trade had flourished in ancient times, but during the barbaric invasions of the fifth century and the succeeding conflicts, this commerce had been largely broken up. A general awakening of economic life in the eleventh century set in motion with renewed vigor the intercourse with the East, a movement greatly aided by the Crusades (1095–1270). Not only did the Crusades enlarge the vision and knowledge of Europeans by introducing them again to the learning and products of Asia, but they laid the foundations for the prosperity of the Italians in this trade.

The bulk of the Levant trade during the 500 years from 1000 to 1500 rested in the hands of the Italians, and the three cities of Venice, Genoa, and Pisa struggled for supremacy in this trade, while Florence became a banking and manufacturing center. From the Italian cities the Oriental merchandise was distributed to northern and central Europe through two main channels. German merchants handled the overland reexport trade from Venice and Genoa.

[1]For a full and skeptical discussion of the connection between Protestant doctrine and the weakening of restraints such as the Catholic "just price" concept, see C. H. Wilson, "Trade, Society, and the State," in *Cambridge Economic History of Europe,* vol. 4 (Cambridge: The University Press, 1967), pp. 487–491.

Through the St. Gothard Pass to Basel, Constance, Strasbourg, and down the Rhine, or over the Brenner Pass to Munich, Nuremberg, or Frankfort: these were the usual overland routes. In addition, a large amount of trade was carried on by sea with Lisbon, Bruges, and London. As far as northern Europe was concerned, it was in the Low Countries—at Antwerp, Bruges, Ghent, and other towns—that the lines of medieval commerce finally crossed. Here the goods of the Mediterranean and the Baltic were sent to be distributed later throughout England and France.

THE COMMERCIAL REVOLUTION

The pivotal role of the Italian merchants in the spice trades, supporting urban population growth in their home city-states, meant profits not only from trading but also from the provision of shipping, financial, and other commercial services in the Mediterranean area. While the Italian merchants thus engaged in capital formation, they were not laggard in taking advantage of other commercial opportunities. Their ships, warehouses, and credit facilities served a diverse and active Mediterranean commerce that included much more than the exotic products carried from the East. The wool and wines of Spain, grain brought from the eastern area of the Mediterranean basin west to the European countries in years of grain shortages, salt from Cyprus and Sicily, fish from Atlantic waters, and hides from North Africa, all played a large part in the overall trade of the region. Taken as a whole, this diversified trade, linked by water and land routes with northern Europe and England, was the principal commercial locus for the European continent of some 60 or 70 million people by 1500. Ravaged by plagues that destroyed a quarter of the population, wars in many parts of the continent, and recurring famines, European society experienced a long economic depression in the late fourteenth and early fifteenth centuries; and the Mediterranean trade shared in these troubles. (One effect of the depression was intensification of trade rivalries among the Italian city-states, with Florence emerging dominant.) But by the 1470s commerce had begun to revive. Population was on the upswing throughout the continent as new food-supply sources were tapped in northeastern Europe (the Baltic grain region), fishing in the Atlantic apparently expanded, and there seems to have been a tendency toward earlier marriages, fecundity, and perhaps a reduced mortality rate.[2]

The sixteenth century carried forward the momentum of economic expansion, culminating in what is known as the Commercial Revolution. Ultimately that fundamental alteration of Europe's economic life was to introduce new trades into a widening commercial world, the plantation of colonies and flourishing of new empires, an influx of products previously unknown and of cheaply produced commodities formerly known but never available except to the wealthiest members of society. Their effects extended beyond the sphere of commercial life, bringing expansion as well in European agriculture and industry.

The shift to the Atlantic

The first great portent of the Commercial Revolution was a shift in the locus of commerce and of expansion from the Mediterranean basin to the Atlantic. In its initial phase, this shift found its chief impetus in the pioneering activities of Portugal in the quest for new, more direct trade routes to the East Indies and Asia. Portugal also sought new sources of gold and other trading commodities along the coast of Africa.

Ultimately the search for a route westward across the Atlantic to the East Indies was carried out by Spain. The discovery instead of a whole new world served to solidify the new importance of the Spanish and Portuguese peninsula as the cockpit of European expansionism. By the mid-1500s, the impetus for expansion had gained a momentum of its own, finally involving all the Atlantic powers of Europe. But for the moment, the shift away from the Mediterranean orientation of the economy was led by Spain and Portugal. Not until the seventeenth century would the span of Atlantic hegemony in Europe's economic expansion extend to England, the Netherlands, and France.

The voyages of discovery

Although early Italian travelers had added much to the European knowledge of Asia, and the Italian cartographers had made further con-

---

[2]Karl F. Helleiner, "The Population of Europe from the Black Death to the Eve of the Vital Revolution," in ibid., pp. 1–40.

tributions to this body of knowledge, the Portuguese enjoyed an advantage of location for purposes of launching voyages of exploration on Atlantic waters. Portugal had always been a seafaring nation, and now its best efforts were mobilized by Prince Henry "the Navigator," a man in whom rare business ability was combined with the instinct of the explorer and the zeal of the missionary. He sent one expedition after another to extend Portugal's influence on the unknown coast of western Africa. By 1420 Portugal had settled the Madeira Islands, and within two decades its flag was planted in the Azores and Cape Verde Islands as well—precursors of European empires and models for the organization of colonizing ventures. The naval expeditions thrust down Africa's western coast with bold daring, but in retrospect also with painful slowness. Not until 1488 did Bartholomeu Dias discover the Cape of Good Hope, and it was ten years more before perhaps the greatest of the Portuguese captains, Vasco da Gama, rounded the Cape, pushed up the east coast, and in 1498 reached India. The new sea route to India was complete and trade was rapidly established. The strategic position of Portugal, combined with the lowered cost of transportation over the new route, threw the Eastern trade into the hands of the Portuguese, who took immediate advantage of the situation by laying the foundations of an Eastern empire that they ruled until the crowns of Spain and Portugal were joined.

THE DISCOVERY OF AMERICA

Portugal was not the only nation where men were dreaming of riches through shortened routes to the Indies. Before Vasco da Gama had made his epochal voyage to India, Ferdinand and Isabella of Spain, fresh from their conquests over the Moors, had paused in their building of a great Spanish state to promise aid to the Italian navigator Christopher Columbus in his projected westward voyage. Columbus, sharing the belief of all educated astronomers and philosophers that the earth was round, thought that by sailing due west he could reach the Indies. The greatness of Columbus lay not in any originality of conception but in his courage in venturing upon the unknown seas and in his pertinacity in pursuing his project. Sailing west in 1492 with his three little ships, he at length ran into what was probably one of the Bahamas. He believed that he had discovered outlying islands of the Indies, and returned three times, only to meet with disappointment in his efforts to get through to India.

The efforts of Columbus were emulated by John Cabot, the Italian navigator in the service of Henry VII of England, who sailed due west in quest of Cipango (Japan), only to land on the barren shore of Labrador. Even after Balboa had discovered the great western ocean (1513) and Magellan's ship *Victoria* had circumnavigated the globe (1519–1522) in that greatest feat of navigation of all time, explorers continued for a hundred years to seek channels that would lead through or around America to Asia. This quest for a passage to the Indies led to the explorations of Verrazano (1524), Cartier (1534), Frobisher (1576–1578), Davis (1585–1587), and Hudson (1609). Although no natural opening through the American continents to Cathay was ever discovered, these voyages gave to Europeans their first knowledge of what is now the coast of the United States and of the two great rivers of the eastern coast, the St. Lawrence and the Hudson.[3]

EFFECTS OF THE COMMERCIAL REVOLUTION

The Commercial Revolution, including as it did the discovery of America, had incalculable effects upon economic history. Only a few of the most important can be suggested here. The

[3]Much earlier, the Scandinavian seafarers had pushed far out into the North Atlantic, and there is gathering evidence that they established fishing bases on American shores. But in any case they did not manage to set up enduring colonizing ventures across the Atlantic. Probably their descendants, together with fishermen in the farthest western islands of England, knew well the fishing waters at least as far as the Newfoundland banks. If this knowledge was a closely kept secret, still it meant that there were probably English sailors who contributed to the early expeditions in search of a northwest passage with their firsthand experience with the ocean lanes traversed.

comparative cheapness of water transportation over the new routes to the Indies reduced the cost of Oriental goods and made possible their more general use. Long ocean voyages developed the construction of stronger and taller ships that could profitably carry to Europe bulky commodities hitherto unknown, such as tea, coffee, Indian corn, and tobacco. All the influences tending to the development of merchant capitalism and economic imperialism were accentuated. The growth in business developed better methods of carrying on trade, new industries sprang into existence, manufacturing increased, all of which tended to break down the antiquated guild system. Even agriculture responded to the stimulus of new crops and the necessity of supporting the greater population that came with enlarged commercial activities. The slave trade was revived to provide the labor necessary to work the plantations of the New World. Not the least effect of the discovery of America was the plunder of Mexico and Peru. The flow of gold and silver from the mines of the New World put Europe definitely on a money economy and gave merchant capitalism a new lease on life. Trade with the Far East, which had been declining as Europe was gradually stripped of its precious metals, revived and flourished. The sudden flow of precious metals pushed prices upward. Since wages and rents lagged behind, enormous profits were reaped by merchants, industrialists, and other entrepreneurs. These profits in turn stimulated commerce and industry, and the results permeated almost every phase of economic and social life.

Little wonder, then, that reflecting upon the history of European civilization in the centuries immediately preceding his own, a famous French cleric and scientist, the Abbé Raynal, should have written in 1770: "No event has been so interesting to mankind . . . as the discovery of the new world, and the passage to India by the Cape of Good Hope"; or that Adam Smith, in the treatise that laid the foundations of modern political economy, should have declared these same two achievements to be "the greatest and most important events recorded in the history of mankind."[4] One modern commentator, K. M. Panikkar, reflecting on the age of discoveries and the Commercial Revolution, argues that the four and a half centuries spanning the period from Vasco da

Gama's arrival in India in 1498 to the withdrawal of the British from India in 1947 constituted a single, great historical epoch. This "Vasco da Gama era" derived what he terms "its singular unity" from the long dominance of European naval power over much of Asia (and, earlier, comparable dominance by maritime power over the American land masses); and also from Europe's continuous exploitation of these distant continents as a vast hinterland for its own economy.[5]

Another valuable perspective is offered by the American historian Walter P. Webb, who viewed the great discoveries as inaugurating an era in which Europe in effect extended its frontiers. By bringing into the European political and economic orbit the 20 million square miles of land in the New World (five times the land mass of Europe itself), the colonizing ventures in the Americas radically altered the ratio of population to land as well as to resources. Thus began a four-century boom in which Europe's "Great Frontier" in the New World offered successive waves of opportunity for enterprise and investment.[6] Elaborating on Webb's bold thesis, another scholar has argued:

> The existence of the New World gave Europeans more room for maneuver. Above all, it promoted movement— movement of wealth, movement of people, movement of ideas. Where there was movement, there were opportunities for people with enterprise, ability, and the willingness to run risks; and they operated in a climate where success bred success. The very achievement of creating great new enterprises out of nothing, on the far side of the Atlantic, was bound to produce a new confidence in man's capacity to shape and control his world.[7]

In sum, the discoveries inaugurated by Spanish and Portuguese seafaring enterprise set in motion a pattern of dynamic change in Europe, the consequences of which did not reach their culmination for centuries. To wrap up four centuries of history, or indeed four decades or four months, in the neat conceptual package termed an "era" or "epoch" ineluctably re-

---

[4]Raynal (1770) and Smith (1776) are both quoted in J. H. Elliott, *The Old World and the New, 1492–1650* (Cambridge: The University Press, 1970), p. 1.

[5]K. M. Panikkar, *Asia and Western Dominance* (1961), quoted in Carlo M. Cipolla, *Guns, Sails, and Empires* (New York: Minerva Press, 1965), Preface. See also Cipolla's own use of the concept, ibid., pp. 147–148.

[6]Walter Prescott Webb, *The Great Frontier* (Boston: Houghton Mifflin, 1953).

[7]Elliott, *The Old World and the New*, p. 78.

quires bending and warping some of the realities of historical change. Granting this risk, still there is a measure of understanding that can be gained only by speculation on this scale.

The view outside Europe

But these conceptual speculations have been formulated from a European or American perspective. Seen in another light, the initial phase of European expansion drew the peoples of other continents into new relationships with Portugal, Spain, and the other powers that set out to enmesh them for Europe's own purposes, in its own sphere, and on uneven terms. The advanced weaponry of Europe, especially the development of the cannon, and European maritime superiority combined to make possible the long historic phase of conquest and exploitation. The extension of Europe's celebrated Great Frontier meant for the native Indian populations of the Americas a genocidal depopulation and engulfment of the survivors in the

tide of expansionism from across the seas. By the seventeenth century the trading posts set up on the ocean rim of Africa in the fifteenth century had become the outlets for a massive slave trade that distorted the whole life and culture of western Africa. As one prominent student of African history has written, "There can be no doubt that on balance the economic effects of European contact worked steady and decisive damage. After about 1650 . . . African production-for-export became a monoculture in human beings," with the effect of bringing economic growth—based before European contact on an elaborate trade system and advanced technologies—to a halt. "In exporting slaves, African states exported their own capital without any possible return in interest or in the enlargement of their economic system."[8] The devastating effect on political life was no less severe. These costs paid by the conquered peoples must also be calculated when one sums up the Great Frontier and its fruits of a four-hundred-year boom.

MOTIVES FOR THE COLONIZATION OF AMERICA

As the idea was gradually brought home to Europeans that the new-found land was not the Indies but two mighty continents, not only did statesmen dream of new empires, and knights and merchants of new sources of riches, but common people began to think of a new home across the seas where they might escape from the religious, political, and economic tyranny of the Old World. The motives for colonization were varied, and religious, political, and economic factors were often inextricably combined.

Religious motives

In the age of the Reformation the religious motive was strong. Prince Henry sent his ships to find not only the Indies but also the fabled Christian kingdom of Prester John. "We come in search of Christians and spices," said Vasco da Gama. In the breasts of the early Spanish conquerors and explorers a consuming passion for gold was fused with a strong crusading spirit.

"Gold is most excellent," said Columbus. "Gold is treasure, and he who possesses it does all he wishes to in this world, and succeeds in helping souls into paradise."[9] French Jesuit priests threaded the lakes and rivers in advance of the fur traders, baptizing as they went. The religious impulse moved even the more prosaic English. Drake and Hawkins scoured the Spanish Main[10] to fight Catholics as well as to collect booty.

Many of the British settlers of the Caribbean and the North American mainland had left their old homes out of a desire to gain freedom from religious persecution. Thus Separatists and Puritans founded New England's colonies to obtain religious liberty; but intolerance there in turn drove others out to found Rhode Island. Puritanism, when ascendant in England during the seventeenth century, drove Anglicans to Virginia and English Catholics to Maryland. French Protestants found refuge in the Carolinas; and

[8]Basil Davidson, *The African Slave Trade: Precolonial History, 1450–1850,* also published as *Black Mother* (Boston: Atlantic–Little, Brown, 1961), p. 278.

[9]Columbus (July 7, 1503), quoted in *The Northmen, Columbus and Cabot,* ed. J. E. Olson and E. G. Bourne (New York: Scribner's, 1906), p. 412.

[10]The term "Spanish Main" properly means the coasts bordering on the Caribbean Sea, but it is sometimes applied

to the Caribbean itself. Considered as a region, writes Carl Ortwin Sauer, its principal historian, the Spanish Main "is the rim of land about a mediterranean sea, it is the double corridor between North and South America; and it is the region of tropical climate . . . that is stirred by the trade winds" (*The Early Spanish Main* [Berkeley: University of California Press, 1966], p. 4). It was also the corridor at the western end of the ocean route between Europe and New Spain.

Quakers, Mennonites, Moravians, and members of other sects found homes in Pennsylvania, New Jersey, and elsewhere.

Political motives

Political motives also played their part. Each nation would secure for itself as much of the new land as possible. Settlements in the thirteen colonies were encouraged to check the northward advance of the Spanish and the southward and eastward pressure of the French. The four-cornered struggle for empire between Spain, France, England, and Holland during the sixteenth and seventeenth centuries contributed much in hastening the occupation of America. Divergence in political ideas, often derived from religious tenets, also sent many to the New World.

Economic motives

Fused solidly with the religious and political considerations were the economic motives. As we have seen, it was the search for new routes to the Far East that led in the first place to the discovery and exploration of America. When gold and silver were discovered in abundance by Cortez in Mexico (1519) and by Pizarro in Peru (1531), the dominating impulse of Spain was the exploitation of this source of income. The foundations of New Spain rested during the early years on the precious metals. Nor was the hope of quick riches through the discovery of gold and silver absent from the minds of the early English explorers, whose appetites had been whetted by the good fortune of their Spanish rivals.

In time Europe came to realize that gold was not the only product of value that might be obtained from America. It is believed that even before the discovery of Columbus fishing vessels from England and France had sailed out to the west close to American shores. Certainly in the fifteenth century the fishing fleets of many nations drew wealth from the Grand Banks. The fur trade came soon to rival in value even that of gold. Sugar, tobacco, cocoa, and many other products, including timber and naval stores (tar, pitch, resin, cordage, masts, and lumber), demonstrated the value of the Americas to Europe as a source of raw materials. As a counterpart to the growth of manufactures in Europe came the appreciation of colonial settlements as markets for the finished products of the looms and workshops of the Atlantic powers. In enumerating the benefits that England would derive from the establishment of colonies beyond the Atlantic, Sir George Peckham wrote that it would revive and promote especially the trades of "Clothiers, Woolmen, Carders, Spinners, Weavers, Fullers, Shearmen, Dyers, Drapers, Cappers, Hatters," and would repair "many decayed towns." A pamphleteer, writing prior to 1606 on "Reasons for raising a fund for the Support of a Colony at Virginia," speaks of it as a place "fit for the vent of our wares."[11]

EUROPEAN VIEWS OF EMIGRATION

Statesmen and contemporary writers on public policy worried, at one time or another, about emigration as a source of damaging "depopulation" in all the expansionist European countries. Before England's great effort to people new colonies in the Caribbean and on the North American mainland, well into the seventeenth century, concern about depopulation through emigration centered in Spain and Portugal, which led the colonizing effort. Ironically, the widespread fears about loss of human resources to the home countries were expressed in the face of fairly small absolute numbers: The leading historian of Portuguese expansion estimates that this country, with a home population of about one million in the sixteenth century, probably never had more than 10,000 men based overseas "in an empire which extended from South America to the Spice Islands."

(This was evidence, too, of the extent to which the Portuguese expansion was maritime and commercial in its main outlines.) Yet the appallingly high death rates suffered in tropical climates by European settlers, the losses of people at sea on the long journeys to distant colonies, and the deaths from wars on land and sea, all did indicate that a sizable annual migration was needed in order to maintain the level of 10,000 overseas.[12]

In sixteenth-century Spain, which suffered serious population losses from a variety of

[11]Sir George Peckham, *A True Report of the Late Discoveries . . .* (1583), a pamphlet reprinted in *Magazine of History with Notes and Queries*, vol. 17 extra no. 68 (1920), p. 43; E. D. Neill, *Virginia Vetusta* (Albany, 1865), p. 30.

[12]C. R. Boxer, *Four Centuries of Portuguese Expansion, 1415–1825* (1961, reprinted Berkeley: University of California Press, 1969), pp. 19–21.

causes at home, there was deep concern about the emigration that had swelled the Spanish populations of Mexico and South America to a level of about 100,000 to 150,000 by the 1560s. The most pessimistic critics of this emigration, fearful of the loss of labor and talent that the outflow meant for Spain, estimated the annual loss to the home country at perhaps 40,000 — and this number included soldiers sent north to fight in the Netherlands. For a country of 8 million, this was a considerable drain, especially since probably 90 percent of emigrants were men in their reproductive years; and since few women emigrated, typically these men married women of the indigenous population, as was true as well of the Portuguese.[13]

The Spanish and Portuguese concentrated their colonizing efforts on areas of the New World and Asia where vast native populations could provide a labor force, and in trading posts on the west African coast, where, at the periphery of African society, they might tap and exploit the flow of slaves and such commodities as gold and ivory as they came to the coast from the interior or via far-flung trade routes. The basic strategy of English expansion, beginning in the early sixteenth century, was different; it was shaped by the nature of the North American territory that was left to England, and it involved planting settlements that would, at least initially, derive their labor forces from the home country. If, as some scholars maintain, the English harbored visions of emulating Spain and using native Indian labor, they were quickly disappointed; ultimately, the southern colonies of England turned to using black slave labor instead. But in the initial period, it was from England itself that the people had to come.[14] Consequently the English chartered colonizing companies, later relying upon royal grants of a proprietary nature to mobilize private energies for the promotion of emigration. In the sixteenth century England was suffering displacement of its agricultural population. Unemployment, a rising problem of poverty (the poor were repeatedly said to be "swarming"), the ravages of civil war and religious persecution, and chronic inadequacies of housing and diet,

as well as recurrent epidemics, all served to make emigration an attractive alternative for many of the people of small property and for the poor. The same factors induced policymakers to consider emigration for purposes of colonization as an attractive means of relieving what they considered population pressure on England's resources and the home economy. Between 1620 and 1642 alone, in the first phase of colonizing by England, some 2 percent of the English population — close to 80,000 people — sought new homes overseas.[15] By 1689 some 210,000 white English lived in the colonies of the North American mainland and perhaps another 50,000 in the Caribbean islands.

English opinion swung back and forth on the depopulation issue. In the seventeenth century, those who welcomed emigration as a relief for "surplus" population spoke of

> our land abounding with swarms of idle persons . . . . It is no new thing but most profitable for our state, to rid our multitudes of such as lie at home pestering the land with pestilence and penury, and infecting one another with vice and villainy worse than the plague itself.[16]

The architect of the Massachusetts Bay Colony's Puritan settlement, John Winthrop, reflected upon such sentiments, no less than upon the condition that had provoked them, when in a treatise on the value of emigration to Massachusetts he wrote that it would offer a productive life to those "swarming" English who were viewed, perversely and in violation of godly precepts, as a waste and a scourge instead of being valued for their humanity.[17] Yet later on, as the tide of emigration rose, English statesmen echoed the refrain heard in earlier times in Spain and Portugal, deploring the loss of human resources that were represented by the movement overseas. In the English case, moreover, from almost the beginning the emigration was of men and women both, families emigrating as units or as parts of large groups, or young people who married other overseas English rather than indigenous people.

---

[13] R. Trevor Davies, *The Golden Century of Spain, 1501–1621* (1937, reprinted New York: Harper & Row, 1965), pp. 264–265.

[14] The English hopes of emulating Spain's model of empire built on exploitation of native Indian labor, and the consequences of their disappointment, are discussed in Edmund S. Morgan, "The Labor Problem at Jamestown, 1607–18," *American Historical Review*, 76 (1971): 595–611, especially pp. 598–599.

[15] Carl Bridenbaugh, *Vexed and Troubled Englishmen, 1590–1642* (New York: Oxford University Press, 1968), pp. 395–400, 464–465, 474–476.

[16] *Nova Britannia* (1609).

[17] Winthrop, "Generall considerations for the plantation in New England," in *Winthrop Papers*, ed. A. B. Forbes, vol. 2 (Boston: Massachusetts Historical Society, 1931), pp. 117–118.

THE HUMAN DIMENSION

All of the foregoing considerations refer to matters of public policy: the interests of commerce, national power, population as a policy concern. But there was also the individual emigrant; there was the human dimension, the motives and aspirations of the people who went. In the Iberian countries, a role in the conquest and settlement of the New World opened a rare opportunity for the younger sons of noble families, for artisans seeking to raise their status in a stratified social order, for farmers and other middling sorts who perceived the chance to find wealth and a place in the colonial elite. There were also servants who went or were taken along. The migration was individual, for the most part, and included a sizable proportion of Jews and other non-Catholics, as well as non-Spaniards, in the case of the colonization of Spanish territory after the Conquest; by evading exclusionist legislation that would have barred them from immigration, they found a more open situation than was their fate in Old World society with its tighter restrictions and status constraints. In the English colonies, the same sorts of motivations attracted thousands to a new start; but there was also substantial group migration, both of religious character and of a looser sort, such as the Scotch-Irish and German migrations into the middle colonies of America in the eighteenth century.

In the American mainland colonies, thousands of others came as indentured servants, or they were "transported" for crimes they were accused of having committed. In either case they were bound by indentures or contracts that required their services for a specified period of years. But millions also came in chains. From 1451 to 1600, according to the best estimates available, some 125,000 blacks were taken from Africa to Portuguese and Spanish possessions in the New World. During the period 1601–1700, 1.3 million Africans were carried across the Atlantic, a sizable proportion of this group to British and French colonies; and in the eighteenth century, the number rose again to almost 2 million. Their fate as a people varied according to the place they were taken. In the Caribbean, they faced grinding and merciless labor in the sugar fields, high disease rates, ruthless discipline; and the charnel house of the Indies meant the need for a constant flow of slaves to replenish the supply of labor, attenuated as it was because of failure under such conditions to reproduce and because of the high death rate. In North and South America,

though their material condition was often much better, the black population suffered what one historian has termed "deculturation": Africans from a variety of cultures, speaking different languages, were thrown together on plantations, and group cohesion was lost.[18] In English North America there was less interracial marriage or widespread miscegenation than in the Spanish and Portuguese colonies; but blacks reproduced, formed families with high birth rates, and increased their numbers by reproduction as well as by replenishment through the slave trade.

Wherever the African was transported, the central reality was enslavement. It is one of the great achievements of human history that wherever black people could survive physically in the New World, they sustained their collective vitality well enough over several centuries to keep constant pressure on the social systems that had enslaved them. In this perspective, the winning of individual emancipation, the intermarriage into many of Latin America's societies of mixed blood, the independence of spirit and self-maintenance won by the "free Negroes" who mastered artisan crafts or became tradesmen, the resistance to various aspects of slavery which forced white society to contend with the black presence in a thousand ways, the sustaining of racial identity itself, all were the enduring measures of achievement—often amid the most appalling conditions of material life, of which scattered instances of slave rebellion were only the most dramatic manifestation. These were a people whose life was outside the conceptual framework of motives for the colonization of America. That the historian of Africans in the New World must take account of "the explosive tensions of slavery . . . knit into the political, social and economic structure"[19] of the New World reflects the continuing vitality of this vast unwilling migration from across the South Atlantic.

It is not easy to determine with any accuracy the proportion of weight to be given to the various influences leading to American colonization. Individuals differed in their motives, and influences that carried weight in one period

---

[18]Charles Gibson, *Spain in America* (New York: Harper & Row, 1966), pp. 114–116. The estimates of numbers of slaves taken from Africa to the New World are from Philip D. Curtin, *The Atlantic Slave Trade: A Census* (Madison: University of Wisconsin Press, 1969), p. 268.

[19]Patrick Richardson, *Empire and Slavery* (1968, reprinted New York: Harper & Row, 1971), p. 13.

may have been of little importance in another. The numerous propaganda pamphlets written to encourage colonization attempted to include all arguments and to appeal to all men. In the end, however, it is safe to say that the underlying motive for interest in America on the part of the great majority—whether king, noble, or commoner—was the economic. On the part of the merchant adventurer it was profit, on that of the humble white emigrant a chance to find in the New World opportunities for a better life.

SELECTED READINGS

*Albion, Robert G., ed., *Exploration and Discovery* (New York: Macmillan, 1965).

*Andrews, Charles M., *The Colonial Background of the American Revolution* (New Haven: Yale University Press, 1924).

*Cipolla, Carlo M., *Guns, Sails, and Empires, . . . 1400–1700* (New York: Minerva Press, 1965).

*Clark, George N., *The Seventeenth Century,* 2nd ed. (New York: Oxford University Press, 1961).

*Davis, Ralph, *The Rise of the Atlantic Economies* (Ithaca: Cornell University Press, 1973).

*Eccles, W. J., *France in America* (New York: Harper & Row, 1972).

*Gibson, Charles, *Spain in America* (New York: Harper & Row, 1966).

Lynch, John, *Spain under the Hapsburgs,* Volume II: *Spain and America, 1598–1700* (New York: Oxford University Press, 1969).

Morison, Samuel Eliot, *The European Discovery of America* (2 volumes, New York: Oxford University Press, 1971, 1974).

Nettels, Curtis Putnam, *The Roots of American Civilization,* 2nd ed. (Englewood Cliffs, N.J.: Prentice Hall, 1963).

*Notestein, Wallace, *The English People on the Eve of Colonization, 1603–1630* (New York: Harper & Row, 1954).

*Nowell, Charles E., *The Great Discoveries and the First Colonial Empires* (Ithaca: Cornell University Press, 1954).

*Parry, J. H., *The Establishment of the European Hegemony, 1415–1715* (New York: Harper & Row, 1961).

*Reynolds, Robert L., *Europe Emerges: Transition Toward an Industrial World-Wide Society, 600–1750* (Madison: University of Wisconsin Press, 1967).

Rich, E. E., and Wilson, C. H., *The Economy of Expanding Europe,* Volume IV: *The Cambridge Economic History of Europe,* M. Postan and H. J. Habakkuk, eds. (Cambridge, England: The University Press, 1967).

*Rowse, A. L., *The Expansion of Elizabethan England* (New York: Harper & Row, 1965).

Sauer, Carl O., *Sixteenth Century North America* (Berkeley: University of California Press, 1971).

The principal competitors in the European struggle for North America were Spain, France, Holland, and England. Each of the four planted colonies in the territory that is now the United States mainland. In addition, other countries— notably Denmark, Sweden, and Russia — at one time or another tried to establish themselves politically or at least commercially in the New World. The Spanish ruled in Mexico and Central America, and they divided control of South America with Portugal, which established hegemony in Brazil. Our focus here will be a comparison of colonization systems and the relative success of the four major powers. But in isolating the Spanish, French, Dutch, and English enterprises for purposes of historical analysis, we must also keep in mind the broader context of maritime and commercial competition, which often brought the European powers into sharp conflict with one another and shaped in large measure the diplomatic and military history of Europe.

THE COLONIAL SYSTEM OF SPAIN

In the first two decades of Spain's colonial effort in the New World, the real base of Spanish power and economic activity remained in the Caribbean. Ranches, mines, and plantations were established on the West Indies islands. A policy of "pacifying" the Indians by force and terror, reducing them to slavery as their population declined with horrifying swiftness by disease, war, and impoverishment, was by 1518 complemented by the introduction of African slaves. Not least important to the future of Spanish America, the Indies, most notably Cuba, became a base from which expeditions set out to explore and probe the Central American coast, Florida, and the northeastern rim of South America.

Then, in 1519, Spain began the second phase of its assault in the New World by launching expeditions to penetrate the mainland and bring its vast native populations under Spanish control. There followed the spectacular conquests in Mexico in 1521 and Peru in 1533. By 1540 Spain had extended its dominance to the entire Mexican mainland and Central America, and by the 1570s Spanish control of the ancient Inca dominions in Peru had also been consolidated. From their mainland colonies the Spanish then moved toward selective control of other areas in South America, concentrating attention on territories with large Indian populations that could be used as labor and on areas with precious metals or other attractive resources.

Colonial economic life

Like the statesmen of all the major European powers, Spain's leaders sought to bring under close governmental regulation the major features of economic life in the colonies. The Spanish brand of mercantilism, a policy of control and regulation designed to make the colonial economies complementary in production to the home country's economy and to generate new wealth on which national power could be built, was a peculiarly thoroughgoing one: The Spanish system of laws and of administration expressed a vision of comprehensive control. From 1503 until 1717, for example, Spain required most of the commerce to and from its colonies to pass through the hands of authorized groups of merchants in Seville who enjoyed an official monopoly. On the American side of the Atlantic there were only limited official ports of entry, at first Vera Cruz on the Mexican coast and Porto Bello on the Panamanian isthmus, the former to be the funnel for all trade with Mexico and Guatemala and the latter for commerce with South America.

The transatlantic trade

As the tide of Spain's trade with America began to rise, carrying sugar, hides, precious metals, and other products to the home country in exchange for manufactured goods and foodstuffs from Spain, the home government imposed increasingly strict regulations upon the ships that carried this commerce. Each year, beginning in the mid-sixteenth century, two fleets of merchant ships—the annual "convoys"—would sail from Spain under the protection of warships, one fleet landing its cargoes in the West Indies and the other proceeding to the mainland ports of entry. Foreign ships and traders were legally excluded from Spanish America, although Genoese merchants and bankers actually exercised a large measure of control from their privileged base in Seville's commerce; and there was persistent "interloper" activity by ships under foreign flags, evading Spain's mercantilist laws.

Commerce was further restricted by the granting of monopolies on gunpowder, salt, tobacco, and quicksilver, by excises levied on goods sold, by export and import duties averaging perhaps 15 percent, and by the king's royalty of one-fifth on the yield of the gold and silver mines. In the colonies the culture of olives, grapes, tobacco, and hemp was forbidden, and intercolonial trade was restricted. The entire system was highly artificial and was seriously undermined by wholesale smuggling after the English and Dutch had obtained footholds in the West Indies and England had, through an agreement reached in 1713, secured the monopoly of the African slave trade with Spanish America.

Mining and agriculture

A disproportionate emphasis may easily be placed on the part played by gold and silver in the economic life of Spanish America. Although they formed the chief items of export, the Spanish government was not indifferent to the establishment of agricultural colonies, nor were the colonists wholly occupied with extracting the precious metals. A great majority of the population lived by farming and ranching, the products of which, including hides, corn, the American aloe or agave, tomatoes, sugar, cocoa, vanilla, and cochineal, were more valuable than those of the mines. Around the two basic industries, mining and agriculture, was built up a prosperous and even wealthy civilization while the English and French to the north were still struggling to maintain a bare existence.

Labor and taxation

Instead of exterminating or driving away the Indians as the English settlers later did, the Spaniards in Mexico, Central America, and South America sought to subjugate the native peoples (though in the process they exterminated a large proportion of them) and force them to work for the Spanish settlers.

The economic unit of early Spanish America was the *encomienda,* a grant of land carrying with it the authority to command the services of a certain number of Indians. Begun by Columbus in the West Indies, the system was later extended and applied almost universally on the mainland. Under this system the Indians were forced to till the crops, tend the cattle, and work the mines for their Spanish overlords. While efforts were made to limit the duration of the *encomienda* system and detailed regulations were issued concerning the treatment of the Indians, forbidding their enslavement and urging their conversion to Christianity, it was to be expected that under such a system the natives would be reduced to serfs and often be subjected to the most cruel treatment.

In addition, the Spaniards used members of the Indian nobility as lower officials in colonial governments, thus penetrating directly into the core of the native society and expediting a system of tribute and taxation that still further drained Indian energies and resources. As Indian labor fell short of Spain's needs, the home country turned to the slave trade. From this source came massive infusions of new workers to carry forward Spanish colonial mining, ranching, and plantation enterprises.

The rise of self-sufficiency

While the result was a vast increase in the production of the New World for purposes of export to Europe, there were also some disappointments for Spanish mercantilist designs.

Hides, gold and silver, sugar, and dyes, as well as more exotic substances such as medicines formerly unknown in Europe, helped Spain's American colonies to fulfill their designated role of supplying the home country with goods complementary to Spain's own economy; this was true throughout much of the sixteenth century. But thereafter, the American colonies became increasingly self-sufficient in foodstuffs (even grain had been imported from Spain in the early period); commerce within and between the colonies increased in volume as cities grew up in the Spanish colonial territories. And, soon, textiles and other goods manufactured by artisans and craftsmen were also available from colonial producers.

The rise of colonial autonomy

The rising degree of economic autonomy in Spanish America was matched by an increasing pressure by the emergent colonial élite to win a greater voice in directing their own societies' public policies. A host of special interests contended with one another for advantages, and the Spanish home government had to make numerous concessions to hold the loyalty of the colonial élite. The colonists, in turn, needed to temporize and compromise in order to retain important privileges, social and political status, and the marketing arrangements that sustained their wealth. In these respects, Spain in the seventeenth century experienced what England would confront at a later time in its dealings with its North American colonies. The Spanish maintained political control partly by what amounted to "salutary neglect" of their own commerical laws: The principles of mercantilism gave way to a pragmatic bargaining relationship in which the colonials were permitted to ignore or evade many trade restrictions. In this sense as well, the relationship between Spain and Spanish America reflected tensions, adjustments, and compromises that the other European nations would, in varying measures, eventually have to accept as the price of their own survival as colonizing powers in America.

Unlike England at the time of the American Revolution, however, Spain in the seventeenth century had to make its imperial adjustments against a background of economic stagnation in the home country, and a staggering decline in even the absolute volume of trade with its colonies.[1] "The sick man of Europe," Spain held onto its American possessions despite additional political troubles at home.

FRANCE IN AMERICA

Almost a century elapsed after the voyage of Verrazano before the first permanent French settlement was made at Quebec in 1608, but the genius of the French for exploration and their talent for dominion were notably demonstrated in the succeeding years. Dominated by patriotism, missionary zeal, and a desire to open up more territory to French traders, priests and explorers pushed their canoes up the St. Lawrence, along the Great Lakes, and down the Mississippi, until by the end of the century French posts extended from New Orleans at the mouth of the Mississippi to Fort Radisson near the western end of Lake Superior, and east to Nova Scotia.

The fur trade

The success of the French as colonizers did not measure up to their attainments as explorers and missionaries. The French as a whole cared little for colonization, and the persecuted Protestants, who might have been eager to emigrate, were forbidden to come. The most important cause of failure, however, probably lay in the source of economic wealth. The economic backbone of New France was the fur trade. To Frenchmen with initiative, the harsh climate and stubborn soil of the St. Lawrence Valley made little appeal. The back country was rich in furs, and in the pursuit of them they penetrated ever farther into the interior. Adaptable in the extreme, these Frenchmen would often affect the manners and dress of the Indians, live with them, and intermarry with them. This won for the French not only the bulk of the fur trade but the friendship of practically all of the Indian tribes, with the exception of the Iroquois. If wealth was to be gained in New France, it must be through furs, and noble and peasant alike engaged in the business. At least a third of the French population was occupied in gathering and transporting furs.

As the fur trade was the principal source of wealth, so it proved also to be the chief cause of weakness for the colony. So long as greater profits were to be made in pelts, it was difficult

[1]See John Lynch, *Spain Under the Hapsburgs,* vol. 2: *Spain and the Americas, 1598–1700* (New York: Oxford University Press, 1969), pp. 184–193.

to interest settlers in agriculture, and the safest basis for a permanent colony was thus lacking. Instead of the 1.3 million inhabitants that the English colonies boasted in 1754, more than nine-tenths of whom were engaged in agriculture, compactly settled along a fringe of seacoast and firmly established, the French had only about 80,000 scattered along the rivers and Great Lakes from the Mississippi to Nova Scotia. Beyond the barest necessities of subsistence, agriculture was neglected. There was some attention to fisheries, but practically no manufactures other than household goods in New France.

Colonial feudalism

From 1600 to 1663 the efforts of the French to colonize and exploit the American mainland were in the hands of commercial companies, the most famous of which was known as the Hundred Associates. After that date the administration was taken over by the crown, and a government characterized by extreme absolutism and centralization was set up. To make complete the replica of the autocratic system of France in the New World, an order of nobility was created by Richelieu in the charter of the Hundred Associates. To induce members of the lesser nobility to remain in America, seigniories were granted them along the lake and river fronts. On the seigniories, the peasant settlers usually lived on a road perhaps a half mile back of the river or lake, with their fields sloping down to the water on one side and back into the forest on the other.

With the seigniories went the rest of the paraphernalia of feudalism. The tenant was expected to pay rent to the seignior (trifling, to be sure, and generally in produce), to work for the lord a certain number of days a year, to patronize his grist mill, to present to him one fish out of every eleven caught, and to render other feudal dues. Although remnants of this system outlasted the English conquest by half a century, the conditions in New France, in contrast to the situation in Spanish America, were not such as feudalism would thrive on. With plenty of vacant land and the fur trade to beckon them on, any attempt to impose a strict feudal system upon the inhabitants was doomed to failure, and the duties of the peasant to the seignior became more nominal than real.

With their trade shackled by petty restrictions and controlled by government monopoly, it is little wonder that private enterprise in industry was smothered and that Canada never prospered under France. This institutional and economic background goes far to explain the eventual conquest of New France by the British.

THE DUTCH IN AMERICA

The efforts of the Dutch to participate in the profits of the American trade led eventually to their settlement of the Hudson Valley. In 1609, in the interests of the Dutch East India Company, Henry Hudson had explored the river that bears his name, and a trading post called New Amsterdam had been established in 1614 by some enterprising merchants of Amsterdam. In 1621 Dutch interests in America were taken over by the Dutch West India Company, a great private corporation to which the States-General of Holland granted a monopoly of the trade not only of the American seaboard but also of the coast of Africa south of the Tropic of Cancer. This corporation, interested in trade in gold, slaves, and tropical products, equipping hundreds of privateers and supporting an army and a large navy with which it made war upon Spain and Portugal, found the fur trade of the Hudson Valley but a small item in its numerous enterprises. The valley consequently absorbed but a small part of the interest of the directors.

Yet in spite of the company's lack of interest in the Hudson Valley, much was done there in the way of trade and colonization. The first Dutch settlers came in 1624 to Fort Orange, site of the present Albany, and to Manhattan Island in 1626; and settlements were made later not only in the Hudson Valley but in the Mohawk Valley, on Long Island, and along Delaware Bay. The West India Company, however, was intent upon accumulating dividends and was not interested primarily in settling the country. The greatest profits were to be made in furs, and upon the promotion of the fur trade the chief energies of the company and its representatives were bent. Later shipbuilding was carried on to some extent, and eventually prosperous agricultural communities grew up.

Patroonships

The first farming in New Netherlands seems to have been done not by tenants but by servants working for the company, which owned both the land and the stock upon it. After trading posts had been established, the company became more interested in stimulating settlement, and a scheme of landed proprietors was introduced in 1629. Any member of the company who would bring over fifty persons at his own expense would receive a large tract of land; and a number of wealthy Dutchmen, including the Amsterdam jeweler Killian Van Rensselaer, carved out huge estates in the Hudson Valley. Upon these grantees, or patroons, were bestowed both proprietary rights and subordinate jurisdiction. The patroons could hold manorial courts, found townships, and appoint officials for them. Upon their estates they had the monopoly of weaving and certain exclusive trading privileges. Here too, as in New France and New Spain, an attempt was made to graft on the New World the feudal system of Europe. Under this system the most influential members of the company soon gained control of the choicest lands in the Hudson Valley. Here we have the origin of the large landed estates that existed in New York until well into the nineteenth century, the cause of the "antirent wars" of the 1830s and 1840s.

Small farmers

The patroon system was exceedingly unpopular from the start, and in 1640 the company attempted to modify it by reducing the extent of the patroonships and introducing a class of smaller proprietor who was to hold 200 acres tilled by five men brought over at his expense. Again in 1650 a further effort was made to increase the number of small farmers. A tract of land with implements and stock was granted to the settler, with the understanding that he pay a fixed rent and return the stock or its equivalent

at the end of six years. In general the agricultural products and life were similar to those found in New England, although the big plantations along the Hudson and Delaware Bay, where tobacco was a favorite crop, resembled those of Virginia. (See below, pp. 52–53.)

The end of Dutch rule

The centralized despotism of the government of New Netherlands in the period before 1629 was modified after the introduction of the patroon system, but the principle of representative government was not recognized in New Netherlands until the closing years of Dutch occupation. At the same time the loss in efficiency and unity of control under a semifeudal patroon system made the colony more susceptible to foreign conquest. Driven like a wedge between the English colonies in New England and the South, the strategic territory of New Netherlands was naturally regarded jealously by Great Britain. In fact, English settlers were beginning to filter in from the east, many seeking the religious toleration that the Dutch were the first to recognize in America and which Englishmen had sought in vain in all of New England except Rhode Island. This influx of English, combined with the lack of interest on the part of the company at home, the corrupt and despotic government in the colony, and the growing sea power of Great Britain, led to the final conquest of New Netherlands in 1664. When the English captured the colony it contained a population of about 5,000, composed of immigrants from France, Germany, and a dozen other nations as well as from Holland and the British Isles.

EARLY ENGLISH COLONIZATION

England in the age of Elizabeth was ripe for exploration and colonization. The strong Tudor monarchy had destroyed the strength of the feudal nobility, broken the political and economic power of the Catholic church, and admitted to titled rank men whose minds were occupied with trade and commerce. With the growing strength of the national government and with a rapidly expanding economic life there developed an independent, self-reliant population eager for gain and commercial development, keen to challenge the maritime domination of Spain, and full of confidence in the destiny of England. While English sea captains like Sir John Hawkins and Sir Francis

Drake roamed the Spanish Main to bait their enemy, capture his bullion, and sack his cities, more serious imperialists were dreaming of establishing plantations in the western wilderness. Men like Richard Hakluyt preserved the voyages of English sailors in print, wrote pamphlets to point out the social, economic, and political advantages to England of foreign possessions, and inflamed the minds of rich and poor with prospects of comfort and wealth to be gained by adventure abroad.

Royal patents

Just as private individuals had borne the burden of propagandizing for English expan-

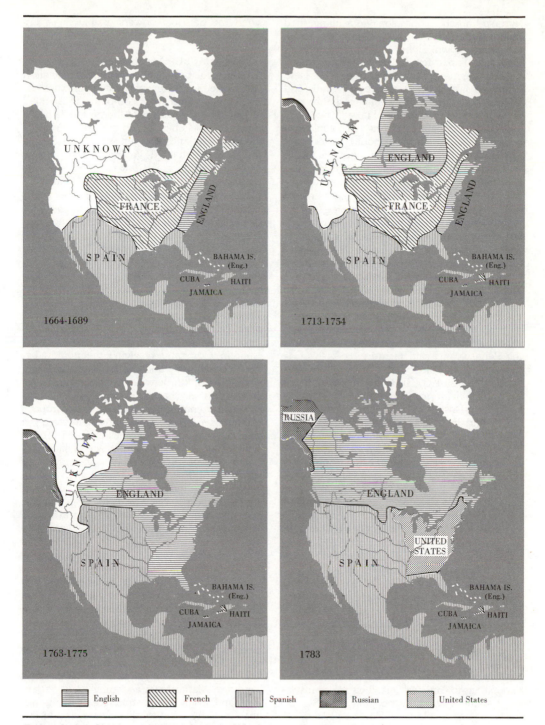

Figure 3–1. Changes in Political Control of North America, 1664–1783.

sion, so English colonization was accomplished by private initiative and with little or no aid from the British crown. Henry VIII and his daughter Elizabeth Tudor favored overseas expansion but did little more. The Stuart kings James I and Charles I were always in need of funds and engaged in a continuous wrangle with their parliaments over the question of taxes. They were nevertheless sincerely interested in colonization if it could be carried on without cost to them. The English kings held to the theory that title to and political jurisdiction over newly discovered or settled lands were vested in the sovereign. To preserve this title, but at the same time to encourage expansion, they were willing to grant to properly accredited persons (usually favorites of the crown) royal patents or charters to settle and exploit the new lands. This arrangement might serve to protect their rights and to increase the power and wealth of the nation and themselves, but at the same time it involved no direct cost to themselves or their government.

From the first patent granted to the Italian captain known as John Cabot in 1496 down to the Pennsylvania settlement in 1682, this was the general policy followed. Cabot, whose voyages (1497–1498) laid the foundation for England's claim to North America, was financed by Bristol and London merchants. To Cabot and his sons and heirs was given the right of a monopoly to whatever trade they might develop with the regions discovered, except that the king was to receive a fifth of the profits. When Englishmen almost a century later (1578) again turned their attention to colonization, Elizabeth granted to that model knight Sir Humphrey Gilbert the exclusive right to "inhabit and possess at his choice all remote and heathen lands not in the possession of any Christian prince," but the crown was to receive "the fifth part of all the oare of golde or silver" that might be obtained. Gilbert made two voyages. His first expedition was scattered by a storm; his second, in 1583, planted a small colony only in Newfoundland which soon disappeared.

In 1584 Elizabeth passed on to Gilbert's half brother, Sir Walter Raleigh, the rights conferred in the early charter. Raleigh dispatched five expeditions to America, but all his efforts resulted in failure. His third expedition, in 1587, actually planted a colony on Roanoke Island, off the coast of Virginia, but this colony vanished because of the failure of England to support the infant enterprise. His efforts demonstrated that the initial stage of colonization was a task beyond the personal powers of any single Englishman.

The joint-stock companies

As a result of Raleigh's failure, the next effort was made by a group of capitalists through the medium of a joint-stock company. These men, inflamed by the success of the East India trade, dreamed of establishing an outpost in America where traders and gold hunters might duplicate the success attained in India. The Virginia charter of 1606 created two companies, one consisting of "certain Knights, Gentlemen, Merchants, and other Adventurers, of our city of London and elsewhere," and the other "Sundry Knights, Gentlemen, Merchants, and other Adventurers, of our cities of Bristol and Exeter, and of our town of Plymouth." These two groups of stockholders—substantial businessmen of the day, many of whom had made similar investments in mercantile ventures organized on a joint-stock-company basis—were known as the London and Plymouth companies. The crown bestowed upon them the Atlantic coast of the present United States, the London Company receiving the portion between parallels 34 and 38, the Plymouth Company the portion between parallels 41 and 45. In issuing their charters, King James I thus followed the common practice of the European monarchs in transferring to private interests the financial risks and responsibilities of an overseas venture. In return for the privilege of title and a large measure of governing power over their territories, the companies were expected to serve as intermediaries for the settlement of their grants (that is, as colonizing agents), which in turn would enhance England's trade and wealth, and extend English power in the world arena.

The Jamestown settlement

The reciprocal relations and obligations of crown and company were spelled out further in 1609. The London Company had encountered great difficulty in development of the settlement it first made, in 1607, at Jamestown in present-day Virginia. Jamestown had experienced an extended time of troubles: the home company was sending large numbers of settlers whom the Jamestown economy could not absorb and sustain, food shortages were chronic, the company failed to obtain much productive labor from the settlers (partly because of undernourishment and sickness, partly because they came, many of them, expecting to rely upon the labor of Indians or servants hired from

England), and the home company ran into money problems. In 1609 the crown agreed to separate the two companies. It converted the Virginia enterprise into a genuine joint-stock venture, the company to raise capital by the sale of shares, the revenues from which would be used to transport settlers and servants under contract. The crown, in turn, exempted the company from certain customs duties and taxes for a limited time.

Virginia became a "charnel house," as the historian Edmund S. Morgan has said: Between 1618 and 1624 death claimed between three and four thousand Englishmen there.[2] The population was only about 1500 in 1624–1625. Moreover, the promoters' hopes of founding a colony where poor and middling sorts of people might live comfortably and enhance the wealth of both England and the company were shattered by persistent shortages of food. Tobacco was the chief cause. The Jamestown settlement became an early-day "boom town" based on tobacco cultivation. People came to make quick fortunes in tobacco, often with no intention of staying permanently themselves; and they generated an insatiable demand for labor. The company attempted to meet this demand by transporting servants to Virginia in large numbers, despite the notorious lack of adequate food supplies and housing there.

An Anglo-American variant of the Spanish *encomienda* system was finally resorted to, as the Virginia company granted to its chief officers in Virginia not only land but also allocations of servants as tenants. The wretched exploitation of these people by ships' captains who packed them into overloaded vessels, by the planters, and by the company itself finally disgraced the whole enterprise.[3] Plunged into bankruptcy even though private fortunes had been made by many individuals, the company folded and lost its charter in 1624. The experiment with company direction was at an end, and the crown took over the whole enterprise.

Virginia's early experience made some enduring contributions to Anglo-American settlement. It witnessed the beginnings of self-government, as in 1619 it had organized the first English assembly in America; it demonstrated the viability of tobacco production for export and helped supply a booming market for that commodity in the home country; and it also laid

the foundations of what became the slave plantation system, first through the grinding exploitation of English indentured servants and then by the mid-1620s through the beginnings of the African slave trade.

The Plymouth settlement

A less melancholy legacy was left by the similar company venture at Plymouth, now part of Massachusetts. This community was settled by a small band of Separatists seeking a religious refuge where they might also sustain themselves economically. In 1620 the Pilgrims, as they came to be called, obtained a charter from the Virginia Company after reorganization of the old London companies. Seventy London merchants subscribed £7000 to finance the venture, and the emigrants themselves were also stockholders who would share in any profits. In addition, the settlers enjoyed substantial rights of self-government, by dint of the compact they drew up for themselves (the Mayflower Compact). The tiny settlement survived by farming and fishing and by the profits of the fur trade. From the time their first group landed on the *Mayflower* until 1624, Plymouth's settlers suffered famines and other troubles, but the abolition of communal landholding in 1623 increased production incentives, and by 1627, when the colonists severed their ties with the original investors in England, Plymouth was well established. By 1660 its population was 3000.

The Massachusetts Bay Colony

Plymouth was eventually absorbed by the strong Massachusetts Bay Company, whose charter had been obtained in 1629 for commercial purposes, and whose stockholders were chiefly Puritan merchants. The pronounced High Church tendency of Charles I and his attempt at tyrannical government, which began in earnest in 1629 with the dissolution of Parliament and the imprisonment of those who opposed his policies, gave a different turn to the activities of the company. To many of the leading Puritans, Massachusetts appeared as an ideal refuge from the hostile policies of the king. Since they belonged to the ruling classes at home, they were unwilling to emigrate as the servants of a plantation company. Consequently they bought up the stock of the Massachusetts Bay Company, took over its charter, and pledged themselves to emigrate. Thus we find Massachusetts Bay settled by the controlling members of the company itself and its form of government in the early years comparing rather

[2]Edmund S. Morgan, "The First American Boom: Virginia, 1618 to 1630," *William and Mary Quarterly*, 3rd ser., 28 (1971): 169–198.
    [3]Ibid.

strikingly to that of a modern corporation. The freemen, for example, may be compared to the stockholders, and the governor, deputy governor, and 18 assistants may be compared to the president, vice president, and board of directors. The place of meeting was not stipulated in the charter, so that it was possible to transfer the whole corporation to America. The great migration of 1630–1640 brought to Massachusetts more than 20,000 settlers, amid religious strife and gathering political troubles in England; some 65,000 English migrated to North America and the West Indies in that decade.

As in Virginia during its early period of settlement, Massachusetts suffered to some degree from food shortages. The colony at first relied upon England for supplies—paid for with the profits of a fur trade that tapped nearly the entire central and western New England region. But the immigration itself drove up prices and opened up handsome opportunities for men of commerce: It was in the 1630s that Boston emerged quickly as the major entrepôt through which English goods were channeled to the newer towns being established in a growing hinterland. Boston's merchants, largely transplanted London tradesmen of middling means, formed a distinct group in a Puritan commonwealth whose citizens came mainly from country districts, and who sought to re-create the village and farming life they had known in the Old World.

In 1640 the great immigration to New England suddenly ended, and in the next decade the Massachusetts economy was forced into a new orientation. The mercantile elite led the way toward a new basis of prosperity, exploiting the market offered by the swiftly growing West Indies sugar plantations for the exports available from New England farms and forests and fisheries. By the 1650s this new trade connection was well established, and New England was also exporting masts cut from giant pine trees to the home country, carrying in American ships the sugar of the British, French, and other West Indies islands to Europe, and providing shipping services for American exports of tobacco and fish as well as garden products and grain. All this, in turn, expedited a process of capital formation out of the commercial profits that accrued to the merchant group; the earnings of trade and shipping became available for reinvestment in ship construction, in the fishing industry, in iron manufacture, and, not least important, in lands of New England's interior.

In sum, New England had carved out a place for itself by 1660 in the commercial revolution that was then gathering momentum in Europe and in the wider world of Atlantic trade and colonization. Provisioning emigrants, supplying the sugar islands of the West Indies, building ships for the rising trade between Europe and the New World, marketing the manufactured goods of the home country in American towns, and carrying the products of the southern colonies' plantations to overseas markets, all would become central elements of the New England regional economy during the century that followed. And all these elements had already become vital components of the region's economic life in the seventeenth century.[4]

LATER ENGLISH COLONIZATION

Virginia and Plymouth were, as we have seen, colonized by commercial companies. They bore the brunt of settling a strange land far from the base of supplies. Subsequent English settlements were founded not only by chartered companies but also by two other agencies: (1) migrating groups from existing colonies and (2) wealthy proprietors. Examples of the first of these are Connecticut, Rhode Island, and parts of New Hampshire and Maine.

The little fishing settlements of Maine and New Hampshire were colonized in part by emigrants from England under the protection of Sir Fernando Gorges and Captain John Mason, who had received patents for this region, and in part by inhabitants of Massachusetts Bay, who by 1652 were successful in extending the government of Massachusetts over the new country. The colonies of Rhode Island and Connecticut were offshoots of Massachusetts Bay, the former settled by religious exiles and the latter by pioneer farmers in search of more fertile land. In 1636, on lands purchased from the Indians, Roger Williams established the democratic commonwealth of Rhode Island, where

---

[4]On economic change and the emergence of the merchant élite, see Bernard Bailyn, *The New England Merchants in the Seventeenth Century* (1955, reprinted New York: Torchbooks, Harper & Row, 1964).

TABLE 3–1. POPULATION OF THE NORTH AMERICAN MAINLAND COLONIES 1630–1770 (THOUSANDS OF PERSONS).[1]

COLONY	1630	1660	1700	1740	1770
Massachusetts (including Plymouth)	1.3	21.9	55.9	151.6	235.3
New Hampshire	0.5	1.6	5.0	23.3	62.4
Connecticut	—	8.0	26.0	89.6	183.9
Rhode Island	—	1.5	5.9	25.3	58.2
New York	0.4	4.9	19.1	63.7	162.9
New Jersey	—	—	14.0	51.4	117.4
Pennsylvania	—	—	18.0	85.6	240.1
Delaware	—	0.5	2.5	19.9	35.5
Maryland	—	8.4	29.6	116.1	202.6
Virginia	2.5	27.0	58.6	180.4	463.0
North Carolina	—	1.0	10.7	51.8	197.2
South Carolina	—	—	5.7	45.0	124.2
Georgia	—	—	—	2.0	23.4
Total Population	4.6	75.1	250.9	905.6	2148.1
Proportion Black	1%	4%	11%	13%	21%

Source: U.S. Department of Commerce, Bureau of the Census, *Historical Statistics of the United States, Colonial Times to 1957* (Washington: U.S. Government Printing Office, 1960), p. 756.

[1]Excludes native Indian population.

for the first time in America religious freedom was put into practice. The settlers of neither Rhode Island nor Connecticut had legal title to the land under English law, but both succeeded eventually in securing charters confirming their occupation.

Proprietary colonies

Under the proprietary system the king granted a single individual (or a group, as in the Carolinas) an estate in America that might be colonized and held by him practically as a feudal lord under the king with very extensive powers and rights, but in most cases with the restraining provision that he must make laws "by and with the consent of the freemen." The most important experiments were those of William Penn in Pennsylvania and the Calverts in Maryland. New York for a time (1665–1685, with the exception of 1673–1674, when it was recaptured by the Dutch) was a proprietary colony of the Duke of York, who handed over New Jersey to his friends Sir George Carteret and Sir John Berkeley. New Jersey, most of which came under the control of the Quakers until it was taken over as a crown colony in 1702, was settled chiefly by men attracted from the surrounding regions by the liberal land offers.

The Carolinas were occupied either by Virginia frontiersmen pushing south or by immigrants direct from England. They were granted (1663) by Charles II to eight proprietors, the most active of whom was Anthony Ashley Cooper, later Earl of Shaftesbury. Proprietary rule in the Carolinas came to an end in 1729. Georgia, the last of the 13 colonies, was founded in 1733, partly as a result of the desire of the British government to set up a buffer state against the Spanish in Florida, and partly through the philanthropic desire to help English debtors commence life anew. For these reasons a charter was given to a group of trustees in 1732, who were to be in control for 21 years. But few of the class for whom the colony was founded came, and the population grew slowly.

LAND TENURE IN THE COLONIES

Despite Indian occupation, European monarchs assumed that the land of the Americas belonged to them. In turn they granted it under certain conditions to joint-stock companies, to individual proprietors, to groups of proprietors as in the case of the Carolinas, or to groups of trustees as in Georgia. It was inevitable, as we have seen in New France, New Netherlands, and New Spain, that attempts would be made to transplant aspects of the feudal system to America. It was the existing land system in Europe and the only system the colonists knew. It was also clear that such a system in the long run was bound to fail in the new settlements. For one thing, the country was too vast; any system that would restrict the amount of land held was certain to be unsuccessful, for there was too much vacant land that could be obtained by mere occupation. Moreover, the competition among proprietors for settlers was so great that it was impossible to impose onerous feudal dues. Furthermore, people who braved the dangers of frontier life demanded actual ownership. As a consequence, the quitrents of the proprietors were collected intermittently and with great difficulty, while laws restricting the amount of land that any single individual might own were generally evaded.

After attempts at cooperative agriculture failed in both Virginia and Massachusetts, they were followed by the parceling out of land. Eventually 100 acres were given in fee simple to each Virginia stockholder for each share owned upon the first division and another 100 acres per share when the grant was settled. A shareholder also received as a "head right" 50 acres for every person he might transport. This privilege was later extended to all residents. After 1705 the crown granted 50 acres for five shillings on condition that a house be built and three acres of land cultivated within three years. Thousands of acres were granted for meritorious service or through favoritism. The Virginia law was so easily evaded that by 1700 the average plantation consisted of 700 acres.

The usual system in New England was settlement under the group plan, in which a number of prospective settlers would secure from the general court a grant commonly of 36 square miles, upon which they would lay out a village, assign plots for homes and gardens, and later divide the arable and the pasture land. The land outside that owned in common was held ordinarily in *fee* simple (absolute ownership).

Penn and Baltimore, motivated by altruistic purposes, imposed small quitrents, but the competition for settlers in any event kept the quitrents low. This form of rent had originated in Europe as a money commutation of other

services, and was looked upon as a boon. In America, small as it might be, it was considered an unjust relic of a hated system. Penn offered 500 acres to anyone who would transport and "seat" his family, and was willing to sell 5000-acre tracts for £100 and to add 50 acres for each servant brought, but he reserved a quitrent of one shilling per 100 acres. In Maryland a settler was given 100 acres for himself, 100 more for his wife and for each servant, and 50 for each child. They were freehold grants subject to a rent of ten pounds of wheat per 50 acres. Anyone who would bring over five settlers was granted 1000 acres, subject to a quitrent of 20 shillings a year. Anyone bringing over more men received a larger grant, which might be divided up and sublet under the manorial usage. A man with a musket and six months' provisions might receive 150 acres in New Jersey, with a like amount for each servant or slave, and 75 additional acres for each woman—conditions so liberal that many came in from the nearby colonies. Somewhat similar offers were made in other colonies.

In spite of quitrents and other feudal regulations, the system of land disposal, as it actually developed, did not greatly hinder the steady expansion of the cultivated area. Nor did it prevent wide ownership of land among the population. It was, nevertheless, a source of much friction and discontent. The rent rolls of the crown and proprietors at the opening of the Revolution amounted to £37,500 annually, and about half of it was actually collected. Fortunately, primogeniture, entails, quitrents, and other appurtenances of the feudal system that prevailed in many of the colonies were all but abolished during or shortly after the Revolution.

The most unfortunate aspect of the colonial land system was the fact that it favored the building of large estates. It was by no means as democratic as it might appear. Early arrivals obtained the best land; the rest had to take what they could get on the frontier. In New England, influential favorites of the legislature often secured the choicest land with little effort or expenditure. This was a great era of land speculation, which favored the man close to the government, particularly if he had some capital with which to start. The ill effects of the land system were particularly accentuated in the South. Here it promoted social inequality, political corruption, and a landed aristocracy, at the same time hindering the westward advance of settlement. Landownership might be widely distributed but it was so uneven in amount that a class society existed from the start.

ON THE EVE OF EXPANSION

At the end of the seventeenth century, the English colonies in North America were at the threshold of a great expansionist period. But the achievements by 1700 were already considerable. The Chesapeake region, Virginia and Maryland, had become a major center of world tobacco production. Its tobacco exports were about half a million pounds in 1628, increased to nearly 10 million by the 1660s, and at the end of the century were averaging 35 million pounds annually.[5] The British West Indies had undergone a "sugar revolution," and so similarly had emerged as a major center for production of one of the chief commodities in world commerce. The rise of plantation agriculture in the sugar islands— by providing a market for foodstuffs and other products, as well as for slaves— in turn stimulated agriculture and trade in New England and the Middle Colonies.

Despite a slackening of immigration from the home country after 1640, the mainland colonies' populations continued to increase, reaching a quarter million by the century's end. Moreover, settlement in all the colonies was spreading gradually inland as the first frontier beyond the coastal region opened up. By 1700 the native Indian nations had been pushed back into the Piedmont region, and the bloody King Philip's War (1675–1676) had crushed Indian power in New England. A foothold of new settlement had been established in the Carolinas, separated by several hundred miles from the Chesapeake tobacco region of Virginia and Maryland.

Farther north, farming settlements surrounded the commercial entrepôts of Philadelphia, New York, and Boston. In those rising centers and in lesser commercial towns, a busy urban life occupied merchants, artisans and craftsmen, shippers and sailors. By the end of the seventeenth century the Anglo-Americans had nearly reached the point— in numbers of people, rising wealth, and diversity of economic activity— from which they could sustain a drive toward rising productivity and economic growth in the century ahead. Moreover, their institutions of government had developed in a direction that gave the colonial élite a significant measure of control over access to land, taxation policy, and other significant aspects of their society's economic life. The prosperity of the colonies was still highly dependent upon the general condition of the Atlantic economy, and, more particularly, upon the way in which English mercantilist regulation shaped the American connection with the Atlantic economy. But colonial institutions of government had already achieved a maturity that gave the Americans by 1700 significant leverage to pursue their own interests within the mercantilist legal framework.

SELECTED READINGS

NOTE: Many of the works listed in the selected readings for the previous chapter also deal with themes treated in this chapter.

*Andrews, Charles M., *The Colonial Period of American History* (4 vols., New Haven: Yale University Press, 1934–1938).

*Bailyn, Bernard, *The New England Merchants in the Seventeenth Century* (1955, reprinted New York: Harper & Row, 1964).

*Cespedes, Guillermo, *Latin America: The Early Years* (New York: Knopf, 1974).

Clowse, Converse D., *Economic Beginnings in Colonial South Carolina, 1607–1730* (Columbia, S.C.: University of South Carolina Press, 1971).

Condon, Thomas J., *New York Beginnings: The Commercial Origins of New Netherland* (New York: New York University Press, 1968).

*Craven, Wesley Frank, *The Colonies in Transition, 1660–1713* (New York: Harper & Row, 1968).

———, *The Southern Colonies in the Seventeenth Century, 1607–1689* (Baton Rouge: Louisiana State University Press, 1949).

[5]Lewis C. Gray, *History of Agriculture in the Southern United States to 1860,* 2 vols. (1933, reprinted Gloucester, Mass.: Peter Smith), vol. 1, p. 213.

*Dunn, Richard S., *Sugar and Slaves: The Rise of the Planter Class in the English West Indies, 1624–1713* (Chapel Hill: University of North Carolina Press, 1972).

*Goodman, Paul, ed., *Essays on American Colonial History,* 2nd ed., (New York: Holt, Rinehart and Winston, 1972).

Gray, Lewis C., *History of Agriculture in the Southern United States to 1860* (2 vols., 1933, reprinted Gloucester, Mass: Peter Smith, 1958).

Greven, Philip J., Jr., *Four Generations: Population, Land, and Family in Colonial Andover, Massachusetts* (Ithaca: Cornell University Press, 1970).

*Henretta, James A., *The Evolution of American Society, 1700–1815: An Interdisciplinary Analysis* (Lexington, Mass.: Heath, 1973).

*Leach, Douglas E., *The Northern Colonial Frontier, 1607–1763* (New York: Holt, Rinehart and Winston, 1966).

*Lockridge, Kenneth A., *A New England Town: The First Hundred Years* (New York: Norton, 1970).

Morgan, Edmund S., "The First American Boom: Virginia, 1618–1630," *William and Mary Quarterly,* 3rd series, XXVIII (1971).

———, "The Labor Problem at Jamestown, 1607–1618," *American Historical Review,* LXXVI (1971).

*Rutman, Darrett B., *Winthrop's Boston: A Portrait of a Puritan Town, 1630–1649* (Chapel Hill: University of North Carolina Press, 1965).

Ver Steeg, Clarence L., *The Formative Years, 1607–1763* (New York: Hill and Wang, 1964).

Waters, John J., "From Democracy to Demography: Recent Historiography on the New England Town," *Perspectives on Early American History,* Alden Vaughan and G. A. Billias eds., (New York: Harper & Row, 1973).

For the first two centuries after the English colonists settled the Atlantic coast, their economic life was heavily based on agriculture. In all the colonies, 85 to 90 percent of the population earned their living on the farms. The immigrants brought from Europe a body of farming technology that basically had not changed for centuries. They took from the native Indian peoples knowledge of American crops and techniques for their cultivation, thus blending the agriculture of the Old World with that of the New. Except for the large plantations that developed in the South, colonial agriculture was organized around family farms, and there was a changing mix of self-sufficient (diversified) production and the commercial production of cash crops. The farm-export trade was large, relative to production and income; intercolonial commerce was small in these relative terms, although the major trading cities on the seaboard provided an expanding domestic market for farm products. Industry was largely confined to hand manufacture in the home, called household manufacturing, and to the artisans' craft industries; production of iron, centering in Pennsylvania, was the major exception.

Economic development

It is difficult to obtain adequate statistics for reconstruction of the structure of income and wealth. But numerous historians have grappled with the documentation that does survive — wills and inventories of estates, tax valuation data, evidence of output trends that can be computed from export statistics or farm and plantation records and the like — and there is general agreement that the living standard of common farmers in seventeenth-century North America was better, on the average, than that of contemporary Europeans. Real per capita income seems to have remained stable, however, during the seventeenth century. In the eighteenth century, at least after 1720, there was probably an increase in the average per capita income of the colonists. Increased shipping earnings in the northern colonies, rising urbanization, and intensified capital formation in southern farming and industrial sectors (especially shipbuilding), all suggest that average real incomes rose, even as population increased.

The major regions varied in the character and rate of income change. Profiting from rising world prices for rice and indigo, and taking advantage of new techniques that probably raised productivity (that is, efficiency of production), the small colonies south of Virginia probably experienced a 15-year period of growth in real income at a 5 percent rate during 1720–1735, after which time income growth slackened until midcentury. The northern colonies seem to have registered equally impressive gains during 1745–1760, when grain prices, the impact of the West Indies market, and expansion of urban-based activities, including shipping, all worked in their favor. The 1745–1760 period also was one in which the large tobacco colonies (Virginia and Maryland) achieved a 2 to 3 percent annual real-income growth rate, as world prices for their export staple rose and a surge in credit extended to planters and merchants by the British enlarged the fund of capital available for agriculture and more efficiently organized commerce in exports. As a whole, during 1710–1775 the British colonies apparently achieved an average increase in per capita real income of about 0.5 percent a year. One informed scholarly estimate makes it as high as 1 percent a year, which would have meant that real income doubled during that period.[1]

Other scholars, however, have found evidence in localized studies of communities in New England and the Middle Colonies that while average real incomes may have risen, a widening gap appeared during the eighteenth century between the earnings of upper and lower income groups. As general prosperity took hold, so did land prices increase. Population had risen swiftly, reducing the ratio of available land in the older-settled areas to the population that the land supported. For persons in the lower strata of white society, therefore, economic opportunities were more restricted than they had been formerly.

Hence by the 1760s the colonists, still largely confined to their settlements on the coast east of the Piedmont, may well have faced the paradox of rising average income levels but (simultaneously) a narrowing range of opportunity for the betterment of those who had failed to share in the rise in average living standards.[2]

In sum, because of rapid population growth, output, foreign trade, and urbanization, the thirteen mainland colonies had achieved within a century and a half of their foundings a high degree of economic maturity, including substantial social and economic stratification. But as this thriving society was confined within the coastal area east of the Appalachian barrier, available land—room for a fresh start—had come under pressures that made the colonial social milieu in essential respects "old, stable, concentrated."[3]

TECHNIQUES OF AGRICULTURE: THE EUROPEAN BACKGROUND

The agricultural techniques brought to the American colonies were extremely primitive. Tools were few and crude; a plow, harrow, hoe, rake, spade, and sickle, with possibly a cart, represented the equipment of the most prosperous farmer. Little was known of stock breeding and this little could be rarely practiced, for cattle and sheep were herded together in a common pasture. Since there was little food for animals during the winter, most of them were slaughtered in the fall. For want of adequate care and knowledge, cattle and sheep were smaller than they are today.

The use of land was likewise primitive. Only the more advanced farmers practiced a crude rotation of crops in a two- or three-field system. Rich virgin soil, with an inexhaustible supply to the west, was no incentive to scientific farming. The value of manure was hardly appreciated and "land butchery" was the usual practice. One observer said that the colonial farmer seemed to have but one object: the plowing up of fresh land. "The case is, they exhaust the old as fast as possible till it will bear nothing more, and then, not having manure to replenish it, nothing remains but to take up new land in the same manner."[4]

Considerable attention was given by farmers in the early years to experimenting with the environment. It was soon found that most of the common grains, vegetables, and fruits of northwestern Europe were suitable to American soil and climate, as were the various farm animals. But efforts to introduce subtropical fruits of the Mediterranean countries failed. The same was true of repeated attempts to raise silkworms. These early efforts were often doomed to failure not so much because the climate was unsuitable as because the scarcity and high cost of labor made production impracticable. Success in some cases came in later years, when knowledge of plant breeding and scientific agriculture had made greater progress.

[1]George Rogers Taylor, "American Economic Growth before 1840," *Journal of Economic History*, XXIV (1964), p. 437; Marc Egnal, "The Economic Development of the Thirteen Continental Colonies, 1720 to 1775," *William and Mary Quarterly*, 3rd. ser., 32 (1975): 191–222.

[2]Kenneth Lockridge, "Land, Population, and the Evolution of New England Society, 1630–1790," *Past and Present*, No. 39 (1968): 62–80; Charles S. Grant, *Democracy in the Connecticut Frontier Town of Kent* (New York: Columbia University Press, 1961), p. 170; V. J. Wyckoff, "The Sizes of Plantations in 17th-century Maryland," *Maryland Historical Magazine*, 32 (1937): 331–339. See also Jackson T. Main, *The Social Structure of Revolutionary America* (Princeton, N.J.: Princeton University Press, 1965), *passim.*

[3]Lockridge, "Land, Population . . . ," p. 62.

[4]Anon., *American Husbandry* (2 vols., 1775), Vol. I, p. 144.

TECHNIQUES OF AGRICULTURE: THE AMERICAN INDIAN BACKGROUND

Throughout the Americas in the sixteenth century, European explorers and colonizers found native Indian peoples that had established widely varying types of economies. Some Indian societies were based on permanent farming settlements, others on a combination of farming with hunting and gathering, still others mainly on hunting or fishing. Generally the native Indians of North America did not oppose by force the initial European incursion. By the 1620s and 1630s, however, the encroachment of white settlers on Indian hunting grounds and farmlands had caused a spread of suspicion and hostility. And as the European powers competed against each other for western territory, they induced the Indian tribes to fight as their allies, setting the Indians against each other as well. The relationship of Indian and white societies was further altered as the exchange of furs for firearms and iron goods increased Indian dependence on the Europeans. All these forces contributed to the increasing turbulence and Indian wars of the seventeenth and eighteenth centuries.

At first, however, as one student of the earliest settlement has written, "the European parties went by Indian trails, commonly with Indian guides, from one settlement to another, and usually depended on food grown, collected, fished, or hunted by natives."[5] All along the Atlantic coast the English established their footholds with vital help from the native inhabitants. Quickly outnumbering the Indians and enjoying superiority of weapons, the Europeans traded with the natives for provisions and obtained from them vital knowledge of crops peculiar to the American continents. "The fruits of immemorial experience with forest life became available to the settlers, almost overnight."[6]

Northeastern Indian agriculture

The agriculture of the northeastern Indians was built up around the cultivation of corn and tobacco, both of them New World products unknown to Europe until the American conquest. The region was heavily wooded, and to clear their forests the Indians first girdled the trees or scotched the roots until they were dead.

The stumps and dead trees, as well as brush, were then burned. Lacking knowledge of ironmaking, the Indians relied upon sticks or simple wooden implements to break the soil for cultivation. Shallow holes were typically dug three or four feet apart, and a few grains or corn or beans were dropped into them. Between the hills were planted pumpkin and squash, also New World crops. As the corn came up it was hilled, and after the harvest much of it was dried and stored away in pits or caves lined with bark or in corncribs, so as to protect it from rotting bacteria and fungi.

Like corn, tobacco was widely used by the Indians from the West Indies to Canada. It was cultivated in separate fields, but it also grew wild along the Atlantic coastal plain. Compared to the present product, the Indian tobacco was of an inferior grade. Nevertheless, Indian methods of cultivation were followed by white farmers, as well as Indian methods of curing by the sun or open fire.

The potato

Another native American plant, destined in the future to be of world importance and to rank as one of the world's four greatest foods (the others are wheat, corn, and rice), was the white potato.[7] It is not possible to locate definitely its original habitat, but it is thought to be Peru or Chile. The potato came to be cultivated in various parts of Europe, but gained popularity first with the Irish; hence the colloquial name "Irish potato." Carried back to the New World, it found little favor in North America until the Irish settlers of the 1840s encouraged its culture. The sweet potato, native to the South, was at once adopted by the English settlers and cooked in many ways. Though white potatoes were produced in very small quantities before the Revolution, large crops of sweet potatoes were characteristic of southern agriculture from the beginning.

Indian agricultural achievements

The tools of the Indians were crude, but in other respects Indian technology was of crucial importance to the European settlers. A prime example was the fishing and hunting of sea animals. The Indians taught the French how to hunt walrus and seal, and they instructed the

---

[5]Carl Ortwin Sauer, *Sixteenth Century North America: The Land and the People as Seen by the Europeans* (Berkeley: University of California Press, 1971). p. 303.

[6]Curtis P. Nettels, *The Roots of American Civilization: A History of American Colonial Life* (2nd edition, New York: Appleton-Century-Crofts, 1963), p. 152.

[7]The world's tobacco and much of its cotton production is today also from plants deriving from those found by Europeans in America.

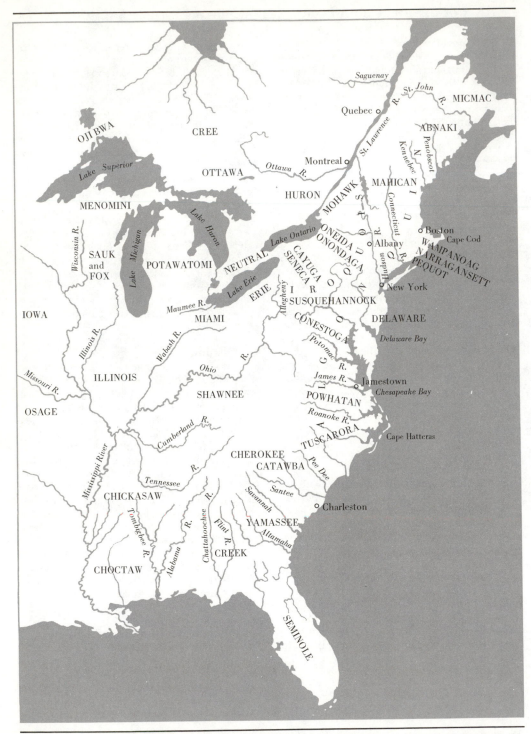

Figure 4–1. Principal Indian Nations of Eastern North America. Source: Rowland Berthoff, *An Unsettled People: Social Order and Disorder in American History* (New York: Harper & Row, 1971), p. 31.

French and English settlers in the gathering of oyster crops. Their techniques for constructing and putting out nets or weirs for fresh-water and tidal fishing were immediately adopted by the colonials. Also invaluable to the settlers from Europe was the knowledge that they gained from the Indians about the edibility of the fruits, nuts, and plants found in great abundance throughout the American forest-lands.

The early English colonists readily exploited the very considerable achievements of the Indian agriculturalists. The native peoples had brought wild plants under control and bred new varieties by seed selection; they had developed excellent cultivation and fertilization techniques, obtaining crop yields not improved much, if at all, by the whites; they had practiced multiple cropping and rotation. The Anglo-American colonial farm, cleared by tree girdling, with its rows of corn twined with bean vines, interspersed with squash and pumpkin and protected by scarecrows, was a direct adaptation of the Indian techniques. The main Indian crops—maize (corn), beans, and squash—became of central importance to the whites' farming in most regions, as did tobacco in the Chesapeake area.

All the contemporary accounts, "Spanish, French, and English, agree that the eastern Indians lived well and at ease in a generous land which they used competently and without spoiling it."[8] Because of limited population—only a million Indians lived in the present-day contig-

uous United States and Canada at the time of the conquest, and perhaps 350,000 at most in the Atlantic seaboard area—less than 1 percent of the arable land area was actually cultivated.[9] Hence the extensive clearing of forest for cultivation by the white colonists represented a shift of vast magnitude in the degree to which human population affected the natural environment.

Indian pharmaceutical knowledge

The transfer and adaptation of the Indian nations' technology, beginning with the Spanish incursions, also included medical and pharmaceutical knowledge. In Central and South America the native Indians taught the Europeans to extract potent drugs from native plants, including quinine from cinchona bark and cocaine from coca. In addition, the white colonists added literally hundreds of other drugs derived from Indian learning to the European pharmacopoeia. Ironically, in the cultural exchange between the native American populations and the Europeans, the conquering armies and permanent settlers visited upon the Indians tuberculosis, smallpox, measles, syphilis, and other diseases, in strains to which the Indians had low resistance or which had been unknown to the New World; and the tragic annals of seventeenth-century Indian life in the Atlantic region are filled with accounts of entire communities wiped out as the result of this aspect of cultural contact.

NEW ENGLAND AGRICULTURE

In addition to the corn, pumpkins, squash, and beans to which they were introduced by the Indians, the New England settlers raised peas, parsnips, turnips, and carrots from seeds they brought with them. Wheat, introduced from England, was not immediately successful, but they had greater success with rye and buckwheat. Barley, oats, and other European grains were introduced generally and thrived, but other products experimented with were found unsuitable. Many berries and fruits grew wild in New England—cranberries, huckleberries, blackberries, raspberries, and cherry and plum trees. Apple trees were imported at once, and were especially successful in New England and the Middle Colonies. Orchards were a part of

every farm, and the large apple crops caused them to be "reckoned as profitable as any other part of the plantation," according to a settler's account in 1642.

Since the Indians had no domesticated animals except dogs, the settlers imported them and they multiplied rapidly. Cattle were brought in as early as 1624 and formed the basis of rapidly increasing herds and successful dairying. Hogs were raised in great numbers in New England, and a considerable export trade was developed in barreled pork. Horses of a very hardy variety were raised, particularly in Rhode Island, and exported in large numbers to

[8]Sauer, *Sixteenth Century North America*, p. 295.

[9]A. L. Kroeber, *Cultural and Natural Areas of Native North America* (1938, reprinted Berkeley: University of California Press, 1963), p. 147.

the West Indies. Sheep were early introduced into Massachusetts and Rhode Island, where they were successfully developed and exported to the other northern colonies.

While the New England farmer of colonial times could with hard work obtain a living from the soil and might even become very prosperous, his methods were of the crudest and most primitive type. The great improvements in English agriculture that eventually led to the introduction of turnips, clover, and better grasses, to the more scientific rotation of crops, and to the abandonment of the three-field system did not come until the eighteenth century and then interested Americans but little. What slight knowledge of improved agricultural methods the immigrant might have he was likely to discard when confronted with an abundance of virgin soil. A harrow, a spade, a fork, all clumsily constructed of wood, were his chief farm tools.

Owing to the small size of the farms and the settlement in villages, "land butchery" was not practiced in New England to the extent that it was in the South, but methods were bad enough. Even to a contemporary observer, tillage in New England was "weakly and insufficiently given: worse ploughing is nowhere to be seen, yet the farmers get tolerable crops; this is owning, particularly in the new settlements, to the looseness and fertility of old woodlands, which with very bad tillage, will yield excellent crops."[10]

Bad as their agricultural methods were, their treatment of livestock was worse. The same observer maintained that in all that concerned cattle the farmers in New England were

the most negligent ignorant set of men in the world. Nor do I know any country in which animals are worse treated. Horses are in general, even valuable ones, worked hard, and starved: they plough, cart, and ride them to death, at the same time that they give very little heed to their food; after the hardest day's work, all the nourishment they are like to have is to be turned into a wood, where the shoots and weeds form the chief of the pasture; unless it be after the hay is in, when they get a share of the after-grass.[11]

During the early days when food was scarce, laws were passed forbidding the feeding of corn to animals.

[10]*American Husbandry,* I, 81.
[11]Ibid., I, 80.

With the exception of a few dollars' worth of salt and iron, many a New England farmer was practically self-sufficing. From his field he obtained grains, from his orchard fruits, and from his pastureland meat and dairy products. Flax from the field and wool from the sheep were spun and made into clothing by his wife and daughters. From honey and maple sap he obtained ingredients to sweeten his food; corn whiskey and cider furnished him with strong drink. Every farmer had to be a Jack-of-all-trades, and his wife had to be just as able to turn her hand to anything.

The New England farmer may have been self-sufficing, but it was not from desire. All who could do so raised a surplus, mainly for export to the West Indian market.

Expansion of farming communities

The early settlements in New England were made under agreements whereby every shareholder or settler was entitled to a certain amount of land. Further expansion usually occurred in the following manner. As vacant land near the seacoast grew scarce, groups or congregations would obtain a grant from the General Court, to which they would move in a body and found a town. The grants, commonly 36 square miles, were owned by these proprietors and eventually divided among them. From the center of the town, where the church or meetinghouse stood, a wide street was laid out, and along it house lots with perhaps six acres of gardenland were assigned. Eventually the rest of the land was distributed, each settler receiving a share in the upland, meadowland, and marshland, and rights in the commons. This system, in combination with the rocky soil, the rigorous climate, and the land laws that allowed division among several heirs, was not conducive to the development of great landed estates. The New England farm continued to be a comparatively small affair; the New Englanders lived in villages and tilled the land with their own hands.

Much of the land was held in common, although it was cultivated separately, and the town meeting was the vehicle by which plans were worked out and the cowherds, swineherds, and other officers who cared for the village property were elected. This system was transitory. As the towns grew larger, as the danger from Indians lessened, and as labor became diversified, the settlers were often glad to sell their scattered strips, and the compact farm with its buildings and land together appeared, resembling rural New England as we know it to-

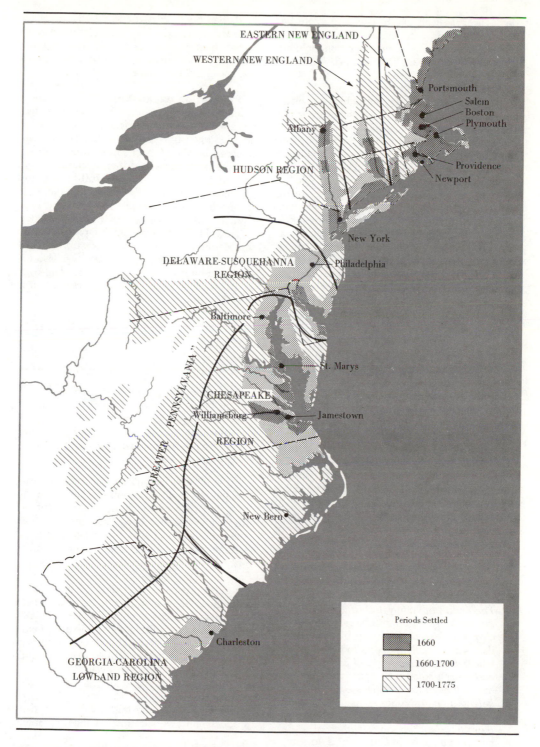

Figure 4–2. Colonial Settlement, 1607–1775. Source: Rowland Berthoff, *An Unsettled People: Social Order and Disorder in American History* (New York: Harper & Row, 1971), p. 25.

day. The ease with which new land might be acquired and an independent living achieved meant that for many years the nonlandholding labor class would be relatively small.

Population pressure

Average landholdings were large at first, with 125 to 150 acres probably the average for each family in the early-seventeenth-century Massachusetts towns. But as the towns' populations increased and as the original proprietors died and their land was parceled out to descendants, the area of village commons available for distribution dwindled and the average size of private holdings began to decline. By the late eighteenth century the inhabitants of the long-settled towns typically held only one-third (or even as little as one-seventh) of the acreage owned by their ancestors in the previous century. Parts of New England, as elsewhere in America, clearly were experiencing an early-day population pressure. Soil was exhausted in many localities, the poorer-quality commons

lands had been divided and put under cultivation, and the range of opportunities open to the poorer members of the society had shrunk—perhaps dangerously, so far as potential or actual social tensions were concerned.[12]

Population expansion

Expansion into hitherto unsettled areas was hastened when the old method of carefully guarded township grants to approved men was replaced by the plan of locating towns in advance of settlement and then auctioning them to land speculators. During 1700–1760 most of the land between the Housatonic and the Connecticut rivers was taken up, and by 1737 Connecticut had disposed of its unsettled lands. In New Hampshire settlement proceeded up the Merrimac and some distance up the Connecticut. The taking up of lands was also encouraged by the grants of Governor Wentworth to 121 new towns west of the Connecticut in what later became Vermont.

AGRICULTURE IN THE MIDDLE COLONIES

With the exception of the Hudson Valley, where the patroon system of large landed proprietors was initiated by the Dutch and perpetuated by the English, the land system of the Middle Colonies resembled that of New England in the sense that the holdings were generally small. There were large plantations on the Chesapeake shore of Maryland, but even in this area the situation was much the same. Between the Hudson and the Potomac the settlers found the soil and climate much closer to those of their native lands than did those of New England. The soil of New Jersey was so rich, said Peter Kalm, a Swedish traveler, in 1749, that it made the settlers careless husbandmen.

They had nothing to do but to cut down the wood, put it up into heaps, and to clear the dead leaves away. They could then immediately proceed to plowing, which in such loose ground is very easy; and having sown their grain, they get a most plentiful harvest. This easy method of getting a rich crop has spoiled the English and other European settlers, and induced them to adopt the same method of agriculture as the Indians; that is, to sow uncultivated grounds, as long as they will produce a crop without manuring, but to

turn them into pastures as soon as they can bear no more, and to take on new spots of ground, covered since ancient times with woods, which have been spared by the fire or the hatchet ever since the Creation.[13]

The Middle Colonies were predominantly agricultural in their economic life. With the exception of furs and lumber, the exports of this section seem to have been almost entirely agricultural. Wheat was the chief export, the average acre yielding from twenty to thirty bushels, a larger crop than was common in England at that time. Corn was raised throughout these provinces, providing the bulk of food for cattle in the winter. Rye, barley, buckwheat, and oats were also generally grown, the latter with great success. Fruits suitable to a temperate climate grew in great abundance—apples in New York, peaches and melons in the sandy soil of New Jersey and Delaware.

Livestock

Both to supply the family with meat, dairy products, and wool and to sell in cash markets,

[12]See note 2, above.
[13]Adolph B. Benson (ed.), *Peter Kalm's Travels in North America* (New York: Dover: 1966), Vol. I, p. 308.

the typical diversified farm in the Middle Colonies raised a variety of livestock. A typical farm of 100 or 125 acres would have cattle, hogs, and horses, sometimes sheep as well. But livestock productivity (judged by yields of meat, milk, and wool) was generally low. Although some upgrading of breeds was achieved by the 1750s, the prevailing methods of handling, feed, and breeding were careless.

Extensive farming

In general, Middle Colonies agriculture was "extensive"; that is, the typical farmer spent little on fertilizers, failed to pursue good field-rotation practices, and tended to rely upon only light tillage of the soil. Some gentlemen-farmers and reformers, aware of contemporary English emphasis on scientific farming, conducted a campaign for more intensive methods of using the land. But because a rude abundance was achieved by the methods then common — not without good reason was Pennsylvania known as "the best poor man's country" — their reforming efforts had little effect. As the leading student of Pennsylvania's colonial agriculture has written: "At bottom, extensive farming was the result of the satisfaction of the average farmer and his response to economic conditions. He produced enough for his family and was able to sell a surplus in the market to buy what he deemed necessities."[14] Moreover, given the relative costs of land and fertilizer and equipment, the scarcity of capital, and the available commercial marketing opportunities, extensive methods were a sensible, economically rational response.

Exports

The income of Middle Colonies farmers increased in the eighteenth century as their exports to the West Indies expanded. Philadelphia was the great entrepôt for their export trade, which included meat, flaxseed, lumber, livestock, and corn; but the largest export, probably half by value in the 1760s and 1770s, was wheat and flour. (All these products were also sold for ships' provisions and for export to the European market.) By 1770 the value of Pennsylvania's grain exports, including flour, was estimated at some £ 27 per farm.[15]

Social stratification

Like the New Englanders, however, Middle Colonies farmers confronted the paradox of intensifying social stratification amidst rising prosperity. Although the growing export trade and the rise of the Philadelphia market for farm products pushed average farm income upward in the eighteenth century, perhaps as much as 70 percent, a gap developed between the top and bottom economic strata in the society. Land prices rose faster than the income of farmers, and the poor were being squeezed. There were complaints of rural poverty, and by the 1770s nearly one-third of the population in some southeastern Pennsylvania towns owned no land. Poverty is a relative condition, and it may not have been synonymous with destitution, to be sure. But it seems clear that "the best poor man's land" was distinctly less than utopia for at least the poorest fifth of the population.

Population expansion

A large and influential element in the advance of the westward frontier was furnished by immigrants from northern Ireland who with questionable accuracy have been commonly termed "Scotch-Irish." The act of 1699 prohibiting the export of Irish wool from Ulster, the enforced payment of tithes to the Anglican church, and the fact that between 1714 and 1718 many of the leases granted to the original settlers in the colonies expired, all contributed in the early years of the eighteenth century to a great migration of Scotch-Irish to America.

Hemmed in by the Catskills to the west and with the Mohawk pass into the interior blocked by the Iroquois, New York during this period showed little expansive vitality. Notwithstanding the richness of the soil, the cultivation of the narrow ribbon of land along the Hudson and the Mohawk rivers proceeded slowly, largely because of the fact that the Dutch system of huge manorial grants was continued under British rule. With millions of acres of the choicest lands under the control of a handful of men who wanted to settle tenant farmers upon their holdings, it was little wonder that the tide of immigration moved elsewhere. Swiss-Germans who came to New York beginning in the 1680s mainly settled in the Mohawk Valley. The Scotch-Irish moving on from New England mingled with the Dutch in the Mohawk region and entered the Cherry Valley in 1738.

Between 1700 and the Revolution, Pennsylvania's reputation as a home for persecuted sects under William Penn's magnanimous rule

[14]James T. Lemon, *The Best Poor Man's Country: A Geographical Study of Early Southeastern Pennsylvania* (Baltimore, Md.: Johns Hopkins Press, 1972), p. 180.

[15]Ibid., p. 181; Lewis C. Gray, *History of Agriculture in the Southern United States to 1860* (1933, reprinted Gloucester: Peter Smith, 1958), Vol. I, pp. 214, 275.

brought as permanent settlers at least 100,000 Germans from the Palatinate and surrounding regions, the ancestors of the present "Pennsylvania Dutch"; 100,000 more were scattered along the frontiers of the other colonies from the head of the Mohawk to Georgia. The Pennsylvania frontier of this period was also the center of the great Scotch-Irish migration, which brought to this country between 1730 and 1770 close to half a million. Probably one-third of Pennsylvania's population at the time of the Revolution was composed of Germans from the Rhineland, and another third of immigrants from northern Ireland.

SOUTHERN AGRICULTURE

The settlers in Virginia soon discovered in tobacco a staple crop upon which they could concentrate their energies. Although prices declined in later years, tobacco cultivation was initially a profitable business, and exports grew to 100 million pounds by 1773. Since tobacco was raised for export, it was necessary for plantations to be located on the riverbanks, where the tiny ships of colonial days could sail up and load a cargo from each farmer's wharf. The land was accordingly rapidly taken up along the many Virginia rivers, then along the Chesapeake inlets, and then south into the Albermarle and Pamlico districts of North Carolina. When the lands near the rivers were entirely occupied, latecomers were forced to establish a tier of farms inland, behind the river plantations, and get the tobacco to their neighbors' wharves as best they might.

The plantation system

Tobacco, it was found, quickly exhausted even the richest soil, and necessitated the continual use of fresh land. Three years under favorable circumstances was the optimal age of a tobacco field, after which it was turned over to other crops. White labor was scarce and costly, and gradually black labor was substituted. Supervision was essential for slave labor, and it was believed that an overseer was too expensive unless he had twenty blacks under him. This situation encouraged large plantations. Sometimes the great plantations had 1000 acres under actual tobacco cultivation, besides land for other crops, a cattle range, and woodland. Many Virginia tobacco plantations covered 5000 acres or more. These factors, combined with the ease with which the title to new land was acquired, are the chief causes for the large holdings in the South. Mere occupation and the payment of a small fee or quitrent were sufficient to establish ownership. "Head rights," or the granting of land to those who imported settlers, grants for meritorious service, and purely personal grants by the governors all contributed to the swelling of the large estates.

The very ease with which land could be acquired, however, tended to make labor scarce and thus to a certain extent retarded the development of large estates. The typical southern holding, while much larger than the New England farm, was still moderate in size, and the average southern white was a small farmer. Methods of agriculture, the emphasis upon the one staple, tobacco, and the geography of the country all tended to a system of settlement that discouraged the growth of towns and promoted a distinctly rural life of scattered plantations, in contrast to New England, where occupation usually began by the founding of a town.

The cattle range

Next in importance to the plantation system, which was undoubtedly the basic feature of southern commercial agriculture, was the cattle range. Shifting arable land and large plantations made enclosures impracticable, and the vast unoccupied regions could readily be utilized for cattle ranges. Cattle, horses, and swine roamed in droves, subsisting on roots and herbage, branded when possible, but wild and often hunted as wild beasts. Each settler had his "right in the woods," which gave him a share in the unbranded cattle. Although the technique of ranching in the West was derived from the Spaniards, the western cattle ranch, with its roundup and brandings, was nevertheless a replica on a much larger scale and at a later date of cattle ranching during the early days in Virginia and the Carolinas.

The Carolinas

Passing south from Maryland and Virginia into the Carolinas, one found different conditions. Although cattle ranching was a feature of both North and South Carolina, in North Carolina farms were likely to be small and products diversified, while the plantations of South Carolina were given over to the production of rice

and indigo on a large scale. The farmers of
North Carolina, most of whom were emigrants
from Virginia—poor men, often former indentured servants or debtors—raised chiefly tobacco and corn on small farms.

Experimentation with rice began in South
Carolina in the late 1600s and it became profitable with the importation of black slaves, who
were able to work in the hot, swampy coast-
lands. By the time of the Revolution, Charleston was exporting annually about 125,000
barrels. After Parliament granted a bounty of
sixpence a pound on indigo (a blue dye) in
1748, indigo also became an increasing source
of wealth until it was displaced by cotton soon
after the Revolution. Other efforts to raise
semitropical products, however, usually failed.

TABLE 4–1. BRITISH IMPORTS OF AMERICAN TOBACCO, 1620–1775 (IN MILLIONS OF POUNDS)

YEAR	VOLUME
1620	0.1
1640	1.3
1672	17.6
1688	28.4
1708	30.0
1723	34.0
1740	41.0
1760	85.0
1770	78.0
1775	102.0

Source: U.S. Department of Commerce, Bureau of the Census, *Historical Statistics of the U.S., Colonial Times to 1957* (Washington, D.C.: U.S. Government Printing Office, 1960), p. 766.

THE ADVANCE INTO THE PIEDMONT

With the tidewater settlements fairly well
secured, colonists pushed into the Piedmont
region to take up the lands between the fall line
and the Alleghenies in the years from 1700 to
1763.

From Maryland to Georgia the story of the
occupation of the Piedmont is much the same.
As population increased and the rich lowlands
were exhausted, more and more land was tak-
en up until the fall line was reached. Then there
moved up into the Piedmont a stream of newcomers, mostly of the poorer classes, to claim
lands under head rights, or settlers brought in
by wealthy speculators to satisfy the requirements for obtaining their vast estates. Efforts
were made by all the colonies, for the purpose
of protection, to lure men to the frontier by the
offer of cheap or free lands and by exemption
from taxation. But an aristocratic planter group
occupied the Piedmont along with a yeomanry
of small farmers. By 1730 settlers from the
coast had spread from 30 to 50 miles into the
Virginia Piedmont, though in the Carolinas and
Georgia the foothills had scarcely been
touched.

After 1730 this westward movement from
the coast was augmented by a steady stream of
Germans and Scotch-Irish from the northeast to
the rich lands in the great valleys of the Appalachians to which ready access could be had
from the north. Impetus was given also by the
fact that the best land in Pennsylvania was already taken up, whereas land in Maryland
could be obtained at a cheaper price and in Virginia it was practically free. Accordingly, a
steady stream of pioneers flowed through the
Cumberland, Hagerstown, and Shenandoah
valleys into the great mountain trough, and finally out through the passes east into North
Carolina or west some years later into Kentucky
and Tennessee. By 1760 they had reached the
uplands of Georgia. In the Piedmont were mingled the settlers of these two converging
streams.

Before the Revolution there had developed
in the back country a society distinct from that
in the tidewater regions. The people of the Piedmont were generally small farmers and trap-
pers. From the beginnings of the westward
advance a distinct antagonism between the interior and the coast seems to have developed,
and during this period it can be clearly seen in
controversies between the plantation owners of
Virginia and the small farmers of the Piedmont,
between the backwoodsmen of Pennsylvania
and the wealthy Quakers of the east, and between the frontiersmen of New England and
the coast-town aristocracy. This antagonism
was evident in the contests between the debtor
class of the interior and the property-holding
class of the coast, in the demands for a more
democratic and representative government in
which the frontier might be more justly represented, and in the dissatisfaction over the defec-
tive administration of government and law
under which the back country suffered.

COLONIAL LABOR

The Europeans who settled North America found a virgin continent still unexploited except by native Indians whose hold on the land was weakened continuously—a continent with a wealth of raw materials and capable of profitable development within the context of an emergent Atlantic economy. But obtaining sufficient labor was a persistent problem. Probably the common glorification of work and the hatred of idleness (exemplified in many colonial laws requiring labor of the unemployed) were responses to American conditions no less than they were manifestations of contemporary English ideals and law. The policies of land distribution that prevailed, especially before the 1730s, were generally liberal. They helped to attract new settlers, therefore, and put labor to the work of exploiting American resources. But the very fact that becoming a free landowner was relatively easy meant that the alternative of making new farms was available to people who might otherwise have become agricultural or urban wage laborers; and the solution to labor shortages on plantations and in shops had to lie in the development of institutions that would expedite the immigration of poor persons and bind them in some way (at least for a period of time) to such work.

In the North, the scarcity of labor was met in the seventeenth and eighteenth centuries by means of "indentures"—contracts between laborers, known as "servants," and an employer or sponsor to whom they were bound.

Voluntary servitude

The indentured servants were of two classes, voluntary and involuntary. The voluntary servant was a worker whose servitude was based upon a contract into which he or she entered without compulsion. Many persons, eager to start a new life in America, sold themselves by indenture for a period of time (usually three to seven years) to shipmasters or brokers who made a business of such traffic. The servant obtained passage money to America, and upon arrival his or her contract would be sold off to an employer looking for labor.

Involuntary servitude

The second class of indentured servants, those suffering involuntary servitude, were usually debtors, vagrants, or criminals deported by the courts. With the courts and prisons crowded with paupers, vagrants, debtors, and petty crim-

inals, it seemed the most humanitarian as well as the most practical policy to ship them over to the colonies. In this way England was relieved of a burden and America was supplied with much-needed labor. If these prisoners could pay their own passage money they were free to do as they pleased; otherwise (and this was true of almost all), they were bound as servants for from seven to ten years.

The group of indentured servants was also recruited by the professional "spirits" or crimps, who picked up thousands of children and adults and sold them to shipmasters engaged in the colonial trade. So extensive was this kidnaping in the later half of the 1600s that Parliament passed legislation to curtail it, but the need for labor in the colonies was so great that the authorities showed little interest in enforcing the prohibition. Their attitude changed somewhat in the 1700s as Britain became a great commercial and industrial power. The desire to deport criminals increased, but Britain preferred to keep its skilled workmen at home. In 1765 Parliament forbade the emigration of skilled workers.

Conditions of servitude

The rights of servants were to a certain extent protected. They were entitled to food, clothing, shelter, and medical attention when sick, and they might own property. At the end of their service they were usually given an outfit and in some cases fifty acres of land. Although they were protected by law from unjust cruelty, the age was a hard one and the lot of the indentured servant, especially the involuntary one, was exceedingly harsh. On the one hand, the cost and need of labor were incentives to considerate treatment, but on the other hand, the desire to obtain as much labor as possible in the number of years covered by the indenture was a spur to excessive driving.

Of the white immigrants to the colonies during the colonial period, probably half came as indentured servants. It is estimated that in Pennsylvania, Maryland, and Virginia possibly three-fourths of the white population at the time of the Revolution were of this origin. Although the population growth during the colonial period came mainly from natural increase rather than from immigration, it is evident that the indentured servants and their offspring formed an important element in the early population of America.

The wages of servitude

For the average European laborer immigration on his own resources was impossible. Transportation to America cost from £6 to £10, and this amounted to three or four years' savings for the pitifully underpaid English laborer. In terms of the wages obtainable in Europe, the indentured servant in America often sold his services at a reasonable price. Free workers in America obtained wages 30 to 100 percent higher than in England. Cruel as the system was, it was not without its defenders. George Alsop, himself an indentured servant, wrote home that "the servants of this Province [Maryland], which are stigmatiz'd for slaves by the clapper-mouth jaws of the vulgar in England, live more like Freemen than the most Mechanick apprentice in London, wanting for nothing that is convenient and necessary, and according to their several capacities, are extraordinarily well used and respected."[16] It should be remembered that the voluntary indentured servants in most cases were the men and women who had the courage and stamina to seek escape from an environment for which they were not responsible and which held out no hope. A good proportion who survived the ordeal in America achieved the better life that they sought, and many rose to positions of importance in their communities.

Other sources of labor

It should be noted, of course, that colonial labor was by no means limited to indentured servants from Europe or slaves from Africa. Families in the colonies were large and child labor was used to the utmost. The common practice in Europe of imprisoning debtors was not uniformly followed in the colonies. Labor was too scarce, and debtors were allowed to work out their obligations to their creditors, while lawbreakers could also work out their fines by indenture. Moreover, the system of apprenticeship, by which youths bound themselves until the age of 18 or 21 to work and live with a master in return for learning a trade and to read and write, was widely practiced.

COLONIAL SLAVERY

The reason that American farmers, chiefly plantation owners in the South, turned from white indentured servants to black slaves was the conviction that they were cheaper than any other form of labor obtainable. An indentured servant cost on an average from £2 to £4 a year in capital investment; an able-bodied slave could be purchased for from £18 to £30. For this the slave owner received a lifetime of service, with the possibility of gain from increase in the slave's family.

During the fifteenth century Portuguese traders began to import into Europe blacks from the "Slave Coast," the part of the west coast of Africa extending from Cape Verde on the north to Cape St. Martha on the south. From the time of the first Portuguese settlement in Africa in 1482 the traffic became regular, lasting for about 350 years. The slaves were purchased from native brokers living in the coast towns, who obtained them from the tribes in the interior. The interior tribes, well supplied with guns and ammunition, turned over their prisoners of war and the fruit of their raiding parties to be imprisoned in the slave pens along the coast until they could be shipped away.

The first African slaves were brought to America and sold at Jamestown in 1619 by a Dutch privateer; within a few years they were to be found in all of the colonies.[17] Slaves were unpopular at first, notwithstanding the scarcity of labor; hence their number grew slowly and for half a century they composed only a small fraction of the total population. The slave trade in the 1600s was largely a monopoly of the Dutch until their power was broken in the 1660s. After that the Royal African Company of England took over until 1698. Then the traffic was thrown open and expanded rapidly. The number of slaves in the American mainland colonies in 1714 has been estimated at 59,000, and in 1754 at 263,000. The first census

---

[16]John G. Shay, *George Alsop, A Character of the Province of Maryland* (New York, 1869) p. 94.

[17]Edmund S. Morgan has recently argued that to solve their labor problem the Jamestown settlers and the Virginia Company relied heavily upon white servants; but these lower-class people soon came into the colony in such large numbers that they were perceived as a serious threat to social order—hence the attractiveness of substituting African slave labor. Morgan, "The Labor Problem at Jamestown, 1607–18," *American Historical Review,* 76 (1971): 595–611.

(1790) showed over 697,000. At this time they formed two-fifths of the total southern population, varying from a small percentage of the total in Maryland and North Carolina to over twice the white population in South Carolina.

The slave trade to the English colonies was soon monopolized by British and American ships. The latter proved to be especially efficient. The usual procedure for the Yankee slaver was to load up with rum and other commodities in New England, sail for the Slave Coast and exchange his goods for slaves, dispose of them in the West Indies or the mainland, and take on a cargo of sugar, molasses, and tobacco for the North. The voyage between Africa and the West Indies, known as the "Middle Passage," shows slavery in its gloomiest aspect and

the slave dealers at their worst. Crowded in the smallest possible space and chained to the ships, the Africans suffered untold agonies during the slow weeks of the Atlantic passage; if they fell sick they were thrown overboard, lest they contaminate their fellows. But the traders were hardened to this and had few compunctions about slavery.

A slave economy was adopted on the tobacco plantations of the South as the easiest way to fill the need for labor, and on the rice plantations of South Carolina as the only labor available for the climatic conditions in the hot, muggy rice fields. Slavery fulfilled an economic need, and as long as this continued, slavery flourished.

GOVERNMENT AND LABOR

If we are to understand colonial agriculture or labor — or, for that matter, any phase of colonial economic life — in a proper perspective, we must keep in mind that the world of that day was dominated by a mercantilist view of government. Laissez-faire was an unfamiliar concept to the people who controlled government, in the colonies no less than in London, just as it was to the population at large. In Chapter 5 we shall consider the reach and impact of mercantilist regulations that shaped the commercial relationship of the colonies and the home country within the Atlantic economy; here, a few examples of legislation adopted by the colonists themselves will illustrate the pervasive influence in America of mercantilist assumptions and techniques.

Laws giving a measure of protection to indentured servants against masters' abuses have already been mentioned. But the reach of the colonial assemblies' power in ordering labor relationships went much further than that. Craftsmen's wages and even those of common laborers were often established, under authority of the legislatures, by the officers of town government. In nearly all the commercial towns of any importance, moreover, certain trades deemed of a quasi-public character — the work of millers, smiths, porters, carters, and others whose services were made available to the public at large — could be practiced only under license. Apprenticeship was closely regulated, and in both rural and entrepôt towns public

markets were also subjected to a wide array of regulations and continuous supervision.

Farmers and artisans alike were affected by laws enacted in all the colonies authorizing local governments to set prices for bread, meat, and other foodstuffs, as well as for other articles of common consumption. Especially in the southern colonies, elaborate laws were put into effect regulating inns and taverns, with official prices established for lodging, drink, and food. The traditional common-law restraints upon conspiracy to fix prices or monopolize commodities in trade were generally complemented by specific legislation against "aggrandizing" and price gouging. Of special importance to farmers were regulation of fencing to keep livestock in (or out of) private holdings, branding regulations, bounties for the killing of predators, and laws that controlled the taking of timber from village commons land.

Usury laws limited interest rates, and occasionally the colonial legislatures provided relief for debtors in periods of economic crisis. In all the colonies, the governments made provision for public authorities to press free laborers into service in emergencies or even to assure the gathering of harvests.

Home-grown mercantilism
Despite the fact that mercantilist policy in the home country was the principal regulator of commerce, each colony undertook to affect trade and production to its own advantage.

Mercantilism of this sort, by and for the colonial people themselves, took many forms. Thus Massachusetts in 1640 provided cash bounties for production of linen, woolen, and cotton cloth, and in 1654 banned the export of ewe lambs in order to foster the home woolen industry. Later in the century Massachusetts banned the export of hides and raw wool, again to stimulate the manufacture of finished goods and to make the colony more self-sufficient. As in many colonies, in Massachusetts frequent attempts were also made to levy the equivalent of protective tariffs (by port duties or taxes) on products from other colonies in competition with its own.

Of particular importance was legislation requiring that commodities that had status as "staples" (goods produced for export to cash markets) be warehoused, inspected, and sometimes graded by public authorities. This was done with grain, flour, tobacco, and other goods that played major roles in colonial trade. Each colony sought thus to assure potential customers in England and elsewhere of the high quality of commodities it permitted to be shipped; there was, in other words, an element of intercolonial commercial rivalry in these efforts at enhancing trade advantages.

Rivalries became most intense when individual colonies sought to limit production. This was done on several occasions in Virginia, where, during periods of depressed prices for tobacco, the legislature mandated crop and output controls. To protect itself against neighboring colonies that did not so limit production, Virginia banned Carolina and Maryland tobacco by embargoes.

The colony and the empire

In sum, mercantilist ideas — fostering of the country's power and wealth by governmental intervention, protection of a favorable balance of trade in which export earnings would exceed expenditures upon imports, control of the labor force, and encouragement of diversification and self-sufficiency — were as readily applied to the colony as to the emergent British empire. The most dramatic manifestation of governmental power in the mercantilist mode, as used by the individual colonies, was currency regulation, which will be discussed later (pp. 63, 71 – 72). But behind the currency acts of the eighteenth century was a long history of intervention in the economy by the colonial assemblies within the broader framework of imperial regulation.

Government control of slavery

For the one in six Americans who lived in slavery, the role of governmental power was of unique importance. Generally speaking, the central authorities in London left each colony free to enact its own laws affecting the relationships of slave and master. The result, especially in the southern plantation colonies, was the emergence of "black codes" — a system of laws relating to slaves and free blacks which by the eighteenth century constituted a separate and much harsher criminal law than was applied to whites. "It was unrelenting fear of the Negro as a potential insurrectionist and constant determination to police his conduct rigidly," as one scholar has written, that produced this system of repressionist law. Apart from inflicting draconian penalties on blacks for such crimes as insurrection and running away, the southern laws "protected to extreme limits the master's privilege of punishing his slaves," even to the point of effectively immunizing a master against prosecution for killing a slave in the course of administering private punishment.[18]

It was remarkable that despite this legitimization of coercive force to maintain the slaves' subservience, still the colonial years witnessed a survival of vigorous black culture and a persistent resistance by blacks to the imposition of total white mastery. There is abundant evidence that the structure and stability of slave families survived, sometimes with the help of the masters and often despite the way in which the system worked against such survival. On every plantation, the owners and overseers were forced to come to terms with the slaves in myriad ways, the specter of violent resistance seemingly always in the background as a restraint against totally arbitrary control; and there was a persistent problem with runaways, despite all the force that the society mustered against this form of subversion and resistance. We are reminded, as Eugene D. Genovese has written, that "although an individual at any given moment may be defenseless, a whole people rarely, if ever, is. It may be on the defensive and dangerously exposed, but it almost invariably finds its own ways to survive and fight back."[19]

[18]Thad W. Tate, *The Negro in Eighteenth-Century Williamsburg* (Charlottesville, Va.: Colonial Williamsburg, 1965), p. 91.

[19]Eugene D. Genovese, *In Red and Black: Marxian Explorations in Southern and Afro-American History* (New York: Pantheon, 1971), p. 108. See also Gerald W. Mullin, *Flight and Rebellion: Slave Resistance in Eighteenth-Century Virginia* (New York: Oxford University Press, 1972).

SELECTED READINGS

NOTE: Most of the works listed in the selected readings for the previous chapter also deal with agriculture and labor.

Bidwell, Percy W., and Falconer, J. I., *History of Agriculture in the Northern United States, 1620–1860* (1925, reprinted Gloucester, Mass.: Peter Smith, 1958).

*Bridenbaugh, Carl, *The Colonial Craftsman: Philadelphia in the Age of Franklin* (New York: New York University Press, 1950).

Carrier, Lyman, *The Beginnings of Agriculture in America* (1923, reprinted New York: Johnson Reprint Corp., 1968).

*Curtin, Philip D., *The Atlantic Slave Trade: A Census* (Madison: University of Wisconsin Press, 1969).

*Driver, Harold E., *Indians of North America* (Chicago: University of Chicago Press, 1961).

Egnal, Marc, "The Economic Development of the Thirteen Continental Colonies, 1720 to 1775," *William and Mary Quarterly,* 3rd ser., 32 (1975).

Gray, Lewis C., *History of Agriculture in the Southern United States to 1860* (1933, reprinted Gloucester, Mass.: Peter Smith, 1958).

Johnson, E. A. J., *American Economic Thought in the Seventeenth Century* (1923, reprinted New York: Russell & Russell, 1961).

Jones, Alice Hanson, "Wealth Estimates for the American Middle Colonies, 1774," *Economic Development & Cultural Change,* XVIII (1970).

——, "Wealth Estimates for the New England Colonies About 1770," *Journal of Economic History,* XXXII (1972).

Land, Aubrey C., "Economic Base and Social Structure: The Northern Chesapeake in the Eighteenth Century," *Journal of Economic History,* XXV (1965).

——, "The Tobacco Staple and the Planter's Problems: Technology, Labor, and Crops," *Agricultural History,* XLIII (1969).

Lemon, James T., *The Best Poor Man's Country: A Geographical Study of Early Southeastern Pennsylvania* (Baltimore: Johns Hopkins Press, 1972).

*Main, Jackson T., *The Social Structure of Revolutionary America* (Princeton, N. J.: Princeton University Press, 1965).

*Morris, Richard B., *Government and Labor in Early America* (New York: Columbia University Press, 1946).

*Nash, Gary B., *Red, White, and Black: The Peoples of Early America* (Englewood Cliffs, N.J.: Prentice-Hall, 1974).

*Nettels, Curtis Putnam, *The Emergence of a National Economy, 1775–1815* (New York: Holt, Rinehart and Winston, 1962), Chaps. 7–9.

Potter, J., "The Growth of Population in America, 1700–1860," in *Population in History,* ed. D. V. Glass and D. E. C. Eversley (Chicago: Aldine, 1965).

Price, Jacob, "The Economic Growth of the Chesapeake and the European Market, 1697–1775," *Journal of Economic History,* 24 (1964).

Smith, Abbot Emerson, *Colonists in Bondage: White Servitude and Convict Labor in America, 1607–1776* (Gloucester, Mass.: Peter Smith, 1965).

Washburn, Wilcomb E., *The Indian in America* (New York: Harper & Row, 1975).

chapter 5

American commerce and industry in a mercantilist world

Until the commencement of the revolutionary crisis in the 1760s, the farmers, rentiers, artisans, merchants, and professional men in the British-American settlements pursued their lives and fortunes as the people of separate but related colonies. Diverse as the economies of the 13 mainland colonies became — and different as they were, in important respects, from the economies of the British West Indies and the settlements in present-day eastern Canada — still, all the colonials were from the outset operating under the common regime of British mercantilism. That is, they were ultimately controlled by the policies that English statesmen fashioned over a century and a half to foster the wealth and power of the home country. Only indirectly did mercantilist aims and policies affect the legal framework and economic development of American agriculture, the pursuit that occupied upwards of 90 percent of the colonials. Mercantilist policy was much more di-rectly concerned with regulating commerce and industry. Parliament and British officialdom designed changing rules and regulations that governed the markets in which the colonists might buy and sell, the routes by which their goods could be carried, the duties and restrictions that could vitally affect the costs and profits of specific commercial relationships, and the competitive structure of shipping enterprises. All these effects, in turn, were transmitted to the agricultural sector of the colonial economy. Moreover, the mercantilist regulation of colonial manufacturing not only went far toward shaping the small but important industrial sector; it also had an impact on the structure of prices that were paid by the colonists for the consumer goods that they bought. Hence to understand why American commerce and industry developed as they did, it makes sense to begin with consideration of England's broad policy objectives in the evolution of its mercantilism.

THE MERCANTILIST THEORY OF COLONIAL TRADE

The basic purpose of mercantilist policy was enhancement of the home country's economy and national power. That the colonies were to be subservient to the home country was a cardinal assumption; this was the consistent and continuous basis of policy — through many changes in scope and detail of the specific regulations enacted — from the beginnings of American settlement to the Revolution. A member of the Board of Trade, the central English agency charged with supervision of the colonies, ex-pressed this assumption succinctly when he wrote in 1726:

> Every act of a dependent provincial government ought therefore to terminate in the advantage of the mother state unto whom it owes its being and protection in all valuable privileges. Hence it follows that all advantageous projects or commercial gains in any colony which are truly prejudicial to and inconsistent with the

*interests of the mother state must be
understood to be illegal and the practice of
them unwarrantable, because they
contradict the end for which the colony
had a being and are incompatible with the
terms on which the people claim both
privileges and protection. . . . For such is
the end of the colonies, and if this use
cannot be made of them it will be much
better for the state to do without them.*[1]

Crown and colonies

"The interests of the mother state," then,
were paramount. Those interests embraced
maximum economic self-sufficiency of Great
Britain and the colonial system, in the sense
that colonies should complement production of
the mother country. It was the business of colonies to produce goods not obtainable at home
except by imports from foreign powers; this
meant, chiefly, raw materials and certain foodstuffs. In addition, colonies should consume
manufactured goods produced in the home
country; that is, they would complement the
home market by enlarging its scope. The two-
way trade that resulted, between home and
colonial ports, would provide an opportunity
for growth of a powerful merchant marine. (In
that day, moreover, merchant ships were readily converted to military purposes; and experienced sailors in merchant service would be the
seamen for navies in wartime.) Profits gained
by shipowners and merchants in the colonial
trade would generate investment capital for a
variety of economic enterprises at home; and
the crown too would profit, by the imposition of
duties and port charges. Mercantilist policy also
postulated that to the greatest extent feasible
and politically advantageous, foreign shippers
and traders would be excluded from the emergent imperial economy. If the colonies needed
market outlets for their surplus beyond those
that the home country could provide, any trade

they undertook with foreign nations would be
watched closely, curbed when necessary, and
taxed as heavily as was practical.

The home economy

The mercantilist policies of England, like
those of the rival European powers, also looked
inward at the governance and ordering of the
home economy. One objective was to protect
and stimulate home industry, to help make the
home country self-sufficient industrially, and—
not least important, in an age of recurrent
economic crises and extensive displacement of
peasant populations—to help provide employment to the poor and the idle.

A related objective was to impose rational
order upon the interlocking interests of the
crown and private centers of wealth and power.
This was to be done by allocating monopolies
in trades and in colonies or plantations, and by
devolving charters upon investors and "adventurers" (as business entrepreneurs were called),
exchanging special privileges for the revenues
and political gains that the government expected. The various special interests were kept
in a delicate balance that was designed to
promote stability amidst plenty at home and
vigorous expansion abroad.

Finally, certain important economic interests
in the home country were to be protected
against actual or potential competition by the
colonies. Occasionally adjustments had to be
made and concessions granted to the colonies,
as when James I in the 1620s enforced a ban
on tobacco planting in England in order to foster its production in Virginia, and when American shipping was given legal status equivalent
to that of English-owned shipping. But more
generally, the colonies were intended to be
developed in ways that would complement the
home country's economy, not duplicate or
compete with home interests.

THE MERCANTILIST LAWS

The coherence and rationality of mercantilist
policy goals in their broad, general terms were
in sharp contrast to actual policy until the
1660s. During the initial decades of English settlement in America, these policies took only
tentative, fragmented form: in the early colonial

[1]Quoted in Louis M. Hacker, "The First American
Revolution," *Columbia University Quarterly*, 27 (1935).

charters, in the activities of the various companies and proprietors and royal officials who
planted and directed new settlement, and in
various royal edicts and parliamentary laws.
Unrest and finally a civil war in England further
militated against coherence of policy in regard
to commercial development of the colonies.

But still, the broad outlines of mercantilism
could be seen. From 1625 to 1631 Dutch and

Spanish tobacco were banned from England, and English production was made illegal, in order to sustain Virginia. Efforts were made to exclude Dutch ships from the English colonies' trade. By the 1630s the chief American staple crop, tobacco, was required to be shipped first to England, where it would pay duties, even if it were ultimately destined for other markets on the Continent. Most important, when Oliver Cromwell turned his attention to colonial problems after his overthrow of the Stuart monarchy, the first so-called Navigation Acts were passed by Parliament in 1651. These laws, aimed at the Dutch, who then carried much of Europe's trade and were the main shippers for American colonial exports, carved out a monopoly for English-controlled shipping. In addition, the home market for fish was restricted to English and English-colonial vessels. But these laws were poorly enforced, and they led to an Anglo-Dutch war that merely sharpened English mercantilist objectives.

Control of colonial exports

English mercantilist regulation, cast in broad and coherent terms in law as well as theory, really began in 1660. In that year, with the Stuart monarchy reestablished, an "Act for the Encouraging and Increasing of Shipping and Navigation" decreed that goods carried to and from England must be transported not only in English-manned ships but in English-built ships or ships built in the English colonies. The act of 1660, besides providing for the protection of shipping and thus the development of the merchant marine, sought to regulate the trade of the colonies so as to add to the monopoly of navigation that of colonial commerce and markets. It was enacted that "no sugars, tobacco, cotton-wool, indigo, ginger, fustick, or other dyeing woods, of the growth, produce, or manufacture of any English plantations in America, Asia or Africa" should be shipped to any place whatsoever except England. This list was expanded in 1706 by the addition of naval stores (tar, pitch, turpentine, hemp, masts, and yards); by rice from 1705 to 1730; by copper ore, beaver, and other furs in 1721; by molasses in 1733; by whale fins, hides, iron, lumber, raw silk, and pearl ashes in 1764. Nonenumerated articles, chief of which were fish, grain, and rum, could be exported anywhere until 1766, but after that date exportation to Europe was confined to south of Cape Finisterre. The latter provision virtually excluded the colonies from direct export trade with any country of northern Europe except England.

Control of colonial imports

Not only did England seek to control colonial exports, but by an act of 1663 it sought to monopolize the handling of imports into the colonies. This act prohibited by high duties the importation into the colonies of any European goods unless they were brought via England and in ships built and manned by the English or by English colonists. The act thus allowed duties and commissions to be collected in England before European goods reached America. Exceptions were made in the case of salt from Spain for the New England fisheries, wine from Madeira and the Azores, and provisions and horses from Ireland and Scotland.

The laws of 1660 and 1663 were both evaded, the former by shipping such enumerated articles as sugar and tobacco directly to European ports without taking them first to England, under the pretense that the commodities were destined for another colony. In an effort to make this practice unprofitable, Parliament enacted a law in 1673 (reaffirmed and interpreted in 1696) levying a tax on enumerated articles shipped from one colony to another equal in amount to the import taxes levied on the articles in England.

Control of colonial manufacturing

The British mercantilist policy was concerned not only with control of the carrying trade and with imports and exports, but also with control of the colonies' manufacturing activities. The British attitude toward manufactures by the colonies was well summarized by the governor of New York, who in 1705 declared in a communication to the Board of Trade that

> all these Colloneys, which are but twigs
> belonging to the main Tree [England],
> ought to be kept intirely dependent upon
> and subservient to England, and that can
> never be if they are suffered to goe on in
> the notions they have, that as they are
> Englishmen, soe they may set up the same
> Manufactures here, as people may doe in
> England. . . .[2]

In actual practice, the English could not completely control manufacturing, or even subject this activity, mainly based as it was in

[2]Lord Cornbury to Secretary Hedges, 1705, in *Documents Relative to the Colonial History of the State of New York*, ed. E. B. O'Callaghan and B. Fernow, 15 vols. (Albany, 1853–1887), vol. 4, p. 115.

households and artisans' shops, to anything like the degree of control attempted over trade and shipping. But two industries were guarded with a jealous eye: woolen goods and iron. Together, woolens and iron were the leading edge of what became England's industrial revolution in the eighteenth century, and crown officials attempted to protect these home industries against damage from the colonial economies. Indeed, half of England's exports to the colonies in the late seventeenth century were woolen goods. So hostile were the home interests to competition that in 1699 England banned the export of colonial woolens or even shipment of these textiles from one colony to another. In a related move, the English government acted to prevent growth of a hat industry in the colonies, where the abundance of beaver gave American hatmakers a decided locational advantage. Hence in 1732 the so-called Hat Act prohibited the export of hats made in the colonies, either to England or to other colonies. The act also sought to limit the extent of colonial hat manufacture by decreeing that no master in this trade might have more than two apprentices.

As for iron, English policy sought to encourage the production of pig and bar iron as raw material for home-country manufactures, but to discourage the colonial manufacture of finished iron products. Hence in 1750 the Iron Act imposed the following regulations: (1) that bar iron might be imported duty-free to London, and pig iron to any port in England; and (2) that no one in the colonies might build a mill for rolling or slitting iron, or any furnace for making steel. In 1757 another law extended duty-free entry of bar iron to any English port.

These restrictions upon manufacturing had a commercial dimension that should not be over-

looked: they limited the possibilities of trade between the colonies themselves in important respects, both as they effectively banned manufacture of finished iron products from colonial metal and as they placed curbs on the woolen and hat trades. Nor were the colonists slow to recognize that England was giving protection to its citizens at home at the expense of the Americans. "A colonist cannot make a button, a horse shoe, nor a hobnail," complained a Boston editor in 1765, "but some sooty iron-monger or respectable button-maker of Britain shall bawl and squall. . . ."[3]

Colonial commerce under mercantilist law

British mercantilism did not, on balance, discourage colonial commerce. For this there were three main reasons. First of all, the colonies, where land and resources were plentiful and labor scarce, were normally producers of raw or semifinished materials. They naturally fitted into the imperial system in which the colonies supplied the raw materials and the home country the manufactured products. In the second place, the colonies that produced commodities competing with those of Great Britain discovered other markets, particularly in the West Indies and southern Europe. Thus they secured means with which to purchase British manufactured goods. Finally, when British laws came in conflict with colonial interests, they were evaded. Despite the British navy, already the most powerful on the sea, smuggling was rampant, and trade with nations forbidden by British law flourished.

As will be seen, however (p. 76), the balance of mercantilism's burdens and benefits would shift markedly after 1763.

THE CONDITIONS OF COLONIAL COMMERCE

In the development of commerce the American colonists were particularly blessed by physiographic conditions. Excellent harbors dotted the coast of New England and the Middle Colonies. Coastal bays, indentations, and rivers in the middle and southern colonies made commerce easy. Numerous small rivers in the South allowed the tiny vessels of the period to sail directly to the private wharves of the planters. "None of the plantation houses, even the most remote," commented a Frenchman traveling in Virginia in 1686, "is more than 100 or 150 feet from a 'crik' and the people are thus enabled

not only to pay their visits in their canoes, but to do all their freight carrying by the same means."[4]

All roads in the colonies were abominable. Most of them were dirt paths that turned to muddy sloughs in wet weather; long-distance highways for coach or wagon travel were practically nonexistent. Only after the 1750s were the larger seaboard urban centers linked by roads that permitted regular stagecoach service. Al-

[3]*Boston Gazette,* April 29, 1765.
[4]Durand, *A Frenchman in Virginia* (n.p., 1923), p. 23.

though travel time between Philadelphia and New York was reduced to a day and a half by 1771, it still took a week in favorable weather to reach Boston from New York City.

Under such conditions, it was natural that most commerce between colonial ports should be carried on by water. Even in this coastal trade, the weather and rocky sections of the coastline posed serious hazards. As for ocean commerce, ships were small and risks high. The ocean crossing to England took eight weeks, and in winter voyages of 14 weeks or more were not uncommon. Nor was navigation aided by many lighthouses on the American coast. And merchant sailors were subject to sickness from scurvy and contagious diseases that could turn a trading voyage into a nightmare of death and suffering.

The currency problem

Other factors also continuously harassed colonial commerce. Not the least of these was the lack of a convenient medium of exchange. As the balance of trade between England and the colonies always favored England, what little currency found its way to British North America was quickly drained away. Such currency as existed came chiefly through trade with the Spanish and French colonies or drifted in through the medium of privateering and piracy. A contemporary writer noted that money from the West Indies "seldom continues six months in the province before it is remitted to Europe." Barter was complicated by the fact that the amount of precious metals in the foreign coins varied, and also by the fact that although English coins were rarely seen, business was carried on in terms of pounds, shillings, and pence.

Efforts by the colonists to provide substitutes for metallic currency and barter were continuous. In Virginia and Maryland warehouse receipts for tobacco that had been deposited were successfully used. In 1690 Massachusetts issued bills of credit to pay the soldiers who took part in the expedition against Port Royal and Quebec, and this experiment in paper money was followed by all the colonies in the hope that such currency would fill a very evident need in commercial life. Acceptable at a premium over silver for the payment of taxes and generally specifying the date for payment, the early issues held up well, but as they became larger and the credit upon which they were based weaker, the result was disastrous. Depreciation followed excessive issue and the numerous emissions with their uncertain value hindered as much as they helped business. So-called loan banks in Massachusetts and Pennsylvania issued loan

bills on real estate, personal security, and merchandise, but little is known of them. English disapprobation of these monetary issues led to an act of Parliament in 1751 forbidding the further issuance of legal-tender bills of credit in New England, a prohibition extended to the other colonies in 1764. Although bitterly resented, this legislation was far from being wholly effective. It is estimated that $22 million in paper was still in circulation at the time of the Revolution.

Piracy and privateering

Another source of more or less continuous annoyance to colonial commerce was the existence of piracy and, in time of war, privateering. Wars were frequent in the seventeenth and eighteenth centuries, particularly after the beginning of the "Second Hundred Years' War" between England and France in 1689. In theory the difference between a pirate (a robber on the high seas) and a privateer (legally commissioned to war upon an enemy) was very wide. In practice it was sometimes exceedingly thin. The famous Captain Kidd started as a privateer and ended as a pirate. Despite the difficulties from pirates and privateers during the long years of warfare, their activities were not a complete loss to the colonists. Their booty and treasure had to be disposed of, and they were often smuggled into the colonies and sold cheaply. Prominent merchants and even government officials connived at the practice. Sober estimates suggest that New York alone for many years thus secured on an average £100,000 in treasure annually, and that up to 1700 much of the supply of specie in the colonies was obtained in this way.

The merchant élite

Of central importance to the successful growth of colonial commerce was the business enterprise of America's merchant class. In New England after 1640, and by the late seventeenth century in all the port towns, there were men and firms risking capital in shipping ventures and trade. Faced with economic stagnation at home during the civil war in England, the American merchants sought out new markets aggressively, and they established new routes and marketing patterns. This did not happen spontaneously, but by the careful knitting together of networks in which the American merchants linked themselves with kinfolk and friends engaged in trade in the English West Indies, the home country, and elsewhere. Each of the major port towns on the Atlantic coast also became a distribution center for a rural hinterland. The network of trade, credit, and enterprise that had reached across the Atlantic thus was extended into the American interior, where farmers provided the agricultural produce for export and purchased the goods brought in from Europe, England, and the West Indies. The export trade in fish, lumber, and ships in the North, and the importation of African slaves, became part of the system as well.

These merchants' activities became the base on which the port towns grew. As their wealth accumulated, the most successful merchants also gained political influence and became a leading element in the colonial élite. They relied on English officialdom for favors and laws that enhanced their success, but they also had a solid economic and political base of their own. By the early eighteenth century in New England and the Middle Colonies, at least, perhaps 200 merchant families had become one of the powerful "interests" within the emergent British empire. As such, they were a force for the home government to contend with. To oppose them on a wholesale basis would be to jeopardize the stability of the empire in America; it would be to taunt the gods of destiny.

ROUTES AND COMMODITIES OF COLONIAL TRADE

The chief markets for colonial products were England, the West Indies, and southern Europe. As we have seen, certain "enumerated" commodities raised in the British mainland colonies were required by law to be sent only to England—tobacco, cotton, wool, indigo, naval stores, rice, copper, iron, lumber, furs, pearl ashes, and other commodities.

As the export staples of the southern colonies were largely tobacco, rice, and indigo, and to a lesser extent naval stores and furs, most of the export trade of these colonies was a direct trade with England. In return they imported drygoods, hardware, furniture, and other types of manufactured goods. The rapid spread of western settlement on the Virginia and Maryland frontiers, together with exhaustion of some tobacco lands in seaboard areas, resulted in a rise (in both absolute and relative importance) of grain exports from the South. By the early 1770s more than half the corn exported by the mainland colonies originated in the South, as did a large proportion of the wheat and flour. New settlement in Georgia and the Carolinas intensified this shift in southern exports toward grain products; in addition, these colonies were major shippers of meat and lumber products. Still, the dominant southern export product by value continued to be tobacco, which, like rice and indigo, was shipped to the English market for consumption there or for reexport.

In New England and the Middle Colonies the situation was quite different. These colonies had certain commodities—such as naval stores, lumber, furs, and metals—that were desired in the mother country, but their great staples— fish, grain, and other foodstuffs—were kept out of England by high tariffs. Their export trade with England was therefore relatively small and they were forced to find other outlets for their chief products. These outlets were primarily in the West Indies and to a lesser extent in southern Europe. To them New England sent mainly pickled and dried fish, pickled beef and pork, horses and livestock, and various kinds of building material. The exports to these regions from New York and Pennsylvania were chiefly flour and wheat. By the opening of the eighteenth century the West Indian islands had been turned largely into sugar and tobacco plantations unable to support themselves without the importation of cheap food for slaves and lumber for homes and for casks to transport sugar, molasses, and tobacco. In return the mainland colonies obtained molasses, which they could turn into rum for the fishing fleet, the slave trade, or domestic use. They also obtained specie or various commodities that could be used to purchase manufactured commodities from Britain. The extent of this trade may be seen from contemporary estimates. One puts the average annual exports from New England (1763–1766) at £485,000, over half of which were products of the sea; from New York at £526,000; and from Pennsylvania at £705,500, more than half of the last two being flour and wheat.[5]

Figure 5–1. Colonial Economy and Trade Routes. (American colonies are shown on a much larger scale than Europe.) Source: Lawrence Leder, *America, 1603–1789: Prelude to a Nation* (Minneapolis: Burgess, 1972), pp. 112–113. © 1972, Burgess Publishing Company. Reproduced by permission.

[5]Anon., *American Husbandry*, 2 vols. (London, 1775), vol. 1, pp. 59, 124, 181.

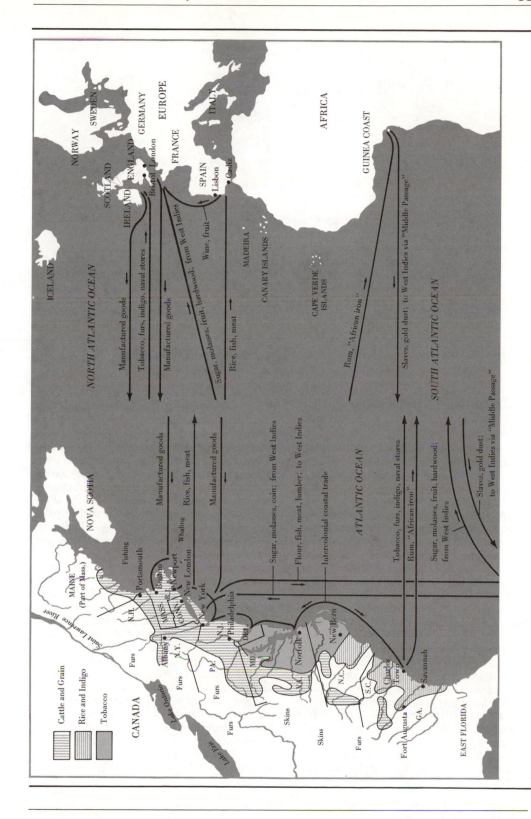

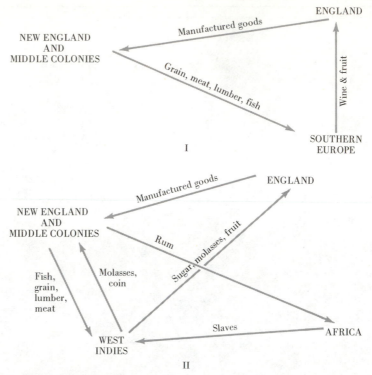

Figure 5–2. Triangular Trade Routes.

The whole course of colonial commerce provides an interesting study in international trade and balance of payments, to say nothing of the ingenuity of the colonial merchant and sea captain in finding an outlet for the products of his region in the face of mercantilist restrictions. In addition to a certain amount of intercolonial commerce and the direct trade to and from Britain and to and from the West Indies, there developed various phases of the famous triangular trade. The imports of New England and the Middle Colonies from Britain were in some years eight or more times their exports. This trade was maintained in various ways. New England and the Middle Colonies exported their grain, meat, fish, and lumber to southern Europe, then carried wine, fruit, and other commodities to England, where they were exchanged for manufactured products. Another triangular route was the carrying of the products of New England and the Middle Colonies to the West Indies, where they were exchanged for sugar, molasses, and other commodities; these were taken to England to be exchanged for manufactured goods that were

brought back to the northern mainland colonies. These manufactured goods from England were in part paid for by coin or bills of exchange on London obtained by the direct trade between the northern mainland colonies and the West Indies, a condition made possible partly by the fact that the exports from the West Indies to Great Britain were almost three times the imports.

Still another phase of the triangular commerce was the African slave trade, which grew enormously during the 1700s. The causes were (1) the demand for cheap labor on the plantations of the islands and mainland, and for household servants in the northern colonies, and (2) the large profits that accrued from the trade to English interests and colonial shipowners. Not only the shipping interests in New England were concerned with the slave trade; so were the rum manufacturers, who supplied the chief commodity used in the purchase of slaves. Until the Revolution, almost all the slaves were taken to the West Indies, and from there a certain portion were later brought to the mainland. An estimated 250,000 African slaves were carried to the North American mainland colonies from 1700 to 1780.[6]

The growth of commerce

At the beginning of the eighteenth century, the American trade with England amounted to about £280,000 in exports to the home country and £140,000 in imports. By the early 1750s the trade had grown to £836,000 in exports and over £1.2 million in imports. In 1774, on the eve of the Revolution, the comparable figures were £1.4 million in exports and nearly £2.6 million in imports. (Since these data are official valuations given in constant prices rather than current market values, they fail to reflect changes in prices; instead they represent the growth in physical volume of goods traded.)

By the middle of the eighteenth century, perhaps 30 percent of colonial exports were being sent out to the West Indies and directly to Europe rather than to England. Moreover, a significant amount of commerce passed between the northern and southern colonies. This intercolonial trade, consisting heavily of foodstuffs, is estimated to have averaged as high as £615,000 in value from 1768 to 1772.[7] How deeply did foreign and coastal commerce penetrate the larger structure of the American colonial economy? The best scholarly estimates suggest that by the early 1770s perhaps 12 to 13 percent of all commodities produced in North America were sent to overseas markets, while an additional 3 percent entered the coastal export trade.[8]

CONDITIONS OF COLONIAL INDUSTRY

The preeminence of agriculture in the colonial economy has been stressed again and again. Factory production as we know it today did not exist. Even the "putting out" system—a method of production in which the capitalist gathered the raw material, distributed it to individual workers in their homes, and later collected and sold the finished products—was rare. Nevertheless, a certain type of crude and somewhat primitive industry was widespread. There was, for example, the typical household manufacturing. On the average farm the housewife spun and wove the wool, flax, or cotton for clothes, smoked and salted meat, dried and preserved fruit and vegetables. She made her own soap and candles and brewed her own beer. Leather for shoes, gloves, and work clothes was produced and processed on the farm. From his own wood lot the farmer procured timber for his house and hardwood for his tools, furniture, and casks. The hard labor involved in manufacturing all these necessities of living was not expended by preference. The colonial farmer, like the farmer of today, would have much preferred to exchange his surplus for manufactured goods. The typical farm of the colonial period was small, however, surpluses were meager, and transportation was poor. The farm family manufactured its own goods by necessity.

Village industries

Another type of manufacturing appeared as communities grew large enough to support it. Most settlements of any size had a sawmill where the farmers could have their lumber prepared, a gristmill where their corn or wheat could be ground, and a fulling mill where cloth could be smoothed and dyed after it was woven. If a community was large enough, it also supported a shoemaker, a tailor, a cabinetmaker, and other highly trained artisans who produced goods on order.

Obstacles to the development of manufacturing

Delay in the development of colonial manufacturing for export and the general trade was not due to lack of resources. These existed or could be produced in abundance. Nor was it due in the last analysis to lack of labor, scarce as that might have been. By 1776 the colonial population was one-fourth that of England. Newly arrived immigrants, deprived of good land in the East, might have been induced to

[6]Philip D. Curtin, *The Atlantic Slave Trade: A Census* (Madison: University of Wisconsin Press, 1969), p. 141.

[7]Figures on exports to England (which include commodities then reexported to Europe's continental market) and colonial imports from England are given in *Historical Statistics of the United States*, p. 757. On the trade among the colonies, see James F. Shepherd and Samuel H. Williamson, "The Coastal Trade of the British North American Colonies, 1768–1772," *Journal of Economic History, 32* (1972): 798–802.

[8]Shepherd and Williamson, "Coastal Trade," pp. 801–802.

enter manufacturing; indentured servants and slaves were available. The lack of development was the result of, among other factors, the belief that greater profits were to be obtained in agriculture, commerce, and land speculation. Above all, it resulted from the opposition of the British government. British mercantilism looked upon the colonies as sources of raw materials and as markets for manufactured goods. Manufactured commodities that came into competition with British goods either in the colonies or in international trade were discouraged.

Even the most cursory survey of the actions of the Board of Trade and other groups in the British government and of their representatives in America during the century preceding the American Revolution bears out this contention. The policy can be seen in specific legislation to curtail the development of a colonial woolen or iron industry. It is also evident in the instructions to colonial governors to prevent the levying of duties on British goods brought to America or anything else that would in any way give preferential treatment to colonial manufactured products. It is apparent in the frequent vetoes of colonial laws passed to encourage local manufacturing. It is clear in the veto of laws passed by southern legislatures to curtail the slave trade, for it was the business of the British government to perpetuate in the colonies the plantation system that was so profitable to the commercial and shipping interests of England.

INDUSTRIES OF THE FOREST

To the pioneer farmers the rich forest lands of America seemed only obstructions to be cleared as quickly as possible in order to open up their farms. It was not long, however, before they discovered in the forests a valuable commodity for trade. Four industries were dependent upon the forest: lumbering, shipbuilding, the manufacture of naval supplies, and the making of potash. In addition, of course, there was the lucrative fur trade. Lumbering and shipbuilding were particularly active in the northern colonies, where the rivers extended well up into the forests and sawmills could be run by water power at the fall line.

There were steady and profitable markets for their products in the West Indies and southern Europe. The northern colonies developed a profitable export trade, mainly to the West Indies, in barrel staves that were used for casks as the sugar trade expanded after 1650. Cooperage also became an important local industry in the North, as the vigorous assault on the heavily forested land went forward.

Ships and naval stores
With an abundance of white pine, fir, and oak close to the water's edge and a ready supply of pitch pine for tar and turpentine, the colonists had at hand the raw products for shipbuilding. The cheapness of the raw materials overcame the high cost of labor, and the need for ships stimulated the industry from the start. Most of the shipbuilding was centered in New England, where construction was 30 to 50 percent cheaper than in Europe. By 1760 the colonies were building from 300 to 400 boats a year, and one-third of the tonnage sailing under the British flag was American-built. Besides lumber and ships, New England produced certain naval stores, notably tar, pitch, resin, turpentine, and water-rotted hemp. Production of these commodities, needed by the British navy and merchant marine, was stimulated, particularly in the Carolinas, by British bounties after 1705.

The fur trade
Throughout the colonial period the fur trade with the Indians was an important and valuable source of income for all of the colonies. Many types of furs were secured, but the basic pelts were beaver skins in the North and deer skins in the South. For these the colonists traded guns, rum, knives, and other commodities. Sale to the Indians of guns and rum was forbidden in most of the colonies, but since it facilitated trade, the laws were generally evaded. The high profits of the early years declined as the Indians grew more knowledgeable and as English colonial traders came into competition with the French and Spanish.

Even as early as the 1720s, furs were of declining relative importance in the Atlantic coastal colonies' exports, their value being about £20,000 or less annually. By then the principal arena of the fur trade had shifted into the continent's interior. Beginning in 1670, a company of merchant adventurers, the Hudson's Bay Company, was given an English monopoly for trade in the region draining into Canada's Hudson's Bay—a direct stroke aimed at the political and economic interests of France in Quebec. From then on, as the new monopoly produced large fur exports for British trade, the principal importance of its activities for the Atlantic coastal colonies was that the rising competition with France played a part in triggering colonial wars, including the great struggle that drove France from Canada in 1763 and established British dominance in eastern North America.

INDUSTRIES OF THE SEA

The demand for fish was increasing in Europe, especially in Catholic countries. New England, close to the fishing grounds and with an abundance of shipbuilding materials at hand, was in a strategic position to profit. After 1650 its prosperity was closely connected with fishing, and by 1675 more than 600 vessels and 4000 men were engaged in cod fishing. By the end of the colonial period the industry was worth £225,000 a year. As the market developed, New Englanders divided their fish into three classes. The largest and fattest, because they were the most difficult to cure thoroughly, were consumed locally. The second class, smaller and more easily cured, was exported to Europe. The third class, too small for the European or American market, was sold in the West Indies as food for slaves, usually in exchange for molasses, which was brought back and converted into rum. In addition to the manufacture of rum, which was thus related to the fish trade, the demand for salt was stimulated, and salt vats were erected at various points along the shore where sea water could be evaporated. Fish, molasses, rum, and salt all contributed to make the cooperage industry one of the liveliest in the northern colonies.

Almost as important as fishing during the last hundred years of the colonial era was the whaling industry. Spermaceti, sperm oil, whalebone, and ambergris were in great demand. Whales were abundant off the New England coast, and after 1700 New England seamen began to harpoon the unwieldy monsters when they came up to breathe. When the whales were driven off the coast, the whalers followed them to other regions. After 1732 an annual bounty of twenty shillings a ton (doubled in 1747) was paid on vessels of 200 tons or upward engaged in whaling, and the consequent increasing values of the products spurred on the hunters. The most skillful whalers in the empire came from New England, and that area practically monopolized the business. More than 300 vessels and 4000 sailors were engaged in it at the outbreak of the Revolution, most of them hailing from Nantucket, New Bedford, Marblehead, and Provincetown.

Upon the basis of spermaceti a candle-making business of some importance grew up. The oil of whales was prized as an illuminant, and was sold throughout the colonies.

INDUSTRIES OF THE HOME AND WORKSHOP

Mention has already been made of household industries, but it is worthwhile to emphasize again the importance of this phase of colonial manufacturing.

Few homes were without a spinning wheel and a hand loom, and the larger part of the textiles used in the colonies was produced in the home. Most of this cloth was either wool or linen or a mixture of the two. Sheep were more commonly raised on farms in this period than in later years and flax was more widely grown. Hemp cloth or linen of varying degrees of fineness was the chief colonial textile; it served nearly all of the purposes for which cotton is used today. While the British government did what it could to discourage the production of woolen goods, which came into competition with its own manufacturing, it was eager to encourage the growth and use of hemp and flax. Several colonial assemblies offered bounties for the growing of these two crops and others required that they be grown. Little cotton was grown in the mainland colonies until after the 1790s. Some was imported, but since it was a difficult fiber to work, it was generally mixed with linen or wool before it was spun. Not only were spinning and weaving universal household industries, but by the time of the Revolution the faint beginnings of the factory system could be seen in the grouping of several weaving machines under the same roof. Such shops could be found in certain of the larger towns such as Philadelphia and Lancaster.

Ironworks

It was impossible to produce iron utensils on most farms. The cost of importing them was so great, however, that ironworks appeared in Massachusetts at Lynn and Taunton as early as the 1640s to exploit the bog iron common in those regions. In the eighteenth century the industry moved farther from the coast to use the rock ores in the uplands of New Jersey and Pennsylvania. Some copper was also mined in Connecticut, New York, and New Jersey.

The purpose of the iron mines was chiefly to supply the immediate needs of the colonists for wagon hardware, mill spindles, anvils, pots, kettles, forged plates, weights, bells, chains, anchors, guns, and cannon. In conjunction with these mines and smelting establishments, casting works were usually found. Slitting mills furnished iron rods from which farmers manufactured nails on winter evenings by means of a small furnace in the chimney corner. The colonial smelting furnaces generally were small and crude, producing from a dozen to twenty tons a week.

The development of iron manufacture was a matter of enormous consequence for British policy makers. By the mid-eighteenth century, some 200,000 workers, and in all at least 600,000 people in the home country, were dependent upon the English iron industry for their employment and support; but the rise of a competing American industry had caused slackening of demand for English iron goods in the colonies. It was to assure England of semi-manufactured iron for the home slitting and rolling mills, hardware and cutlery manufacturers, and similar firms — iron from its own possessions, enough to free England from persistent dependence upon Swedish suppliers — and to stifle the rising colonial competition that the famous Iron Act of 1750 was made law. This act, banning the building of any rolling, plating, or other specialized ironworks in the American colonies somewhat discouraged American investment in iron works, but not because the law was actually enforced: there is no surviving record of a single prosecution in America under this act, though scores of blatant evasions of its terms are well known. In any case, a very substantial iron industry already existed in America in 1750. Together with new iron works built illegally after the Iron Act became law, these forges and furnaces exceeded the number in

England and Wales combined by the 1770s, and American crude-iron output was greater than that of England's furnaces. The output of American iron producers in 1775 was three times that of 1750, when the Iron Act went into operation — obviously, an attenuated and ineffective sort of operation at best.[9]

Distilling

An almost universal industry was the making of liquor, both in households and in distilleries. It thrived in the coastal towns of New England, where molasses from the West Indies was distilled into rum. Beer, ale, and cider as well as rum were exported to the West Indies, and rum was in constant demand for provisioning ships and for trading on the African slave coast. The colonial Americans were hard drinkers, and a large volume of rum was consumed at home. For fishermen, loggers, sailors, and laborers in the northern colonies, a generous daily rum ration was commonly regarded as indispensable to fortify oneself against the rigors of climate and hard toil, and it was considered to have medicinal powers as well. The million gallons a year estimated to have been distilled in Massachusetts alone by the 1750s also found use in household cooking.

The growth of manufacturing

A useful impression of the extent to which colonial manufacturing had grown, despite British regulatory efforts, was given by an English commentator who wrote in 1774:

> *The inhabitants in the Colonies . . . do make many things, and export several manufactures, to the exclusion of English manufactures of the same kinds. The New England people import from the foreign and the British Islands very large quantities of cotton, which they spin and work up with linen yarn into a stuff, like that made in Manchester, wherewith they clothe themselves and their neighbours. Hats are manufactured in Carolina, Pennsylvania and in other Colonies. Soap and candles, and all kinds of wood-work, are made in the Northern Colonies and exported to the Southern. Coaches, chariots, chaises, and*

[9]Lawrence H. Gipson, *The British Empire Before the American Revolution,* vol. 3 (revised): *The British Isles and the American Colonies: The Northern Plantations, 1748–1754* (New York: Knopf, 1960), pp. 206–208, 227–229; Oliver M. Dickerson, *The Navigation Acts and the American Revolution* (Philadelphia: University of Pennsylvania Press, 1951), pp. 47–49.

chairs, are also made in the Northern Colonies and sent down to the Southern. Coach harness, and many other kinds of leather manufactures, are likewise made in the Northern Colonies, and sent down to the Southern; and large quantities of shoes have lately been exported from thence to the West India Islands. Linens are made to a great amount in Pennsylvania and cordage and other hemp manufactures are carried on in many places with great success: and foundry ware, axes, and other iron tools and utensils are also become articles of commerce, with which the Southern Colonies are supplied from the Northern.[10]

Industries that were characterized by relatively heavy investment in equipment and that included numerous firms with large work forces for that day were shipbuilding, leathertanning, glassmaking, sugarrefining, and candlemaking. To be sure, small shops and individual crafts-

men were also engaged in these trades. Female artisans were important in millinery shops, ladies' tailoring, and household manufacturing of textiles. Flour mills, lumber mills, and paperworks were widely dispersed; many of the country mills were small and involved only a few hundred dollars in capital and a handful of workers at each site. But at Philadelphia especially, and in the other Atlantic port towns as well, there were also some large-scale milling establishments. Individual artisans, working alone or with a small force of apprentices and journeymen, engaged in scores of old-line crafts: not only the classic occupations such as harness-making, smithing, carpentry, printing, ropemaking, and the like, but also highly specialized crafts emblematic of the rich diversity of urban and rural life in colonial America. Thus the specialist in codfishing hooks or ornamental glass birds and the plaster-forms artist also contributed to the larger complex of economic activity that is subsumed under the phrase "colonial manufacturing."

THE PROBLEM OF A COLONIAL CURRENCY

Not least of the problems confronted by colonial political leaders and English officialdom was that of providing an expanding, vigorously active American economy with an adequate supply of currency. In the seventeenth century the gold and silver coin that was obtained in foreign commerce was rapidly drained off because of the unequal trade balance with England. The ordinary needs of commerce, in any case, made it desirable for paper money of some sort to be provided. With specie in short supply, it was difficult to settle balances, carry on domestic commercial transactions, or even meet merchants' current obligations on customs duties and taxes.

Land banks

Massachusetts, Pennsylvania, Delaware, New York, and Maryland resorted to land banks, also called loan banks, which issued paper on the collateral of mortgages and real estate. Although Maryland's paper issues on mortages declined in value, thus creating the problems that accompany a depreciated cur-

rency, the other land banks were generally successful in their dual purpose of getting needed credit into the hands of farmers and helping to provide the larger community with paper currency.

Fiat money

The colonial governments also resorted to the issuing of fiat money (non-interest-bearing paper), which passed as common currency at face value or less, depending upon public confidence in the revenue-raising capacity of the government. Beginning with Massachusetts in 1690, fiat-money issues were resorted to regularly in times of extraordinary governmental burdens, particularly during periods of war. Future taxes were customarily pledged for the redemption of the debt that the fiat issues represented, and the currency was meanwhile accepted for payment of taxes.

Currency policy in peace and war, 1754–1764

In many colonies, such paper-money issues resulted in only mild depreciation. But there were some dramatic instances of irresponsible currency policy, most notably in Rhode Island. In all cases, British governors and colonial offi-

[10]*Interest of the Merchants and Manufacturers of Great Britain in the Present Contest with the Colonies Stated and Considered* (London, 1774), p. 12

cials in London reviewed the legislation and attempted to keep the currency emissions within moderate limits, often to the distress of various American interest groups. Although historians have often portrayed the currency policy question as one that pitted poor debtor-farmers against the wealthier creditor elements in American society, in fact merchants and the largest planters had a stake in providing the economy with a circulating medium and maintaining the flow of credit; hence they were usually found on the side of those who favored paper issues within reasonable bounds.

The restraints of prudence broke down during the French and Indian Wars (1754–1763), when enormous demands were made upon the colonial governments to meet the expenses of recruiting, outfitting, provisioning, and paying troops. Pennsylvania resorted to paper issues that swelled its outstanding currency from £80,000 to £540,000; New York issued £535,000, and Virginia £440,000. Serious depreciation of currency valuation resulted, and English creditors of American tobacco planters and merchants stood to lose heavily, especially as Virginia and other colonies had

moved toward making their paper currency legal tender; that is, to require its acceptance at face value for payment of private obligations. There had always been abundant difference of opinion on both sides of the Atlantic as to what in fact constituted "reasonable bounds" for colonial paper-money issues. But by 1763 the debate had assumed crisis proportions, and the result was a move in England to clamp rigid controls on the colonial legislatures. This was accomplished with the Currency Act of 1764, which extended to all the colonies a prohibition (imposed on New England in 1751) against the issue of bills of credit as legal tender. The British did continue to grant permission for limited issues of paper acceptable for payment of taxes. In the political atmosphere of the late 1760s and early 1770s, however, such concessions by the British were deemed much less significant than the 1764 Currency Act. The Americans viewed that measure as a crippling impairment of the colonies' autonomy in their fiscal and business affairs. It appeared to be yet another effort to subordinate the colonies to British interests.

RESISTANCE TO AUTHORITY AND "SALUTARY NEGLECT"

It had never been the intent of British mercantilist policy to cripple the colonial economy, but only to channel economic development and align it with the mother country's needs and interests. But one political reality that became evident rather early in the game was the readiness of the American colonies to resist mercantilist laws that they found damaging. Indeed, the threshold at which the Americans considered British legislation to have become "intolerable" was remarkably low, and the degree of resistance they proved willing to mount was remarkably high.

This was true even in 1660, when the English government under Charles II moved to regularize the laws of trade and navigation. The new enactments were accompanied by a reform that placed customs officers in America under the direct control of crown officials in London for the first time. (As a parliamentary act of 1673 read, this was done so that "this whole Business" of customs-duty collection might be "ordered and managed," instead of being left to people who had proved themselves more dedicated to the colonies' than to

the crown's interests.) Resistance in America was both immediate and widespread. The assemblies of several colonies—including that of Virginia, the leading exporting colony—voiced official protests and denials of English authority. There was turmoil in many towns, with outbreaks of violence that killed three of the royal customs collectors. Two other collectors were thrown into prison, and one was even tried for treason.

In 1696 Parliament responded by ordering the enforcement of the trade laws in Admiralty courts, under direct control of London, thereby bypassing the American colonial governments. But again resistance in America made it impossible for royal officials to function, and there were both official remonstrances by the legislatures and outright mob violence in the streets.

The price of strict enforcement, it had become clear, was political disaffection and perhaps much worse. For the Whigs, who dominated English politics from 1725 to the early 1760s, this seemed too high a price to pay. Being closely allied with the merchant interests, the Whigs were dedicated to prosperity, and they did not wish to risk loss of the empire and its markets. Hence the home government adopted a calculated policy of looking the other way, permitting colonial evasion of many trade regulations. The result was what has been called the policy of "salutary neglect." The colonists were allowed to pursue their economic destinies; and while mercantilist laws remained on the books, government officials and colonists alike understood that they were not to be enforced vigorously.[11]

The Molasses Act of 1733

Salutary neglect, which, as we have seen, made the Iron Act a virtual dead letter, was even more important with regard to the trade in sugar and molasses. The Molasses Act of 1733 placed a high duty upon sugar imported to the mainland American colonies from the Spanish, French, and Dutch islands in the West Indies. Had the Molasses Act been enforced strictly, it would have undermined the vital trade in sugar and molasses on which New England's rum distilling industry was dependent. But New England's illicit trade with the foreign islands (whose sugar was much cheaper than that produced in the English islands) was also a matter of deep concern to other powerful interests within the imperial economy. The British families that owned land in the West Indies wanted the colonial trade with the foreign islands cut off entirely, while the American merchants and shippers wanted to keep their foreign sources of supply and to evade payment of the official duties. London grocers and merchants were primarily interested in protecting their position in the reexport trade to continental Europe; and merchants who refined and marketed sugar for the domestic English market wished to see prices held down, so they could expand their market at home. This multiple clash of divergent interest groups created endless headaches for the British administrators who presided over a diverse, far-flung imperial system; some balance had to be struck. And so they decided to permit American shippers to smuggle vast quantities of foreign sugar and molasses. In that important respect, the home government was not yet prepared to translate formal law into operative policy. What a leading American historian has written of mercantilist policy as it was applied to iron manufacturing reflected a similar

dilemma in the case of enforcement of the Molasses Act:

> The mother country's unsuccessful attempt to regulate production and sales of colonial iron in the middle of the eighteenth century . . . served to make clear that— even with the best of motives— it was no easy task to shape by legislation the complex economic forces of the Empire. It also made clear that the government could not guide these forces, as had been hoped, toward realizing the ideals of imperial self-sufficiency and planned economy based on mutual advantages. . . . Economic sectionalism within the Empire, based upon particular and important sectional divergent interests, in the end served to defeat every effort put forth in this direction.[12]

The costs of empire

Apart from the political risks that constantly bedeviled enforcement of the mercantilist laws, there were increasingly serious revenue problems. The cost of subsidies paid by the British to support selected activities such as indigo cultivation and of rebates on duties designed to encourage colonial production of naval stores and lumber was of no small importance: an estimated £1.7 million was paid in bounties on American products from 1706 through 1774.[13] In addition, the British calculated as major costs of empire the protection of the home market for the benefit of colonial interests, as with tobacco, foodstuffs, crude iron, and other products.

Not least important was the continuing cost of naval and military protection for American trade and colonial defense. This last item of expenditure became enormous—and indeed an overriding consideration that would soon shape nearly the whole of British colonial policy—during the nine-year conflict with France known as the French and Indian Wars (1754– 1763). England emerged from that conflict with an increased burden of national debt: some £137 million of funded debt, requiring annual expenditures for interest alone that were equivalent to the entire governmental budget of a decade earlier.

The fiscal crisis ineluctably led Parliament and crown officials to seek new means of taxing

---

[11]See Thomas C. Barrow, *Trade and Empire: The British Customs Service in Colonial America, 1660–1775* (Cambridge, Mass.: Harvard University Press, 1967).

[12]Gipson, *British Empire*, vol. 3, p. 229.
[13]Dickerson, *Navigation Acts*, p. 14.

the colonies. The urgent question of new sources of revenue coincided, however, with the advent to power of new royal officials who were determined to make British rule in America more centralized and effective. Their new determination led the British government to adopt a series of measures that again triggered resistance and defiance; but this time, the two sides were on a collision course that culminated in the Revolution.

SELECTED READINGS

Barrow, Thomas C., *Trade and Empire: The British Customs Service in Colonial America, 1660–1775* (Cambridge, Mass.: Harvard University Press, 1967).

Bining, Arthur C., *Pennsylvania Iron Manufacture in the Eighteenth Century* (Harrisburg: Pennsylvania Museum and Historical Commission, 1938).

Bridenbaugh, Carl, *Cities in the Wilderness: The First Century of Urban Life in America, 1625–1742* (New York: Knopf, 1955).

———, *The Colonial Craftsman* (New York: New York University Press, 1950).

Carroll, Charles, *The Timber Economy of Puritan New England* (Providence: Brown University Press, 1973).

Clark, Victor S., *History of Manufactures in the United States,* Volume I: *1607–1860* (1929, reprinted New York: Peter Smith, 1949).

Davis, Ralph, "English Foreign Trade, 1660–1700," *Economic History Review,* 2nd series, VII (1954).

*Dickerson, Oliver M., *The Navigation Acts and the American Revolution* (1951, reprinted New York: A. S. Barnes, 1963).

Farnie, D. A., "The Commercial Empire of the Atlantic, 1607–1783," *Economic History Review,* 2nd series, XV (1962).

Gipson, Lawrence H., *The British Empire Before the American Revolution,* Volume II (revised): *The British Isles and the American Colonies: The Southern Plantations, 1748–1754;* and Volume III (revised): . . . *The Northern Plantations, 1748–1754;* and Volume X: *The Triumphant Empire, . . . 1763–1766* (New York: Knopf, 1960, 1961).

Harper, Lawrence A., *The English Navigation Laws: A 17th Century Experiment in Social Engineering* (New York: Columbia University Press, 1939).

Jensen, Arthur L., *The Maritime Commerce of Colonial Philadelphia* (Madison: State Historical Society of Wisconsin, 1963).

Johnson, Victor, "Fair Traders and Smugglers in Philadelphia, 1754–1763," *Pennsylvania Magazine of History and Biography,* LXXXIII (1959).

*Kammen, Michael, *Empire and Interest: The American Colonies and the Politics of Mercantilism* (Philadephia: Lippincott, 1970).

Malone, Joseph J., *Pine Trees and Politics: The Naval Stores and Forest Policy in Colonial New England, 1691–1775* (Seattle: University of Washington Press, 1964).

Nettels, Curtis Putnam, *The Money Supply of the American Colonies Before 1720* (Madison: University of Wisconsin Press, 1934).

Price, Jacob M., "Economic Function and the Growth of American Port Towns in the Eighteenth Century," *Perspectives in American History,* VIII (1974).

Shepherd, James, and Walton, Gary M., *Shipping, Maritime Trade, and the Economic Development of Colonial North America* (Cambridge, England: The University Press, 1972).

Sheridan, Richard B., "The Molasses Act and the Market Strategy of the British Sugar Planters," *Journal of Economic History,* XVII (1957).

Spruill, Julia C., *Women's Life and Work in the Southern Colonies* (1938, reprinted New York: Norton, 1972).

Tryon, Rolla M., *Household Manufactures in the United States, 1640–1860* (New York: Johnson Reprint, 1972).

the American revolution and the new nation, 1763–1789

The American economy had fared well, on the whole, under British mercantilism up to 1763. There had been persistent tension between the colonies and the home country over the issue of revenue laws and their enforcement, and this tension had sometimes produced violent resistance in America. There were other significant areas of conflict as well, such as British policy with respect to the colonies' revenue laws and the policies governing land distribution in the West. Nonetheless, Americans in the eighteenth century enjoyed an economic and political situation described well enough by the Scots economist Adam Smith (no friend of mercantilism) when he contended that British rule in America had been "less illiberal and oppressive than that of any other European nation."

The explanation of colonial prosperity up to 1763 rests primarily upon three facts. In the first place, the colonists occupied the rim of a continent rich in agricultural, forest, ocean, and mineral resources. Hence they enjoyed a comparative economic advantage in devoting themselves to extractive industries — activities generally consistent with British mercantilist aims. Moreover, by a process of "forward linkage" — exploiting comparative advantage in primary activities such as lumbering by using the resources so acquired in related secondary and tertiary activities such as shipbuilding and commerce — the colonists were able to accumulate savings to develop certain manufactures and to build up their own commerce.

In the second place, British mercantilist laws had frequently benefited special interests in the colonial economy. Thus preferential tariff treatment had been given in England to the "enumerated" commodities such as tobacco, lumber, crude iron, whale oil, and pot and pearl ashes. The British paid substantial bounties, moreover, on American naval stores and indigo. In some instances, the colonists could purchase commodities imported via England from the Continent more cheaply than could Englishmen in the home islands, since the duties were partially refunded.

In the third place, mercantilist regulation had not pressed too harshly because of salutary neglect; many of the laws had been easily evaded.

On the negative side were the well-known disadvantages of colonial status within a mercantilist system geared to the economy of the home country and the larger interests of a diverse empire. These disadvantages included the need to pay middlemen's charges to English merchants on colonial products required to pass through the home country prior to sale in ultimate markets on the Continent. Monopoly of the carrying trade by English and colonial ships may have tended to make freight rates higher than they would have been in a more competitive regime, perhaps partially offsetting the gains to the colonial economy of American shipping earnings. And finally, the colonists' supply of gold and silver with which to meet adverse trade balances was small, yet Britain had chosen to close to them one of the greatest sources of specie, the French, Dutch, and Spanish West Indies markets. Colonial efforts to ease the currency and credit situation were closely controlled — unfairly, as many colonists thought — by the home government in England.

Empire's new context, 1763

In the 1760s the balance of burdens and advantages began to shift markedly. By their victory over France in the war that ended in

1763, the British had acquired control of a vast American empire that included former French Canada and the entire western territory to the Mississippi River. In addition, Great Britain emerged from that war with an enormous national debt and serious governmental financing problems. With a new king, George III, coming to the British throne just as the war with France was ending, leadership of the home government in London became infused with the ideas of new men—men who perceived their role as that of imperial reformer. Their self-appointed mission was to put their government's fiscal affairs in better order, to assert the need (and the power) of Great Britain to control the American economy more effectively, and to derive large additional revenues from America.

To accomplish these reforms the British adopted a three-pronged strategy. First, they designed new revenue laws that proved to be so provocative as to threaten outright revolution in the colonies. Second, they redesigned British imperial administration so as to render royal officers free of effective control by the colonial governments. And finally, to ensure the security of the enlarged empire in America, but also (at least as the colonists saw it) to back up the civil authority of their officials, they placed a standing army of 10,000 men on permanent duty in North America and stood ready to support them with the Royal Navy. These measures were received in the colonies with alarm and a sense of outrage. An atmosphere of impending crisis and turmoil quickly prevailed.

REVOLUTIONARY CRISIS: 1764 to 1776

George Grenville, the new British prime minister, who took office at the end of the great war with France, together with Charles Townshend, president of the Board of Trade, the principal agency in charge of colonial affairs, determined to end the old policy of salutary neglect. The first step they took to force the colonies to pay a "fair" share (as the British saw it) of the war debt and current expenses was to impose a "realistic" duty on sugar and molasses. Their basic strategy was to lower the Molasses Act duties, but simultaneously to crack down on smuggling and thereby increase total revenues.

The Sugar Act
This strategy was carried out in the Sugar Act of 1764, which lowered the duty on foreign molasses from sixpence to threepence a gallon. British naval officers were ordered to aid in enforcement, and cases arising from indictments for smuggling would be tried by British Admiralty courts. In addition, the 1764 act placed duties on sugar, indigo, coffee, wines, silks, and calicoes, while the number of "enumerated" articles was increased.

The Stamp and Quartering Acts
The Sugar Act was supplemented in 1765 by the Stamp Act, which provided that stamps varying in cost from a halfpenny to £10 be affixed to licenses, contracts, deeds, wills, newspapers, pamphlets, almanacs, and other papers. The Stamp Act, following the Sugar Act so

closely, created an excitement unparalleled in the colonies. When petitions and remonstrances failed, a boycott of English goods was inaugurated, merchants binding themselves to import no British goods until the act was repealed. In England merchants and manufacturers were affected to such an extent that in 1766 the Stamp Act was repealed and the Sugar Act revised downward, although the concessions were accompanied by a "declaratory act" asserting the legal right of Parliament to legislate for the colonies "in all cases whatsoever."

Rejoicing followed the repeal of the Stamp Act, and opposition to the British government might have subsided had not the imperial authority in 1765 passed a quartering act, declaring that the colonists must provide for the light, lodging, and fuel of garrisons to be placed in specified districts.

The Townshend Acts
In 1767 Charles Townshend, who was now the leading spirit in the cabinet, forced through Parliament the Townshend Acts, one of which imposed duties on glass, paper, painters' colors, red and white lead, and tea. Though not high, these tariffs fell on articles of general consumption and raised the cost of living. More dangerous than the duties were other features of the Townshend Acts which called for a reorganization of the customs service, with Admiralty courts established in the colonies to expedite cases of smuggling, and which provided that the money raised be used to pay the expenses

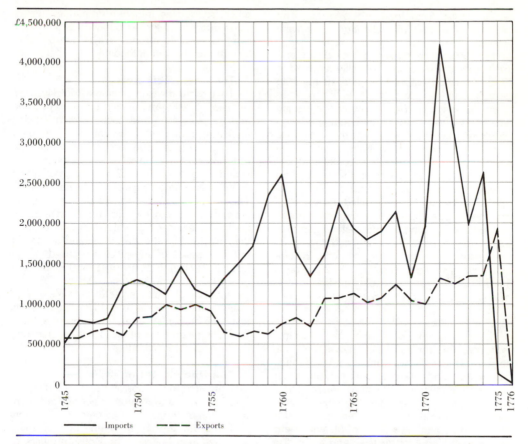

Figure 6–1. **Trade Between Great Britain and the American Mainland Colonies, 1745–1776.** Source: U.S. Department of Commerce, Bureau of the Census, *Historical Statistics of the United States, Colonial Times to 1957* (Washington, D.C.: U.S. Government Printing Office, 1960), p. 757.

of the civil government. The latter provision was particularly obnoxious because it would have removed from the colonists their chief weapon in their conflict with British officials.[1] A special act suspended the New York Assembly because it had refused to comply with a law of 1765 calling for the adequate quartering of soldiers. Irritating also was a part of one of the acts that reaffirmed the legality of the writs of assistance.[2]

The colonists responded to the Townshend Acts with a policy of "nonintercourse." The boycott of 1768–1769 was more than a voluntary movement; it was backed and encouraged by the colonial legislatures. It was enforced, too, by vigilante groups whose activities were coordinated by "committees of correspondence" and whose membership, as in the organization called the Sons of Liberty, included both wealthy men of prominence and (increasingly)

[1] In many instances when customs officials—who often had simply allowed the trade laws to go unenforced—did attempt rigid enforcement, colonial courts had actually prosecuted them for violations of provincial law.

[2] Writs of assistance were general search warrants that gave law-enforcement officials a virtually free hand in searching for and taking smuggled goods. In 1760 the British government, outraged by American merchants' trading with the enemy, had ordered American customs officers to employ writs of assistance. In Massachusetts the brilliant lawyer James

Otis argued in a widely publicized court test that the writs were unconstitutional because they violated inalienable rights—"fundamental principles of law" that even Parliament could not violate. "Then and there," John Adams later wrote, "was the first scene of the first act of opposition to the arbitrary claims of Great Britain. Then and there, the child Independence was born" (quoted in Lawrence H. Gipson, *The Coming of the Revolution, 1763–1775* [New York: Harper & Row, 1962], p. 37).

people drawn from lower walks of life. The makings of a true revolutionary cadre were present.[3]

The British were forced to back down, and the Townshend Acts were partially repealed in 1770. A tax on tea was retained, as much to assert in principle the authority of the crown as to obtain revenues. Now many of the leading merchants who had advocated nonimportation withdrew their support from the resistance movement. They did so either because they feared the growing turmoil in colonial society or, as contemporary critics and some modern scholars have asserted, because they had succeeded in selling off their piled-up stocks of imported goods and were ready to resume their profitable trade with England.[4] After a period of persistent economic uncertainty and stagnation, the prosperity of commerce returned and colonial imports soared, exceeding £4.2 million in 1771. This was roughly double the import level of any year since 1764. (See Figure 6–1.)

The Tea Act

If the defection of prosperous merchants from the militant resistance movement indicated that the steam was running out of the radicalism that had prevailed since 1765, other causes for continuing turmoil appeared. There was no cessation of revolutionary activity on the part of the most militant leadership faction—men such as Samuel Adams of Massachusetts and Patrick Henry of Virginia. And the British government continued to take measures that frustrated the possibility of reconciliation. One such measure was the Tea Act of 1773, giving a full monopoly of the American market for tea to the East India Company, which was then facing bankruptcy. Although this monopoly act actually made tea cheaper in America than ever before, it also deprived the American merchants of a valuable branch of their trade.

If such a monopoly could be granted on one commodity, why assume that other, similar monopolies would not follow? Instantly the most powerful merchants in the seaport towns were aroused to action, and when the East India Company's first ships arrived, the "Boston Tea Party" was staged: A group of Boston citizens disguised as Indians dumped the entire cargo into the water. At other ports, the ships carrying tea were turned back or persuaded to lie offshore, without unloading.

The Intolerable Acts

Then other measures followed quickly, each of them widening the breach between England and the colonies—and each of them forcing increasing numbers of the colonial élite, many of them conservatives driven reluctantly to it, to endorse the radical cause. Parliament responded to Boston's challenge by passing four coercive laws known as the "Intolerable Acts." These acts closed the port of Boston until the tea should be paid for; they removed some of the liberal features of the Massachusetts charter; they provided for the trial in England, instead of in the colonies, of any officials accused of violence in executing their duties; and Parliament revived the hated Quartering Act of 1765, for the purpose of stationing soldiers in Massachusetts. In short, Boston would be brought to its knees by draconian economic punishment and by placing a garrison of the British regular army in the midst of its citizens.

The Quebec Act of 1774

Unrelated to the Boston situation but equally inflammatory was another act of Parliament in 1774 known as the Quebec Act. This law annexed the territory between the Ohio River and the Great Lakes to the British province of Quebec. At a single stroke the British seemed to be slamming the door against any further westward settlement by the Atlantic coast colonies, making permanent an official ban to new settlement beyond the Appalachians which they had put into effect in 1763. They abandoned the traditional policy of substantial self-government in America, since royal officials and courts in Quebec had been given autocratic powers greatly exceeding those they exercised in the thirteen American colonies.

The colonies move toward revolution

With the enactment of these laws, the revolutionary crisis came to a climax. The Continental Congress, representing all the colonies, issued a Declaration of Rights that substantially denied the authority of Parliament to enact any of the laws that had sparked resistance since 1763. Still another boycott went into effect against British goods, and imports fell off in 1775 to only a tenth of the level they had

---

[3]Pauline Maier, *From Resistance to Revolution: Colonial Radicals and the Development of American Opposition to Britain, 1765–1776* (New York: Knopf, 1972), pp. 78–91, 116–117.

[4]Ibid., p. 118; Marc Egnal and Joseph A. Ernst, "An Economic Interpretation of the American Revolution," *William and Mary Quarterly,* 3rd ser., 29 (1972):11–23.

reached the previous year. Military preparations were made, as the new militant coalition established revolutionary councils in all the colonies, seizing power from loyalist officials, and forcibly threatened those who refused to pledge allegiance to their cause. Then, in March 1775, Parliament declared Massachusetts to be in a state of rebellion, and the revolutionary leaders had a price put upon their heads. New England fishermen were banned from the Grand Banks, American trade with the British West Indies and the home country was interdicted, and England moved toward effective all-out war against its colonies. The Revolution had begun. The guns sounded at Lexington and Concord in April 1775, and the official declaration of independence lay ahead.

THE ECONOMY AND THE REVOLUTION

It remains for us to examine more closely some of the major economic factors in the imperial conflict and in the political situation within the colonies.

The diversity of American society

Most scholars recognize that the very diversity of American society militated against abiding American loyalties to Great Britain. This diversity was the result of economic opportunity in America during the eighteenth century: the seaboard colonies had proved a magnet for immigrants not only from England but also from the Netherlands, Germany, Ulster, and southern Ireland. None of these non-English elements, who comprised one-fourth of the white population in the colonies generally and a much higher proportion in some of them, felt ties of sentiment and tradition to England. Distance, too, worked against the old Anglo-American connection.

Revenues and rebellion

Economic considerations played a large part in motivating both colonial revolutionary groups and the British government's leadership in the ministries and Parliament. To some extent, of course, motivation was purely political. One cannot easily discount the testimony of such men as George Mason of Virginia, who claimed that he had risked his life and standing "to rescue our Country from the Oppression and Tyranny of the British Government, and to secure the Rights and Liberty of ourselves, and our Posterity."[5] On the British side, the government's leaders had "law and order" in mind when they decided to reassert their authority in America. They recognized that there was a strong drift toward insubordination and defiance of their authority, and they decided to employ such measures as placing a large standing army on American soil because it "might be particularly necessary for awing the Colonists" and to "secure their dependence" on the home country.[6] But libertarian ideology on the American side and authoritarian notions of crown authority on the British side surfaced and assumed new importance because of a confrontation that had some vital economic dimensions.

In essence, the British grand design for reordering the empire in 1763 had a consistency of purpose. It was:

1. To raise revenues independently of the colonial legistatures.
2. To use those revenues partly to help finance the costs of British government generally and partly to maintain civil, military, and naval forces in America.
3. To meet any defiance or resistance by the colonists with intimidating force.[7]

Once intimidating measures were resorted to by the British, principled constitutional objections came forth from American leaders who defended the notion of inalienable liberties. But such intimidation had seemed necessary in the first place because of Britain's concern to in-

[5]Mason to Patrick Henry, May 6, 1783, *The Papers of George Mason, 1725–1792*, ed. Robert A. Rutland (Chapel Hill: University of North Carolina Press, 1970), vol. 2, pp. 771–772.

[6]"Hints Respecting the Settlement of Our American Provinces" (MS, 1763), quoted in Thomas C. Barrow, "A Project for Imperial Reform . . . 1763," *William and Mary Quarterly*, 3rd ser., 24 (1967):122, 125. This 1763 manuscript report was prepared by a British official, probably William Knox, a former colonial official in Georgia, and (as Barrow demonstrates) appears to have had considerable influence in shaping government policy in 1763 and 1764.

[7]Thomas C. Barrow, "Background to the Grenville Program, 1757–1763," *William and Mary Quarterly*, 3rd ser., 22 (1965):93–104.

crease its revenues and to maintain its control, through mercantilist regulation, over the colonial economy.

The imperial system
vs. American interests

At a more specific level, each British measure to reform and consolidate the imperial system was a definite blow to well-developed American economic interests. For instance, the policy adopted in 1763 of placing a ban upon new settlement west of the Appalachian fall line thwarted the ambitions of wealthy merchants and planters who regarded the West as a field for profitable speculative investment. When the 1763 ban was effectively made permanent by the 1774 Quebec Act, the British threatened to hem in colonial population on the seaboard. This was a time when pressure on available land was already becoming severe in the seaboard region. A declining proportion of settlers owned their own farms, and many people of small means were already concerned that lack of land meant lack of opportunity for a better life.

Similarly, the Currency Act of 1764 removed one of the critically important instruments available to the colonists in the ordering of their own economy. The new revenue and commercial measures such as the Stamp Act and the Townshend Acts also represented serious challenges to the colonists' sovereignty in controlling their economic affairs. As one recent scholarly study has contended, these challenges made various interest groups within colonial society "more aware of the identity of economic and political goals."[8] For the Americans felt the effects of the new laws on their trade, were asked to pay higher taxes, and witnessed the reduction of their power over lands and currency: it became increasingly clear that the prosperity of the colonies was at the mercy of a distant and seemingly hostile government. Hence the political goal of independence seemed to be the indispensable key to protecting their economy.

The Revolution
and cost-benefit analysis

It has been argued that in fact the economic burdens of colonial status within the British empire were not severe. For example, one scholar has calculated the dollar value of services (such as protection afforded by the British

army and navy) and of specific burdens (such as the Navigation Acts); and he concludes that during 1768–1772 the net "per capita cost to the colonist of being an Englishman" was only 26 to 42 cents per year![9]

Such statistical calculations are seductively appealing if only because they appear to be so precise. But we think they do not advance very usefully our understanding of the revolutionary situation or the dynamics of the post-1763 crisis. Consider, for example, the following:

1. Economic self-interest: The colonists believed that their economic interests were threatened *potentially,* not only immediately, by such measures as the Quebec Act. In responding to this and other post-1763 British policy initiatives, the Americans were concerned that the home country not only was imposing immediate "burdens" but was also foreclosing the anticipated benefits of enterprise and economic growth.

2. The nature of "benefits": The British services, or "benefits," to the colonies that figure in such statistical calculations were not uniformly viewed by the colonists in that light. This was true especially of the British army stationed in North America after 1763. The army was perceived as a threat by the Americans because it was available for use against them in times of civil disorder; that is, the army was an instrument, potentially, of political repression. And this was precisely how the army was in fact employed by the British in 1774. The same was true of the Royal Navy, which became an instrument for enforcing new trade laws unfavorable to the colonies.

3. Oppressive measures not susceptible to quantitative analysis: The dynamics of the revolutionary crisis were deeply affected by some British policies that cannot be reduced to statistical terms.

[8]Egnal and Ernst, "Economic Interpretation," p. 21.

[9]Robert Paul Thomas, "A Quantitative Approach to the Study of the Effects of British Imperial Policy upon Colonial Welfare," *Journal of Economic History,* 25 (1965): 636–638. The pioneering study employing quantitative analysis is Lawrence A. Harper, "The Effect of the Navigation Acts on the Thirteen Colonies," in *The Era of the American Revolution,* ed. Richard B. Morris (New York: Columbia University Press, 1939), pp. 3–39; Harper's study reached conclusions contrary to those of Professor Thomas.

A particularly dramatic example was the policy of impressment, which the British customarily used to man the ships of the Royal Navy. Periodically, British Navy units would sweep through the streets and taverns of colonial port towns to impress sailors (that is, draft them, involuntarily, for service on Navy ships). Apart from its arbitrary and brutal character, impressment had major economic effects; for it could strip an American port town of the men who were relied upon to sail on colonial merchants' vessels, so vital to the prosperity of the community. Repeatedly, impressment raids produced mob violence in reaction to the Navy's action in colonial towns—violence that mobilized respectable merchants and shipowners as well as the towns' common laborers.[10] It seems highly unlikely that any American who joined these mobs would have stayed his hand had he realized that being an Englishman cost him only 26 or 42 cents a year!

Nonimportation

The dynamics of the revolutionary movement were greatly influenced by the British economic connection at the time of the nonimportation and boycott movements against the Townshend Acts. The colonial economy was constantly exposed to the effects of imported goods from England; and when the nonimportation effort began, urban artisans and craftsmen quickly joined it, for they perceived a chance to sell their products in the home market free from the competition of similar goods imported from England. Many colonial merchants may well have been motivated to join in the nonimportation agreements because during the 1760s British trading firms had increasingly tended to market their exports to America through auctions and direct sales, bypassing the American merchant houses. Here again, nonimportation offered a chance to sell off stockpiled goods free (at least for the moment) of such British competition.[11] But the larger significance of these incidents may have been political in nature: the nonimportation movement served to mobilize resistance to the British and to increase colonial consciousness of the need for economic sovereignty.

The plantation economy

In the South a comparable situation prevailed, with similar political effects. In Virginia and Maryland after 1763 the tobacco planters became increasingly dependent upon a marketing system controlled by Scottish and English merchants. The planters' debt to these merchants rose steadily and became a source of alarm in those colonies; periodic gluts of the tobacco market and credit crises such as occurred in 1772 served to intensify planters' concern that they were becoming caught in a web of indebtedness to "monopolistic" merchants: a situation that they regarded as a form of economic dependency.

Many of the Virginia and Maryland elite sought at first to escape from this dependency by diversifying their agricultural production or experimenting with home manufactures; George Washington was a leader in this effort. But by 1774 the question of planter debts had become embroiled in the larger controversies that brought on the Revolution. There is little doubt that debts and economic dependence were one source of tensions that prompted Virginia to take a strong stand against England at the time of the Intolerable Acts.[12]

Internal conflicts

Economic self-interest also played a part in the internal conflicts within each American colony—conflicts that assumed new prominence in the post-1763 period. Throughout the eighteenth century, artisans in the cities, the small farmers in the countryside, middling sorts of property owners, and even the urban poor had become increasingly active in colonial politics. This was the case both in formal political activity, as the less wealthy elements participated directly in politics through voting and officeholding, and in activity beyond the limits of formal

[10]Jesse Lemisch, "Jack Tar in the Streets: Merchant Seamen in the Politics of Revolutionary America," *William and Mary Quarterly*, 3rd ser., 25 (1968):371–407; Pauline Maier, "Popular Uprisings and Civil Authority in Eighteenth-Century America," ibid., 27 (1970):12–13. In rural areas of New York and New Jersey, mob violence had flared up over the harsh treatment of tenants and the poor by rural landlords; in New Hampshire against Crown enforcement of laws restricting colonists' use of forest timber; and in the South against the authorities' policies toward the Indians and frontier representation.

[11]See note 4.

[12]Egnal and Ernst, "Economic Interpretation," pp. 23–28; Richard B. Sheridan, "The British Credit Crisis of 1772 and the American Colonies," *Journal of Economic History*, 20 (1960):184–186.

political structure (most notably in mob activity, which by the 1760s had become institutionalized as a regular part of American political culture).

Even before the imperial crisis, lower-class and middle-class groups had begun to pose a serious challenge to the rich and well born who controlled the colonial assemblies and councils. But the events that led toward revolution produced new instabilities after 1763; and when small farmers, artisans, and urban mobs mobilized, their attacks upon British and colonial leaders often "became an attack upon men of wealth generally."[13] In short, the turmoil that accompanied mounting resistance to British measures opened up new opportunities for those in American society who were agitating for social and political change. The political situation differed in each colony, but everywhere radical elements and mobs expressed their opposition to various aspects of élite rule within colonial society as well as to repressive actions of the British government.

Mercantilism in America

As historian Curtis P. Nettels has contended, it must be recognized that by 1763 the Americans, living as they did in a world of competing mercantilist powers, had themselves "become imbued with mercantilist ideas." In that context, it is readily understandable that independence from England should have had strong appeal, especially after elimination of the French menace from North America. And in a context of intensified political repression, independence was an obvious remedy for the damaging and confining economic dependence that had held American economic interests within the British orbit.

> If the British imperium would not allow them to grow and expand, if it would not provide a solution of the central problem of the American economy, the colonists would take to themselves the right and the power to guide their economic development. They would find it necessary to create a new authority that would foster American shipping and commerce, make possible the continued growth of settlement, and above all, stimulate the growth of domestic manufacturing industries.

What followed, Professor Nettels argues, was "the creation of a new mercantilist state on this side of the Atlantic."[14] Whether or not it is strictly correct, in view of certain laissez-faire features of the policies adopted, to speak of the newly independent American government as "mercantilist," there can be no doubt of its determination to purposefully foster economic growth and development.

THE DIVIDED SOCIETY

The Loyalists

Bitter divisions of opinion, and soon bloody clashes, pitted neighbors and relatives against one another.

The Loyalists, or Tories, who supported continued allegiance to England even though many of them had complained of specific British measures and supported limited forms of resistance, undoubtedly still formed a majority when the hostilities broke out. But after 1776, probably less than one-third of the colonists remained overtly loyal.

The alignment of political forces shifted with the fortunes of war—it was not difficult to remain a Loyalist in towns occupied by British troops or in areas where revolutionary committees were not able to build up strong support. But certain groups were most prominent in the Loyalist ranks. One leading element was composed of those who were closely associated with the royal governors, including many who held crown offices. Another embraced the clergy of the Anglican church (the Church of England), together with many Anglican church members. Prosperous members of the professional groups in the towns, especially in the Middle Colonies, and many of the influential and "cultivated" upper-class urban rentiers and merchants also remained loyal to England.

In some localities, long-standing rivalries

[13]Merrill Jensen, "The American People and the American Revolution," *Journal of American History*, 57 (1970): 20. See also Gary B. Nash, "The Transformation of Urban Politics, 1700–1765," ibid., 60 (1973): 605–632.

[14]Curtis P. Nettels, "British Mercantilism and the Economic Development of the Thirteen Colonies," *Journal of Economic History*, 12 (1952): 113–114.

between élite factions persisted into the war period, as in New York and Virginia, where those allied with one group became Loyalists while a rival faction of precisely the same socio-economic group became Whigs (those who favored independence). In North Carolina, on the other hand, a similar division among people of identical class and property interests occurred in the *lower* orders of society. There the crown had granted pardons to back-country small farmers who had taken up arms in protest against the seaboard gentry, and so they remained loyal to the British while those of similar status in the seaboard region became Whigs.

More generally, there were many who remained loyal to England because they were understandably reluctant to be branded as traitors. Fear and expediency doubtless were controlling influences, in many cases, on both sides of the Loyalist-Whig conflict.

From 30,000 to 50,000 Tories enlisted in the British army and navy, New York alone furnishing 15,000. Those to whom regular service did not appeal organized companies of militia under commission from the crown, which cooperated with the Indians in cruel and useless warfare, of which the leading examples were the Wyoming and Cherry Valley massacres. Wherever Patriots confronted Tories, there the fighting was fiercest.

The lot of the Tories not under the protection of the British army was likely to be hard. Denounced and deprived of citizenship under the new state consitutions, they had no legal redress for their troubles. Laws forced them to pay for a cause they hated and at the same time denied them liberty to speak or write their opinions. Tarring and feathering, imprisonment, banishment and the appropriation of property, death—any of these might await the person whose loyalty to the Patriot cause was suspected. Whole communities of Loyalists were driven into the back country to prevent them from giving aid to the British army on its approach. Eleven hundred Tory refugees sailed away with Sir William Howe's army to Halifax in March 1776, and 3,000 left with Sir Henry Clinton from Philadelphia in 1778. At least 35,000—some contend 100,000—eventually reached Canada and laid there the foundations of a new English community: The makers of British Canada were the Tories who left the thirteen colonies during the war.

The Patriots

Mass support for the Revolution came from all ranks of the social order. To be sure, the Whigs, who dominated the Continental Congress in 1774, and who held sway in the state legislatures as new governments were formed, were led by people of property and standing. Hence rich merchants, the great majority of tobacco planters who could be termed wealthy, and some of the colonies' most prosperous lawyers formed the Patriot leadership. But common farmers, poorer groups of urban workers, and many middle-class politicians who were radical democrats, all were prominent enough in the revolutionary movement to explain why the more moderate and conservative leaders feared demagoguery and possible "leveling" or social revolution. Nor was this sort of fear paranoid, or even mildly misguided. Democratic ideas and hatred of the established élites were widespread. The impulse toward social revolution was a force of real moment.

The disunited states

To carry on a war efficiently with such a division of sentiment was impossible. Not only was there no unanimity in regard to separation from England; there was little unity among the colonies. Thirteen provinces jealous of one another and with separate interests made impossible a close political union or the formation of a body with sufficient powers to carry on a revolution. Only a common cause and a common enemy developed enough cooperation to keep an army in the field. The Continental Congress took over the prosecution of the struggle, but it had little authority. It could not impose taxes; it simply voted levies and asked the states to meet them. Efforts to draw up a plan for a united government that would grant legal power to a central body were blocked until 1781.

ECONOMIC AND SOCIAL CHANGES

The American Revolution effected important economic as well as political changes. As the French Revolution of 1789 and the English civil wars of 1640–1660 broke up landed estates and brought radical changes in the agrarian economies of these two nations, so the years from 1775 to 1781 in some of the 13 states introduced changes in the land system as radical if not as thoroughgoing.

The great estates

For a century and a half European rulers had endeavored to transplant to America the feudal system of the Old World, and vast estates were to be found in most of the colonies. As late as 1769 five-sixths of the population of Westchester County, New York, lived on manor lands. The exodus of the Tories not only removed the most conservative class in the country, thereby throwing the local governments into the hands of a new group, but made possible the breaking up of the large landholdings. In November 1777 Congress recommended that the states confiscate and sell the Loyalists' property and invest the proceeds in Continental loan certificates. The idea found immediate favor. New Hampshire confiscated 28 estates, including that of Governor Wentworth. Massachusetts confiscated the land of all who fought for England, including the Pepperell estate, which contained 30 miles of coastland. In New York State the 50,000-acre manor of Sir John Johnson, the Philipse manor of 300 square miles, the Morris estate, and many other large holdings were broken up and sold, usually in parcels of not over 500 acres. Everywhere royal and proprietary properties were confiscated. The Penn estate taken over by Pennsylvania was valued at nearly £1 million sterling, and the state of New York received about 3.16 million Spanish dollars for forfeited real estate.[15]

Land speculation

Although the confiscation of crown and Tory estates did something to break up large landholdings, it by no means eliminated great estates. Nor did it end the mania for land speculation so widespread in the years before the Revolution. This was true in both East and West. States with western lands gave land bounties to soldiers, which in turn were bought and consolidated into large holdings. Virginia's practice of selling vacant lands as a means of paying state debts increased during the war and

also stimulated speculation. Bending the state laws to their purpose,

> *promoters obtained great tracts in the West. They purchased at a discount the bounty warrants of soldiers unable or unwilling to migrate; they sent out servants to secure preemption rights; and they converted state certificates of indebtedness (which represented the values of depreciated currency) into claims upon the land. Estates as large as 140,000 acres came into being.*[16]

So much land, in fact, had thus been obtained beyond the Alleghenies that settlers pushing westward found it difficult to secure titles for reasonable prices.

Land tenure

Along with the confiscation of land and its division into smaller parcels came vital legal reforms effected by a change to more democratic land tenure. Quitrents were the first to disappear. By 1786 every state but two had abolished entail, and by 1792 primogeniture had gone, the new laws providing in some form or other for equality of inheritance. An act of 1776 probably released from half to three-quarters of the entire "seated" area of Virginia.[17] The significance of these laws in the development of a democratic society is, of course, obvious; one should also note the fact that this action was taken in many cases after the fighting had ceased. The war might be over, but the American Revolution, in a sense, had just begun.

The state constitutions

The Revolution had been ushered in with much condemnation of the autocratic methods of the British government. Consequently the new state constitutions tended to vest little power in the executive branch, reducing the authority of governors and councils while they

---

[15]The social effects of confiscation varied greatly from state to state. In Dutchess and Westchester counties of New York, sites of enormous estates dating from the Dutch patroonships, confiscation resulted in acquisition of relatively small holdings (under 500 acres) by hundreds of purchasers. In Long Island and the areas adjacent to New York City, the result was simply to channel large holdings of Loyalists to equally wealthy Patriots. In Virginia a somewhat wider distribution of land resulted from confiscation.

[16]Curtis P. Nettels, *The Roots of American Civilization: A History of American Colonial Life,* 2nd ed. (New York: Appleton-Century-Crofts, 1963), p. 684. Yet large numbers of common soldiers did acquire small farms with Virginia bounty warrants. See W. A. Low, "The Farmer in Post-Revolutionary Virginia," *Agricultural History,* 25 (1951).

[17] The "seated" lands were those vested in individuals by the royal government, lands that under earlier law passed automatically to the heirs and were not permitted to be sold. In a letter to John Adams (October 28, 1813), Jefferson asserted that the Virginia laws abolishing entails and primogeniture, "drawn by myself, laid the ax to the root of pseudo-aristocracy" (Paul L. Ford, ed., *Writings of Thomas Jefferson,* 10 vols. [New York, 1892–1899], vol. 9, p. 427).

placed the bulk of formal authority in the legislatures. Frontier districts and areas long underrepresented by malapportionment received fairer shares of legislative seats. And, since these regions tended to elect representatives of lower economic and social status, the social composition of the states' legislative bodies tended to become more truly representative. New, loosely organized parties emerged, with popular grass-roots support. Although the gentry, the wealthier lawyers, and the planter and merchant élites retained a considerable share of power, there was a decline in political deference — the respectful attitude toward the "better sorts" which had once permitted popular forces to be subordinated in American political affairs. This popularization of politics accelerated during the 1780s.

The abolitionist movement

The antislavery movement grew during the war, and initiatives were begun in the northern and middle states to end the slave trade and even to abolish slavery. In Virginia, on the other hand, British authorities embittered planters and other whites, who feared a black insurrection, by offering emancipation to slaves who deserted their masters. In the South generally there was no relaxation of slavery either as a labor system or as the essential component of a racist social system.

The new men

The uncertainties and turmoil of an extended war also gave openings to "new men" — people of small means who found a chance through privateering, speculation in confiscated estates, trading in arms imported through the British blockade, and supplying the armies with food and supplies — to make themselves fortunes and places in the sun. Shrewd country merchants gained enormously from the opportunity to sell goods badly needed by citizens and by the revolutionary army (or the British, for that matter) in areas where local economies had been disrupted by fighting or blockade. Hence Henry Laurens, a leading Charleston merchant, could complain of "Knaves and fools" now found to be "building enormous estates";[18] and a Massachusetts county meeting condemned the "avarice and extortion, which, like a resistless torrent, has overspread the land,"[19] with merchants and farmers reaping the profits of war-born monopolies over vital goods. "The course of the war," wrote Robert Treat Paine of Boston in 1777, "has thrown property into channels where before it never was. . . ."[20]

Turmoil itself did not necessarily denote social revolution, nor did the rise to wealth of new men at the expense of some older élites necessarily denote anything more than a game of winners and losers. But the prolonged conflict, the establishment of new governments, the struggles for power involving not only men of new wealth but broadly based popular constituencies, all indicate some sweeping changes in the social, economic, and political orders. Nor did the momentum or importance of these changes lose force with the war's end; they became the basis of a deeply rooted political conflict during the 1780s.

THE WAR'S EFFECTS: AGRICULTURE AND INDUSTRY

The population of the United States at the opening of the Revolution is estimated to have reached approximately 2.5 million persons. There were about 700,000 men between ages 18 and 60, but at no time during the war was more than one-eighth of this number under arms, and during most of the period probably no more than one-sixteenth. There was widespread apathy concerning the war, and the agricultural and industrial work of the people went on much as usual. New England was free from the British after the first year, with the exception of the occupation of Newport and a few minor raids upon towns on Long Island Sound.

Agriculture

Agriculture was hardly affected. In New York, New Jersey, and Pennsylvania the depredations of both armies were to a great extent compensated for by the liberal prices the French and British paid the farmers in gold for supplies of all kinds; the farmers seemed only too willing to double their prices for the export

[18] Quoted in Evarts B. Greene, *The Revolutionary Generation, 1763–1790* (1943, reprinted New York: Quadrangle, 1971), p. 270.

[19] Quoted in Green, *Revolutionary Generation*, p. 270.

[20] Paine quoted in Robert A. East, *Business Enterprise in the American Revolutionary Era* (New York: Columbia University Press, 1938), p. 213.

trade or sell produce to Howe, while Washington's men shivered and starved at Valley Forge. That the colonies must have been plentifully supplied with profiteers and "sunshine patriots" we may gather from the words of George Washington:

Such a dearth of public spirit and want of virtue, such stockjobbing, and fertility in all the low arts to obtain advantage of one kind or another . . . I never saw before, and I pray God I may never be a witness to again. . . . Such a dirty mercenary spirit pervades the whole that I should not be at all surprised at any disaster that may happen.[21]

Blockade runners were always ready to carry the tobacco of the Virginia plantations to waiting markets in Europe. Yields of leaf tobacco rose from 101.8 million pounds in 1774 to 130 million in 1790, when probably one-third of the southern population was either engaged in or dependent on its production. In the Carolinas the cultivation and export of rice went on, apparently with little interruption. In 1778 the first water mill adapted to cleaning and preparing rice for the market was erected on the Santee River. While it is true that many phases of southern agriculture was not fundamentally affected by the war, at the same time it should not be forgotten that Patriot plantation owners suffered from British raids and lost heavily by the confiscation of slaves. And the cessation of British bounties on indigo marked the beginning of the end of an important industry.

The interference in trade caused by nonimportation agreements and the first years of the war stimulated the production of wool throughout the colonies and of cotton in the South. The legislatures of Maryland, Virginia, and South Carolina urged upon their farmers the growing of cotton so effectively, apparently, that Hamilton, writing in 1775, said, "Several of the Southern colonies are so favorable to it that, with due cultivation, in a couple of years they would afford enough to clothe the whole continent."[22] Knowledge of improved European agricultural techniques was spread by the foreigners whom the war brought into the country, and on the whole, American agriculture was stimulated rather than injured by the war.

Industry

American manufacturing was more directly affected than agriculture by the war. The Revolution enfranchised American industry by ending the annoying restrictions that Parliament, under the influence of mercantilism, had imposed when it sought to confine the colonies to the production of raw materials. During the boycotts preceding the outbreak of hostilities, the colonists refused to purchase English goods, and great efforts were made to stimulate the manufacture of such necessities as woolens and linens, which had formerly been imported in large amounts. Large numbers of people pledged themselves not to eat lamb or mutton or to buy from butchers who sold it, in order to discourage the slaughtering of sheep so that their wool might be harvested for clothing. Women of all classes turned to the production of cloth as a domestic business. This activity in spinning and weaving during the early years of the war declined after the cargoes captured by the privateers began to be thrown on the market and importation was resumed.

The manufacture of munitions and other necessities of war was, of course, stimulated, and small gun factories sprang up in Massachusetts, Connecticut, and Rhode Island. In 1778 Congress founded works in Springfield, Massachusetts, where cannon were cast, and the predecessor of the present national armory was established there in 1794. The casting and forging of guns and camp kettles was carried on in Pennsylvania and on the Hudson, and new furnaces were built in many places in New England and the Middle Colonies. Rhode Island and Maine granted bounties for the manufacture of steel. It is claimed that Jeremiah Wilkinson of Cumberland, Rhode Island, turned out the first cold-cut nail in the world in 1777. Massachusetts offered bounties on sulphur extracted from native ores, and Rhode Island for powder, but most of the powder used was imported. Attempts at mining and refining lead were made in Connecticut and at Cheswell, Virginia, but most of the lead used was obtained from abroad or from melting down lead roofs, window weights, and other objects.

A very real shortage of many of the necessities was felt until 1777 in all parts of the country, but it was in part overcome. The increase in newspapers and other printing during the war brought an increase in paper mills. Small establishments were set up to manufacture various commodities formerly imported. But shipbuilding, an industry that had been stimulated by the Navigation Acts, was greatly restricted during the war.

    [21]W. C. Ford, ed., *Writings of George Washington,* 14 vols. (New York, 1889), vol. 3, pp. 246–247.
    [22]Henry C. Lodge, ed., *The Works of Alexander Hamilton,* 9 vols. (New York, 1885–1886), vol. 1, p. 153.

Labor, always scarce and expensive in the colonial period, became increasingly so during the war. Enlistments in the army and on privateers, and the emigration of Loyalists with their servants, decreased the supply. Wages of skilled and unskilled labor doubled from 1774 to 1784, not only because of scarcity of labor, but also because of the rising cost of living and the increased amount of money in circulation.

COMMERCE AND PRIVATEERING

The Revolution favored maritime activity in two ways: first in the opening of colonial ports to the world, and second in stimulating privateering.

Imports and exports

The nonimportation agreements of the years preceding the war had exhausted the supply of English goods; as a consequence, the merchants of Spain, Holland, and France eagerly welcomed the new markets, discovering means of evading the British warships and privateersmen so successfully that by 1777 there was little lack of foreign merchandise. Lists of imports during the war reveal items distinctly in the class of luxuries—such finer textiles as velvets, linens, silks, and broadcloths, as well as teas, coffees, spices, and wines. Ports occupied by the British were opened to English goods and considerable quantities were imported through New York. The articles were paid for mainly by exports of flour, tobacco, and rice, and by the money that found its way to the colonies through the medium of foreign loans and British quartermasters. These exported staples also had to run the gauntlet of the British fleet and privateersmen. Although the British admirals reported the capture of 570 vessels between 1776 and 1779, exportation was sufficiently lucrative to continue with little abatement throughout the war. Twenty-four million pounds of tobacco alone were recorded in 1777 and 1778 by the British customs officials, about one-third of the ordinary consumption, received possibly under the pretense that it came from neutral ports, for the Dutch island of St. Eustatius and the French island of Martinique served as ports where cargoes could be transferred and neutralized.

Privateers

Of almost equal magnitude with wartime commerce were the operations carried on by privateers. It has been estimated that 2000 privateers were commissioned, of which the great majority came from Massachusetts. With his usual routine voyage cut off, the American seaman found a natural outlet in privateering. Daring was necessary and the risk great, but the spice of adventure and the lure of profits drew the keenest and coolest. It was customary for the owners to split half and half with the crew, according to rank. Captured prizes were either taken to European ports, sold, and the money invested in merchandise to be brought home, or else, if the capture was effected off the American coast, brought in at once. More than 445 prizes were brought in by the Salem fleet. Elias Hasket Derby, the chief shipowner and the enterprising genius of this port town, was worth about $1 million when he died in 1799—a stupendous fortune in those days—most of it realized by privateering. "Probably as many as ninety thousand Americans were, first and last," says Jameson, "engaged in these voyages, a number of men almost as great as served in the army, and greater than that of the army in any single year save one."[23]

A witness before a special parliamentary inquiry in 1778 stated that the losses suffered by British merchants from American privateers "could not be less than two million two hundred thousand pounds." Privateering served the purpose not alone of harassing the enemy but of keeping alive the maritime spirit and holding capital in the shipping industry. It also increased the unpopularity of the war in England.

WAR FINANCE AND INFLATION

If any single step was decisive in the complex dynamics of the events that led to independence, it was the decision of the Continen-

[23]J. Franklin Jameson, *The American Revolution Considered as a Social Movement* (Princeton: Princeton University Press, 1926), p. 103.

tal Congress, in June 1775, to raise an army of 15,000 men. By this time revolutionary resistance groups and committees were displacing the regular colonial authorities as the effective governments of the states, and the Congress moved immediately in other ways to assume the functions of a central government. Hence a postal service was formed, a military code of laws was adopted, commissioners were appointed to handle relations with the Indian nations, and—a measure emblematic of Congress's determination to serve as the legitimate government, assuming the traditional high prerogatives of sovereignty—a currency act was passed, providing for the issue of paper money.

Neither then nor when the Articles of Confederation were drawn up and submitted to the states for approval in 1776 (not to be finally ratified until 1781) did the new central government obtain the power to levy taxes directly upon individual citizens. The Articles provided for "levies" upon the states; that is, Congress could call upon them to pay their share of the costs of government. But if a state chose not to comply—as most of them did most of the time—Congress had no power to enforce payment. It did, however, have exclusive power to coin money, and was authorized to obtain loans or issue bills of credit, so long as nine states assented.

Paper currency

Beginning in June 1775 the Congress issued bills of credit that passed for currency much as our paper money does today, and these fiat issues were used to meet the expenses of the revolutionary government. The value of the money rested ultimately upon the success of the struggle for independence. Congress relied upon the states to meet future levies for their redemption, and it also depended upon them to make the currency legal tender.[24] Even before the Declaration of Independence was issued in July 1776, some $12 million in Continental currency had been printed, mainly in small denominations. Up to November 1779 a total of $191 million in this currency had been issued.

Inflation

Instead of levying taxes to help take the Continental paper out of circulation, the state legislatures—many of them not taxing at all, at

least initially, for fear of losing popular support—complicated the situation further by printing their own paper currencies. A classic monetary inflation ensued, given additional impetus by the chaotic swings in the revolutionary army's military performance and prospects, by pervasive waste and corruption, and by scarcities of many vital goods. The resultant decline—a disastrous one—in the specie value of the Continental paper brought the currency's standing down to $3 for $1 specie in late 1777, to $5 a year later, and to $16 by the spring of 1779. Then the spiral accelerated. By late 1780 the specie value of one Continental paper dollar was at a ratio of 1:77, and by mid-1781 it took $167.50 in Continental currency to buy $1 of specie.[25] By then it took $100 of the paper currency to buy a pair of shoes, $90 for a pound of tea, and over $1500 for a barrel of flour. "Not worth a Continental" became a synonym of worthlessness.

Domestic loans and indebtedness

Although the printing press was the main instrument of Congress in financing the war until late 1779, other expedients were attempted. Quartermasters seized produce and other property to supply the armies, issuing certificates of indebtedness to the hapless citizenry, and an abortive effort was made to obtain loans at home ("domestic loans," as opposed to loans from foreign governments). Only speculators with capital could afford to gamble on the loan certificates, which could be purchased with the Continental currency. And the real interest rate on this loan paper was as high as 30 percent, payable in specie—the specie being made available to Congress by subsidies from France and Spain in 1777, then by foreign loans from those countries amounting by 1780 to the equivalent of $2.2 million in specie value.

The retirement of continental currency

Finally Congress faced the hard necessity of giving up exclusive reliance upon paper issues, and from the end of 1779 onward it turned to the states for financial support sufficient to sustain the costs of the conflict. A massive devaluation was approved by Congress in 1780, the currency in circulation being revalued at 40 to

---

[24]The June 1775 act also instituted a new unit of value, the dollar (which derived its name from the Spanish milled dollar or piece of eight), and abandoned the British pound sterling.

[25]Although inflation and prices varied from one locality to another, it has become common to use the detailed data compiled by Anne Bezanson on Philadelphia and other port towns to illustrate these fluctuations. See Bezanson and others, *Prices and Inflation During the American Revolution: Pennsylvania, 1770–1790* (Philadelphia: University of Pennsylvania Press, 1951).

1. Meanwhile the state governments, which by then had finally dared to enact taxation programs, made the Continental paper legal tender, leading to retirement of the currency by 1781. But during these last years of the war, the principal means by which the American armies were supplied and the government kept going was outright impressment of goods from the citizenry. Even after foodstuffs had been taken from farmers and merchants in exchange for debt certificates by army quartermasters, enormous problems of transportation and distribution to the troops remained. So vast numbers of horses and wagons were also seized, and the principle prevailed (as one military officer wrote) that "those who are nearest to where the scene of action is to be, must expect to give up everything they have which is wanted for the enterprize."[26] When France finally committed military forces to the American cause in 1781, the pressures of impressment eased slightly.

Price regulation

From 1774 to the war's end, Congress exhorted the states to impose price-fixing laws and to punish speculators and engrossers. Popular outrage over extortionate profits being made in the midst of suffering and monetary derangement sometimes led to tar-and-feathering or other mob action, as well as to more formal sorts of action by local revolutionary committees. But on the whole, the laws regulating prices went unenforced. Hence people with fixed incomes, including soldiers in the army and the militias, people whose property was taken by the quartermasters, and those who were caught with holdings of Continental currency or other government paper carried a disproportionate burden of the real fiscal costs of the Revolution.

Robert Morris and war financing

In the final phase of the war, 1781–1782, foreign loans from France were also of crucial importance, and a Dutch syndicate also arranged valuable credits. These foreign funds became the key to badly needed fiscal and administrative reforms engineered by Robert Morris, a leading Philadelphia merchant who became superintendent of finance in 1781. Morris's brilliant direction of treasury affairs was of enduring importance not only because he was instrumental in helping the Congress weather the final period of the war, but also because he pointed it toward the assumption of the leading role in postwar finance instead of permitting the states to retain all initiatives. In this sense, his political accomplishment was supreme: He required the states to pay all requisitions in cash to the central government and he established the clear responsibility of Congress itself for the domestic debt of nearly $40 million (after devaluation) and the additional accumulated foreign debt of $12 million. The ultimate triumph of Morris's goal of a powerful central government, with independent revenues and centralized management of the debt as well as budgeted expenditures, had to await a later day, when Secretary of the Treasury Alexander Hamilton would give substance to these ideas under a new constitution.

POSTWAR ECONOMIC REORGANIZATION

With the successful conclusion of the Revolution, a period of economic uncertainty and readjustment followed. Many problems of the economy and governance were solved by the weak central government under the Articles of Confederation and by the states, but other problems lingered or assumed new urgency. The reabsorption of the disbanded army required some time, as did propping up the slave plantation system in areas of the South ravaged by the war and loss of slaves.

[26] Quoted in E. James Ferguson, *The Power of the Purse: A History of American Public Finance, 1776–1790* (Chapel Hill: University of North Carolina Press, 1961), p. 62.

Foreign trade regulation

New England had seen its fishing industry and the West Indies trade badly disrupted. The peace treaty of 1783 with England, moreover, failed to do anything more for American commerce than guarantee that navigation of the Mississippi River should be forever open to the United States; there were no reciprocal trade provisions to assure American vessels a renewed role in the British West Indies or in trade with other British ports. Indeed, in the period 1783–1787 the British government enacted revisions of its navigation acts that banned American ships from the Indies and put them under severe liabilities in other aspects of trade with England. Although new direct trading routes to other European countries were opened up in ensuing years, the progress of commercial treaty negotiations was slow. The weakness of Congress under the Articles of Confederation prevented effective retaliation or other measures to aid American commerce. Each state adopted its own regulations of trade, and from 1783 to 1788 ten states levied tonnage dues upon British vessels or discriminatory tariffs. But these duties were not uniform, so the British ships simply went to the free ports or those that were cheapest.

Chaos in currency and trade

There was also disunity among the states, which had not overcome their old provincialisms. Boundary-line disputes, conflict over the disposition of western lands won from Britain by the peace treaty, and even some instances of discriminatory tariff duties levied by one state upon another, all bedeviled efforts to achieve integration of the national economy. Most serious of all was continued chaos in the currency. Congress and the states had issued nearly $440 million in paper money during the war years. Much of the depreciated currency had become practically worthless for purposes of trade, simply paper in the hands of speculators. Business thus became dependent upon English, French, Spanish, and Portuguese coins, and adverse trade balances drew off the specie. "When hostilities ceased," one contemporary wrote, "the floodgates of commerce were opened; and an inundation of foreign manufactures overflowed the United States; we seemed to have forgot, that to pay was as necessary in trade as to purchase."[27] Foreign taxes on American tobacco hurt returns from this important source of foreign earnings; naval stores and indigo no longer enjoyed British subsidies; shipbuilding and whaling suffered, at least briefly, from loss of preferred status in English markets. These and other problems meant that in New England, whose economy was deeply reliant upon the carrying trade, the West Indies, and industries related to shipping, suffering was intense.

The revival of agriculture

Yet the economy was not altogether disrupted. Outside New England, the revival of agriculture was achieved through development of direct trade with markets formerly made inaccessible by British mercantilism. In the South, the major exports had recovered to prewar levels within three or four years, surging again to much higher levels by 1792. Meanwhile, domestic population grew rapidly in the 1780s. Interstate trade probably exceeded former levels significantly and widened market opportunities for southern producers, especially with the great shift toward wheat and corn production in older coastal areas where tobacco lands had worn out.

Although prices for farm products fell sharply in 1785, prompting widespread demands by agrarians for easier credit and debt relief, still prices did not fall substantially below the level of 1770.

Commerce in the 1780s

Despite trade stagnation in New England, the general picture of commerce in the 1780s had positive features. Tonnage of shipping that cleared American ports, for example, registered substantial increases: Clearances from New York had averaged 26,000 tons from 1770 to 1772, whereas 30,000 tons of foreign-owned shipping alone cleared the port in 1789; Philadelphia's clearances, which had been 45,000 tons from 1770 to 1772, rose to 72,000 tons in 1789; and Virginia and Maryland ports, with 83,000 tons of clearances in 1769, reported an estimated 166,000 tons during the year ending September 1790.[28]

Economic readjustment

Historians differ sharply on the question of economic readjustment in the 1780s: Was it a success or largely a failure? Some scholars, viewing the evidences of rising population, production, interstate trade, and the like, conclude that one must accept Benjamin Franklin's assertion in March 1786 that "America was never in higher prosperity, her produce abundant and bearing a good price, her working people all employed and well paid. . . ."[29] Other historians view the 1780s as a period of persistent economic distress. Granting year-to-year fluctuations in American welfare, they give principal weight to the fact that despite evidence of recovery in trade volume, foreign exports fell below prewar levels in per capita value. They stress also that persistent foreign-trade imbalances, with accompanying domestic currency problems, aggravated the social unrest already

---

[27]James Wilson, quoted in Merrill E. Jensen, *The New Nation: A History of the United States During the Confederation, 1781–1789* (New York: Knopf, 1950), p. 190.

[28]Jensen, *New Nation*, pp. 215–217.
[29]Quoted in ibid., p. 249.

sparked by high taxes, widespread debt, and the damage suffered by some occupational groups disadvantaged by the loss of British imperial subsidies or preferences. Moreover, they point to the severe price decline of 1785–1786, which continued until at least 1788, possibly mid-1789, as evidence of severe dislocations that formed the background of the movement for a new constitution and a central government strong enough to deal with serious economic problems and rising social disorders.[30]

NEW LINES OF ENTERPRISE

Whether or not the 1780s truly comprised a "critical period" (as historians once generally termed it), this immediate postwar era witnessed vigorous pursuit of economic opportunities by the new nation's entrepreneurs. As the revival of trade to its prewar volume indicates, a considerable degree of enterprise was present in the commercial sector. It is true that under the British Navigation Act of 1783 the British West Indies were closed to American ships, but the demand for lumber and foodstuffs in these islands was so great that ways of evading the act were quickly discovered. One method was to ship products to the French, Dutch, or Spanish islands, from which they found their way to the British islands. The fact that half of the shipments to the West Indies from the United States reached Jamaica is ample proof of evasion. By the middle 1780s the navigation acts of the French, Spanish, and Dutch had been sufficiently relaxed to allow an active trade with their colonies. Moreover, trade with France and Holland developed beyond prewar levels, since these nations took certain "enumerated" products that could be shipped only to Great Britain during the colonial period. By 1787–1789 the trade with Holland had become more than 50 percent as valuable as that with England, with a balance probably in favor of America. This revival of commerce brought in its wake, of course, a revival of the fishing and lumbering industries and a demand for foodstuffs, tobacco, and other agricultural commodities.

The China trade

During the Revolution the slave trade passed into the hands of other nations and the three-cornered route became a thing of the past. Yankee merchants, however, soon found other opportunities for trade in the Baltic countries, the Near East, and the Far East. It was in 1785 that the *Empress of China* entered New York from Canton and in 1787 that the *Grand Turk* sailed into Salem from the same port; of 46 foreign vessels entering Canton in 1789, 18 were American. It was also during these years that the first New England mariners reached the northwest coast in search of furs. Captain Robert Gray's famous voyages to Oregon and from there to China (1787–1793) opened the New England–Northwest–China trade, a lucrative traffic whereby the New Englander traded manufactured products to the northwest Indians for furs, and then sailed for China to trade the furs for tea, silk, and other Asian goods.

Banking and chartered companies

Commerce was by no means the only field in which a vigorous spirit of business enterprise was evident. With British restrictions now lifted, the Bank of North America was established in 1781, the Bank of New York and the Massachusetts Bank of Boston in 1784. Throughout the country merchant capitalists, hitherto held in restraint by British mercantilism, were pooling their capital and organizing companies to exploit the West, to build turnpikes, bridges, and canals, and to promote manufacturing. The issuing of charters to American concerns was almost unknown in the colonial period, but between 1781 and 1785 state legislatures issued 11 and between 1786 and 1790 at least 22 more.

Industrial growth

Americans were particularly loath to sacrifice such gains in manufacturing as they had made during the war. Many of these industries kept going. During this period the first cotton factory in the United States was built (1787) at Beverly, Massachusetts, and three years later Samuel Slater built his cotton mill at Pawtucket. In 1788 a woolen factory was established at Hartford,

---

[30]Merrill Jensen, in *The New Nation*, portrays economic conditions as sound over the decade as a whole, despite short-term fluctuations. The contrary view is best represented by Curtis P. Nettels, *The Emergence of a National Economy, 1775–1815* (New York: Holt, Rinehart and Winston, 1962), pp. 45–88. See also Gordon C. Bjork, "The Weaning of the American Economy: Independence, Market Changes, and Economic Development," *Journal of Economic History*, 24 (1964): 541–560, and Albert Fishlow's "Comment", ibid., pp. 561–566.

and by the mid-1790s carding machines were coming into use. Before the end of the period many of the New England mill towns had commenced their manufacturing careers. At Philadelphia John Fitch and others who were experimenting with the steamboat built one in 1790 that ran 80 miles a day. It was a period when society was alive not only to political changes but to the economic possibilities of the new nation.

The country suffered a depression in 1785 and 1786, but the letdown was due as much to overtrading and expansion as to any weakness of government. It did not last long, and by late 1786 economic activity was again on the rise. Commenting on this activity, a leading authority on the period writes:

> High rentals, building activity, and luxurious living actually impressed Franklin on his return to America in 1785. Stagecoach routes and facilities were steadily being increased in various regions. The paper industry continued to grow, and important companies were organized for iron and woolen manufactures in 1786 and 1788. Above all, it is significant that capital was much sought after everywhere during the "critical" years. Interest rates were high in 1784. New York merchant-capitalists were even invited to New Jersey and Connecticut, being promised liberal treatment. . . . And if it be argued that all this merely emphasized a great lack of capital, rather than a general demand for it, it can be pointed out in reply that there was no difficulty in securing subscriptions of specie value for large amounts of bank stock in 1784 in Philadelphia, Boston and New York.[31]

THE STRUGGLE FOR THE CONSTITUTION

That the economic and social conditions of the 1780s presented many reasons for a stronger central government there can be no doubt. American economic expansion needed a more unified economic program, freedom of interstate commerce, a more stabilized currency, and other benefits that a strong central government could provide. Yet the student of American history must be cautioned not to overemphasize the effects of the weak government under the Articles of Confederation. To no small extent it was the economic conditions that prevented government from functioning, rather than poor government that caused the depression.

Nevertheless, the movement for a constitution was supported most eagerly by those whose economic interests were most seriously affected by the weakness of the central government under the Articles of Confederation. It was also supported by many of the new ruling class, who were frightened by the restlessness of the small farmers, particularly after Shays' Rebellion.[32] Moreover, investors in manufacturing and shipping desired a government strong enough to protect them against foreign discrimination, in order to sustain the expansion of the 1780s. The debtor class was endeavoring to push stay laws and paper-money acts through the legislatures. While shipowners and manufacturers wanted tariff protection from a strong government, domestic merchants were anxious to demolish the barriers to interstate traffic and longed for a stable and uniform currency.

But among the most ardent advocates of the Constitution were naturally those who held claims against the Confederacy. These included owners of Continental bonds, certificates of indebtedness, and paper money, who knew that a strong central government would be able not only to redeem its own securities but to tone up the state paper. Much of this paper, of course, was no longer in the hands of the original owners but had long since shifted into the possession of speculators.

The Constitutional Convention

Concern about the basic rights of citizens — issues over which the Revolution had been

---

[31]East, *Business Enterprise*, p. 242.

[32]Massachusetts was one of the three states — the others were Pennsylvania and North Carolina — in which radical political elements gained a substantial degree of power with the outbreak of the Revolution. The noted uprising in 1786 led by Daniel Shays expressed the outrage of small farmers in western Massachusetts at policies of their state government, which by 1781 had once again fallen under control of conservative mercantile-oriented elements. Widespread imprisonment for debt among small farmers, high taxes, and a general unrest stemming from economic depression in New England all contributed to the situation. The rebellion had to be put down with force by the state.

fought—and about the very survival of republican government were also prominent in the minds of those who met in Philadelphia in 1787 to frame a new constitution. Economic unrest and resultant class antagonisms had reached a climax with Shays' Rebellion in 1786; but the hard-pressed farmers who had followed Daniel Shays in Massachusetts expressed grievances that were common elsewhere. Men such as James Madison of Virginia, deeply committed to republicanism, believed that the fragile national system under the Articles of Confederation could not survive many such blows. Either social disorder would engulf the individual states or tyrannous majority interests in each state would adopt measures oppressive of beleaguered minorities, whether religious, political, or social. A more powerful central government could ensure not only the security of property rights, but also the strength of the nation in dealing with foreign threats.

Although strong convictions about the survival of the American experiment in self-government on republican principles certainly motivated many of the framers, there is no denying that the Constitutional Convention was dominated by men who were at least equally dedicated to the rights of property and were sympathetic to the interests of both landed and commercial interests. No neat and firm division placed upper-class people on one side in favor of the Constitution, with middle- and lower-class people (as some historians have argued) solidly opposed. Yet the *leadership* did divide to no small degree along these lines. Prominent among the leading spokesmen for the Constitution were the holders of Continental securities, leading merchants and financiers, and northern merchants. The opposition, though it included some wealthy persons from all of these groups, drew its leadership more heavily from politicians who had been associated with debtor causes or agrarian political factions in the states. They perceived the movement for a stronger central government as authoritarian, designed to move the locus of political power farther from the people and into the hands of a small national élite.[33]

The Constitution and the economy

The most important contributions of the 1787 Constitution to congressional power bearing upon the economy were the provisions concerning finance and commerce. It enabled the central government to levy taxes; to regulate domestic trade, impose customs duties on imports, and coin money; and, as events later proved, to establish the national credit securely and provide for redemption of the Revolution's debt. These prospective benefits had been explicitly applauded by the framers and those who championed the Constitution in the ratifying debates, and adequate powers were granted. In addition, the Constitution included a ban on importation of slaves after 1807 and provided for a patent system.

A constitutional foundation was also laid for enactment of American navigation acts, fostering the shipbuilding and shipping industries. Independent revenues could be employed to secure American control of the West, to expedite that region's settlement and economic development, and to build a national navy adequate to defend the nation's merchant shipping. The Constitution provided negative checks against state legislation damaging to the climate of business enterprise, most notably in the contract clause and in the ban upon *ex post facto* legislation that might abridge commercial and debt obligations. That these benefits could become the underpinning of governmentally aided and protected economic growth beneficial to all sectors of the society was a point made repeatedly by those who favored ratification. Along with a widespread concern to bring about greater political stability and enhanced national power in foreign affairs, the breadth of this appeal probably goes far toward explaining why the Constitution finally won broad popular support, despite the sort of class and interest-group alignments that divided the leadership.

As was intended, the Constitution established a firm basis for an independent American mercantilism. A government with "independent energy" had been provided for, and it was given the authority necessary to make an autonomous and unified national economic policy a reality.

[33]No interpretive issue of the period has been so much debated by historians as this one, concerning the cleavages in the country as a whole (and to a lesser extent the interests and motives of political leaders) over the adoption of the 1787 Constitution. The classic view, pioneered by Charles Beard, arguing that national cleavages broke across class lines, was challenged by Forest McDonald in *We the People: The Economic Origins of the Constitution* (Chicago: University of Chicago Press, 1958). McDonald's thesis was in turn subjected to a close critique by Jackson T. Main (with rebuttal by McDonald) in the *William and Mary Quarterly*, 3rd ser., 17 (1960): 86–110.

SELECTED READINGS

NOTE: Many of the works listed in the selected readings for the previous chapter also deal with mercantilism and its impact, and some with the Revolutionary crisis.

*Beard, Charles A., *An Economic Interpretation of the Constitution of the United States* (New York: Macmillan, 1913).

*Bridenbaugh, Carl, *Cities in Revolt: Urban Life in America, 1743–1776* (1955, reprinted New York: Capricorn, 1964).

*Dickerson, Oliver M., *The Navigation Acts and the American Revolution* (1951, reprinted New York: Barnes, 1963).

East, Robert A., *Business Enterprise in the Revolutionary Era* (1938, reprinted Gloucester, Mass.: Peter Smith, 1964).

Egnal, Marc, and Ernst, Joseph A., "An Economic Interpretation of the American Revolution," *William and Mary Quarterly,* 3rd series, XXIX (1972).

Ferguson, E. James, "The Nationalists of 1781–1783 and the Economic Interpretation of the Constitution," *Journal of American History,* LVI (1969).

*Gipson, Lawrence H., *The Coming of the Revolution, 1763–1776* (New York: Harper & Row, 1957).

Henretta, James A., *"Salutary Neglect": Colonial Administration Under the Duke of Newcastle* (Princeton, N.J.: Princeton University Press, 1972).

Higginbothom, Don, *The War of American Independence . . . 1763–1789* (New York: Macmillan, 1971).

Jensen, Merrill E., *The Founding of a Nation: A History of the American Revolution, 1763–1776* (New York: Oxford University Press, 1968).

*———, *The New Nation, . . . 1781–1789* (New York: Knopf, 1950).

Main, Jackson Turner, *The Social Structure of Revolutionary America* (Princeton, N. J.: Princeton University Press, 1965).

*Nettels, Curtis Putnam, *The Emergence of a National Economy, 1775–1815* (New York: Holt, Rinehart and Winston, 1962). (This work contains a full bibliography of the period.)

Ransom, Roger L., "British Policy and Colonial Growth," *Journal of Economic History,* XXVIII (1968). (See also works cited in note 9 in this chapter.)

Ver Steeg, Clarence L., "The American Revolution Considered as an Economic Movement," *Huntington Library Quarterly,* XX (1967).

Anthologies

The following works are collections of important articles on the Revolution, including many on economic aspects of the post-1763 conflict and the war period.

Agricultural History, XLIII (January 1969), Symposium on 18th-Century Agriculture.

*Greene, Jack P., ed., *The Ambiguity of the American Revolution* (New York: Harper & Row, 1968).

*Jacobson, David L., ed., *Essays on the American Revolution* (New York: Holt, Rinehart and Winston, 1970).

*Morris, Richard B., ed., *The Era of the American Revolution* (New York: Columbia University Press, 1939).

*Wright, Esmond, ed., *Causes and Consequences of the American Revolution* (New York: Quadrangle, 1966).

agrarian america

the role of government, banking, and finance

In the modern industrial countries of our own day, and also in the less developed countries that are struggling to achieve economic growth, we regard it as normal to find government playing a large role in the economy. Taxation of private income at rates of 40 percent or higher is common in socialist and mixed capitalist economies alike. We have come to expect that governmental expenditures will constitute one-fourth or more of national income and investment flows in the modern United States. But when we examine the role of government in the American economy from 1790 to 1860, a very different picture emerges. State and local governmental expenditures were only about 3 percent of national income, and the federal government's spending accounted for only 1 to 2 percent. In contrast with our own day, when one out of six workers is employed by government, from 1790 to 1860 only perhaps 2 percent were public employees. In sum, early American government was extremely frugal and small in scale.

FEDERAL GOVERNMENT: THE POLICY MIX

Another major contrast with modern American government was the decentralized nature of governmental power in the Republic's early era. Many responsibilities and powers now exercised by the federal government were exclusively the province of state government before the Civil War. But our modern perspective should not lead us to conclude that from 1790 to 1860 the federal government's powers were of small importance. On the contrary, the constitutional foundations of strong central government were laid in the Republic's early days; and when the federal government did intervene in the economy, it was often with major effects upon economic institutions and the direction of development.

Federalist policies
The decade of the 1790s was crucially important because of legislation by Congress that assured a fiscally viable central government.

Greatly influenced by the ideas of Alexander Hamilton, the first Secretary of the Treasury, the Federalist party, which dominated national politics under George Washington's leadership, moved quickly and effectively to render the central government independent of the states for its revenues. In addition, the Federalists enacted major legislation instituting a protective import tariff, national excise taxes, a federally chartered Bank of the United States, and a policy to control trade and shipping within the great tradition of mercantilism. A national army and navy were built up and supported by federal revenues; and — over the objections of many anti-Federalists, who feared that such centralization bore the seeds of tyranny — Congress established a separate system of federal courts to enforce national laws, instead of leaving such enforcement to the state judiciaries. Finally, in one of the most controversial measures of all, the first Congress enacted a program to fund the national debt, transferring obligations to pay from the states to the central government, on terms highly favorable to the holders of securities.[1]

Republican policies

All of these measures drew fire from the emergent anti-Federalist party organization, which was to become the first Republican party under the leadership of Thomas Jefferson. Above all, Jefferson and his supporters distrusted the centralization of power that the Federalist Congress had achieved. They charged that the funding of the debt, the establishment of a national bank, and various forms of aid and protection to special economic interests, such as manufacturers, were "a mere scramble for so much public plunder." There was a real danger, wrote Jefferson's closest collaborator, James Madison, of a government that was monarchist in spirit if not in form. Such a government would retain its power by purchasing the support of special interests by wanton distribution of subsidies, privileges, and favors.[2] The doctrines propounded by the Jeffersonians have often been termed "agrarian," in the sense that they favored a simple society and an economy based upon agriculture. While such a view exaggerates Jefferson's suspicion of emergent modern capitalism, it is certain that he and his party did consistently advocate limited government at all levels, a doctrine of states' rights, and frugality in the public sector.

Ideological cleavage

The ideological debates of the 1790s were important not only at the time but also in subsequent years. They did much to establish the lines of political cleavage in the United States

until the very eve of the Civil War in 1861. Whenever land policy, banking policy, the protective tariff, the federal debt, or any other leading issue was debated, there were echoes of the original Federalist-Republican division over questions of limited versus strong government and of states' rights versus centralism.

In later sections of this chapter, and in subsequent chapters, we shall return to some of the leading policy issues that divided statesmen and animated American politics in the antebellum years. Keeping in mind the ideological divisions so firmly established in the Republic's earliest period, however, we can consider here the role of the federal government in the nation's developing economy in general terms that embrace the whole period from 1790 to 1860.

Federal intervention

Viewed in the most general terms, federal economic policy was certainly not one of perfect laissez-faire, which would have left the allocation and use of resources exclusively to market forces, with government reduced to a role of exercising only the most basic police powers. Nor was it aggressively interventionist, which would have meant governmental supervision of economic life in a manner comparable to that found in the modern fiscal and regulatory state. Rather the central government intervened with considerable intensity and regularity in a few — but only a few — key sectors of the economy, on the premise that governmental policy should stimulate private energies and provide a legal framework conducive to growth in the private sector generally.

Three areas of economic activity in which federal intervention was most important were the land market, foreign trade, and banking. National legislation affecting these sectors of the economy (treated in more detail on pp. 108–112 and in Chapter 8) took various forms. Through its policies for disposal of the public lands, Congress established the basic conditions for use of natural resources. It also influenced profoundly the availability and price of real estate, especially farmland, in the national economy as a whole. In the realm of foreign trade, the tariff programs not only raised revenues for the government but also gave varying measures of protection to producers of specific commodities, fostering some types of economic activity and leaving others to the mercy of international market forces while also influencing the level of consumer prices. And in the field of banking, the federal government, which twice

---

[1] In his Report on the Public Credit (January 1790), Hamilton showed that the foreign debt of Congress amounted to nearly $12 million (owed France, Spain, and the Netherlands); the congressional domestic debt was $27 million plus some $13 million interest in arrears; and accumulated, unpaid debts of the states were another $25 million. His plan — which was finally accepted by Congress after a heated debate — was to consolidate the entire debt, asking the holders of securities to accept scaled-down back interest. As it was notorious that the domestic debt was held largely by speculators who had obtained the paper at a fraction of its face value, opponents of the measure denounced it as corrupt. But the plan worked, as it was designed to do, to restore the credit of the new nation. By the end of 1790 the federal securities were selling at par value in the open market. The U.S. government thus embarked on its new programs with a debt of $20 per capita.

[2] *Writings of James Madison,* ed. Gaillard Hunt (New York: Putnam, 1906), vol. 6, p. 116.

chartered national banks, influenced the supply of credit and, more generally, affected the course of the business cycle at critical periods.

The federal government also intervened by providing social overhead capital — that is, facilities such as roads and educational institutions, which private capital could not or would not undertake, and the benefits of which were diffused widely in the economy. Thus the federal government constructed the National Road, beginning in 1806; granted lands to aid western states in building canals in the 1820s and railroads in the 1850s; and supported the construction of lighthouses and harbor facilities. As each new western state entered the Union, moreover, Congress granted it land that could be sold to raise funds for transport and for schools. The federal government supported the postal system, sponsored scientific explorations, built military roads in frontier areas, and collected and published statistical data, notably in the census that was taken every ten years.

Subsidies and privileges

Another major type of federal intervention consisted of grants of subsidies and privileges to private economic interests. Protective tariffs amounted to indirect subsidies of favored industries. In the 1790s Congress inaugurated a system of discriminatory duties that favored American shipping interests, and it granted domestic shipowners a virtual monopoly of the coastal trade between American ocean ports. The fostering hand of government was extended to shippers again from 1845 to 1858, when Congress gave out over $14 million in subsidies to American ship lines that carried the mails. In 1843 Congress also paid a cash subsidy to help the nation's first telegraph service. Other interests that received similar assistance included the cod-fishing industry, subsidized with cash bounties of $11 million from 1819 to 1859; the manufacturers of small arms, who received liberal cash advances on government contracts; and trans-Mississippi stagecoach lines and various railroad companies, which received generous mail contracts.

In comparison with these forms of promotional intervention, designed to foster specific business interests, there was little regulatory legislation or intervention by the federal government. Congress did regulate trade with the Indians, and it enacted quarantine and other laws to protect public health in the port cities where commerce and immigration were centered; and

in 1838 a system of federal inspection of steamboats on inland rivers was instituted. But otherwise, direct federal regulation was negligible.

The Supreme Court

No less important than direct action by Congress was the role played by the federal judiciary, especially the Supreme Court. Constitutional decisions by the Supreme Court went far toward establishing the legal framework within which investment and business enterprise functioned. And on the whole, the Supreme Court encouraged development of the private sector and a high degree of entrepreneurial liberty, for many of its landmark decisions served mainly to prevent the state governments from exercising their power in ways that would have hampered freedom of interstate commerce or hindered new investment.

Among the major decisions of the Supreme Court that had an impact on the economy, especially noteworthy was the *Dartmouth College Case* of 1819. In an opinion written by Chief Justice John Marshall, a nationalist who tended to favor both private property rights and centralized public power, the Court ruled that corporate charters were contracts. As such, a corporation charter was inviolable unless the state government that issued it had expressly reserved the right to alter its terms. Some years later the Supreme Court softened the impact of the *Dartmouth College* decision when Chief Justice Marshall's successor, Roger B. Taney, speaking for a court that by then reflected the rising influence of Andrew Jackson, declared in the *Charles River Bridge* decision (1837) that corporate charters should be interpreted very strictly. That is, corporations should not be viewed by the courts as having privileges beyond those explicitly granted in their charters. This left the state governments more room to protect the public interest against powerful business interests.

The legitimate constitutional power of the states was also contested in *McCulloch* v. *Maryland* (1819), in which Marshall's court ruled that a state might not levy taxes upon a federal instrumentality such as the first Bank of the United States. This decision was also important for its "broad construction" of the Constitution, as Marshall ruled that the "necessary and proper" clause made it possible for Congress to charter a bank, as it had done. Equally important was the case of *Gibbons* v. *Ogden* (1824), which reserved to Congress the power to regulate interstate commerce. Although the states

continued to pass laws that imposed discriminatory taxes, and also hampered freedom of
internal commerce with their schedules of state
canal tolls favoring local producers, still the

Marshall court assured that in broadest terms
the American internal national economy would
comprise a "common market."

THE EFFECTS OF LIMITED INTERVENTION

The limited range and types of federal intervention in the economy had two major effects
that need further comment. First, there was the
fiscal impact. When Congress did choose to intervene, it was usually by means of indirect subsidy (as with the protective tariff) or by use of
land grants. Seldom were cash subsidies employed. Moreover, few of the policies adopted
by the national government required costly
bureaucracies to administer them. In fact, as
late as 1860 the federal government's civilian
employees numbered only about 50,000. As a
result, nothing comparable to modern-day income taxation was necessary. Revenues from
the sales of public lands and from tariff collections, together with some excise taxes, were
sufficient to support the government's operations. Moreover, with federal spending only 2
percent or less of national income, governmental programs did not have the effect of redistributing the society's resources in ways that be-

came possible when public spending rose to
much higher relative levels and when adjustments in tax policy could have major effects
upon the level of private investment and upon
private incomes generally.

The second important effect of limited federal intervention in the economy was the remarkably persistent decentralization of decision-
making power. Much greater discretion was left
to the state governments in the nineteenth century than in the twentieth. Thus basic property
law remained under the states' control, within
the broad boundaries established by the Supreme Court to assure the protection of vested
property interests. Each state adopted its own
code of laws defining obligations under commercial contracts and with regard to tenants'
improvements, mechanics' liens, bankruptcy
relief, disposition of tax-delinquent property,
and inheritance and trusts.

"STATE MERCANTILISM" AND RIVALRIES

Each state's legislature pursued its own
"mercantilist" policy for promoting economic
development. Active intervention by state government was justified on several grounds. First,
the state courts characteristically based their decisions on a broad definition of state sovereignty, declaring that, within reasonable constitutional limits, the states retained large powers to
impose regulations on property that were in the
common interest. Second, there was a wide
acceptance of the "commonwealth" idea on
grounds of policy — a belief that the people of
each state comprised a true community, and
that its general interests required intervention
for the purpose of guiding and hedging the
strictly private uses of property. Third, there
was a high degree of rivalry evident in the way
that lawmakers defined their programs within
each state. In the same manner as the nation-
states of the eighteenth century had sought to
make themselves more self-sufficient in rivalry

with other nations for control of a limited pool
of resources, so did the state governments of
antebellum America compete with one another
for the available investment capital, labor, and
other resources that could foster economic
development.

Public enterprise
The spirit of rivalry lay behind many of the
state projects that took the form of "public
enterprise" — undertakings financed, planned,
and managed by the states themselves. The
principal enterprises in this category were the
great road and canal projects built by the states
from the 1820s through the late 1840s. There
was also widespread public enterprise in the
field of banking. Even in those states that left
banking to private interests, there were distinct
differences as to the liberality of the prevailing
banking laws. State-to-state variation meant
that the nation was a mosaic of distinctly sepa-

rate legal jurisdictions, each one having its own policy. Thus, uniformity was lacking. In the attempt to give their own people an advantage over competing interests located elsewhere, many states undertook subsidy programs: New York paid bounties to salt producers, Louisiana and Alabama to shipbuilding firms, and many other states to farmers who were experimenting with new techniques such as silk culture.

Labor relations and public welfare

Labor relations, including the status of slavery, also remained under virtually exclusive state control. Some northern states enacted legislation setting maximum hours for factory workers, but enforcement was seldom effective. In the South, all the states maintained strict controls—which were gradually made more severe in the late 1840s and the ensuing decade—over free blacks, in addition to enforcing elaborate slave codes designed to maintain discipline over the labor force on plantations.

Consistent with the English and colonial American traditions, local government had nearly exclusive responsibility for the alleviation of poverty and for public health. Not until the 1830s did the states spend much on support of homes for the indigent, and confinement in a miserable county or city workhouse was the fate of most people who fell into poverty. Imprisonment of debtors was common. The influx of immigrants and the sharp rise in factory employment in the 1840s put a severe strain upon the private charitable agencies and local government efforts to deal with unemployment and poverty. That it "corrupts a people, even in starvation, to be fed by a government" was a sentiment fairly typical of early-nineteenth-century attitudes.[3] Even if prevailing popular attitudes had been different, the ability of state and local government to relieve poverty and

unemployment was limited by the fact that state and local revenues (mainly derived from property taxes) typically fell off during periods of economic crisis.

State and local finance

There was a marked upswing in the level of local governmental expenditures during the 1850s, chiefly, it would seem, because urban governments were finally providing public fire protection, more adequate police forces, schools, and some welfare and health facilities. The 1850s also witnessed an increase in state expenditures for education, while reform movements were gaining new legislation for the construction of prisons, state-supported poorhouses and orphanages, and similar facilities.

Estimates of combined state and local government spending indicate that in the 1830s New England was expending 50 cents to $1 per capita; by the 1840s the region's public expenditures ranged from 85 to 93 cents per capita; and in the 1850s they were $1.08 to $1.55. The national average for state and local public spending from 1840 to 1860 was in the range of $1 to $3 per capita, as compared with federal expenditures averaging about $2 per person.[4] These funds were acquired largely by means of property taxation, mainly on real estate. Like the federal customs tariffs, such property taxation tended to be regressive, falling hardest on lower-income groups and on consumption rather than savings. It is worth noting, however, that in many states a principal item of state expenditure was support of the public debts incurred to aid in building of canals, railroads, and other social-overhead capital improvements whose benefits were widely diffused. Still, the main thrust of nineteenth-century fiscal policy was to maintain a high private savings rate and a high private investment level.

THE FIRST BANK OF THE UNITED STATES

One of the first major policy problems confronted by Congress in 1790 concerned banking. How should the new federal government act to assure the national economy of the credit that was needed to expedite commercial transactions and keep the flow of trade going? And

to what extent should government, either directly or through the intermediary services of one or more large financial institutions, seek to assure a measure of stability in an economy constantly subject to short-term market pressures?

In his famous *Report on the Constitutional-*

---

[3]Contemporary quotation, in Samuel Rezneck, "The Influence of Depression upon American Opinion, 1857–1859," *Business Depressions and Financial Panics* (New York: Greenwood, 1968), p. 122.

[4]Lance E. Davis, Jr., and John Legler, "Government in the American Economy, 1815–1902," *Journal of Economic History,* 26 (1966):514–552.

ity of the Bank, in February 1790, Secretary of the Treasury Hamilton set forth a theory of the "implied powers" of Congress, arguing that because of the general responsibilities that the Constitution devolved upon the federal government, Congress might properly charter a bank or indeed any other sort of corporation deemed necessary to the national economy. On the basis of Hamilton's recommendations, Congress moved to set up the first Bank of the United States under a federal charter. This was to be modeled after the Bank of England, an institution owned privately but managed with a view toward exercising control over the country's banking system. Hamilton deviated from the English model by suggesting that the federal government subscribe to one-fifth of the capital stock. The Bank, he declared, would

1. provide a much-needed paper currency through issue of its notes;
2. furnish a safe place for keeping federal revenues;
3. offer benefits to both the government and private commercial interests by financing short-term loans on goods in transit to market or in storage;
4. act as the government's fiscal agent in such matters as the sale of bonds, payment of interest, and transfer of funds from one region to another.

There was a critical need for such a bank, for in 1791 there were only five privately owned chartered banks in the United States. Furthermore, under the Constitution the states were not permitted to issue money in the form of bills of credit. Merchants needed paper money, which banks could issue in the form of notes or credit bills on goods in trade, which in turn served as collateral. Lacking such sources of liquidity, commerce had to be conducted on a restrictive basis. On the other hand, the bank as proposed by Hamilton had little to offer agrarian interests. No provision for mortgage lending was envisioned, nor could farmers obtain the long-term or intermediate-term loans they might need for the purchase of stock and equipment or the financing of improvements.

Jefferson vs. the Bank
Hamilton's scheme drew fire from Jefferson, who declared that congressional chartering of the Bank of the United States exceeded the express constitutional powers granted to the federal government. He feared too that the bank, capitalized at $10 million, would become

a monopoly in the hands of seaboard capitalists, so powerful that it would dominate entirely the state-chartered banks' operations. The bank would become still another "lottery," Jefferson said; it would produce fortunes for a favored few at the expense of the many. To him, bankers were "hornets" whose manipulations of paper credit would produce "confusion and ruin." He preferred "an ordinary circulation of metallic currency" — gold and silver — which he regarded as sufficient to meet the needs of farmers and artisans who sold their goods in local markets.

Over the long run, in both policy making and party controversy, Jefferson's antibank views became important as a fully developed expression of constitutional doctrine, as a reflection of his deeply rooted prejudice against all banks (not just Hamilton's bank), and as a position in favor of "hard money" (specie) over any form of paper currency. President Andrew Jackson was to subscribe to all these positions forty years later; and from Jackson's time until the Civil War, many Democratic leaders would regard limitation of federal power, suspicion of all banks, and hard money as articles of political orthodoxy.

Hamilton's triumph
In the short run, however, Hamilton triumphed over the Jeffersonians. The Bank of the United States operated as he had envisioned it, aided by the credit and resources of the federal government. Notes of the BUS were limited in total issue to the amount of capital stock ($10 million) and were made receivable for taxes and other debts due the government. Hamilton hoped that foreign capital would be attracted to the United States, and in fact there was extensive foreign investment in BUS stock, growing to 18,000 shares of $400 each by 1809. To the Republicans, the foreign investment provided further evidence of a decadent, monarchistic European influence in every policy proposed by the Federalists.

The Bank served the government well. Its management was conservative, and it performed as had been planned in its operations as fiscal agent. Occasionally the BUS provided short-term loans to the Treasury Department, amounting in all to $13.5 million during its 20-year career; and it provided a safe paper currency for the nation. As a creditor of many state banks, and by pursuing a policy of refusing the notes of banks that did not redeem their paper in specie, the Bank drove out fiat money and thereby helped to keep the economy's money supply stable.

State banks

The Bank's responsibilities in maintaining stability of the currency were heavy, as during the years 1781–1798 some 22 banks were operating in individual states, with capital amounting to about $15 million. Generally these early state banks served the commercial community in a conservative manner, and during the 1790s there were no major instances of insolvency or "suspension" (failure to pay specie on demand). But from 1799 to 1811, a new and more vigorous phase of banking growth began. The number of banks in operation grew to about 90, and their capitalization to $52 million. Unlike the early banking institutions, many banks chartered after 1799 were controlled by Republicans. A few were wholly owned by the state governments, and some were given exclusive banking power in their states, despite the inherited Jeffersonian hatred of monopolies. A large number of the banks chartered after 1800 were linked with projects for other developmental purposes—insurance, manufacturing, water works, canals. Together with the BUS, these state banks provided the currency of the country. Notes were issued to borrowers of funds, almost always for a short term (up to six months or so) on the collateral of goods in transit or in storage. The notes, especially if they consisted of small denominations, were passed widely and served as the circulating medium in the economy's daily transactions.

Metallic currency

The country also developed a gold and silver coinage. The metallic currency system was inaugurated by Congress in 1794 when a coinage act established the dollar as the basic monetary unit. Silver was to be minted into smaller coins, at a ratio to gold of 15 to 1; the dollar was set at $24\frac{3}{4}$ grains of pure gold. But the open-market price of silver fell relative to gold in the 1790s, when new silver mines were opened in Mexico. As a result, owners of gold bullion did not turn in their metal for minting, and the domestic coinage of the country was almost exclusively silver. In 1806 President Jefferson terminated the minting of silver, but comprehensive federal coinage reform was not effected until 1834.

The death of the BUS

So useful did the first Bank of the United States prove to be that by the time its charter expired in 1811 many Republicans had been won to its support. Secretary of the Treasury Albert Gallatin strongly advocated its renewal, and the House voted by a single-vote majority to continue the Bank; but the Senate vote was a tie, and Vice-President George Clinton cast the deciding vote against it. Only a few of the state-chartered banks used their political influence in its favor. Most of the state bankers were jealous of their giant rival, it seemed, and consequently representatives in Congress from the commercial centers generally opposed renewal. As one senator charged, the "avarice" of the commercial states and their banking interests did as much to defeat recharter as continued doubts concerning the Bank's constitutionality.

Pressures on the banking system

The restraining hand of a specie-paying national bank was now removed, and numerous new state banks sprang up. With the growth of population and with rising demand for bank credit to finance new enterprises, it was not surprising that the number of state banks should have increased from 89 in 1811 to nearly 250 five years later. Money in circulation rose rapidly. Because many of the new banks had been established on a slim basis of paid-in capital or specie reserves, the resultant instability of the currency had become troublesome even before the War of 1812. The war put new pressures on the banking system as federal expenditures rose steadily from $8 million in 1810 to $35 million by 1814. Congress balked at new taxes, and the Treasury was forced to borrow at high interest rates. Not until the war was nearly half over did Congress increase customs duties and impose new excise taxes. The war was paid for largely by loans, with a resultant increase in the national debt from $45 million in January 1812 to $120 million in late 1815. With specie in short supply and the currency (consisting largely of depreciated bank notes) badly deranged, the Treasury had to accept bank paper of all kinds in order to keep the revenues from drying up. This in turn merely fed the inflation that was already under way.

THE SECOND BANK OF THE UNITED STATES

The disastrous fiscal experience during the war and persistent currency problems caused a reconsideration of banking policy by Republican leaders. They decided that the crisis was serious enough to warrant reversing the party's traditional position on a national bank. A coalition of southern and western congressmen, predominantly Republican in party affiliation, pushed through Congress a charter for the Second Bank of the United States in 1816.

The new BUS was in most respects comparable to the first. The charter, to run for 20 years, called for one-fifth of the $35 million capital to be subscribed by the government; it provided that the BUS should be the government's principal fiscal agent, to hold and transfer revenues as needed, pay interest to bondholders, and the like; and it was to have 25 directors, with five to be appointed by the President of the United States. The notes of the Bank were to be accepted in payment of both debts and taxes owed the government. It was also understood by the friends and opponents of recharter that the BUS would serve as a check on state banks, forcing them to resume specie payments through its operations or else replacing them by driving their notes out of circulation. The new institution began operations in January 1817.

The Bank's first three years were marked by something less than distinguished service. Its president, William Jones, at first pursued a policy of overindulgent tolerance toward the state banks. Then he abruptly shifted gears in 1818 and subjected them mercilessly to pressure for immediate specie settlement of accounts.

Langdon Cheves, who became the Bank's president in 1819 and served until 1823, adopted a more conservative course. Under Cheves the loans of the BUS were sharply reduced from over $40 million to $28 million—rendering the Bank widely unpopular in the West,

where this contractionist policy hit hardest and brought down many banks.

The branch banks

During most of the Bank's subsequent history it adequately fulfilled its manifold functions as commercial bank, governmental fiscal agent, and protector of "sound currency." Under Cheve's successor, Nicholas Biddle, the Bank moved vigorously to expand the number of its branches—eventually 29 were opened—and to give the branch cashiers discretion in issuing credit. This expansion of branch business encountered the hostility and militant opposition of state bankers throughout much of the country. "I consider the U.S. Bank as it respects the States Banks, as a caged tiger," wrote a prominent New York banker in 1831, "and I should be afraid to be within his reach whenever the bars are removed and the chain extended."[5]

The strategy that Biddle pursued also posed a challenge to bankers in the major commercial cities, especially New York and Baltimore, where some local banking leaders may well have feared that Biddle and his bank, with its main office in Philadelphia, would use the institution's rising strength to rival their own cities' commercial ambitions. In the interior districts there was considerable resentment of the BUS as a symbol of "monopoly," some of it stemming from widespread popular belief that the Panic of 1819 was caused by the Bank's policies. The political leaders who were gathering under the banner of Andrew Jackson for president in the mid-1820s included many who harbored no great friendship for the Bank.

JACKSON'S "BANK WAR"

Andrew Jackson's election to the Presidency in 1828 set the stage for the fatal embroilment of the BUS in partisan politics. Jackson, who was suspicious of all banks, regarded Biddle as arrogant and believed that the Bank had become dangerously powerful. Confrontation became inevitable when, in 1831 or 1832, Jackson also became convinced that the BUS was confronting bankruptcy. At that time, supporters of the Bank in Congress prevailed upon Biddle to petition for renewal of the charter (four years prematurely), and Jackson angrily vetoed the measure. Unwisely seeking to turn public opinion against Jackson in hopes of building support for recharter, Biddle ordered a severe contraction of loans by his bank in 1833.

This precipitated a major credit crisis, popularly known as "Biddle's panic." Jackson countered by removing the government's deposits from the Bank in the fall of 1833. The deposits were placed in selected state banks, known derisively as "pet banks" because they were thought to be closely associated with the interests of Democrats in the business community. But over the next few years the number of deposit banks was gradually enlarged, and Jackson's Treasury Department selected many that were controlled by opposition-party Whigs.

[5]Henry Dwight, letter of August 25, 1831, "Some Documents on Jackson's Bank War," ed. H. Scheiber, *Pennsylvania History,* 30 (1963):51.

Jackson's pet-banks policy is commonly viewed by historians as a crass political move, or at best as a misguided effort to replace the system of controlled banking that the Bank of the United States had assured with a policy of virtual laissez-faire. But there is an alternative explanation, which interprets the pet-bank policy as a move toward tighter federal regulation of banking and restoration of truly public control, supplanting the irresponsible private control that Biddle had exercised. This latter view is based upon evidence that Jackson's Treasury Department in 1833–1835 required the new deposit banks to accept guidelines for keeping their specie reserves in a conservative ratio to note issues, to reduce the issue of small-denomination notes, and to provide the government with personal bonds by their directors as security for the deposits they held.[6]

Expansion and panic

Despite the restraining influence of these Treasury guidelines, other forces encouraged the state banks generally, and the pet banks as well, to expand their loans, discounts, and note issues and thus encourage expansion of the currency in the economic boom conditions that prevailed in 1835 and 1836. As the national debt was retired in 1834, and as federal land sales soared, the level of federal deposits rose fivefold between 1834 and 1836. A self-reinforcing cycle set in, whereby expansion by the banks further stimulated the land boom and the pace of business activity generally.

Jackson viewed this cycle of expansion with alarm, and in July 1836 he issued his famous Specie Circular, an executive order that required purchasers of government land beyond a small quantity to pay in gold or silver. At nearly the same time, Congress adopted a new policy of distributing the federal surplus revenues to the states. These two measures placed the government deposit banks under enormous pressure because of increased demand for specie and transfer funds. Soon afterward there was a rise in demand for specie to pay for American imports from England.

A credit contraction resulted, and in May 1837 nearly all American banks stopped redeeming their notes in gold and silver. The Panic of 1837 had thus begun, and Jackson's critics laid blame for it at his doorstep. The Jacksonians, on the other hand, bitterly denounced the machinations of corrupt bankers and a fundamentally unsound credit system.

The crisis conditions of 1837 merely confirmed many Democrats' conviction that the government ought to sever all connections with banks, and instead put the country on a hard-money basis. Both in Congress and in the state legislatures, Jackson's Democratic party moved toward an ideological, or antibank, radicalism.

BANKING AND CURRENCY, 1839–1862

After a brief recovery, a prolonged depression began in 1839. It was the worst the nation had experienced up to then, and it resulted in the bankruptcy of thousands of businesses and, in many states, the complete restructuring of banking. Loans and discounts by American banks fell by half, to $255 million, during the long downswing of 1837 to 1843. Congress enacted a special national bankruptcy law in 1841 to aid in providing relief to debtors; and the Treasury Department, faced with rising budgetary deficits, resorted to the issue of non-interest-bearing government notes. Whig spokesmen in Congress attempted to charter a third Bank of the United States. But Jackson's successor, Martin Van Buren, held solidly to the radical antibank position.

The independent treasury system

Van Buren's most enduring accomplishment in the realm of economic policy was the Independent Treasury System, by which the government collected, held, transferred, and disbursed its own revenues. No banks were used for depository or transfer functions. Inaugurated in 1840 and repealed by the Whigs when they regained power in 1841, the Independent Treasury was reinstated by the Democrats in 1846. It continued in effect thereafter, and no major reform was undertaken until the Civil War. During the 1837–1843 depression, the number of state banks declined. Also, bank expansion was hindered by the enactment of regulatory laws in many states. But after 1843 the divorce of banking from governmental fi-

---

[6]Scheiber, "The Pet Banks in Jacksonian Politics and Finance, 1833–1840," *Journal of Economic History*, 23 (1963):196–214; John McFaul, *The Politics of Jacksonian Finance* (Ithaca, N.Y.: Cornell University Press, 1972), chap. 6.

nances probably stimulated the private banking institutions, whose number rose from 700 in 1844 to over 1500 in 1860, while their note circulation increased from $75 million to $207 million.

State banking regulation

With the federal government effectively removed from the field after adoption of the Independent Treasury, banking progressed under regulatory rules established by the states. During the post-1840 period the states adopted a wide variety of policies to govern banks and other financial institutions. Nearly every state had usury laws that set upper limits on the interest rates charged on loans. Some states also established specie-reserve requirements, restricting the note-issue practices of their banks; others banned banking under corporate charters altogether; a few states, notably Missouri, Indiana, and Ohio, set up banks owned by the state itself and operated under the control of appointed public directors. There was an abundance, too, of "wildcat banks," which operated on slender or nonexistent specie reserves. New York, Michigan, and other states instituted "free banking"—an important innovative policy under which the field of banking was opened to any firm that had the requisite capital. New York, however, linked its free banking policy with a system of regulatory controls. The states that did impose well-enforced regulations on their banks often suffered temporary disadvantages, however, since the notes of out-of-state banks could circulate at heavy discounts. Sometimes altogether worthless notes easily crossed over state lines.

Banking development and innovation

The great variety of state laws regulating bank practices and charters from 1834 to 1860 meant that banking was subject to all the difficulties of a complex legal framework. But even lacking the advantage of national uniformity, there was considerable institutional development and innovation. By 1860, bankers had introduced clearinghouses for daily settlement of demands and balances among institutions in major cities; they had successfully mobilized private savings and invested these funds in state bonds and private securities, to aid in financing internal improvements such as canals and railroads; and they had spawned related forms of financial institutions such as insurance companies. Indeed, in the Northeast there arose what amounted to a system of regional "central" banks operating in the large commercial cities.

By the 1850s, moreover, the use of checks had become common in business transactions, and banks had begun to use "created deposits" as instruments for making loans—an important complement to currency in the nation's money supply. Despite persistent evidences of instability, such as the widespread bank failures associated with the Panic of 1857, the nation's financial institutions made a positive contribution to the processes of economic growth by expediting capital formation and commercial transactions.

LAND POLICY AND DEVELOPMENT

Throughout the early nineteenth century, expansion of the nation's territorial boundaries was a major feature of American development. The United States acquired the vast territory of Louisiana from France in 1803, pushing the area of American hegemony west to the Rocky Mountains and giving the nation entire control of the Mississippi Valley. Acquisition of Florida from Spain in 1819 and the annexation of Texas in 1845 extended the potential domain of King Cotton and southern slave society generally. Oregon, with its rich resources in furs, farmland, and waterways, was acquired from Great Britain in 1846, following which California and the present-day southwestern states were taken by military force from Mexico.

Hence a combination of good fortune, aggressive expansionist designs, military strength, and a population growing quickly enough to people newly acquired lands with a European-American settlement base, all contributed to a vast extension of U.S. territory and of the economy's pool of resources. In the earliest days of independence, therefore, Congress found it necessary to hammer out a policy for disposal of land and natural resources.

Indian policy and creation of new states

Two elements of American policy regarding the western territories were fashioned initially in the 1780s and 1790s and became permanent features of national policy thereafter. The first was the policy of reducing the native Indians' hold over their ancestral lands, and ultimately of pushing the Indians out of any areas where European-Americans wanted to farm, prospect for mineral deposits, or settle for other purposes. In many instances the Indian peoples were subjected to military action; in others, typically devious and corrupt means were used to deprive them of their lands by treaty.

The second element of American policy that dated from the Confederation period was the granting of self-government and entry into the Union as new states to the western communities of American settlers. First instituted in the Northwest Ordinances of 1784 and 1787, the plan provided for stages by which territories were organized with rising degrees of popular political participation, culminating in their admission to the Union as new states. In addition, the 1787 ordinance banned slavery in the Old Northwest, north of the Ohio River. In later years Congress permitted slavery to be extended into the new territories of the South. The Missouri Compromise of 1820 demarcated free territory from slave territory west of the Mississippi River, but the slavery issue was destined to become the vortex of critical sectional controversies following the war with Mexico.

The objectives of land policy

Even before the Ordinance of 1787 had been passed, the Congress of the Confederation was giving attention to the problem of land disposal and laying the foundations of an American land policy. Despite a century and a half of experience, the problem was a difficult one. The Congress had two objectives: It was eager to promote settlement but at the same time it wished to derive income from the public land sales. As most settlers were people with little or no capital, the two desires were hardly compatible. If the land was to be sold, should it be disposed of in large tracts or small ones? Sale in large tracts would play into the hands of wealthy land speculators; sale in small lots would benefit bona fide settlers, who were generally poor. From the point of revenue, however, there were arguments against small sales. Buyers would purchase only the good land and leave the rest, and the small-scale arrangement would tend to scatter the settlers. There was also the problem of settlement requirements. Should actual occupation of the land be required? Such a regulation would minimize speculation and favor the small buyer, but it might depress the

value of the land. There were, of course, the important problems of price, of whether the land should be sold for cash or for credit (or both), and of where the land offices should be set up.

The Ordinance of 1785

Since all this involved the method by which a large part of the American continent was to be transferred from the government to private ownership, it was obviously a matter of primary significance. To the westward-moving settler the land policy of the government was of fundamental importance. Forced by necessity to tackle the problem, the Congress under the Articles of Confederation made a beginning in the Land Ordinance of 1785. This provided (1) for a rectangular land survey by the government, (2) for the setting aside of one-thirty-sixth of the land for educational purposes, and (3) for the establishment of land offices for the sale of public lands at low prices. After a north–south line, known as the "prime meridian," had been established (the first one set up being the present boundary line between Ohio and Indiana), an east–west base line was laid down to intersect it at right angles. From the intersection of the prime meridian and the base line the surveyors ran out perpendicular lines at six-mile intervals. The crossing of these lines divided the land into squares containing 36 square miles. Each of these squares was to be a township and was subsequently to be subdivided into 36 squares each one mile square (640 acres), known as sections, Section 16 being reserved for the support of common schools. Most of the states admitted after 1842 also reserved Section 36 for school purposes, thus setting aside for education one-eighteenth of the land surveyed. An attempt was made to reserve Section 15 from each township for religious purposes, but it was voted down. In the history of American land policy the Ordinance of 1785 proved as fundamental as the Ordinance of 1787 did in the political life of the new West. The method outlined in 1785 was generally followed during the next century.

Changing terms of land disposal

It was in the methods of disposal rather than survey that policies changed. Uncertain whether to follow the New England system of grants by townships or the Virginia system of individual sales of grants, Congress in 1785 provided for both; half of the townships were to be sold entire and the other half in sections of 640 acres.

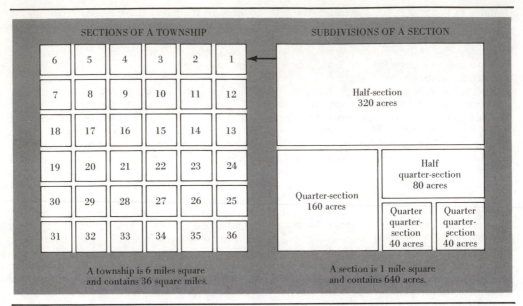

Figure 7–1. Land Division by Township and Section. Adapted from *History of the American Way* by Faulkner, Kepner, and Merrill © 1950 with permission of Webster/McGraw-Hill.

The land was to be sold at auction, with a minimum price of $1 an acre. An act of 1796 raised the price to $2 an acre but introduced a credit system that allowed a year for payment. As few pioneers could command $1280, the demand arose immediately that the law be changed to favor the settlers. As the political power of the West increased, this demand was successful. In 1800 the minimum amount of land that could be purchased was reduced to 320 acres and in 1804 to 160 acres. The time for payment in the latter act was extended to five years. New legislation in 1820 again reduced the amount to 80 acres and cut the price to $1.25 an acre. Inordinate speculation culminating in the Panic of 1819, however, influenced the Congress to abolish the credit system.

Perhaps the most important concession obtained by the West in the years before the Civil War was the right of preemption, secured permanently in 1841. For years settlers had moved onto the public lands, cleared the forest, and laid out farms without the formality of a purchase, only to find that they were illegal intruders on government land; sometimes the land was sold over their heads or they were driven off by federal troops. Settlers demanded the right to take up the land that they wanted, whether it had been surveyed or not, and then purchase it at the minimum price free from

competitive bids. In practice they had sometimes succeeded in doing this before the law of 1841 made it legal. Settlers would select their land and improve it and then organize squatters' protective associations. Members of these protective associations would appear at the land auctions and make perfectly clear to any outsider that he had better not bid on their land—that is, if he valued his personal safety. The Preemption Act of 1841 was an important concession, but it was by no means the ultimate goal of the western spokesmen. But the next step, free land to actual settlers, was not taken until the famous Homestead Act of 1862.

Settlers and speculators

From this brief résumé of the more important land acts, it is evident that the land policy of the federal government became more liberal as time went on. Nevertheless, the whole policy was by no means as just or as democratic as it might appear. The chief weakness was the fact that in actual practice the laws tended to favor the wealthy speculator rather than the poor settler.[7] Three factors (until the Homestead Act of 1862) were responsible: The government

[7]Paul Wallace Gates, *History of Public Land Law Development* (Washington, D.C.: Public Land Law Review Commission, 1968), chaps. 7–10.

charged a price for the land beyond the capacity of the average settler, it set no limit on the amount that could be acquired, and it did not require actual settlement on or improvement of the land.

It is true that the government gave some land away — large grants to transportation companies, as in the case of the Illinois Central Railroad, and land bounties to veterans of Indian wars and soldiers of the War of 1812 and the Mexican War. But most veterans did not actually settle the land, instead selling their warrants to speculators. Indeed, twice as much federal land purchased during 1847–1854 was paid for with warrants (that sold at 70 cents to $1.10 an acre) as was paid for in cash. The average settler needed to borrow to buy warrants or to pay cash, and prevailing interest rates were extremely high: 10 to 36 percent in most areas of the West and South. Also, the best land was often in the hands of speculators — both large-scale capitalists and petty speculators — by the time many potential settlers reached the area

where they wanted land. There were many localities where the pattern of speculation and high interest charges made it difficult for many settlers to acquire their own property, so that they had to take up a life as tenant farmers or farm laborers.[8]

In sum, the land system of the United States before 1862 offered considerable advantages to individuals and firms with abundant capital. For people of slender resources, the way to gaining status as an independent landholder and prosperity through commercial farming was seldom an easy one. Still, despite a resultant pattern of landownership that fell far short of Jeffersonian ideals, in most of the Northeast and upper Mississippi and Ohio valley regions the great bulk of land came into the hands of independent small farmers. In the South, the best land went to the large-scale slave plantations (see pp. 132–133). But even there a substantial American yeoman–farmer element constituted an important segment of the region's population.

PRIVATISM AND THE SPECIAL USES OF LAND

While Congress continually readjusted land policy, it gave relatively little attention to the wide variety of uses to which private interests actually put western land. Congress tended to think only of arable farming as the norm in the use of federal lands. The states generally formulated their own land policies on the same premise. But in fact, in many areas of the West, it was for minerals, grass, or timber that control of the land was sought.

Mining

Although Congress under the Confederation, in 1785, had required a one-third royalty for the government on the value of metals mined on public land, this provision was not reenacted when the new government was established under the Constitution. Loosely drafted laws did make provision for some leasing of mineral lands, and for about twenty years beginning in the late 1820s the federal government controlled lead mining in the rich Galena district of Illinois and southwestern Wisconsin. But generally mineral-bearing lands were not treated much differently from agricultural lands: They were sold outright (though often at higher prices than the $1.25-per-acre minimum), without limitation as to amount of land that

might be bought by one purchaser. Hence large areas of rich copper and iron deposits were sold off cheaply to the first takers. Apparently the national lawmakers were far more interested in releasing private entrepreneurial energies than in realizing revenues for the national Treasury, and they let the race go to the swiftest. The idea of imposing conservationist principles in oversight of mineral production was never even seriously considered.[9]

Even when incredibly rich gold deposits were discovered in California, triggering the fabulous Gold Rush of 1849, Congress permitted mining to go forward without requiring royalties or indeed imposing any form of active legal controls. The California legislature thus came by default to regulate gold-mining practices. The state's lawmakers generally validated local codes adopted on a voluntary basis in the mining districts. But California also gave miners priority of right to enter public lands that were being used by others for farming or grazing, and state law permitted the mines to pollute the state's rivers with effluent, in effect subordinat-

[8]Gates, *The Farmer's Age, 1815–1860* (New York: Holt, Rinehart, and Winston, 1961), pp. 70–98, 398–413.
[9]Gates, *History of Public Land Law*, chap. 23.

ing all other interests to that of the miners.[10]
Mining in the Far West, as President Millard Fillmore said approvingly, thus remained "a common field, open to the enterprise and industry of all our citizens."

Ranching and lumbering
Congress adopted no policy, either, for control or leasing of public lands used for the grazing of livestock. Wherever grasslands existed beyond the areas of compact settlement, cattlemen were left free to use the public domain. Like the California miners, the cattle interests made informal agreements of their own and adopted local codes. And, as happened in California, a comparatively few first arrivals often preempted the public resources and excluded others.

The lumber industry, too, developed in the United States by drawing heavily on low-priced or free resources for which Congress neglected to design special policies. Timber was cut fairly freely from the public lands, and whenever population began to drift into a timbered area for permanent settlement, the lumbermen bought up huge tracts at the $1.25 minimum price that had been instituted to favor potential farmers.

In sum, antebellum America was virtually without systematic resource management by public authorities. It was an era in which "the public interest" was equated with giving private enterprise cheap or free access to the nation's natural resources—that is, an era whose policies reflected clearly laissez-faire preferences.

SELECTED READINGS

Broude, Henry W., "The Role of the State in American Economic Development," in *United States Economic History: Selected Readings,* Harry N. Scheiber, ed. (New York: Knopf, 1964).

*Bruchey, Stuart, *The Roots of American Economic Growth, 1607–1861* (New York: Harper & Row, 1965). (This is a valuable survey and guide to the literature of that period.)

*Goodrich, Carter, *The Government and the Economy, 1783–1861* (Indianapolis: Bobbs-Merrill, 1967). (Essay and documents.)

*Hammond, Bray, *Banks and Politics in America from the Revolution to the Civil War* (Princeton: Princeton University Press, 1957).

*Hurst, James Willard, *Law and the Conditions of Freedom in the 19th Century United States* (1956, reprinted Madison: University of Wisconsin Press, 1964).

*Miller, John C., *Alexander Hamilton and the Growth of the New Nation* (New York: Harper & Row, 1959).

*———, *The Federalist Era, 1789–1801* (New York: Harper & Row, 1960).

*Nettels, Curtis P., *The Emergence of a National Economy, 1775–1815* (New York: Holt, Rinehart and Winston, 1962).

Redlich, Fritz, *The Molding of American Banking* (1951, reprinted New York: Johnson Reprint Corp., 1969).

Reznick, Samuel, *Business Depressions and Financial Panics* (New York: Greenwood Publishing Co., 1968).

Rothbard, Murray, *The Panic of 1819: Reactions and Policies* (New York: Columbia University Press, 1962).

Scheiber, Harry N., *The Condition of American Federalism: An Historian's View* (Washington, D.C.: 89 Cong., 2nd Sess., Senate, Committee on Government Operations, print, 1966).

Smith, Walter B., *Economic Aspects of the Second Bank of the United States* (Cambridge, Mass.: Harvard University Press, 1953).

Studenski, Paul, and Krooss, Herman, *Financial History of the United States,* 2nd ed. (New York: McGraw-Hill, 1963).

*Taylor, George Rogers, *The Transportation Revolution, 1815–1860* (New York: Holt, Rinehart and Winston, 1951).

---

[10]Rodman W. Paul, *Mining Frontiers of the Far West, 1848–1880* (New York: Holt, Rinehart and Winston, 1963), pp. 161–175; H. Scheiber and Charles W. McCurdy, "Eminent-Domain Law and Western Agriculture," *Agricultural History,* 49 (1975):112–130.

*Wright, Benjamin F., *The Growth of American Constitutional Law* (Chicago: University of Chicago Press, 1967).

Studies of Individual States

Handlin, Oscar, and Handlin, Mary F., *Commonwealth: A Study of the Role of Government in the American Economy—Massachusetts, 1774–1861,* revised edition (Cambridge, Mass.: Harvard University Press, 1969).

*Hartz, Louis, *Economic Policy and Democratic Thought: Pennsylvania, 1776–1860* (Cambridge, Mass: Harvard University Press, 1948).

Heath, Milton, *Constructive Liberalism: The Role of the State in the Economic Development of Georgia to 1860* (Cambridge, Mass.: Harvard University Press, 1954).

Nash, Gerald D., *State Government and Economic Development . . . in California, 1849–1933* (Berkeley: University of California Press, 1964).

Scheiber, Harry N., *Ohio Canal Era: A Case Study of Government and the Economy, 1820–1861* (Athens, Ohio: Ohio University Press, 1969).

Soltow, James H., "American Institutional Studies," *Journal of Economic History,* XXXI (1971). (Bibliographic essay.)

Studies of Land Policy

*Carstensen, Vernon, ed., *The Public Lands: Studies in the History of the Public Domain* (Madison: University of Wisconsin Press, 1963).

*Bogue, Allan G., *From Prairie to Corn Belt: Farming on the Illinois and Iowa Prairies in the 19th Century* (Chicago: University of Chicago Press, 1963).

*Gates, Paul W., *The Farmer's Age: Agriculture, 1815–1860* (New York: Holt, Rinehart and Winston, 1961).

———, *History of Public Land Law Development* (Washington: U. S. Government Printing Office, 1968).

Le Duc, Thomas, "History and Appraisal of U.S. Land Policy to 1862," in Howard W. Ottoson, ed., *Land Use Policy and Problems in the United States* (Lincoln: University of Nebraska Press, 1963).

Swierenga, Robert P., *Pioneers and Profits: Land Speculation on the Iowa Frontier* (Ames: Iowa State University Press, 1968).

Studies of Law and the Economy

*Friedman, Lawrence M., *A History of American Law* (New York: Simon & Schuster, 1973).

*Kutler, Stanley I., *Privilege and Creative Destruction: The Charles River Bridge Case* (Philadelphia: Lippincott, 1971).

Wright, Benjamin F., *The Contract Clause of the Constitution* (Cambridge, Mass.: Harvard University Press, 1938).

"Our commerce is freed from those shackles it used to be cramped with, and bids fair to extend to every part of the globe without passing through the medium of England, that rotten island."[1] So wrote a Massachusetts editor in 1784, in a private declaration of commercial independence that expressed the high optimism prevailing in America about the national economy when the burdens of English mercantilism were thrown off. Looking outward across the Atlantic sea-lanes they knew so well, American merchants and shippers anticipated prosperity from new trade. And in the 1780s the Continental Congress attempted to advance these ambitions by seeking special privileges and immunities for the United States from every nation in Europe.[2] But the humiliations of national weakness under the Articles of Confederation proved to be a hindrance to successful commercial diplomacy. To be sure, France opened its doors to American tobacco and admitted American ships on favorable terms. A few of the lesser trading nations made comparable concessions. Ironically, however, the real key to American commercial prosperity had to be the maintaining of a profitable trade with England; and the British were not disposed to reward rebellion with commercial favors. Cal-

culating correctly, the British government was confident that superior British credit facilities, their advantages over the Continent in efficient manufacturing of export articles, and the very force of habit and old trading relationships would retain for them much of the U.S. market. His Majesty's government thus for more than a decade after the Revolution barred American ships from the West Indies islands—once kingpin of the colonial trade for the North Americans—and the United States was treated simply as another nation outside the imperial system of British trade protected by the Navigation Acts.

Developing new commerce

The Yankee shipping magnates thus had to seek new markets and sources of supply to maintain their commerce. With a vigor and enterprising spirit that built some great fortunes in Boston and Salem, the merchants turned first to East Asia. As we have seen (p. 91), a lucrative trade with China was initiated in 1785, and trade with the French, Dutch, Spanish, and Danish West Indies islands expanded throughout the 1780s. However, England still remained the principal supplier of goods imported into the United States, and the newer trades were only makeshift substitutes for what had been lost.

Conditions of American trade

When the Constitution was adopted, one of the first questions that Congress considered was the requirements of American trade. In this policy debate, as in others, Secretary of the Treasury Hamilton took the lead, recommending a policy of nondiscrimination and equal treatment of all foreign nations, with tariff and other advantages extended to domestic shippers.

---

[1]Quoted in Merrill Jensen, *The New Nation: A History of the United States Under the Articles of Confederation, 1781–1789* (New York: Knopf, 1950), p. 154.

[2]As Merrill Peterson has argued, the Continental Congress's effort to open up freer trade among all nations was as revolutionary a departure from Europe's *commercial* order as the decision for American independence had been with respect to the Old World's established *political* order. See Peterson, "Thomas Jefferson and Commercial Policy, 1783–1793," *William and Mary Quarterly*, 3rd ser., 22 (1965): 588.

Opposed to his position was, predictably, Secretary of State Jefferson and his right arm in Congress, James Madison. They were appalled at Hamilton's unwillingness to reward America's true friends, such as France, which had already granted ample trade concessions; and they sought to retaliate against Great Britain for its posture of hostility. They scornfully rebutted Hamilton's view that trade ties with England should be cemented because British capital would be important to American development. The flow of credit from England to America, Jefferson declared, merely rendered the southern planters "a specie[s] of property annexed to certain mercantile houses in London."[3]

Hamilton won this fight, as he did nearly all the policy confrontations of the day. In the Tariff and Tonnage Acts of 1789, Congress adopted a policy of nondiscrimination respecting foreign nations. Protective tariffs were levied on imports, but no special advantages were awarded to France or any other trading partner. In a move to encourage American shipping, Congress gave a 10 percent discount on all duties to imports carried to this country in ships built and owned by American citizens. The newly developed trade with East Asia was also encouraged, as tea carried in American ships directly was subject to a tariff of only half the tariff on tea brought from any European port. The Tonnage Act imposed a duty of 6 cents a ton on cargoes brought from foreign ports by American ships, but 50 cents a ton on cargoes carried by foreign-built, foreign-owned vessels.

At the same time, American ships in the coastwise trade (from one American port to another) were required to pay tonnage duties only once, whereas foreign ships paid at each entry. This act set the stage for a virtual monopoly on coastwise commerce for American shipping. But British and French ships, like other foreign vessels, were put on an equal footing with each other in American ports.

In March 1792 a new revenue law adjusted tariffs and incorporated some 18 of the increases of duties recommended by Hamilton for purposes of protection to manufacturers. In all cases, however, duties were moderate, with a range of 5 to 15 percent on value prevailing on nearly all commodities imported.

Master-seaman relations

An act of 1790 regulating seamen provided a code of law well in advance of its time. It stipulated that a written contract must be entered into between master and seaman, specifying the voyage and rate of wages, and bound the ship itself as a guarantee of performance. Masters were liable to severe penalties if they abandoned American sailors in a foreign country, whereas seamen who signed articles and then deserted were subject to forfeiture of wages and return by compulsion. Though this law was widely evaded, it established an important constitutional precedent for congressional exercise of power over labor relations as an instrument for regulating commerce.

TRADE AND GROWTH, 1790–1819

America's foreign trade set the pattern for expansion for the national economy throughout the period 1790–1819. Never since that time has foreign commerce so thoroughly absorbed the energies of the people. Income generated by foreign trade had been approximately $7 per capita throughout the 1780s. By 1807 (the peak of the trade expansion) it had soared to about $21 to $24 per capita, equivalent to more than a sixth of per capita income. Though the West has traditionally been considered the great frontier of the United States, an equally vital frontier of enterprise during this

early period was the Atlantic coast's string of ports and the decks of American ships.

War and trade

The central fact of the period was war in Europe, as England and France engaged in a protracted clash of arms that involved nearly all of the Continent. When the contest began in 1793, French shipping was nearly driven out of the Atlantic by the British navy, and the United States merchant fleet became the ocean carrier to a world at war. In addition to trading directly with both the principal belligerents, American ships reaped handsome profits from transporting the products of the European colonies. Consequently, the shipping earnings of the United States rose from $6 million in 1790 to

[3]Quoted in John C. Miller, *Alexander Hamilton and the Growth of the New Nation* (New York: Harper & Row, 1959), p. 222.

TABLE 8–1.   COMPOSITION OF U.S. MERCHANDISE EXPORTS, 1790–1860 (MILLIONS OF CURRENT DOLLARS)

YEAR	TOTAL EXPORTS[1]	REEXPORTS	UNMANUFACTURED COTTON	LEAF TOBACCO	WHEAT
1790	$ 20	$ –	$ –	$ 4	$ 1
1800	71	32	3[2]	8[2]	–
1807	108	60	14	5	–
1820	70	18	22	8	–
1830	72	13	30	6	–
1840	124	12	64	10	2
1850	144	9	72	10	1
1857	294	15	132	20	22
1860	334	17	192	16	4

Source: U.S. Department of Commerce, Bureau of the Census, *Historical Statistics of the United States, Colonial Times to 1957* (Washington, D.C.: U.S. Government Printing Office, 1960), pp. 538, 547.

[1]Includes reexports.
[2]Estimated.

TABLE 8–2.   COMPOSITION OF U.S. MERCHANDISE EXPORTS AND IMPORTS, 1820/1821–1860 (MILLIONS OF CURRENT DOLLARS)

YEAR	TOTAL VALUE[2]	CRUDE MATERIALS AND FOODSTUFFS	MANUFACTURED FOODSTUFFS	SEMI- AND FINISHED MANUFACTURES
1820, 1821[1]				
Exports	$ 52	$ 33	$10	$ 8
Imports	55	9	11	35
1830				
Exports	59	40	10	9
Imports	63	12	10	41
1840				
Exports	112	81	16	16
Imports	98	27	15	55
1850				
Exports	135	92	20	23
Imports	174	31	21	121
1855				
Exports	193	120	33	40
Imports	258	60	34	164
1860				
Exports	316	229	39	49
Imports	354	86	60	207

Source: U.S. Department of Commerce, Bureau of the Census, *Historical Statistics of the United States, Colonial Times to 1957* (Washington, D.C.: U.S. Government Printing Office, 1960), pp. 544–545.

[1]Exports, 1820; imports, 1821.
[2]Exports *exclude* value of reexports.

$42 million in 1807. Reexports (goods brought to American ports, then shipped out again as neutral commerce) increased in value from only $300,000 in 1790 to $6.5 million in 1794 and $60 million in 1807, at the climax of the boom.[4]

The European war also gave a powerful stimulus to domestic production for the export trade. Exportation of domestic products more than doubled from 1805 to 1808, with about half the increase accounted for by cotton. American wheat, flour, corn, meat, and live-

[4]Douglass C. North, "The U.S. Balance of Payments," in National Bureau of Economic Research, *Trends in the American Economy in the Nineteenth Century* (Princeton: Princeton University Press, 1960), pp. 590–600; John G. B. Hutchins, *The American Maritime Industries and Public Policy, 1789–1914* (Cambridge: Harvard University Press, 1941), p. 227; Curtis P. Nettels, *The Emergence of a National Economy, 1775–1815* (New York: Holt, Rinehart and Winston, 1962), chap. 10.

stock also went into the international market, as high wartime food prices attracted a vast migration into the farmlands of the Ohio Valley. The British West Indies islands were now occasionally opened to American vessels, and livestock, fish, lumber, and grain went to these Caribbean ports as well as to French and other colonial possessions in the West Indies and South America.

Trade restrictions

Great Britain soon became concerned, however, about the role of American commerce in supporting the war effort of its rival, and the French were likewise troubled. Eager to cut off vital supply lines, England imposed a blockade of all northern Europe from 1804 to 1807, and forbade the landing of neutral vessels at ports of France or its allies without first touching at English harbors. Napoleon replied with decrees that declared the British Isles under blockade, and from 1803 to 1811 some 900 American ships were seized by the British and another 760 by French privateers. The French actions came after the United States had waged an undeclared war against France in 1798. But after 1800 American outrage was focused increasingly on the British navy and its depredations against American commerce. Most galling of all was the policy of seizing from United States ships sailors who were deemed to be British subjects, and impressing them into service with the Royal Navy. The State Department claimed that in 1806 and 1807 some 6000 sailors who were American nationals had thus been illegally impressed by the British.

Anxious to preserve the peace, President Jefferson decided on economic sanctions as the only weapon short of war that could protect America's national interest. On his advice, Congress passed an embargo act in December 1807, prohibiting American ships to sail to any foreign port. The act also permitted coasting trade only under condition that the shipowner give bond double the value of the cargo for its delivery at a United States port. Instead of starving the European powers into submission, however, the embargo dealt a hard blow to the American economy itself. Exports (at least those legally registered) sank to one-fifth their previous level. Imports dropped back by half. "Not a box, bale, cask, barrel, or package was to be seen upon the wharves," a British traveler in New York declared.[5] Ships were laid up

everywhere, and the docks and streets of the port cities, normally teeming with men and vehicles, were ghostly quiet.

The losses sustained by shipping interests were colossal, especially in New England. Smuggling was rampant, and it became a major occupation on the border with Canada. In addition, innumerable ships allegedly bound for coastal ports encountered "storms" and other "calamities" that forced them off course, and it just happened that the West Indies islands were the only safe harbors available! Finally the protests of merchants and shippers grew so insistent that Congress was forced to yield. In March 1809 the Embargo Act was repealed and replaced by the Nonintercourse Act, which prohibited trade only with Great Britain, France, and their possessions. The diplomatic deadlock over America's neutral rights continued, and in 1810 Congress repealed the Nonintercourse Act and passed the so-called Macon Bill. This provided that as soon as either England or France withdrew its decrees against American shipping, the Nonintercourse Act would be reimposed against the other country. Napoleon — who had little to lose, since England dominated the seas — complied in August 1810. Now the American government gave England until February 1811 to withdraw its own trade restrictions promulgated by orders-in-council.

The War of 1812

As the ultimatum date went by, war fever rose in Congress. Pressure was all the greater, perhaps, because of depressed agricultural prices in the South and West as the result of the embargo and continued trade restrictions. President James Madison, who finally delivered a war message against Great Britain on June 1, 1812, declared that the principal causes of war were Indian attacks inspired by England, the obnoxious orders-in-council, and the impressment of seamen.[6]

Although the War of 1812 was fought primarily on the sea, a U. S. invasion of Canada was attempted; the British did invade the American coast and take Washington; and Jackson defended New Orleans in 1815, after the official end of the war, in the only American land victory of any consequence. Mobilization of manpower was limited, and the immediate eco-

---

[5]John Lambert, *Travels Through Canada and the United States, . . . 1806, 1807, and 1808* (London, 1810), vol. 2, p. 65.

[6]Many years later, Madison said privately that had Britain withdrawn its orders-in-council sooner, only the impressment question would have been left as a critical diplomatic issue and the war might have been avoided. See Roger H. Brown, *The Republic in Peril, 1812* (New York: Columbia University Press, 1964), p. 209 n.

nomic effects were felt mainly on the seaboard. The British successfully blockaded the Atlantic ports, and some 1400 American ships were captured. But U.S. privateers themselves took about 2000 ships as prizes, and many wartime fortunes were made in this manner on the high seas.

Foreign trade was hard hit by the war. The combined value of imports and exports declined from $133 million in 1811 to only $20 million in 1814, and American ships—which had carried 95 percent of the nation's foreign commerce before the war—lost half the total tonnage to foreign shippers. In the domestic economy, the major impact of the war was the impetus given to manufacturing. British competition for the American market was temporarily removed, and emergency wartime requirements and inflation induced a rise in household manufactures and factory production throughout the nation. Even Jefferson, witnessing the enthusiasm for manufacturing, was willing to admit by 1815 that there could be no turning back to an agrarian economic order.[7]

The postwar economy

The war was ended by a treaty signed at Ghent on December 27, 1814. Ironically, issues that Madison had cited as among the main causes of war (impressment, the right of search on the seas, and the blockade of neutral commerce) were not mentioned in the treaty. What immediate gains the war provided came to the West, where Indian power was effectually

broken and the way prepared for the annexation of Florida in 1819. In fact, the post-Napoleonic settlement written in Europe in 1815 had the more enduring effect on the United States. The powers that had crushed France vowed to keep the peace through a classic balance-of-power arrangement, and not until 1914–1917 would America again play the role of neutral carrier in wartime sea-lanes. The long years of peace also provided favorable commercial conditions for acceleration of the factory-production phase of the Industrial Revolution in Europe; and as British and Continental manufacturing flourished, the demand for American cotton rose apace, with sweeping effects on the U.S. economy.

Immediately following the war, the foreign-trade sector once again paced the economy and dictated the course of boom and crisis. British goods were dumped in the American market in unprecedented volume, and accounted for much of the import increase from $13 million in 1814 to $147 million the next year. American demand for such products had been built up by the war, and imports found a ready market at such low prices that many war-born manufacturing establishments in the United States went under. It took several years for England and the continental countries to restore their own agricultural sectors after the long wars, and so American exports of foodstuffs (and cotton as well, of course) led an economic boom.

TARIFF POLICY

Protection of the nascent manufacturing sector now came to be of deep concern in Congress. The spirit of nationalism was evoked, perpetuating wartime feelings against Europe, to justify new protective tariffs. Even John C. Calhoun, later the bellwether of southern opposition to protectionist policies, supported a bill introduced in 1816 by William Lowndes of South Carolina, establishing a duty of 25 percent on cotton and woolen textiles to protect an American industry that promised most rapid development and was then being exposed to drastic foreign competition. In addition, a minimum valuation was set on cotton goods, with

the practical effect of barring their importation altogether, in effect reserving the American market for low-grade cotton fabrics to the American factories. This first explicitly protective tariff bill was regarded in Congress as temporary, and so it provided for an automatic reduction of the textile tariff to 20 percent in 1819. Iron and other products were made subject to rates averaging about 20 percent—a modest rate, not sharply protectionist.

The next tariff was enacted in 1819, just as the country was plunging into a depression crisis. When the European countries had adjusted to peacetime needs and production, aided by bumper crops in 1818 and 1819, the foreign market for American staples suddenly contracted. The value of U.S. exports in the ensuing

[7]·Nettels, *Emergence of a National Economy,* pp. 338–340.

downswing fell sharply, from $93 million in 1818 to a low of $55 million in 1821. As cotton prices collapsed, the value of cotton export earnings declined by one-third in 1819 alone. Cotton prices never recovered to the 1819 level, though in subsequent years the *quantity* of cotton exported would rise dramatically.

Protectionism

From enactment of the 1816 tariff onward, protectionist sentiment grew steadily in the North but met with intense enmity in the South. Henry Clay became the leading spokesman in Congress for higher tariffs. He continued to champion the protection of infant industries, but he also took a more comprehensive view of the tariff as one component of a program that also embraced federal aid to transportation and the distribution of any surplus federal revenues to the states for development of social overhead facilities. This program, which Clay termed the "American system," emphasized that manufacturing would provide expanding home markets for the products of farm, mine, and forest. Clay won support from most of the West and from many congressmen from the middle Atlantic states when the tariff was debated in the early 1820s. New England was divided, however, as the old maritime and mercantile interests feared damage to trade, whereas newer interests in textile manufacturing joined Clay.

In the South, Clay confronted growing opposition. The more fully the South became committed to cotton and the plantation system, the more dangerous Clay's views appeared to the planters. By 1830, with the South unifying on the proposition that high tariffs would be intolerable, Daniel Webster had helped swing the New England votes in Congress over to a protectionist view as a counterweight to the Cotton Kingdom's influence.

After a tariff debate distinguished by passionate nationalism expressed on each side of the issue, Congress in 1824 granted additional protection to manufacturers of woolen goods, lead, glass, and iron. Hemp, principally raised in Clay's own Kentucky, was given 25 percent protection; and, to please the West and some rural areas of the East, high tariffs were levied on raw wool. Four years later, in 1828, further tariff increases were voted in an omnibus bill supported by many Jacksonian politicians who sensed the possibility of electing their presidential candidate that year. The 1828 bill increased the duties on raw wool, hemp, flax, sailcloth, and molasses; raised tariffs as well on all types

of iron; and set an unprecedented 45 percent levy on woolen goods. The 1828 tariff was therefore a mélange of disagreeable restrictions that transcended all former notions of the acceptable upper limits for protection. It was quickly termed the Tariff of Abominations and was denounced even in many areas normally favorable to high tariffs.

The nullification controversy

The 1828 tariff precipitated the most dangerous crisis of the Union since 1798: the nullification controversy between South Carolina and the central government. Throughout the South, the high tariff of 1828 raised fears that planters, already suffering from a fall in cotton prices greater than the decline in general living costs, would be saddled permanently with higher costs on consumer goods, both imported and domestic. The legislature of South Carolina voted to nullify the terms of the 1828 tariff within its borders. Underlying South Carolina's extremism was fear of northern power to undermine the slave system. Nat Turner's slave revolt in Virginia, which had resulted in the death of some 60 whites, occurred in 1831, following a period of sporadic slave rebellions in South Carolina. The simultaneous emergence of a militant abolitionist movement in the North resulted in a wave of hysteria in South Carolina, which now challenged the very authority of Congress to impose so unfavorable a tariff on any state, and implicitly challenged congressional authority to control race relations and slavery.

President Jackson reacted quickly, thundering against the doctrine of nullification. While denouncing the nullifiers' pretensions, however, Jackson shrewdly worked for revision of the tariff. The result was a new tariff law in 1832, which added several items to the free list (though it kept hemp and iron, both vital to the South, at high protective levels) and brought average rates back to 25 percent. "The people must now see," wrote Jackson, "that all their grievances are removed, and oppression only exists in the distempered brains of disappointed ambitious men."

In 1833 a compromise tariff was introduced by Henry Clay. As finally enacted, the 1833 tariff law reduced protective duties over a ten-year period until a maximum of 20 percent was reached on all items. Simultaneously Congress passed a "force bill," affirming the President's power to use the army and navy to put down any insurgent resistance to federal authority.

When the lower, 1833 tariff rates went into effect, however, the nullification crisis quickly receded.

The Walker tariff

When the Whig party took power after defeating Martin Van Buren in the 1840 presidential election, Congress was again decisively controlled by friends of a protectionist policy. With the Democrats taking an increasingly hard line in favor of low tariffs, favorable to the South, the Whigs pushed through a tariff bill in 1842 that restored duties almost to the 1832 levels. Another major turnabout came in 1846, however, after James K. Polk had led the Democrats back into a position of national control, having run in 1844 on a platform that promised a low tariff, for revenue purposes only. The 1846 tariff bill, called the Walker Tariff for its principal sponsor, a congressman from Mississippi, reflected on this side of the Atlantic Ocean the same spirit that motivated the anti–Corn Law reformers in England. It reflected as well, to be sure, the economic interests of the Democrats' influential southern wing. After a bitter debate, in which the Whigs warned repeatedly that the proposed rates would wipe out American manufacturing industries, a single-vote majority was won for the Walker Tariff in the Senate, and the House also approved the bill. The new tariff law introduced a major reform in the structure of duties by classifying all goods by categories—a 100 percent duty to be levied on luxuries, a lower rate on semiluxuries, and still lower duties on ordinary commercial commodities. Though some protective features were thus perpetuated, the general effect was a sharp reduction from 1842 levels, with an average duty of just over 20 percent.

The 1846 Walker Tariff set the standard for American trade policy until the Civil War. The low 1846 tariff probably served its main purpose by aiding in attaining a reduction of prices for many everyday items. But the protective duties were not inconsequential, and the 1846 tariff apparently had no adverse effect on cotton manufacturers and little on the producers of woolens. From the standpoint of America's agrarian interests, both Northern and Southern, the 1846 tariff was an important move because it threw the nation's weight on the side of free trade at a time when England and other major trading countries were undertaking basic reforms of commercial policy. Freer trade in international markets generally was essential if exporters of American cotton and foodstuffs were to obtain less restrictive terms of entry into foreign markets.

The 1857 tariff

In 1857 Congress enlarged the free list and instituted a further reduction in rates in response to the Treasury surplus that had accumulated during the continuous business expansion since 1854. From 1857 until the Republicans enacted their Civil War tariff, then, the United States was closer to a genuine free-trade policy than at any other time since the War of 1812.

TRADE AND GROWTH, 1820–1845

From 1820 to 1845, the foreign-trade sector was a less important contributor to national income than it had been earlier. But the impact of European industrialization was transmitted to the United States through the export trade in raw cotton. The American South became the chief supplier of cotton to industrial England; consequently, the role of cotton in total U.S. exports rose dramatically, from 10 percent of exports in 1807 to more than half by the mid-1830s. Cotton held this position until the Civil War.

The role of cotton in the U.S. economy

The mechanisms whereby cotton exporting affected the pattern of overall economic growth in the United States have been described as follows:[8]

First, the sheer volume of the cotton trade created an enormous demand for shipping, attracted capital into insurance and other trade-related activities, and had a direct impact on New York and its sister ports in the North by providing a flow of exports that supported the growth of import commerce and the merchant fleet.

Second, foreign demand for cotton was the main impetus for southern expansion into the

---

[8]The following model draws heavily from the work of Douglass C. North, especially his major study *The Economic Growth of the United States, 1790–1860* (Englewood Cliffs, N.J.: Prentice-Hall, 1961).

TABLE 8–3. BRITISH IMPORTS OF COTTON FROM THE UNITED STATES AND OTHER SOURCES, 1821–1855

FIVE-YEAR PERIOD	IMPORTS FROM U.S.A.	IMPORTS FROM ALL OTHER COUNTRIES
	(MILLIONS OF POUNDS)	
1821–1825	596	46
1826–1830	868	38
1831–1835	1230	36
1836–1840	1841	59
1841–1845	2491	69
1846–1850	2494	68
1851–1855	3425	166

Source: U.S. Commissioner of Patents, *Report: Agriculture, 1857* (Washington, D.C., 1858), p. 416.

Southwest, and rising cotton production in the expanding South not only contributed to national income directly, but also stimulated foodstuffs production in the upper South and the West.

Third, the earnings of the cotton trade (like those of exports generally) helped to finance imports and to sustain the flow of foreign capital that came into the United States to build canals and other transport facilities that proved vital to internal development.

Fourth, the cotton trade was so large that both short-term and secular (long-run) changes in cotton supply, demand, and prices were major determinants of cyclical fluctuations. Moreover, American cyclical fluctuations were closely tied to those of the British economy. The United Kingdom took two-thirds to three-quarters of American cotton exports, and overall the British provided the market for a third to a half of American exports each year from 1815 to 1860. The special Anglo-American relationship was also evident in American import accounts, as some 40 percent of all imports were from Britain during this period. Thus, while both political and emotional impulses to make the United States economically free of British influence were manifest in many ways, there was continuing, mutually profitable interdependence between the United States and England. This was reinforced further in 1830, when the British opened their West Indies market permanently to American shipping and trade.

Fifth, Anglo-American commercial ties were also strengthened by financial interdependence. British capital available for overseas investment outlets was attracted heavily to the United States, amounting to $125 million from 1821 to 1837. This long-term capital aided in financing social overhead facilities in America: canals before the mid-1840s, rail-roads afterward. Shorter-term credit from London bankers underwrote American purchases in England and also the export trade from the United States. Hence "this British backing," as one scholar writes, "not only financed North Atlantic commerce . . . but sustained a chain of credit, through New York jobbers and country wholesalers to remote storekeepers, farmers, and planters, which made possible a rapid expansion of the continental hinterland."[9] For these reasons, it can be said, Friedrich Engels was right when he asserted that "England and the United States are bound together by a single thread of cotton, which, weak and fragile as it may appear, is, nevertheless, stronger than an iron cable."[10]

This analytic model of Anglo-American trade and the relationship of cotton exports to national growth is not intended as a single-cause explanation of American development. For it must be acknowledged that abundant natural resources, governmental policies designed to maximize the flow of credit and mobilize capital for transport building, urbanization, the early development of food-processing manufactures, and America's own Industrial Revolution—manifest by the 1820s in the spectacular rise of the New England textile industry—also were major determinants of domestic economic change.

The Anglo-American trade relationship

The close linkages between the trade sector and domestic development were evident in the expansion of the U.S. economy from 1825 to 1837, when British textile factories were absorbing fast-rising American exports. Export

[9]Frank Thistlethwaite, *America and the Atlantic Community* (New York: Torchbooks, Harper & Row, 1963).

[10]Friedrich Engels, as reported in U.S. Commissioner of Patents, *Annual Report for 1857: Agriculture* (Washington, D.C., 1858), p. 412.

earnings supported both the heavy public transport investments of the states in that period and the expansion of American banking facilities. The post-1839 depression, on the other hand, was deepened and prolonged largely because the London money market cut back so decisively on the flow of credit, as English textile production fell and the declining price of cotton led a disastrous price deflation in the United States. Similarly, the strength of the recovery in the United States after 1846 was closely related to shifts in the British economy: famines and crop failures that stimulated unprecedented imports of grain from America, and recovery of the British cotton textile industry.

The close trade relationship with the United Kingdom did not comprise the whole of American commerce, to be sure; and so later in this chapter we shall consider the larger dimensions of America's world trade.

TRADE AND GROWTH, 1846–1860

By the mid-1840s the cotton trade was no longer quite so important an independent variable in the overall pattern of growth. Influences internal to the American economy had by then begun to achieve a new prominence, the most important factor being the growth of domestic commerce.

Internal commerce
Over 2000 miles of main-line canals had been constructed in the 1830s and early 1840s, and the Great Lakes were linked to both the Mississippi Valley and the eastern seaboard by artificial waterways; by 1830 the country had also built 3300 miles of railroad line; and both on the rivers of the interior and on the Great Lakes and Lake Champlain, steamers had greatly augmented the tonnage in domestic trade. A dramatic decline in transport rates occurred in the 1840s—a much greater drop than in the general price index—and by 1851 the value of domestic commerce was estimated at nearly $3 billion. This was seven times the value of total foreign commerce at that time.[11] In the 1850s, internal trade became even larger in relation to imports and exports.

The discovery of gold in California in 1848 gave the United States an ample domestic supply of specie to expand domestic bank credit and to support a consistently negative balance of trade in commodity shipments. (Throughout the pre–Civil War period, American commodity imports consistently exceeded exports, the balance being made up by shipping earnings, long-term capital loans, and "invisibles" such as immigrants' savings.) A great surge of new settlement and immigration in the 1850s contributed further to the autonomy of economic change, as did a boom in railroad construction that began in the mid-1840s and climaxed in 1854.

Foreign trade
The United States underwent a spurt of growth in the 1850s (output per capita rose from 1849 to 1859 by 20 percent), and the foreign-trade sector made a significant contribution to development. During the Crimean War, American farmers shipped their surpluses into European grain markets, and throughout the decade the domestic production that was increasing so phenomenally supported a rise in total imports from $220 million (1851) to $362 million (1862). Cotton exports continued to expand, reaching a value of almost $200 million on the eve of the Civil War. Because this traditional segment of foreign commerce remained so vigorous, the pattern established in the South in the 1820s—continual expansion of plantation agriculture and single-crop concentration—persisted to 1860. This persistence explained much of the southern political intransigence that threw the country into civil war in 1861.

COMMODITIES AND PAYMENTS

Cotton was not the only southern product among the leading exports of the United States. Rice, tobacco, and sugar all found markets in Europe throughout the antebellum period, and

[11]Domestic trade was estimated at $2.8 billion in value, the combined value of imports and exports at $400 million. The figure for domestic trade includes, of course, foreign goods in transit to markets and goods destined for export.

See George R. Taylor, *The Transportation Revolution, 1815–1860* (New York: Holt, Rinehart and Winston, 1951), pp. 173–175.

in fact approximately three-fourths of all exports were from the southern states.

Foodstuffs other than rice and sugar, particularly grain and packed meat from the northern states, found only a small market in Europe except during the unusual periods of crop failure and war. American advantages were more pronounced in the markets of the West Indies and South America, and these areas generally were the principal outlets for foodstuffs.

Of industrial exports, which comprised only 6 percent of the export trade in 1820 and 11 percent in 1860, the principal commodity was cotton goods. They were sold primarily in China, Mexico, and the West Indies. Other important exports were pot and pearl ashes, wood, iron and ironware, distilled liquors, and manufactured tobacco. Overall, Europe purchased three-fourths of American exports.

Trade with Canada

One notable feature of U.S. foreign trade in the 1850s was a dramatic increase in the tonnage of commerce with British Quebec, Upper Canada, and the Maritime Provinces. This redirection of trade was attributable, first of all, to the very rapid pace of both Canadian and American agricultural expansion in this period. But gains in output that swelled trade flows were closely related to policy changes. In 1845 Congress acted to remove customs duties on imports to the United States that were reexported to Canada; and in 1846, tariffs were also waived on imports from Canada that were reexported from the United States. Far from being expressions of American altruism, these new trade laws were designed to strengthen New York's bid to serve as the main entrepôt for the Canadian market.[12]

In 1854 Great Britain and the United States signed a reciprocity treaty under which Canadian tariff restrictions were lifted on U.S. tobacco, naval stores, and other products, and American tariffs were removed on Canadian coal, fish, grain and flour, lumber products, and meat. As a result, there was a further increase in trade volume in both directions across the Canadian-American border. The new laws permitted American grain to be exported via the Great Lakes–St. Lawrence River route when shipping rates there were favorable. Even larger quantities of grain from both the American midwest and Canada's own wheat-growing district in present-day Ontario passed through canals and Lake Champlain, to be shipped overseas from New York. Canadian merchants meanwhile were able to import English and European merchandise from wholesalers at New York, Boston, and other Atlantic ports in the United States. This freed them from the need to buy (generally in much larger minimum quantities) directly from Europe. New York benefited most from these new trade arrangements, garnering about three-fourths of the reexport trade with Canada by 1860.

MARITIME REVIVAL AND DECLINE

The years from the mid-1820s to the late 1830s were another period of remarkable prosperity for the U.S. merchant marine. American shipbuilders enjoyed advantages that permitted them to construct vessels at lower cost than comparable European shipping. Although busy yards clustered along the port waters at Baltimore, Philadelphia, and New York, the chief center of shipbuilding was the New England coast. Located close to rich forests of white pine and oak, the New Englanders could also draw upon a labor force of highly skilled artisans. In 1852 more than half the nation's tonnage in the coastal trade was comprised of New England–built "cotton ships," and American vessels made up 60 percent or more of tonnage engaged in foreign trade each year throughout the pre–Civil War period.

Taking advantage of their city's banking resources, their fine transport facilities (via the Erie Canal) to the growing western market, and the aggressive initiatives of their mercantile community, the capitalists of New York took a leading role in the transatlantic trade. From 1818 till the 1840s their packet lines ran on a regular schedule to England, their schedules coordinated with a coastwise service to southern ports. The climax of the wooden sailing ship's hegemony came in the late 1840s with the clipper-ship boom. Speed was the foremost consideration in their design, and these ships, fitted for heavy sail, were especially suited to the long-distance Australia, China, and California trades. Although the clippers were certainly emblematic of a romantic era of sail, they repre-

---

[12]Prior to tariff reform in Britain in 1846, much American wheat and flour went to Canada for export, to take advantage of the tariff preference given Canadian exports in the British market.

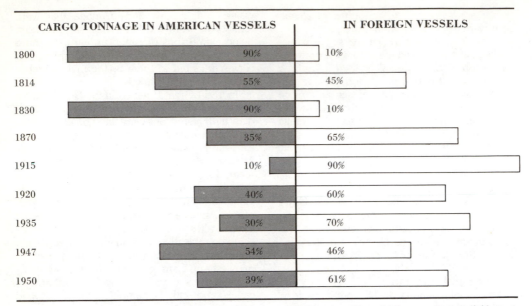

Figure 8–1. Cargo Percentage of Exports and Imports in American Vessels. Source: *Statistical Abstract,* 1952, p. 535.

sented a tardy investment in a nearly obsolete technology. For by the 1840s the British shipbuilders were experimenting intensively with the use of steam power for oceangoing vessels. Aided by government subsidies, the British pressed their advantages hard, and the proportion of American trade carried in U.S. vessels began to decline (see Figure 8–1). By 1853 one-fifth of U.S. shipping tonnage constructed was for steam, but still the American builders lagged behind their transatlantic cousins in substituting iron for wood in hull design. When the Panic of 1857 bankrupted the only major American steamship line, the Collins line, its ships were sold to British companies, dramat-

ically underscoring American failure in this competition.

When the Civil War ended in 1865, the American merchant marine had been reduced in tonnage from its prewar level, and only about 25 percent of American imports and exports were being carried in the nation's own maritime fleet. No longer were ocean vessels typically owned by merchants who used them for their own cargoes, as had been the case in the clipper era. Now large firms ran fleets of ships, specialized in contract haulage, and used steam-driven vessels built with much iron and, typically, manned by foreign labor.

THE LEADING PORT CITIES

Indicative of the close relationship between trade and early urbanization was the fact that in 1830 the four leading Atlantic seaport cities (Boston, New York, Philadelphia, Baltimore) had nearly half the total urban population of the nation—800,000 urban residents out of 1.8 million. Of the port cities, New York was dominant, becoming a distribution center for both imported goods and domestic products through heavy mercantile investments in warehouse and other facilities. Specialized wholesaling

became the hallmark of New York's mercantile life, and the Erie Canal route to the West gave the city, with its magnificent harbor, a jump on its rivals. The agglomeration of marketing facilities, with capital and banking, regular shipping schedules, and the rest, helped perpetuate New York's dominance. Much of the cotton-export trade of the South was thus funneled through New York.

As an export center, New Orleans was a leading challenger despite the disadvantage of a harbor that could not accommodate the largest oceangoing ships. Until the new canal routes of the western states offered alternative outlets for regional exports, the foodstuffs of the Ohio Valley as well as the lower Mississippi trade in cotton poured down the river to New Orleans.

On a smaller scale than New Orleans, all of the ports on ocean waters from Texas around the coast to New England performed as commercial "hinges," linking America's agricultural regions of the interior with Europe. By 1860, moreover, San Francisco was on the list of America's fifteen largest cities, serving similar functions for the mining and farming regions newly opened in California.

WHALING AND FISHING

The history of the American whaling industry provides a poignant but telling example of the way exploitative attitudes toward valuable resources can encourage rapid exhaustion of those resources and bring ruin to an industry that has thrived on relentless enterprise. In the New England region, whaling ranked third in value of product among the area's industries (after textiles and boot and shoe production). Shipping used in whaling rose from 35,000 tons in 1820 to nearly 200,000 tons in 1858. The profits to be made from this dangerous trade stemmed largely from the use of whale oil for illumination by lamps; whalebone was also valuable.

In the late eighteenth century, whaling from the Northeast had been confined to the Atlantic, but during the 1830s American vessels began to venture into Pacific waters. After 1850 the whaling fleets were, as Herman Melville wrote, "penetrating even through Bering's Strait, and into the remotest secret drawers and lockers of the world," as the hunters found it increasingly difficult to run down the declining herds. Depletion of whale stock was thus increasing risks and reducing profits at the very time that substitutes for the oil (in the form of mineral oils and gas) became available in the domestic market. By 1860 the refining of petroleum had rung the death knell for whaling as it was then organized, and thereafter the industry's decline was steady.

New England also dominated the nation's fishing industry. The tonnage of shipping used in commercial fishing rose steadily, especially as the market for fresh fish expanded with introduction of the use of ice to preserve the cargoes in the 1840s. By the 1850s, commercial fishing, especially for salmon, was also developing on the west coast. Despite growth in the volume of catches, however, the fisheries industry did not keep pace with growth in the economy generally. At no time from 1790 to 1860 did fishing attain again the relative economic importance it had held during the colonial period.

SELECTED READINGS

Albion, Robert G., *The Rise of New York Port, 1815–1860* (New York: Scribner's, 1939).

Bjork, Gordon, "The Weaning of the American Economy: Independence, Market Changes, and Economic Development," *Journal of Economic History*, XXIV (1964).

Bruchey, Stuart, "Success and Failure Factors: American Merchants in Foreign Trade," *Business History Review*, XXXII (1958).

Gilchrist, David, ed., *The Growth of the Seaport Cities, 1790–1825* (Charlottesville: University Press of Virginia, 1967).

Hutchins, John G. B., *American Maritime Industries and Public Policy, 1789–1914* (Cambridge: Harvard University Press, 1941).

Johnson, Emory R. et al., *History of Domestic and Foreign Commerce of the United States* (Washington: Carnegie Institution, 1915).

*Nettels, Curtis P., *The Emergence of a National Economy, 1775–1815* (New York: Holt, Rinehart and Winston, 1962).

*North, Douglass C., *Economic Growth of the United States, 1790–1860* (Englewood Cliffs, N.J.: Prentice-Hall, 1961).

Potter, J., "Atlantic Economy, 1815–1860: The U.S. and the Industrial Revolution in Britain," in *Studies in the Industrial Revolution,* L. S. Pressnell, ed., (London: Athlone Press, 1960).

*Taussig, F. W., *The Tariff History of the United States* (1931, reprinted New York: Capricorn Books, 1964).

*Taylor, George Rogers, *The Transportation Revolution, 1815–1860* (New York: Holt, Rinehart and Winston, 1951).

Woodruff, William, *The Impact of Western Man: A Study of Europe's Role in the World Economy, 1750–1960* (New York: St. Martin's Press, 1967).

Specialized Studies

Baughman, James P., *The Mallorys of Mystic: Six Generations in American Maritime Enterprise* (Middletown, Conn.: Wesleyan University Press, 1972).

Chappelle, Howard I., *The Search for Speed Under Sail, 1700–1855* (New York: Norton, 1967).

Coatsworth, John H., "American Trade with European Colonies in the Caribbean and South America, 1790–1812," *William and Mary Quarterly,* 3rd ser., XXIV (1967).

*Freehling, William W., *Prelude to Civil War: The Nullification Controversy in South Carolina, 1816–1836* (New York: Harper & Row, 1968).

Lamb, Robert K., "The Entrepreneur and the Community," in *Men in Business,* ed. William Miller (Cambridge: Harvard University Press, 1952).

*Morison, Samuel Eliot, *The Maritime History of Massachusetts* (1941, reprinted Boston: Houghton Mifflin, 1961).

Rothstein, Morton, "The Cotton Frontier of the Antebellum United States," *Agricultural History,* XL (1971).

Scheiber, Harry N., "America and the World Economy: A Retrospect," in *America: Purpose and Power,* ed. Gene M. Lyons (New York: Quandrangle, 1965).

Sterns, W. P., "The Foreign Trade of the United States From 1820 to 1840," *Journal of Political Economy,* VIII (1900), two parts.

chapter 9
the agricultural
era

During the period from the Revolution to the Civil War, the availability of frontier land permitted a vast increase in the area of land under cultivation at the same time as early industrialization took hold. In the Old World it was common for a nation's agricultural sector to diminish rapidly in relative importance during the industrialization process. Typically a fairly stable area of farmland was put into more intensive, efficient production, and the number of workers required on the land would be reduced. But in the early United States pattern of development, there was a steady increase in the area of land put into cultivation, in the number of farm workers, and also in the output of the agricultural sector. The product of America's farms increased at least sevenfold from 1800 to 1860. The settlement of the West and Southwest brought an increase in the farm labor force from about 1.4 million in 1800 to nearly 5 million in 1850, then to nearly 6 million by 1860. At the latter date, more than half the nation's workers were still engaged in farming, as compared with 14 percent in manufacturing, and some 80 percent of the American population were still living in rural areas. At the same time, however, farm-labor's share of the total labor force declined.

Both the sheer magnitude of the farm sector and its continuing growth through early industrialization indicate that agriculture must have played a central role in the overall process of economic growth. In the first place, the vast farm population was the principal market for American manufactured goods. The building of improved transport facilities in the post-1815 period provided early manufacturing industries with access to this extensive, growing market; and the reduced costs of transport, together with the improvement of marketing facilities, encouraged efficiencies through *large-scale* manufacturing that depended on a wide market. In the second place, the farm sector made a direct contribution to total output increases, supplying the urban population with its foodstuffs and also producing fibers, animal products, and tobacco for the manufacturing industries. Besides, agriculture contributed more than half—in some periods up to 70 percent—of the nation's foreign-export earnings. Third, agriculture achieved improved efficiency in production as the result of the movement onto more fertile lands in the West and the adoption of labor-saving machinery, the development of new plant varieties, and the systematic breeding of livestock. Productivity increases in agriculture went forward less rapidly than in the other sectors of the economy; they were sufficiently important, however, to have comprised a major contribution to per capita growth of output in the economy as a whole. According to one recent estimate, gross farm product per worker (expressed in 1910–1914 prices) was $292 in 1800 and about the same until 1830. It rose to $311 in 1840 and had reached $332 by 1860.[1]

[1]Marvin Towne and Wayne Rasmussen, "Farm Gross Product," in *Trends in the American Economy in the Nineteenth Century* (Princeton: National Bureau of Economic Research, Princeton University Press, 1964), p. 269.

THE FRONTIER'S EXPANSION AND AGRICULTURE

Territorial acquisitions, the subjugation of the Indian nations, and the consequent spread of European-American control over the continent's full westward reach resulted in major additions to the national economy's stock of natural resources. But resource additions alone did not mean inevitable increases in total output or economic growth: labor, capital, entrepreneurial talent, and adaptations in technology had to be brought to bear for successful resource exploitation. Because the availability of western lands and the process of new settlement was such a major factor in the overall agricultural development of the United States, we need to look closely at some of the leading features of the interaction between expansion and growth.

Opportunity costs

In the first place, it is well to recognize that the frontier farm-making process involved certain opportunity costs to the economy: Opening up new lands required inputs of labor and capital that might otherwise have gone into alternative economic activities that, at least in the short run, would have produced greater returns. Indeed, some scholars have argued that a more compact and orderly pattern of national economic growth — with settlement more concentrated, with resources dedicated to sustenance of older lands through use of fertilizers and better cropping practices, and with the capital used for new farm making devoted instead to manufacturing investment and the like — would have produced considerably higher returns. Whether these returns would have been equal to or greater than the production gains achieved through expansion into new territory is a difficult question. An estimated 12 percent of total farm labor was dedicated to the work of land clearing alone in the 1850s; the cash equivalent value of the heavy labor in removing timber and preparing new soil in wooded areas was between $8 and $15 per acre.[2] On the other hand, such expenditures, including the sums expended on buildings and improvements, constituted an important form of capital formation: new units of production (western farms) were being created, an important element in the society's overall capital-formation activity.

Regional specialization

A second feature of western resource exploitation was the contribution of newly settled lands to the emergence of internal commerce based upon regional specialization. The Northeast, the South, and the new western regions of both the Northwest and Southwest, all exploited their comparative advantages by undertaking production of commodities for which their respective climates, soils, and other resource endowments suited them. So long as goods could be exchanged at low transfer costs, overall efficiency in the national economy and per capita income were increased. Thus the South specialized in cotton and other semitropical staples (tobacco, sugar, hemp) while the northwestern region went heavily into production of grain products and grain-fed livestock. In the East, agriculture shifted to specialty production, such as dairying and orchard crops, while at the same time manufacturing took hold in the region, led by textiles and then iron, until by the late 1840s a generalized pattern of manufacturing specialization had become established.

Exploitative farming techniques

Another much-noticed effect of relatively abundant new land was the perpetuation it fostered of exploitative, essentially wasteful methods of cultivation and land use. In the Atlantic seaboard region, farmers who confronted competition from western producers operating on more fertile land readily pulled up stakes and themselves moved west. Although such a relocation of farm labor was rational, given market realities, it meant abandonment of lands that could have been conserved and replenished by more scientific crop rotation, fertilizers, and similar intensive-cultivation and conservationist measures. Commenting on Missouri farming in 1848, for example, one observer wrote: "Farming is here conducted on the regular skinning system. . . . Most of the farmers in this country *scratch* over a great deal of ground but *cultivate* none."[3] Similar complaints were heard in every region.

Although some eastern farmers, hit by western competition, did readjust by shifting to new, more intensive forms of agriculture, farm abandonment had devastating effects on many lo-

[2]Martin Primack, "Land Clearing Under 19th Century Techniques," *Journal of Economic History*, (1962) 22: 492–493.

[3]*Cultivator* (1849), quoted in Percy W. Bidwell and J. I. Falconer, *History of Agriculture in the Northern United States* (1925, reprinted Gloucester, Mass.: Peter Smith, 1958), p. 272.

calities. Nor was the West immune to such pressures. By the 1850s farmers in Ohio and Indiana were relinquishing and abandoning their land in many localities as they met competition in wheat growing from Illinois, Wisconsin, and Iowa. The other side of the same coin, however, was that the newer areas farther west were in fact capable of more efficient farming than the regions facing out-migration, and settlement of the more fertile areas contributed in a major way to rising agricultural productivity in the national economy.

"Boom-stage" expansion and the national economy

Development of the West was not smoothly continuous over time. Rather it was characterized by a series of booms— surges of new in-migration, speculation, and social overhead capital investment in railroads and other facilities. The great boom periods were 1800–1807, 1815–1819, 1835–1837, and 1844–1857. Each boom was both the result of changes in national and international market conditions, on the one hand, and a partial determinant of cyclical responses to such changes on the other. For example, in the period down to the 1850s, wars, famines, and surges of industrialization in England and on the European continent all sparked western expansion booms.

When slowdowns or crises occurred in the Atlantic economy, as happened from 1839 to 1843 and in the late 1850s, they had an immediate dampening effect on the western economy. Because agriculture was so early and so thoroughly commercialized in both the southwestern cotton area and the northwestern foodstuffs region, economic conditions in the West were always highly sensitive to international market changes. As western producers (agricultural, extractive, and later industrial) became a larger and larger factor in the national economy, peculiarly *regional* economic changes— for example, new resource additions such as California gold and the opening of the prairies in the 1850s— had commensurately greater effects on the national business cycle and on the world economy.

Thus from 1844 to 1854 it was *western* railroad building that required heavy borrowing of capital from Europe and created a large domestic demand for iron products and other manufactured goods; it was *western* lands, together with urban-based jobs for migrants, that led the national economy. When the economy slowed down and finally went into an extended depression in 1857, the enormous burden of surplus

western farm products lacking sufficient markets to sustain price levels, and also western mortgage borrowing, stood out as leading obstacles to recovery and renewed growth.

The western impact on manufacturing

The effects of the westward movement on the rising manufacturing industries and on labor are more difficult to determine. Eastern manufacturers were generally persuaded that the exodus of potential factory labor to the West served to keep American wages high and thus to discourage industrial development by depressing profits. Scholarly research has supported this point of view to the extent that most analysts grant that *potential* industrial wage earners did leave the East, with an inevitably supportive effect on wage scales. But there was another side to the western impact on manufacturing.

First of all, western growth broadened manufacturers' markets. In the Northwest, income distribution supported a relatively wide market for consumer goods and for farm equipment and other durables; and concentration on agricultural pursuits made the Southwest dependent on the East and Northwest for manufactured goods. Moreover, the western state and local governments heavily subsidized the construction of transport facilities that by the mid-1840s were giving eastern factories inexpensive access to an extended national market.

Second, the opportunities that continually unfolded in the western regions were magnets for immigration. This was especially so in the 1840s and 1850s, when war, famine, and revolutions in Europe and Ireland stimulated emigration at the very time that such calamities were increasing European demand for American cotton and foodstuffs, thus making the West more attractive to immigrants. The many immigrants who settled in seaboard cities rather than going directly West were a source of industrial labor, and indeed were willing to accept lower wages than native workers demanded and to take on bottom-of-the ladder occupational employments.

Third, the very fact that wages tended to be higher in the United States than in Europe—a difference attributable in part to western opportunity—created an incentive for American manufacturers to adopt labor-saving technology and over the long run contributed to their efficiency. Their capacity to invest capital in labor-saving technology was in turn enhanced by the widening market for their goods, to which western settlement made an important contribution.

Urbanization

The last feature of western development that should be noted was the growth of towns and cities (and of urban-based service and industrial occupations) concurrently with agricultural, mining, and forest-industry advance. The cotton regions of the Southwest did not develop urban centers or manufacturing, except for the port cities that warehoused and shipped cotton exports and handled the region's imports. In the Northwest, however, town-based processing industries such as flour mills, distilleries, meat-packing plants, and lumber mills appeared simultaneously with agricultural settlement. The prevailing techniques for these processing industries were capital-intensive techniques by contemporary standards. This meant important productivity gains, and significant regional income was generated by such forms of manufacturing.[4]

The process of industrial growth was greatly expedited, moreover, by the early start that manufacturing thereby enjoyed in the Northwest. New industries were spawned: for example, the meat-packing industries produced by-products such as soap, candles, tallow, and bristles. But more important, the entrepreneurial experience gained and the capital accumulated in these industries moved fairly readily into heavier manufacturing such as iron and ironware manufacturing, furniture making, and consumer goods industries (clothing, boots and shoes, and so on). The very pace of urban growth in the Northwest similarly gave impetus to development of such construction-related industries as the manufacture of paints, turpentine, varnishes, plumbing equipment, and stoves.

In California and other mining districts of the Far West, the urban character of early settlement was even more dominant. Mining towns were themselves urban-type communities, of course. These towns quickly established trade links with such port cities as San Francisco, where the profits of mercantile establishments moved readily into banking, the financing of capital-intensive mining ventures, and the like. The foodstuffs needs of urban settlers and miners served as a stimulus to agricultural production, and California's ranches and extensive wheat farms alike sold their products primarily in these local markets at first; only later in the 1850s did California agriculture look to the East and to Europe for the marketing of surplus crops.

Entrepreneurship and the West

Related to all these factors was the cultural impact of successive community-building experiences on the frontier. Recently, some historians have argued that the spatial, occupational, and (to some extent) social mobility that westward expansion fostered contributed to entrepreneurial drive and innovation: "A business started in almost any community would grow if it merely held its competitive position. The usual western promoter would have agreed with [one resident] of Hudson, Ohio, that it was safe continually to add new business ventures, since as the town grew each would 'support the other.' "[5] Western attitudes reflected accurately the characteristic national desire for business growth, and to an extent caricatured it because they sanctioned exploitative policies that mined their resources ruthlessly in the race for economic growth. The public programs of transport–construction and the policies for resource use that westerners undertook further reinforced the pattern of innovation and cyclical expansion.

THE RISE OF COTTON

The most important single development in the history of agriculture during the antebellum period was the rise of cotton as a staple commercial crop, to become the main basis of the southern regional economy and the major American export commodity. Little progress had been made in cotton culture during the colonial era, mainly because wool continued to

---

[4]See Albert Fishlow, *American Railroads and the Transformation of the Antebellum Economy* (Cambridge: Harvard University Press, 1965).

[5]Richard Wohl, "Henry Noble Day," in *Men in Business* ed. William Miller (New York: Harper & Row, 1962), p. 187. 187. Cf. Leslie Decker, "The Great Speculation," in *The Frontier in American Development,* ed. David M. Ellis (Ithaca: Cornell University Press, 1969), pp. 357–381.

be the principal fiber used in textile production and because growers had to contend with serious practical difficulties in separating cotton seeds from the fiber, a costly process even with slave labor. After the Revolution many planters hoped that cotton might help bring them out of an agricultural depression. The tobacco lands of the coastal region were wearing out, and the markets for indigo and rice had been injured by the separation from Great Britain. Hence the South desperately needed a new staple.

The British market

In the years 1790–1830 cotton became not only a major export of the South but also the region's most valuable cash crop and the largest component of total American exports. Lying behind this development was the rise of the British textile industry, which opened a rapidly expanding market for raw cotton. After 1760 water and then steam were applied as motive power to eliminate hand spinning in British textile production; then in the early 1800s technological progress was pushed forward another step with the spread of power weaving. The resultant improvement in efficiency and the rapid transfer of labor from households to factories spurred England's Industrial Revolution. Cotton manufacturing, which in 1775 had been deemed "amongst the humblest of the domestic [household] arts," had by 1797 taken the lead over all other manufactures in Britain. In 1809 the cotton textile industry gave employment to 800,000 persons in Britain. Obtaining its cotton mainly from the West Indies, England imported 9 million pounds in 1783 and fully 28 million in 1790.[6]

Sea island and green-seed varieties

Coinciding with industrialization in England was the fortuitous introduction of Sea Island cotton to the United States. Brought in from the Bahamas, this long-staple strain of cotton thrived in the seacoast lands of the South and in the outlying islands. Georgia farmers found that the Sea Island plant's fibers were easily separated from seeds by running the uncleaned cotton between two wooden rollers.

Although the Sea Island strain became a boon to the coastal region's planters, it did not lend itself to extensive cultivation in most interior areas, where soil and climate were unfavorable for its production. In the upland South, farmers could raise only the "green-seed" strain

of cotton, a shorter-stapled plant that could be cleaned only by hand. Therefore green-seed cotton was grown in only small quantities, and was used mainly for homemade clothes.

The cotton gin

Hence the impetus for widespread cotton cultivation was undoubtedly present by 1790. The needed innovational breakthrough was provided by Eli Whitney, a young Yale graduate who produced a machine that overnight made the green-seed upland cotton a commercial crop. His contraption was a cotton gin that consisted of a cylinder equipped with teeth projecting through strips of metal that drew in the cotton fiber, leaving the seeds behind, and a second roller, equipped with brushes to free the lint from the teeth, which revolved in the opposite direction. Operated by hand, the gin would clean fifty pounds a day, and with waterpower a thousand pounds. Within three years, Whitney and his business partner were operating thirty of the machines by horsepower or waterpower at eight locations in Georgia. It was, however, a testimony to the beautiful simplicity of his design — "declared by a number of the first men in America," Whitney wrote, "the most perfect & valuable invention that has ever appeared in this country" — that it was easily copied. Rival manufacturers violated the Whitney patent with impunity, and bootleg machines were soon in use throughout the cotton region.[7]

Petit Gulf cotton

The progress of cotton culture was given a further boost by the introduction of a new strain from Mexico about 1805. Called Petit Gulf cotton, the plant was comparatively immune to disease, had a longer staple than green-seed cotton, and was suitable for cultivation in the uplands. The plant could be picked by hand twice as fast as the older strains, making possible a major upward shift in labor productivity at the harvest. Ease of picking was crucial for another reason, too: Cotton rots quickly if it is not taken from the plants when ripe, so that time savings in the harvest meant reduced loss from spoilage. By 1820 the Mexican strain had been widely adopted throughout the upland region and the Gulf coast.

The expansion of cotton growing

Southern planters recognized opportunity when they saw it. In Georgia, the original site of

[6]Adam Seybert, *Statistical Annals . . . of the United States* (Philadelphia, 1818), p. 92.

[7]Jeanette Mirsky and Allan Nevins, *The World of Eli Whitney* (New York, Collier, 1966), p. 79.

**TABLE 9–1.   OUTPUT OF LEADING U.S.
AGRICULTURAL PRODUCTS,
1839–1859**

CROP	1839	1849	1859
Cotton (thousand bales)	1976	2469	5387
Corn (harvested for grain) (million bushels)	378	592	839
Wheat (million bushels)	85	100	173
Tobacco (million pounds)	219	200	434
Rice (million pounds)	81	215	187
Sugar (thousand hogsheads)	–	237	231

Source: Agricultural censuses of 1839, 1849, 1859.

**TABLE 9–2.   NUMBER OF LIVESTOCK IN
THE UNITED STATES,
1839–1859**

TYPE	1839	1849	1859
Cattle (million)	15.0	18.0	26.0
Sheep (million)	19.0	22.0	22.0
Horses and mules (million)	4.3	4.9	7.4
Hogs (million)	26.0	30.0	33.0

Source: Agricultural censuses of 1839, 1849, 1859.

Sea Island production, cotton output soared from 500,000 pounds in 1790 to 20,000 tons in 1801 and 40,000 tons in 1811. Cotton-growing spread quickly from Georgia and South Carolina into North Carolina, Virginia, and Tennessee. As planters recognized that the Gulf coast's rich alluvial soil was even better suited than the uplands to cotton cultivation, they moved by the thousands into the Southwest, pushing before them the Indians, cattle ranchers, and American pioneer settlers. The depletion of older soils quickened the movement to new land. Output of cotton soared, rising from 533,000 bales in 1825 to 2 million in 1839, then to over 3 million bales annually in

the late 1850s, and meanwhile the center of production shifted.

The periods of most rapid expansion in the Southwest were 1815–1819, the late 1830s, and the period immediately following the war with Mexico. Each new settlement boom was followed by expanded cotton output. By 1850 Alabama was the leading state in cotton crop. In 1860 three southwestern states—Alabama, Mississippi, and Louisiana—raised half the total product.

The absorbing interest in cotton, which dominated southern agriculture, shaped a regional identity that helped set the South apart within the nation. The profitability—and, in a sense, the tyranny—of cotton established a distinct way of life. What some had feared would happen—"the making of cotton to purchase everything else"—became for a large segment of southern society a daily reality.[8]

THE PLANTATION SYSTEM

"Planter capitalism" and "the plantation system" are phrases used synonymously—and appropriately so, since the leading feature of plantation organization is the application of capitalistic methods to agricultural production in large, unified, highly rationalized farm units. On a plantation, tasks are reduced to routine as far as possible, whether labor or machinery is relied upon, and whether slave or free labor is employed. There is a strict calculation of production economies, to maximize the output and profits of a cash crop. In the twentieth century we have seen plantation organization applied in various ways, ranging from large-scale rubber-planting operations in Southeast Asia to corporation-owned farms using migrant labor in American garden crops to highly mechanized, integrated "agribusinesses" producing livestock and dairy products in the Midwest. But in the

pre–Civil War United States, plantation agriculture became dominant only in sugar, rice, and cotton culture, all based in the South and reliant upon slave labor.

The pre–Civil War southern plantation system had special attributes of time and place: (1) Planters in the South accepted, and in a calculating manner perpetuated, soil-depleting practices, largely in response to the presence of unoccupied or newly settled (potentially competing) lands to the west. (2) There was a considerable degree of absentee ownership in the antebellum South. Hence actual management of the larger plantations was left to the overseer, a professional whose performance

[8]Grievance petition of 1841, quoted in Ralph B. Flanders, *Plantation Slavery in Georgia* (Chapel Hill: University of North Carolina Press, 1933), p. 68.

**TABLE 9–3.   NUMBER AND AVERAGE SIZE OF FARMS IN THE SOUTHWESTERN STATES,
1850–1860**

STATE	NUMBER (THOUSANDS)		AVERAGE SIZE (ACRES)	
	1850	1860	1850	1860
Alabama	42	55	289	346
Arkansas	18	39	146	245
Louisiana	13	17	372	536
Mississippi	34	43	309	370
Texas	12	43	942	591
United States	—	—	203	194

Source: *Eighth Census of the United States, 1860: Agriculture* (Washington, D.C., 1864), p. 222.

was assessed by the farm's production. He thus had an incentive to maximize output even if it meant a grinding exploitation of the labor force. (3) Most centrally important, black slave labor was employed on the plantations, permitting coercive mobilization of women, children, and the aged among the slaves.

For each of the three major southern staples, the growing season was long and the tasks of cultivation fairly simple, with primitive tools used. Cotton cultivation was highly labor-intensive; this meant that slave workers could be closely supervised, being organized for field work in gangs under the overseer and his subordinates, the latter often being slaves who were regarded as "reliable."

Whatever its staple crop, degree of mechanization it achieved, or its type of labor force, the plantation enjoyed important advantages over the family farm, especially in production of the South's staple crops. Large planters had the cash to buy out smaller farmers in order to extend their operations or obtain the better lands in a particular locality. The plantation also produced on a scale large enough to justify the purchase of baling machinery, cottonseed presses, and other heavy equipment used in cotton cultivation, or comparable equipment for processing sugar. The unit cost of clothing, foodstuffs, and other supplies was lower when these things were purchased in quantity for a large slave labor force. Moreover, in dealings with cotton factors and other middlemen, the large planter had more leverage than the small farmer—not only to obtain favorable interest rates on loans, but also to get a crop into available cargo space when shipping was in short supply at the ports.

Consolidation of holdings

As shown in Table 9–3, the average size of farm units in the cotton states shifted over time, with a distinct tendency toward the consolida-

tion of landholdings in Alabama, Mississippi, and Arkansas. During the 1850s the proportion of small farms in Mississippi's Delta lands declined sharply, as large plantations displaced them. Of all farm units in the region, plantations with 500 acres or more of improved land were 11 percent of the total in 1850 but 22 percent in 1860. This rapid change in the Southwest reflected a similar pattern of experience in older cotton-producing localities farther east.[9]

In 1850 the Mississippi counties along the rivers and in the Delta, comprising the most productive cotton lands, contained half the state's slaves but only one-fifth of the white population. In many Mississippi and Alabama cotton-growing counties in the 1850s, as in Georgia during a slightly earlier period, there was an absolute decline in the number of white farmers, coinciding with the trend toward larger plantations holding more slaves.[10]

Slave prices

One plausible explanation of this dramatic shift toward larger-scale cotton plantations in the 1850s lies in the effects of the trend of slave prices. Though the number of Afro-Americans held in slavery rose from 698,000 in 1790 to almost 4 million in 1860, the increase was not

[9]Herbert Weaver, *Mississippi Farmers, 1850–1860* (Nashville: Vanderbilt University Press, 1945), p. 36. In three Georgia counties that concentrated heavily on cotton production, there were trends toward larger plantations and more slaves per farm unit. Their average number of slaves per farm was 5 to 6 in 1800, but 10 to 12 in 1835, and by 1860 had risen again to as high as 17. In each of the three counties, moreover, there was an *absolute decline* in the number of white farm families (Ulrich B. Phillips, *The Slave Economy of the Old South*, ed. E. D. Genovese [Baton Rouge: Louisiana State University Press, 1968], pp. 109–113).

[10] In one Mississippi county the average number of slaves held was 82, in another 64. Statewide, the ratio of white to black population was about 1:1, but in two Delta counties there were 10 or more slaves to every white resident. Data are from Fabien Linden, "Economic Democracy in the Slave South," *Journal of Negro History,* 21 (1946): 140–189.

rapid enough to meet the demand; in addition, the birth rate of the black population apparently fell off from 1850 to 1860. Although the border and Atlantic coast states regularly sold their slaves to traders for resale in the Southwest, supply ran behind demand. A long-term upward trend in the price of slaves reflected this slackening in slave supply for the seemingly insatiable needs of American cotton culture. This change meant that the capital require-

ments for purchase of slaves rose, and plantations that realized savings in operating costs because of large-scale operations were better able to justify the investment now required to obtain slaves for larger output. Finally, the stagnation of cotton prices during the 1850s, when output soared, put pressure on cotton producers at the market end of the production process, pressure that large planters probably could withstand best. (See Chapter 12.)

OTHER ASPECTS OF SOUTHERN AGRICULTURE

Tobacco

In the colonial period, tobacco had been the leading southern crop. The 1790s saw tobacco at the height of its relative importance, as it headed the list of all American exports and was the source of income for roughly half the population of Virginia, North Carolina, and Maryland. After 1800, tobacco's importance declined because of the disastrous effects of the Embargo Acts and the War of 1812, the competition of Cuba, Colombia, and Sumatra, and the high tariff barriers in foreign countries. Land exhaustion in the older tobacco regions was meanwhile causing a decline in yields. Not until 1840 were American tobacco exports equal to the amount shipped in 1800. But by then the home market had begun to widen markedly, and southern planters had improved their processing to turn out a better product. Flue curing was substituted for the old-fashioned charcoal fire and a new yellow-leaf species was introduced.

Like cotton, tobacco culture also marched westward, and by the 1820s Kentucky and Tennessee were expanding their production rapidly; later, tobacco became a crop of some importance in Ohio and Missouri as well. Virginia, North Carolina and Maryland—the older, established tobacco states—suffered soil depletion and by 1840 were producing only half the nation's total output; by 1860 their production amounted to less than 40 percent.

Each of the tobacco-raising states meanwhile developed manufacturing industries dedicated to the production of snuff, plug, and twist products for the consumer market.

Between 1849 and 1859, tobacco culture underwent a burst of expansion: output doubled, with about half the crop raised at this time being exported to England and Germany. (See Table 9–1.)

Sugar

Sugar-cane production in the South was centered in Louisiana. The refining machinery required heavy capitalization, and many slave plantations that produced sugar were unusually large in acreage and size of labor force. Sugar-growing expanded continuously until 1854, with a fourfold increase in production in the ten years from 1843 to 1853. This great surge of output put pressure on sugar prices in the domestic market, and throughout the 1850s smaller plantations in Louisiana either quit sugar production or were consolidated into larger holdings. Although some of the planters experimented with diversified crops, the sugar country exhibited the same stresses as the other staple-producing regions: soil depletion, a decline in yields, and a ruthless exploitation of the 180,000 black slaves who worked the Louisiana plantations.

Rice

Rice, which had been a leading colonial crop along the seacoast in South Carolina and Georgia, continued to be grown successfully, with production more than tripling from 1820 to 1850. During that 30-year period rice prices did not suffer the same unfavorable decline relative to the general price index as cotton. The rice crop was cultivated with the most primitive of implements, but the rice plantation was also the site of some of the most complex and expensive processing equipment used in American agriculture. Concentrated in Georgia and South Carolina, the rice-growing industry was characterized by large slave plantations. Unlike other staple crops of American agriculture, rice suffered a large absolute decline in output from 1849 to 1859. (See Table 9–1.) By the late 1850s, many Carolina rice growers were obtaining much, perhaps most, of their income by

TABLE 9–4. PER CAPITA PRODUCTION, PRINCIPAL FOOD CROPS, 1860 (BUSHELS)

PRODUCT	NORTH	SOUTH
Wheat	5.57	4.78
Corn	25.55	31.05
Oats	7.03	2.18
Rice	—	0.35
Rye	0.87	0.24
Potatoes (white and sweet)	5.97	4.35

Source: Paul Wallace Gates, *Agriculture and the Civil War* (New York: Alfred A. Knopf, 1965), p. 9. Reprinted by permission.

selling their slaves off to cotton and sugar planters in the Southwest.

Hemp
The beginnings of the hemp industry date from the settlement of Kentucky, where hemp production became almost as predominant as tobacco had been in Virginia earlier. Hemp was in demand for use in bagging and rope for cotton bales, and also for common cordage. In the 1850s hemp production began to slump as declining yields and soil exhaustion in Kentucky led farmers to shift to corn and other crops; but Missouri and Arkansas took up much of the slack. Tariff protection was of crucial importance to this industry.

Other crops
Although the economic life of the South was dominated by these commercial crops, other farm products were raised, chiefly for home consumption. Most prominent was corn, grown on small farms and cotton and tobacco plantations throughout the region. Because of its hardiness, the ease and cheapness of its cultivation, and its adaptability to livestock feeding and use as bread, meal, and table food, corn was a universal crop throughout the United States. But yields were generally much lower in the South than in the Northwest. In terms of acreage planted, corn was the South's "leading crop," and the South as a region (partly because it was so little urbanized) exceeded the North in corn output per capita. But corn never became the basis for a diversified and commercialized agricultural-industrial complex in the South, as it did in the Middle West, where urban-based slaughtering and related industries emerged to process the livestock that were fed on corn.

Wheat
Wheat was another crop grown widely in the South. In 1859 some 50 million bushels were raised (compared with 433 million bushels of corn), but again the region-wide statistics may be misleading. For despite high total southern output, the region's commercial wheat production was confined largely to the Atlantic coast and the upland border states. In the Gulf coast region, the urban populations and large-scale cotton and other staple-producing plantations relied on interregional imports of grain from the West, augmented by imports from the border states.

Livestock
In livestock production, the South had high animal-human ratios (the hog ratio was 1.85, compared with 0.9 in the North), but again this was attributable in part to the low degree of southern urbanization. Besides, the quality of southern cattle and hogs was notoriously poor everywhere except in Kentucky, Virginia, and Maryland, where systematic stock breeding advanced steadily in the antebellum period. Mules and hogs were driven regularly from the border states into the lower South, and horses were driven from Kentucky and Ohio. Despite some planter interest in improved livestock, the handling of stock by slaves was said to be generally abusive—a subtle technique of subversion against the system of bondage—and in the scrub-pine districts of the interior, stock raising was largely a matter of turning the animals loose in the woods.[11]

AGRICULTURAL ADVANCE IN THE NORTHWEST

Whereas agriculture in the South was distinguished by a landowning system that concentrated much of the best land in the hands of large-scale, slave-owning staples planters, in the North the pattern was mainly one of small-scale independent farm owners. Moreover, unlike the South, as northern farming moved west, it spawned urban centers that underwent rapid industrial growth by processing the products of farm and forest. The early rise of commercial and industrial cities, in turn, made it profitable

[11]See Eugene D. Genovese, *The Political Economy of Slavery* (New York: Knopf, 1962).

for older-settled farming regions to specialize in dairying, sheep raising, meat production, orchard crops, and garden vegetables. The distilling, flour-milling, meat-packing, tanning, and other industries that took hold in the western cities became the industrial base for expansion into other manufacturing activity, leading to further regional economic diversification with beneficial spillover effects on agriculture.[12]

It is important to note also that in the North the pattern of income distribution, with wider diffusion of income than in the more stratified society of the South, resulted in broadly based local markets for diversified manufacturing production.[13] Finally, northern agriculture, especially in the 1850s, was characterized by wide adoption of new technology that improved farm-production efficiency. Especially during the spectacular spread of grain cultivation on the prairies in the 1850s, the new settlers applied large amounts of capital to bringing each new farm into production. Although cropping and soil-use practices certainly left much to be desired, farm machinery was brought into widespread use on smaller as well as large-scale commercial farms. By 1860 the entire process of wheat cultivation had been subjected to labor-saving mechanization.

In short, northern agriculture was part of a larger developmental process, closely linked with canal and railroad construction, with urbanization, and with a pattern of industrialization led by food processing. The whole thrust of changes in production methods was toward application of labor-saving machinery. There was no pattern of systematic, self-perpetuating exploitation of human capital, as prevailed in such extreme form in the South.

The agricultural surplus and its markets

Such interregional exports of foodstuffs as there had been in the trans-Appalachian West prior to 1825 consisted of flour and whiskey sent south on flatboats, and of pork, beef, and mutton sent eastward on the hoof through the mountains. But with the advent of western canals, beginning in 1830 in Ohio, there was a massive influx of population; and the new set-

tlers themselves provided a sizable steady market for a provisioning trade while they were clearing land and were not yet self-sufficient. By the mid-1830s the Ohio country was shipping a flood of surplus flour and grain eastward to New York; and as the western canals proliferated during the 1830s and 1840s, the flood tide continued to rise. In addition to consumption of western foodstuffs by the growing eastern cities, there was a regular market for pork products and corn at the river towns along the Mississippi and at the New Orleans export market.

Foreign demand for grain products in the 1840s, when European crops failed and the British repealed their Corn Laws, gave a boost to prices and commercial production of wheat and livestock; and also in the late 1850s, as the result of the Crimean War grain exports rose sharply.

Western transport construction, typically bringing thousands of laborers into formerly isolated farming districts, had an immediate impact on foodstuffs production and virtually overnight introduced many areas into a cash economy. Throughout the post-1840 period, moreover, the costs of transportation between East and West declined markedly. Tonnage of shipping on the Great Lakes grew rapidly and overland transport routes were multiplied, resulting in more intensive competition for the region's traffic. (See p. 152.)

Wheat and corn

By this time the specialized wheat culture and farmers' concentration on corn and hog production had led to emergence of a distinct wheat belt and also a corn belt in the Northwest, stretching from Ohio to the Mississippi River. The western states as a whole, which raised 7.4 bushels of wheat per capita in 1840, brought their production to 13.3 bushels in 1860. Corn output also rose in the West, from 33 bushels per capita in 1840 to 45.7 bushels in 1860.[14]

Livestock and dairying

As wheat cultivation moved westward into Illinois, Iowa, Wisconsin, and Michigan, the eastern and older-settled western states took up the production of livestock and also went into dairying. They introduced specialized crops as well to supply their thriving urban centers. In

---

[12]Harry N. Scheiber, *Ohio Canal Era: A Case Study of Government and the Economy, 1820–1861* (Athens: Ohio University Press, 1969), pp. 338–343.

[13]There is considerable dispute among scholars on the regional differences that prevailed in income and wealth distribution. See Gavin Wright, "Economic Democracy and the Concentration of Agricultural Wealth in the Cotton South, 1850–1860," *Agricultural History,* 44 (1970): 63–94.

[14]Overall northern average wheat production was brought down by the dramatic decline of wheat growing in the Northeast. In New England, for example, wheat output was only 1 bushel per capita in 1840 and 0.3 in 1860.

Ohio and New York in particular, cheese making became a prominent specialty. In 1860 the North as a whole was producing 99 percent of the nation's cheese and 86 percent of its butter. Much of the land once devoted to wheat in Ohio was shifted over to dairy and livestock forage crops during the 1850s, and sheep raising became a prominent western agricultural specialty.

The advent of the railroads in the 1850s forced a dramatic readjustment on the western livestock industry. The long drives of stock overland to eastern markets ended overnight as railway stock cars carried cattle and hogs to the coast much more rapidly and with less loss of weight. In addition, however, the railroads caused a slowdown in the formerly spectacular growth of western meatpacking, as farmers could choose between local slaughterhouses and sending their stock on the long railroad routes to competing meat-packing centers in the East.

In the West, as in the South, pork was the meat mainstay of the common diet. A large proportion of bacon and other pork products was consumed either locally or in the southern market, with extensive exports to Europe and the West Indies as well. But beef was more in favor in the East, and the western beef packers shipped much of their product to the coastal market for final consumption. The supplying of beef was a far-flung system: The grass-feeding (range) areas of "stock cattle" moved westward as the margins of the frontier shifted from Ohio in 1800 to a western base in Missouri and western Iowa by the 1850s; the range-fed cattle were shipped or driven to corn-raising centers farther east, where they were kept in pens, to be fed on corn and other grains; and then slaughter took place at either eastern or western urban centers. Throughout the period from 1820 to 1860, moreover, in all phases of livestock raising in the Northwest, improvement of breeds and feeding practices, as well as rising investment in buildings and pens for livestock, led to steady increases in productivity, as reflected in average weights and yields. This was in striking contrast to the sorry condition of contemporary livestock raising in most of the Deep South.

PROGRESS IN THE 1850s

The decade of the 1850s witnessed a great increase in farm output and agricultural productivity. Both land values and the value of farm machinery in use rose sharply in this decade.

The prairies

Western settlement had reached the fertile prairie soils of northern Indiana, Illinois, Iowa, Kansas, and Nebraska. The heavily glaciated prairie soils were of high organic content, but their complex grassy root structure made plowing difficult. By the late 1840s, pioneers understood that such land was superbly fertile, and new plows, including the steel plow, came onto the market specifically designed for breaking such land.

There were many problems to be solved before a working farm could be carved out of prairie land: The wood that was essential for fencing, buildings, and fuel had to be taken from scattered groves or purchased at commercial prices; drainage was difficult and expensive in some areas; and, overall, the migrant accustomed to farming eastern land had to adjust to a new set of environmental factors. Nonetheless, the settler could usually get a wheat crop onto fifty acres or more by his second year. Although farmers constantly complained that wheat was "the great impoverisher" of prairie country, still a market could always be found for this crop. And wheat required far less capital than the available alternatives (especially livestock raising, which meant construction of outbuildings as shelter and also a longer wait before the farmer could realize cash in the market). "The wheat crop," wrote an Illinois farm journalist in 1850, is "the great crop of the Northwest for exchange purposes. It pays debts, buys groceries, clothing and lands, and answers more emphatically the purposes of trade . . . than any other crop."[15]

Hence, not only did a large area of fertile farmland come into production for the first time in the 1850s, but it was land that was devoted heavily to commercial wheat production from the start, with high yields and crop value. Taken together with the surge in the South's cotton production, this rise in wheat output meant that

---

[15]Quoted in Paul W. Gates, *The Farmer's Age: Agriculture, 1815–1860* (New York: Holt, Rinehart and Winston, 1960), p. 166.

overall American farm output would advance substantially in the 1850s.

Railroads

A second major force operating on agriculture in the 1850s was the intensive construction of midwestern railroads, which permitted newly settled farmers on the prairies to be absorbed into the commercial economy almost from the start. Just as the railroads carried the West's surplus crops to coastal markets, they brought into the frontier or near-frontier areas the farm machinery, lumber, consumer goods, and other needs of commercial farmers and the rural towns. The railroads also expedited migration into the newly opened areas and were instru-

mental in forcing shifts in agricultural patterns in older-settled areas.

Mechanization

Farm productivity was given a further boost in the 1850s by the introduction of new labor-saving machinery. The most important single innovation was the mechanical reaper, used especially on the prairie farms. The decade also witnessed technical improvements in seed-drilling equipment, plows, threshers, and mowers. In many wet areas in the North there was heavy new investment in tile drainage; and southern rice and sugar planters were adopting larger-scale, more capital-intensive processing with new machinery designs.

THE READJUSTMENT OF EASTERN AGRICULTURE

The Northeast

New England agriculture underwent several major shifts as the result of both westward expansion and the East's own industrialization. In rural New England during colonial days many districts had been largely self-sufficient in their production, and farming tended to be general (a mix of livestock, corn, some wheat, grazing, and some garden and specialty crops). But after 1810 the urban market began to affect the area's agriculture. The growth of Boston and secondary cities, under the impact of rising foreign trade, provided cash markets that stimulated a higher degree of specialization in farming. Wool growing began to assume new prominence in the hilly country, and the Connecticut Valley went heavily into production of beef cattle. Garden crops were grown in the areas around all the port cities. Agricultural societies sprang up and a scientific "spirit of improvement" was manifest in farmers' attention to crop and animal breeding, crop rotation, and introduction of new farm implements, the most important being the iron plow.

The growth of western New York and later the Old Northwest states after the opening of the Erie Canal in 1825 forced a new kind of adjustment on New England. Cheap transportation brought into the region western wool, grain, and even meat products. Beginning in the late 1830s the completion of new railroads linking the Erie Canal with Boston further intensified the competitive impact of the West. As railroad development went forward, the pro-

duction of beef and pork in New England declined. Farmers turned their attention to dairying and truck gardening, and after 1840 in the Connecticut Valley there was a spectacular extension of tobacco culture.

The concurrent industrialization of New England, as early as 1820, gave farm children reaching adulthood an opportunity for employment in the region's factories. It also helped ease the adjustment from labor-intensive field crops to wool and dairying. But industrialization meant that domestic (household) production of manufactured goods quickly declined as a source of supplemental farm income. In the more remote and less fertile hill country of Vermont and New Hampshire, meanwhile, the lure of the West led to an exodus of thousands of farm families. Many farm villages there reached their historic high point of population in 1835 or 1840, thereafter suffering farm abandonment and steady out-migration of their young people.

The Middle Atlantic states

What happened in New England was duplicated, with some differences, in many parts of the Middle Atlantic states. Pennsylvania and New York had some especially rich soils, and they remained among the leading agricultural states throughout the pre-1860 period. Livestock production, especially dairying, had displaced arable crops by 1840 as the main activity of many farmers. There was an extensive shift away from corn and wheat in the face of western competition, and farmers turned to production of potatoes, oats, barley, buckwheat, and forage crops. Supplying the breweries, distilleries, and urban dairies was a major activity of eastern farmers. Throughout the region, urban demand for food made orchard crops and truck gardening another major source of farm income.

TECHNICAL ADVANCES IN AGRICULTURE

In a national economy that had plentiful land but relatively scarce labor, it was to be expected that the first great advances in farm technology would come in labor-saving rather than in land-saving devices. As of 1790, the farmer's implements typically consisted of a crude wooden plow, harrows, hoes, shovels, forks, and rakes. By comparison, the variety and designs of farm equipment available in 1860 were astonishing. A technology that in 1790 had been, in its fundamentals, close to that of the medieval period had now given way to a mechanization that was the hallmark of the Industrial Revolution.

The diffusion of farm machinery accelerated greatly in the 1850s—a fact that goes far toward explaining why a sharp rise in farm-labor productivity occurred during that decade, in contrast to a slight decrease during the 1840s. Accompanying rapid mechanization was an increase in the number of horses and mules on American farms (see Table 9–2, p. 132). Horses and mules were more adaptable for use with the new machinery than were draft oxen, relatively clumsy animals formerly used for plowing and other field tasks.

The plow

The first great improvement was the metal plow, which came into general use after 1825. Colonial plows had been covered with strips of iron, and as early as 1790 Charles Newbold of New Jersey was working on the idea of a cast-iron plow, which he finally patented in 1797. But Newbold's plow was ineffective and many farmers would have none of it. Eventually Newbold's plow—one solid piece of cast iron—was improved by others, including Jethro Wood of New York, who in 1819 patented a plow whose parts interlocked and could be replaced if broken. Manufacturers and inventors infringed his patents, but the farmer profited. Eventually moldboards were designed that were more adaptable to breaking the matted grasses of the prairies, the sticky soil of which also necessitated a smoother surface. This was provided by the all-steel plow of John Deere

and the chilled-steel plow of James Oliver, which eliminated blowholes and made the metal less brittle. Following 1850 the steel plow was adopted rapidly, particularly after quantity production lowered prices. Improved plows not only effected a saving in the labor of men and animals but by stirring the soil more deeply lengthened its productivity.

Mowers and reapers

Simultaneously with the improvement in plows came the invention of the mowing and reaping machines to keep pace with the increased production that the new plows made possible. Just as in manufacturing, the improvement of one stage of agricultural production forced the development of others. The grain cradle had come into use about 1800 and had considerably facilitated both the cutting and the gathering of the grain, but harvesting was still a painfully slow process. Many men experimented during the following years on the problem of a reaper, and many minds contributed to the eventual machine. A patent for a mowing machine had been granted to William Manning of New Jersey in 1831, but the two men who succeeded in building a practical reaper were Obed Hussey and Cyrus McCormick, whose patents were dated, respectively, 1833 and 1834. Hussey's machines, which could mow 15 acres a day, were good enough to demonstrate the possibilities of a reaper, and he had little competition for almost a decade. His poverty and mistakes in policy, however, prevented large-scale production, and in the end other manufacturers were to reap greater fame and fortune.

The greatest success was gained by Cyrus McCormick, of Scotch-Irish ancestry, who had emigrated from Pennsylvania into the Shenandoah Valley. Turning his attention to the development of a practical reaping machine, he continued, after securing his first patent, to manufacture reapers in his workshop on the Virginia farm and to perfect further improvements. Believing his machines would be more practical on the level land of the West, he moved in 1845 to Brockport, New York, on the

Erie Canal, and three years later to Chicago, where by 1860 he was turning out 4000 machines a year.

The principle of these early mowers and reapers was the same: A number of blades or "wipers" swept the grain against the cutting surface, after which it was pushed onto a receiving table and automatically shoved off when enough had been gathered to make a sheaf. Laborers following the machine tied the sheaves. These early machines, clumsy as they were, were clearly superior to hand labor, and improvements came rapidly. By 1855 nearly 10,000 were in use. At the International Exposition at Paris in that year an American reaper cut an acre of oats in 21 minutes, one-third of the time consumed by the foreign makes. By this time also the most serious disadvantages, such as side draft, clogging, and inability to begin in standing grain, had been practically eliminated. Moreover, new features such as the header, invented by George Esterly of Wisconsin, were being added to increase the usefulness of the machines. In the succeeding years the reapers were widely introduced, a fact that explains the great crops in spite of the labor shortage during the Civil War.

The thresher

A necessary further improvement was furnished when a satisfactory thresher was added to the mechanical devices upon which the farmer could depend. With the old-fashioned hand flail, progress was painfully slow; from 8 to 16 bushels a day was the average production per man. Experiments went on in both Europe and America in an attempt to devise flails that could be attached to cylinders and driven by horse or steam power, but it was not until 1850 that the separator was attached to the thresher and the whole process of threshing and winnowing was carried on in the same machine. In America Hiram and John Pitts took the leadership in developing a successful thresher, securing their first patent in 1837.

Other farm machinery

The invention and improvement of other farming implements accompanied the greater inventions. The horse hay-rake, which did the work of from eight to ten men, came into use about 1820, and the curing of hay was aided years later by the invention of the tedder. In the decade of the 1840s seed drills for sowing wheat were introduced, followed by the corn planter and various types of cultivators that were widely adopted by 1860.

Farmers of the time were not unaware that a revolution in agricultural methods was under way. As early as 1839 Jesse Buel, a prominent agitator for scientific farming, wrote:

> *The disparity between the old and new implements of culture is great, not only in the time employed, but in the manner in which they do their work, and in the power required to perform it. The old plow required a four-cattle team, and two hands, to manage it, and the work ordinarily was but half executed. The improved plow is generally propelled by two cattle, requires but one man to manage it, and, when properly governed, performs thorough work. Harrows and other implements have undergone a like movement. Besides, new implements, which greatly economize the labor of tillage, are coming into use, as the roller, cultivator, drill-barrow, etc., so that a farm may now be worked with half the expense of labor that it was wont to be worked forty years ago, and may be better worked withal.*[16]

This remarkable development was only the beginning. A much more important period of agricultural transformation came in the next two decades, the years that witnessed the introduction of seed drills, corn planters, cultivators, and many other types of machinery, particularly the mower and the reaper. Said the Census of 1860:

> *By the improved plow, labor equivalent to that of one horse in three is saved. By means of drills two bushels of seed will go as far as three bushels scattered broadcast, while the yield is increased six to eight bushels per acre; the plants come up in rows and may be tended by horse-hoes. . . . The reaping machine is a saving of more than one-third the labor when it cuts and rakes. . . . The threshing machine is a saving of two-thirds on the old hand flail mode. . . . The saving in the labor of handling hay in the field and barn by means of horserakes and horsehayforks is equal to one-half.*

It was of course this saving in labor that made possible the great added expense of the new machinery to the farmer.

---

[16]*The Farmer's Companion* (1839), p. 123.

SCIENTIFIC AGRICULTURE

Along with movement into new western lands and adoption of labor-saving techniques, scientific agriculture, including development of new breeds of crops and livestock, conservationist land-use techniques, and the like, also contributed to increased productivity in farming before 1860.

Livestock breeding

The improvement of livestock breeds was a leading activity of agricultural reformers and innovators. The wealthier southern plantation owners, gentleman-farmers in the North, and the more innovative common farmers all recognized the importance of increasing their yields from livestock.

Throughout the pre-1860 period, for example, there was steady concern with raising wool yields. Breeding stock was imported from England, Germany, Spain, and France, and sheep raisers gave attention to fodder crops, stock management, and pasturage techniques, with a consequent increase of nearly 50 percent in average yield per animal between 1839 and 1859. There was similar improvement in the size and quality of cattle, which were bred variously for use as draft animals, for dairy production, and for meat. With horses the main reliance for overland travel until the 1840s, there was also keen interest in riding, carriage, and work-horse breeds. Upgrading of hog stock in the pre-1860 period was proably more the result of improved feeding and handling practices than of breed improvement.

As American agriculture expanded rapidly after 1840, the number of stock on farms also rose dramatically. Horses and mules numbered 4.3 million in 1840 and over 7 million in 1860. Cattle increased from 15 to 26 million in the same period, hogs from 26 to 33 million, and sheep—in an industry that suffered great fluctuations in demand for wool—only from 19 to 22 million.

Agricultural education

Reformers disseminated information on superior breeds, new types of farm implements, and resource-management improvements by a variety of mechanisms. The most important institutions for diffusion of agricultural technology were agricultural societies and fairs, farm journals, advertising and demonstrations by the farm-machinery manufacturers, and educational efforts by government and the schools. Although the states and the local governments supported agricultural improvement by subsidies to societies, fairs, and educational institutions, the federal government was relatively inactive. In 1839, however, Congress did authorize the commissioner of patents to collect statistics on agriculture. Southerners' constitutional objections to a national university, and also the jealousies of the private colleges, thwarted efforts to institute federal patronage of agriculture and the industrial arts. On the eve of the Civil War, formal agricultural education in the United States thus lagged far behind institutionalized instruction in the professions. The great surge of growth in research and teaching in agriculture had to await enactment of the Morrill Land Grant Act of 1862, by which Congress granted each state lands or land scrip to aid in the financing of agricultural and mechanical colleges. From this beginning stemmed the system of state land-grant colleges, which would play a crucial role in scientific agriculture from that day forward.

AGRICULTURAL TRENDS TO 1860

The rising output of the farm sector during the pre-1860 period has already been illustrated (Tables 9–1 and 9–2, p. 132), but the relative importance of individual farm commodities and the mix of diverse specialties that marked American agriculture in 1859 may be illustrated also by the value of output. In that year, wheat was valued at over $150 million, cotton at $217 million. Total corn production was $385 million, although only one-fifth of the total was sold in primary form; the remainder was used as feed for livestock. Beef and dairy production were valued at $318 million, and hog output at over $300 million. Sugar and tobacco were valued at nearly $40 million each. Other crops worth $20 million or more included hay, potatoes, orchard fruits, and truck vegetables.

Several main characteristics of agricultural development to 1860 stand out. First of all,

TABLE 9-5. EXPORTS AS PROPORTION OF OUTPUT, BY VOLUME (PERCENT)

YEAR	WHEAT	CORN (1)[1]	CORN (2)[2]	COTTON
1839	6.6	—	1.0	86.7
1849	14.0	1.8	8.4	80.1
1859	16.7	0.8	3.9	48.9

Source: William N. Parker, "Agricultural Commodities," in *Economic Change in the Civil War Era*, David Gilchrist and W. D. Lewis, ed., (Wilmington, Del.: Eleutherian Mills-Hagley Foundation, 1965), p. 74. Reproduced by permission. Copyright 1965, Eleutherian Mills-Hagley Foundation.

[1]Percent exported of total output.
[2]Percent exported of output distributed outside the U.S. farm sector (that is, not consumed on farms for stock feed and family consumption).

there was a great expansion of the nation's farming areas and a steady rise in the number of people occupied in agriculture. Second, there was rapid development of regional specialization, as identifiable crop belts emerged in both North and South. Third, a process of agricultural readjustment was forced upon older-settled regions in succession as the nation expanded. In the North, such readjustment led to adoption of specialty crops, livestock feeding, and dairying geared to the urban market; in the South there was a more general trend toward soil exhaustion and abandonment in many areas, while small-scale farmers often were pushed down on the social ladder, reduced to near-subsistence or below-subsistence living in the backwoods districts. Fourth, the agricultural sector had a major impact on foreign trade, mainly through cotton exports from 1820 onward, but also, especially after the mid-1840s through the export of grain products and meatstuffs. (See Table 9-5.) Finally, the pre-Civil War period witnessed the beginnings of scientific agriculture and mechanization. By the 1850s a thoroughgoing technical revolution in farming had commenced. This was an era of confident expansion, and widening markets in Europe and at home opened opportunities for expanding farm production in the United States.

SELECTED READINGS

NOTE: See also selected readings in Chapter 12.

*Aitken, Hugh G. J., ed., *Did Slavery Pay? Readings in the Economics of Black Slavery in the U.S.* (Boston: Houghton Mifflin, 1971).

Bidwell, Percy W., and Falconer, J. I., *History of Agriculture in the Northern United States, 1620–1860* (1925, reprinted New York: Peter Smith, 1941).

*Bogue, Allan G., *From Prairie to Corn Belt* (Chicago: University of Chicago Press, 1963).

*Bruchey, Stuart, ed., *Cotton and the Growth of the Southern Economy* (New York: Harcourt Brace Jovanovich, 1967).

Clark, John G., *The Grain Trade in the Old Northwest* (Urbana: University of Illinois Press, 1965).

Danhof, Clarence H., *Change in Agriculture: The Northern United States, 1820–1870* (Cambridge: Harvard University Press, 1969).

*Gatell, Frank O., and Weinstein, Allen, eds., *American Negro Slavery: A Modern Reader*, 2nd ed., (New York: Oxford University Press, 1973).

Gates, Paul W., *Agriculture and the Civil War* (New York: Knopf, 1965).

*————, *The Farmer's Age: Agriculture, 1815–1860* (New York: Holt, Rinehart and Winston, 1960). (This book contains a full annotated bibliography of pre-1860 farming.)

Gray, Lewis C., *History of Agriculture in the Southern United States to 1860* (1933, reprinted Gloucester, Mass.: Peter Smith, 1958).

Kelsey, Darwin P., ed., *Farming in the New Nation: Interpreting American Agriculture, 1790–1840* (Washington: Agricultural History Society, 1972).

Klingaman, David C., and Vedder, R. K., eds., *Essays in 19th Century Economic History* (Athens: Ohio University Press, 1975). (Includes studies of agriculture by Richard Easterlin and Robert Gallman, and of transport's impact, by Roger Ransom.)

Olmstead, Alan L., "The Mechanization of Reaping and Mowing in American Agriculture, 1833–1870," *Journal of Economic History*, XXXV (1975).

Parker, William N., "Agriculture," in Lance E. Davis et al., *American Economic Growth: An Economist's History of the United States* (New York: Harper & Row, 1972).

Parker, William N., ed., *The Structure of the Cotton Economy in the Antebellum South* (Washington: Agricultural History Society, 1970).

Rogin, Leo, *The Introduction of Farm Machinery in Its Relation to the Productivity of Labor in Agriculture of the United States During the 19th Century* (Berkeley: University of California Publications in Economics, IX, 1931).

Rothstein, Morton, "The Antebellum South as a Dual Economy," *Agricultural History,* XLI (1967).

———, "Antebellum Wheat and Cotton Exports," *Agricultural History,* XL (1966).

Scarborough, William, *The Overseer: Plantation Management in the Old South* (Baton Rouge: Louisiana State University Press, 1966).

Schob, David, *Hired Hands and Plowboys: Farm Labor in the Midwest, 1815–60* (Urbana: University of Illinois Press, 1975).

*Stampp, Kenneth, *The Peculiar Institution: Slavery in the Antebellum South* (New York: Knopf, 1956).

Whitaker, James, ed., *Farming in the Midwest, 1840–1900* (Washington: Agricultural History Society, 1974).

Wright, Gavin, "Economic Democracy and the Concentration of Agricultural Wealth in the Cotton South, 1850–1860," *Agricultural History,* XLIV (1970).

Technical innovations and new capital investment in transportation were of basic importance to the pattern of American economic growth from 1790 to 1860. Technological advances in both water and overland transportation reduced transfer costs dramatically. Because it became progressively less costly and less risky to ship commodities — even low-value bulk commodities — over long distances, the more recently settled western regions could be integrated fairly quickly into the national and international channels of commerce. Low transfer costs made it possible for manufacturers to serve a progressively wider market, and this in turn enabled them to achieve economies of scale in production.

The revolution in transportation also was an essential causal factor in the emergence of regional specialization: Just as the Northeast could move heavily into manufacturing activity, so could the South concentrate on staples production and the western regions on foodstuffs. Low transport costs enabled shippers to haul coal and raw materials over progressively greater distances to cities and factories, giving still further impetus to industrialization. Moreover, the process by which the society built its new transport facilities meant that millions of dollars in European investment capital were attracted to the United States. Finally, the American experience in building and operating transport facilities of increasing complexity and extent provided the society with expertise in the management and control of large-scale entrepreneurial organizations, experience that proved crucial to the subsequent development of corporations in American industry.

In road and turnpike construction, the period of most intense activity was 1815–1840, with perhaps 12,000 miles of toll roads built. In canal construction, also, the period prior to 1840 witnessed rapid and extensive building: The nation had perhaps 100 miles of canal in 1816, just under 1300 miles in 1830, and over 3300 miles by 1840, with only 400 miles or so additional built in the 1850s. Another major innovation in inland transport, the steamboat, had its principal impact in the 1830s and 1840s, though addition of steamer tonnage in the Great Lakes and Mississippi Valley trades continued up to the Civil War. Finally, the introduction of the railroad — though it dated, in its beginnings, from a much earlier period — culminated in a great extension of the rail network from 1845 to 1854. Railroad mileage was 3328 by 1840 (some 60 percent of it in the Northeast), but the great railway construction boom that followed had given the nation over 30,000 miles of line by 1860.

Transportation technology and economic integration

These overlapping waves of canal, steamer, and railroad investment based on new technologies had an enormous impact on the pace and character of American economic growth. They did much to shape the contours and timing of business cycles, especially after 1835; they speeded the settlement and growth of the West; they greatly improved the West's terms of trade; they made and broke the fortunes of cities and regions, as well as untold thousands of business firms; and, overall, they transformed many of the basic conditions of economic life. Together with the telegraph, which introduced instantaneous communication over vast distances in the mid-1840s, the new transport facilities provided the basic social overhead industries necessary for a truly integrated national economy.

Initiative and financing

Where did the initiative for these sweeping innovations and waves of promotion originate? The technologies were in the international domain of ideas, although in road and canal technology major advances had been registered in England and continental Europe before extensive construction began in the United States. In the application of steam energy, American inventors kept pace with and interacted with English innovators. So far as promotional initiative was concerned, a mixture of public and private energies was involved. The state governments built most of the nation's canal lines, and railroads relied heavily upon state subsidies in the early period. But by the 1850s both promotion and financing of railroads were mainly in the private sector. Large injections of British and European capital stimulated both public canal and private railroad development throughout the period to 1860.

Pressures for new transport projects

The problem of transport was particularly acute for settlers in the nation's interior. On the seaboard, the coastwise shipping routes and the Atlantic sea-lanes had long served the needs of commerce. But as the extent of American settlement widened, the merchants of the great seaboard cities, and also of major inland towns such as Pittsburgh and Cincinnati, became no less eager than isolated western agriculturalists to have new lines of transport built. There was a strong dose, too, of disinterested nationalism and parochial state loyalties in the early movement for internal improvements: Political leaders were dedicated to binding the nation's remote sections together and to establishing the necessary foundations for economic growth that better transport could foster.

The resultant political pressures came to focus on both Congress and the state governments. From the states, transport promoters wanted public enterprise—governmental construction and operation of new projects—and liberal corporate charters for private companies. From the federal government, promoters sought programs of public construction and also various forms of subsidy. Even when the private sector itself took principal responsibility for transport improvement in the 1850s, promoters pushed hard for subsidies from government at all levels.

LIMITED FEDERAL PROGRAMS

Congress generally did not respond favorably to such pressures until the 1820s, and even then the federal role in providing improvements was limited.

Road construction

From the start of the new government in 1790, there were annual appropriations for post roads and some military roads. In addition, when Ohio attained statehood in 1802, Congress decided that 5 percent of revenues from land sales within the new state should be set aside for the financing of roads. As other new states entered the Union, similar provisions were made for them. But the principal contribution of the federal government in the early period was construction of the National Road, authorized in 1806, to link the older-settled eastern region with the West. All the major Atlantic port cities regarded selection as the road's eastern terminus as a treasured prize, and the political infighting was keen. Congress finally decided to sidestep the problem by building the road westward from little Cumberland, Maryland. Surveys and construction went slowly, and the road did not reach the Ohio River (at Wheeling) until 1818. And not until 1825 were further appropriations made to continue this major east-west overland route farther west.

The Gallatin plan

Despite his devotion to the idea of limited government, Thomas Jefferson became an advocate, when he was President, of a larger federal role in transportation. Among the "foundations of prosperity and union" Jefferson numbered "the improvement of roads, canals, rivers," and similar projects that we term today social-overhead capital facilities: productive facilities that generate large external benefits and whose social importance therefore warrants construction at public expense. Jefferson's secretary of the Treasury, Albert Gallatin, authored the celebrated *Report on Roads and Canals* in 1808, setting out a proposed program of specific road and canal projects. The report championed federal investment for facilities that private enterprise, with its shorter investment horizon and lack of capital, would not undertake. Gallatin also recommended federal aid for numerous major canal projects linking the Atlantic Coast with the interior—projects that in fact by 1850 would be largely completed by state governments and private enterprise.

Obstacles to federal programs

Some of the same practical obstacles that were obstructing the progress of appropriations for the National Road stood in the way of congressional adoption of Gallatin's program. They were:

1. Rivalries among the major cities and the states: Every project evoked the jealousies of rival centers, making it impossible to put together coalitions of any strength to vote through major measures.
2. Constitutional objections: Many of Jefferson's own followers feared powerful national government, and southern congressmen saw an indirect threat to state control of slavery if they permitted federal power in other areas to expand.
3. Reasons of economy: There was widespread concern that tariff duties might have to be raised if federal expenditures rose. This was of urgent moment because of the burdens put upon the Treasury by the War of 1812.

Meanwhile, however, the rising population of the West, where demand for nationally sponsored improvements was strongest, became reflected in congressional voting strength as new states were admitted to the Union. As population and government revenues grew after 1820, Congress did take several steps toward a greater federal role in transportation.

The General Survey Act

In 1824 Congress passed the General Survey Act, authorizing the President to help relieve the critical shortage of trained civil engineers by assigning Army Engineers to survey road and canal routes deemed of national importance. Under this law, their

services were made available until 1838 to the states and private enterprises.

Land grants and cash subsidies

Those who believed that the General Survey Act might be the first step toward comprehensive federal aid were to be disappointed, for Congress granted only piecemeal aid to selected enterprises of the state governments and private promoters. From 1824 to 1828, land grants were made to several western states (Ohio, Indiana, Illinois) to help subsidize canal and road projects sponsored by the state governments, and Congress also voted some cash subscriptions to the stock of private canal companies.[1]

During Andrew Jackson's administrations (1829–1837) Congress also stepped up its modest annual appropriations, generally ranging from $500,000 to nearly $900,000, for federal construction of river and harbor improvements planned by the Army Engineers. But in 1830 Jackson jolted the advocates of governmental activism with his famous veto of the Maysville Road Bill, which had authorized aid to a turnpike company's project, on grounds that the road was of merely local, not national, importance. Jackson promised in his veto message that once the federal debt was retired "a general system of improvement" might be warranted. But this came to little. Although annual river and harbor bills continued to be voted, for the most part Congress left to the individual states the chief responsibility for developing the nation's transport system.

Overbuilding and spill-over effects

Hence a score of separate governments, motivated by rivalries with their sister states, was left in charge of policy making. However,

---

[1]From 1825 to 1828 Congress voted nearly $2 million in cash subscriptions to four canal companies: the Chesapeake and Delaware, the Louisville and Portland, the Dismal Swamp, and the Chesapeake and Ohio. The land grants to states consisted of a total of 3 million acres to aid canal construction in Ohio, Indiana, and Illinois. These canal grants were made on the "prodent proprietor" principle, by which sections were granted to the state and alternate sections were retained for sale at double the usual minimum price (or $2.50 an acre) by the federal government. The result was a checkerboard pattern within the land-grant area along the lines of the canals for which aid had been granted. In theory, the federal government protected its interest in revenues by charging double the minimum price. In practice, the higher price discouraged many settlers (despite advantages of proximity to the canal lines) and probably retarded development of the canal regions. See Harry N. Scheiber, "State Policy and the Public Domain," *Journal of Economic History*, 25 (1965).

the result was not to stymie social-overhead investment. Instead of carefully fashioned national priorities, state and local development of internal improvements became marked by considerable overbuilding; that is, by construction of competing routes that cut into one another's commerce. Localistic pressures on state legislatures often led to irrational decisions to build dense networks of transport facilities that could not generate revenues sufficient to pay interest on the bonds issued to finance them. From another standpoint, however, the decision to decentralize transport policy probably resulted in cyclical stimulation of the economy — and especially in the force-feeding of regional and local economies because of spill-over effects of public investment and new transport lines.

ROADS AND TURNPIKES IN THE STATES

At the close of the Revolution, the main towns and cities along the Atlantic seaboard were connected by very primitive roads, many of them hardly passable in bad weather. The technology of road building had been well advanced in Europe, especially in England and France, but capital and engineering expertise were lacking in America. Besides, the citizens of the new nation were notoriously resistant to taxing themselves for such projects.

The Lancaster Pike
Nonetheless, the 1790s witnessed the beginnings of a turnpike movement of some importance. It was led by a private company's construction of a $500,000 road, the Lancaster Pike, between Philadelphia and Lancaster in Pennsylvania. Built through rich farming country, the pike prospered. Its remarkable success stimulated expectations elsewhere that similarly high profits could be realized, and throughout New England and the Middle Atlantic states hundreds of small-scale capitalists, especially tavern operators and others who could hope for indirect profits as well from their investments, helped to finance turnpike ventures. But most of the new roads were poorly built, many not even paved. In the West and in the region south of Virginia, lack of local capital resulted in little turnpike construction at all prior to about 1810.

Private projects and the law
The early turnpike movement also stimulated projects for toll bridges and ferries. As with the turnpikes, their construction was accomplished by the formation of chartered corporations. Because the projects were regarded as public in their purpose, though not in their ownership, legislatures felt justified in granting the companies exceptional privileges and immunities in their charters. Thus the lawmakers gave tax exemptions, authorized the corporations to seize land for rights of way under the states' power of eminent domain, and made any evasion of payment of tolls by users subject to legal sanctions. In this manner the fabric of traditional law was stretched, and a precedent was established for similar grants of corporate power when private companies undertook canal and railroad construction at a later time.

Mixed enterprise
During the War of 1812, a lack of improved roads hampered military and supply operations. This experience stimulated new interest in turnpikes. In the decade after 1816, Virginia undertook an important experiment in "mixed enterprise." Under this Virginia system, state funds were invested in the stock of private road companies, and state directors were appointed to represent the public interest. This style of state aid was later to be copied in Kentucky and Ohio, and variants of it would mark other state programs of aid to railroads.

Beginning in the 1830s, state and local governments rather than private corporations began to carry nearly the entire burden of road building. But private turnpike companies, operating both with and without public aid, continued to build new projects in the West well into the 1840s, after the turnpike enthusiasm had died out in the older states.

RIVER NAVIGATION

The use of America's rivers became a hotly contested political and constitutional issue in 1807, when Robert Fulton piloted a new design of river vessel, the steamboat, on a trial run from New York to Albany on the Hudson River. Fulton's boat, the *Clermont,* was a 160-ton sidewheeler. To encourage his experiments, he was given a monopoly privilege for steam navigation on New York waters by the state legislature. Other states, and also the Territory of Orleans, which controlled the Mississippi, granted similar monopolies to Fulton and rival experimenters. Among the latter was Henry Shreve of Pittsburgh, who made the first successful steam voyage upstream on the Mississippi in 1817.

The constitutional issue

The legitimacy of such monopoly grants came before the U.S. Supreme Court in the case of *Gibbons* v. *Ogden* (1824), testing the constitutionality of New Jersey laws designed to challenge the New York monopoly grant to Fulton. In a landmark decision written by Chief Justice John Marshall, reflecting Marshall's strongly nationalistic views, the Court ruled that only Congress might properly control interstate commerce, including navigation on the nation's inland waters. Often termed "the emancipation proclamation of American commerce," *Gibbons* v. *Ogden* opened wide the doors of competitive private enterprise in steamboat development.

Steamboats on the western waters

The most spectacular growth of steamer navigation took place on western waters, where farmers and merchants throughout the Mississippi–Ohio Valley region sought more reliable transport to and from New Orleans. Although farm products continued to be shipped downstream in the traditional way, by flatboats and other primitive vessels powered by the currents, steamers were used for upstream hauling of passengers and merchandise; and their speed and comfort also captured for them the downstream trade for valuable cargoes and passenger carriage. Hence the tonnage of steamers on the Mississippi and Ohio rivers rose from 3,300 tons in 1817 (when 17 boats were running) to nearly 40,000 tons in 1834. By 1842 there were over 450 boats of 90,000 tons.[2] In addition, steamboats came into wide use on the Great Lakes, where shipping of over 20,000 tons was operating in the mid-1840s in competition with sailing vessels.

The average freight rates on steamboats, though subject to navigational conditions and seasonal demand, generally were far lower than on overland roads or turnpikes.[3] Introduction of the steamboat was thus crucial to the rise of New Orleans as a major export center for western foodstuffs as well as cotton, and as the fastest growing American city in the 1830s. Growing western steamer traffic also became a powerful force behind a popular movement for federal river improvement. Heavy losses to boats on the bars and snags of the Mississippi excited widespread protest in the West. Congress responded by appropriating about $3 million between 1822 and 1860 for improvement of traffic conditions on the western rivers, and the federal government purchased and operated the Louisville and Portland Canal, which bypassed the treacherous falls of the Ohio River at Louisville.

THE CANAL ERA: FIRST PHASE

By the late eighteenth century, England and France had built efficient networks of canals, and the superiority of canals over roads for hauling heavy freight under favorable conditions of terrain and water supply had been well demonstrated. The chief advantage was savings of motive power: A horse could pull through dead water a load 50 times or so heavier than it could over even an improved road. Offsetting disadvantages were the greater complexity and cost per mile of canal construction; the need for heavy and reliable flows of water to supply canals, especially where rough country required frequent changing of levels through locks; and the winter closing of canals by ice. Moreover, the shortage of skilled engineers and the lack of sufficient domestic capital were formidable obstacles to canal-building in America.

[2]Thomas Senior Berry, *Western Prices Before 1861* (Cambridge: Harvard University Press, 1943), p. 34. In 1840 an estimated 20 percent of freight on the lower Mississippi was still carried by flatboat. Arrivals of flatboats at New Orleans numbered about 3000 annually in the 1840s, thereafter falling to about one-third that level; but probably an equal number of flatboats coming down from the Ohio and other streams terminated their trading voyages at points on the Mississippi above New Orleans.

[3]In the mid-1830s the cost of shipping merchandise by wagon between Philadelphia and Pittsburgh was $3.50 per hundred pounds. By the more circuitous route via New Orleans, by river and coastwise shipping, the cost was only $1.50 (Berry, *Western Prices*, p. 81).

The Erie Canal

There had been scattered efforts in the late colonial period to improve rivers and undertake canal construction, and by 1815 small canal lines were in operation in Virginia, North Carolina, and Massachusetts. But the modern canal era did not open in America until 1816, when a coalition of New York City merchants, upstate farmers, and other political allies of Governor De Witt Clinton pushed through the New York State legislature a bill authorizing state construction of both the Erie Canal and a second canal to be built between the Hudson River and Lake Champlain.

The Erie Canal was completed and opened for its entire length from Buffalo to Albany in 1825 — an event that opened a new era in American transport history, as it stimulated many rival and complementary projects in other states. Financing was accomplished partly by mobilizing private New York capital, but foreigners took at least $2.4 million of the bonds issued by the state. This was the first major foreign investment in the U.S. economy since organization of the first Bank of the United States. The Erie Canal was successful from its first days, producing revenues in excess of carrying charges on the debt that New York State incurred to build it. Optimistic predictions of similar success elsewhere inevitably followed, fueling the canal enthusiasm — or "canal mania," as it came to be called.

Apart from inspiring imitators, the Erie Canal also provided a model for other states in the organization of their public enterprises and served as a training ground for the education of civil engineers. It also gave experience to canal contractors and laborers, many of whom moved elsewhere when their work was done in New York State. No less important were technical innovations developed in the course of construction, especially in the design of aqueducts and water-supply systems.

Pennsylvania and Ohio projects

Pennsylvania soon emulated New York, authorizing in 1825 the construction by the state of a complex canal-and-railroad system (the Pennsylvania Main Line) to link Philadelphia with Pittsburgh. This $10 million project, completed in 1834, tapped the Ohio Valley directly and offered an alternative marketing route to settlers on the Ohio, who were formerly dependent upon the New Orleans outlet.

Although the young state of Ohio commanded only a small fraction of New York's and Pennsylvania's fiscal resources, nevertheless it undertook major public canal construc-

tion in 1825. The $4.5 million Ohio project, like the eastern canal ventures, attracted both domestic and foreign investment. Unlike Pennsylvania, however, Ohio could boast an enterprise ably managed and built; there was nothing like the administrative incompetence and corruption that had plagued the Quaker State's undertaking. Ohio's first major line was completed in 1834 over a 300-mile route between Portsmouth, on the Ohio River, and Cleveland, then a tiny port town, on Lake Erie. It was the first all-water link between the Mississippi—Ohio river basin and the Great Lakes, serving in effect to extend the trade route opened up by New York via Buffalo.

Other major canals

Other major canals inaugurated before the mid-1830s included the Chesapeake and Ohio line through Maryland, which was not finally completed until 1850; canal projects into the coal region of northeastern Pennsylvania; several major short lines in New Jersey; and one across the neck of land separating Chesapeake Bay from Delaware Bay, the latter serving the coastal commerce on the Atlantic seaboard.

New Jersey's Delaware and Raritan Canal was the only one to be completed by a private company with no state subsidy. Running from the Delaware River north to New York's harbor, it provided a direct route between Philadelphia and New York. Private operation was made possible on this $4 million undertaking by the rich trade it would instantly command. Few of the other lines built prior to 1834 could have attracted private risk capital, as they did not exploit established lines of commerce, but rather were designed to build new ones almost from scratch. Despite promoters' high hopes, however, none of the other state projects enjoyed the success of the Erie Canal.

In all, just under $60 million was invested in canals from 1815 to 1834; and 70 percent of the total was governmental investment, mainly by the states, as shown in Table 10–1. The states accomplished this financing by pledging canal and tax revenues to back up bonds that were sold abroad and in the commercial cities of the East. It was America's good fortune that its early state canal ventures coincided with a period of peace abroad, when European capital was seeking new investment opportunities.[4]

[4]Data on canal investment and the governmental share, here and later in the text, are from Carter Goodrich, *Government Promotion of American Canals and Railroads* (New York: Columbia University Press, 1960); and Goodrich, ed., *Canals and American Economic Development* (New York: Columbia University Press, 1961).

TABLE 10–1. CYCLES OF CANAL CONSTRUCTION, 1815–1860

CYCLES	PEAK YEAR OF CYCLE[1]	COMPLETED MILEAGE	INVESTMENT OVER CYCLE ($ MILLION)	SHARE OF PUBLIC FUNDS IN INVESTMENT[2]
1815–1834	1828	2,188	$58.6	70.3
1834–1844	1840	1,172	72.2	79.4
1844–1860	1855	894	57.4	66.2

Source: Harvey Segal, "Cycles of Canal Construction," in *Canals and American Economic Development,* Carter Goodrich, ed. (New York: Columbia University Press, 1961), pp. 172, 215. Reprinted by permission of the publisher. Underlying data on investment are by Jerome Cramner and originally appeared in *Trends in American Economy in the Nineteenth Century* (National Bureau of Economic Research, *Studies in Income and Wealth,* Vol. 24. Princeton: Princeton University Press, 1960), pp. 555–556. Copyright 1960, The National Bureau of Economic Research. (Used by permission.)

[1]Year of greatest investment in each distinct cycle (trough years were 1834 and 1844).

[2]Includes cash investments, mainly financed through bond issues. In addition, three states (Ohio, Indiana, Illinois) financed cash investments partially through sale of lands granted by Congress.

THE CANAL ERA: SECOND PHASE

The inflow of foreign capital, the Erie Canal's success, and the long upswing in the business cycle that lasted from the mid-1820s until 1837, all fed a spirit of optimism and enthusiasm for canal building. Rivalries between states and cities contributed to the mania, and in 1835 a new wave of canal construction began. In Ohio, Indiana, and Illinois, major canal projects were undertaken to link the waters of the Great Lakes by new routes to the Mississippi and Ohio rivers. All of these states threw aside cautious planning and respect for systematic priorities, and they approved giant, costly programs designed to give nearly every county new transport facilities. So did New York State, with the important difference that New York's treasury could easily carry the burden of such expansion. In Pennsylvania, too, the construction of lateral canals from the Main Line had already begun prior to 1834. In Virginia, the state government and several municipalities voted large subsidies for canalization of the James River. North Carolina and Georgia, too, expended state funds on major river improvements. Elsewhere in the South, and also in Michigan, state programs that required heavy bond issues concentrated mainly on subsidizing railroad projects.

Financial difficulties

The total length of canals built from 1834 to 1844 was nearly 1200 miles, bringing national canal mileage to 3360. But because the new canals were built of larger dimensions than earlier ones, the nation's capacity for carrying canal traffic was probably doubled in the decade after 1834. Government expenditures

were responsible for about 60 percent of the new construction, which cost some $72 million. The Panic of 1837 and the four-year business depression that began in 1839 cut off investment capital, and delay or abandonment of construction became necessary in many states. By 1843, several states—Illinois, Indiana, Michigan, Maryland, and others, including the mighty Commonwealth of Pennsylvania—had defaulted on interest payments to bondholders. Three southern states repudiated their debts outright.

By struggling through the depression years, reorganizing their debts, and renegotiating contracts for construction, however, the states completed most of the main-line canals. Ohio's second Lake Erie–Ohio River canal (the Miami and Erie) was completed in 1845; the Wabash and Erie was completed from Toledo, Ohio, to Terre Haute, Indiana, in 1848; and the Illinois and Michigan Canal linked Chicago by an all-water route with the Mississippi River in 1848. In the East, Pennsylvania brought into operation its system of feeder lines, and New York State enlarged the Erie Canal system, tripling its total mileage.

Expansion and competition

This second wave of American canal construction had a number of distinct effects. First of all, the physical transportation network was greatly extended, with effects especially important in the West. Four new canals connected the Great Lakes with the interior basin of the Mississippi–Ohio system. These canals gave most of the Old Northwest access to the Atlantic coast by several alternative routes, and they

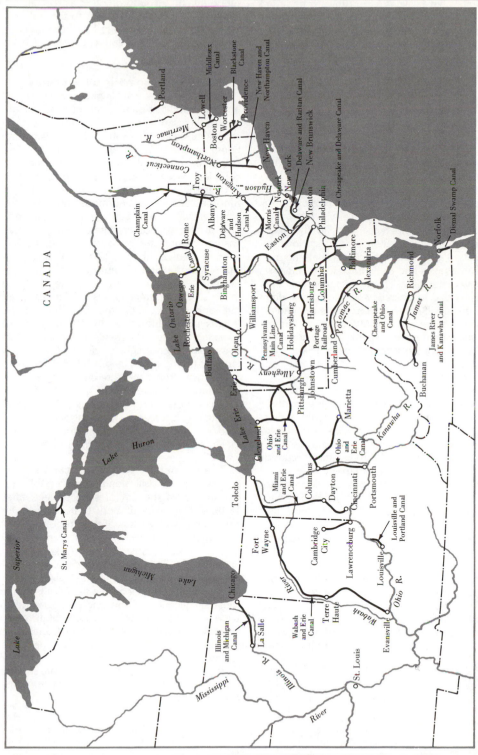

Figure 10–1. Principal Canals Built by **1860**. Source: George Rogers Taylor, *The Transportation Revolution, 1815–1860*, vol. 4, *The Economic History of the United States* (New York: Holt, Rinehart and Winston, 1951), p. 35.

also improved facilities for southward trade to New Orleans. Moreover, the very proliferation of canals intensified competition upon all routes, forcing a general decline in interregional transport charges. As private operators and state canal officials struggled for a share of the trade, rates came down.[5]

Disillusionment with state enterprise

Second, the new canals were important for their impact on contemporary public opinion concerning active governmental enterprise. The decline in freight rates proved to be a source of grief to the states, making it impossible for them to increase their toll revenues in proportion to traffic-volume increases. There had been corruption and incompetence, too, in the state governments' construction of canals. Now, as the costs of maintaining the older canals mounted, higher taxes had to be imposed to support the new waterways. This convergence of difficulties tended to discredit state enterprise after 1837. Especially in the defaulting and repudiating states, there was a revulsion against further state-sponsored improvements. Many constitutions revised by the states in the late 1840s contained provisions that banned debt-financed improvements.

Whether the people's disillusionment with state enterprise was justified is another matter. In fact, the states' administrative record during construction was generally no worse than that of private railroad promoters in the same period. But the reversal of public views occurred nonetheless; and it forced a transfer of responsibilities for subsequent transport development to local governments, which in the 1850s began to subsidize railroad companies with local tax funds.

Not least important, the discrediting of public enterprise helped open the transport field to private enterprise still more fully. Indeed, one scholar has termed the pattern of pre-1860 governmental action as one of "state in, state out," with government called upon to build and operate transport facilities when the private sector was young and the prospects of profits were slim, but then reduced to a subsidizing role

supportive of private promotion as soon as private capital became adequate to the task and the economy's productivity had become sufficient to hold out the early prospect of good profits.[6]

Canals and the national economy

Finally, the new canals had a major impact upon the development of the national economy. In the short run, the heavy construction expenditures of the 1830s fed the inflationary boom of 1834–1837; and the difficulties encountered by the states in obtaining funds to complete construction after 1839 had the effect of deepening depression conditions. In the long run, the canals gave enormous impetus to the commercialization of agriculture in Ohio, Indiana, Illinois, and other states. They permitted eastern manufacturers to reach the growing western market; they linked coal-mining regions with the iron-manufacturing centers at Pittsburgh and Cleveland; and they reduced the cost of consumer goods (including sugar, salt, and merchandise imported through the Atlantic ports) throughout the West. In light of these major external benefits, it is obvious that many canals that might be deemed failures in terms of the revenues they produced (or failed to produce) from tolls were eminently successful in terms of social savings generated for private consumers and producers. This was so despite the fact that many canals were quickly rendered obsolescent by the competition they met from the railroads built in the 1850s.

The financially successful canals

The popular disillusionment with public enterprise ended the era of state projects after 1845, except in New York State, where the continuing fiscal success of the Erie Canal produced revenues sufficient to sustain some $60 million of new construction in the form of branch lines. The great era of canal construction had come to an end by the 1850s. Of the remaining canals built before the Civil War, the most significant was the one-mile long deepwater ship canal connecting Lake Huron with Lake Superior, the Sault Ste. Marie Canal. Built by a private company, which received a lavish federal grant of valuable mineral and timber lands, the "Soo" line was an immediate success and was vital to the exploitation of the Lake Superior iron-ore deposits.

---

[5]Ohio's canal tolls on merchandise carried on 250 miles of line between Cincinnati and Toledo were $7 per ton in 1845 but had fallen to $3 in 1850. In New York, the Erie Canal charges on flour were 2.7 cents per ton-mile in 1832, 1.6 cents in 1845, and 1.3 cents in 1851. On the Pennsylvania Main Line, flour was carried at 3.8 cents per ton-mile in 1838, but at only 1.8 cents in 1848 (Harry N. Scheiber, *Ohio Canal Era* [Athens: Ohio University Press, 1969], pp. 259–263, 300, 380–386).

[6]Carter Goodrich, "State In, State Out: A Pattern of Development Policy," *Journal of Economic Issues, 2* (1968): pp. 365–383.

THE EARLY AMERICAN RAILROADS

Even before completion of the Erie Canal in 1825, popular interest in railroads was keen. Whereas some $60 million in bonds were sold to finance canals prior to 1838, $43 million were marketed to finance railroad construction in the same period. With the end of the 1839–1844 depression, the railway movement gained full strength. A period of intensive construction followed, increasing the nation's railway network to more than 30,000 miles of line by 1860.

Railroads were cheaper to build than canals in most terrain. The transportation they provided, although still slow in the early years, was far more rapid than the three to five miles per hour attained by canal boats, which were towed by horses or mules following towpaths alongside the canal waters. Moreover, railroads did not require an extensive water supply, and they did not rely upon locks that slowed navigation. They offered, too, the supreme advantages of flexibility: They could be built to factory doors, and they were free from seasonal closing by ice or drought. Even so, many prominent American canal engineers were at first prejudiced against railroads, considering them practical only for passenger transport and light freight. There was also some popular distrust, based on the notion that since railroads were by nature monopolies, they were dangerous to the public interest.

Eastern railroads

On July 4, 1828, Charles Carroll of Carrollton, a signer of the Declaration of Independence, turned the first spadeful of earth for the track of the Baltimore and Ohio Railroad. This was the first modern railway built in America (a few others had been constructed with wooden rails or for use by horse-drawn trains), and its first division, 13 miles long, was opened in 1830. Not until Peter Cooper's engine, "Tom Thumb," had made the 13 miles from Baltimore to Ellicott's Mills in an hour in 1830 did the management decide definitely to use steam instead of horsepower.

The Baltimore and Ohio had been organized by a small group of Baltimore's leading merchants. Concerned because the city's growth had slowed perceptibly since 1815, they recognized that the Erie Canal threatened them with further commercial disappointments. Though the Baltimore promoters anticipated (correctly, as it proved) receiving public aid from the city, they conceived of the project as a private corporation from the first. And they expected to make it pay.

Boston's response to the Erie Canal was similar to that of Baltimore: a railroad project rather than a canal, and reliance upon private enterprise bolstered by government aid rather than state construction. The strategy in Massachusetts was to build initially the Boston and Worcester Railroad (under construction from 1830 to 1834) through settled country where manufacturing firms and farms could provide traffic, and then, with a separate corporation, the Western Railroad, to continue the line to Albany.

Charleston, South Carolina, also adopted a railroad plan to penetrate the interior. The Charleston and Hamburg, completed in 1833, covered 136 miles and was then the world's longest railroad under a single management. In New York the legislature granted a charter in 1826 to the Mohawk and Hudson, which would later become part of the New York Central. It was completed in 1831, when its first train ran the 17 miles from Albany to Schenectady in one hour. The initial link in what later would become the Pennsylvania Railroad system was a strip of road from Philadelphia into the Susquehanna region, built in 1834.

Once the practicability of railway transport technology had been established, entrepreneurs in all the eastern states undertook railroad construction on an expanding basis. By 1840 the nation boasted some 3,328 miles of railway, of which a third was in New York and Pennsylvania alone. Nearly all the early eastern roads were sturdily independent of water routes; that is, they either were competitors of major canals or were built in regions not already served by canals.

Railroads to the West

There was only limited construction west of the Appalachians, about a hundred miles in all, before 1840.

After the business recovery of the mid-1840s, another (much larger) wave of new construction began, as railroad promoters responded to the growing opportunites afforded by a sharp rise in the volume of East-West trade. But by then a grand strategy had emerged of linking or consolidating railroad lines between the Atlantic coastal cities and the major western commercial centers. In the mid-1850s, several long-line systems penetrated the Appa-

TABLE 10–2.   RAILROAD MILEAGE BY REGION, 1830–1860

REGION	1830	1840	1850	1860
New England	3	436	2,633	3,660
Middle Atlantic[1]	70	1,510	2,972	6,353
West[2]	—	199	1,307	11,055
South[3]	—	1,183	1,967	9,535
Pacific[4]	—	—	—	23
U.S. TOTAL	73	3,328	8,879	30,626

Sources: Data on 1830, 1840, and 1850 in "Pacific Railway Survey," in *Hunt's Merchants' Magazine,* 25 (September 1851):381–382; and data on 1860 in Henry V. Poor, *Manual of the Railroads of the United States for 1868–1869* (New York, 1868), pp. 20–21. Total mileage for 1860 corrected. For a full discussion of the varied reliability of the data, see George R. Taylor, "Comment," in National Bureau of Economic Research, *Trends in the American Economy in the Nineteenth Century* (Princeton: Princeton University Press, 1960), pp. 524–544, and tables of alternate estimates of mileage in ibid., pp. 526–527.

[1]New York, New Jersey, Pennsylvania, Delaware, Maryland, and the District of Columbia.
[2]Ohio, Michigan, Indiana, Illinois, Wisconsin, Iowa, and Missouri.
[3]Virginia, North Carolina, South Carolina, Georgia, Florida, Alabama, Mississippi, Louisiana, Texas, Kentucky, Tennessee, and Arkansas.
[4]California and Oregon.

lachian barrier all the way to central Indiana, Chicago, and beyond: the New York Central in 1853; the Erie, which reached Pittsburgh and connecting roads westward from New York about the same time; the Baltimore & Ohio, which reached St. Louis in 1858; and the Pennsylvania Railroad, which, through operating agreements and stock subscriptions in numerous western lines, pushed through to Chicago in 1859.

Both Boston and Portland also established connections through to Chicago during the 1850s, at first by way of New York State and later by connections with railroads through Montreal and across Canadian soil to Michigan, and from there to Chicago. By 1858 the Central Virginia, running west from Richmond, and a sister road from Petersburg had made connections with the Southwest, and in 1859 they reached the Mississippi River. As shown in Figure 10–2, however, the South was much less well provided with railroad lines than other sections of the country in 1860.

RAILROAD FINANCING AND REGULATION

Though many of the eastern railroad companies paid handsome dividends from the start, the prospect of returns on railroad stock was at best uncertain in the more sparsely settled portions of the West and South. The investor might need to wait for years before dividends could be paid, if indeed they ever were. But in spite of this fundamental difficulty, more than $1.2 billion had been invested in railroads by 1860. Nearly all the railroad ventures of the time were built by private companies. New York, Philadelphia, and Boston were the principal sources of capital at first. While common and preferred stocks were sold mostly in the United States, a large proportion of railroad bonds (many guaranteed by state or local governments) was sold abroad, mainly in England. In addition, railroad promoters commonly obtained short-term credits by importing British rails with funds loaned by the manufacturers or by banking houses in London.

State and local funds
Where private capital was insufficient, public aid was freely given. In New England, Massachusetts was the only state to provide heavy cash subsidies. But elsewhere—Pennsylvania, South Carolina, Georgia—the state governments financed the first railroads. Other states subscribed public funds in the equity stock of private companies (as Maryland did, in the Baltimore and Ohio Railroad), or else made public construction or state aid to railway projects a component of general programs of internal improvement (as Michigan did) in the 1830s. In the 1840s popular disillusionment caused state support to be cut back in many places. But in the 1850s there was extensive municipal and county aid to railroad corporations, as private promoters commonly promised to build through communities that aided them and threatened to bypass places that extended no public support. In all, perhaps one-third of all

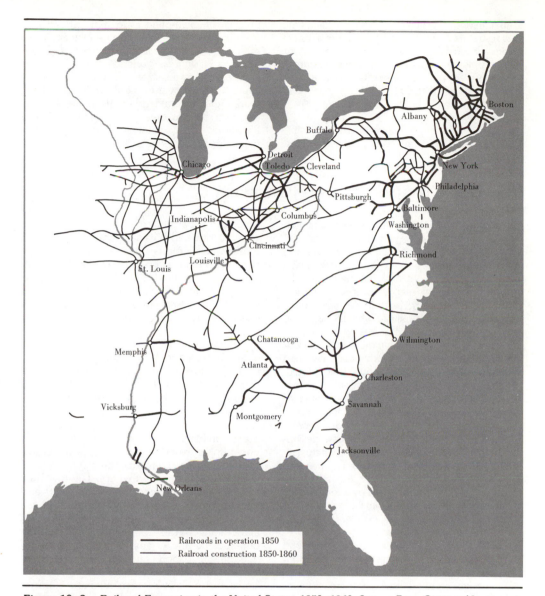

Figure 10–2. **Railroad Expansion in the United States, 1850–1860.** Source: From *Cities and Immigrants: A Geography of Change in Nineteenth-Century America* by David Ward. Copyright © 1971 by Oxford University Press, Inc. Reprinted by permission.

railroad investment prior to 1860 represented public funds.

More generally, state-government action helped shape railroad promotion and finance through grants of corporate charters. Corporate status included many benefits, usually including limited liability for stockholders, the right to condemn land under the power of eminent domain, and the like. In addition, many states exempted railroads from taxation; some even exempted them from effective rate regulation,

at least for a specified period of years. These privileges and others served to reduce costs, and so constituted an important form of indirect subsidy.

State regulation

While private entrepreneurs thus largely built the American railroad system with very substantial aid and support from government, they were not much troubled by state regulation. New York, concerned about protecting Erie

Canal revenues, was the only state to place serious restraints upon railroad corporations' operations or profits. Elsewhere some regulatory laws prohibiting rate discrimination or cutthroat practices were put on the books, but they were enforced loosely if at all.

Federal aid

Aid from the federal government was minimal. Indirect subsidy effects did derive from the practice of exempting European railroad iron from import duties, and army engineers made many of the early railroad surveys. In 1850, however, Congress granted over 2.5 million acres of land to the state of Illinois, whose legislature turned it over to the Illinois Central Railroad. Other federal land grants to western and southern states followed, amounting by 1861 to 25 million acres, generally worth at least the federal minimum price of $1.25 per acre.[7]

RAILROAD TECHNOLOGY AND MANAGEMENT

Continuous technical experimentation marked the pre-1860 period of railroad development. The earliest engines were small and could not negotiate steep grades with heavy loads; rails were light and roadbeds typically poorly built; and passenger cars were the last word in discomfort, essentially stagecoach bodies outfitted with railway wheels. But some of the larger railroad corporations and equipment builders (most notably the Baldwin Locomotive Company of Philadelphia) financed experimentation with locomotive design, brake and coupling devices, roadbed design, and cars for specialized cargoes—an early example of research and development by private firms. Among the greatest achievements of the pre–Civil War railroad builders were new designs in bridges, both of the iron-truss variety (pioneered by James Warren and Thomas and Caleb Pratt in the 1840s) and the cable-suspension type (whose principal developers were Charles Ellet and John Roebling).

Nonconnecting lines

True physical integration of the railroad network was not accomplished before 1860, despite the proliferation of new lines. For one thing, gauges were not uniform; there was considerable variation from one state to another, so that long-haul shipments could not always be carried without transfers between the lines of "connecting" companies. For another thing, the major railroad terminals in most cities were not located at a common point, and some were even constructed outside municipal limits, like modern-day airports. In a famous instance of parochialism run rampant, the State of Pennsylvania even required a break in gauge of lines passing through Erie's town limits in order to protect the existing investments of local merchants, warehousemen and haulers.

Management problems and innovations

The first railroad companies also faced perplexing management problems. Unlike canals and turnpikes, which were open to private operators of their own boats and vehicles, the railroad was run as a single system. Track, equipment, buildings, and repair shops were all under unitary ownership and control. Moreover, the larger railway companies employed workers in numbers unique for that era. The Erie Railroad, for example, had more than 4000 employees, whereas few industrial firms of that day had as many as 500. Hence the railroad managers pioneered in development of corporate bureaucracy and organization, instituting staff departmentalization and specialization, cost accounting and price administration. The divisional and multilevel organizational systems of management that were to be adopted by giant American industrial corporations in the late nineteenth century owed much to the precedents established by the pre–Civil War railroad operators.

ECONOMIC CONTRIBUTION OF THE RAILROADS

During the 1850s, railroad mileage increased fivefold, from about 6,000 miles to more than 30,000. The east–west trunk lines that were built and consolidated under joint or unified management, often in combination with

[7]The additional land grants used for aid to railroads went to Mississippi, Missouri, Michigan, Wisconsin, Minnesota, Iowa, Arkansas, Alabama, Florida, and Louisiana. Kansas was the site of a particularly lurid struggle over lands by competing railroad promoters. See Paul W. Gates, *Fifty Million Acres* (Ithaca: Cornell University Press, 1954).

steamer lines on the Great Lakes and the Ohio River, greatly increased railroad efficiency and helped drive down rates. Average railway rates did not fall below canal rates during the 1850s, partly because canal operations were in many cases heavily subsidized with state tax money. But in periods of exceptional competition, combined water-rail routes did carry long-distance freight at charges comparable to those of all-water facilities. Above all, the railroad offered the shipper speed, year-round transportation, the flexibility to respond quickly to short-run market changes, and relative safety and reliability.

Social returns

The changing market patterns that resulted affected agriculture, industry, and commerce in every region of the country. Of special interest here is the question of social utility. The key issue is whether or not the railroads generated social returns (direct savings to shippers and related indirect savings) that exceeded their operating costs and the costs of maintaining interest on funds invested in them. Clearly, had the free-market economy been allowed to operate independently, with no public subsidies or other aid to railroads, fewer lines would have been built. The majority of companies were overcapitalized: Funds were wasted on poorly designed construction; financing was loose; and corrupt managers manipulated stock sales, watered equity capital, and gave out contracts to favored construction firms at inflated prices.

One scholar's estimate of the *direct benefits*—that is, savings realized in shipping by railroad over the cost of shipping via alternative means of transport—is $175 million for 1859. This was about 4 percent of gross national product in that year, when the railroads carried some 2.5 billion ton-miles of freight and had passenger traffic of 1.5 billion rider-miles.[8] Compounded annually, a social-savings level of 4 percent for a single innovation constitutes a major contribution to the growth of the national

economy. But, in addition, the railroads generated *indirect benefits* such as the production that was stimulated by railway investment in locomotives, rolling stock, and other equipment, which amounted to an estimated 15 percent of total capital outlays in the economy during the 1850s. By fostering regional specialization, extending the market for manufacturers, speeding up product flows, making possible year-round shipment of goods when ice closed the northern waterways, and the like, the railroad was a powerful force for economic growth.

Risk and competition

At the same time, however, the very rapidity and geographic reach of new railroad construction also increased elements of risk and uncertainty in the economy, not least for the railroad firms themselves. Railway managers responded by trying to reduce uncertainty through private rate-setting agreements, pools for divisions of traffic between competing lines, and formation of operating agreements between lines or consolidation and merger. A few railroad companies bought out competing canal lines and closed them down; many railroads acquired their own steamers and port facilities to expedite lake-and-rail or river-and-rail combined shipping. Not least important, it became common practice for the railroads to charge discriminatory high rates at localities served only by themselves in order to support low rates at points where competition was intense. Hence by the mid-1850s, farmers, shippers, and merchants were complaining of "Wall Street profiteering," and there were movements in many states to enact strong state laws to prohibit rate discrimination and other "robber baron" tactics. But they met with little success until a later day, for on the whole public sentiment toward railroads was enthusiastic and benevolent. The railroad remained, for the time, the goose that had laid the golden egg; and in the 1850s, neither state regulation nor the railroadmen's efforts at self-regulation had much success.

SELECTED READINGS

Berry, Thomas Senior, *Western Prices before 1861* (Cambridge: Harvard University Press, 1943).

Fishlow, Albert, *American Railroads and the Transformation of the Antebellum Economy* (Cambridge: Harvard University Press, 1965).

[8]Albert Fishlow, *American Railroads and the Transformation of the Antebellum Economy* (Cambridge: Harvard University Press, 1965), p. 52. A different view, arguing that the railroads did not in fact constitute a source of major social savings, is to be found in Robert William Fogel, *Railroads and American Economic Growth* (Baltimore: Johns Hopkins University Press, 1964). See also Harry N. Scheiber, "On the New Economic History and Its Limitations," *Agricultural History*, 41 (1967): 383–395.

*Fogel, Robert William, *Railroads and American Economic Growth: Essays in Econometric History* (Baltimore: Johns Hopkins Press, 1964). See also review essay by Harry N. Scheiber, "On the New Economic History and Its Limitations," *Agricultural History,* XLI (1967).

Gates, Paul Wallace, *The Illinois Central Railroad and Its Colonization Work* (1934, reprinted New York: Johnson Reprint, 1971).

Goodrich, Carter, ed., *Canals and American Economic Development* (New York: Columbia University Press, 1961).

————, *Government Promotion of American Canals and Railroads, 1800–1890* (New York: Columbia University Press, 1960).

Gray, Ralph D., *The National Waterway: A History of the Chesapeake and Delaware Canal* (Urbana: University of Illinois Press, 1967).

Haites, Erik F., James Mak, and Gary M. Walton, *Western River Transportation: The Era of Early Internal Development, 1810–1860* (Baltimore, Md.: Johns Hopkins University Press, 1975).

Hunter, Louis C., *Steamboats on the Western Rivers* (Cambridge, Mass.: Harvard University Press, 1949).

Jackson, William Turrentine, *Wagon Roads West: A Study of Federal Road Surveys and Construction in the Trans-Mississippi West, 1846–1869* (Berkeley: University of California Press, 1952).

Johnson, Arthur M., and Supple, Barry E., *Boston Capitalists and Western Railroads: A Study in the Nineteenth-Century Railroad Investment Process* (Cambridge: Harvard University Press, 1967).

Kirkland, Edward Chase, *Men, Cities, and Transporation: A Study in New England History, 1820–1900* (Cambridge: Harvard University Press, 1949).

*Kutler, Stanley I., *Privilege and Creative Destruction: The Charles River Bridge Case* (Philadelphia: Lippincott, 1972).

Miller, Nathan, *Enterprise of a Free People: New York State During the Canal Period* (Ithaca: Cornell University Press, 1962).

*Nettels, Curtis Putnam, *Emergence of a National Economy, 1775–1815* (New York: Holt, Rinehart and Winston, 1962).

Ransom, Roger L., "Interregional Canals and Economic Specialization in the Antebellum United States," *Explorations in Economic History* (Second Series), V (1967).

————, "Public Canal Investment and the Opening of the Old Northwest," *Essays in Nineteenth Century Economic History: The Old Northwest,* D. C. Klingaman and R. K. Vedder, eds. (Athens, Ohio: Ohio University Press, 1975).

Salsbury, Stephen, *The State, the Investor, and the Railroad: The Boston & Albany, 1825–1867* (Cambridge: Harvard University Press, 1967).

Scheiber, Harry N., *Ohio Canal Era . . . 1820–1861* (Athens, Ohio: Ohio University Press, 1969).

————, "Property Law, Expropriation, and Resource Allocation by Government: the U.S., 1789–1910," *Journal of Economic History,* XXXIII (1973).

Shaw, Ronald, *Erie Water West: A History of the Erie Canal . . . 1792–1854* (Lexington: University of Kentucky Press, 1966).

Taylor, George Rogers, "The Beginnings of Mass Transportation in Urban America," *Smithsonian Journal of History,* I (1966).

*————, *The Transportation Revolution, 1815–1860* (New York: Holt, Rinehart and Winston, 1951).

Taylor, George Rogers, and Neu, Irene D., *The American Railroad Network, 1861–1890* (Cambridge: Harvard University Press, 1956).

Thompson, Robert L., *Writing a Continent: The History of the Telegraph Industry in the United States, 1832–1866* (Princeton, N.J.: Princeton University Press, 1947).

Up to this point in our study of pre-1860 economic change, we have examined the pattern of development in the major sectors of the economy. But it is vital to recognize that agriculture, commerce, and transportation underwent change as part of a larger process that we term industrialization. Also traditionally called the Industrial Revolution, this process included the introduction of powerful new sources of energy (especially steam power) and a new technology of production in the manufacturing sector, with the rise of factory organization making it possible to achieve enormous productivity gains. The shifts in manufacturing interacted with changes in other sectors: Transport extended the market and stimulated shifts toward larger-scale production, commercialization of agriculture was encouraged by the growth of an urban industrial work force, the earnings of foreign commerce were available for investment in manufacturing and social overhead capital facilities, and the efficiencies realized in all sectors generated savings that could be reinvested to take advantage of new technologies.

Although the Industrial Revolution reached high tide in the United States only after 1870, the industrialization process had already become a leading force in the national economy's development well before the Civil War. Value added by agriculture increased from $800 million in 1839 to $1.5 billion in 1859, while in the same period value added by manufacturing rose from less than $200 million to $860 million.[1] In the 1840s, a decade of spectacular growth for the manufacturing sector, its output rose by over 150 percent. The trend of industrialization was also reflected in the basic structure of commodity output in the economy. Agriculture's share, though farm output was rising absolutely, declined from 72 percent in 1839 to 56 percent in 1859; manufacturing's share, on the other hand, rose in the same period from 17 percent to 32 percent.[2] Distribution of workers in the labor force also indicated the magnitude of the shift that was under way. In 1820 nearly 8 out of 10 workers were in agriculture, and in 1840, 63 to 69 percent. But in 1860, agricultural workers constituted only 53 to 60 percent of labor force; 18 percent of workers were in manufacturing and construction, while the rest were engaged in other nonfarm occupations.[3]

Industrialization, in this era when the modern economy was taking shape, brought with it rising productivity and incomes largely because efficiency gains in manufacturing were outrunning the pace of similar gains in agriculture. The value of output per worker increased from $244 in 1839 to $268 in 1849, and to $330 in 1859.[4] As a growing share of total commodity output came from the manufacturing sector, the pace of productivity gains quickened.

---

[1] Stuart Bruchey, *The Roots of American Economic Growth, 1607–1861* (New York: Harper & Row, 1965), p. 80. The values are given in 1879 (constant) prices, and therefore indicate a real increase.

[2] Robert E. Gallman, "Commodity Output, 1839–1899," in National Bureau of Economic Research, *Trends in the American Economy in the Nineteenth Century* (Princeton: Princeton University Press, 1960), p. 26.

[3] Stanley Lebergott, "Labor Force and Employment, 1800–1960," in National Bureau of Economic Research, *Output, Employment, and Productivity in the United States after 1800* (New York: Columbia University Press, 1966), p. 118; and *Historical Statistics of the U.S.* (1960), p. 74, provide differing estimates.

[4] Gallman's data, in 1879 prices (*Trends*, p. 16).

STAGES OF INDUSTRIALIZATION

The development of the Industrial Revolution before 1860 may be divided, as the economic historian Victor S. Clark has suggested, into three periods.[5] The first, 1790–1815, witnessed the beginnings of factory production in American manufacturing, concentrated in the New England textile industry. But in this period, what Clark terms "foreign contingencies" — international crises, European wars, and the consequent vicissitudes of foreign trade — dominated the basic market environment.

In the second period, 1815–1840, the Transportation Revolution and its effects tended to weaken the impact of foreign contingencies. Also, technical advances in ironmaking, spreading adoption of steam power, and the absorption of European immigrants into the labor force all had important stimulative effects on manufacturing. This second period was also characterized by considerable geographic dispersion of industry, especially as manufacturers remained close to sources of energy (coal and waterpower sites) and of raw materials. But of no less impact was the rise of a "manufacturing interest": a class of capitalists principally involved in industry, not commerce or other pursuits.

The third period was 1840–1860, when, as we have seen, manufacturing output increased at an accelerating rate.[6] The rise of the railroad, innovations in metallurgy (especially iron manufacture), and rapid development of machine technology permitting use of stronger, more precise tooling, all stimulated heavy industry, especially manufacture of producers' durables (machinery, railway equipment, and so on). The small water-driven mill now gave way decisively to factory organization on an ever larger scale and to the use of steam power. Meanwhile, though foreign trade (especially the competition of imported goods) continued to influence manufacturing, autonomous internal developments became more controlling.

[5]Victor S. Clark, *History of Manufactures in the United States,* vol. 1 (Washington, D.C.: Carnegie Institution, 1929), pp. 233–262.

[6]Walt W. Rostow has termed the years 1843–1860 as the time when the U.S. economy entered its "takeoff" into sustained economic growth, by which he means a stage in which "the scale of productive economic activity reaches a critical level and produces changes which lead to a massive and progressive structural transformation in economies and the societies of which they are a part, better viewed as changes in kind than merely in degree" (Rostow, *The Stages of Economic Growth* [Cambridge: The University Press, 1960], pp. 38, 40).

Obstacles to industrialization

When we take a broad view of manufacturing development across these three distinct periods, certain stimuli and obstacles to industrialization can be identified. The difficulty of successfully competing with England — the workshop of the world, with a long lead as a manufacturing nation — was a persistent problem. Another was the relative shortage of capital in the United States, especially with western lands, commerce, and transportation competing for investment funds. Relative labor scarcity was also a problem for early manufacturers. In periods of expansion and boom, therefore, the Americans had to pay higher wages than prevailed in Europe for similar work, or else, as happened after 1840, institute new methods of production that substituted machinery for human labor and reduced the level of skills necessary on the part of workers employed.

Stimuli to industrialization

The offsetting advantages and stimuli were numerous. For one thing, the rich resource endowments of the nation offered a treasure store on which manufacturers could draw. Waterpower sites abounded; there were large iron and coal deposits; forest resources were abundant; and processing of both cotton and food products, being produced in rising quantity by a burgeoning agricultural sector, offered major opportunities for profitable manufacturing.

Social and cultural factors cannot be neglected, either. Americans, as many contemporary observers remarked, were quick to accept manufacturing and careers in industry as a positive good; and workers were, especially in the North, well educated, generally healthy by comparison with those in Europe, and highly motivated, many of them believing that they could rise in life and become capitalists themselves.

Government at all levels did much to channel capital and human energies into the industrialization process. Federal patent laws protective of rights to inventions, bounties and tax exemptions offered by state governments, a liberal policy at the state level of granting corporate charters with valuable privileges, a favorable federal protective tariff policy through much of the pre-1860 period, and a system of taxation that fell lightly on savings, all played their parts.

In sum, no revolution in social values or in the basic social institutions of the society was necessary; there was no established church, vast governmental bureaucracy, or entrenched landed gentry or nobility to contend with. To be sure, there was social conflict, and men and women whose lives were made bleak by industrial work and industrial cities did not passively accept every feature of industrialization. But on the whole, the social environment was no less favorable than the other aspects of American life and resources to the growth of a vigorous manufacturing sector.

Of course, all these stimuli to industrialization operated on the supply side. On the demand side was the fact that as per capita incomes rose, the proportion of the increment spent on industrial goods was very high.

BEGINNINGS OF THE AMERICAN FACTORY SYSTEM

Household manufacture for family needs was general everywhere in the United States at the end of the eighteenth century, except, perhaps, in some plantation districts, and this type of manufacture continued in the frontier regions long after it had disappeared from the seacoast. Household manufacture for the general market was also carried on at this time, the craftsman sometimes working on the raw material supplied by the merchant capitalist. The manufacturing artisan who had confined his energy to custom work was extending his operations to a general market, and some mills and furnaces were operating on a scale that approached factory production. At the same time itinerant artisans wandered from house to house making shoes and doing other skilled work beyond the ability of the family. In other words, all these stages of industry—the household, the domestic, the small mill or shop, and their various modifications—were contemporary in America on the eve of the Industrial Revolution. Although the United States passed from "mother and daughter power" to water and steam power in a short period of some 70 years, almost all phases of the household and domestic stages continued during these years. Rapid as the transition was, it would have come even more quickly had not the poverty and remoteness of the frontier held it back.

Since the Industrial Revolution had taken place first in England, that country had become the workshop of the world. This advantage it was loath to lose, and attempts were made to keep the secrets of the new machinery from spreading. Between 1765 and 1789 laws were passed prohibiting the emigration of skilled workers in textiles and machinery and the exportation of textile machinery, plans, or models. But these measures did not materially delay the introduction of such machinery into this country after interest had once been aroused.

The years from the close of the Revolution to 1800 were a period of experimentation. Factories in which the jenny was used were established in 1787 in Philadelphia and in Beverly, Massachusetts, and in succeeding years in other places in New England and New York—undoubtedly the first cotton mills in America. None of them survived long. The first successful Arkwright cotton mill was built in 1789 by Samuel Slater, an English emigrant who had served an apprenticeship in one of Arkwright's factories at Belper and had been induced to come to America by bounties offered here for the improved machinery. Through the influence of Moses Brown, a Quaker merchant of Providence, Slater came to Rhode Island, and in 1790 his mill, erected at Pawtucket, spun the first machine-made cotton warp in America. The beginnings of the American factory system can truly be traced to Slater and his Pawtucket mill.

Sources of power

The first spinning machines set up were run either by hand or by horsepower. Later, waterpower was used extensively, and for a while almost exclusively, both for spinning and weaving and for other types of production.

Steam was probably first used in America for pumping mines in New Jersey and Rhode Island during the last decades of the eighteenth century; it is believed that it was first applied to mill machinery in a sawmill in New York in 1803. In the years following, either the imported low-pressure engines of the Boulton-Watt type or the high-pressure engines of Evans were introduced in sections where waterpower was inadequate or fluctuated greatly, as it did in the Ohio Valley. It was in this region that steam power was first widely used in manufacturing. Steam power was also superior in the heat-using industries, such as glass and iron making, centered in western Pennsylvania and Ohio.

Another impetus to the use of steam engines was provided as good waterpower sites in New England were no longer obtainable and as manufacturing was urbanized. Although steam power increased rapidly after 1840, water remained the chief source of power as late as 1860.

Inventions

When manufacturing by machinery was firmly established, American inventors enthusiastically took up the ideas of European engineers, adapted them to conditions here, and contributed new improvements. Labor scarcity did much to stimulate inventions, but ignorance as to what had been done in England led to duplication.

Of American contributions, perhaps the most famous was that of Eli Whitney, who not only invented the cotton gin but in the late 1790s applied — at least in rudimentary form — the principle of standardization and interchangeability of parts in the manufacture of firearms. Another notable American advance was the Goulding condenser, which greatly simplified and quickened the carding of wool. The first successful power loom for weaving in America was constructed by a Boston merchant, Francis Cabot Lowell, who on a trip to England from 1810 to 1812 had made a careful study of textile machinery. With the aid of a mechanical genius, Paul Moody, Lowell designed and constructed a new set of spinning machinery and a power loom, which were set up at Waltham in 1814. Here, for the first time in the world, it is believed, all the processes of spinning and weaving were brought together in the same factory. In concentrating all the processes in one factory, the "Waltham system" took a long step toward modern factory production. In the succeeding years many American inventors, of whom John Thorp, Samuel Batchelder, and William Mason are the best known, invented the "ring spinner," which raised spindle speed to three times that of the Arkwright spindle, and perfected machines for knitting and lace making, and for manufacturing linen and cotton in figured designs.

Not only in textiles were American machinists making progress. Oliver Evans of Philadelphia invented a high-pressure steam engine that was used successfully. James Rumsey, John Fitch, and Robert Fulton made notable experiments in the application of steam to water transportation, and John Stevens of Hoboken did pioneer work on the railroad engine. Frederick Geissenhainer in 1830 successfully smelt-

ed iron ore with anthracite coal, and in 1851 William Kelly of Kentucky independently discovered the principle of the Bessemer method of decarbonizing molten metal by forcing air through it. Elias Howe in 1846 invented the sewing machine, a machine equally suitable to the home and the factory, and one that not only proved an immense boon to women but revolutionized the clothing and shoe industries. The work of Samuel Morse in introducing the magnetic telegraph effected a similar revolution in methods of communication. The Patent Office, which reported an average of 77 inventions annually from 1790 to 1811, recorded 544 patents in 1830. In the decade 1841–1850 it issued 6,460 patents, and in the next decade 25,250.

Entrepreneurs

Recognition should also be accorded that remarkably large and brilliant group of entrepreneurs and capitalists who built upon the labors of the technicians, men who planted little factories in out-of-the-way places which became the foundations for important industries and thriving cities. Among the many who come to mind are Nathan Appleton and Abbott Lawrence, who were leaders of the group responsible for the manufacturing development of Lowell and Lawrence, Massachusetts; Edmund Dwight, who played a similar role in Chicopee and Holyoke, also in Massachusetts; and the visionary industrialist and publicist William Gregg, who innovated in textile manufacturing in Graniteville, South Carolina.

One of the ablest of them was Patrick Tracy Jackson (1780–1847), whose activities exemplify the entrepreneur at his best. Apprenticed to a Newburyport merchant at the age of 15, he became a sea captain in his early 20s, retired from the sea at 28 to engage in the exporting and importing business, and with the curtailment of his shipping interests by the War of 1812 found an outlet for his energy in the manufacture of cotton. Joining his brother-in-law, Francis C. Lowell, he aided in the establishment of the famous Waltham factory and managed it in its early years. When the local power resources were exhausted, Jackson and his associates moved to the Merrimac and erected mills around which grew the city of Lowell, the "Manchester of America." Finding transportation facilities from his new mills to Boston inadequate, Jackson turned a ready ear to the reports of steam railroads and was chiefly responsible for the first one in New England. Sailor, merchant, manufacturer, railroad builder, he epitomizes the economic history of New England during the first half of the nineteenth century.

Factory development

The development of the Industrial Revolution, of course, followed no fixed rule. Some factories were merely the extensions of tiny mills already in existence; some were the work of inventors or technicians who also had capital, as in the case of Lowell; others were established by businessmen who had little or no technical knowledge but could obtain capital. Some were personally managed by the owner or his friends, while many, particularly in the large centers of New England, were controlled by absentee owners and conducted by resident managers. Each type of industry had to develop its particular technique of production and distribution. In some industries the expanding market produced by the Industrial Revolution was met by the expansion of old methods rather than by new machinery. The shoe industry, for example, did not introduce new machinery until the 1860s, but in the meantime the little hand shop increased in size until a more minute division of labor became possible. In the shoe centers of New England there appeared the main "factory," where the cutting, packing, and shipping were done, and many little shops or even private homes about the town where specialized operations, such as binding, stitching, soling, and lasting, were carried on—an excellent example of an industry that predated nineteenth-century technology expanding to meet changed market conditions without new machinery. Not until development of the sewing machine in the 1850s and the application of power to shoe machinery did this branch of manufacture become a factory industry.

Variant paths of industries' development

The student of American manufacturing needs to keep in mind the conclusion of a leading British business historian, Sidney Pollard, that one cannot "[treat] all industries as if they belong to a single process called the 'industrial revolution.'"[7] Extractive industries necessarily developed where the resources were located, whereas processing industries were not necessarily tightly bound by resource location. Thus, lumber mills characteristically were located near the forests and the streams that carried the cut

timber down to the mills, and the iron industry was at first located at places near mineral deposits and forests. But as transport costs declined iron mills tended to cluster near coal mines and to carry their ore by water and (in the 1850s) by rail to those locations. The finished products of the iron industry (stoves, farm implements, machinery, and the like) were often manufactured in the cities near iron mills. Yet even in this industry important exceptions were to be found; for instance, the town of Springfield, Vermont, became a center of skilled machine workers and the machine-tool industry thrived there.

Technological innovation occurred in different ways as well. In industries such as flour milling and other *processing* types of manufacture, successive technological advances relied heavily upon applications of water and steam power; and they led to increasing scale of production. In the *assembly* industries, such as those which produced firearms, clocks and watches, and farm implements, the impact of technical changes was felt mainly through routinization of manufacturing in the factories (a rudimentary assembly-line process became prominent by the 1850s), specialization of machine tools that turned out precision components, and standardization and interchangeability of parts.

Even in the legal forms adopted for industrial organization there were significant differences according to region or industry. Thus in the Massachusetts textile industry, entrepreneurs organized limited-liability corporations very early in the nineteenth century. But in Rhode Island's textile industry, the partnership remained the characteristic form of organization much longer. And even when Rhode Island's legislature authorized corporate organization, the textile manufacturers there viewed limited liability with disfavor.

Finally, some of the major industries that shifted from household to factory production were developed from established products, with new firms entering the industry on a specialized basis; for example, at Cincinnati, Chicago, and other meat-packing centers, there emerged in the 1840s and 1850s specialized firms to process on a mass-production basis such byproducts as candles, brushes, and leather goods. But other new firms—for instance, those that produced gas for illumination in the 1830s and 1840s—had no counterparts in older household-based industries; they were organized on a relatively large scale, and they employed entirely new technologies from their beginnings.

---

[7]Sidney Pollard, *The Genesis of Modern Management* (Baltimore: Penguin Books, 1965), p. 126.

SOME PATTERNS OF MANUFACTURING GROWTH

An examination of a few specific industries will afford a sense of the varying importance of technology, markets, entrepreneurial innovation, and other factors in the rise of American manufacturing.

The textile industry

The textile industry introduced factory-organized production in America. The textile firms, as we have seen, also were major innovators in the application of machine techniques. Their industry was the first in manufacturing to reach a size sufficient to permit it to transcend the limitations of local and regional markets, to serve the entire national market. In short, textile manufacturing was at the "frontiering" edge of American industrialization.

The power looms installed at Waltham and other plants organized upon the Lowell model provided the advantage of cost-reducing efficiency in production of coarse fabrics. And it was precisely these cheaper fabrics that were most in demand in the American market. In the 1820s and early 1830s, having weathered the challenge of import competition from British mills, the New England textile manufacturers began to increase in size and capitalization, gaining economies of scale in the process. Aided by tariff protection and concentrating on the coarse cottons, the New England firms increased their spindlage from about 80,000 in 1811 to about 1.3 million by the early 1830s. Further technical advances in weaving then converged with another innovation, calico printing — a cheap technique for printing a design on the fabric — to give a fresh push to the industry's development. From 1840 to 1860 the number of spindles again doubled.

Several other factors were also important in the spectacular success of cotton textile manufacturing. One was the linkage with the machinery industry. The very rapidity of growth in textiles created a profitable market for machinery, and by the 1850s a specialized machinery industry had grown up in New England, at first dedicated mainly to producing equipment and new designs for the textile mills. Initially, its importance lay in the cost savings it effected in the production of cotton fabrics. These savings, in turn, lowered fabric prices and helped widen the market. The rise of the machinery industry was also important because the machine firms became a seedbed for transfer of new ideas and techniques to problems of machine design in industries other than textiles.

Another major factor stimulating growth was the availability of capital in New England: Savings that accrued to merchant capitalists in foreign trade and shipping were transferred to investment in manufacturing.

Finally, the cotton-textile industry successfully exploited the labor market. It attracted farm girls from the New England countryside; skilled workers came from English mills; and by the 1840s, as machinery became more versatile and the need for specialized labor skills was reduced, it employed women, children, and unskilled immigrants willing to work for relatively low wages.

In 1860, capitalization and value of product in woolens production were only about half those in cotton manufacture. Unlike the manufacturers of cotton goods, who benefited from the vast expansion of raw cotton supply in the South, woolens manufacturers did not enjoy a long-term reduction in the cost of their raw materials. In fact, they relied to some degree upon imported wool throughout the pre-1860 period. Because they could not reduce the costs of their materials, the woolens producers depended upon tariff protection to sustain profits.

Food-processing and tobacco

The agricultural processing industries followed a different line of development. Only in flour milling was there a major breakthrough in technology: the inventions of Oliver Evans in the 1780s and 1790s, put machinery to work on many of the tasks formerly done by hand, from cleaning to final barreling. Even flour milling, however, remained widely dispersed, and many small-scale mills continued to flourish throughout the northern states and the West, in competition with more heavily capitalized mills in Rochester, Baltimore, Cincinnati, and other urban centers.

Traditional techniques, small scale of operations, and dispersion characterized leather tanning until after the Civil War. In meat packing, there were only gradual technological changes. The larger cities were able to provide a seasonal labor force and capital, and so the urban packing plants grew in scale, especially after 1845. Manufacturers soon took advantage, too, of the opportunity to produce by-products such as bristles, lard oil, candles, soaps, fats, and fertilizer. But despite the growth of some large packing firms in the major cities, especially Cincinnati, a great share of the nation's meat was still smoked and packed on farms even in the

TABLE 11–1. UNITED STATES MANUFACTURES, 1860

INDUSTRY	RANK[1]	NUMBER OF EMPLOYEES	VALUE OF PRODUCT ($ MILLION, CURRENT)	VALUE ADDED ($ MILLION, CURRENT)
Cotton goods	1	114,955	$107.4	$54.7
Lumber	2	75,595	104.9	53.6
Boots and shoes	3	123,026	91.9	49.2
Flour and meal	4	27,682	248.6	40.1
Men's clothing	5	114,800	80.8	36.7
Iron (cast, forged, rolled, and wrought)	6	48,975	73.2	35.7
Machinery	7	41,223	52.0	32.6
Woolen goods	8	40,597	60.7	25.0
Carriages, wagons, and carts	9	37,102	35.6	23.7
Leather	10	22,697	67.3	22.8

Source: *Eighth Census of the United States (1860): Manufactures*, pp. 733–742.
[1]Rank by value added.

1850s. By contrast, geographic concentration marked the cigar-making and plug-tobacco industry. Richmond, Virginia, had some 40 tobacco houses employing 2500 slaves in 1860, and other major centers developed in Philadelphia, St. Louis, and Louisville. Cotton ginning and sugar crushing were done on the plantation site. In food canning, though the technology was available at an early period, significant commercialized activity was concentrated mainly in eastern and Pacific-coast fish-packing plants.

The iron industry

The pattern of development in the iron industry was shaped both by market factors and by basic changes in technology. On the supply side, the industry was dependent upon local sources of wood (for charcoal) and iron ore. Until development of canals and railroads, the iron smelters had to be located close to their raw materials. On the demand side, in the early period the iron makers were dependent on an essentially agricultural market: They turned out wrought iron for blacksmiths and bar iron for the craftsmen who made finished metal products. Gradually industrialization basically transformed their market. By the 1850s the iron makers were producing on a large scale for independent factory-organized industries such as machinery manufacturing, locomotive building, and agricultural implement production. Among the technological innovations that made the shift possible were improvements in puddling and rolling; the use of anthracite coal in furnaces, beginning in the 1840s; and specialization in production of such products as rails and structural iron. Thus in iron making, as in textiles, a dramatic increase in the capitalization of mills and in the scale of production by the leading firms took place.

Meanwhile, railroads, canals, and lake ships carried Ohio and Great Lakes iron ores to Pittsburgh and other milling centers, freeing the industry to concentrate in a few locations. In turn, the availability of inexpensive iron — produced by new techniques, in specialized forms, and on an ever increasing scale by large firms — served as a stimulus to American manufacturing generally, in competition with foreign industrial producers.

LEADING INDUSTRIES AND THE INDUSTRIAL REGIONS

The three leading industries in 1860, ranked by value of their products, were flour and meal ($249 million), cotton goods ($107 million), and lumber ($105 million). A slightly different rank order is obtained when the basis is *value added by manufacture:* the difference between cost of raw materials and value of final product. Table 11–1 illustrates rank by the value-added measure, with data also on the number of employees as reported in the 1860 census—a source only partially accurate, but still the best summary of data for that period available.

TABLE 11–2. MANUFACTURING REGIONS, 1860

SECTIONS	NUMBER OF ESTAB- LISHMENTS	CAPITAL INVESTED	NUMBER OF LABORERS	ANNUAL VALUE OF PRODUCTS
New England	20,671	$ 257,477,783	391,836	$ 468,599,287
Middle states	53,387	435,061,964	546,243	802,338,392
Western states	36,785	194,212,543	209,909	384,606,530
Southern states	20,631	95,975,185	110,721	155,531,281
Pacific states	8,777	23,380,334	50,204	71,229,989
Territories	282	3,747,906	2,333	3,556,197
Total	140,533	$1,009,855,715	1,311,246	$1,885,861,676

Source: *Eighth Census of the United States (1860): Manufactures*, p. 725.

The location of industries

The location of American industries was determined by chance in some cases, but more commonly by economic factors. The Northeast asserted its leadership in manufacturing in colonial times and continued to hold first rank. New England, with little good agricultural soil but gifted with abundance of waterpower, an active commerce, and a thrifty, energetic, closely settled population, was especially fitted for manufacturing, though the area lacked important raw materials. The Middle Atlantic states were favored by more varied mineral resources, by direct routes to the interior, and by a greater supply of capital and labor, but were handicapped by competing agriculture and the constant draining off of their population to the West. Nevertheless, important centers for textiles and other manufactures arose near the waterpower furnished by the Mohawk, the Hudson, and the Delaware, and in New York, Newark, Paterson, Philadelphia, Rochester, and Pittsburgh, which were located on routes of travel or accessible to coal and iron. The early years of the century also gave promise of considerable manufacturing in the Piedmont regions of Virginia and the Carolinas, but the absorbing interest in agriculture prevented any great development until after the Civil War, although such successful enterprises as Gregg's cotton mills at Graniteville, South Carolina, and the Tredegar ironworks at Richmond proved that this handicap might be overcome.

Far more important than the South was the region of the Ohio River, where considerable manufacturing existed prior to 1860. Pittsburgh specialized in many forms of ironware; Cincinnati, until 1850 the only town west of the Alleghenies with a population of 100,000, was a great center for meat packing and the manufacture of machinery, clothing, whiskey, and other commodities; Louisville produced cordage, bagging, and clothing; and Chicago was developing large milling and packing interests. The products of New England and the middle states in general were of a type requiring detailed manufacturing with finer mechanisms and involving higher labor costs. Thus textiles, boots and shoes, rubber goods, clothing, glassware, pottery, and cutlery were centered there. Data on regional distribution of manufacturing in 1860 are given in Table 11–2.

INDUSTRIAL WORKERS

A developing country still settling a vast frontier, the United States experienced a relative scarcity of labor despite its high rate of population growth. The rise of the factory-organized industries and the expansion of economic activity generally created demands for new skills, on the one hand, and, on the other, rendered some old skills obsolete. In some localities, workers organized fairly successfully to maintain their wages and status; elsewhere they failed. For some occupational groups, industrialization and economic growth meant a rise in opportunity; for others it brought a measure of grinding hardship. Hence the historian finds it difficult to generalize about "the worker," a task made all the more perplexing by the lack of statistical data that would reliably help tell the story of wages, employment, and union organization.

Mill workers

Foreign observers often commented that workers were generally enjoying a higher level of living in America than in contemporary Europe. Of particular interest to them were the mill towns of New England, which were lauded as model communities offering a happy contrast with dreary factory towns in the Old World. Initially the Massachusetts mill owners attracted young farm girls by providing them with lodging in supervised boardinghouses and access to libraries, organized religious and educational activities, and other trappings of a contrived gentility. The point at which the provision of amenities verged over into an intolerable paternalism is hard to discern. In any event, it is known that from the start the hours of work were long (sunrise to sunset); and after artificial lighting came into wide use in the 1830s, many workers were required to be at the machines 14 hours a day. By the 1840s the boardinghouse atmosphere and services had begun to disappear, and workers complained widely of the "speedup": Machines were run at ever higher speeds or the girls were each required to tend a greater number of looms.

The speedup was only the most dramatic among many management practices that fell hard on workers. Owners held the laborers to tight schedules, and insubordination was punished with fines. Chronic "troublemakers" were blacklisted; that is, their names were circulated among nearby factories to make certain they could find no other employment when they were discharged. Workers often were paid in cash only at long intervals, up to several months' time, or they were paid in scrip that could be used only in company stores.

By 1850 the golden age of paternalism was dead. The girls were departing the mills, to be replaced by Irish immigrants who came into New England in great numbers after the famine in Ireland in 1846. Skilled textile workers were displaced as machines took over their work, and wages were forced down. In short, the mill towns began to reflect the harsh mores of an impersonal marketplace.

Child labor

Although children commonly worked (and were worked hard) on family farms, their treatment in American factories reflected vividly the increasing severity of industrial life. In some New England factories, children made up between 20 and 40 percent of the work forces, and some as young as ten years of age were required to stay at the machines all day. In the eastern industrial cities in the 1840s, mortality rates for immigrant children were twice as high as the rate for the native born, a result of disease in the tenement districts and of the taxing work typically done by such children in dirty, unsanitary factory buildings.

Traditional skills

The depersonalization of work, the skilled laborers' loss of status and ultimate displacement, and the harsh discipline of the large mills were portents of what the factory system and modern industrialization held in store for rising numbers of workers. But even in the 1850s the great majority of the labor force was not in the mills. There were still a great variety of skilled crafts, semiskilled and unskilled jobs, and local job-market differences from place to place. Technological revolution had not yet displaced the traditionally skilled laborers in the building and printing trades, sailmaking and shipbuilding, carriage making, and a large number of other trades in which the apprenticeship system, sturdy independence, and a chance to make good wages still persisted. In every town and city there were workers who found employment in small family shops. As late as 1820 it was still possible to characterize urban society as one in which "the lines between worker and owner were blurred despite an obvious coexistence of rich and poor."[8]

Opportunity did not die out overnight for the skilled workers. In many crafts, the technology did not change enough to threaten the status of skilled workers before the Civil War. Indeed, a persistent shortage of trained persons during good times was what attracted British and other European skilled workers to American shores:

> Lancashire cotton printers came to new centers of their trade such as Lowell; thread spinners from the mills of Ulster and Paisley came to Newark . . .; iron puddlers and rollers from Germany and the English Back Country found work in Pittsburgh; Scottish and English "engineers" became American "machinists"; Staffordshire potters made Trenton and East Liverpool [New Jersey] the American centers of their trade. . . . [There were also] the English, German, and French woolen spinners of Lawrence, the Kilmarnock and Kidderminster carpet weavers and Nottingham hosiery spinners at Philadelphia, the Macclesfield silk weavers of Paterson, English and German cutlers in Connecticut, English paper-

[8] Sam Bass Warner, Jr., *The Urban Wilderness: A History of the American City* (New York: Harper & Row, 1972), p. 79.

makers and glovers, and—all across the country when new mills and cities were going up—English and Scottish bricklayers, masons, and other building tradesmen.[9]

Together with traditional craft trades, traditional modes of industrial organization, styles of work, attitudes toward work, and status relationships also survived. For example, in Pennsylvania mining towns, the miners' families grew vegetables and raised some livestock to help maintain a decent standard of living. Down in the mines themselves, the men typically had similar backgrounds; kinfolk worked side by side, and common ethnicity (most of them were Scottish and English) was an important social bond. Workers of this sort usually dealt with a manager or owner of similar ethnic background even of common social origins in the working class.

Wages and social mobility

There was a significant gap between skilled workers and common labor—a gap that was evident in their ways of thinking about themselves and their status, in their wages, and in their responses to industrialization.[10] Wages alone can tell much of the story. Whereas women and girls in New England mills earned as little as 25 cents a day in the 1830s, and male mill workers were paid $5 a week from 1830 to 1860, skilled craftsmen in the building trades could count on $10 a week or more in times of full employment. (For skilled workmen with the means to own homes there was also the possibility of extra income from taking in boarders.)

Whether *real wages*—money wages adjusted for changes in the buying power of the dollar—actually rose after 1830 is a subject of much dispute among historians. The best estimates available to us suggest rising real wages, perhaps even a doubling, from 1800 to 1830 or to the late 1830s. But after the Panic of 1837 the situation changed, and deterioration of workers' standard of living seems to have been general. For most of the skilled crafts, for factory work, and certainly for common labor, average real pay in the years just before the Civil War probably was not much above the levels of 1835.[11]

And so we confront a paradox: From the mid-1840s to 1860, the very period when industrialization and the economy's output were on a sharp upswing, slippage in wages and a decline of living levels beset many workers. Several factors accounted for this development. First, the average size of plant in many industries increased, and employees now were subjected to factory discipline, instead of retaining a degree of autonomy as workers in small shops. Second, many industries adopted new types of labor-saving machinery, reducing the demand for skilled labor and forcing many workers in traditional crafts down into the ranks of common labor. Third, the acceleration of economic activity and the ongoing technological revolution caused wide resort to wage cutting, speedups, and the like as instruments of survival for businesses caught in a competitive squeeze. Fourth, there was an enormous influx of new immigrants, including a vast number of unskilled Irish workers, increasing the available pool of the unskilled. Their presence in turn may well have increased manufacturers' incentives to adopt labor-saving machinery that permitted them to shift from use of skilled workers to use of common laborers.

The result was not only the weakening of wage scales generally, but also a growing gap between the wages of common labor and wages of the surviving skilled craftsmen.[12] Also, while some native-born workers moved up into expanding white-collar employment, life for the lower-class urban citizen, especially the immigrant, grew far worse in the years after 1845. Boston, for example, was converted from "a densely settled into an overcrowded city" in the

---

[9]Rowland Berthoff, *An Unsettled People: Social Order and Disorder in American History* (New York: Harper & Row, 1971), pp. 165–166.

[10]On working-class culture and cleavages, see generally Herbert G. Gutman, "Work, Culture, and Society in Industrializing America, 1815–1919," *American Historical Review*, 78 (1973): pp. 531–588. On the way the differing attitudes of skilled and common laborers affected the contemporary efforts to form effective unions, *see* pp. 169–170.

[11]The best data we have on urban wages are for Philadelphia, where industrialization had advanced farther than in most cities prior to 1830. Common labor in Philadelphia enjoyed a doubling of real wages from 1790 to 1830, although this 40-year period embraced several short-term downward fluctuations. Real wages for the Philadelphia skilled worker increased by 50 to 100 percent from 1800 to 1830 (Donald R. Adams, Jr., "Wage Rates in the Early National Period: Philadelphia, 1785–1830," *Journal of Economic History*, 28 [1968]:420).

[12]This gap between skilled and unskilled was reflected in the wealth of occupational groups. Again Philadelphia data are most complete. The 1860 data for that city show the wealth of bricklayers, carpenters, and coach makers averaging from $3371 to over $4000; but wealth holdings of common laborers averaged only $180 and of domestic servants only $328 (Stuart Blumin, "Mobility and Change in Antebellum Philadelphia," in *Nineteenth-Century Cities,* ed. Stephen Thernstrom and Richard Sennett [New Haven: Yale University Press, 1969], pp. 168–169, 198).

space of a decade, and slums appeared in all the major industrial centers,[13] (White-collar workers and other higher wage groups could afford to move out to the burgeoning suburbs, whose expansion was expedited by introduction of the streetcar in the 1820s and the railroad later on. The central city meanwhile deteriorated.) Inevitably the quality of management-labor relations was affected by such changes. The growing social gulf between common workers and managers, the fracturing of ethnic homogeneity, and the growth in scale of firms all fostered new, harder attitudes toward the worker and working families' welfare.

There was still a measure of upward social mobility. The proud tradition of apprenticeship, which allowed a young man to become a journeyman and then a master, continued to flourish in skilled crafts. And doubtless many who could not realistically hope to escape the lower class still waited for a better future. But the more common prospect for many skilled workers was loss of status. Hence urban workers flocked into new organizations of all kinds — benevolent societies, church groups, lodges, and clubs — in a quest to maintain their sense of community. Among these organizations, labor unions were one important type, as workers sought to arm themselves more effectively in an increasingly tense confrontation with the new industrial order.

EARLY LABOR ORGANIZATIONS

The early American labor movement, down to the mid-1830s, involved only the skilled craftsmen, was localized in only a few industrial towns, and was slow to gain strength. As late as 1834, only some 30,000 workers were union members, in a work force of over 3 million free laborers. Moreover, many of the men who held membership in the local unions — printers, cordwainers, carpenters, and other skilled workers — were essentially small businessmen seeking to institute minimum prices at which they would contract their services; they were not wage employees in the same sense as modern factory workers, or as mill workers of their own day. The organizations they formed, which often were benevolent associations as much as unions, were typically ephemeral, lacked continuity of leadership, and proved weak in confrontations that involved strikes or boycotts.

Obstacles to unionization

One serious obstacle to successful organization was the uncertain legal status of labor's two most powerful weapons, the strike and the boycott. Frequently local and state courts ruled that such actions constituted criminal conspiracy, as defined in the common law. Then a Massa-

chusetts decision, *Commonwealth* v. *Hunt* (1842), ruled that unions as such were not conspiracies; they could do anything that the individual worker legally could do. The Massachusetts ruling was widely adopted in other states, and not until the 1880s did conspiracy law reemerge as a leading weapon of employers against unions. But other obstacles to successful organization were no less serious. Among them were these:

First, employers could easily use the classic technique of "divide and conquer." Skilled workers scorned cooperation with the unskilled, and in many industries employers could shift over to use of unskilled labor when they were confronted with strikes or alleged unreasonable demands by the skilled. Such organization as there was involved the skilled; and as machine technology displaced this group in many industries, the best-organized element in the labor force lost leverage in the marketplace relations with employers.

Second, the frequent recessions and depressions that hit the economy made it difficult for labor organizations to sustain internal unity or to control their local labor markets. The influx of immigrants after 1845 had the same effects.

Third, it was a complex and difficult matter to achieve effective internal organization. The early local unions failed to form alliances across craft lines, and they did not succeed in allying themselves (even within craft lines) with sister unions in other cities than their own. The employment before 1830 of full-time union offi-

[13]Oscar Handlin, *Boston's Immigrants,* rev. ed. (Cambridge: Harvard University Press, 1958), p. 89. The heavy Irish immigration into Boston in the decade after 1845 brought 230,000 foreigners into the city, pushing Boston's population up by a third. Meanwhile, Boston's suburbs were growing in population even more rapidly than the central city. Thernstrom and Sennett, eds., *Nineteenth-Century Cities,* p. 249.

cials, the pooling of strike funds, and other techniques that later became common were virtually unknown.

Political action

The boom conditions of the mid-1830s placed laboring men in a stronger bargaining position, and this period witnessed a sudden growth of union membership to perhaps as many as 100,000 by 1837. But the depression of 1839–1844 virtually wiped out the gains just accomplished. Thus the pattern was established: trade-union membership rose in periods of prosperity, declined in periods of depression. The ensuing years found workers adopting a new strategy, geared to achieving their goals through political action in alliance with reformers interested primarily in other problems, such as public schools, land reform, and equal taxation. These early unions also strove to extend the franchise and end imprisonment for debt. There were also numerous utopian movements, which sought to reorganize workers in producers' cooperatives, new communitarian settlements, and the like. In the eastern cities, moreover, some leaders of the skilled workers formed political alliances with the Jackson Democratic party or organized their own Workingmen's parties, seeking strict regulation of corporations, control of banks, hard money, and wider opportunity for small-scale enterprises. None of these movements enjoyed more than transitory success, and many never got off the ground.

The ten-hour day

Meanwhile there was a movement to institute the ten-hour day, which won greater popular support than utopian schemes. The ten-hour movement initially gained impetus from the efforts of mill girls and other factory workers in New England. By the mid-1840s many states had enacted laws mandating the ten-hour day, but they were only partially responsive to labor demands: Most of them covered only women and children, and in no state was enforcement vigorously pursued.

National unions

In the 1850s organized labor entered a more aggressive phase of development. As had been true 20 years earlier, general prosperity stimulated labor organization, and again the emphasis was on old-line unionism in the skilled crafts, with narrowly focused bread-and-butter issues brought to the fore. Many local craft unions were revitalized, and some determined strike efforts were launched to gain higher pay. Workers also supported the organization of national unions, at least ten of which were launched, including the Typographical Union (1850), the Hat Finishers (1854), the Stone-Cutters (1855), and national unions of both machinists and iron founders (1859). These groups put aside utopian goals and concentrated on wages, hours, seniority, working conditions, and demands that employers engage on an industry-wide basis in collective bargaining. Craftsmen who were themselves employers of others were often excluded from the new unions, and there was a new concern with building up strike funds and other elements of organizational strength. But hard times following the Panic of 1857 dealt these organizations a serious blow. Their unity and strength eroded as craftsmen had to compete with unemployed and immigrant workers amidst widespread unemployment in every industrial city. Thus only a few national unions survived in 1860. Vital experience had been gained, however, in militant craft unionism.

THE BLACK WORKER

Although the vast majority of Afro-Americans lived as slaves before the Civil War, the numbers of blacks who attained free status were hardly negligible: From fewer than 100,000 in 1790, the number of free blacks rose to 348,000 in 1830 and some 600,000 by 1860. As the northern states moved toward abolition of slavery, there began a northward migration of free blacks; even by 1830, about half their number lived in the North. In the South as well as other regions, the free blacks tended to cluster in towns and cities.

They were heavily concentrated in domestic service, common labor, and the crafts in the South. But there was also a free-black labor aristocracy in the skilled trades: blacksmithing, barbering, and other crafts. In the 1840s and 1850s most of the southern states imposed restrictions upon blacks' admission to certain trades, in addition to imposing severe codes

TABLE 11–3. POPULATION OF THE UNITED STATES, 1790–1860

YEAR	WHITE	NONWHITE	TOTAL
1790	3,172,006	757,208	3,929,214
1800	4,306,446	1,002,037	5,308,483
1810	5,862,073	1,377,808	7,239,881
1820	7,866,797	1,771,656	9,638,453
1830	10,537,378	2,328,642	12,866,020
1840	14,195,805	2,873,648	17,069,453
1850	19,553,068	3,638,808	23,191,876
1860	26,922,537	4,520,784	31,443,321

Source: U.S. Census of 1910, vol. 1, p. 127.

affecting the right to meet with slaves, to be on the streets after a curfew hour, and so on. Black craftsmen in the North began to suffer from similar measures against them in the 1850s, the result of racial prejudice and competition with white workers. Especially resented by the whites was the near-monopoly position that free blacks had attained in the restaurant, hotel, and barbering trades. European immigrants who entered the urban labor markets after 1845 were often involved in hostile encounters with blacks, who meanwhile were subject to increasingly severe housing segregation.

Black labor and the unions

Organized union labor everywhere in the North was exclusively white. Whether native-born or immigrant, the union leaders seemed uniformly antagonistic to black laborers. Bitter attacks on blacks culminated in race riots in Phil-

adelphia, where, as W. E. B. Du Bois has written, white workers' hostility forced blacks out of the skilled and semi-skilled trades and by the mid-1830s had "pushed the black artisans more and more to the wall."[14] The labor unions were frequently in the vanguard of efforts to obtain legislation barring black immigration to northern states, and in 1863 (in the midst of the Civil War) Irish and native-born blue-collar workers were prominent in mobs that ran riot when black strikebreakers came to New York, with resultant casualties running perhaps as high as 10,000. Among labor spokesmen, only utopian socialists, German radicals, and a tiny minority of native-born white laborers were willing to espouse the cause of racial equality as a labor goal.

Limits of the American dream

In all the places where free blacks clustered, there were a few professional people among their ranks who joined with those who had managed to build successful businesses and who became leaders of their communities. This élite group provided black leadership in the formation of benevolent societies, social organizations of other types, and black schools, joining the black churches in helping to sustain their cultural life and institutions. While the Afro-American communities certainly harbored their own version of the American dream—acquisition of property, social standing, and legal equality—it was a remote prospect for all but a few in the years before 1860.

POPULATION AND LABOR

Population increase and the coming and going of a mobile work force were constant elements in the pre-1860 American labor scene. The threefold growth in population between 1790 and 1830 (see Table 11–3) was attributable mainly to a high birth rate in this new land, where large families meant more hands to work the farm or take wage employment to supplement the parents' income. The birth rate has been estimated at 50 to 55 per 1000, which is about twice the rate of the 1960s in the United States and even higher than in most of the less developed countries today. The death rate was about 20 to 25 per 1000 in the period before 1830.

There was apparently a gradual decline in the birth rate after 1835, probably to the low 40s by 1860, and there was a slightly lesser

death-rate decline. Probably delay of marriage to later average age played a considerable part in bringing down the birth rate. Meanwhile, rising numbers of immigrants helped to maintain the overall population growth rate of about 34 percent each decade: a doubling of population every 25 years (see Figure 11–1). This rate was sustained despite an apparent rise in mortality in some of the larger cities, where slum conditions, poor sanitation, and crowding among the urban poor bred epidemics. "Consumption" (tuberculosis), smallpox, and cholera were all major killing diseases. Malnutrition probably took a toll as well, not only

[14]W. E. B. Du Bois, *The Philadelphia Negro* (Philadelphia, 1899), p. 33.

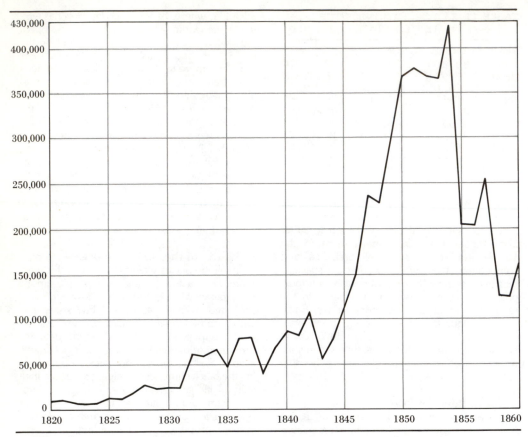

Figure 11–1.   **Immigration into the United States, 1820–1860.** Source: Eighth Census, 1860, *Preliminary Report.*

among the urban poor but also fairly widely in the backwoods South. Advances in public health before 1860 were not impressive, and probably 25 percent of deaths resulted from infectious diseases.

Mobility and urbanization

Two major population trends of the pre-1860 period were the continual westward shift of the population center and the rising concentration in cities. Americans moved from place to place at astonishingly high rates: Some careful local studies of local urban work forces have shown that 75 percent or more of sample groups moved within two decades' time. By 1850 about half the total population lived in the region west of the Alleghenies, with an estimated 4 million eastern-born people having moved beyond the mountains. Farm people also left the older rural areas for the cities, and the great bulk of the post-1845 Irish immigration settled

in the eastern urban centers. The proportion of total American population living in urban places (2500 or more residents) rose from only 5 percent in 1790 to 9 percent in 1830, and then to 20 percent in 1860. The 1840s saw the highest urbanization rate in American history.

Immigration

Immigration amounted to less than 10,000 a year until 1825, then rose gradually until 1845, when the potato famine in Europe caused a sudden increase (see Figure 11–1). In fact, never in the nation's history since 1790 had the number of immigrants been so high in proportion to American population as during the late 1840s. The Irish who poured in during the great migration were largely from agricultural areas or had worked as common laborers. This was in sharp contrast to earlier immigrants, dominated by Britons, who had included a large proportion of skilled workers. An important characteristic of the immigration as a whole was the large proportion of young, working-age people who immediately entered the labor market. In short, the immigrants who were attracted by employment opportunities and higher wages in America, or who left the old country because of the "push" factors, such as the famine or the revolutions on the European continent in 1848, offered the United States a great fund of muscle and skills to fill labor needs.[15]

Those immigrants who came with little education or to escape grinding poverty found their opportunities restricted to the lowest paying, lowest status jobs. Thus by 1860 the foreign-born comprised the majority of common laborers in the industrial cities. They also constituted most of the labor force on the crews that built canals and railroads and in other types of backbreaking heavy work. The young women in the immigrant populations of the cities mainly obtained jobs as domestic or personal servants. Paid little and working long hours, these women staffed many middle-class homes as well as virtually all upper-class residences in an era when housework was aided by few mechanical devices.

For the people who found only this kind of labor in the Promised Land, after a long journey across the Atlantic, the cycle of poverty was hard to break, and hard to bear. And as the industrial cities grew rapidly in the 1840s and 1850s, so too did the slums and urban blight that became a seemingly permanent part of the American urban landscape. At the same time, immigration represented a vast transfer of growth-stimulating human capital from Europe to America.

SELECTED READINGS

General works

*Bruchey, Stuart, *The Roots of American Economic Growth* (New York: Harper & Row, 1965).

Davis, Lance E., et al., *American Economic Growth* (New York: Harper & Row, 1971).

*North, Douglass C., *Economic Growth of the U. S., 1790–1860* (Englewood Cliffs: Prentice-Hall, 1961).

*Taylor, George Rogers, *The Transportation Revolution, 1815–1860* (New York: Holt, Rinehart and Winston, 1951).

Industry before 1861

Clark, Victor S., *History of Manufactures in the United States,* Volume I: *1607–1860* (Washington: Carnegie Institution, 1929).

Chandler, Alfred D., Jr., "Anthracite Coal and the Beginnings of the Industrial Revolution in the United States," *Business History Review,* XLVI (1972).

*Cochran, Thomas, *Business in American Life: A History* (New York: McGraw-Hill, 1972).

*———, *The Inner Revolution* (New York: Harper & Row, 1964).

Coleman, Peter J., *The Transformation of Rhode Island, 1790–1860* (Providence, R.I.: Brown University Press, 1963).

David, Paul, *Technical Choice, Innovation, and Economic Growth* (Cambridge, Eng., Cambridge University Press, 1975).

Gibb, George S., *The Whitesmiths of Taunton* (Cambridge, Mass.: Harvard University Press, 1943).

Gilchrist, David, and Lewis, W. David, eds., *Economic Change in the Civil War Era* (Greenville, Delaware, Eleutherian Mills-Hagley Foundation, 1965).

*Habakkuk, H. J., *American and British Technology in the Nineteenth Century* (Cambridge, England: Cambridge University Press, 1962).

Kranzberg, Melvin, and Purcell, C. W., Jr., eds., *Technology in Western Civilization* (New York: Oxford University Press, 1967), Volume I.

*Rosenberg, Nathan, *Technology and American Economic Growth* (New York: Harper & Row, 1972).

---

[15]Of 2.8 million immigrants during 1846–1854, some 44 percent were from Ireland and 32 percent were from Germany.

Strassmann, W. P., *Risk and Technological Innovation* (Ithaca: Cornell University Press, 1959).

*Struik, Dirk J., *Yankee Science in the Making,* rev. ed. (New York: Collier Books, 1962)

Temin, Peter, *Iron and Steel in 19th-Century America* (Cambridge: MIT Press, 1964).

Ware, Caroline F., *The Early New England Cotton Manufacture* (1925, reprinted New York: Johnson Reprint Corp., 1972).

Zevin, Robert Brooke, "The Growth of Cotton Textile Production after 1815," Robert W. Fogel and Stanley Engerman, eds., *The Reinterpretation of American Economic History* (New York: Harper & Row, 1971).

Urbanization and Demography

*Callow, Alexander B., ed., *American Urban History,* 2nd ed. (New York: Oxford University Press, 1972).

Gilchrist, David, ed., *The Growth of the Seaport Cities, 1790–1825* (Charlottesville, Va: University Press of Virginia, 1967).

*Handlin, Oscar, *Boston's Immigrants* (Cambridge: Harvard University Press, 1959).

Pred, Allan R., *The Spatial Dynamics of U.S. Urban-Industrial Growth, 1800–1914* (Cambridge, Mass.: MIT Press, 1966).

*Thernstrom, Stephan, and Sennett, Richard, eds., *Nineteenth-Century Cities: Essays in the New Urban History* (New Haven: Yale University Press, 1969).

*Ward, David, *Cities and Immigrants: A Geography of Change in Nineteenth-Century America* (New York: Oxford University Press, 1971).

Warner, Sam Bass, Jr., *The Urban Wilderness: A History of the American City* (New York: Harper & Row, 1972).

Williamson, Jeffrey G., "Antebellum Urbanization in the American Northeast," *Journal of Economic History,* XXV (1965).

The American Worker

Berthoff, Rowland, *British Immigrants in Industrial America* (Cambridge: Harvard University Press, 1953).

Commons, John R. et al., *History of Labour in the United States* (New York: Macmillan, 1918).

Gutman, Herbert G., "Work, Culture, and Society in Industrializing America, 1815–1919," *American Historical Review,* LXXVIII (1973).

Knights, Peter R., *The Plain People of Boston, 1830–1860* (New York: Oxford University Press, 1971).

Montgomery, David, "The Working Class of the Preindustrial American City, 1780–1830," *Labor History,* IX (1968).

Sullivan, William, *The Industrial Worker in Pennsylvania, 1800–1840* (1955, reprinted New York: Johnson Reprint, 1972).

Taft, Philip, *Organized Labor in American History* (New York: Harper & Row, 1964).

Walker, J. E., *Hopewell Village* (Philadelphia: University of Pennsylvania Press, 1966).

*Ware, Norman, *The Industrial Worker, 1840–1860* (1924, reprinted Chicago: Quadrangle Books, 1964).

Warner, Sam Bass, Jr., *The Private City: Philadelphia in Three Periods of Its Growth* (Philadelphia: University of Pennsylvania Press, 1968).

Deeply rooted sectional differences between the North and the South had existed since colonial days — differences in regional economies, social structures, political attitudes, and cultural preferences. The spread of the Cotton Kingdom and the rising importance of the slave plantation served to intensify these differences. And the issue of whether slavery should be permitted in the vast new territory taken from Mexico in 1848 intensified still further the already dangerous divergence of sectional views.

When the militant demands of the northern abolitionists began to win favor in the 1850s, weakening existing party organizations and leading to new coalitions, spokesmen for the South began to watch the census returns with a growing sense of foreboding. The rising industrialization of the North, together with an immigration influx and natural population increase, indicated that the passing of time could destroy the balance of political power between North and South. When the new Republican party forged an alliance in 1860 between northeastern industrial interests (who favored high tariffs) and northwestern farmers (who wanted free land under a homestead law), southern pro-slavery leaders were appalled. The Mississippian Jefferson Davis, soon to become leader of the secessionist South's new government, declared that the Republicans' real motive was a desire "that your section . . . grow in power and prosperity upon treasures unjustly taken from the South."[1] Similarly, other southern leaders predicted the triumph of abolitionism, along with a high-tariff policy that would build up the North at the South's expense.

Consistent with this sort of evidence, many scholars have argued that economic differences made a civil war inevitable. The war, as one has written, was "nothing less than a conflict between two different systems of economic production." The election of Lincoln in 1860 represented the triumph of "the young industrial capitalism of the North and Middle West."[2] For the southern states, only secession and (if necessary) war remained — their only recourse for defending the very fabric of their unique social and economic system, based upon agrarian institutions and slavery.

Before accepting so sweeping an economic interpretation of the Civil War, we must recognize that despite the intensity and long standing of sectional differences, the federal union did endure for 70 years. The recurrent conflicts were resolved through normal political and constitutional processes, even in serious crises such as the confrontation over the tariff and nullification in 1831 and 1832. It is doubtful that economic self-interest alone can explain why the South became increasingly belligerent and prone to resist national power in the secession crisis. In fact, a plausible explanation of the Civil War, and of the popular fears and beliefs that heated the fires of rebellion, must take account of moral, ideological, and political attitudes, including an element of the irrational.

[1] Quoted in Charles Beard and Mary Beard, *The Rise of American Civilization* (New York: Macmillan, 1930), vol. 2, pp. 5–6.

[2] Louis Hacker, "Revolutionary America," in *The Causes of the Civil War*, ed. Kenneth M. Stampp (Englewood Cliffs, N.J.: Prentice-Hall, 1959), p. 64.

SOUTHERN ECONOMIC DEPENDENCE

One economic reality of the antebellum period that was perceived and resented by many southerners was their region's dependence—what some of them bitterly termed economic vassalage—in relation to the North. Northern financial institutions provided credit to southern planters; the manufactured goods consumed in the South were mainly produced in the North or imported by northern mercantile houses; the marketing of cotton was largely in the hands of middlemen (jobbers, factors, and commission merchants) who depended upon northern merchants or were themselves northerners. The cotton exports of the South were generally carried in northern-owned ships; the cargoes were insured by northern firms; and the cotton—like imports from Europe—usually passed first through northeastern ports.

In reality, this was a condition of regional interdependence, not one-way dependence. The northern business interests profited handsomely from these relationships—so handsomely that they were heavily in favor of reconciliation with the South when secession came in 1861. Moreover, to depend upon northern mercantile, shipping, and banking services was rational economic behavior for southern planters: Their capital was probably better invested, and certainly more easily watched, when it was devoted to the production of their staple export crops. But in a real sense, the North–South economic relationship did tie the planter to cotton in a way that could be perceived as entrapment. If cotton prices fell, the planter had to borrow to carry on his operations until the next year's crop came in; and if he was to be assured of future cash returns with which to discharge the debt, more cotton had to be planted. If prices were high, as was more usual from 1843 to 1857, planters tended to put their earnings into more land and slaves in order to increase production. Either way, the drift was toward ever-increasing investment in plantation agriculture.

Southern options

Certainly one alternative to this reliance, or dependence, upon the North was diversification of the South's commercial farm production. But only a few of the larger planters had the leisure, the capital, and the operating margin to experiment; and in fact they usually did so mainly when cotton prices were depressed. As soon as prosperity returned, southern efforts were typically redirected to the staples that were sure to bring profitable cash returns.

Another option was for the South to diversify its economy more broadly by promoting investment in manufacturing. In fact, commercial men and planters in the South held numerous meetings and formal conventions to urge just such a course. But they ran up against the fact that the region's capital was heavily tied up in land and slaves, as southern investors exploited the region's comparative advantage in production of staples.

An even more serious long-run problem was the nature of the consumer market in the South: A large proportion of southerners were black slaves kept at the subsistence level, "poor white" farmers and herdsmen, and yeoman farmers with only small cash incomes. The development of towns and cities—with their labor forces, their capital for industrial investment, and their advantages of agglomeration—required a society in which income and buying power were more broadly distributed than they were in the South.[3] Whereas a third or more of the population in New England and the Middle Atlantic states lived in cities in 1860, in the South urban residents comprised less than 10 percent of the regional total.

THE PECULIAR INSTITUTION

Lying behind the lack of flexibility that might have stimulated regional economic diversification of some kind was slavery, an institution that set the South apart from the rest of the nation and indeed most of the Atlantic world. The South's political leaders were always concerned that any basic reorientation of the southern economy would put in motion a set of social changes that would jeopardize a fixed, inherited system of race relations as well as a massive propertied interest.

In cotton the South found a crop especially

[3]Eugene D. Genovese, "The Significance of the Slave Plantation for Southern Economic Development," *Journal of Southern History,* 28 (1962):422–437.

well suited to slave labor. The implements used in its cultivation were simple, and slaves could be worked in gangs under constant supervision. The long growing season meant profitable exploitation of the labor force, which had to be fed and housed year round. Maintenance costs for slaves were kept at a minimum, and rural isolation of the large plantation was advantageous in controlling and disciplining the slaves.

The varieties of slaves' work

On the plantation there was some diversity in the slave-labor force and the way it was used. Some of the more fortunate blacks were made household servants. Among the rest, some were employed at such crafts as carpentry or blacksmithing, and on the larger plantations a small number were used as drivers in charge of slave gangs, mediating between the field hands and the white overseer. Work in the fields was carried on by the task system, in which a specified amount of work was assigned to each slave daily, or by the gang system, in which minute-by-minute supervision assured that the pace of work would be kept up. On smaller plantations and farms whose owners held only a small number of slaves, the field hands might simply be sent to work with no organization and no incentive other than fear of the lash.

The overseer

As the size of plantations grew and absentee ownership became more common, the role of the hired overseer became increasingly important. There were about 19,000 overseers in the South in 1850 and 38,000 a decade later. Many were of the poor-white class and were treated with contempt by other whites. But there was also an overseer élite, which generally enjoyed high social status and provided the entrepreneurial talent needed to sustain the growth of the plantation system in the staple-crop areas. Judged chiefly by his ability to produce a large crop, the overseer was likely to drive slaves to the limit and abuse the land.

Blacks and the law

The cruelties inflicted upon slaves on the plantations to keep them subordinate were part of a larger complex of social and racial controls in the southern states. As we have seen, "black codes" were enacted in nearly every southern state, setting restrictions on the movement of slaves and black freedmen, requiring passes or other identification, imposing penalties for resistance to authority, and more generally expressing vividly the fear with which the white population confronted the possibility of slave

TABLE 12–1. PERCENTAGE INCREASE OF POPULATION, WHITE AND SLAVE, 1840–1850

STATE	WHITES	SLAVES
Virginia	20.8%	5.2%
Maryland	31.3	0.7
Kentucky	29.0	15.8
Arkansas	110.2	136.3
Mississippi	65.1	58.7
Louisiana	61.2	45.3

Source: John F. Cairnes, *The Slave Power*, 2nd ed. (1863), p. 130.

uprisings. Laws were enacted to put severe legal limits upon manumission, and capital punishment was mandatory for many crimes of blacks against whites. Vigilante action and lynchings were also common during the scares such as those which followed Nat Turner's rebellion in 1831.

The slave trade

The demand for slaves to work the South's land was met both by natural increase and by importation from Africa, though the latter was illegal after 1807. In the border states and the eastern Carolinas, slaves were regularly shipped to the Southwest for sale to the planters in the new states. The rising prices of slaves after 1845 gave new impetus to the internal slave trade, and exportation of blacks from the border states probably well exceeded 25,000 a year during the 1850s. For the older coastal areas and the border states, slavery continued to be economically feasible during the pre-1860 decade at least in part because it was possible to realize income through such sales.[4] In the course of the slave trade, black families were broken up and the inherent degradations of bondage were intensified. Tables 12–1 and

[4]Seeking to demonstrate that slavery was a profitable form of investment for planters, Alfred H. Conrad and John R. Meyer estimate as part of returns on investment the profits and costs of rearing and selling slave children ("The Economics of Slavery," *Journal of Political Economy*, 66 [1958]: 95–122). Recently Robert W. Fogel and Stanley Engerman, in *Time on the Cross: The Economics of American Negro Slavery* (Boston: Little, Brown, 1974), have minimized the importance of the sizable slave trade from the Old South to the Southwest; but on this, as on other main interpretive issues, their contention flies in the face of the evidence adduced by other scholars. See Kenneth Stampp, *The Peculiar Institution* (New York: Knopf, 1956); Clement Eaton, *The Growth of Southern Civilization, 1790–1860* (New York: Harper & Row, 1961), pp. 49–55; and two critiques of Fogel and Engerman, "Slavery: The Progressive Institution?" by Paul David and Peter Temin, in *Journal of Economic History*, 34 (1974):739–783; and Richard Sutch, "The Treatment Received by American Slaves," *Explorations in Economic History*, 12 (1975):335–448.

TABLE 12–2. SLAVE POPULATION AS PERCENTAGE OF TOTAL POPULATION, 1790–1860

STATE OR REGION	1790	1810	1830	1840	1850	1860
Border states	32%	30%	29%	27%	25%	22%
Delaware	15	6	4	3	3	2
Maryland	32	29	23	19	16	13
Virginia	39	40	39	36	33	31
North Carolina	26	30	33	33	33	33
Kentucky	16	20	24	23	22	20
Missouri	—	15	18	15	13	10
Tennessee	10	17	21	22	24	25
Lower South states	41	45	46	46	45	45
South Carolina	43	47	54	55	58	57
Georgia	36	42	42	41	42	44
Alabama	—	—	38	43	44	45
Florida	—	—	45	47	45	44
Mississippi	—	36	48	52	51	55
Louisiana	—	45	51	48	47	47
Arkansas	—	—	15	20	22	26
Texas	—	—	—	—	27	30
All southern states	34	33	34	34	33	32

Source: U.S. Census, 1860, *Population*, pp. 599–604.

12–2 illustrate the dimensions of this trade as it affected population-growth patterns in the older states and the new.

Nonagricultural slave labor

Not all slaves lived in rural areas or worked on plantations or small farms. It has been estimated that in the 1850s about 5 percent of the South's slaves, or about 200,000, were employed as construction workers and industrial laborers. Though most of them were located in rural towns, some 15,000 were urban industrial workers. Tobacco factories, hemp plants, brickmaking establishments, mines, and railroad labor crews sometimes were racially integrated; more often, the Old South industrialist who maintained slaves operated with an all-black work force. Railroad-construction firms, white master artisans, and farm owners seeking extra seasonal labor all resorted extensively to slave hiring as well, usually at a rate of 10 or 15 percent of the going price for slaves for a year's work.[5]

Black freedmen

The few slaves who gained their freedom by manumission or by purchase—there were only 262,000 freedmen in the South in 1860, of a black population of 4.4 million—lived under trying conditions, which grew worse in the 1850s. In 1820 some 37 percent of urban residents in the South were blacks, but in 1860 the proportion was down to 17 percent. The decline in relative numbers was the result of deliberate policies adopted by many municipalities to discourage urban living by free blacks, who were feared because they developed their own churches and other associations, formal and informal, and their own social life. Many cities adopted ordinances barring blacks from various urban occupations. These deliberate policies had the intended impact: Many urban slave-holders sold their slaves out into the countryside, while the attractions of the city were much diminished for the freedmen.

THE ECONOMICS OF SLAVERY

The census of 1860 gave the white population of the slave states as 8 million and the slave

[5]Clement Eaton, "Slave-Hiring in the Upper South," *Mississippi Valley Historical Review*, 46 (1960):663–678; Edward Phifer, "Slavery in Microcosm," *Journal of Southern History*, 28 (1962).

population as nearly 4 million. But the distribution of slave ownership revealed a startling concentration of this human property: Fewer than 400,000 whites were slave owners, so that if one takes an average slaveholder's family as five persons, only about 2 million whites were directly interested in slavery through proprietorship. Furthermore, only a small minority of white families were directly involved in the economy of the large-scale plantations. About 107,000 owned ten or more slaves, and of these 11,000 held 50 or more. At the top of this hierarchy were the slightly more than 300 families that owned 200 slaves or more each. The median slaveholding in the South as a whole in 1860 was 23, and in the lower South it was 33.

Within individual states, the areas of large plantations and concentrated slave ownership tended to be restricted. On the coast of Georgia, for example, slaves comprised 70 to 80 percent of total population, whereas inland in Georgia the proportion ranged from 11 to 60 percent. In Mississippi, the 1860 census showed that five-sixths of the farm units with 200 or more slaves were concentrated in a few river counties. In the alluvial district of Louisiana, seat of cotton and sugar production, lived only a fourth of the state's white population, "but this minority owned half the wealth, two-thirds of the slaves, and nearly half the plantations [farms of 50 acres or more] in Louisiana."[6]

The plantation aristocracy

The wealthy planters with large slaveholdings, therefore, constituted a tiny minority of southern society. But their influence in the politics, the social life, and the shaping of the region's self-image was pervasive and controlling. The lawyers, urban businessmen, and others who held public office in the region recognized full well how heavily the South's economic welfare depended upon the vitality of King Cotton. If this were not enough, the suffrage laws and districting of legislative representation served for many years to assure control by the plantation aristocracy. There was also a manifest tendency in the South for poorer whites to follow a pattern of political deference, leaving control of government to the "better people." Moreover, the planters were expert at playing upon racial prejudice and fears. In a hundred ways they conveyed the message that any crack in the solid wall of black slavery might topple the whole system that gave even the poorest white higher status than any black. Controlling the political system, the plantation aristocracy made southern law responsive to its needs; both the statutes and the judges functioned to maintain discipline and control over the slave population.

Voices of dissent

There were a few dissenting voices in the South that argued against slavery on moral or economic grounds. Among the most prominent dissenters was Hinton R. Helper of North Carolina, who wrote that slavery was impeding economic progress in the South, causing poverty among the white population, and hampering efforts at diversification. The Lexington, Kentucky, newspaper editor Cassius M. Clay asserted that slave labor was more expensive than wage labor: Slaves were inefficient because they were denied formal education as a matter of policy; the billion-dollar capital they represented was tied up, "a dead loss to the South;" and, finally, Clay declared, slavery was hindering the growth of manufacturing. Other critics of southern society echoed these themes.

Slavery: profitable or unprofitable?

Charges of this sort, condemning slavery as an economically inefficient labor system, have long intrigued historians. Indeed, at one time many prominent historians of the South believed that slavery was unprofitable and probably would have died out without the trauma of civil war and emancipation by presidential proclamation. Analytically, there are two separate questions to be considered: whether slavery profited the planters as individual business proprietors and whether slavery was a burden or a benefit to the southern regional economy. Recent research confirms an assessment that *for the individual planter* slavery was a rational investment, as the average return on an investment in slaves (about 10 percent) compared favorably with what the investor could have realized from placing the capital in alternative forms of enterprise.[7] Of course, the profitability of slave investment on a particular farm or plantation depended upon that unit's other fixed costs, its distance from markets, the fertility of its land, its efficiency in using slave labor, and related factors; but *average* returns support the notion of profitability.

The second analytical question, whether slavery constituted a burden or a benefit to the southern economy, is more complex. Here the focus shifts from the private profitability of slaveholding to slavery as a labor system, as an instrument to govern race relations, and as the central issue in southern political life. This larger issue requires a different perspective, embrac-

---

[6]Roger W. Shugg, *Origins of Class Struggle in Louisiana* (Baton Rouge: Louisiana State University Press, 1939), p. 7; Charles Sydnor, *Slavery in Mississippi* (New York: Appleton-Century, 1933), p. 193. In several of the Louisiana parishes, median size of slaveholdings was between 117 and 175.

[7]See Conrad and Meyer, "Economics of Slavery", and Stanley Engerman, "The Effects of Slavery upon the Southern Economy," *Explorations in Entrepreneurial History,* 2nd ser., 4 (1967).

ing matters such as education and immigration as well as narrow questions of profit and loss on the annual balance sheet of individual farm units. It also requires consideration of slavery and cotton culture on the long-run potential of the South for regional economic development.

The dynamic South

It would be incorrect to view the South as stagnant or hopelessly behind in the process of economic growth prior to 1860. On the contrary, the region's economy was dynamic. Both cotton culture and the slave-plantation system spread vigorously into the Southwest; the region's agricultural output rose steadily, and in boom periods spectacularly, in response to world demand for cotton; and southern per capita income rose at nearly the same rate as income in the national economy from 1840 to 1860. Despite economic dependency, the South's plantation aristocracy lived well and indeed lavishly—witness high consumption of imported luxuries—and there is no reason to assume that a region's dedication to cash-crop staple production will, in itself, necessarily cause output or average per capita incomes to lag.

The unbalanced South

There were, however, several features of the regional economy and southern social structure that reflected an unhealthy lack of balance. First of all, personal income on a per capita basis in the South was only 77 percent of the national average in 1840, and only 80 percent in 1860. Second, there was a persistent concentration of wealth in relatively few hands. Thus in 1860 the top 1.2 percent of the South's white population (a group that included planters with 40 or more slaves) garnered 20 percent of the region's income.[8] This degree of wealth concentration was not radically different from distribution of wealth in other regions and at other times. What made it a problem, so far as long-term development of the South was concerned, was the fact that members of the South's élite tended to reinvest their capital in further expansion of the plantation system within their own region, or—more ominous still for the South—in railroad and bank stock, mortgages, and other forms of investment *in the North.* Hence reinvested earnings tended heavily either to fix the plantation system even more firmly on the South or to drain funds out of the South alto-

gether. In either case, the investment pattern did not operate to broaden economic opportunity or enhance the welfare of the vast numbers of small white farmers and poor whites who produced only marginally for cash markets (to say nothing of the slaves or their welfare, damaged in much more devastating ways).[9]

There was lack of balance, too, in regional economic structure, as manufacturing and commercial activity remained at low levels. Finally, there was an imbalance within the region as a whole that revealed how slender a base plantation agriculture provided for vigorous economic development over the long run. In the North generally, the longer an area had been settled, the higher the average income level. In the South the pattern was reversed. There the older Atlantic coastal regions consistently lagged behind the fast-growing Southwest, where new plantations were being put into production. Growth rates were slower in the South Atlantic states from 1840 to 1860, and absolute dollar income per capita was lower.[10]

There seems little doubt that this dismal economic legacy was functionally related to slavery, for slavery was an obstacle to immigration into the region (the South's foreign-born population in 1860 was only one-fifth the proportion of immigrants in New England), since most newcomers did not wish to compete with slave labor or even live and work in a slave society. The conscious policy of keeping slaves uneducated had militated against expenditures for public education generally; and indeed the general level of public spending on social-overhead facilities of all kinds was lower in planter-dominated slave states than elsewhere in the nation. Finally, the lack of manufacturing and commerce, and the consequently low level of southern urbanization, provided little in the way of a viable base for further development once the heyday of agriculture had passed in the older regions and the soil was worn out. The tragedy of this legacy may be seen in the fact that the South Atlantic region's income would probably have been even lower than it was had there not been a steady trade in sale of its slaves to newer plantations in the Southwest.

"There is a kind of rapid growth that produces the conditions for successful growth in a

[8]Engerman, "Effects of Slavery," 88–89, 96 n. But see Gavin Wright, "Economic Democracy and the Concentration of Agricultural Wealth in the Cotton South, 1850–1860," *Agricultural History,* 44 (1970): 79–85.

[9]Morton Rothstein, "The Antebellum South as a Dual Economy," *Agricultural History,* 41 (1967):381.

[10]M. Fischbaum and J. Rubin, "Slavery and the Economic Development of the American South," *Explorations in Entrepreneurial History,* 2nd ser., 6(1968): 123, 125. See also the extended commentaries on Fogel and Engerman by Bertram Wyatt-Brown and William N. Parker, in *Reviews in American History,* 2 (1974):457–474.

later period," one recent study contends, "while there is another kind of rapid growth that produces precisely the conditions for later stagnation."[11] It is obvious which type the South experienced, and the central importance of the slave system in fixing a pattern of growth on the South that led to stagnation seems equally manifest, as will be seen below (p. 212).

Southern politics and perspectives

By the 1850s the question of the South's adherence to the slavery system was no longer negotiable. The entire political and social life of the region was dominated by the slave interest. One of slavery's costs, as Douglas Dowd has written, was "the suppression of that kind of social rationality which has been, for better or for worse, associated with the development of industrial capitalism."[12] By the same token, the obsessive southern concern to maintain slavery as an institution led ineluctably to a rising aggressiveness and intractable political postures whenever white supremacy seemed to be even remotely threatened. Southern spokesmen viewed the extension of free labor into the West as a menacing development in the 1840s and 1850s, and the editor of the leading southern commercial journal, *DeBow's Review*, warned of an ominous "contest for the wealth and commerce of the great valley of the Mississippi." Jefferson Davis's accusation that the northern Republicans sought to "grow in power and prosperity upon treasures unjustly taken from the South" (quoted earlier in this chapter) was but one example of many that some historians cite as evidence of a growing southern paranoia that excited hysteria in the 1850s, and ultimately pushed the South to secession and war.

Whether or not one accepts literally the notion that southern fears were paranoid, certainly southern reactions to a host of specific issues—especially constitutional issues—had the effect

of escalating conflicts, transforming policy matters into confrontational traumas. And perhaps the very nature of slavery made such a transformation of issues inevitable. For abolitionist sentiment gained in respectability and acceptance in the North, despite continuing attacks on its legitimacy, throughout the turbulent 1850s; and its moral fervor understandably aroused deep fears on the part of southern proslavery leaders that any compromise or concession on their part would prove to be a step on the road to abolition by congressional fiat. It may well be true, also, that southern leaders were pushed into irrational behavior by their own inability to back down. As late as the 1830s, southerners had been seriously debating abolition in the constitutional conventions of several states. Now, as the historian Charles Sellers contends, southern spokesmen were

> forced to smother and distort their most fundamental convictions by the decision to maintain slavery; and goaded by criticism based on these same [liberal Christian] convictions, southerners of the generation before the Civil War suffered the most painful loss of social morale and identity that any large group of Americans has ever experienced.

According to this view, slavery had involved the southern mind so deeply "in its contradictions that [southerners] could neither deal with it rationally nor longer endure the tensions and anxieties it created."[13]

To be sure, such excursions into the realm of abnormal social psychology may appear out of place in an economic history of the Civil War era. But they are highly relevant if, as seems to have been true, the strictly economic dimensions of both the slavery system and of the conflict between North and South were only a fragment of the realities as they were then perceived.

THE CIVIL WAR

When the guns were fired at Fort Sumter in 1861, neither President Lincoln's administration nor the newly forming government of the Confederacy was prepared for the kind of pro-

tracted conflict that would follow. Nor, of course, were the profound consequences of the war for the national economy and its long-term course of development anticipated.

---

[11]Fischbaum and Rubin, "Slavery," p. 125.

[12]Douglas F. Dowd, commentary on Conrad and Meyer, "Economics of Slavery," *Journal of Political Economy*, 66 (1958):441.

[13]Charles G. Sellers, Jr., *The Southerner as American* (Chapel Hill: University of North Carolina Press, 1960), pp. 51–52, 71. See also David Brion Davis, *The Slave Power Conspiracy and the Paranoid Style* (Baton Rouge: Louisiana State University Press, 1969).

The population of the eleven states that formed the Confederacy was under 9 million, of whom 3.5 million were slaves. The population of the states remaining in the Union numbered over 22 million, and the northern labor force was augmented by continuing immigration during the war. Of crucial importance to the North's ability to fight a long war was the fact that it controlled 90 percent of the nation's manufacturing industries, as well as most of the merchant ships and fighting ships of the U.S. Navy. Southern leaders based their hopes upon (1) the fact that many of the most experienced regular army officers and Mexican War veterans cast their lot with the Confederacy; (2) the prospect of a defensive war on southern territory, at least initially, which would help to neutralize the North's advantage in men and resources; and (3) the importance of cotton, which the South expected would finance the war effort and, if necessary, bring British intervention on the side of the Confederacy because Britain required American cotton to keep its textile industry going.

Mobilization of manpower

The early mobilization, in 1861, was accomplished in the same manner as in America's earlier wars. That is, both in the North and in the South volunteers were accepted individually or in organized units to serve in the regular armies, while militia calls were made upon the states. But after the first flush of enthusiasm for war evaporated, and a protracted struggle loomed ahead, volunteering proved inadequate to the needs of both sides. With only about a million men between the ages of 15 and 40, the South had to resort first to conscription, in April 1862. Exemptions were granted to men in occupa-

tions deemed essential to the war effort, including government officials, large-scale planters and their overseers, and technical personnel on railroads and steamboats; but labor shortages nevertheless appeared in the industrial sector. By the end of the war the Confederacy was conscripting partially disabled men to work in government-controlled mines and factories; slaves were "impressed" (that is, drafted for government service); and women and children were widely used in jobs formerly filled by men. By 1864 the southern government—often over vigorous objections by state governors and legislatures, and in the face of some strong popular resistance—was also seizing foodstuffs and other supplies for use by the beleaguered armies.[14]

By contrast, the manpower policies of the Union represented only modest governmental intervention for the allocation of labor. The North never had to resort to conscription or impressment to maintain mines, factories, and transport facilities, and it supplied its armies with horses, food, and industrial products by purchases from private firms. Whereas the South called into its fighting forces about 90 percent of the able-bodied white men under age 40, the Union drafted at most 60 percent of such men. Nonetheless, the Union did have to resort to national conscription in 1863, but the law permitted any draftee to arrange to pay a substitute to fight in his place—giving substance to the charge that it was a rich men's war but a poor men's fight. Some 20 percent of the Union soldiers were immigrants, and about 220,000 of them were blacks. In the last months of the war, the Confederacy authorized the use of blacks as soldiers, perhaps the ultimate paradox of the tragic conflict.

THE NORTHERN ECONOMY

The secession crisis created a panic and depression in the North in mid-1861, because of the uncertainties it threatened and especially the immediate loss of some $400 million owed to northern merchants and bankers by southern firms and individuals. But in 1862 there was a strong revival of the economy in the North and West, stimulated by Union spending to supply a growing army.

Agriculture

Domestic and foreign demand for foodstuffs was a stimulus to northern farming and contin-

ued new farm making in the West. Under the 1862 Homestead Act, granting 160 acres of land to actual settlers, a million acres of land were brought into farms: there was active homesteading in Minnesota, Wisconsin, Iowa, Nebraska, California, and Kansas. Prices of the major cash crops rose 50 to 100 percent during

---

[14]A total of 60,000 civilians was employed directly by the Confederate government in industrial and mining facilities. (Paul P. Van Riper and Harry N. Scheiber, "The Confederate Civil Service," *Journal of Southern History,* 25 [1959]: 457–458).

TABLE 12–3. STATISTICS OF AGRICULTURE DURING THE CIVIL WAR

	1859	1863	1864	1865
Wheat from northern farms (million bushels)	139	191	161	149
Corn from northern farms (million bushels)	547	451	530	704
Value of pork, beef, corn, and wheat products exported by the North ($ million, current)	28[1]	128	94	82
Wool production in the North (million pounds)	60[1]	–	–	140
Exports of southern cotton to Britain (thousand bales)	2,581	132	198	462
Number of reapers on wheat farms (thousands)	125[2]	–	–	375

Sources: Emerson D. Fite, "Agricultural Development of the West During the Civil War," *Quarterly Journal of Economics,* 20 (1906), for all data except those on northern exports, which are found in Paul W. Gates, *Agriculture and the Civil War* (New York: Knopf, 1965), p. 227.

[1]Data for 1860.
[2]Data for 1861.

the first two years of the war, because of both monetary inflation and rising European and American demand. With more than 600,000 new farms having been established in the West during the 1850s, the northern farmers responded with significant advances in output and capital input. (See Table 12–3.) Moreover, in the older farming regions of the North, many producers shifted to specialty crops, increasing the region's production of tobacco, wool (which was in great demand by the army for blankets and uniforms, and was substituted for cotton), dairy products, and orchard crops. Unexpected surges in European demand—the result of crop failures there—caused swift price increases for wheat, corn, and meat products.

Although women and children often took the place of men called from their farms to the armies, it was the rapid progress of mechanization that accounted for the North's ability to meet wartime demands at home and simultaneously sustain the outflow of foodstuffs from 1861 to 1865. Agricultural prices reached their nineteenth-century highs during the war years, and farm prosperity was evident. Higher farm incomes supported extensive new purchases of labor-saving equipment. Sales of reapers and mowers, for example, rose from an average of 16,000 machines annually in the five years before the war to an average of 50,000 annually during the years of fighting.

Manufacturing

The Union government gave out enormous private contracts for arms, clothing, blankets, wagons, gun-carriages, and other goods required by the military forces. For the industrial sector in the North, the war years brought hectic change, expansion in some segments of manufacturing and contraction in others, numerous opportunities for spectacular profits, the introduction of new products, and significant increases in the scale of production in many factories.

For the cotton textile industry, reliant upon the South for its raw material, there was a decline in production as soon as surplus stocks were exhausted. But trouble in the cotton mills worked to the benefit of the woolen firms. Many woolen companies paid dividends of 25 to 40 percent to stockholders during each year of the war, and by 1864 over 200 million pounds of wool per year were being woven, as against less than half that amount in the late 1850s.

Rising foreign and domestic demand for meat induced a rise of output in the packing plants, and Chicago emerged during the war as the leading center of pork packing. The leather industry, too, was stimulated by wartime needs for shoes and boots, harness leather, belts, and other products. In the machinery industries, farm implements manufacturing made probably the most spectacular gains, but the needs of expanding factory output aided the machinery industry as a whole. Nevertheless, the war years were not a time of expansion for norther manufacturing overall; indeed, the 1860s saw the slowest rate of manufacturing growth for any decade between 1840 and 1900.

The petroleum industries and mining

A new branch of industry that had its beginnings in the war period stemmed from the oil strikes at Titusville, Pennsylvania, in 1859 and the development of new oil-refining processes. By 1865 oil had become the sixth-ranking item in the nation's foreign exports. The use of kerosene for illumination immediately spread, too, in every major city of the North; but despite the vast expansion of the domestic market, more kerosene was exported than was sold at home, a unique phenomenon in American manufacturing. During the war, new mineral resources were also discovered in the Far West, as Nevada's Comstock Lode of gold and silver and Colorado's Gregory Lode were opened up; and perhaps 200,000 people flocked to the Rocky Mountain mineral areas during the war years.

Railroads, the telegraph, and urban construction

The war gave impetus to the process of consolidation in the railroad and telegraph industries. Although new railroad mileage constructed fell off from peacetime levels, military traffic meant increased railroad profits; and several major lines used their new revenues to integrate operations and buy up connecting roads. The Pennsylvania railroad companies began to tighten their grip on coal production in the anthracite region, and both New York City and Philadelphia improved their rail connections by consolidating lines in the midwestern region. Among the new lines planned or financed in the war years, the most important was the transcontinental railroad, aided by congressional land grants and cash. The Union Pacific laid its first rails in 1865, heralding a new era in American transport and resolving a long-time conflict between northern and southern interests on this question.

There was also extensive urban construction during the war years. Large investments in new building, both of housing and of industrial or commercial structures, took place in Chicago, San Francisco, and other cities, as well as in specialized manufacturing centers.

Shipping

The stream of capital that went into new enterprises during the war contrasted with a decline after 1861 in American merchant shipping, which was hurt by the sharp drop in cotton exports, the damage inflicted on Union vessels by Confederate ships, and rising insurance rates. Scores of ships were sold to European firms, and registered U.S. tonnage in foreign trade declined from 2.5 million tons in 1861 to 1.5 million at the war's end.

The war and northern business

The decline in merchant shipping and in the cotton textile industry while railroads and woolen mills prospered, the swift rise of petroleum, and the replacement of King Cotton with food-stuffs in foreign trade, all indicated the range of business vicissitudes brought about by the war. Scores of individual fortunes were made, and many an industrial statesman (or robber baron) of the postwar years made his start by being in the right business in the right place during the Civil War. Also, established companies reinvested their wartime profits in the introduction of assembly-line processes or new lines of products; and in many industries, rising scale of production raised the cost of entry for potential competitors seeking to make a start. There was also a distinct trend toward greater coordination within industries. Among the national trade associations that were newly organized or which greatly expanded their activities during the war were the American Iron and Steel Association, the National Association of Wool Manufacturers, and the National Woolgrowers Association. Some historians have argued, moreover, that the war gave a whole generation of industrial entrepreneurs invaluable experience with the techniques of modern large-scale organization in production, distribution, and finance.[15]

Inflation, fiscal policy, and wages

Structural changes in American industry were accompanied by a significant shifting of the government's financial burdens. Federal expenditures rose from $66.5 million in 1861 to $474.8 million in 1862 and reached $1.3 billion in 1865. Although new excise taxes and an income tax (1863) were levied, the conflict was financed mainly through borrowing and the issue of paper money. Under a law of February 1862, the Treasury embarked upon the issue of "greenbacks"–non-interest-bearing notes backed by the general credit of the United States. The greenbacks were made legal tender, and over $400 million of them were issued. Metallic money practically disappeared, and banks generally suspended specie payment on their paper in December 1861. The greenback issues were supplemented by interest-bearing bonds, sold in government loan drives on varying terms and redeemable at various future dates. Only a fourth of war expenditures were met by taxation, and in September 1865 the public debt stood at $2.8 billion, the high point of federal debt until World War I.

[15]Chester McA. Destler, "Entrepreneurial Leadership Among the Robber Barons," *Journal of Economic History,* 6, Supplement (1946): 28–49; Allan Nevins, *The War for the Union,* vol. 2: *War Becomes Revolution* (New York: Scribner, 1960), chap. 19.

TABLE 12–4. NORTHERN WAGES AND PRICES DURING THE WAR

	1861	1862	1863	1864	1865
Index of wholesale prices (1850–1859 = 100)	103	120	152	221	211
Consumer price index (1851–1859 = 100)	102	114	141	178	177
Index of real wages, skilled workers (men) (January 1860 = 100)	98	88	74	67	85
Index of real wages, unskilled workers (men) (January 1860 = 100)	98	87	79	79	86

Source: U.S. Congress, *Employment, Growth, and Price Levels*, 86th Cong., 1st sess., Joint Economic Committee, *Hearings*, April 7–10, 1959, pt. 2: "Historical and Comparative Rates of Production, Productivity, and Prices" (Washington, D.C.: U.S. Government Printing Office, 1959), pp. 395, 397; *Historical Statistics of the United States, Colonial Times to 1957* (Washington, D.C.: U.S. Government Printing Office, 1960), p. 90.

Some historians have argued that this heavy government borrowing "crowded out" private borrowing for capital investment during the war years, thus reducing the rate of private capital formation. But this is a controversial view—much of borrowed public funds went into paying for contracts that, in turn, generated private profits that could be reinvested by business firms in new plant. (We know, for example, that some northern railroads were able to make considerable new investment in track and equipment by using wartime profits instead of borrowing.) Because we lack year-by-year data on capital formation for the war period, this interpretive question remains in dispute.

Coming into circulation under the impact of federal deficits and simultaneously with sharply rising demand in the economy, the greenbacks contributed to an inflationary price situation.

(At no time during the war were the greenbacks traded at par with gold; in the summer of 1864 they fell to 39 cents in relation to the gold dollar.) As prices soared, labor was hard put to keep real income from falling behind. The cost of 60 articles of prime necessity, weighted according to quantities of such articles consumed, is estimated to have increased 125 percent during the war years. The consumer price index, shown in Table 12–4, went from 102 to 177 during the war period. Entry of 800,000 immigrants into the northern labor market also kept pressure on wages. Finally, militating further against workers' real income was the wide range of protective tariffs newly instituted during the war, as the Republicans delivered on an 1860 campaign promise. The plight of wage earners is illustrated by the data in Table 12–4.

THE SOUTHERN ECONOMY

A major influence upon the South's wartime economy was the blockade that the U.S. Navy threw around the entire Atlantic and Gulf coast perimeter. The blockade successfully cut off the cotton trade with Europe, and immediately the traditional basis of the region's economy was jeopardized. As Union armies pushed south and east after 1862, the navy drew the iron ring tighter, subjecting the Confederacy to relentless economic pressure. At every southern port, blockade runners challenged the war fleet of the Union, carrying both imports and exports in small quantities for soaring prices and profits. But despite smuggling through Union lines and Mexico, and despite blockade running, the real hopes of the Confederacy had to rest on a massive reorientation of its entire economy.

Manufacturing

Up to the opening of the Civil War, practically all the region's industrial machinery had been produced in the North, and the rich coal and iron deposits of the South had scarcely been tapped. Consequently, from nearly the very start of the war, the Confederate government had to undertake centralized control and ownership of manufacturing, together with allocation of labor and raw materials. There were no precedents for this in American history. Except for war-related goods, such manufacturing as the South enjoyed went into decline. Government plants manufactured guns and small arms, powder, salt, clothing, blankets, and other goods. Raw cotton was carefully allocated to privately owned textile mills, which were scattered throughout the Southeast in small numbers. Military conscription laws provided for exemption of enough workers to assure that the factories could work full-time. There was a massive return to simple household production and hand industry for the manufacture of many goods formerly imported from the North or Europe and now unavailable or in short supply. Household workers, mainly women, also improvised substitutes for coffee and other products whose importation was cut off by the blockade.

By 1864 a succession of military defeats and chaotic inflation were disrupting the South's manufacturing efforts. Rapid devaluation of Confederate paper currency made it virtually impossible for the government to purchase goods in the open market, and so forcible impressment (confiscation, in effect) became imperative. This removed all profit incentives, of course, leaving only southern patriotism to motivate producers. And patriotism eroded disastrously: for southern morale disintegrated amidst widespread suffering, mass desertions by Confederate troops (many of whom received no pay, even in the worthless government notes, because of disrupted Treasury operations), and news of southern losses on the battlefields. In the last months of the war, the vicious cycle of demoralization and the increasingly harsh onslaught by the Union armies undermined any coherence that was left in the Confederacy's economic support of the war effort.

Agriculture

The Confederacy's initial diplomatic strategy was based on King Cotton diplomacy: the belief that Europe's need for southern cotton would force intervention by Great Britain on the side of the Confederacy, or at least that the loss of cotton supplies would cause enough economic distress in the North to make the Union sue for peace. Hence in May 1861 the Confederate congress prohibited exportation of cotton to the North. Meanwhile the central government urged cotton planters to diversify their production, and especially to increase output of foodstuffs. At first the planters resisted. But by 1863 food shortages had forced a new emphasis on corn and livestock, while stockpiled cotton rotted or was burned to prevent capture by Union forces. The distribution of food was badly disrupted by the destruction of southern railroad facilities, and when Union forces closed the Mississippi in mid-1863, they cut off the meat

and other food supplies of Texas from the eastern half of the Confederacy.

To protect their citizens against sharply rising prices, Richmond and other cities undertook regulation of markets and prices. Some southern states forbade the distilling of liquor, in order to conserve grain. But as the invading and defending armies alike seized farmers' and planters' stores, cut off distribution lines, and impressed livestock for their forces, the local food shortages grew worse and contributed to the loss of southern morale, both military and civilian.

Finance and the currency

From the outset of the war, the South's central government resorted to the printing press to meet its obligations. By 1864 the Confederacy had put over $1 billion of paper money into circulation. The currency fell to $1.20 to the gold dollar in 1862, then to $7 in 1863, and to $21 in 1864. Finally, in the war's last months it circulated at 60 to 1 or worse. Rendered totally worthless by the South's surrender in 1865, the vast currency issues left a legacy of confusion and contributed to economic disruption in the war's immediate aftermath.

Only stringent taxation could have offset the fiscal pressures on the Confederacy, but the government did not turn to taxes until 1863, when it was already too late to stabilize the public finances. Official devaluation of the currency and the desperate expedient of confiscation in 1864 and 1865 did little to restore order. Total borrowing, by domestic bond issues and a loan floated in Europe in 1863, amounted to more than $2 billion, and tax revenues covered only an eighth of this amount.

Inflation

The impact of inflation was staggering. Whenever possible, wage workers sought to be paid "in kind" (in commodities) rather than in paper money, at least late in the war. Money wages rose approximately tenfold during the war, but the cost of living, in terms of representative price indices, rose at least thirtyfold; and in many areas of the South, shortages made it impossible to obtain some goods, even basic foodstuffs at times, at any price. As shortages of skilled workers occurred in 1864 and 1865, there was increasing use of hired or conscripted slaves in manufacturing and construction. Complaining of inadequate pay, inflated prices, speculators' activities, and disruption, one worker wrote the Confederate treasury secretary in late 1863: "We are literally reduced to destitution."[16] By late 1864 the complaint could have been voiced, with entire credibility, by civilians and Confederate soldiers throughout the South.

DID THE WAR RETARD INDUSTRIALIZATION?

The costs of war are difficult to measure, and for the Civil War this problem is especially difficult because of massive social changes that were among the war's major effects. The loss of life was enormous, with over half a million soldiers dead—equivalent to 5 percent of the nation's gainfully employed workers in 1860. Military operations in the South also left a path of destruction so terrible that southern farm output did not regain prewar levels until nearly 1880. (The South's manufactures recovered more quickly, but they had been small in scope in 1860.) Even the termination of slavery had its ironic side: The poverty and wartime losses suffered by southern planters gave the region's whites an incentive to reestablish control over the black labor force by any means. And so even before the Reconstruction military occupations had ended in 1877, most of the South's black workers had become entrapped and tied to the land under an elaborate new legal system of sharecropping, tenancy, crop liens, and labor control amounting to peonage. In turn, this exacted economic costs over the long run, perpetuating many of the effects of slavery as obstacles to industrialization.

The war also exacted costs in the North. We have already considered specific industries adversely affected. In addition, commerce with the South was cut off and inflation contributed to further derangement. But some scholars have argued that in the long run as well the Civil War retarded American industrialization. Their argument pivots on the following data: National commodity output during the Civil War decade (1860–1870) grew by only 23 percent, as compared with growth of 60 percent or more during the preceding decade of the 1850s and also during the succeeding decade, 1870–1880.[17] Further support for the argument that the war retarded growth is derived from the fact that labor productivity in manufacturing did not rise in the 1860s, as it had been rising before and would rise again after 1870. Finally, specific output data for mining, pig-iron, and certain other industries show a slowdown in the rate of increase during the war period. But in ensuing decades (after 1870 and until the end of the century), not only did increases in output of specific commodities accelerate, but the overall production growth rates exceeded the rate of the Civil War decade.

There is another way of interpreting the long-term growth data, however, which suggests instead that the Civil War contributed to an acceleration in the economy's growth during the last 35 years of the nineteenth century. From 1839 to 1859, commodity output per capita rose 16 percent, on the average, during each ten-year period. From 1869 to 1899, however, the comparable growth rate for each decade was 24 percent. Because the destruction wrought in the South was so devastating that slowness of economic recovery there acted as a drag on the overall national economy, it is remarkable that such large average gains should have been registered after 1869. In addition, the wartime advances in scale of production, size of firms and consolidation, and profits available for reinvestment were probably crucial to the basic structural shifts of the post-1865 economy, which in turn stimulated industrialization, integration of many of the heavy industries, and large-scale factory organization.

---

[16]Letter quoted in Eugene M. Lerner, "Money, Wages, and Prices in the Confederacy," *Journal of Political Economy,* 62 (1955): 20–40. Lerner's article is the source of the estimates of Confederate wages and price changes in this text. See also Richard Todd, *Confederate Finance* (Athens: University of Georgia Press, 1954).

[17]Thomas C. Cochran, "Did the Civil War Retard Industrialization?" *Mississippi Valley Historical Review,* 48 (1961): 191–210. The following discussion in the text draws on material in Harry N. Scheiber, "Economic Change in the Civil War Era," *Civil War History,* 11 (1965): 396–411. The case for viewing the war period events as a retardative influence is found in Stanley Engerman, "The Economic Impact of the Civil War," in *The Reinterpretation of American Economic History,* ed. Stanley Engerman and Robert Fogel (New York: Harper & Row, 1971), pp. 369–378.

The new political economy

The war years also brought fundamental changes in certain key national economic policies. The Republican party, assured of control of Congress by withdrawal of the southern representatives, seized its opportunity to write a program of legislation that favored industrialization and stimulated economic growth.

In place of the low-tariff policy that had prevailed since 1846, the Republicans instituted high protective tariffs. Starting in 1862 Congress provided lavish subsidies to railroads, mainly in the form of land grants but also with supplementary loans of credit and cash. The 1862 Homestead Act, together with the railroad-aid measures, assured that the process of westward settlement (and with it extension of the domestic market) would continue as manufacturing developed. Also, in 1862 Congress instituted federal land-grant subsidies for agricultural education and research and for university support of "mechanical arts" under the Morrill Land-Grant College Act (see p. 141).

In 1864 Congress enacted a contract-labor law that legalized the subsidizing of immigrants by manufacturers, who were permitted to bind an immigrant to service in their firms for a specified period of time. Perhaps most important of all, the inauguration of a national banking system, centralizing in the national government the power to charter and regulate banks and imposing a prohibitive tax on state-chartered banks' notes, provided a more stable banking structure than the nation had known. This was an important change from the standpoint of financing the flow of commerce, capitalizing new enterprises, and furnishing a uniform currency.

The new economic program was also notable for what Congress did *not* do: it did not institute regulatory or conservation measures over the use of grassland by ranchers or timberland by lumbering firms, and it did not stand in the way of aggressive private exploitation of mineral resources. Taken as a whole, this program suggests that during the war period Congress took "a long step forward in placing the services of the state at the command of private enterprise."[18]

The reorientation of congressional economic policy was accompanied by a significant shifting of the financial burdens of government. Throughout the period 1790–1860 the main sources of revenue for the national treasury had been customs receipts and the sale of public lands. Nearly overnight the Civil War taxation measures adopted by Congress instituted a revolution in government finance: Stamp and excise taxes were enacted in 1863, and these new sources of revenue, together with an income tax and special taxes on manufactures, accounted for two-thirds of Treasury receipts by the war's end. Both the protective tariff and the new excise taxes worked to the disadvantage of low-income workers during the war, contributing to a sharp downward shift in real wages as inflation pushed prices steadily upward.[19]

Immediately after the war, Congress ended the income tax, which had been mildly progressive (that is, graduated according to income level), and the taxes on manufacturers were rescinded. But the lawmakers kept in effect the excise levies, thereby putting the burden of government costs more solidly onto consumers in general and especially low-income workers. By protecting manufacturers with high tariffs, by keeping natural resources cheaply accessible to entrepreneurs in lumbering and mining, and by shifting the burden of government costs away from producer interests, government policy aided business in its efforts to reinvest earnings in new capital goods. That these same policies contributed to inequalities of income distribution was probably considered a reasonable, and not especially troubling, tradeoff by the congressional policy makers who engineered the new economic program.

To contend that the war retarded the industrialization process in the long run requires an assumption that changes in the 1860s in industrial structure, income distribution, and public economic policy bore no functional relationship to the quickened pace of industrialization in the post-1869 period. Such an assumption hardly seems tenable. Much more compelling is the evidence for the contention that "the Civil War did indeed induce a profound economic disequilibrium and much of the subsequent economic performance (including retardation) in the North can be interpreted as a gradual return to normality."[20]

[18]Louis M. Hacker, *The Triumph of American Capitalism* (New York: Simon & Schuster, 1940), p. 361.

[19] Reuben Kessel and Armen Alchian, "Real Wages in the North During the Civil War," *Journal of Law and Economics,* 2 (1959): 111. See Alfred H. Conrad, "Income Growth and Structural Change," in *American Economic History,* ed. Seymour Harris (New York: McGraw-Hill, 1961), pp. 48–54, on post-1869 intensification of capital formation.

[20]Jeffrey G. Williamson, "Watersheds and Turning Points: Conjectures on the Long-Term Impact of Civil War Financing," *Journal of Economic History,* 34 (1974):661.

SELECTED READINGS

*Andreano, Ralph, ed., *The Economic Impact of the American Civil War,* revised edition (Boston: Schenkman, 1962). (Contains essays, statisitcs, and topical bibliographies.)

Cochran, Thomas C., "Did the Civil War Retard Industrialization?" *Mississippi Valley Historical Review,* XLVIII (1961). (Reprinted in Andreano)

Conrad, Alfred H., and Meyer, John R., "The Economics of Slavery in the Antebellum South," *Journal of Political Economy,* LXVI (1958).

Eaton, Clement, *History of the Southern Confederacy* (New York: Macmillan, 1954).

Engerman, Stanley, "The Economic Impact of the Civil War," in Fogel and Engerman, *Reinterpretation of American Economic History* (New York: Harper & Row, 1971). (Also printed in Andreano)

Fite, Emerson D., *Social and Industrial Conditions in the North During the Civil War* (New York: Macmillan, 1910).

*Fogel, Robert William, and Engerman, Stanley, *Time on the Cross: The Economics of American Negro Slavery* (Boston: Little, Brown, 1973). See the highly critical review essay, "Slavery: The Progressive Institution?" by Paul David and Peter Temin, *Journal of Economic History,* XXXIV (1974). (See also Gutman, Scheiber entries, below.)

Gates, Paul W., *Agriculture and the Civil War* (New York: Knopf, 1965).

*Genovese, Eugene D., *The Political Economy of Slavery* (New York: Knopf, 1964).

Gilchrist, David, and Lewis, W. D., eds., *Economic Change in the Civil War Era* (Greenville, Del.: Eleutherian Mills-Hagley Foundation, 1965).

Gutman, Herbert G., *Slavery and the Numbers Game* (Urbana: University of Illinois Press, 1975). (Critique of Fogel and Engerman.)

*Hacker, Louis M., *The Triumph of American Capitalism* (New York: Columbia University Press, 1940).

Nevins, Allan, *The War for the Union* (New York: Scribner, 1959, 1960).

Parker, William, ed., *Structure of the Cotton Economy* (Washington, D.C. Agricultural History Society, 1970).

Randall, J. H., and Donald, David, *The Civil War and Reconstruction,* 2nd ed. (Boston: D. C. Heath, 1961). (Contains a full bibliography.)

Scheiber, Harry N., "Black Is Computable: The Controversy Over *Time on the Cross* and the History of American Slavery," *American Scholar,* 44 (1975).

——, "Economic Change in the Civil War Era: An Analysis of Recent Studies," *Civil War History,* XI (1965).

"Slavery as an Obstacle to Economic Growth in the United States" (Symposium), *Journal of Economic History,* XXVII (1967).

*Stampp, Kenneth, *The Peculiar Institution* (New York: Knopf, 1956).

*Starobin, Robert, *Industrial Slavery in the Old South* (New York: Oxford University Press, 1970).

Woodman, Harold D., "The Profitability of Slavery: A Historical Perennial," *Journal of Southern History,* XXIX (1963).

Woodman, Harold D., ed., *Slavery and the Southern Economy: Sources and Readings* (New York: Harcourt Brace Jovanovich, 1966).

Wright, Gavin, "New and Old Views on the Economics of Slavery," *Journal of Economic History,* XXXIII (1973).

NOTE: See also works on slavery and the South listed in Selected Readings for Chapter 9.

the early industrial age

part 3

chapter 13
expansion, new frontiers, and economic development after 1865

By the 1860s the United States had already assumed an important position in the world scene as a manufacturing nation. By 1870 this country was producing one-fourth of the world's manufacturing output, and only Great Britain (which produced over 30 percent) was more important. By the mid-1880s the United States had successfully challenged the British lead. In 1900 American industry was producing some 30 percent of world manufactures, compared with 20 percent for Great Britain, 17 percent for Germany, and 7 percent for France. Hence the central question before us, when we confront the experience of American economic growth after 1865, is why the United States became an industrial colossus.

THE CONTOURS OF GROWTH

During the period 1865–1914, population rose from 33 to 100 million. But in the same period, real gross national product (termed "real" GNP because the data are adjusted for price changes) rose approximately sixfold. The rise in output and income was not uninterrupted, of course; there were periods of depression within the 1870s, 1880s, and 1890s, and other cyclical slowdowns. But in the long run, the pace of growth was impressive indeed. The following data provide a fairly reliable indication of the growth pattern, showing real annual GNP per capita expressed in 1929 prices:[1]

1874/1883	*$263*
1879/1888	*$384*
1892	*$457*
1900	*$502*
1910	*$611*

Underlying these gains in GNP were major *structural transformations* in the economy; that is to say, shifts in the basic organization of the economy and the relative roles of various types of production. There was a shift in the sectoral location of the labor force, with a decline in the proportion of agricultural workers and a rise of nonagricultural labor, and there was a dramatic change in the sectoral distribution of income. These major changes are shown in Table 13–1. Expressed in terms of commodity-output shares, the contribution of the agricultural sector fell from more than 50 percent in 1869 to 33 percent in 1899. Meanwhile, the share represented by manufacturing rose from about one-third (1869) to 53 percent (1899). Hence a trend already well established before the Civil War was continued. In absolute measures, the output and income of both agriculture and manufacturing rose; indeed, they both rose spectacularly. Both sectors also increased their efficiency; that is to say, their productivity (output per unit of labor input). But manufacturing

[1]Robert Gallman, "Gross National Product in the United States, 1834–1909," in National Bureau of Economic Research, *Output, Employment, and Productivity in the United States After 1800* (New York: Columbia University Press, 1966), pp. 8–9; U.S. Department of Commerce, Bureau of the Census, *Long-Term Economic Growth, 1860–1965* (Washington, D.C.: U.S. Government Printing Office, 1966), p. 166.

TABLE 13–1. PERCENTAGE DISTRIBUTION OF NATIONAL INCOME AND THE LABOR FORCE, BY SECTOR, 1839–1940

	1839–1859	1869–1879	1889–1899	1919–1940
Labor force				
Agriculture	56.9%	51.9%	41.5%	21.5%
Manufacturing and mining	14.1	20.7	21.8	24.7
All other	29.0	27.4	36.7	53.8
Totals	100.0	100.0	100.0	100.0
National income				
Agriculture	25.8	21.6	15.2	10.4
Manufacturing and mining	14.0	17.5	24.7	26.2
All other	60.2	60.9	60.1	63.4
Totals	100.0	100.0	100.0	100.0

Source: Robert E. Gallman and Edward S. Howle, "Trends in the Structure of the American Economy Since 1840," in *The Reinterpretation of American Economic History*, ed. Robert W. Fogel and Stanley Engerman (New York: Harper & Row, 1971), data underlying Tables 1–3, pp. 26–28. Computations above appear in Lance Davis et al., *American Economic Growth: An Economist's History of the United States* (New York: Harper & Row, 1972), p. 55.

outstripped agriculture. While the number of people engaged in farming, the area of land in farms, and the production of agricultural commodities were making the United States one of the world's leading farming nations, gains in the manufacturing sector (especially after 1890) far surpassed agriculture's record of growth.

SOME OBSTACLES TO RAPID GROWTH

It is a remarkable feature of the growth pattern from 1865 to World War I that enormous growth, at a rate of 4 percent annually, was attained despite some serious obstacles.

Recurrent depressions

The first problem in the way of growth was the impact of business depressions. Unemployment, major declines in output, and widespread social unrest accompanied the two most serious depressions of the nineteenth century, those of 1873–1878 and 1893–1897. Yet in each case the forces impelling economic growth pulled the economy out of crisis, and the long-run pattern was sustained.

Declining prices

A second major problem was the long-term decline in price levels that marked the period from 1865 to the late 1890s. Price deflation was so severe that from the Civil War's end (1865) to 1879 alone there was an estimated 50 percent decline in prices, caused both by monetary factors (movements in money supply, partly in response to governmental fiscal decisions) and by the pattern of technological advances and high investment rates that was pushing produc-

tivity out ahead of demand. Each new advance that brought a cheap substitute product into competition with an established one displaced older occupational skills, drove prices down, and put business firms under intense competitive pressure.

The lag in Southern development

A third problem that served as an obstacle to growth (already considered in Chapter 12) was the persistent lag in the South's regional economy throughout much of the late nineteenth century. Even after the southern farm sector recovered to pre-1860 levels of production (which occurred about 1880), the region's generally underdeveloped institutional structure prevented the South from enjoying its full share of American industrialization or raising its per capita regional income to near the national average. At the end of the nineteenth century, southern per capita income was only 51 percent of the national level.

Foreign competition

Fourth, the world market as a whole was becoming more competitive in the late nineteenth century. American producers of both farm and manufactured commodities had to face the rival efforts of their counterparts in other nations. France and Germany were both industrializing rapidly, and American producers felt the pressures of competition for those markets. Except for England, the European nations raised tariffs and other barriers to freedom of trade—just as the United States did, with its protective tariff policies. Even as the wheat and corn belts spread westward, and as ranching reached out over extensive grasslands in the West, the American producers of foodstuffs and meat found themselves rivaled in the world market by rising production in other countries that had expanding frontiers: Argentina, Russia, Australia. World demand was also expanding, to be sure. But the prosperity of American farmers was hardly uniform, continuous, or very certain in these years of hectic expansion.

Social unrest

Finally, it can probably be argued that periodic social unrest and disorder served to disrupt the pattern of growth. The spirit of the day was one of buoyant optimism, and growth was celebrated as part of the "American way." But a persistent, wide gap separated the rich and the poor in America: Even amidst general optimism it was evident that rising income averages did not mean a uniformly improved quality of life for all groups. The United States experienced a large number of industrial strikes during both the 1870s and the 1890s. Labor radicalism challenged the social fabric in the western mining industries; farm-based Populism shook the political framework in the West and South, and indeed in the nation as a whole, at least indirectly, in the 1890s; and many regions and particular industries suffered stagnation for short or long periods.

THE DYNAMICS OF GROWTH

A major factor underlying American economic growth was the sheer good luck of nature's bounty, a fabulously rich resource base. From the end of the Civil War to about 1910 that resource base was expanded enormously. Settlement moved into the vast western regions; new railroad lines knitted together the national economy and linked new sources of supply with distant markets; and new technologies such as petroleum refining and hydroelectric power production enlarged the potential of the nation's stock of resources. The most direct evidence of how the rapidly expanding resource base affected production is the output data for the major extractive industries: agriculture, mining, lumbering, and fishing. Agricultural output tripled between 1850 and 1890. This increase was achieved partly because of new techniques and machines, but it was also the result of expansion into a vast western region richly endowed with pasture- and cropland. Other measures of extractive industries' growth are given in Table 13–2.

An autonomous growth pattern

One major effect of the vast resource-base expansion that occurred after 1865 was an increasingly *autonomous* pattern of growth. That is, the timing and direction of growth were shaped by new resource exploitation and other factors internal to the American economy. The U.S. economy was now reacting to de-

velopments in the international marketplace to a much lesser degree than it had done before 1860.

Also contributing to the autonomous growth pattern was the process of new investment in capital goods such as urban housing, transportation facilities, machinery, farm buildings, and factories. This investment process, termed *capital formation,* required savings from the society's current income for investment purposes. Domestic savings were augmented by foreign investments in the U.S. economy. So rapid was capital formation in the course of post-1865 development that the total stock of capital goods grew at a rate of approximately 45 to 60 percent during each decade, two to three times the rate of population increase. Gross capital stock per capita, in constant (1929) dollars, was as follows:[2]

1869	*$1,120*
1889	*$1,860*
1899	*$3,250*

Producers' durables and construction

Throughout the years from 1865 to 1914, gross capital formation was at the astonishingly

[2]Simon Kuznets, *Capital in the American Economy: Its Formation and Financing* (Princeton, N.J.: Princeton University Press, 1961), pp. 64–65. Data in the text on gross capital formation as a proportion of GNP are from ibid., p. 95.

TABLE 13-2.   OUTPUT OF SELECTED EXTRACTIVE INDUSTRIES

Product (Units)	1865	1880	1900	1913
Lumber (billion board-feet)	12.8[1]	18.1	35.1	44.0
Iron ore (million tons)	2.2	9.1	27.6	62.0
Copper (thousand tons)	12.8	30.5	303.1	617.8
Lead (thousand tons)	14.7	95.7	367.7	483.1
Bituminous coal (million tons)	12.3	50.8	212.3	478.4
Crude petroleum (million barrels)	2.5	26.2	63.6	248.4
Fish yield (million pounds)	n.a.	1598.0	1831.0	2153.0[2]

Source: *Historical Statistics of the United States from Colonial Times to 1957*, pp. 312–313, 324, 362–370. The 1865 estimate of iron-ore production is from National Bureau of Economic Research, *Output, Employment, and Productivity in the United States After 1800* (New York: Columbia University Press, 1966), p. 323. Used by permission of the National Bureau of Economic Research.

[1]Data for 1869.
[2]Data for 1915.

high level of 22 to 25 percent of GNP during each decade, as shown in Table 13–3. A sectoral breakdown of capital formation indicates the way in which American society was allocating its savings to increase the economy's productive capacity. Table 13–4 provides Professor Kuznets' estimates of increases in the economy's capital stock during three periods from 1880 to 1912. As seen from that table, the total increase in producers' durables was only slightly larger in the 1890s than it was in the previous decade; but while capital formation in the transportation and public utilities sector remained nearly the same, there was a substantial increase in the manufacturing sector and in agriculture. In the period from 1900 to 1912, there was a massive overall rise in capital formation. But producers' durables surged ahead of residential and government construction, pacing the rise. Within the producers' durables segment of capital formation during 1900–1912, all sectors achieved impressive increases over the previous period. But noteworthy after 1900 was the rise in new investment for electric power and light production and distribution. Also railroads (which in 1880–1890 had accounted for nearly half of all producers' durables), fell off to only one-fourth in 1900–1912.

New energy sources

Another internal factor that helped to shape a more autonomous pattern of growth in this period was the succession of innovations in energy production. In 1870 American manufacturing drew upon primary sources of energy amounting to 2.4 million horsepower capacity, about equally divided between water power and steam power. By 1890 the total capacity of primary power sources had increased to nearly 6 million horsepower (1.3 million water power

and 4.5 million steam power). Then, in the 1890s, the introduction of electrical power production—the most important advance since steam power was first harnessed in the eighteenth century—basically changed the sources and distribution of energy. By 1910, total capacity had risen to 18.5 million horsepower—eight times the level of forty years earlier. In millions of horsepower, manufacturers' sources of energy in 1909 were as follows:

Water	*1.8*
Gas	*0.7*
Steam	*14.2*
Electric (purchased)	*1.7*

And electric power accounted for one-third the total capacity of 29.4 million horsepower by 1919.[3] At the same time the internal-combustion engine was also being developed, further revolutionizing energy uses and their impact. Of course, this type of engine became most important in transportation, for it inaugurated the age of gasoline-powered engines for use in trucks and tractors, automobiles, and later aircraft.

Technology and productivity gains

We have already referred to the revolution in energy production that so greatly expanded available energy sources during the post–Civil War period, and throughout the following chapters we shall examine more closely the major technical innovations in manufacturing, agriculture, transport, and other sectors of the economy that drove the level of productivity steadily higher. Here we shall note the general

[3]Allen H. Fenichel, "Growth and Diffusion of Power in Manufacturing, 1838–1919," in *Output, Employment, and Productivity in the U.S. After 1800*, p. 460.

TABLE 13–3. GROSS NATIONAL PRODUCT AND GROSS CAPITAL FORMATION 1869–1916 (IN BILLIONS OF DOLLARS; 1929 PRICES)

PERIOD[1]	GROSS NATIONAL PRODUCT (GNP)	GROSS CAPITAL FORMATION (GCF)	GCF AS PERCENTAGE OF GNP
1869–1873	$ 9.1	$ 2.1	23%
1872–1876	11.2	2.6	23
1877–1881	16.1	3.7	23
1882–1886	20.7	4.5	22
1887–1891	24.0	5.9	25
1892–1896	28.3	7.4	26
1897–1901	35.4	8.7	25
1902–1906	45.0	10.8	24
1907–1911	52.5	11.7	22
1912–1916	59.7	13.1	22

Source: U.S. Department of Commerce, Bureau of the Census, *Historical Statistics of the United States, Colonial Times to 1957* (Washington, D.C.: Government Printing Office, 1960), p. 144.

[1]5-year periods are annual averages.

TABLE 13–4. SECTORAL DISTRIBUTION OF INCREASES IN CAPITAL STOCK, 1880–1912 (BILLIONS OF DOLLARS; 1929 PRICES)

SECTOR	1880–1890	1890–1900	1900–1912
1. Agriculture	$ 0.7	$ 1.5	$ 4.7
2. Mining	0.5	0.7	1.9
3. Manufacturing	2.6	3.2	8.1
4. Transportation and Public Utilities	4.7	4.5	12.0
Railroads	{4.1}	{3.1}	{6.9}
Electric power and light	{0.1}	{0.5}	{2.3}
TOTAL Producers' durables	$ 8.5	$ 9.9	$26.7
Nonfarm residential, private institutional, and government construction	14.0	15.5	22.2
TOTAL CAPITAL FORMATION	$22.5	$25.3	$48.9

Source: Simon Kuznets, *Capital in the American Economy: Its Formation and Financing* (Princeton, N. J.: Princeton University Press, for the National Bureau of Economic Research, 1961), pp. 610–611. Copyright 1961, The National Bureau of Economic Research. Used by permission.

trend of productivity; that is, of the output obtained for each unit of labor input (output per worker-hour) in the American economy. It is estimated that productivity rose at an average rate of about 1.6 percent annually during the period 1889–1919. Moreover, in the longer period from 1865 to 1914, productivity gains accounted for about 20 percent of overall growth, which may be compared with the still more impressive 44 percent of growth attributable to productivity gains from 1900 to the present day.[4]

[4]Lance E. Davis, Richard Easterlin, et al., *American Economic Growth: An Economist's History of the United States* (New York: Harper & Row, 1972), pp. 38–39; Edward F. Denison, *Accounting for U.S. Economic Growth, 1929–1969* (Washington, D.C.: Brookings Institution, 1974), pp. 128–129; and John Kendrick, *Productivity Trends in the United States* (Princeton, N.J.: Princeton University Press, 1961). (See Table 1–3, p. 14.)

Immigration and the labor force

Although up to now our discussion has stressed autonomous elements of the dynamics of growth, it is important to recognize that America's place in the international economy continued to be of crucial importance as well. Even the new technologies being introduced through rapid capital formation owed much to foreign inventors' ideas and contributions, and the continued strength of international trade helped sustain new investment and productivity gains both in the extractive industries and in manufacturing. But one very direct link to the international economy was the flow of immigration, amounting to nearly 30 million persons, mainly from Europe, from 1865 to 1914. Immigration was highly sensitive to cyclical fluctuations in the American economy. Immigrants poured in during periods of economic expansion, and in depression years there was often a net outflow. As an addition to the labor force, as a factor in the growth of the major cities, and as a major factor in the general population trend that created the enormous mass market of the United States by the end of the nineteenth century, immigration reinforced the more purely internal factors that generated economic expansion.

Trade and the international economy

The creation and sustained expansion of a vast internal market had a far greater impact than foreign trade on the pattern of U.S. growth after 1865. And yet from the Civil War to the 1880s the foreign trade of the United States represented an increasing share of world trade, rising from about 8 percent to about 10 percent of the total. Then, although domestic production was accelerating, the U.S. share of world trade leveled off until World War I.

In the farm sector, cotton continued to depend heavily upon foreign markets, and exports of foodstuffs were also important determinants of farm income. Over the long run, industrial exports grew steadily in value relative to agricultural exports, and by the 1890s American manufacturers were conducting an aggressive export drive. Still, despite massive increases in the value of exports (which rose seven-fold from the 1860s to 1910–1915), foreign trade comprised only about 10 percent of GNP in the United States. This level of dependence upon foreign trade was in marked contrast to the other major industrial countries' dependence on their foreign-trade sectors: between 38 and 54 percent in France, England, and Germany on the eve of World War I.

Government policy

The economic policies of government at all levels (state, local, federal) in post-1865 America reflected the values of a society dedicated to material growth and private capitalism. There was very little intervention by government for "planning" of growth, involving conscious allocation of goods and mandating of priorities; and until the 1880s there was little systematic regulation of private interests, either. To this degree, *laissez faire* prevailed. But government did extend significant support in many ways to the productive efforts of private enterprise. Among the major supportive policies (which are discussed more fully in Chapter 19), most prominent were the high protective tariffs that insulated sections of American industry from foreign competition; generous land grants to some railroads, both by the federal government and by many states; a policy of ruthless, unremitting pressure against native Indian land claims and the virtual elimination of those Indian nations that sought to resist by force the incursions of white settlement.

There was a tendency to give strong preference to business interests over the claims of organized labor and workers generally. Even regulatory legislation, such as the railroad rate laws of the states and the establishment of the Interstate Commerce Commission in 1887, usually was designed to stabilize competition within the industries regulated. In addition, most of the individual state governments enacted tax, resource-use, and other legislation favorable to dominant interests such as the mining companies, manufacturers, and railroads.

Entrepreneurship

In an age when the very rapidity of economic growth, the introduction of new products and technologies, and the expansion of market opportunities gave wide play to creative individual energies, the role of the entrepreneur was crucial. The society and its legal system gave relatively free play to the people who mobilized its capital, developed new markets, created giant business corporations, and generally speaking were the principal agents of economic innovation and economic change. Men such as John D. Rockefeller in oil and Andrew Carnegie in steel have been celebrated as "industrial statesmen" whose genius built an industrial order in which improved standards of living were ultimately realized. But these same entrepreneurs have also been condemned as "robber barons," morally equivalent to those land pirates who exacted tribute from all who passed by their castles on the trade routes of medieval Europe. They built enormous fortunes at considerable cost to human welfare; they often seemed oblivious of ethical constraints or morality; and they launched relentless attacks upon the nation's natural resources in the quest for production and profits. In the perspective of a century's time, however, it is important to recognize that in their own day they were widely admired. And although they certainly did their part in corrupting the political process with "bought legislators" and the like, they did not lack for popular acclaim or support from the churches and from the universities, where Social Darwinists proclaimed them as the "fittest" who had survived in life's ruthless competition. Neither, however, did they lack for critics or enemies, not least the millions who were dependent upon the business order for their survival and welfare.

NEW TERRITORIAL AND RESOURCE FRONTIERS

The spread of white settlement into the trans-Mississippi area occurred swiftly. More than two centuries had passed from the time the first permanent European settlements were planted on the Atlantic coast until the frontier line reached the 97th meridian. But only 30 years were needed to occupy the rest of the territory that comprises the contiguous United States today. And after 1865 western settlement and development were integral parts of the industrialization then transforming the national economy.

The West, as one economist has written, "was never a region faced with a development *problem*. It developed as an outcome of the needs of the rest of the nation."[5] And although settlements were initially often small and the conditions of life hard, commonly only a very brief period of time passed before the most modern techniques and even large-scale capitalist organization were employed to exploit the resources of the region. Eastern capital and foreign investment poured into the cattleman's frontier and the miner's frontier, close on the heels of the first adventurers. The farmer's frontier was characterized by small-scale investments, and the family farm dominated the scene. Yet the West's family farmers quickly moved into production for national and world markets. Aided by railroads, warehousing enterprises, and organized futures trading in the commercial cities, they were linked almost immediately with the American and world economies. The word "frontier" no longer could properly be used to convey an image of self-sufficiency and economically independent units. The markets for western grain, cattle, mineral products, lumber, and processed goods were often thousands of miles distant.

The mining frontier

Both before and after the Civil War, the West developed in a series of spectacular booms, nowhere so dramatically as in the mining areas. Within a year of California's fabled Gold Rush of 1849, the tiny population of perhaps 14,000 *Californios* (of Mexican heritage) was swamped by an influx of nearly 100,000 whites seeking gold. Chinese and South Americans joined the influx, though the vast majority of newcomers were Anglos, and the population

of California reached 380,000 by the time of the Civil War. Both federal and state laws gave prospectors for gold first-priority claims on the land, and successive new gold strikes in the Sierras generated a series of local rushes. The peak year was reached in 1852, when $81 million in gold was produced. As the easily worked placer deposits gave out, large-scale mining companies moved in with new capital-intensive techniques for digging ore out of the land, and by the 1870s the typical miner was not a prospector but a wage-earning employee of a corporation.

Meanwhile, the mining economy gave rise to urbanization. San Francisco grew rapidly as northern California's commercial and banking center, as well as a transport entrepôt. And thousands settled the land to engage in farming, first to supply the mining camps but by the 1860s to export rising quantities of wheat for eastern and European markets.

A second great gold rush centered on Colorado's Pike's Peak in 1859. Other strikes in Colorado began a boom that produced fully $300 million in precious metals during the three decades after 1860. Both there and in Nevada the ore could be reached only by sinking deep shafts, requiring large investments in equipment. And so there emerged quickly a highly capitalized form of mining, dominated by a few large corporate firms employing the latest in technology. In this respect, at least, the gold and silver mines were no primitive frontier. They were emblematic of an advanced capitalism.

Additional mineral discoveries brought population into Montana and Idaho soon afterward. There too the trend, especially in the copper mines, was toward large-scale enterprise employing wage labor. The bitterness of life in the company towns and beneath the ground in the copper district led to some of the bloodiest uprisings in American labor history at the end of the century. Other mining rushes took place in Utah, Arizona, and New Mexico. But the last great western rush was in the Black Hills of South Dakota, on land belonging to the Sioux Indians, in 1875. Unwilling to keep white prospectors out, the U.S. Army instead ordered the Sioux to come in from the hills and concentrate at specified agency sites. Resistance sparked the bloody Sioux War of 1876, following which the miners poured in and founded a score of boom towns.

In some of the West's mining areas, boom towns were abandoned and the mining camps

[5]Douglas F. Dowd, "A Comparative Analysis of Economic Development in the American West and South," *Journal of Economic History*, 16 (1956): 562–563.

were deserted as soon as the ores were exhausted. Where the finds were large enough to sustain production, quartz mining conducted by large corporations maintained the local economies. In a few favored places, the camps became the nuclei of more diversified local economies, and ranching and farming developed alongside mineral extraction. By the 1890s irrigation projects for arid-land farming and, a decade later, the development of hydroelectric power facilities provided the basis for regional economic growth. By the mid-twentieth century the West's growth had become so accelerated, building on those slender remote beginnings, that the entire national economy was given a "westward tilt."

The ranchers' frontier

Lying between the margins of farming settlement spreading from the East into the Mississippi — Missouri basin and the western mining camps in the Rockies was a vast country of flat and gently rolling land, grass-covered but lacking in rivers and streams and with less rainfall than the fertile East. Many believed that the High Plains region, because it was only semi-humid, would never be occupied by permanent white settlers. But in the 1860s cattle raisers discovered that their stock could survive the region's cold winters and thrive on the wild-grass pasturage. And so, during the 1870s and 1880s, this western area was a cattle ranchers' frontier, on which livestock were fed on the government's land and range wars were fought over water rights. The livestock were rounded up in the summer, shipped on the railroads to the stockyards of Kansas City or Chicago, and then sent on to consumer markets both in America and in Europe.

Beginning in 1866, cattle ranchers in Texas drove their stock northward to the railheads at Abilene, at Dodge City, Kansas, and at Ogallala, Nebraska. Within a few years cattlemen had begun to winter their herds in the rich grass-covered country of Wyoming and Colorado, later spreading out into Montana as well. Because access to the grass was free, overhead costs were low. This fact, together with rising demand for meat in foreign and domestic markets, generated enormous profits for some of the livestock operations. The state governments further aided their leading industry by giving the livestock growers' associations a high degree of control over matters such as fencing requirements and quarantine regulations — in effect establishing a sort of private government, which

later became a powerful instrument with which the ranchers harassed small farmers seeking land in the range country.

The cattlemen's associations were one facet of "giantism" in the western economy, comparable to the organized power of the mining companies in states farther west. Another was the emergence of a few ranching companies capitalized at $4 million or more, several of them controlling as much as 2 million acres of government land. Both English and Scottish investors became deeply involved in these ventures. With an ample supply of feeder stock and capital in such enormous amounts available, it was not surprising that the western ranges became overstocked. With both water and grass becoming short, the advent of competing sheep ranchers made matters worse. Then disaster struck, as terrifying blizzards in the 1880s killed vast numbers of livestock, and many of the ranching outfits went bankrupt.

Meanwhile thousands of new settlers were putting pressure on the land. They homesteaded or bought land from the government and put up enclosures, thus threatening to end the era of free grassland. The ranchers responded in some places with use of force. More generally, they sought to stop new settlement by putting up their own fences on government land. By 1888, such illegal fences enclosed 8 million acres. But the federal officials ordered them taken down, and the way was open to a more orderly process of settlement by farmers.

The farmers' frontier

One of the most significant trends of the post-1865 economy was the continuing westward spread of agriculture. In 1870 the trans-Mississippi West contributed only about 16 percent of the value of farm products. But by 1890 — the year the census director announced there was no longer "a frontier line," in the sense that settlement exceeding 2 persons per square mile had reached all the cultivable areas — the West contributed 33 percent of farm products. And in 1910 the West's share was 45 percent.[6]

Of basic importance in the interpretation of this rapid spread of farming westward was the growing demand in domestic and foreign markets. But settlement was also encouraged and speeded by other factors. First of all, the na-

[6]Harvey Perloff et al., *Regions, Resources, and Economic Growth* (Baltimore: Johns Hopkins University Press, 1960), p. 138.

tion's land laws made the land available and permitted farm making on a generally profitable basis. The Homestead Act of 1862 represented the culmination of years of agitation by reformers who saw free land as a means of keeping economic opportunity open. This law granted free a quarter section (160 acres) to any adult single person or head of a family. Residence of five years on the homesteaded land was required before ownership was established; good faith was to be proved by actual cultivation. After six months, however, the homesteader had the right to "commute" the claim; that is, obtain full legal title by payment of $1.25 an acre.

The Homestead Act proved badly adapted to the needs of new farmers in the arid and semiarid states of the West. But in many portions of the states lying just east and along two tiers west of the Mississippi River, a family could hope to make a good living on a 160-acre farm, as ample rainfall and good soil afforded high crop yields. Thus in Kansas, Nebraska, Minnesota, and the Dakotas, more than half of the 240,000 new farms established between 1863 and 1880 were on land acquired under the Homestead Act.

Elsewhere in the heartland of the continent, results were similar. But west of the 100th meridian, the lack of rainfall made the 160-acre farm impracticable, and so the land laws were amended to enable farmers to acquire larger tracts cheaply. The Timber Culture Act of 1873 allowed a homesteader to acquire an additional 160 acres if he or she planted trees on a fourth or more of the tract. The Desert Land Act of 1877 gave an applicant title to 640 acres in the Great Plains region upon initial payment of twenty-five cents an acre, proof of irrigation within three years, and payment of an additional dollar an acre. The Timber and Stone Act of 1878 was designed to dispose of land valuable for timber or quarries; it provided for sale of such land in 160-acre tracts at $2.50 an acre.

The Dawes Act of 1887 applied to lands owned by the American Indians; it provided for allotment of individual tracts to members of each Indian nation, and under it much land passed at low prices to white settlers, either through honest sale or through defrauding of the Indians. Revisions of the Homestead Act itself from 1909 to 1912 enlarged the homestead to 320 acres of nonirrigable land. And the Taylor Grazing Act of 1916 permitted grants of 640-acre homesteads if the land was useful only for grazing stock. Finally, the federal lands in Louisiana, Arkansas, Mississippi, Alabama,

and Florida were covered by the 1866 Southern Homestead Act. This law, pushed through Congress by reformers who hoped to see freed slaves get the land, provided for free grants of 80 acres, but also made the 1862 Homestead Act's provisions inoperative in those southern states.

Although the principle of homesteading worked well in the midcontinent region, the land system as a whole did not work to the advantage of small-scale actual settlers. Certainly it did not provide them with "free farms" in the arid and semiarid regions of the West.[7] This was true for several reasons:

First of all, the 1862 Homestead Act did not render earlier land laws inoperative. Hence lands could be obtained through cash sales at auction and through preemption, without any upper limit on what an individual or company might acquire. As each new land district was opened, therefore, early buyers with capital in hand could gain control of much of the best land. Not only large-scale speculators but also people of relatively small means were thus permitted to get and hold land for a profit, with no intention of farming it themselves.

Second, much of the public domain never came under the terms of the Homestead Law. In the 1860s and 1870s Congress granted more than 125 million acres to railroad companies, and in addition it made enormous grants to the state governments for various purposes. Both the railroads and the states sold this land for $2.50 cash or more—much more, in many cases. Some 140 million acres were held by state governments in the West in 1862; they disposed of this treasure in real estate at prices averaging about $10 an acre, and some states averaged as much as $16 to $35. Third, widespread fraud badly corrupted the original purposes of settler-oriented legislation. Vast areas of land were taken, under all the land laws, by people posing as actual settlers who in fact were acting as the agents of land speculators, cattle ranchers, lumber companies, and mining firms.

Promotion of settlement

If land was not commonly free, it was nonetheless certainly readily available to those with

[7]Paul W. Gates, "The Homestead Act: Free Land Policy in Operation, 1862–1935," in *Land Use Policy and Problems in the United States,* ed. H. W. Ottoson (Lincoln: University of Nebraska Press, 1963); Gates, "The Homestead Law in an Incongruous Land System," *American Historical Review,* 41 (1936).

the capital or the guile to obtain title to it.[8] Reinforcing the effects of the land laws in attracting people to the agricultural districts of the West were the railroads built in the western states during the post-1865 period. Not only did they provide farmers with transportation services; they also promoted settlement actively, and those lines that held government land grants typically organized elaborate recruitment campaigns to lure purchasers to their parts of the country. The state governments of the West also maintained active promotional bureaus that advertised widely in the United States and Europe. In addition, the railroad companies offered credit to purchasers of their land. These promotional efforts did much to nurture the land boom of the 1880s, a decade in which the population of the trans-Mississippi region doubled.

Agricultural technology

Innovations in farming technology were also of crucial importance in sustaining the westward march of agriculture. In the dry lands west of the 100th meridian, farmers faced conditions unlike those they had been familiar with in the East. Shortages of water and timber were the foremost difficulties. The windmill provided one answer. By harnessing a resource abundant on the Great Plains—the wind—to pump subsurface water to ground level, the western farmer could supply irrigation ditches and water crops. American manufacturers responded to this need with quantity production of small metal windmills. Another crucial innovation was the development of barbed wire for fencing. Without forested land, the pioneer farmer was hard put to find cheap material for fencing. Barbed wire, developed in the mid-1870s by Joseph Glidden and Jacob Haish of Illinois, was light, easy to work, and inexpensive. Seldom have inventors found so receptive a market. By 1880 more than 80 million pounds of barbed wire were sold annually. Lack of wood also led to the use of sod houses on the prairies of Kansas, Nebraska, and the upper Mississippi Valley. Even for the farm family that obtained its land under the Homestead Act, the cash requirements for getting a farm into production (the costs of buildings, fencing, a well, machinery,

stock, feed, and seed) ran to at least $1000. Hence the incentives to improvise and to try the unfamiliar were high.[9]

Irrigation

Trans-Mississippi agricultural settlement and growth were also expedited by innovations in the irrigating of dry lands. The individual farmer was seldom able to afford the kind of investment needed to acquire water rights, build reservoirs and ditches, and water much land in a dry country. Therefore, collective organization marked irrigation efforts, and from the beginnings of settlement in Utah, Colorado, New Mexico, and other states with irrigable land the farmers sought help from government. Each state developed a system of legal rights in water. The laws were of two main types. Colorado's system provided for "prior appropriation," by which the first white person to use water gained a property right in it. Other states, including California, adopted the "riparian" system, which assured each landowner along a stream of some right to use of the water. But eventually most of the states introduced a degree of regulatory control, by which commissioners measured water and ruled on rival claims. The states also authorized formation of special-district governments—called irrigation districts—with power to assess taxes and build large-scale irrigation facilities.

Despite the vaunted individualism of the farmer, there was no lack of pressure in the West for federal aid to irrigation. A campaign for government assistance culminated in the enactment by Congress of the Carey Act of 1894. Under its terms, any arid-land state could qualify for a grant of up to one million acres of land, to assist either state or private construction of irrigation projects. When this proved to be of only limited usefulness, Congress in 1902 passed the Newlands Reclamation Act. It set aside the proceeds of all federal land sales in the arid regions, earmarking the funds for water projects. Despite provisions of the Newlands Act designed to assure that its benefits would be distributed to small-scale individual farmers, its administration by the U.S. Department of the Interior actually permitted large-scale landowners and corporations to harvest a rich crop of profits from its operation.[10] With the enact-

---

[8] Even in California, where litigation over old Mexican land titles covering much of the state's potential farmland and grazing country had long made it nearly impossible to gain clear title by direct purchase from the government, by the mid-1870s the government land offices were offering land regularly.

[9] Gilbert Fite, *The Farmers' Frontier, 1865–1900* (New York: Holt, Rinehart and Winston, 1966), passim.

[10] Paul S. Taylor, "Reclamation: The Rise and Fall of an American Idea," *The American West,* 7 (1970):31. See Paul Wallace Gates, *History of Public Land Law Development* (Washington, D.C.: U.S. Public Land Law Review Commission, 1968), chap. 22.

ment of this legislation, moreover, the federal government's reclamation and irrigation activities became a permanent feature of agricultural development in the West.

Transportation and agricultural development

Finally, the establishment and growth of commercialized agriculture in the trans-Missis-sippi West after 1865 was greatly facilitated by the railroads. Dramatic reductions in transport costs—despite policies of rate discrimination that evoked farmers' complaints—enabled the spreading railroad network to make national and international markets readily accessible to western farmers. (See Chapter 17, pp. 264–265.). The influence of the railroad was critical in opening the West to agriculture.

THE FRONTIER IN PERSPECTIVE

Enormous new areas of natural resources were drawn into the national economy from 1865 to 1914, and new foci for settlement and economic activity were established. The westward shift in population and production was great enough to constitute a major reorientation of the nation's economic geography. Of the 40 million Americans in 1870, only 14 percent lived in the trans-Mississippi West; by 1900, when national population was 76 million, the West held nearly 25 percent of the total.

The boom in the Plains

The boom pattern of western development—mining rushes, surges of in-migration into newly opened farming areas, new regions suddenly made desirable sites for farming by irrigation projects—was reflected in the irregular rate of growth of the western states. During the 1860s, most of the people who left the eastern region to take up residence in the West moved to Iowa, Kansas, and Missouri. In the 1870s, Kansas continued to gain population rapidly (it received nearly 350,000 in-migrants), and Texas, Iowa, and Colorado were also major gainers. Illinois lost nearly a third of a million people, who "hedge-hopped" to make new homes farther west. Meanwhile, the Pacific Coast states also registered heavy gains of in-migrants. The 1880s were a decade of land-rush booms for the Great Plains region. Unusually high rainfall coincided with the introduction of improved flour-milling processes that made it economically feasible to cultivate hard spring wheat on the Plains. The 1880s were also a period when the "push" factors in the East—especially rising land values as urbanization progressed, increasing taxes on farms, and the competition of western agriculture—induced many dirt farmers to rush westward. The wheat belt thus spread west in this decade, as the Dakotas, Kansas, Nebraska, Colorado, and Washington all experienced a massive influx of homesteaders.

The boom in the Plains states peaked out after 1890, as new farmers there learned to their sorrow, from a series of dry years, what the region's normal climate was like. Farm prices, especially of wheat, slumped in the early 1890s and drove many recent agricultural settlers off the land they had so recently occupied. Population in the East rose steadily in the 1890s, under the impact of the new immigration from southern and eastern Europe. But population growth in the Rocky Mountain, Pacific, and southwestern states nearly kept pace. Oklahoma underwent its famous land rush in April 1889, when lands formerly reserved to the Indian nations were thrown open to white settlement. California too underwent a surge of expansion in the 1890s, as diversified farming and urban-based activity grew.

The environment

The process of frontier development after 1865 also altered the relationship between the society and the North American environment. Exploitative farming methods, with concentration on soil-exhausting cash crops, had long been characteristic of American agriculture in the East. After 1865 this type of farming spread westward. But the exploitative character of resource use was greatly extended beyond agriculture to other types of economic activity as the heavy technology of a modernizing industrial nation was unleashed on the landscape. Thus in mining, lumbering, and even fishing, methods for tearing resources loose from nature's hold put immense pressure on the environment. Cattle ranchers overstocked the western ranges, mining companies in California washed down hillsides and filled the rivers with silt and debris, and lumber companies stripped the forests, all in much the same manner as the western bison herds had been slaughtered (perhaps 100 million head in 40 years) to the verge of extinction.

Alarmed by the swiftness of this assault on resources, and mindful of continuing population increases from a high birth rate and mass immigration, many Americans had developed and begun to articulate a new concern for conservation by the turn of the century. Among the first results were actions by Presidents Benjamin Harrison, Grover Cleveland, and William McKinley to set aside some 46 million acres of western land as forest reserves in the 1890s. During Theodore Roosevelt's presidential administrations, 148 million additional acres were set aside. Together with the Carey Act and the Newlands Act, these measures foreshadowed a more comprehensive federal role in public management of resources in the west.

The Indians

For the American Indians, the process of frontier development was one of dispossession and tragedy. In the 1860s the spread of cattle ranching and the completion of the nation's first transcontinental railroad line (the Union Pacific in 1869) signaled an end to the Plains Indians' way of life. Wherever miners, ranchers, and land-hungry farmers wanted to penetrate lands formerly assured to the Indians by treaty, the government demanded that the Indians yield. Resistance was put down ruthlessly. Meanwhile the slaughter of the bison went on, by the mid-1880s eliminating the great herds around which the Plains Indians' cultures centered. The remnants of Indian civilization were reduced, finally, to life on reservations. About 50,000 had survived the wars and devastation, only a third of their former numbers in the West.

The Mexicans

When the United States took control of Mexican territory in California and the Southwest in 1848, most of the approximately 75,000 Mexicans living there suffered a dolorous fate. About three-fourths of them, mainly *mestizos* (of mixed Spanish and Indian descent), lived in New Mexico. There they worked as *peones*— nearly as slaves, though the traditional Mexican law give them status and personal protection greater than American black slaves enjoyed— under the dominant control of a small group of rich Mexican landowners. A large number of the peasantry and the rich alike, however, lost title to their lands as the Anglo-Americans penetrated their territory: Swindling, corruption in judicial settlement of titles, and unconscionable bargaining divested the *mestizo* people of their landed heritage. A small number of the upper-class New Mexicans, however, intermarried with the Anglos, entered into joint business ventures and land dealings with them, and man-

aged to dominate the politics and public offices of territorial New Mexico for a generation while their compatriots sank into more desperate poverty. The few thousand Mexicans living in Arizona were less successful in developing their own assimilated upper class; most of them succeeded only in obtaining poorly paid, unskilled work in the mines, on ranches, and as teamsters.

In California, still another group—culturally distinct in many respects from the Mexican populations of the Southwest—confronted a different set of problems in the struggle for economic and cultural survival. Above all, they faced an unprecedentedly massive influx of Anglos (and also of Chinese and South Americans) as the result of the 1849 gold rush. The upper-class Californios were overwhelmed by the numbers, wealth, and political power of the new Anglo-American majority; hence they were unable to strike the bargains that the wealthy Mexicans managed in New Mexico, where for several decades they continued to be numerically dominant. An antiforeign miners' tax drove the California-born people out of the mining industry, thus robbing them of any share in the new state's boom sector. Meanwhile, frauds and corrupt judicial decisions, together with rising tax and mortgage burdens, cost most of the Californios their rancho lands. In the southern region of the state, where Anglos poured in only in the late 1870s, the native-born Californios were better able to hold onto their means of making a living, whether in the crafts, in ranching, or in small-scale farming. By the end of the nineteenth century, however, large numbers of Californios had drifted into the cities to seek employment as common laborers, or worked at menial jobs for the railroads, or eked out a sparse existence on poor land in the back country. Only a tiny number of the rich landowners (*ricos*) succeeded in holding onto their estates and being socially accepted by the dominant Anglo society.[11]

In sum, while the Mexican population escaped the tragic fate of the majority of native Indians—outright extermination—their diverse

[11]Leonard Pitt, *The Decline of the Californios: A Social History of the Spanish-Speaking Californians, 1864–1890* (Berkeley: University of California Press, 1966); Rodman W. Paul, "The Spanish-Americans in the Southwest, 1848–1900," in *The Frontier Challenge: Responses to the Trans-Mississippi West,* ed. John G. Clark (Lawrence: University Press of Kansas, 1971); Julian Samora, ed., *La Raza: Forgotten Americans* (South Bend: Notre Dame University Press, 1966).

local cultures experienced intensive destructive pressures. They were largely dispossessed of their property, pushed down (or down further) into poverty, and finally absorbed by the developing western economy as menial workers and the victims of unremitting racial prejudice in addition to economic exploitation. To this degree, at least, the stunning Anglo-American assault on the resources of the West was an economic triumph gained at high human cost to other peoples.

SELECTED READINGS

General Works

*Bruchey, Stuart, *Growth of the Modern American Economy* (New York: Dodd, Mead, 1975). (Includes detailed general bibliography.)

*Higgs, Robert, *Transformation of the American Economy, 1865 – 1914* (New York: Wiley, 1971).

National Bureau of Economic Research, *Output, Employment, and Productivity in the U. S. After 1800* (New York: Columbia University Press, 1966).

—— *Trends in the American Economy in the 19th Century* (Princeton, N.J.: Princeton University Press, 1960).

*Niemi, Albert W., Jr., *U.S. Economic History: A Survey of the Major Issues* (Chicago: Rand McNally, 1975).

*Perloff, Harvey S. et al., *Regions, Resources, and Economic Growth* (Baltimore: Johns Hopkins Press, 1960). (Includes historical articles by Eric Lampard.)

*Vatter, Harold G. *The Drive to Industrial Maturity: The U.S. Economy, 1860 – 1914* (Westport, Conn.: Greenwood, 1975).

Land Policy and Frontier Development

*Billington, Ray A., *America's Frontier Heritage* (New York: Holt, Rinehart and Winston, 1966).

Briggs, Harold E., *Frontiers of the Northwest: A History of the Upper Missouri Valley* (1939, reprinted New York: Peter Smith, 1950).

Ellis, David M., ed., *The Frontier and American Development* (Ithaca, N.Y.: Cornell University Press, 1969).

*Fite, Gilbert C., *The Farmers' Frontier, 1865 – 1900* (New York: Holt, Rinehart and Winston, 1966).

Frink, Maurice et al., *When Grass Was King* (Boulder: University of Colorado Press, 1956).

Gates, Paul Wallace, *History of Public Land Law Development* (Washington, D.C.: Government Printing Office, 1968).

Gressley, Gene M., ed., *The American West, A Reorientation* (University of Wyoming Publications, XXXII, 1966).

*Hurst, James Willard, *Law and the Conditions of Freedom in the Nineteenth Century U.S.* (Madison: University of Wisconsin Press, 1956).

*Osgood, Ernest S., *The Day of the Cattleman* (Minneapolis: University of Minnesota Press, 1929).

Paul, Rodman Wilson, *Mining Frontiers of the Far West, 1848 – 1880* (New York: Holt, Rinehart and Winston, 1963).

Paxson, Frederic L., *The Last American Frontier* (New York: Macmillan, 1910).

*Pomeroy, Earl, *The Pacific Slope* (New York: Knopf, 1965).

*Turner, Frederick Jackson, *The Frontier in American History* (New York: Holt, Rinehart and Winston, 1921).

*Webb, Walter Prescott, *The Great Plains* (Boston: Ginn, 1931).

Specialized Studies

Fels, Rendigs, *American Business Cycles, 1865 – 1897* (Chapel Hill: University of North Carolina Press, 1959).

Goldsmith, Raymond W., *Income and Wealth in the United States* (Cambridge, England: Bowes and Bowes, 1952).

Kuznets, Simon, *Capital in the American Economy: Its Formation and Financing* (Princeton, N.J.: Princeton University Press, 1961).

———, Miller, Ann R. and Easterlin, Richard A., *Population Redistribution and Economic Growth: United States, 1870–1950* (Philadelphia: American Philosophical Society, 1960).

Williamson, Jeffrey G., *Late Nineteenth-Century American Development: A General Equilibrium History* (Cambridge, England: Cambridge University Press, 1974).

While the United States underwent industrialization and urbanization after 1865, agriculture was experiencing some sweeping changes. But some of the major trends in the farm sector were a continuation of patterns established earlier in the century. The family farm continued to be the basic unit of production in most of the country; cotton remained the staple cash crop of the South, exported to foreign markets in enormous volume; and there was a persistent expansion of the area of land devoted to agricultural production. The quest for higher productivity went on as farmers experimented with stock and plant breeding, new management practices, and mechanization of field and yard tasks.

The post – Civil War era also witnessed departures from earlier patterns, some of them transforming in their impact. In the South, of course, slavery was abolished. And immediately after the war there were new movements to accomplish more effective organization of farmer interests both within the political arena and outside it. We have already noted the importance of arid-land farming techniques and irrigation in the western states. The pace of mechanization quickened, especially in the midwestern wheat and corn regions. And while regional specialization persisted from the pre-1861 years, the major crop belts extended farther westward. There was also a rising number of highly capitalized, large-scale farms in the North, foreshadowing modern agribusiness. In the marketing of farm products, a genuine revolution of technique took place. In all respects, agriculture shared in the accelerating rate of change that industrialization brought with it. In fact, the farm sector can best be described as itself undergoing industrialization, or at least absorption in the larger industrialization process.

THE PACE AND STRUCTURE OF CHANGE IN AGRICULTURE

Gross farm product is the most useful measure of economic activity in the farm sector. This includes not only crop and livestock sales by farmers, but also the value of improvements (fencing, buildings, land clearing, and so on) and the value added in manufactured goods produced by farm workers. As shown in Table 14–1, gross farm product rose from $2.2 billion in 1860 to $3.9 billion in 1880, then to $5.8 billion in 1900. These data are given in constant dollar values, hence they represent real volume changes.

Accounting for the great rise in agricultural product was expansion in the number of workers, in the land area in farms, and in the efficiency or productivity of farming. The gains in productivity were achieved on the one hand through technical innovations — the application of machine technology, the use of new breeds, and (to a lesser degree) soil-replenishment techniques; and, on the other hand, through the shifting of production to newer lands. Not all the new land brought into arable production in the West was more fertile than eastern farmlands, to be sure; but some gains were attributable to this shift.

TABLE 14–1. STATISTICS OF AMERICAN AGRICULTURE, 1860–1910

	1860	1870	1880	1890	1900	1910
Number of farms (millions)	2.0	2.7	4.0	4.6	5.7	6.4
Land in farms (millions of acres)	407	408	536	623	839	879
Persons engaged in agriculture (millions)	6.2	6.9	8.6	10.0	10.7	11.3
Gross Farm Product, including improvements and home manufactures (billions of constant 1910–1914 dollars)	2.2	2.6	3.9	4.6	5.8	—
Gross farm product per worker (1910–1914 dollars)	332	362	439	456	526	—

Source: U.S. Department of Commerce, *Historical Statistics of the United States, Colonial Times to 1957* (Washington, D.C.: U.S. Government Printing Office, 1960), pp. 74, 278, 284. The data are analyzed fully in Marvin W. Towne and Wayne D. Rasmussen, "Farm Gross Product and Gross Investment," in National Bureau of Economic Research, *Trends in the American Economy in the Nineteenth Century*, vol. 24 of *Studies in Income and Wealth* (Princeton: Princeton University Press, 1960), pp. 255–311.

As the data in Table 14–1 show, land in farms rose 106 percent from 1860 to 1900, while the farm-labor force increased by 72 percent. But farm product per worker rose only 58 percent.[1] This pattern for the United States conformed to that in other "frontier" agricultural areas of recent European settlement in the late nineteenth century (Australia, Canada, and South America): among the factors contributing to a dramatic rise in farm output, additions of land and labor were *relatively* more important than productivity gains achieved by applying technical innovations.

From 1860 to 1910 the area of lands newly brought into production by American farmers and ranchers was almost as large as the area of western Europe. As for population, in 1860 the

United States contained about 31 million people, all but 6.2 million living on farms and in small rural towns. In 1910, when national population was 92 million, the farming and rural population still numbered fully 50 million. (However, we should note that ten years later the American farm population and labor force would enter a long period of absolute decline, continuing to the present day.) The rapid increase in city population meant expansion in the domestic market for food products and fibers; and the spread of the transportation network, tying the national economy together, made it possible for farms to enter into commercial production almost from the start of modern settlement, even in the remoter western regions.

MECHANIZATION OF THE FARM

Large farms and scarcity of labor, the two forces that previously had impelled the development of farm machinery, continued to be influential after the Civil War. The first great improvements in the plow, reaper, and thresher had already demonstrated their practicability

[1]Most of this 58 percent increase in worker productivity doubtless derived from technical innovations, especially mechanization. But to some degree it was attributable as well to the rise in land per agricultural worker (in the newer areas of farming particularly), with attendant economies of scale. For this and all other interpretations of Table 14–1, however, it must be stressed that there were large variations according to the particular region and crop (or other farm product) that is being considered. (Compare, for example, Table 14–2.) Also, it is worth reiterating that the quantitative data are well-informed estimates; like most nineteenth-century economic statistics, they are less reliable than comparable data available on today's economic activities.

before 1860, but it was the war that widened their use. When the federal government mobilized the largest army that the world had yet seen, those who remained on the farm turned of necessity to labor-saving machinery. The rapid adoption of farm machinery was also encouraged by the fact that the type of country occupied during these years was adaptable to large-scale farming and to machine operation. It is therefore correct to say that the agricultural revolution in America, as far as machinery is concerned, came in the half century after 1860.

Harvest and cultivation machinery

The climate in the wheat regions of the Middle West necessitated rapid harvesting when the crop was ripe, and the amount planted was dependent upon the farmer's ability to harvest the grain before it spoiled. Consequently the attention of inventors was directed most of all toward methods to speed up harvesting. Already in 1858 C. W. and W. W. Marsh had patented the "Marsh harvester," a reaping machine that, by means of an endless apron, delivered the grain upon a table where two men could bind it. This reaper almost doubled the amount of grain that could be harvested in a given time. Even more important was the invention in 1878 of a "twine binder," a machine that took the place of the crude and unsatisfactory wire binders in use and increased eightfold the speed in harvesting.

The invention of the twine binder, therefore, by increasing the amount which a farmer could harvest, increased by that precise amount the quantity which he could profitably grow. In other words, it was the twine binder more than any other single machine or implement that enabled the country to increase its production of grain, especially wheat, during this period. The per capita production of the country as a whole increased from about 5.6 bushels in 1860 to 9.2 bushels in 1880.[2]

Further improvements were made by the addition of a bundle carrier and, in dry climates, of a header. On the great wheat farms of the West were to be found "combines" drawn by a score or more of horses (later propelled by gasoline tractors) that could cut, thresh, clean, sack, and weigh the grain without the touch of human hands.

Improvements in machinery for planting and cultivating appeared simultaneously with those for harvesting. During this period there came into use the straddle-row cultivator, the sulky plow, spring-tooth sulky harrows of various types, and seeders that planted, covered, and fertilized at the same time. This type of agricultural machinery, which helped to speed up the process of planting and thus put it on a par with harvesting, was rapidly adopted after 1875 in the Red River wheat country and the Far West. The lister, which plowed and planted the seed at the same time, was introduced in 1880. The mowing machine was perfected, and improvements in haying included the spring-tooth sulky rake and machines for loading, stacking, and baling. Hand shelling of corn gave way after 1850 to machine shelling. The failure of the hay crop several times in the 1880s, when the dairy-

ing industry was being rapidly developed, directed attention to corn raising, and the combined work of many inventors resulted in a machine with which one man could cut and bind from six to ten acres a day. This enabled farmers to cut their fodder corn green, with the juice still in the stock, and store it in a silo for winter food, whereas before they were often forced to leave it standing in the fields to dry.

Motive power

The first stage in the mechanization of the farm was the general displacement of men by horses as the motive power for agricultural energy. This commenced long before the Civil War but developed most rapidly between 1850 and 1910. It was accompanied by a tremendous increase in the number of draft animals on the farm. The substitution of horsepower for manpower, however, had hardly begun before manufacturers of farm machinery were considering the possibility of substituting mechanical power for that of animals. On the large prairie farms, experiments were soon being made with steam tractors for planting and preparing the land. By 1910 the gasoline engine had been applied to farm machinery and was so obviously superior to either steam or horsepower that in the next decade it rapidly replaced both on large farms. Almost as revolutionary in its effects was the use of the gasoline truck and pleasure car, which brought the farmer into closer touch with urban life and thus facilitated both marketing and purchasing. Not only the automobile but gasoline pumping and lighting outfits helped to bring the advantages of the city to the farmer and to decrease household drudgery.

Machines and laborers

As a result of mechanization, the value of farm machinery and equipment more than doubled between 1860 and 1890, then rose even more dramatically from $494 million in 1890 to $1.7 billion in 1914. The amount of power used on farms is estimated to have risen from 605,000 horsepower in 1879 to over 10 billion horsepower in 1910 (exclusive of work animals). These technological changes contributed to the major gains in overall productivity of farm labor. An indication of the magnitude of labor savings is given by the data for three crops in Table 14–2. It should be noted that the reduction of man-hours per unit of output between 1880 and 1920 was much smaller in southern cotton than in the other two crops.

One of the social consequences of mechanization was a rise in the number of wage-paid

[2]T. N. Carver, *The Principles of Rural Economics* (1911), p. 99.

TABLE 14–2.   MAN-HOURS USED IN PRODUCING SPECIFIED AMOUNTS OF WHEAT, CORN, AND COTTON, 1800–1920

CROP	1800	1840	1880	1900	1920
Wheat					
Man-hours per acre	56	35	20	15	12
Man-hours per hundred bushels	373	233	152	108	87
Yield per acre (bushels)	15	15	13	14	14
Corn					
Man-hours per acre	86	69	46	38	32
Man-hours per hundred bushels	344	276	180	147	113
Yield per acre (bushels)	25	25	26	26	28
Cotton					
Man-hours per acre	185	135	119	112	90
Man-hours per bale	601	439	318	280	269
Yield per acre (lbs. lint)	147	147	179	191	160

Source: U.S. Department of Commerce, Bureau of the Census, *Historical Statistics of the United States, Colonial Times to 1957* (Washington, D.C.: U.S. Government Printing Office. 1960), p. 281.

laborers in agriculture relative to the number of owners and tenants who operated their own farms. The farmer with capital had special advantages in the grain-growing states—the wheat and corn belts—where expensive machinery was becoming essential for production at competitive cost. As the following data show, in seven leading grain states (Illinois, Iowa, Kansas, Nebraska, Minnesota, and North and South Dakota), a rising proportion of the people who worked the land in mid-America were wage laborers:

	1880	*1900*
Proprietors (including tenants)	*838,967*	*1,073,911*
Agricultural laborers	*363,233*	*631,740*

Summarizing, we may say that mechanization on the farms (1) released labor force for work in industrial occupations; (2) increased the production of agricultural products and output per capita; (3) eliminated a certain amount of the drudgery of work on the farm; and (4) contributed to real-income gains for farmers in periods when expanding markets maintained price levels.

On the negative side of the ledger, in a social cost accounting, mechanization made it more difficult for people to become farm owners by increasing capital requirements. In the periods when farm prices were in decline it contributed to the overproduction that was a basic cause of the American "farm problem" in the late nineteenth century.

AGRICULTURAL REGIONS

Regional specialization continued to be a leading feature of agriculture after 1865, as had been true since the early nineteenth century. The lines demarcating the areas of specialized production were not precise and exclusive: Grain crops were widely grown; livestock (including draft animals, dairy stock, stock raised for meat, and sheep) was found in all regions; and some areas, especially near the larger cities, had highly diversified agriculture. But still, the intensive specialization in cash crops long familiar in the nation's farming did lead to emergence of "belts" where individual crops' production was concentrated.

The wheat belt

In 1860, most of the nation's wheat was grown east of the Mississippi River. But after the Civil War the wheat belt shifted steadily westward. The giant midcontinent area from northern Texas to the Dakotas grew a large proportion of the wheat produced in the late nineteenth century. In addition, the Pacific Coast states emerged as major wheat producers. Mixed in with wheat were other grain crops, including barley, oats, and rye. In the 1880s the Red River Valley of Minnesota became the site of a wheat-growing boom, marked by the operation of enormous "bonanza farms." The largest covered more than 30,000 acres, employed 1000 or more laborers in harvest season, and used large-scale equipment for heavily mechanized production. Another seat of similarly modern, large-scale wheat production was California. There too the vast acreage of individual farms—in the tens of thousands of acres—and use of gang labor made it profitable to use heavy equipment of unprecedented size and cost. The mainstay of wheat production, however, was the family farm in the spring and winter wheat belts of the Midwest.

The corn belt

The central states from Ohio to Iowa were well adapted to corn, and formed an area of concentration in growing of that staple, mainly for feeding to hogs, even before 1861. The corn belt did not move westward to the extent that the wheat belt did, though Nebraska and Missouri were added to the traditional corn-and-hog region in the immediate postwar years. Corn was also widely used for feeding of cattle, both for meat and for dairy production. Relatively easy to plant and cultivate, corn was a favorite initial crop for pioneer farmers in the West more generally. Even when some areas, such as the Kansas wheat country, moved into commercial production of other grains, farmers continued to mix corn in their crop pattern. This feed grain was also grown widely in the South and on the Pacific coast. Rapid development in the midwestern corn belt, however, was the mainstay on which American per capita production of hog products rose by 50 percent during the 1870s. Though it leveled off below the peak of the late 1870s in the last decades of the nineteenth century, per capita hog products output was sustained at forty to fifty pounds per person in the later years of that period.

Diversified farm regions

Even before the Civil War, New England imported nearly all its grain products from other regions. Between 1860 and 1914 there was a 42 percent decrease in the area of farmland under cultivation in New England, with a drastic decline as well in sheep (on a per capita basis) and a somewhat lesser decline in cattle. Dairying, some commercial tobacco production

(centering in Connecticut), orchard crops, and truck crops were raised for the large urban markets of New England's industrial states. In New York, New Jersey, and Pennsylvania, general agriculture prevailed, with truck gardening, dairy products, and fruits comprising the largest part of agricultural production; a few rich wheat-growing districts did, however, continue to specialize in the production of grain. By the early twentieth century, California's agriculture had also become highly diversified, with fruit and vegetable production stimulated by the introduction of the refrigerated railroad car in the 1880s. In all the Pacific coast states, livestock, wheat and small grains, and fruit were important components of farm production.

Farm readjustment

It has been typical of the growth of American agriculture since the early nineteenth century that older-settled regions adjusted by turning to new specialties when more efficient, newly opened regions came into competition with them. The 1865–1914 period was no exception. Even California and some of the major wheat districts of the 1870s, for example, declined in their output of wheat from 1900 to 1910. In this period, the Great Plains states boomed in wheat output, under the impact of irrigation. Also influential was "dry farming"—a technique calling for deep plowing of the land after harvest and following rains, and maintenance of fields in fallow in alternate years—which became important in the semiarid regions during this decade. Later, declining rainfall drove many farmers out of business in the dry-farming districts.

Wisconsin provides another interesting example of readjustment. The scene of intensive wheat growing in the 1870s, Wisconsin had shifted heavily to production of cheese and other dairy products by 1900, exploiting the expertise of European farm immigrants and the opportunities offered by growth of urban markets such as nearby Chicago. Somewhat earlier, the former wheat-growing centers in Illinois had shifted cropland use to vegetable gardening, orchard fruits, and diversified farming on wet lands that had been drained, requiring large investments of capital.

COTTON CULTURE AND THE SOUTH

Cotton moved westward, as did wheat. Between 1880 and 1900, Texas tripled its out-

put of cotton, leading the Southwest to new prominence as the South generally expanded its cotton production enormously (see Table 14–3). But older regions of the South did not demonstrate a capacity for successful readjustment of farming on the lines of dairying in Wisconsin and truck gardening in Illinois. Instead of diversification, there was a relative decline in the older southern states' output of grain products. This region, the old slave-plantation South, became ensnared in a vicious circle of concentration upon the traditional staples: cotton, sugar, tobacco, and rice. In the lower Mississippi Valley, farm readjustment after 1865 consisted mainly of the fastening of tenants and sharecroppers on small tracts of land. To assure themselves of cash returns, landlords used a variety of tactics to keep the people on the land, concentrating on cash-crop production of cotton, even if it meant they were forced to sell that crop at prices which kept the farm families in abject poverty. Thus the landlords used loan contracts and outright physical coercion to keep labor on the farms once the black labor force was free of slavery. Similarly, the merchants—who provided most of the credit in the South, a region desperately short of commercial banking facilities—legally required small-farm borrowers to keep their land in cotton or another cash staple crop, so as to assure the safety of their loans. Consequently, as cotton output rose, overall southern production of foodstuffs and the number of livestock per capita remained well below 1860 levels until the end of the century.

Thus the South was still locked tightly into a single-crop economy. The old plantation system, meanwhile, was supplanted by a system of small-scale farms mainly worked by tenants, most on a sharecropping basis. Moreover (and quite apart from economic considerations), racist attitudes made it nearly impossible for blacks to buy land; the white person who dared to sell land to a black would face not only community disapproval, but also a strong chance of harm from personal violence.[3]

The results were ruinous for the southern economy. "The evils of land monopoly, absentee ownership, soil mining, and the one-crop system, once associated with and blamed upon slavery, did not disappear with that institution but were, instead, aggravated, intensified and

multiplied."[4] Vast numbers of blacks were kept in debt peonage, in effect assuring their continuing poverty, and depriving the South of both the institutional flexibility and the sort of educated labor force that would have encouraged economic diversification, expansion of social and economic opportunities, and a process of vigorous industrialization. To be sure, some politicians and journalists in the South did champion the idea of a "New South," with a regional economy that fostered change through diversification, farm ownership by the people who worked the land, and opening up of opportunity for poor blacks and poor whites alike. But continuous expansion of the world market for southern cotton, despite disruptive cyclical fluctuations and a long-run downward trend in cotton prices in the South, reinforced the social status quo.

It should also be noted, however, that the rate of growth of cotton production and exports after 1880 was distinctly slower than before the Civil War. The South—quite apart from the devastation wrought by the war itself, with its effects on the region's income—had finally lost the primary demand stimulant that formerly had afforded it a high growth rate of total regional product. From 1880 to the end of the 1920s the South did gain in *absolute* per capita income, but it did not regain its position *relative to the national level.* This had been 77 percent of national average per capita income in 1840, but was only 55 percent in 1930. Thus, in the post-Civil War era the staple economy of the South was confronting a pattern of relative stagnation and lag, born of dependence on cotton; it also now confronted the need to find other means of economic development if it was to close the gap between its own and the national average income levels.

Tenancy was not confined to the South. In fact, in all regions of the country the proportion of farms operated on a tenancy basis was increasing in the late nineteenth century. But in the North, tenancy tended to be a commercial arrangement not necessarily very closely correlated with low-income status: Many midwestern farmers who made a good living remained ten-

[3]Roger Ransom and Richard Sutch, "Debt Peonage in the Cotton South After the Civil War," *Journal of Economic History,* 32 (1973):657; Sutch and Ransom, "The Ex-Slave in the Post-Bellum South: A Study of the Economic Impact of Racism in a Market Environment," *Journal of Economic History,* 33 (1973): 135–136.

[4]C. Vann Woodward, *Origins of the New South, 1877–1913* (Baton Rouge: Louisiana State University Press, 1951), pp. 182, 179–180. Recent scholarly research based on 1880 census returns and other sources relating to southern agriculture, shows that sharecroppers were generally paid only 25 to 50 percent of the crop—indicative of the high exploitation rate that was one of the "evils" mentioned above. *Cf.* Stephen J. DeCanio, *Agriculture in the Postbellum South* (Cambridge, Mass.: MIT Press, 1974).

TABLE 14–3. ACREAGE, OUTPUT, AND PRICES OF FARM STAPLES, 1859–1915

CROP AND YEAR	ACREAGE HARVESTED	PRODUCTION	PRICE (CURRENT)
Cotton	(Millions of Acres)	(Thousand Bales)	(Cents per Pound)
1859	–	5,387	11.5
1866	7.7	2,097	–
1873	11.0	4,168	14.1
1880	15.9	6,606	9.8
1890	20.9	8,653	8.6
1900	24.9	10,124	9.2
1910	31.5	11,609	14.0
1915	30.0	11,172	11.2
			(Cents per Bushel)
Corn	(Millions of Acres)	(Million Bushels)	
1859	–	839	46
1866	30	730	66
1873	44	1,008	48
1880	63	1,244	63
1890	75	1,650	49
1900	95	2,662	35
1910	102	2,853	52
1915	101	2,829	68
			(Dollars per Bushel)
Wheat	(Millions of Acres)	(Million Bushels)	
1859	–	173	1.02
1866	15	170	2.06
1873	25	322	1.16
1880	38	502	0.95
1890	37	449	0.84
1900	49	599	0.62
1910	46	625	0.91
1915	60	1,009	0.96

Source: U.S. Department of Commerce, Bureau of the Census, *Historical Statistics of the United States, Colonial Times to 1957* (Washington, D. C.: Government Printing Office), pp. 296–297, 301–302.

ants because it freed their capital for other sorts of investment such as mechanized equipment. In the South, however, tenancy and sharecropping were generally associated with poverty, debt peonage, and dependence on the plantation store at high credit charges.

PERSISTENT FARM PROBLEMS

For some fortunate American farmers, the years 1865–1893 were generally prosperous. This was so especially of those who shifted successfully to dairy production, orchard crops, garden vegetables and truck farming, and diversified farming in areas near the growing industrial cities. Their markets expanded at a rate sufficient to keep prices buoyant and to sustain their incomes. And of course there were periods of genuine prosperity for the livestock raisers and those who specialized in staple-crop production in the corn, wheat, and cotton belts. But for these cotton, grain, and livestock producers, the long-run trend of farm prices—though not *necessarily* real farm income—was relentlessly downward in the late nineteenth century.[5] For them, the rapid ex-

[5]Wholesale prices generally declined in the world economy from 1867 to 1897, with the American farm sector particularly hard hit after 1873. Of course, care must be used in any analysis of price declines for particular goods (such as farm products) or services (such as railroad transport), in order to take account of *relative* price changes as well as aggregative shifts.

pansion of farm output came to mean over-production, declining real incomes relative to trends in other sectors of the economy, and persistent problems that impelled what became known as the American "farm revolt."

Natural disasters

Some of the realities that dashed the optimistic hopes of people who made their lives on the land, especially in the newly opened western regions and in the South, appeared in the form of natural disasters. Blizzards in the mid-1880s wiped out many of the ranchers, large and small, in the western grazing regions. In the Midwest, the 1870s brought a succession of locust invasions that devastated the wheatfields and cornfields, leaving a harvest of human distress; and epidemics of hog cholera took a high toll in the corn belt in the 1880s and again in the 1890s. In the Southwest, the newer cotton-growing region suffered staggering losses, beginning in 1892, from boll-weevil invasions. Droughts, windstorms, and killing frosts periodically wrought havoc with farmers' lives and fortunes, as they always had.

Price fluctuations

The cyclical fluctuations in farm prices also created serious problems. In periods of good prices, farmers invested in land, machinery, and improvements, thus increasing their mortgaged long-term indebtedness and also their "intermediate"-term debts (3 to 4 years) for equipment bought on credit. Then a drop in prices made it difficult for them to keep up interest payments and to pay the taxes on their land. One solution was to increase the farm's production; but if the price slump carried over into a second or third year, it became harder still to meet debt-carrying charges. A mortgage foreclosure on the farm or a sheriff's sale to meet overdue taxes was often the result. The long-term deflation of the period 1867–1897 fell hard on the farmer. Interest rates in the South and West tended to be higher than in longer-settled regions, and debts had to be paid off in the face of the secular (long-term) price-decline pattern.

Middlemen and speculators

Farmers also complained widely of middlemen and commodity speculators who handled their crops, standing between them and the final consumer. The warehouse operators, speculators in futures, and marketing firms all took an unfair proportion of their products' value, farmers contended. One farm newspaper declared in 1890:

> There are three great crops raised in Nebraska. One is a crop of corn, one a crop of freight rates, and one a crop of interest. One is produced by the farmers who by sweat and toil farm the land. The other two are produced by men who sit in their offices and behind their bank counters and farm the farmers.[6]

The crop of freight rates was mainly harvested by the railroads. In many regions farmers had no choice except to ship on a railroad line that had a local monopoly of traffic. In localities where there were competing lines, freight rates tended to be lower; but even so, the railroads often joined in pools or rate agreements, forcing small shippers to bear the burden of high freight charges. The railroads were then forming gigantic mergers, and were typically controlled by city financiers who seemed to care little for the customers they served on distant farms. These facts increased the bitterness that was felt toward them by many of the nation's farmers. Similar resentment was directed against the land speculators, the mortgage-lending companies, and the bankers, whom farmers regarded as being responsible for the heavy burden of interest rates.

The roots of agrarian unrest

Some historians have argued recently that the farmers' angry complaints were in fact misguided. The railroads and middlemen did, after all, successfully get American products from the farms across enormous distances to markets in the United States and Europe. Indeed, one historian of the middlemen in grain marketing has shown that "with all its imperfections, it was the highly developed and tightly organized grain business, along with additional advantages in transportation, that accounted in large measure for the unique position of the American wheat trade" in the period 1870–1900.[7] Other scholars emphasize that *average* railroad rates declined in the post-1865 period, with obvious advantages to at least some farmers.

[6]*Farmers' Alliance,* August 23, 1890, quoted in John D. Hicks, *The Populist Revolt* (Minneapolis: University of Minnesota Press, 1931), p. 83.

[7]Morton Rothstein, "America in the International Rivalry for the British Wheat Market, 1860–1914," *Mississippi Valley Historical Review,* 47 (1960):411.

Together with the middlemen's introduction of bulk-handling techniques, increasing size of lake and oceangoing vessels, and new methods of organizing the trade in farm commodities, declining transport rates contributed to maintaining farm incomes at levels that became the envy of farmers in other countries.

Even the land speculator and mortgage lender have lately received highly positive appraisals, on the grounds that these businessmen extended credit when it was not forthcoming from banks or other sources, helped to channel capital into new frontier districts, and expedited settlement and farm-making. "These entrepreneurs," writes one historian, "were as essential to the economic development of the West as were their clients, the frontier farmers."[8] On different lines, some scholars have recently argued that the farmers who protested their conditions so loudly, condemning "conspiracies" of railroad corporations and others, in fact did so because they were frustrated by their loss of social status in an industrializing society. In essence, according to this view, farmers were irrational and even "paranoid."[9]

Where does the truth lie? How realistic were farmers' complaints? First, it must be recognized that if farmers were beset with anxieties, those anxieties were often well founded. It is an objective fact that railroads did form pools and otherwise exact high charges from farmers. It is also true that middlemen often engaged in shady practices and fraud, and that warehouse operators were often guilty of manipulating futures markets. It is true as well, that interest rates were staggeringly high in frontier areas, often running 15 to 20 percent or even more. These were no chimerical products of "paranoid minds." They were realities for many American farmers. And with regard to alleged paranoia, many urban businessmen and politicians, journalists, and other commentators spoke in precisely the same terms about "conspiracy" and "exploitation." Although we certainly must allow the possibility of rhetorical excess, it would seem far-fetched to label so many elements of the society paranoid, or even

subject to status anxiety to the point where their perceptions of farm problems were hopelessly distorted. In sum, the positive contributions of the speculators, lenders, middlemen, and railroads to the process of farm-sector expansion do need to be recognized; but the readiness of these capitalists to charge what the traffic would bear must not be written off as insignificant.

The independent farmer and foreign sales

Two basic problems of post-1865 American agriculture have not been disputed. One was the fact that the millions of farmers could not rely on combination, merger, market control, production cutbacks, and the other devices by which manufacturing firms and transportation companies coped with intensifying competition, price decline, and the distress accompanying periods of general business contraction. The other was the enormous expansion of production of the staple crops (shown in Table 14.3). This expansion put severe pressure on the price structure in agriculture. Moreover, wheat, cotton, and corn were all highly sensitive to world market fluctuations. Although some 80 percent of all U.S. farm output was consumed in the domestic market from 1870 to 1900, the situation for the staple crops was very different. In 1870 over 80 percent of cotton farmers' income was derived from *foreign* sales; and even in 1900, by which time U.S. textile production had increased enormously, still two-thirds of the American cotton crop was sold abroad. On a less dramatic scale, wheat producers were also highly subject to world market forces. In some years in the late nineteenth century, one-fourth of the wheat crop was sold in foreign markets. Similarly, the prices received by U.S. livestock raisers and corn farmers were influenced significantly by the prices received abroad by that portion of American meat products exported.

Staggering rises in output of corn, wheat, and cotton in the United States were only one part of the story. The other was intensifying competition from producers in other countries who served the same world markets as did American farmers. Russian wheat exports rose dramatically in the 1880s, and by the next decade Australia and Canada were also competing with U.S. farmers in the European grain market. Further pressure on grain prices came from sales of Argentine and Indian exports. In the 1890s, both Egypt and India were giving American cotton producers formidable competition in the European market.

[8]Robert Swierenga, *Pioneers and Profits: Land Speculation on the Iowa Frontier* (Ames: Iowa State University Press, 1968), p. 227.

[9]In the 1950s particularly, revisionist social scientists seeking to explain the origins of disturbing contemporary political trends fastened on a view of the agrarian Populists of the 1890s as irrational, demagogic, paranoid, obsessed, and the like. See the discussion of this literature in C. Vann Woodward, "The Ghost of Populism Walks Again," *New York Times Magazine,* June 4, 1972, p. 64.

Fortunately for American farmers, a favorable shift in market forces expanded demand for their products and set the stage for a golden age of agriculture after 1900. (See p. 217.) But (See p. 217.) from 1867 to 1897 there had been hard times aplenty; the golden age was a long time coming.

THE FARM REVOLT

By the early 1870s, the precipitous decline in agricultural prices impelled farmers to seek greater power in national politics. Farmers' concern over their plight led to repeated efforts to organize farm interests more effectively, both then and later in the century. From those efforts came the first massive social attack on private market mechanisms in post-Civil War America. By its setting of political and legal precedents for other aggrieved groups in the society, it was a movement of enormous long-run significance.

Early farm movements

Between 1869 and 1875, cotton fell from 16.5 cents to 11 cents a pound, corn from 72 to 41 cents a bushel, and wheat and other grain prices also fell though not so far as they would in the 1880s. Farmers thus became prominent in the organization of the Greenback party, which in the mid-1870s pressed for inflationary monetary policies. The Greenback movement lost strength when farm prices turned upward temporarily in 1880 and 1881. But meanwhile western and southern farmers had also built up a new organization, the Patrons of Husbandry (the Grange), which attained a membership of 800,000 by the mid-1870s. The Grange became an active voice in midwestern politics, pushing for state regulation of railroads and warehousing. The main thrust of the Grange, however, was to encourage local farmers to form cooperatives, and also to relieve the loneliness and isolation of rural life for farm families.

The Farmers' Alliances

As the crisis of farm prices became acute after 1881, groups far more radical than the Grange began to gather strength: the Wheel and the Farmers' Alliances. The Alliances were composed mainly of dirt farmers. Unlike the Grange, they generally excluded from membership such elements as rural merchants and lawyers, and they did not include large-scale farmers or gentleman-farmers. The Alliances pressed militantly for antitrust laws, government ownership of the railroads, a progressive income tax, and an inflationary monetary policy (especially free coinage of silver). In the early 1890s, cotton and corn prices fell to half the level of 20 years earlier, and wheat, which had been $2 a bushel in 1867, fell as low as 49 cents. As mortgage default and tax foreclosures caused thousands of farmers to lose their land, militancy reached new heights in the cotton, corn, and wheat belts.

The climax of the farm revolt was reached when the People's party (known as Populists) emerged as a major force in national politics in 1890. The political backbone of the new party was formed by the Northwestern and Southern Alliances, together with the southern Colored Farmers' Alliance. They joined forces with socialist and radical intellectuals, the remnant of Knights of Labor industrial unionists, advocates of free coinage (including the mining interests in the Rocky Mountain area), and other disparate groups—what one reformer, Henry Demarest Lloyd, called "a fortuitous collection of the dissatisfied."[10] Populist and Alliance candidates won many state offices and congressional seats, and the 1892 Populist candidate for President, James Weaver of Iowa, polled over a million votes, or 9 percent of all ballots cast. Although Grover Cleveland won the election and the Democrats controlled Congress, they had clearly been put on notice that farm interests were determined to be heard.

McKinley vs. Bryan

As general business conditions became severely depressed after 1893, and unemployment in the cities matched farm-region distress, the Democratic party took up some of the insurgents' causes. In 1896 the Democrats nominated the fiery young orator William Jennings Bryan of Nebraska for the presidency, and Bryan worked valiantly to forge a winning coalition of farmers and urban working-class voters. He based nearly his entire campaign upon free coinage of silver, a policy of monetary inflation; other reform concerns (taxation, banking practices and interest rates, railroad regulation, and so on) were subordinated. The Republicans, who were opposing Bryan with the Ohio con-

[10]Quoted in ibid., p. 17.

servative William McKinley, argued that a "sound currency," high tariffs, and business confidence were needed to combat the depression. Pressed to choose, mainstream American urban middle-class voters and urban workers voted heavily for McKinley; Bryan's appeal was mainly in the cotton and wheat belts and in the silver-mining states of the Far West.

The 1896 election was a turning point for the nation's farmers. McKinley's victory was doubtless aided greatly by an upturn in the business cycle during the election campaign months. After 1897, farm prices moved up from their depressed levels, taking some of the steam out of agrarian radicalism. In the South, moreover, disillusionment with the politics of protest—and also abiding racial prejudice, which could easily be directed against the farm radicals for their alliance of the black and white poor—led to legal disfranchisement of the black voters and a new alignment of the major parties. More generally, American farmers tended to abandon the evangelical style of the Populists and the 1896 Bryan campaign, at least until renewed agricultural depression in the 1920s revived that style. In the period from 1897 until 1920, farm groups tended to concentrate upon narrowly focused programs that met specific farm needs: cheaper credit, more efficiency in marketing farm products, support of farm-export efforts, and other policies of a technical nature. The free-wheeling agrarian commitment to free silver yielded to a much more sober demand for essentially conservative technical reforms of the monetary and banking systems.[11]

FARM PROSPERITY: THE GOLDEN AGE

In the period from 1897 until World War I, agriculture experienced a general prosperity unmatched since the mid-nineteenth century. There was a slowdown in the rate at which new lands were settled and brought into farm production, and output of some major crops, notably corn and cotton, tended to level off (see Table 14–3). Meanwhile, industrial output expanded at an enormous rate; population increased in the cities under the impact of massive immigration from southern and eastern Europe; and farm prices tended to rise more rapidly than the prices farmers had to pay for products they consumed, leading to greatly improved real farm income.[12] The vastly improved status of the farm sector was reflected in the rise in value of crops, from $3 billion in 1899 to $5.5 billion in 1909, then to $6 billion in 1914. Also supportive of farm income and reflecting farm prices was the doubling in the value of farmland from 1900 to 1910 alone. The continued success of American farm exports was also a factor in the agricultural prosperity that made this a "golden age" for farmers.

Changes in dietary tastes, shifting market opportunities, and the availability of investment capital in the farm sector as incomes rose also had major effects on the farmer's economic role. While output of grains rose (1897–1914) only 0.6 percent annually and meat animals 0.7 percent, there were other newly popular crops whose output increased much more rapidly: cottonseed, flaxseed, and peanuts by nearly 4 percent, citrus fruits by 9 percent, and poultry and eggs by 3.1 percent. Urban workers' incomes were also rising markedly during this period of rapid economic growth. Hence consumers could take advantage of refrigeration in transport to consume more eggs and dairy products. California and Florida became suppliers of citrus fruits to the whole nation, and there was a general rise in consumption of fruits and vegetables (based also on spreading knowledge of their importance for sound diets) that set the stage for a vast expansion of American orchard and garden crops in the early twentieth century.

GOVERNMENT AND SCIENTIFIC FARMING

The transformation of American farming after 1865 was influenced by continued progress in scientific agriculture and by various forms of limited government intervention. The involvement of government took three main forms:

---

[12]Richard Hofstadter, *The Age of Reform: From Bryan to F.D.R.* (New York: Knopf, 1955), pp. 109–110.

[11]See pp. 218 and 346–347.

research and education, the protection of farm interests through technical reforms, and irrigation and reclamation aid.

Research and education

The 1862 Morrill Act, which provided land grants to the states for colleges of agriculture and the mechanical arts, afforded a great stimulus to new activity. Colleges were founded or expanded in every state, and in 1887 the Hatch Act provided new Federal funds for experimental stations and research. The resultant research in the state land-grant colleges was marked by a rich diversity that matched the diversity of agriculture itself. Beginning in 1914, when Congress enacted the Smith-Lever Act, annual federal grants were also provided for "extension work," by which the land-grant colleges carried the results of their research directly to the farmer through correspondence, publications, lectures, and demonstrations of new farm equipment and techniques.

The agricultural colleges also produced a growing supply of skilled personnel who became available to staff an increasingly professionalized Department of Agriculture. In 1889 the department attained full-fledged cabinet status, and in ensuing years the USDA's activities proliferated. New bureaus and divisions were established for research and regulation in such areas as inspection of meat for export, quarantine of animals, importation and distribution of new plant varieties, control of agricultural pests, and improvement of fertilizer and soil-management techniques. When Congress enacted the Pure Food and Drug Act (1906), authority to enforce this legislation was given to the USDA, which by then commanded the expertise of a developed bureaucracy sufficient to handle the complex job of carrying out inspections in thousands of plants.

The state governments also aided farming through their own activities. Occasionally the states offered subsidies to encourage production of specific commodities. In 1919, for example, North Dakota launched a project for state control and ownership of flour mills, terminal elevators, and agencies for giving credit to farmers. Efforts such as this were short-lived. The more enduring contributions of the states included sponsorship of agricultural fairs, support of university and extension research and dissemination of technical information, and sponsorship of farmers' education in the schools.

Technical reforms

Another main focus of special-interest farm legislation was the problem of farm credit. High interest rates in the West and South and growing farm debt led to widespread demands for government aid. Until failure of the 1896 Bryan campaign, the organized farm groups concentrated on demanding inflationary monetary policies. But then the focus shifted to more technical reforms, with specific focus on credit; and when the Federal Reserve System was inaugurated in 1913, national banks were permitted for the first time to lend money on farm mortgages.[13] In 1916, during Woodrow Wilson's presidency, the Federal Farm Loan Act also provided for the founding of twelve federal land banks, which lent funds to cooperative farm marketing groups. Not until 1923, however, did somewhat more adequate federal funding for intermediate credit become available.

Farm groups were continuously active in political struggles for the regulation of railroads' and warehousemen's rates and practices, beginning with the midwestern Grange movement of the 1860s and 1870s. Typically, farm interests formed coalitions with groups of nonfarm businessmen and political-reform factions that represented the consumers' interest in more favorable retail prices. Over the long run, the pressure of farm organizations for more active government regulation, reform of the nation's banking and monetary systems, and free rural mail delivery and other innovations in government's role had a major impact upon the stance of the two national parties on these issues.

Irrigation and reclamation

The third major area of government intervention was in the field of irrigation and reclamation. Activities in this field centered, of course, in the arid and semi-arid regions of the West. (See Chap. 13.) The struggle for water in the dry regions produced extensive litigation and intense conflicts over riparian law in all the Rocky Mountain and Pacific states.

Colorado's state government led in a type of intervention that imposed more orderly distribution and use of water resources. In 1879 and 1881, the state enacted laws that established regional districts, with a water commissioner appointed to allocate the available flow and courts empowered to adjudicate conflicting claims based on prior rights. California followed suit in 1887, with its Wright Act, empowering local voters to set up irrigation projects to be financed through special taxes.

After enactment of the federal Newlands Act in 1902, providing for greatly increased funding of western water projects (see page 202

---

[13]See p. 309.

above), the total acreage under irrigation began to climb steeply. Sixteen western states were aided by the law; and although some of the early projects were poorly conceived or designed, still within five years provision had been made for the eventual irrigation of some 2.5 million acres. This represented a one-third increase in the area that had been provided with irrigation facilities by private enterprise and the state governments over a period of more than three decades.[14]

Meanwhile, in the midwestern and eastern states, similar legislation was passed for intervention by the state governments for purposes of organizing and administering drainage districts in wet areas. The scope of such projects and the capital investments involved were, however, but a small fraction of what was being undertaken in the irrigation projects of the West.

Although other forms of government intervention on behalf of farm interests were of some importance, as has been noted, it was the reclamation and irrigation projects that were to emerge as the true predecessors of public policy toward agriculture in future years. For in three respects the Newlands Act foreshadowed modern farm policies: (1) It shifted the locus of decision-making power and policy responsibility to the federal level, (2) it set up a new federal agency (in this case, the Reclamation Service) with extensive administrative power in day-to-day operation of the program, and (3) it involved massive cash subsidies and capital expenditures to meet farmers' needs. As actually administered, moreover, the irrigation and reclamation program foreshadowed twentieth-century American farm policy in another vital respect. Its benefits accrued heavily to the large-scale farmers, including emergent corporate-style "agribusiness," while concern for the small family farm and its survival was at best severely diminished.[15]

SELECTED READINGS

NOTE: See also works listed in selected readings for Chapter 13.

Barger, Harold, and Landsberg, Hans, *American Agriculture, 1899–1939* (New York: National Bureau of Economic Research, 1942).

*Bogue, Allan, *From Prairie to Corn Belt* (Chicago: University of Chicago Press, 1963).

*———, *Money at Interest* (Ithaca: Cornell University Press, 1955).

Bogue, Margaret B., *Patterns from the Sod: Land Use and Tenure in the Grand Prairie, 1850–1900* (Springfield: Illinois State Historical Society, 1959).

Cox, LaWanda F., "The American Agricultural Wage Earner, 1865–1900," *Agricultural History,* XXII (1949).

*Daniel, Pete, *The Shadow of Slavery: Peonage in the South, 1901–1969* (New York: Oxford University Press, 1973).

DeCanio, Stephen J., *Agriculture in the Postbellum South: The Economics of Production and Supply* (Cambridge, Mass.: MIT Press, 1974).

Ellis, David M., ed., *The Frontier in American Development* (Ithaca: Cornell University Press, 1969).

*Fite, Gilbert C., *The Farmers' Frontier, 1865–1900* (New York: Holt, Rinehart and Winston 1966).

Gates, Paul Wallace, *Landlords and Tenants on the Prairie Frontier: Studies in American Land Policy* (Ithaca: Cornell University Press, 1973).

Hayter, Earl, *The Troubled Farmer, 1850–1900* (DeKalb, Ill.: Northern Illinois University Press, 1970).

*Hicks, John D., *The Populist Revolt* (Minneapolis: University of Minnesota Press, 1931).

[14]Gilbert C. Fite, *The Farmers' Frontier, 1865–1900* (New York: Holt, Rinehart and Winston, 1966), pp. 166–170, 183–192; Paul Wallace Gates, *History of Public Land Law Development* (Washington, D.C.: Government Printing Office, 1968), pp. 643–666.

[15]This was so despite a provision of the Newlands Act that limited provision of water to farms of 160 acres or less. The provision was blatantly ignored by federal officials down to the 1960s, and it was ingeniously evaded by large-scale agri-business interests. Cf. Paul S. Taylor, "Reclamation: The Rise and Fall of an American Idea," *The American West,* 7 (1970):27–33, 63.

Lampard, Eric E., *The Rise of the Dairy Industry in Wisconsin* (Madison: State Historical Society of Wisconsin, 1963).

Mayhew, Anne, "A Reappraisal of the Causes of Farm Protest in the United States, 1870–1900," *Journal of Economic History,* XXXII (1972).

Miller, George H., *Railroads and the Granger Laws* (Madison: University of Wisconsin Press, 1971).

Rasmussen, Wayne D., "The Civil War: A Catalyst of Agricultural Revolution," *Agricultural History,* XXXIX (1965).

———, "The Impact of Technological Change on American Agriculture, 1862–1962," *Journal of Economic History,* XXII (1972).

Rothstein, Morton, "America in the International Rivalry for the British Wheat Market, 1860–1914," *Mississippi Valley Historical Review,* XLVII (1960).

*Saloutos, Theodore, *Farmer Movements in the South, 1865–1933* (Lincoln, Neb.: Bison Books, 1960).

Schlebecker, John T. *Whereby We Thrive: A History of American Farming, 1607–1972* (Ames: Iowa State University Press, 1975).

*Shannon, Fred, *The Farmer's Last Frontier: Agriculture, 1860–1897* (New York: Holt, Rinehart and Winston, 1945).

Shideler, James H., ed., *Agriculture in the Development of the Far West* (Washington, D.C.: Agricultural History Society, 1975).

Sitterson, J. Carlyle, *Sugar Country: The Cane Sugar Industry in the South, 1753–1950* (Lexington: University of Kentucky Press, 1953).

Towne, Marvin W., and Rasmussen, Wayne D., "Farm Gross Product and Gross Investment in the 19th Century," in National Bureau of Economic Research, *Trends in the American Economy in the 19th Century* (Princeton, N.J.: Princeton University Press, 1960).

U.S. Department of Agriculture, *Yearbook, 1962* (Washington, D.C.: 1963). (A history of the USDA.).

Woodward, C. Vann, *Origins of the New South, 1877–1913* (Baton Rouge: Louisiana State University Press, 1951).

Wright, Gavin, "Slavery and the Cotton Boom," *Explorations in Economic History,* XII (1975).

manufacturing and the modern industrial nation

In any statistical portrayal of growth in the American economy from 1865 to 1914, the picture must be dominated by the sharp upward-sweeping curve that depicts the rise of manufacturing. A retrospective view reveals that in 1865, when America was already a major industrial nation, the manufacturing sector was producing only 17 percent of what it would produce by 1900. In 1880 the curve had reached 42 percent of the 1900 level. It continued upward in the 1880s, rising to 70 percent by the decade's end. Despite a long and severe depression in the mid-1890s, output leaped forward again, and from the 100 mark at the century's end, the upward course continued. The index of industrial output nearly doubled in only 15 years. (See Figure 15–1).

Other quantitative measures of manufacturing indicate that by 1900 the modern industrial order had taken shape in the United States. Capital invested in manufacturing facilities rose from $3 billion in 1880 to over $8 billion in 1900, then soared to nearly $40 billion by 1914. As shown in Table 15–1, manufacturing accounted for more than half of total value added in the economy's commodity output by 1900, while agriculture, despite immense absolute increases in production since 1865, had dropped to a one-third share. By 1900, one-fifth of all American workers were directly engaged in manufacturing—not much below the 25 percent level that has generally prevailed from 1920 to the present day.[1]

[1]Computed from Stanley Lebergott, *Manpower in Economic Growth: The American Record Since 1800* (New York: McGraw-Hill, 1964), p. 510.

The giant corporation

In the organization of business enterprise, the dramatic rise of manufacturing created a new order, one presaged by the giant railroad corporations of the 1850s but that came to fruition only with the spread of giantism into the manufacturing sector. In 1865 the typical American business concern was still owned by an individual entrepreneur, a family, or a partnership; and it did its business locally, in the main, while its management was based on relatively simple organization. But by the 1890s the basic structure of the American business system had been transformed. Although small businesses persisted, and in great numbers, the dominant form of enterprise in the economy, measured in terms of economic power, was the giant corporation. Increasing scale of operations, ownership-management separation, complex management structures, and increasing concentration of business in the hands of a few firms, all were distinctly established trends. In 1900 corporations employed some 70 percent of all production workers outside of agriculture; by 1919 the proportion had risen to 87 percent. American society had become "a citizenry of wage-earners."[2]

Firms controlling assets of 10 million or more each numbered nearly a hundred at the turn of the century. They accounted for the major part of iron and steel capacity, of farm-machinery production, of processing of many farm products. In addition, the giant manufacturing firms were forming close links with

[2]William Letwin, "The Past and Future of the American Businessman," *Daedalus*, 98 (Winter 1969):11.

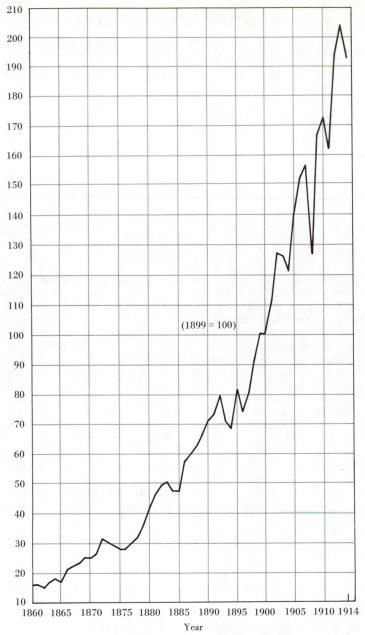

Figure 15–1. **Edwin Frickey's Index of Production for Manufacture, 1860–1914 (1899 = 100).** Source: U.S. Department of Commerce, Bureau of the Census, *Historical Statistics of the United States, Colonial Times to 1957* (Washington, D.C.: U.S. Government Printing Office, 1960), p. 409.

investment banking firms that within a decade would control several billions of dollars in assets. Apart from the strictly economic dimensions of big business's power by 1900, the giant corporations exercised great influence in the nation's public policies, both domestic and foreign.

It was in the manufacturing sector that the Industrial Revolution generated its most far-reaching, transforming effects. The locus of

TABLE 15–1. VALUE ADDED IN COMMODITY OUTPUT, BY SECTORS 1840–1900: PERCENTAGE SHARES (CONSTANT, 1879 PRICES)

YEAR	AGRICULTURE	MINING	MANUFACTURING	CONSTRUCTION
1839	72%	1%	17%	10%
1849	60	1	30	10
1859	56	1	32	11
1869	53	2	33	12
1879	49	3	37	11
1889	37	4	48	11
1899	33	5	53	9

Source: U.S. Department of Commerce, Bureau of the Census, *Historical Statistics of the United States, Colonial Times to 1957* (Washington, D.C.: Government Printing Office, 1960), p. 139.

power resided principally in this sector, and by examining the dynamics of change in manufacturing we can gain important insights into how big business emerged to a position of dominance in American capitalism in the post-Civil War period.

THE GROWTH OF MAJOR INDUSTRIES

Manufacturing and the larger process of industrialization had already taken hold in America well before the Civil War, and the shift to factory-organized production was well under way in many key industries by the 1850s. Table 15–1 shows the percentage of value added in commodity output by manufacturing and other sectors—a good measure of each sector's importance, since value added represents the value of product minus the cost of materials used.

As shown in Table 15–2, there were some major changes in the rank and importance of manufacturing industries. Whereas in 1860 the leading industries by value added had all been dependent upon either agriculture or lumbering (see Table 11–1, page 166), by 1904 iron and steel manufacture had advanced decisively to first place. In 1919 this branch of heavy industry had increased its value added more than fourfold over the 1904 level. (Moreover, the tenth ranked industry group was composed of firms producing metals and metal products other than iron and steel.)

Meanwhile the development of the automobile launched a major new industry, and by 1919 the manufacture of land-transport vehicles had attained eighth rank among the leading groups. Indicative of the enormous aggregate advance in manufacturing was the fact that in 1914 the 25th ranking industry (silk goods), with a value of total output of $254 million, exceeded the production of the industry that had ranked first in 1860.

TECHNOLOGICAL ADVANCE: METALLURGY

As indicated by the data on leading industries, post-1865 advances in metallurgy, especially iron and steel, were of basic importance to the entire manufacturing sector. Metals offered durability, strength, and malleability; they could be used for stronger bonding, as with rivets and welding; and they could be used to build machinery capable of running at high speeds, of being designed to very close tolerances, and of being adapted to the new sources of power. In sum, metals became the basic materials from which the machinery of the modern industrial revolution was built.

Railroads had been major users of iron in the pre–Civil War period. Metal had also begun to replace wood in machinery construction, and iron was widely used for stoves, farm implements, and a wide variety of common goods. But in the late nineteenth century, metal production and consumption were of an entirely different order of magnitude. Steel production soared from less than 400,000 tons in 1875 to 4.3 million in 1890, over 10 million in 1900, and 23.5 million in 1914. Abundant natural resources, including iron ore and coal deposits, together with improved transportation

TABLE 15–2. VALUE ADDED BY LEADING MANUFACTURING INDUSTRY GROUPS, 1904 AND 1919 ($ MILLION, CURRENT PRICES)

	1904	1919
1. Iron and steel and their products	$1009	$4588
2. Textiles and their products (clothing, etc.)	908	3834
3. Lumber and lumber products	702	1710
4. Paper and printing	550	1706
5. Food products	539	2327
6. Miscellaneous	491	3313
7. Chemicals and related products	442	1863
8. Liquors and beverages	361	381
9. Stone, clay, and glass products	268	677
10. Metals and metal products other than iron and steel	263	850
11. Leather and leather products	244	896
12. Tobacco manufactures	205	529
13. Railroad repair shops	167	807
14. Vehicles for land transport	143	1561

Source: U·S. Department of Commerce, *Statistical Abstract*, 1909, 1921.

systems and major innovations in the production process itself, all contributed to the rising output of metals. (See pages 228–229.)

The machine-tool industry

Advances in metallurgy and the use of petroleum lubricants stimulated the progress of design and development of machine tools: the machines that cut, thread, grind, and shape metals. Machine tools were of crucial importance in the advance of technology because they produced parts and fittings to standard shapes and sizes. Thus the components of manufactured products became standardized, and this meant that the manufacturing process in an industrial plant could become one of *assembly:* Instead of shaping, fitting, and otherwise using highly skilled specialized techniques at the workbench, the industrial laborer now engaged in the assembly of machine-tooled parts based on a continuous-production technology. The machine-tool industry itself was composed of numerous highly specialized firms. Typically they might solve a problem in the manufacture of machinery for one sort of product, then apply the technique to solution of problems in very different areas of production in other industries. As the economic historian Nathan Rosenberg has written, the machine-tool firms

> played the role of a transmission center in the diffusion of the new technology. . . . The existence of a well-developed machine-tool industry induced a higher rate of technological change by lowering the cost of innovation throughout the metal-using sectors of the economy.[3]

MANAGEMENT CONCEPTS: MASS PRODUCTION

Machine tools provided the essential features of mass production: interchangeability, standardization, and assembly. These features were hardly unknown to the American manufacturing scene, for standardized parts and assembly had been applied since before the Civil War to the manufacture of small firearms, watches and clocks, sewing machines, and some agricultural machinery. But in the post-1865 era, the assembly system of production became much more general, spreading to the production of typewriters, bicycles, coaches and carriages, and other consumer products.

According to Henry Ford, whose automobile firm became a pioneering developer of the technique,

> Mass production is the focussing upon a manufacturing product of the principles of power, accuracy, economy, system, continuity and speed . . . and the normal result is a productive organization that delivers in quantities a useful commodity

[3]Nathan Rosenberg. *Technology and American Economic Growth* (New York: Harper & Row, 1972), p. 102.

of standard material, workmanship and design at minimum cost.[4]

Note that in contrast to the factory system of fixed stations, mass production involves continuous production; also, modern mass production is almost inconceivable—given the principles of "system, continuity, and speed"—without electrical power.

The mass market

To deliver "in quantities" and to minimize costs through mass assembly, the manufacturer requires a mass market; and the U.S. economy provided a highly favorable basis for mass consumption in the years from 1865 to 1914. Population increase, as we have seen, was steady and impressive, so that the population reached nearly 80 million—twice that of Great Britain or France—even before 1900. Urbanization brought large numbers of consumers together in dense market concentrations. Because the mass-produced product could be placed in the consumer's hands at minimum cost, the consumer had an incentive to buy and forego any aesthetic values or other qualities attached to more individualized designs, such as were available from craftsmen at higher prices. With incomes rising, the American public proved willing to maximize its purchasing power through use of standardized goods. The manufacturers built up their own wholesale systems and resorted to intensive advertising and other marketing techniques to foster mass consumption. In sum, the American market provided fertile ground in which mass-production manufacturing could flourish.

The assembly line

The assembly-line method required detailed coordination of the flow of materials and supplies to the assembly floor, where components were carried to the workers. To maintain maximum control of flow, therefore, the firms that undertook mass production through assembly techniques often sought to acquire control of raw-material supplies, so they could free themselves of dependence upon other firms for the supplies they needed to produce finished goods. In this drive for "vertical integration," as it was termed, as in the introduction of assembly-line technique, Ford was an innovating firm.

Scientific management

In Ford's auto plants an essential characteristic of mass production appeared, beginning in 1913, in the form of the "moving assembly." The auto frame was put on a moving track or belt; each worker along the line had one simplified task to perform, and the frames were delivered to workers at speeds controlled by foremen and managers (later by control instruments).

Assembly technique stimulated other efforts to organize the individual worker's labor more efficiently. The theory and development of "scientific management" was largely initiated by Frederick W. Taylor, who conducted studies of workers' physical motions and uses of time in the 1890s. The moving assembly provided an opportunity for Taylor to apply his ideas for stimulating productivity through repetition of simple body and hand motions and through tight control over the laborer's minute-to-minute activity. Understandably, many assembly workers bitterly denounced the contributions of scientific management as dehumanizing and punishing. "Speedups" reduced the laborer to the status of a cog in the impersonal machinery of production.

INVENTION AND THE PATENT SYSTEM

The rate of technological advance and innovation was influenced by numerous factors in the dynamics of growth after 1865. First, the great size and diversity of the economy, with new products being introduced continuously and economies of scale stimulated by growing market size, created important incentives for invention. The intensity of competition and the high capital formation rate—indicating that

business firms were plowing back earnings into new equipment—also stimulated the advance of technology. Moreover, the United States has had a liberal patent law, which provides inventors with legal monopoly rights for a period of 17 years from the date of grant—often 20 years or more from the date of application. (President Lincoln once said that the patent laws added the fuel of self-interest to the fire of genius.) The number of patents issued ranged narrowly around the 12,000 mark from the Civil War until the 1880s, when the number doubled;

[4]Henry Ford, "Mass Production," *Encyclopedia Britannica*, 13th ed. suppl. vol. 2 (London, 1926), p. 821.

then it reached 30,000 in 1904 and more than 40,000 by 1914. The industries in which capital investment rates were highest tended to attract the greatest attention from inventors.

Until late in the nineteenth century, the typical operation of the inventor was individual work in a small shop. But by the 1890s some of the larger corporate firms were organizing large, well-coordinated laboratories and concentrating team research efforts on the solution of problems they encountered in the quest for greater efficiency. Meanwhile, professionalization of engineering and research in government laboratories, especially in the Department of Agriculture, gave research activity additional impetus.

The sources of invention

Since the commencement of American industrialization in the early nineteenth century, the United States had enjoyed what has been termed "the advantage of the late starter." That is to say, American industry was able to borrow from technology developed earlier in Great Britain—then the world's most advanced manufacturing nation—as well as to draw from the inventive work of innovators in the field of technology internationally. In the late nineteenth century the United States continued to borrow and adapt ideas for its own purposes. Many of the major American inventions, so called, were based squarely upon prior advances in basic science or engineering of other nations. Moreover, the vast immigration from Europe brought to American shores a rich variety of individual talents that—in an atmosphere that encouraged individual initiative and gave considerable play to inventors—directly contributed to the growing pool of technical knowledge. Among the major advances of the post-1865 period were these: the loading coil for long-distance telephony and telegraphy, developed by Michael Pupin, of Serbian extraction; the alternating current (AC) motor, designed by Nikola Tesla, Croatian; the ironclad ship and screw propeller, first advanced in the pre–Civil War years and fully developed after 1865, the work of John Ericsson, a Swede; and design of improved AC generators, pioneered by the German immigrant Charles Steinmetz.

Among the major innovations in technology in the years after 1865 to which American inventors and firms made major contributions, but in nearly all of which European inventive activity was also vital in advancing the technology, were these: In *agriculture:* barbed wire, the automatic twine binder, the harvester combine, application of nitrates for fertilizer, the milking machine, and the gasoline tractor. In *mining:* the diamond drill, compressed-air power transmission, and petroleum-refining technique. In *transportation:* the high-pressure boiler, navigational equipment, use of wireless telegraphy, automated bulk-loading, and refrigerated transport equipment. In *manufacturing:* the list of new techniques and products was immense; the accelerating pace of the Industrial Revolution caused enormous proliferation of innovations with basic effects on the structure of production in the manufacturing sector. Of prime importance were developments in metallurgy, larger-scale and fuller automaticity of textile-manufacturing equipment, and introduction of new sources of power, including electricity and the internal-combustion engine.

The following analyses of specific industries will illustrate the diverse effects of technological innovation and other factors that shaped industrial development.

FOOD PROCESSING

The processing of meat, grinding of grains, and preservation of fruits and vegetables were still mainly household or neighborhood industries at the beginning of the nineteenth century. Meat packing and milling were first to become more heavily concentrated in urban centers, but even they were still fairly dispersed until the 1850s. Urbanization, with its concentrations of population dependent on the rural hinterland for food, increased the incentives at midcentury for moving these food-processing activities into centralized factories. The commercial market for these products was expanded also by the desire to escape the drudgery of household tasks such as canning and preserving, and by foreign demand for American meat and foodstuffs.

Meat packing

New technology revolutionized meat packing after the Civil War. Beginning in the 1870s, refrigeration was introduced for both meat storage and transportation by railroad and waterway. Pioneering packers, including Philip and Herman Armour, Gustavus F. Swift, and Nelson Morris, greatly increased the scale of their operations in Chicago, the principal packing center. Rising scale of production expedited the simplification of labor tasks, including the grotesque slaughtering process contemptuously known as the "disassembly line." The large packing firms also built up their own marketing organizations to carry their products directly to retail outlets, bypassing the traditional wholesalers. This too tended to increase efficiency and cost savings in the production and distribution processes.

Another source of savings, as packers struggled for a share of the widening market, was the manufacture of by-products such as glue, leather, soap, and fertilizer. By the 1880s the pork packers were also rendering lard, and some of the packing firms were using fats and other waste to manufacture pharmaceuticals. The westward spread of the corn belt and the rise of livestock ranching in the West tended to lead the meat-packing industry westward. In 1914 the leading packing centers included Omaha, Sioux City, St. Louis, Kansas City, Denver, and Fort Worth. But Chicago still remained the largest.

Flour milling

A similar pattern of development characterized the flour-milling industry. On the demand side, there was an expanding market both domestically and abroad; on the production side, numerous technological innovations encouraged concentration of the industry in large firms, and midwestern urban centers gained dominant positions in the industry. In 1870 the leading states in value of flour produced were New York, Pennsylvania, and Illinois; but in ensuing years, the milling industry followed the spread of wheat production westward. New techniques were introduced for grinding: "new process" milling (1871), which involved multiple grinding of the hard spring wheat grown in the northern Plains region and Minnesota, and "roller milling" (1878), which substituted hard steel rollers for grinding stones. These techniques had their most dramatic impact in Minneapolis and St. Paul, where large-scale mills, using an assembly-line technique employing gravity, pioneered in their use. The tendency toward concentration in heavily capitalized firms was reinforced by the brand-name packaging and marketing of flour. In 1914 Minnesota was the leading flour-milling state, New York second, and Kansas third.

Canning and other food-processing industries

New techniques for the mass-production canning of fish, vegetables, and fruit came into use in the 1880s. From 1890 to 1913, the value of output from factory canning rose from about $100 million to $243 million. Other important food-processing industries included sugar refining, liquor distilling, and baking. The trend in all these industries, as in milling and meat packing, was toward larger-scale operations, with control of a large portion of the market by a few large firms.

THE CONSUMER GOODS INDUSTRIES: TEXTILES, SHOES, AND CLOTHING

Cotton textiles

The manufacture of cotton textiles had been the first branch of American industry to use factory-organized production on a large scale. After the Civil War the industry continued to expand, with spindlage increasing from 8 million in 1867 to 31 million in 1913; and it underwent major changes as its output rose. The following data on raw cotton consumed by the textile mills illustrate the industry's growth:

1860	845,000 bales
1880	1,501,000 bales
1900	3,687,000 bales
1914	5,885,000 bales

So revolutionary were the improvements in textile technology in this period that the leading firms scrapped obsolescent plant to install new "generations" (designs) of machinery two or three times in less than fifty years. Indeed, the new technology would have penetrated the industry even more quickly had management been less conservative in its outlook. The industry preferred progressive modification, it seems, to fundamental redesign.[5]

Among the basic innovations that were adopted were the ring spinner, first introduced in the 1830s, which permitted continuous spinning of yarn at high speeds, and the Northrop automatic loom, which changed bobbins automatically when the shuttle ran out of yarn, and which was adopted widely in the 1890s when it

[5]W. Paul Strassmann, *Risk and Technological Innovation: American Manufacturing Methods During the Nineteenth Century* (Ithaca: Cornell University Press, 1959), pp. 90–93.

had proved its ability to reduce labor by two-thirds. There were dramatic gains in worker productivity generally as machinery was adapted first to steam power, then to electric power, permitting great increases in the speed of operation.

Textile production had been heavily concentrated in New England during the early nineteenth century. But in the 1880s, the South, offering proximity to cotton supplies, cheap labor, and good water power sites to manufacturers who had to adopt new machinery and invest in new plant anyway, began to emerge as a new textile center. By 1905 South Carolina was the second-ranking cotton textile state. New plants were built throughout the southeastern region, especially to produce coarse goods. The trend toward movement of the industry southward would continue vigorously into the 1920s, encouraged by state and local governments that held out tax incentives. Absence of laws regulating child and female labor was also a factor in the southward movement.

Woolens and carpets

Manufacture of woolens and carpets enjoyed vigorous growth after the Civil War, thanks in part to high tariff protection throughout the 1865–1915 period. High-speed spindles, automated strippers, and the Northrop automatic loom all contributed to productivity gains in the woolen industry. The most rapid advance in woolen textile production came in worsted fabrics. Developed in response to changing tastes and standards, worsteds were produced in new, modern mills using the latest designs. While the worsted mills' use of raw wool rose ninefold from 1869 to 1909, raw wool used in the output of more traditional varieties of woolens declined. As in other branches of manufacturing, in the woolen and carpet industries production became more heavily concentrated in a small number of large firms.

Ready-to-wear

The ready-made clothing industries had already gained substantial importance by the 1850s. After 1865 these industries too were able to exploit the vastly growing domestic market, as urbanization went forward and efficiencies in factory production encouraged purchase of ready-mades in place of hand-sewn clothing. The sewing machine, mechanization of cloth cutting and steam pressing, and other technical innovations spurred the growth of the industry. From 1879 to 1914, capital invested in the clothing industries rose sixfold. The value of their sales rose from $230 million in 1869 to $817 million in 1900, then to nearly $1.6 billion in 1914. The clothing and furnishings industries were characterized by a multitude of relatively small firms and intensely competitive conditions—as they still are. An archaic mixture of factory, workshop, and household labor prevailed. Immigrants provided both the skilled and unskilled labor, as most of the workers after 1870 were from Italy and eastern European countries. Many of these workers were employed in miserable urban sweatshops. But much of the sewing was done at home, in big-city tenement houses, where typically the children as well as parents spent long hours at the sewing table.

Boots and shoes

In boot and shoe manufacture, as in the clothing industries, the basic technical innovation was the sewing machine. In the 1860s Lyman Blake and Gordon McKay adapted the machine for sewing the soles of shoes to the uppers. Further work by Charles Goodyear in the 1870s led to adaptation of the machine to welt-stitching.

With the application of steam and electrical power, the speed of factory manufacture increased phenomenally, and the cost of production consequently declined by some 80 percent during the period 1865–1895. By 1910, as the industrial census of that year declared, American machine-made shoes had become "the standard production of the world." The industry was concentrated in New England, especially Massachusetts. Sales rose from under $100 million in 1860 to over $500 million in 1914, then to over $1 billion in 1919. American world leadership is illustrated by the fact that the industry flourished without protective tariffs. By the 1890s, moreover, rising quantities of shoes were sold in foreign markets; by 1908, exports had reached a level of 6.5 million pairs shipped.

THE BASIC INDUSTRIES: IRON AND STEEL

Until after the Civil War, steel was a rare commodity that was used chiefly in cutlery and the finer grade of tools. Iron was the chief metal in use, and until 1839, when anthracite coal was introduced, it was for the most part smelted with charcoal. After the Civil War, bituminous coal, chiefly in the form of coke, was introduced in smelting, a factor that enabled the industry to distribute itself so widely that in 1880 iron was manufactured in thirty states. The greatest event in the history of iron and steel occurred in the 1850s, when an American, William Kelly, and an Englishman, Henry Bessemer, independently discovered a method, known as the Bessemer process, by which a blast of cold air is forced through the molten pig iron to oxidize the foreign substances; after this such quantities of carbon and other elements may be introduced as will make the desired quality of steel. By cheapening production, the Bessemer process made the use of steel universal and relegated iron to a position of comparative unimportance.

The Bessemer process had its limitations. It is not suitable for ore of high phosphorus content, and this led to its being supplanted by the open-hearth, or Siemens-Martin, process, which makes possible the use of lower-grade ores. Because the ore in the Lake Superior region was of high grade, the Bessemer method was widely used until 1906, but afterward it was largely superseded by the open-hearth method.

Automaticity

The iron and steel companies pressed technological innovations forward in all stages of manufacture. New gains in productivity were attained through design of larger furnaces. The largest furnaces in 1860 produced 40 tons of pig iron per day, but by 1900 the *average* furnace capacity in the steel industry was about 500 tons. Hotter blasting also served to increase efficiency, and automaticity marked *every* step of the steel-making process. There was mechanized digging of ore with power shovels in the Lake Superior open-pit mines, mechanized loading and handling, powerized lifting and handling of ore at the furnaces, and use of hydraulic presses in the rolling mills. In all these respects, the American steel industry was well in advance of techniques in the other industrial countries, except for Germany.

Forward and backward linkages

Steel output rose enormously, from under 100,000 tons in 1871 to over 1.2 million in 1880, then to 10 million in 1900 and to 32 million in 1915. In addition to the 250,000 workers in iron and steel plants around 1910, another million were employed by industries that manufactured consumer goods and producers' durables from iron and steel: plumbing supplies, hardware, stoves, cutlery, machinery. Expansion of all these lines of manufacture, and the spreading use of steel for bridges and building construction, gave impetus to development of coal and iron mining, railroads, Great Lakes shipping, and other activities that were affected by "backward linkage."

The "forward linkages" associated with iron and steel included gains in productivity by steel-using industries. The steel firms provided them with new alloys and with new forms of steel such as relatively low-cost wire for barbed wire, improved boiler plate, and structural steel for building construction.

Andrew Carnegie

Rapidly changing technology and rising scale of production made steel a prime example of the domination of an industry by a handful of highly capitalized, enormous corporations. Andrew Carnegie's steelworks in Pennsylvania was capitalized at $750,000 when he organized it in 1873. During depression periods Carnegie was able to pour additional capital into new plant of the latest design; he pursued cost-cutting policies relentlessly; and he sought to integrate vertically, by gaining control of mines and transportation. In 1894, Carnegie's firm had a steel-making capacity of 1.1 million tons, a fourth of the entire industry's capacity. High protective tariffs, combinations and consolidations with other firms, and the imposition of long hours and low wages on workers under his control, all played their parts in Carnegie's success. The culmination of his work came in 1901, when the United States Steel Corporation, a holding company capitalized at nearly $1.5 billion, was organized. The giant new firm, with Carnegie's steel empire its largest component, controlled 80 blast furnaces, 150 steelworks, a gigantic fleet of Great Lakes ore vessels, and vast reserves of iron and coal deposits. The company had half the nation's pig-iron and rail-milling capacity; a virtual monopoly on barbed-wire production; and control of 60 percent of structural steel and wire markets.

Even prior to the formation of U.S. Steel, the basic competitive conditions within the steel industry had been transformed by large-scale production, technology, and vertical integration. The largest firms typically acquired control of raw-materials sources and were in a position to invest the necessary capital in large-scale equipment. And they also developed their own wholesaling and marketing organizations, by-passing independent wholesalers and cutting their middleman costs. In order to compete with firms of this sort, the new entrant into the industry had to command an estimated minimum of $10 million in capital by 1901, when U.S. Steel was organized. "Cost of entry" at this level was a massive barrier to new competition.

Andrew Carnegie — onetime messenger boy, clerk, and supervisor for the Pennsylvania Railroad — had masterminded his own firm's development in the steel industry on the basis of his personal knowledge and competence in the manufacturing end of the business. Ironical-ly, with cost of entry driven upward even more dramatically by the formation of U.S. Steel, the era of industrial capitalism personified by Carnegie went into eclipse. Now Carnegie had elected to share — and ultimately to yield — control of his industrial empire to the titan of New York investment banking, J. P. Morgan, with actual management of the steel firm falling to former lawyer and judge Elbert H. Gary. The age of management and finance capitalism had dawned in the industry that epitomized the modern industrial thrust of the post — Civil War era.

NEW MAJOR INDUSTRIES: AUTOMOBILES AND ELECTRIC POWER

Automobiles

As the iron and steel industry illustrates, giantism — the dominance of the large firm — had already become well established by 1900. But at this time the automobile industry was still characterized by a multitude of small-scale firms, including those of mechanics, bicycle craftsmen, and engine builders working in small shops. All of them shared the dream of developing a horseless carriage that could provide personal, mechanized transport free of the fixed track and other limitations of the railroad and the streetcar. At least fifty firms were building experimental vehicles powered by steam, electricity, and internal-combustion engines. The first American car had been designed by Charles Duryea in 1892, followed the next year by Henry Ford; both inventors were applying designs for lightweight internal-combustion engines first worked out by Dr. Otto Nathan, a German, in the mid-1870s.

Henry Ford and mass production

Competition was intense, and the number of firms in auto-making grew swiftly, but at the price of an average firm life of only seven years during the period 1903–1926. Designs were numerous, and with competition so keen, bankers who could provide capital were not interested in this sort of investment. Out of this competitive scene emerged Henry Ford, who succeeded in perfecting simplified designs and rudimentary mass-production techniques. (See pp. 224–225.) By 1913, Ford was producing half the nation's output (250,000 cars), and the age of big business was well established in automobile manufacturing.

The manufacturers developed gasoline tractors and trucks as well as passenger autos, and by 1917 nearly 2 million vehicles were being produced annually. Building a product totally unknown a quarter century earlier, these vehicle firms had brought their industry to sixth place in value of output among the nation's manufacturing industries. A new consumer durable, one that would take a large part of many American families' durables budgets, had become a permanent part of the industrial scene.

The auto manufacturers exploited mass-production assembly techniques to capture this mass market. Meanwhile, as had happened in other industries, the larger firms lengthened their lead in domination of the market. By 1920 Henry Ford's position in the motor-vehicles industry had rendered that industry similar in competitive structure to others whose origins dated from the early nineteenth century or even earlier. In short, industrial maturity and big business were not functions of longevity alone. The rapid pace of American industrialization and expanding mass consumption served as a hot-house for emergence of large firms and concentration.

Electric power and machinery

Useful comparisons with the auto industry may be made with the history of the electrical industries, which similarly arose swiftly from a technology that was new in the late nineteenth century. Just as automobiles became a major consumer commodity, the use of electricity gained wide, nearly immediate acceptance. Within 20 years of the building of central power stations in the 1890s, the electric utility companies had captured much of the urban market for lighting, were providing power to manufacturers, and were powering the street railways, which became the chief means of intracity passenger transportation. By the 1890s, appliances such as the electric flatiron were also becoming major items of household use.

The manufacture of electrical machinery was concentrated in the Northeast, just as automobile manufacturing centered in the Detroit region. (Of course, production of electric power was by its nature dispersed widely throughout the nation.) Only a few firms—General Electric, Westinghouse, Thompson-Houston, Edison— early gained dominant positions in the production of machinery and appliances. They did so not so much because of manufacturing assembly technique (as was typical in the auto industry) but because of their control of patent rights, the highly specialized nature of their products, and successful consolidation with smaller firms. In the communications branch of the electrical industry, Western Electric emerged as the dominant firm, both because of its uniquely well-organized research and development activity and because of its special relationship to its parent firm, the Bell System of telephone companies.

BIG BUSINESS AND INDUSTRIAL CONCENTRATION

The pervasive tendency toward bigness and concentration was evident after 1865, as we have seen, in new and old industries alike. Although a few major industries—for example, clothing manufacture—were not so much affected by the trend, the tendency was general enough to constitute a genuinely basic change in manufacturing structure. By 1914, manufacturing establishments that produced $1 million or more comprised 2.2 percent of the total. But this tiny percentage employed more than one-third of all industrial wage earners, and it accounted for 49 percent of the value of products in manufacturing. By 1920 the shift toward bigness had become even more pronounced. (See Table 15–3.) Consolidation and concentration were by no means confined to manufacturing. Among the financial-intermediaries, insurance companies and investment banks with assets on a scale that dwarfed the largest firms of the 1860s were dominant by the 1890s. In 1912 the three leading investment banking houses in New York had assets of $632 million. Their partners sat on the boards of over 100 corporations capitalized at $22 billion. New York State's eleven largest insurance corporations increased their combined assets from $328 million in 1881 to nearly $2.4 billion by 1907. Consolidation and bigness also characterized the railroad industry, whose mergers of large firms dated back as early as the 1850s. An estimated 90 percent of the nation's entire railway mileage had been consolidated under the control of six financial groups by 1904. Similar magnitudes of capitalization on a vast scale were also evident in the public utilities sector, embracing electric, telephone, telegraph, and streetcar corporations.

Vertical and horizontal integration

Until the mid-1890s, the large firms that emerged as the prominent big-business corporations followed two paths toward giantism. One was vertical integration, by which a firm moved out from functioning exclusively as a production organization to take control of raw-materials sources and processing (backward integration) or to acquire control of marketing facilities that routed the firm's products to ultimate consumers (forward integration). Vertical integration was particularly attractive to firms that offered highly specialized products, adaptable to unique marketing facilities such as refrigerated transport and warehousing of meat, or specialized steel products and electric-power generating equipment, sold to a relatively small number of purchasers. Another motivation to vertical integration was the desire to control sources of supply in order to maintain continuous-flow production on assembly-line facilities (as in autos) or in extremely large-scale plants (as in steel) requiring systematic allocation of supplies.

The other major path toward consolidation was horizontal integration: acquiring control of firms producing identical or similar product lines. Like vertical integration, the horizontal type served as a means of attaining economies of scale in production and marketing. But probably the leading motivation was the

TABLE 15–3.   MANUFACTURES: ESTABLISHMENTS CLASSIFIED BY VALUE OF PRODUCTS, 1914–1929

CLASS OF ESTABLISHMENTS ACCORDING TO VALUE OF PRODUCTS	ESTABLISHMENTS		WAGE EARNERS		VALUE OF PRODUCTS	
	NUMBER	PER-CENT DISTRI-BUTION	NUMBER	PER-CENT DISTRI-BUTION	AMOUNT	PER-CENT DISTRI-BUTION
$5,000 and over[1]						
1929	210,959	100.0	8,838,743	100.0	$70,434,863,443	100.0
1925	187,390	100.0	8,384,261	100.0	62,713,713,730	100.0
1921	196,267	100.0	6,946,570	99.4[1]	43,653,282,833	99.7[1]
1919	214,383	100.0	9,000,059	99.5[1]	62,041,795,316	99.8[1]
1914	177,110	100.0	6,896,190	98.2[1]	23,987,860,617	99.1[1]
$5,000 to $20,000						
1929	69,423	32.0	202,958	2.3	771,417,436	1.1
1925	55,876	29.8	156,373	1.9	628,373,403	1.0
1921	71,075	36.2	224,852	3.2	782,977,433	1.8
1919	79,699	37.2	227,977	2.5	866,086,290	1.4
1914	86,587	48.9	423,829	6.0	893,459,166	3.7
$20,000 to $100,000						
1929	75,225	35.7	693,155	7.8	3,587,697,276	5.1
1925	68,951	36.8	660,309	7.9	3,272,196,872	5.0
1921	72,251	36.8	746,024	10.0	3,330,350,409	7.6
1919	75.627	35.3	773,701	8.6	3,487,756,280	5.6
1914	56,557	31.9	995,743	14.2	2,540,949,405	10.5
$100,000 to $500,000						
1929	44,153	20.9	1,672,983	18.9	10,023,771,653	14.2
1925	42,209	22.5	1,675,911	20.0	9,576,090,022	15.3
1921	38,027	19.4	1,629,573	23.3	8,405,758,540	19.2
1919	39,477	18.4	1,712,854	18.9	8,929,364,110	14.4
1914[2]	30,147	17.0	3,000,612	42.7	8,759,391,117	36.2
$500,000 to $1,000,000						
1929	10,395	4.9	1,121,547	12.7	7,294,860,945	10.4
1925	9,771	5.2	1,131,439	13.5	6,870,112,293	11.0
1921	7,581	3.9	966,559	13.8	5,296,720,583	12.1
1919	9,197	4.2	1,112,815	12.3	6,457,485,019	10.4
1914[2]						
$1,000,000 and over						
1929	11,763	5.6	5,148,100	58.3	48,757,116,133	69.2
1925	10,583	5.7	4,760,229	56.7	42,366,941,140	67.5
1921	7,333	3.7	3,379,562	48.4	25,837,475,868	59.0
1919	10,413	4.9	5,172,712	57.2	42,301,103,617	68.0
1914	3,819	2.2	2,476,006	35.3	11,794,060,929	48.7

Source: *Statistical Abstract, 1933,* p.693.
[1]Small percentages for establishments doing a business of less than $5,000 omitted.
[2]Figures include data for two groups, $100,000 to $1,000,000.

desire to abridge competition and thereby control the prices at which goods were offered to buyers.

Mergers

As one would expect, specific firms might first take one path or the other — vertical or horizontal integration — and then shift strategies. A leading example is the National Biscuit Company, initially formed in 1898 in a merger of three firms. As the corporation itself reported in 1901, the merger was sought because "it was thought that we must control competition, and that to do this we must either fight competition or buy it." Having "bought it," the company's management then swiftly adopted the alternative strategy of making the firm more efficient through creation of special departments for raw materials, production, finance, and marketing and sales. Each of the new departments expanded its activities in what amounted to vertical integration.[6] In other leading firms, too, initial integration through mergers of similar businesses was followed by vertical integration; they include Standard Oil, American Sugar Refining, and American Tobacco. The growth strategies of some other giant businesses reversed the order, with horizontal integration following an initial vertical strategy.

Pools and cartels

American business firms used other mechanisms as well to extend their control over markets and prices. One variant of the merger technique was the pool, an organization of business firms in a specific industry whose members sought to restrict output or else to divide and apportion the available business, either by sales quotas or by regions. Railroad firms had formed pools and price-fixing agreements in the 1850s, and some industries (especially salt and cutlery) even earlier. But the high-water mark for manufacturing pools came in the 1870s. Because they were based on voluntary compliance—their terms were not enforceable in the courts, since in most states the courts found pools to be in conflict with common-law conspiracy prohibitions—many of these agreements fell apart almost immediately. Even the more enduring ones tended to weaken in periods of low prices and depressed markets. From 1887 to 1893 the steel companies worked out an uneasy but persistent pool in the market for rails, and the meat packers agreed on several pools from the mid-1880s to 1902.

In 1902 a *cartel* (in effect an international pooling agreement) was formed by the giant American Tobacco Company and the comparably dominant British firm, the Imperial Tobacco Company. Under its terms, Imperial left the American, Cuban, and U.S. colonial markets exclusively to American Tobacco, which in turn stayed out of the British market. Similar international cartels were attempted before 1920 in the thread, glass bottle, aluminum, gunpowder, chemical, and meat industries. And no doubt informal pooling and cartel agreements, usually secret, have prevailed in certain markets down to the present day.

Trusts

From the mid-1880s until 1897, the trust, a mechanism more efficient than the pool and certainly of less dubious legality, came into wide

[6]Alfred D. Chandler, Jr., *Strategy and Structure: Chapters in the History of the Industrial Enterprise* (Cambridge: MIT Press, 1962), pp. 32–33.

use. By this mechanism, the stockholders in two or more firms deposit a controlling portion of their stock in the hands of trustees, receiving trust certificates in return; hence, unlike the pool, the trust is an actual consolidation of ownership. The most successful early trust was John D. Rockefeller's Standard Oil venture of 1882. Other notable trusts were formed in whiskey distilling, sugar refining, lead smelting, and cotton-oil production. Their effectiveness became notorious, and intense public criticism led to efforts by state authorities to curb trust activities. Common-law actions against trusts as conspiracies in restraint of trade brought them before the courts of Ohio, New York, and other industrial states. In many instances the big trusts were successfully challenged. Meanwhile the Panic of 1893 and the long depression of 1893–1897 held up for the time being further aggressive moves toward consolidation.

Holding companies

Antitrust legislation in the states, and also new federal restraints as the result of the 1890 Sherman Antitrust Act, led businessmen to favor a new form of consolidation: the holding company. A holding company is an organization created to dominate other corporations by owning or controlling a portion of their stocks. The laws favorable to such organization adopted by several states, most notably New Jersey, West Virginia, Delaware, and Maine, expedited the spread of the holding company.

Whether a holding company, even if it was legal under state law, was operating in restraint of trade—or was so large as to constitute by its very size a restraint of trade under terms of the Sherman Antitrust Act—was difficult to know, given the broad and vague language of the federal statute. In 1895, however, the Supreme Court removed the uncertainty with its decision in *United States* v. *E. C. Knight Company,* popularly known as the Sugar Trust Case. The Court ruled that the trust, which controlled 95 percent of American sugar refining, did not violate the Sherman Act because it affected only manufacturing, not commerce or trade. The nice casuistry of the Court's decision seemed to undermine the whole force of the Sherman Act so far as industrial corporations were concerned. Hence, when business conditions turned upward once again in 1897, a new wave of consolidations began to gather strength.

There followed an incredibly rapid merger movement, centering on the years 1898–1902, when hundreds of American business firms disappeared by merger each year, absorbed by other firms. An economy already undergoing rapid transformation, as giantism

and industrial concentration were already well advanced by the mid-1890s, suddenly accelerated the momentum of institutional change.

THE MERGER WAVE OF 1895–1904

Prior to the 1890s, the stock and trust certificates of a few large industrial firms and trusts had begun to find markets on the New York Stock Exchange and other cities' exchanges. A few small banking houses had pioneered in the business of inducing the public to invest money in industrial stock, just as the public had been investing funds in federal and state bonds and in railroad and some mining stocks and bonds for many years.

When the merger wave of the late 1890s began, public sale of industrial securities began to dominate the exchanges. Large banks were attracted to industrial securities by the impressive business success of many merged corporations during the difficult depression period. Confident that a broadly based public market for industrial securities could be tapped, the wealthiest and most widely reputed investment bankers (including J. P. Morgan and Company) became deeply involved in merger reorganizations and the public sale of stock in the newly created corporations.

The largest firms formed by merger did issue stock to the public. Though representing only one-fifth of the absolute number of consolidations, the firms whose shares were admitted to trading on the New York Stock Exchange represented three-fifths of the authorized capitalization involved in all mergers from 1895 to 1904. Enormous fortunes were made, both by the industrialists who merged their firms and by the bankers who underwrote their stock issues. Investors in the stock of the newly merged corporations proved willing and eager to pay high prices, beyond the current actual value of assets, in the expectation of future growth and profitability.[7]

The emergence of a broadly based investor market for merger stock, with the brokerage role being played by the giant banking firms, together with the optimism generated by the

economy's rapid recovery and expansion after 1897, gave further momentum to the merger wave. Also important was the continuing quest of business managers for market control. Economist Ralph L. Nelson, in his study of post-1895 mergers, found that

a substantial share of total 1895–1904 merger activity did result in securing a leading and often dominant share of the market. Almost one-half of firm disappearances and seven-tenths of merger

TABLE 15–4.   FIRM DISAPPEARANCES BY MERGER AND MERGER CAPITALIZATION, 1895–1920

YEAR	NUMBER OF FIRMS DISAPPEARING BY MERGER	MERGER CAPITALIZATIONS (MILLIONS)
1895	43	$ 40.8
1896	26	24.7
1897	69	119.7
1898	303	650.6
1899	1208	2262.7
1900	340	442.4
1901	423	2052.9
1902	379	910.8
1903	142	297.6
1904	79	110.5
1905	226	243.0
1906	128	377.8
1907	87	184.8
1908	50	187.6
1909	49	89.1
1910	142	257.0
1911	103	210.5
1912	82	322.4
1913	85	175.6
1914	39	159.6
1915	71	158.4
1916	117	470.0
1917	195	678.7
1918	71	254.2
1919	171	981.7
1920	206	1088.6

[7]Thomas R. Navin and Marian V. Sears, "The Rise of a Market for Industrial Securities," *Business History Review, 29* (1955): 106–115; Fritz Redlich, *The Molding of American Banking: Men and Ideas* (1951, reprinted New York: Johnson Reprint, 1972), pp. 381–396.

Source: Ralph L. Nelson, *Merger Movements in American Industry, 1895–1956* (Princeton: National Bureau of Economic Research, Princeton University Press, 1959), p. 37. Copyright 1959 by The National Bureau of Economic Research. Reprinted by permission.

capitalizations were accounted for by mergers that gained a leading position in the market.[8]

The annual number of merger-caused disappearances of firms from 1895 to 1920, together with the capitalization involved, is shown in Table 15–4.

Concentration ratios
Students of industrial organization have used "concentration ratio" as a measure of concentration; this ratio represents the per-

centage of total sales in an industry accounted for by the four largest sellers in that industry. By 1901, before the great merger wave had reached its climax, nearly one-third of the value added in manufacturing was accounted for by industries with concentration ratios of 50 or higher. For certain industries the 1901 figures show ratios as high as 78.8 (steel), 71.0 (paper and allied products), 57.3 (transportation equipment). By 1901, then, the purely quantitative dimensions of structural change had become eloquent testimony to the depth of qualitative change in economic life.

THE STANDARD OIL COMPANY

The history of the oil business is of particular significance in the study of industrial combinations, for the rise and progress of the Standard Oil Company illustrates practically every phase in the development and methods of monopoly under American conditions. It serves, in fact, as the classic story of monopoly in this country.

Successful drilling for oil began in 1859 in the vicinity of Titusville, Pennsylvania. While the business of drilling wells and refining oil expanded rapidly during the Civil War, production in 1865 was behind demand and the whole industry was severely handicapped by lack of transportation facilities and efficient refining machinery. The fact that transportation was the great problem and the chief expense of the expanding oil industry made it evident that success would come to the large concern with enough capital to install the best machinery for large-scale production and sufficient output to force favorable railroad rates. In 1867, while the industry was still in its infancy, John D. Rockefeller united several refineries in the firm of Rockefeller, Andrews and Flagler. "The cause leading to its formation," he said, "was the desire to unite our skill and capital in order to carry on a business of some magnitude and importance in place of the small business that each separately had theretofore carried on."[9] Further capital was needed, and in 1870 the company was reorganized into the Standard Oil Company of Ohio, with capital of $1 million

and a refining capacity in its Cleveland plant of about 600 barrels a day. This amounted, however, to only 4 percent of the oil refined in the United States, and the Standard Oil plant was not even then the largest in the country.

Standard Oil and the railroads
Up to 1879 competition among oilmen had been confined largely to production.[10] In the succeeding years they competed for transportation facilities and favorable rates in a bitter war that left the Standard Oil Company in complete control. This victory may be attributed largely to the business acumen of Rockefeller and his associates, to favorable freight rates, and to the unscrupulous methods to which these men resorted to destroy competition and win favorable concessions from railroads and legislatures. Their efforts to secure low transportation rates were aided by the railroads, chiefly the Erie, the New York Central, and the Pennsylvania, which were in competition for the oil business. In keeping with the policy of the time, the roads lowered their rates at competitive points and to promising concerns. In all the dickering with the railroads, no group of refiners was so successful as Standard Oil. Its favorable location at Cleveland was a factor in this success, since it freed the concern from complete dependence

---

[8]Ralph L. Nelson, *Merger Movements in American Industry, 1895–1956* (Princeton, N.J.: Princeton University Press, 1959), p. 102.

[9]*Preliminary Report of the Industrial Commission* (Washington, D.C., 1900), p. 95.

[10]Until the 1880s both Rockefeller's company and its competitors relied upon independent commission merchants and jobbers to market their products to retailers. Up to then, Standard Oil's strategy focused on "bringing refining and transportation under [its] control" (Harold F. Williamson and A. R. Daum, *The American Petroleum Industry: The Age of Illumination, 1859–1899* [Evanston: Northwestern University Press, 1959], p. 535).

on the railroads by affording water transportation to the seaboard by way of the Great Lakes and the Erie Canal.

The South Improvement Company

The most notorious of the rate agreements was made through the South Improvement Company, chartered by the Pennsylvania legislature in 1871 with the widest powers, including authority "to construct and operate any work, or works, public or private, designed to include, increase, facilitate, or develop trade, travel, or the transportation of freight, livestock, passengers, or any traffic by land or water, from or to any part of the United States."[11] This company, 900 of whose 2000 shares were held by Rockefeller and his close associates, was actually initiated by the railroads in search of business, not by the refiners in search of cheap transportation. Nevertheless, the company contracted with the Pennsylvania, the New York Central, and the Erie to ship 45 percent of all the oil transported by it on the Pennsylvania Railroad and to divide the remainder between the other two roads. In return the railroads agreed to allow rebates on all petroleum shipped by the company and to charge all others the full rates, and in addition to furnish the South Improvement Company with waybills on all petroleum and its products transported over their lines. Each road also agreed

> at all times to cooperate, as far as it legally may, with the [South Improvement Company] against loss by injury or competition, to the end that [the Company] may keep up a remunerative, and so a full and regular business, and to that end shall lower or raise the gross rates of transportation over its railroads and connections, as far as it legally may, for such times and to such extent as may be necessary to overcome such competition.

The South Improvement Company aroused such a storm of opposition that its charter was revoked after three months. The story is told here simply to point out how far the system of rebating might go.

Pipelines

Despite the end of the South Improvement Company, rebates and favorable discriminations were continued. Standard Oil gradually extended its operations to include the owner-

ship of pipelines; by 1879 it controlled from 90 to 95 percent of the oil refined and was able in turn virtually to dictate its rates to the roads. The Hepburn Committee, reporting to the New York legislature in January 1880, said:

> It owns and controls the pipe lines of the producing regions that connect with the railroads. It controls both ends of these roads. It ships 95 per cent of all oil. . . . It dictates terms and rates to the railroads. It has bought out and frozen out refiners all over the country. By means of the superior facilities for transportation which it thus possessed, it could overbid in the producing regions and undersell in the markets of the world. Thus it has gone on buying out and freezing out all opposition, until it has absorbed and monopolized this great traffic, this great production which ranks second on the list of exports of our country. The parties whom they have driven to the wall have had ample capital, and equal ability in the prosecution of their business in all things save their ability to acquire facilities for transportation.[12]

The Standard Oil trust

In order to dominate the situation more completely, Standard Oil of Ohio worked out a scheme in 1882 by which the stockholdings of 14 companies and the majority of holdings of 26 others were placed in the hands of nine trustees having irrevocable powers of attorney. The stockholders received trust certificates in return. The par value of these certificates amounted to $70 million, of which $46 million was owned by the nine trustees who dictated the policies of the constituent companies. The public in general had no difficulty in understanding the purpose of this new organization. A wave of state anti-monopoly legislation followed, and the courts of Ohio in 1890 broke up the Standard Oil Trust into twenty constituent companies. Trust certificates were replaced by proportionate shares of stock in the new companies.

The holding company

In 1899 a second attempt was made to bring the entire properties under single control by the formation of the Standard Oil Company of New Jersey, a holding company as well as an operating company, formed with the intention of transferring to it the stock of the various corporations so that in time one concern might own

---

[11]*Preliminary Report of the Industrial Commission,* p. 608.

[12]*New York Assembly Documents, 1880,* No. 38, "Report of the Special Committee on Railroads."

and direct the whole industry. The new company's position as a holding company was gravely imperiled by the decision in the Northern Securities Case (1904) and was finally made untenable by a Supreme Court order of dissolution in 1911.[13] Since then the business has been carried on by corporations chartered by the several states.

Standard Oil's role in the market

By 1904 Standard Oil controlled about 85 percent of the domestic market and 90 percent of the export trade. Earnings of Standard Oil ranged from 11 to 15.4 percent of net assets from 1883 to 1891, rising to a range of 21 to 27 percent from 1900 to 1906.

Standard Oil achieved its long-lived hegemony in the oil-refining business at first through tactics that permitted it to obtain a large portion of the crude oil produced by others. Throughout the late 1870s and the 1880s the firm's continuing preeminence was maintained through its control of transportation and pipeline facilities; indeed, operation of those facilities generated a large portion of Standard's total income.

After 1904 the market share controlled by Standard Oil declined. This occurred partially because of successive discoveries and regional development of oil reserves in new locations. Pennsylvania's petroleum output had risen to a historic high of 31 million barrels by 1891, but four years later Ohio had displaced Pennsylvania as the leading oil producer. Ohio in turn was passed by California in 1903. By 1910, with Texas and other southwestern oil fields opening up, California was producing only a third of national output.

The opening of each new oil region posed a challenge to Standard Oil. Not only was total national output rapidly on the rise, soaring from 51 million barrels in 1899 to 379 million barrels 20 years later, putting pressure on oil prices; but the westward movement of oil production also reduced Standard's advantages in the control of transport and pipelines. Hence by 1909 Standard was controlling 66 percent of refined petroleum output in the United States, a considerable decrease from the nearly 90 percent that it controlled at the turn of the century.

Vertical integration

As competition developed, Standard redoubled its efforts to perfect vertical integration, moving into retailing as well as wholesaling (and so appeared the Standard Oil gasoline stations on American roads), and into aggressive

[13]See p. 313.

exploration and crude-oil production. Standard Oil had not obtained its dominant position by developing a superior technology, although Standard did, of course, attain important economies of scale. By the 1890s rival oil companies were modeling their own tactics and organizations on those pioneered by Standard.[14]

New challenges to Standard Oil

Its greatest rival, the Pure Oil Company, successfully challenged Standard on its home territory in Pennsylvania. Pure Oil flourished by controlling its own pipeline in competition with Standard's, and so the way was cleared for Pure Oil's emergence as a fully integrated firm in 1900.

Meanwhile in Kansas and other new oil-producing states, the small-scale producers banded together to challenge Standard's methods of organization and competition through numerous law suits charging restraint of trade (under the common law) or violation of state statutes. The rival firms also pressed their state legislatures for new laws that would make Standard's aggressive tactics clearly illegal. This appeal to law by competing business interests—a case of conflict within an industry, with the weaker group of business firms trying to bring the state's power to bear to their advantage against a stronger rival—was a scenario duplicated in many other industries and other states. Laissez-faire, no matter how much it was admired as a theory, was not allowed to stand in the way when beleaguered business groups perceived that state intervention would serve their own interests.[15]

Efficiency vs. social costs

Admirers of Standard Oil pointed to its size and scale of operations as the source of efficiencies that ultimately helped consumers. What portion of the decline in refined-oil prices from 45 cents per gallon in 1863 to about 6 cents in

[14]Williamson and Daum, *American Petroleum Industry,* p. 729; Henrietta M. Larson, "The Rise of Big Business in the Oil Industry," in *Oil's First Century,* ed. *Business History Review* Staff (Cambridge, Mass.: Harvard University Press, 1960), pp. 27–42.

[15]Arthur M. Johnson, "Public Policy and Concentration in the Petroleum Industry, 1870–1911," in *Oil's First Century,* pp. 43–56; Johnson, *The Development of American Petroleum Pipelines . . . 1862–1906* (Ithaca: Cornell University Press, 1956), pp. 243–251. Of the small independent producers' successful drive to defeat the South Improvement Company scheme, one historian has said: "In the first great conflict between free enterprise and the new spirit of aggressive, ruthless industry monopoly, the free enterprisers had won" (Chester M. Destler, *Roger Sherman and the Independent Oil Men* [Ithaca: Cornell University Press, 1967], p. 40).

the late 1890s was attributable to Standard's efficiencies of scale, and what portion to the great technological advances in exploration and refining technology, in use of pipelines for bulk shipment, and so on — technological advances that were achieved by scientists and innovators in the industry as a whole, not primarily associated with or pioneered by Standard — is difficult to say.

On the other hand, had the costs of entry into the industry been lower, and had Standard's great size and massive assets not been so intimidating to actual or potential competitors, what efficiencies might then have been achieved? And how can one measure the social costs of ruthless price cutting by Standard in local markets, followed by price increases once competition was eliminated? Or the tremendous waste of natural resources in oil that characterized the ruthlessly exploitative methods used during the highly competitive early period of the industry's history? Questions such as these underline the difficulty of assessing the "efficiency" of monopoly enterprise in an era of hectic, rapid change. Such questions also echo the kinds of inquiries and issues that racked the country when "antitrust" became a leading policy question in the age of giant enterprise.

SELECTED READINGS

General Works

Clark, Victor S., *History of Manufactures in the United States,* Volume II: *1860–1893,* Volume III: *1893–1928* (Washington, D.C.: Carnegie Institution, 1929).

*Faulkner, Harold U., *The Decline of Laissez-Faire, 1897–1917* (New York: Holt, Rinehart and Winston, 1962).

*Kirkland, Edward Chase, *Industry Comes of Age: Business, Labor, and Public Policy, 1860–1897* (New York: Holt, Rinehart and Winston, 1961).

Kranzberg, Melvin, and Purcell, C. W., Jr., eds., *Technology in Western Civilization* (New York: Oxford University Press,1967).

Williamson, Harold F., ed., *The Growth of the American Economy,* 2nd ed. (Englewood Cliffs, N.J.: Prentice-Hall, 1951).

Specialized Works

Adams, Walter, *The Structure of American Industry,* 3rd ed. (New York: Macmillan, 1961).

Carossa, Vincent, *Investment Banking in America* (Cambridge, Mass.: Harvard University Press, 1970).

Chandler, Alfred D., *Strategy and Structure: Chapters in the History of the Industrial Enterprise* (Cambridge. Mass.: MIT Press, 1962).

Chandler, Alfred D., and Galambos, Louis, "The Development of Large-Scale Economic Organizations in Modern America," *Journal of Economic History,* XXX (1970).

Eichner, Alfred S., *The Emergence of Oligopoly: Sugar Refining as a Case Study* (Baltimore: Johns Hopkins Press, 1969).

Hacker, Louis M., *The World of Andrew Carnegie, 1865–1901* (Philadelphia: Lippincott, 1968).

Hidy, Ralph W., and Hidy, Muriel, *Pioneering in Big Business, 1882–1911* (New York: Harper & Row, 1955).

Johnson, Arthur M., *The Development of American Petroleum Pipelines . . . 1862–1906* (Ithaca: Cornell University Press, 1956).

Jones, Eliot, *The Trust Problem in the United States* (New York: Macmillan, 1921).

Nevins, Allan, and Hill, Frank E., *Ford: The Times, the Man, and the Company* (New York: Scribner's, 1954).

Niemi, Albert W., Jr., *State and Regional Patterns in American Manufacturing, 1860–1900* (Westport, Conn.: Greenwood, 1974).

Passer, Harold C., *The Electrical Manufacturers, 1875–1900* (Cambridge, Mass.: Harvard University Press, 1953).

*Porter, Glenn, *The Rise of Big Business, 1860–1910* (New York: Crowell, 1973).

Porter, Glenn, and Livesay, Harold C., *Merchants and Manufacturers: Studies in the Changing Structure of 19th-Century Marketing* (Baltimore: Johns Hopkins Press, 1971).

Rae, John B., *American Automobile Manufacturers: The First Forty Years* (Philadelphia: Chilton, 1959).

Rumelt, Richard P., *Strategy, Structure and Economic Performance* (Boston: Division of Research, Harvard University Graduate School of Business Administration, 1974).

Temin, Peter, *Iron and Steel in 19th Century America* (Cambridge, Mass.: MIT Press, 1964).

Wall, Joseph Frazier, *Andrew Carnegie* (New York: Oxford University Press, 1970).

White, Gerald T., *Formative Years in the Far West: A History of Standard Oil Company of California* (Englewood Cliffs, N.J.: Prentice-Hall, 1962).

Williamson, Harold F., and Daum, Arnold, *The American Petroleum Industry: The Age of Illumination* (Evanston, Ill.: Northwestern University Press, 1959).

Williamson, Harold F. et al. *The American Petroleum Industry: The Age of Energy, 1899–1959* (Evanston, Ill.: Northwestern University Press, 1963).

The rushing pace of changes generated by post–Civil War industrialization caught the American worker in a net of uncertainties. Rapid development of new technologies meant that old products and traditional labor skills might be displaced almost overnight. The coming into production of new resource areas could threaten the stability of business firms in older, less productive areas of the country, also threatening the jobs of workers in those older regions.

And the intensive business quest for productivity, profits, and market control meant new pressures on the labor force — pressures to work more efficiently, to adapt to machine processes, to accept lower wages. And with the emergence of big business, growing numbers of workers were faced with the necessity of dealing with employers who commanded vast power and wealth.

POPULATION CHANGE

Population continued to rise after 1865, but the leading features of demographic change were different from those prevailing earlier in the century. Traditionally, American families had been large, young people had married early, and (at least until 1846) population had increased mainly as the result of fertility among the American-born rather than from immigration. In the late nineteenth century there were basic changes in all these respects. As employment opportunities beckoned in the cities, young farm people who were attracted to urban areas tended to postpone marriage, and when they did marry they tended to have smaller families. Longer life expectancy and a slight decline in death rates after 1890 did not much offset the downward shift in fertility of the native-born population.

What kept the average rate of population increase at levels of 1.5 to 2.8 percent, instead of the 1 percent level that fertility of the native-born would have sustained, was immigration. (See Figure 16–1.) Until 1880 the major sources of immigration were Great Britain, Ireland, and Germany, the same countries that

had provided most of the nation's immigrants earlier in the century. They were joined by the Scandinavian countries after 1865. But the massive increase in immigration occurred later, reaching flood-tide proportions in the 1880s, remaining high in the 1890s, and again expanding vastly from 1900 to 1914 when more than 13 million persons came to the United States. The source of this mass of humanity was mainly eastern Europe: From 1891 to 1910, Poland, Russia, Austria-Hungary, and Italy furnished more than half the total immigrants. During 1910–1914, eastern and southern Europeans comprised some 85 percent of those who immigrated. (See Figure 16.2.) They were known as the "new immigrants."

The new immigrants
The new immigration's impact on population change was magnified by the fact that some 85 percent of them were between 14 and 44 years of age. In other words, they were of working age, and of marrying and childbearing age; and they tended to have more children than the native-born.

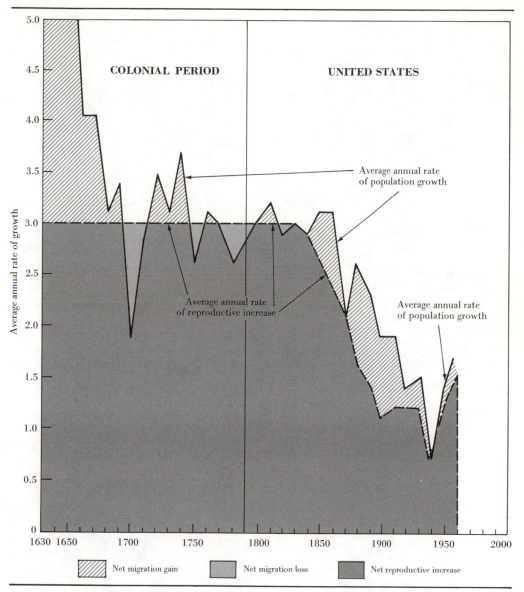

Figure 16–1. Estimated Components of the Population Growth Rate in the United States, 1630–1960. Source: Donald J. Bogue, *Principles of Demography* (New York: John Wiley & Sons, 1969), p. 130. Copyright © 1969 by John Wiley & Sons. Reprinted by permission.

Although most of the new immigrants came from rural towns or peasant farms in Europe, they settled mainly in cities when they reached America. It was in the urban centers that un-skilled industrial jobs could be found for the men, and work as domestic servants for the women. In the ethnic neighborhoods of the large cities, moreover, immigrants could find friends from the old country, or at least neigh-

bors who spoke their own language. Many newly arrived workers found jobs in the smaller urban-industrial centers: in steel towns, mill towns, and mining districts. (See Figure 16–3.)

By 1910 immigrants comprised more than a third of the labor force in manufacturing and a fourth of the labor force in both construction and transportation. Whether they were em-ployed in the cities or in the mills and mines, the

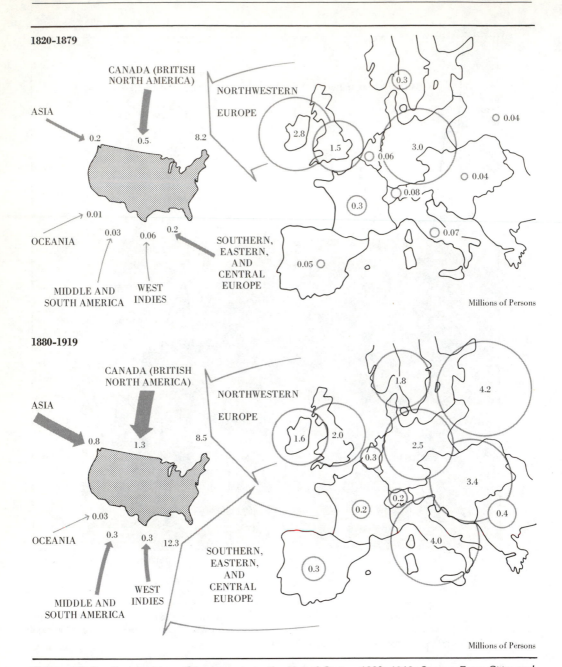

Figure 16–2. **Source Areas of Immigrants to the United States, 1820–1919.** Source: From *Cities and Immigrants: A Geography of Change in Nineteenth-Century America* by David Ward. Copyright © 1971 by Oxford University Press, Inc. Reprinted by permission.

foreign-born tended to occupy the bottom of the job ladder. In the woolen mills, coal mines, iron and steel mills, and quarries, immigrants made up half or more of the work force in 1910. In copper mining, the clothing industries, and iron mining, they provided two-thirds of the labor force or more. But the proportions of foreign-born in the managerial and other white-collar groups within these industries were negligible. The immigrant provided the muscle.

TABLE 16-1. GROWTH OF CITY POPULATION, 1790-1930

YEAR	TOTAL POPULATION	PLACES OF 8,000 INHABITANTS OR MORE		
		POPULATION	NUMBER OF PLACES	PERCENT OF POPULATION
1790	3,929,214	131,472	6	3.3
1800	5,308,483	210,873	6	4.0
1820	9,638,453	475,135	13	4.9
1840	17,069,453	1,453,994	44	8.5
1860	31,443,321	5,072,256	141	16.1
1880	50,155,783	11,365,698	285	22.7
1900	75,994,575	25,018,335	547	32.0
1920	105,710,620	46,307,640	924	43.8
1930	122,775,046	60,333,452	1208	49.1

Source: Fifteenth census, 1930, vol. 1, *Population*, p. 9.

From the standpoint of native-born workers and earlier arrivals, the inflow of immigration threatened to keep wages down for all of them. But the downward push on wages was partly, at least, offset by the cyclical character of immigration. The massive inflow of Europeans came during years of expansion and prosperity. Besides, immigrants were consumers as well as workers: They generated demand for housing, food, and consumer goods generally. Certainly some of the extensive growth patterns of American development prior to 1914 — the rapid filling up of newly opened western regions, the expansion of mining and lumbering, the vast increase in the size of the urban markets — could not have occurred on the scale they did without the high levels of immigration that were experienced.

The vast pool of foreign-born workers included many who spoke no English and lacked modern industrial skills. Some scholars contend that their availability in the American labor market was an incentive to manufacturers to adopt new technology rapidly — to simplify and mechanize factory processes, making them adaptable to unskilled, cheap labor. If so, immigration may have worked indirectly to accelerate the pace of productivity gains through technological innovation.[1]

URBANIZATION

It was not only immigrants, but the industrial work force as a whole, that became concentrated after 1865 largely in a few urban centers with massive populations. The number of "urban" places — towns and cities with 8000 population or more — rose rapidly, as shown in Table 16-1; and even as early as 1900, some 25 million out of 76 million Americans lived in these urban locations. As we have noted, the rise in urban population was derived in considerable part from the clustering of new immigrants in the major cities. In New York, Boston, Chicago, Milwaukee, and many other cities with manufacturing centers, upwards of 70 percent of the residents by 1910 were of "foreign stock"; that is they were born overseas or had at least one foreign-born parent. Taking total U.S. urban population in 1910, we find that one resident in four was an immigrant.

But urbanization was also given impetus by a steady movement of farm and small-town people into the major cities. For many native-born younger sons on farms, for the artisans and mechanics of the rural areas, and for young rural women who decided to seek jobs in industry, offices, and shops, the American city was the great frontier of employment — the magnet that lured them away from home, usually permanently. As farming became mechanized, the need for children to stay close to home declined; many older farming areas, and even some newly settled ones, became depopulated under pressure of competition from more productive areas; and the seriousness of agricultural depressions periodically drove rural people to search for alternatives.[2] By 1910, native-born people who had moved cityward from rural areas comprised one-fourth of the nation's urban residents.

[1]Brinley Thomas, *Migration and Economic Growth* (Cambridge: The University Press, 1954), p. 165.
[2]See Sam Bass Warner, Jr., *The Urban Wilderness* (New York: Harper & Row, 1973).

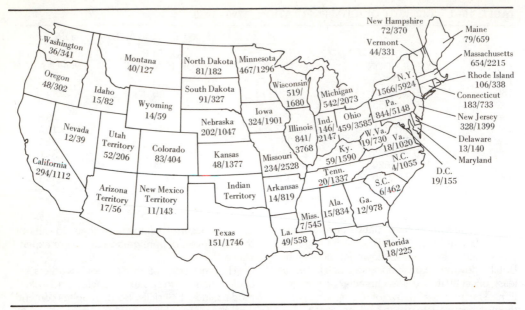

Figure 16–3. Foreign-Born in Relation to White Population of the United States, 1890 (in thousands).
Source: Philip Taylor, *The Distant Magnet: European Emigration to the U.S.A.* (New York: Harper & Row, 1971), p. 177. Copyright © 1971 by Harper & Row.

THE BLACK MIGRATION

As late as 1910, the black population of the United States was still predominantly southern and rural. The two occupations that in 1900 employed almost 90 percent of black workers were farming and work as domestic servants. But shortly after 1910, southern black workers began to join the migration to the cities in massive numbers. Both push and pull factors induced this great migration, much as similar factors had conditioned the new immigration from southern and eastern Europe.

Push factors, working as an expulsive force on blacks in the South, included the intensification of Jim Crow legislation and social practices, the discrimination against the black population by public school authorities, the rising incidence of lynching and other forms of overt violence against blacks, and the drudgery and grinding poverty of life as tenants or sharecroppers on the land. Also, in those few urban and industrial occupations where black urban residents in the South had found work, they came under increasing pressure of competition for jobs from poor whites.

Pull factors, attracting blacks northward, included the beckoning opportunity of industrial jobs, especially after war broke out in Europe in 1914, generating a boom in American manufacturing. This led many northern firms to promote black migration actively through agents sent to the South, advertisements in newspapers circulated among the black community, and arrangements for paying the costs of transportation northward. After America's entry into the war, labor shortages opened up industrial jobs formerly held exclusively by whites, inducing further migration. At the same time, boll weevil blights were making it impossible for blacks to earn even a minimal living in many rural areas of the South. By 1920, more than 1.5 million blacks—nearly a third of those gainfully employed—were engaged in manufacturing or other urban-based occupations outside of domestic service.

The great migration had taken on a new regional dimension as well, for black population rose in cities of the South itself. By 1920, one in four southern blacks lived in urban places. But the degree of urbanization was far greater in the North, where by 1920 some 84 percent of the region's black population lived in the cities, with over a third of all northern black people in just six places: New York, Chicago, Philadelphia, Detroit, Cleveland, and Pittsburgh.

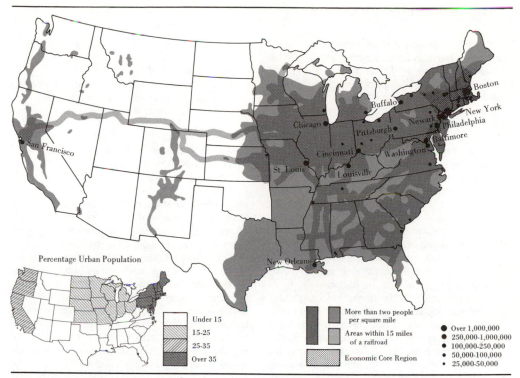

Figure 16—4. **Urbanization in the United States, 1870.** Source: *Cities and Immigrants: A Geography of Change in Nineteenth-Century America* by David Ward. Copyright © 1971 by Oxford University Press, Inc. Reprinted by permission.

Racial tensions

Moving north was a bittersweet experience for black Americans. If employers sought them out, white co-workers resented their coming; and to the irritations of competition in the job market were added the social tensions that arose from the settlement of southern-born blacks in ghetto areas that became bases from which they moved out into adjoining neighborhoods, where they met with white hostility and pressures to keep them back in the ghettos. As a result, rents rose in the segregated districts, and living conditions deteriorated.

The explosive social effects of consequent crowding, crime, and deterioration of buildings and neighborhoods served to intensify the already powerful fears and hostility of white fellow citizens. Tensions finally bred catastrophe. In East St. Louis in 1917 a bloody race riot broke out, sparked by the in-migration of 10,000 southern blacks, including many brought in as strikebreakers. Frenzied white mobs lynched at least 40 blacks; some estimated blacks' deaths at 250 or more.

As migration continued during the war, racial tensions in other cities became more volatile. When the war ended, with unemployment widespread among white workers and especially returned veterans, the explosion finally came. Washington, D.C., and Chicago experienced bloody riots, marked by atrocities against blacks. Ironically, these riots led to a rising demand by whites that tighter legalized segregation be imposed, to keep the races apart. The riots also intensified prejudice against blacks in the major labor unions, which virtually shut their doors to Afro-Americans. Hence, at the very time that the status of the black worker was shifting from that of a "labor reserve" to that of "a regular element in the labor force of nearly every basic industry," organized labor was institutionalizing racial prejudice and barring the Afro-American worker more firmly than ever from the union movement.[3]

[3]Sterling D. Spero and Abram L. Harris, *The Black Worker* (1931, reprinted New York: Atheneum, 1968), p. 461; George W. Groh, *The Black Migration: The Journey to Urban America* (New York: Weybright & Talley, 1972).

THE INDUSTRIAL IDEOLOGY

For the common American worker—whatever his or her skin color, whether immigrant or native-born—laboring in the industrial metropolis meant a harsh depersonalization of life. There was a breakdown in the sense of community in the larger cities, as residential segregation by ethnic group and economic status became a regular feature of urban life. One source of depersonalization and loss of community was the sheer massiveness of numbers. Life was no longer lived in a milieu in which workers' neighbors included those who owned the stores where they shopped, taught in their children's schools, and staffed the city's municipal offices. There were neighbors aplenty, in a life of crowded tenements—but they tended to be people who felt (and were) trapped in the same box, compartmentalized from other aspects of life in the city and the nation.

The immigrant family might hold together, and ethnic loyalties could provide another source of cohesion in the immigrant worker's life, but in other vital respects life was inchoate, even incomprehensible: Jobs disappeared as the result of impersonal market forces operating through a vast international economy, all the power of corporate ownership was arrayed against workers in the major cities, machinery was brought into factories to displace skilled workers and replace them with unskilled men, women, and children.

These aspects of mass society in urban centers were only part of a situation that seemed to erode the dignity of the individual. Equally important was the new sort of work discipline that modern industrial society imposed upon its labor force. In preindustrial society, farmers and craftsmen timed their tasks according to the seasons of nature; the very rhythm of life was shaped by natural forces, and the constraints of time tended to fall upon the worker in ways that left room for leisure and release of time pressure, what one scholar has called the "alternate bouts of intense labour and of idleness, wherever men were in control of their working lives."[4] But in modern industrial society, as Daniel Bell has argued,

the world has become technical and rationalized. The machine predominates, and the rhythms of life are mechanically

paced: time is chronological, methodical, evenly spaced. . . . It is a world of organization—of hierarchy and bureaucracy—in which men are treated as "things" because one can more easily coordinate things than men.[5]

Workers who began their lives in preindustrial communities, whether in farms and small towns in America or other farms and small towns in Europe, did not surrender their whole cultural baggage to accommodate the industrial order. As Professor Herbert Gutman's studies have shown, the workers resisted the demands of modern industrial discipline in surprising ways, holding onto old customs like paying one of their fellow workers to read to them while the rest rolled cigars or made shoes in the shop, or seeking through strikes and other forms of resistance to keep up the tradition of the two-day weekend. Although they fought a losing battle in the large industrial cities, in some of the smaller industrial and mining centers they did win the sympathy of the local power structure—shopkeepers, policemen, the people who served on juries—when they clashed with absentee owners of corporate mills or mines.[6] But even in those places, the pressure of the new industrial discipline was unremitting. The direction that pressure took was eloquently provided in the simplistic propagandist rhetoric of a brochure prepared by the International Harvester Corporation to be used by its Polish-born workers in their English-language lessons:

I hear the whistle. I must hurry.
I hear the five minute whistle.
It is time to go into the shop.
I take my check from the gate board
    and hang it on the department board.
I change my clothes and get ready for
    work.
The starting whistle blows.
I eat my lunch.
It is forbidden to eat until then.
The whistle blows at five minutes of
    starting time.

[4]E. P. Thompson, "Time, Work-Discipline, and Industrial Capitalism," *Past and Present,* 38 (1967): 73.

[5]Daniel Bell, "Labor in the Post-Industrial Society," *Dissent,* Winter 1972, pp. 165–166.

[6]Herbert G. Gutman, "Work, Culture, and Society in Industrializing America, 1815–1919," *American Historical Review, 78* (1973):567; Gutman, "The Worker's Search for Power," in *The Gilded Age: A Reappraisal,* ed. H. Wayne Morgan (Syracuse: Syracuse University Press, 1963), pp. 38–68.

I get ready to go to work.
I work until the whistle blows to quit.
I leave my place nice and clean.
I put all my clothes in the locker.
I must go home.[7]

The imposition of such a work discipline, or industrial ideology, was nothing new in American life. Similar sentiment, if not rhetoric, had been read as lessons to the Lowell mill girls early in the nineteenth century. In the post–Civil War industrialization, as Gutman has written, another wave of first-generation indus-trial workers, this one from eastern and southern European peasant origins instead of from Yankee farms, confronted the demands of an industrial discipline: "It is as if a film — run at a much faster speed — is being viewed for the second time: primitive work rules for unskilled labor, fines, gang labor, and subcontracting were commonplace."[8] Except, as the film was run at the faster speed this second time, the cast of actors had become larger by many orders of magnitude; and further screenings at yet faster speeds lay ahead, a harsh fact that was obvious to the workers themselves.

WAGES AND THE STATUS OF LABOR

To estimate "real wages" — money wages adjusted to take account of changing prices and cost of living — is a difficult task for the historian of nineteenth-century labor. For one thing, the data on money wages are scattered and of dubious reliability. Even when we have reliable data about what was paid to workers in a given factory, locality, or industry, we still must inquire as to how typical the data actually are. It is well known, however, that there were large differentials in wages from region to region, especially between the South and the rest of the nation; and there were also large differentials in the wages paid men and women for the same or comparable work.

Several recent efforts to compute the trends in real wages have been made by economists and historians of labor. The data problems notwithstanding, some reasonably supportable generalizations (and some areas of agreement, too) have emerged from their efforts at statistical reconstruction. First, it is well accepted that during the Civil War prices rose much faster than wages, so that workers in nonfarm occupations suffered perhaps an average 25 to 30 percent loss of real income. Second, it is manifest that *prices* underwent a sharp decline from 1865 to 1871, then continued on a more gradual downward course until 1896. But the degree to which this great price deflation benefited workers is a matter of dispute among scholars. In some occupations real earnings apparently rose by 100 percent from 1865 to 1890. But the average gain was probably in the range of 35 to 50 percent. One authoritative recent study, for example, estimates annual earnings of industrial workers (in constant 1914 dollars) to have risen as follows:[9]

1865 – 1869	$347
1875 – 1879	$395
1885 – 1889	$503
1895 – 1899	$532

From 1901 to 1905, average real earnings (1914 dollars) were $606, rising further to $685 from 1911 to 1915.

There also was probably a decline in the number of hours required of workers paid by the day in the skilled trades. At the time of the Civil War, the average day for all labor was about eleven hours. There was a gradual reduction in manufacturing to ten hours in 1890. Skilled craftsmen probably averaged about nine hours. But there was enormous variation in the hours required of wage workers. In the textile mills of the Southeast, for example, 13 or 14 hours were not uncommon. In the steel mills, the standard day in 1903 was still 12 hours; and in many mills a seventh day on overtime was normal, accepted by the men because a shift from daily to hourly wages had caused them to fall behind in real earnings. (Money wages in the steel mills fell steadily from 1880 to 1897.) Among those groups that worked the longest hours were women and children.

Many factory workers, miners, and others

[7]*Harvester World*, 3 (1912):31, quoted in Gard Korman, "Americanization at the Factory Gate," *Industrial and Labor Relations Review*, 18 (1965):402.

[8]Gutman, "Work, Culture, and Society," p. 546.
[9]Stanley Lebergott, "The American Labor Force," in *American Economic Growth*, ed. Lance E. Davis (New York: Harper & Row, 1972), pp. 212–213; cf. Albert Rees, *Real Wages in Manufacturing, 1890–1894* (Princeton, N.J: Princeton University Press, 1961).

were not paid entirely in money: Mining and other corporations typically paid wages partly in scrip to be used in company stores, and the paternalistic practices of some large firms involved provision of housing or services in ways hard to measure accurately.

Child labor

Perhaps one-sixth of children aged ten to fifteen were employed in the late nineteenth century. Nearly two million children worked and they were some 5 percent of the labor force in 1910. A majority were in agriculture or other nonindustrial pursuits, but still the number doing factory work or employed in mines was high and attracted much attention. Both social reformers and labor unions objected to this use of children, and they pressed for legislation to prohibit it. Led by Massachusetts, which had long been in advance of other states in child-labor legislation, many states in the 1880s and 1890s made school attendance compulsory for at least 20 weeks a year, restricted use of children in factory and other indoor work, and raised the age for compulsory schooling.

As late as 1914, however, six states (all of them in the South) still had no laws making school attendance mandatory, and several states had only minimum legal restraints upon employment of young children. Generally the southern states provided the core of resistance to efforts toward obtaining federal child-labor legislation. Manufacturers in more progressive states, such as those in New England, sought minimum federal standards in hopes of equalizing the competition with low-wage southern manufacturers who employed many children in their mills. Though Congress responded favorably on two occasions, the Supreme Court overturned these child-labor laws; and so by 1914 a national drive, well supported by organized labor as well as northern manufacturers, was under way to gain a constitutional amendment.

Women at work

Concern about women in the labor force stemmed from two sources. First, there was genuine popular feeling that women were ruthlessly exploited by employers in low-wage industries such as ready-made clothing, as well as in the harsh regimen of work in the mills. And second, male workers and labor unions were particularly concerned that general wage scales were imperiled by the low wages offered to women.

As the traditional home occupations, such as clothes making and food preserving, passed to factories in the late nineteenth century, many women sought paid employment outside the home. (See Table 16–2.) The average age of marriage shifted upward as urbanization progressed; in 1900, half the women under 22 were single. A rising divorce rate by the 1870s also led many women to seek jobs.

Between 1880 and 1910, the number of women in the total labor force rose from 2.6 million (15 percent of all workers in 1880) to 7.4 million (20 percent in 1910). Women formed a much higher proportion of the labor force in nonfarm occupations. The relationship between marital status and women's employment was different from that which prevails in our own day. In 1890, for example, only 14 percent of women holding jobs were married, and only about 5 percent of women listed by the census as "married, husband present," held paid employment outside the home. The labor-force participation rate (that is, percentage of the population over 14 years of age holding jobs) was gradually climbing for women generally. In 1890, nearly 16 percent of white women held jobs; in 1900 it was 17.3 percent; and in 1920 it reached 20.7 percent. But for nonwhite women, the participation rate was much higher in that era, as it is today: 37.7 percent in 1890, rising to 40.6 percent by 1920.

Beneath the statistics of general employment, there is evidence of the shifting character of jobs available to women. Increasingly these jobs were in the white-collar category: Burgeoning corporation bureaucracies, expanding service industries such as insurance and advertising, and government agencies all generated demand for clerical and secretarial workers. Educated women found employment as well in nursing, teaching, and social work; but they made only slight gains in the fields of law, medicine, and business management. A large proportion—probably half—of the women who did enter professional life remained single.

The attention of reformers focused mainly upon the deplorable conditions of factory work and the destitution of many female workers, especially in the large cities. The extent of these problems was illustrated by a survey conducted in 1914, which showed that half the women in nonfarm jobs (other than professional work) earned less than $6 a week, with one in five earning less than $4. And at this time, the minimum subsistence wage for a single woman was estimated as $7 weekly. Women's wages generally averaged about half those of men in similar jobs. A Consumers' League survey of New

TABLE 16–2. MAJOR OCCUPATIONAL GROUPS IN THE ACTIVE U.S. LABOR FORCE,[1] BY SEX, 1900–1920 (MILLIONS OF PERSONS)

MAJOR OCCUPATIONAL GROUPS	1900		1910		1920	
	MALE	FEMALE	MALE	FEMALE	MALE	FEMALE
Total workers	23.7	5.3	29.8	7.4	33.6	8.6
White-collar workers	*4.2*	*0.9*	*6.0*	*1.9*	*7.2*	*3.4*
Professional, technical, etc.	0.8	0.4	1.0	0.7	1.3	1.0
Proprietors, managers, officials	1.6	0.1	2.3	0.2	2.6	0.2
Clerical and sales	1.7	0.4	2.7	1.0	3.3	2.2
Manual and service workers	*9.7*	*3.4*	*13.5*	*4.3*	*16.2*	*4.1*
Craftsmen, foremen, etc.	3.0	.1	4.2	.1	5.4	.1
Operatives and laborers	6.0	1.3	8.0	1.7	9.5	1.7
Private household workers (service)	0.1	1.5	0.1	1.8	0.1	1.4
Other service workers	0.7	0.4	1.1	0.6	1.2	0.7
Farm workers	*9.9*	*1.0*	*10.4*	*1.2*	*10.2*	*1.2*
Farmers and farm managers	5.5	0.3	5.9	0.3	6.2	0.3
Farm laborers	4.4	0.7	4.5	0.9	4.1	0.9

Source: U.S. Department of Commerce, Bureau of the Census, *Historical Statistics of the United States, Colonial Times to 1957* (Washington, D.C.: U.S. Government Printing Office, 1960), p. 74.

[1]Includes only self-employed, salaried, and wage workers. This table does not reflect numbers in household unpaid work (mainly of urban housewives, farm wives, children).

York City employment in 1919 concluded that in that city only one out of fourteen industries that employed large numbers of women paid a decent living wage. For those single women who did not live with a family group and pool their earnings to meet expenses of living, the specter of poverty was immediate and real.

Under pressure from women's groups, labor unions, and social reformers, numerous states enacted laws to protect female workers. By 1897 some 15 states had adopted laws limiting the hours of women workers in factories or mines, or forbidding female employment in certain hazardous occupations (especially in mining). In addition, laws requiring safety inspection of shops and factories, and establishing minimum sanitation standards, often were enacted in response to special concern about women workers.

The Progressives

One of the reasons social-reform legislation designed to improve working conditions won approval in the first two decades of the twentieth century was the success of the Progressive movement in American politics. The Progressives, so-called, constituted a reform element of great significance in both the Republican and

Democratic parties. There was great variation from one state to another in the social composition of Progressive reform leadership, in their specific reform goals, and in their main party affiliations. In a few states, such as Wisconsin, Progressives formed close association with the craft unions in seeking social legislation. Elsewhere, they were basically hostile to the principles of organized labor and to the strategies of the AFL or workers' groups outside the AFL; indeed Progressive leadership tended to be distinctly upper middle class and upper class in social origins and orientation. And in the South, the Progressives regarded disfranchisement of blacks as a worthy "reform" goal.

Nonetheless, the Progressives did stand generally for reforms that were designed to curb the power of private business interests, particularly the giant corporations. Even in states where these reformers were clearly hostile to collective bargaining and strikes, or where they condemned the unions as yet one more "special interest" whose political influence must be curbed, the Progressives usually supported factory safety and inspection laws, maximum-hour legislation for female workers, abolition of child labor, and other reforms that were readily supported by organized labor.

UNIONIZATION AFTER 1865

American workers needed labor unions for the same reason that the successful organization of unions was extremely difficult: Employers enjoyed tremendous power over their employees. Never until after 1900 did membership in labor unions include more than 2 or 3 percent of wage earners, and the primary reason was not lack of willingness to organize on the workers' part, but the power of employers to resist unionization.

The specific objectives of the unions that did manage to get a start offer an accurate guide to the plight of American workers. First, of course, was the objective of collective bargaining, a means of bringing the united strength of a firm's or an industry's workers to bear in the negotiation of wages and working conditions. Lacking organization, the individual worker had to accept the employer's best wage offer or else find other employment; collective bargaining held out the chance, at least, that the issues might be discussed.

Second was the typical union concern with what they called "benevolent" functions; that is, group insurance against injury or death on the job, unemployment and loss of income, and other disasters. These benevolent activities were of crucial importance because under American law and prevailing practice, employers shouldered none of these responsibilities. The workers in a shop or mill might pass the hat for the family of one who had died, and the company might contribute something as well. But typically such charity carried a distressed family for only a few weeks or months. Workers had no *right* to such financial help and no legal claim even for injuries sustained on the job. (Under the fellow-servant rule that prevailed in American law until after 1900, an employer was relieved of responsibility for an employee's injury so long as no negligence could be proved.)

Third, the unions typically concerned themselves with forming ties to similar organizations in other cities and other trades. In the national economy of the late nineteenth century — tied together with an expanding railroad system, characterized by large firms that could transfer their production from plants in one city to plants elsewhere, and served by a mobile labor force — workers' organizations could not be truly effective until they were no longer limited to a single locality. To be most effective they also needed to rely upon support from workers in allied trades, especially when they put up picket lines during strikes. And ideally, large unions or federations of unions, embracing great numbers of dues-paying workers, could build up strike funds and organizational treasuries capable of lending aid to individual member unions in times of stress.

Finally, all the unions made provision for payment of dues to support at least modest leadership bureaucracies. Union leaders in the nineteenth century did not command handsome salaries, nor were they afforded the kind of staff and office support that became common in a later time. But workers did understand that some degree of full-time staffing was necessary if union interests were to be defined and pursued with any vigor.

Unions and politics

Some of the union efforts of the late nineteenth century were marked by heavy emphasis upon political strategy. Under the leadership of William H. Sylvis, for example, the National Labor Union was organized in 1866 and functioned essentially as a political reform group. Its leaders rejected militant trade unionism, with its emphasis on bread-and-butter issues such as wages, and even deplored the strike as a weapon of laboring people. Although some of them were trade-union leaders (Sylvis, for example, was president of the Iron Molders Union), they favored a coalition of unions with reformers who agreed to seek the eight-hour day, exclusion of Chinese immigrants, and other objectives that the NLU thought required legislation. After it had organized the dismally unsuccessful National Labor Reform party in 1872, the NLU disappeared from the scene.

During the discouraging depression years of the 1870s, extensive unemployment and some desperate strikes — like the great railroad strike of 1877, which was crushed with the help of federal troops — worked to demoralize and break up the trade unions. Only about one in five of the unions survived these years, as workers turned to political action and also to secret societies. One of the latter that was destined to play a major role in the history of American unions was the Noble Order of the Knights of Labor.

The Knights of Labor

Originally founded in 1869, the Knights of Labor had general benevolent purposes but also were dedicated to the radical view that through "agitation, education, and organization" they might successfully "banish that curse of modern civilization—wage slavery," as an early leader of the Knights, Terence Powderly, declared in 1880.

The Knights were not principally a federation of craft unions, but rather sought to make themselves "one big union," as they said, to bring workers of all crafts and degrees of skill into one great organization. They even reached out to organize the unskilled, men and women, white and nonwhite, in "local assemblies." These assemblies, together with the craft unions, were directly affiliated with the national governing body of the Knights.

Although they had probably needed secrecy to grow in their initial stages—secrecy being a means of defense against employers who might get rid of known union people—in 1881 the Knights abandoned it and inaugurated a remarkably successful membership drive. Political reform was an essential part of the strategy. The Knights demanded an eight-hour day, land reform, tax reform, child-labor prohibitions, and the like. The local assemblies also set up some cooperative shops and buying co-ops.

Until 1884, the Knights discouraged strike activity. But then a wave of wage cuts on the railroads forced the Knights to support strike action by trainmen in their craft-union wing. A strike against Jay Gould's powerful Wabash Railroad followed, which in 1886 brought a spectacular temporary victory for the Knights; and immediately their membership shot up from 100,000 to 700,000.

The basic conflict between craft-union goals and broad reform goals, however, split the Knights' leadership and undermined the gains of 1886. Powderly was opposed to lending the Knights' support to further strikes, and even his endorsement of the eight-hour day proved lukewarm.

By 1888 this organization had had its day in the sun. The Knights had pumped life and funds into some struggling local unions and even a few of the craft unions, and they had certainly brought the message of dignity, self-respect, and the need for organization and solidarity to American workers. But the future lay with a rival group, the American Federation of Labor.

THE AMERICAN FEDERATION OF LABOR

The AFL, as its name implied, was distinctly a federation of craft and industrial unions. It made relative autonomy of its member groups a cardinal principle of organization, and its leaders were committed to "pure and simple" trade unionism. Yet the founding convention, held in Columbus in 1886, also adopted demands for anticontract immigration laws, the abolition of conspiracy laws as applied to trade unions, compulsory education for children, and other essentially political reforms. The growth of the AFL was slow for several years, its membership numbering only 100,000 in 1890. Further membership growth was as follows:

1898	278,000
1900	548,000
1904	1,676,000
1914	2,020,000
1920	4,078,000

During the period of spectacular growth, from 1898 to 1904, the union received vital support from such middle-class organizations as the National Consumers' League, the National Civic Federation, and the National Child Labor Committee, groups that accepted the ideal of collective bargaining and that also wanted progressive social legislation. The AFL needed such help, for this was a period of stiffening employer resistance to unionization. The business antiunion campaign was led by the National Association of Manufacturers, founded in 1895, and was joined by large corporations and associations of business firms ready to spend large sums in legal action against unions. In addition, antiunion employers used the lockout, the blacklist, labor spies, and similar tactics in mines, shops, and factories where AFL organizers appeared.

AFL leadership

The quality of AFL leadership contributed much to its successes. Perhaps the most brilliant of craft leaders was John Mitchell, who at the age of 29, having already worked in the coal mines for 16 years, became president of the United Mine Workers of America. He led his union through the successful coal strike of 1902, and during his presidency, from 1898 to 1908, he directed the miners in an uphill fight for membership which carried it from 43,000 to over 400,000. It was probably the largest trade union of its day.

National leadership of the AFL was provided by Samuel Gompers. Born in London in 1850 of Dutch-Jewish parentage, Gompers emigrated to America in 1863 and joined the first cigar makers' union formed in New York. He became president of his local of the Cigar Makers' Union in 1877, and he was elected chairman of the committee on the constitution of the AFL's predecessor union in 1881 and served continuously (except for one year) as AFL president from 1886 until his death in 1924. Gompers hoped to steer clear of political entanglements. He was even more dedicated to keeping the unions free of radical strategies urged upon them by socialists both within and outside organized labor, and keeping them free as well of what he viewed as excessively utopian or general reform concerns. This kind of pragmatism was the essence of "pure and simple" unionist philosophy.

Exclusive jurisdiction

Gompers championed "exclusive jurisdiction" — the principle that only one national union would be recognized and admitted to the federation in each trade or craft. The AFL's devotion to exclusive jurisdiction was based on bitter experience with jurisdictional conflicts in the history of the Knights of Labor. Repeatedly the craft unions found that workers who had acted as strikebreakers or in other ways undermined their union activities were given Knights of Labor cards by the local assemblies, with the approval of the Knights' national leadership. Indeed, this grievance had been the chief issue that brought the craft unions together in 1886 to form the AFL. In the organizing convention of that year, the federated unions issued this declaration against the Knights:

> The K. of L. have persistently attempted to undermine and disrupt the well established Trades' Unions, organized and encouraged men who have proven themselves untrue to their trade, false to the obligations of their union, embezzlers of moneys, and expelled by many of the unions, and conspiring to pull down the Trades' Unions, which has cost years of work and sacrifice to build; therefore, be it Resolved we condemn the acts above recited, and call upon all workingmen to join unions of their respective trades, and urge the formation of all under one head, the American Federation of Labor.[10]

[10]Quoted in Philip Taft, *Organized Labor in American History* (New York: Harper & Row, 1964), p. 115.

The strike as a labor weapon

In addition to remaining faithful to the trade unions' commitment regarding exclusive jurisdiction, Gompers and the AFL leadership did not hesitate to use the strike. In contrast with Powderly's and the Knights' squeamishness about supporting strike activity, and their belief that unions should avoid the "folly" of strikes by all means, the craft union leaders in the AFL saw this form of militant action as a vital means of putting pressure on employers. "No strike is a loss or a failure to the workers," declared Peter McGuire of the Carpenters' Union. "If naught else, they at least teach the capitalists that they are expensive luxuries to be indulged in."[11]

Labor issues, 1898–1904

The Federation pursued a determined strategy in regard to obtaining contracts from employers that recognized their unions' standings as negotiators in collective bargaining for member workers. Whereas only 10 to 20 percent of strikes in the 1880s and 1890s concerned union recognition, as opposed to wages or other specific issues, during the great organizing drive of 1898–1904 at least one-third of all strikes were concerned with recognition. Other issues that the AFL unions pushed to the forefront were: hours of work, powers of foremen in the shops, formulation of grievance procedures, assignment of union shop stewards, workers' seniority, rules for assignment of helpers to skilled workers, use of apprentices, policies regarding nonunion materials, and the relations between union and nonunion workers.

The AFL also used the union label, or mark, on products made by its workers. This was a means of identifying such goods to encourage their purchase, but also to expedite boycotts against non-union-made products. Moreover, as the member craft unions became stronger and better financed, Gompers organized campaigns to obtain the eight-hour day, a cause that attracted wide popular sympathy and served as excellent publicity for the AFL. Typically, as in the 1889–1891 drive that Gompers engineered, one or more of the strongest unions would spearhead the pressures, and the gains they achieved might then be extended to other workers. Thus the Carpenters' Union succeeded in winning the eight-hour day in over 100 cities in 1891, and claimed that thou-

[11]Quoted in ibid., p. 110.

sands of workers in the building trades who belonged to other unions gained the benefits as well. Indicative of the rising strength of the trade unions was the fact that AFL sponsorship of the 1891 Carpenters' campaign involved a paltry $12,000 contribution from the central organization; by 1907, however, a Typographers' Union campaign for the eight-hour day was financed by a $4 million special assessment on its members.

The skilled vs. the unskilled

Power of the sort that could produce a $4 million special fund to support a strike for the eight-hour day was the essence of Samuel Gompers' dream: that labor should consolidate its resources to launch the sort of financial and organizational effort that could move and shake the business establishment. And the AFL, by building on the strongest unions and organizing the best-paid, most highly skilled workers, did succeed in extending its power and dominating organized labor in the United States from the 1890s until the 1930s.

But if Gompers and the AFL strategy served the craft unions' own constituency well enough, for the majority of American workers—90 percent of whom were not union members, even in 1910—the AFL was a remote, élite group. It was composed of the skilled and semiskilled, and its constituent unions were opposed to spending funds and effort trying to organize unskilled factory workers or common laborers—what they viewed as the fatal error of the Knights of Labor. Moreover, when technological change in a given industry reduced the proportion of skilled workers in that industry, the AFL principle of exclusive jurisdiction often resulted *not* in bringing more of the less-skilled workers into the organization, but rather in reducing the proportion of the industry's workers who were unionized.

Exclusionist policies

The AFL was explicitly exclusionist so far as nonwhite workers were concerned. Gompers himself was committed to racial integration in the unionization movement, at least early in his career. But in the late 1890s he and the AFL leadership bowed to pressure from the craft unions on the race question. In 1900 the council did declare it to be AFL policy to encourage the chartering of separate "colored locals," but this was an empty gesture. Thus, in 1900 only nine of the 60 craft unions had any black members, and two-thirds of all black unionized workers were in the United Mine Workers of America.

The exclusionist strategy of the AFL, which won major gains for the skilled but excluded racial minorities and the great mass of unskilled workers from its ranks, was in the union's early years a controversial issue. Some historians accept Gompers' own view that only the skilled workers had the market power, cohesion, unity, and organizational base that could ensure a successful labor movement. Moreover, those sympathetic to the AFL can cite the spillover gains that unorganized labor undoubtedly enjoyed as the result of union successes, especially the reduced working hours won in many cities—and, of course, the general pressure that the AFL exerted on wage scales, at least in times of prosperity and expansion. But on the other side, critics and historians argue, the true measure of success in unionization is the proportion of the labor force that the unions actually bring into their membership. And by this standard the AFL record was probably not what a more aggressive, less exclusionist strategy might have produced. For even in 1900, only 4.8 percent of American nonfarm workers were in unions, and in 1920, after a wartime period of enormous AFL expansion, still only 1 worker in 6 held a union card.

INDUSTRIAL UNIONISM

Although craft unionism dominated the labor scene, industrial unionism—organization of all workers within an industry, regardless of craft, into a single industry union—did persist even in some of the AFL's constituent unions. It was most notably the organizing principle in the United Mine Workers of America, in which every worker from slate picker to engineer was eligible to join a single organization. Industrial unionism was the most practicable form of organization for an industry with workmen in many trades, or for an industry like mining, which was typically isolated from large, diverse population centers. In addition, industrial unionism was most compatible with the new mass-production industries in which skilled craftsmen were being displaced.

The Western Federation of Miners

The AFL's "pure and simple" unionism, with its stress of bread-and-butter issues, its conservative acceptance of the capitalist system itself, and its élitist tone, repelled some labor leaders and great numbers of workers who subscribed to more radical principles. One dissident group was the Western Federation of Miners. Briefly affiliated with the AFL in the mid-1890s, the WFM stood for industrial unionism. It staged a series of bitter and costly strikes in the West from 1894 to 1904, often calling skilled workers off the job to strike on behalf of the unskilled; they opened their membership, too, to all who worked in mining, regardless of race or craft.

The IWW

In 1905 the WFM helped launch a serious national challenge to the AFL, organizing a convention in Chicago, together with elements of the Socialist and Socialist Labor movements, and founded the Industrial Workers of the World. The IWW's charter manifesto denounced craft unionism, declared the necessity of class struggle, and, in an amendment adopted in 1908, asserted that workers must "take possession of the earth and the machinery of production and abolish the wage system." Committed, like the Knights of Labor, to "one big union," the IWW advocated the general strike; and, in the face of employers' use of force in such industries as mining and lumbering, they advocated the use as well of sabotage and armed resistance to private detectives and government troops. The IWW gained diverse followings in the western region, in the mill towns of New England and New Jersey, and in the ranks of Socialist and anarchist groups. The most notable successes of the Wobblies, as they came to be called, were in overcoming the ethnic animosities and differences in craft skills that had divided workers in Lawrence, Massachusetts, and Paterson, New Jersey — but not well enough to win enduring victories in the mills. The IWW also sustained organizations of workers against some of the most unscrupulous, most heavy-handed corporations in the country, in the mining districts and lumbering regions of the Far West.[12]

Factionalism weakened the IWW. Its militancy and radicalism frightened property-conscious middle-class people and workers, who looked to the AFL for their future betterment. Finally, the IWW opposed American participation in World War I, triggering a devastating attack upon the organization by the federal government itself, as well as by employers who had long waited for a chance to discredit and eliminate the Wobblies. Never having had more than 100,000 members, the IWW emerged from the war in 1918 a badly crippled organization. Although it persisted in a few localities in the 1920s, even launching some important strike movements, it was no longer a force of major moment in the national labor scene.

In an era when the aristocracy of American labor, epitomized by the AFL council, pursued a pragmatic course in paying respect to what Carl Sandburg once called "the dictates of the belly," the IWW had taken an entirely different direction. Its revolutionary outlook, militant tactics, and tenacious organization in areas of the country and the labor force that were hardest to organize, against the nation's toughest anti-union business firms, kept "pressure from the left" on the business interests and on the political establishment. In retrospect, some of the social legislation designed to ameliorate the worker's lot in the Progressive era may well have been motivated by fear of IWW-style alternatives to reform within the system.

LABOR STRIFE

In the late nineteenth century, industrialists' resistance to the unions was adamant, the power of government was repeatedly mobilized against striking workers, and the advances that labor gained were hard-won.

The 1870s were marked by widespread strikes, particularly in the mining industry, in response to wage cuts and layoffs. The depression of 1873 – 1877 also triggered a series of railroad strikes, which culminated in public disorder and rioting in many cities in 1877. In the mining districts of Pennsylvania, meanwhile, an Irish immigrant labor organization, the Molly Maguires, had organized miners; there ensued three years of violence, both from the labor group and from Pinkerton detectives and other armed agents of the mine companies. Violence also flared up in San Francisco in 1877, as a

---

[12]A full and rich history is provided by Melvyn Dubofsky, *We Shall Be All: A History of the IWW* (New York: Quadrangle Books, 1969).

union-led political movement turned furiously upon the Chinese immigrants in the city, who were cast as scapegoats for unemployment and wage cutting.

The intensity of labor strife did not diminish in the 1880s. Over 6000 strikes were reported from 1886 to 1890, involving nearly 2 million workers. Railroad strikes occurred on some of the major lines—five of them from 1884 to 1886 involved the Knights of Labor and the Jay Gould lines—and in 1889 the AFL launched its first great strike effort for the eight-hour day.

The Haymarket affair

The most notorious incident of the 1880s was the Haymarket affair in Chicago, where a workers' meeting, called to protest the McCormick Harvester Company's actions against striking workers and to consider deaths of strikers reported at the hands of police, became the scene of a bombing that took seven lives. Antilabor spokesmen used the incident to discredit union leaders generally and anarchists in particular. A number of Chicago anarchists, probably wholly innocent, were found guilty and executed. Governor John Altgeld of Illinois later pardoned other defendants, condemning the trails as a travesty of justice. Employers meanwhile exploited the Haymarket affair to launch a devastating attack on the Knights of Labor.

The Homestead and Pullman strikes

In the 1890s nearly 4 million workers participated in some 10,000 strikes. Of particular note was a strike in 1892 against Carnegie steel mills in Homestead, Pennsylvania. The company brought in hundreds of private police in an effort to drive the Association of Iron and Steel Workers out of the mills. They largely succeeded, but not before extensive violence had aroused public opinion on both sides of the issues.

In 1894 a strike against the Pullman Company widened into a railroad strike involving thousands of workers in the Chicago area. The federal government intervened in what organized labor universally condemned as "union breaking by injunction." The attorney general, Richard Olney, obtained court orders enjoining the workers from interfering with the railroads; the American Railway Union leader, Eugene V. Debs, was imprisoned; and federal troops were used to get the trains running again. From that day forward, it became a leading political objective of organized labor to obtain legislation banning such injunctions.

The 1902 coal strike

From 1900 to 1905 there were nearly 3000 strikes annually, on the average, and more than 3 million workers were involved. Widely publicized was a United Mine Workers' strike against the anthracite companies in 1902. Led by union president John Mitchell, whose eloquent appeals to the public awakened much sympathy for labor, the strikers demanded recognition of their union, as well as other bread-and-butter objectives. President Theodore Roosevelt established a precedent by intervening personally, gaining consent for mediation by commissioners whom he appointed.

The employers' counter-offensive

Employer interests and government alike were displaying new antiunion weapons and using older techniques more vigorously in these turn-of-the-century labor conflicts. In Homestead, in the railroad strikes, and (initially, at least) in the coal district, the employers seemed determined not only to resist workers' demands but also to drive the unions themselves into the ground. Use by the business firms of undercover agents, including *agents provocateurs*, the arming of private police and detective forces, strong-arm tactics by hired hoodlums, and similar techniques seemed to be gaining legitimacy throughout the industrial world, wherever unions rose up.

Colorado labor war

Nowhere was the level of violence so high for so long as in the Colorado labor war of 1903–1904. Miners' strikes in the copper region were led by the Western Federation of Miners. The mining companies reacted with a massive show of force, and the state governor responded at the behest of the companies by mobilizing the militia, declaring martial law, suspending civil liberties, and deporting more than 200 union men, who were rounded up and held in bullpens before being thrown on trains to be taken out of the state. Dynamitings, shootings, mysterious accidents, all took a high toll in lives. Ironically, the major issues in the strike were over the mining companies' open refusal to honor the laws of Colorado, which required safety measures in the mines, uniform weighing procedures, recognition of workers' rights to form a union, and abolition of the scrip system of paying miners. "IS COLORADO IN AMERICA?" the WFM asked in a famous circular that featured union slogans written across the American flag. The response by the authorities made the question worth repeating: for the union's leader was jailed for desecrating the American flag, and habeas corpus was refused when the state failed to prosecute formally. The U.S. Supreme Court upheld the governor's power to imprison him without trial or other recourse, on grounds that in an "insurrection" the public authorities' good faith must be assumed.[13]

The courts

Menacing new ways of twisting the law to legitimize and accommodate antiunion measures by employers and a hostile government continued to appear in the decade after 1900. In 1902, when the AFL unions struck against a hat-making firm in Danbury, Connecticut, they organized a national boycott against the firm's products. In a series of important decisions on this case, the Supreme Court ruled that the union's boycott was a violation of the Sherman Antitrust Act of 1890, which barred conspiracies in restraint of trade.[14] Federal courts gave prison terms (never served, because of legal maneuvers) to Samuel Gompers and other AFL leaders for their violation of a sweeping court injunction against their national boycott activities. The federal court of appeals that passed sentence on Gompers and his colleagues denounced them as demagogues leading "the rabble," and as dangerous characters who would "smite the foundations of civil government" and subordinate the law to "anarchy and riot."[15]

State police forces

In addition to confronting stiffening employer resistance and new legal doctrines, the unions had to deal with still another government innovation: state police. Until about 1900, few states maintained even small forces of this kind. But at the turn of the century, Pennsylvania and several other industrial states created state police forces, mainly to deal with labor unrest. Business interests avidly supported this innovation, for they had found that local police and other officials in small towns and rural areas (such as the mining districts) were too sympathetic with the workers during strikes.

"Violent encounters"

There were numerous additional strikes in the years from 1900 to the outbreak of World War I: IWW strikes in the mill towns, seamen's actions at the Great Lakes ports and on the Pacific coast, widespread strikes by employees of municipal and franchised street railways, and a series of episodes involving many thousands of garment workers in a great organizing drive in New York and other cities. The period from 1911 to 1916 has been termed a time when "violent encounters . . . attained a virulence seldom equaled in industrial warfare in any nation."[16] In the face of stiffening opposition, the AFL could not sustain the momentum of the expansion achieved in the boom years 1898–1904; and when the European war began in 1914, organized labor was struggling to hold its ground in the United States. The war-induced economic boom, and the involvement of this country in the war, would provide the AFL with a new opportunity to extend its organizing reach.

IMMIGRATION RECONSIDERED: RESTRICTIONISM TRIUMPHS

Many of the craft-union leaders, as well as rank-and-file members, were English, Irish, Scottish or northern Europeans by birth or recent extraction. In some areas of the country around 1900, foreign-born workers comprised half or more of all union members. Nonetheless, the trade unions were among the most ardent advocates of immigration restriction. In 1880 the craft unions had joined in agitation for exclusion of Chinese immigrants, which Congress mandated in 1882 in the first significant restriction of free immigration ever adopted by the United States. By the turn of the century, the new immigration had become an object of concern for the unions. The language barriers

[13]James Edward Wright, *The Politics of Populism: Dissent in Colorado* (New Haven: Yale University Press, 1974), pp. 238–239; Vernon H. Jensen, *Heritage of Conflict: Labor Relations in the Non-Ferrous Metals Industry up to 1930* (Ithaca: Cornell University Press, 1950), pp. 118–159.

[14]Loewe v. Lawlor, 208 U.S. 274 (1908); Lawlor v. Loewe, 235 U.S. 522 (1915). Cf. Harold U. Faulkner, *The Quest for Social Justice, 1898–1914* (New York: Macmillan, 1931), pp. 60–61.

[15]Quoted in Faulkner, *Quest for Social Justice,* pp. 62–63.

[16]Philip Taft and Philip Ross, "American Labor Violence," in U.S. National Commission on the Causes and Prevention of Violence, *Violence in America* (Washington, D.C.: U.S. Government Printing Office, 1969), vol. 1, p. 248.

posed problems for union organizers. Besides, many of the recently arrived workers viewed themselves as transients; they intended to return to the old country as soon as they had saved enough, and so they had a detached, uncommitted attitude when it came to unions, strikes, and politics. Employers' frequent use of immigrants as strikebreakers naturally tended to reinforce the ethnic antagonisms and distrust that already were directed against the new immigrants.

Business interests had traditionally supported open immigration. But in the 1890s, seething unrest in the industrial cities, the popular association of recent immigrants with radical (especially anarchist) ideas and episodes of violence, and fears of general social chaos engendered by the depression conditions of the decade, all gave new impetus to efforts to restrict immigration. Deep suspicion of the foreign-born seemed to grip much of middle-class America.[17] Hence by 1915 the combined pressures of the craft unions, businessmen, and nativist groups generally led Congress to consider restriction of immigration. In 1917 a literacy test for immigrants became law.[18] Meanwhile, the European war suspended immigration from the Old World. During the war years there was intensified anti-immigrant feeling. Wartime patriotism became an instrument with which enemies of the labor unions could attack them and alien radicals as well. As the war neared an end, fears grew that the United States might be deluged with refugees from Europe. And so Congress reversed the nation's historic immigration policy: In the early 1920s strict quotas were placed upon new entries, discriminating against the people of southern and eastern Europe. Immigration restriction must be acknowledged as a "reform" objective successfully attained by, or with the support of, organized labor. But in light of the immigrant worker's importance in America's labor movement, it was at best an ironic triumph.

SELECTED READINGS

*Brody, David, ed., *The American Labor Movement* (New York: Harper & Row, 1971). (Excellent collection of essays.)

*————, *Steelworkers in America: The Nonunion Era* (New York: Harper & Row, 1969).

Cantor, Milton, ed., *Black Labor in America* (Westport, Conn.: Negro Universities Press, 1970).

Commons, John R., *History of Labour in the United States* (New York: Macmillan, 1935).

*Dubofsky, Melvyn, *Industrialism and the American Worker, 1865–1920* (New York: Crowell, 1975). (Includes bibliographic essay.)

————, *We Shall Be All: History of the IWW* (New York: Quadrangle Books, 1969).

Easterlin, Richard A., "The American Population," in Lance Davis et al., *American Economic Growth* (New York: Harper & Row, 1972).

Erickson, Charlotte, *American Industry and the European Immigrant, 1860–1885* (Cambridge, Mass.: Harvard University Press, 1957).

*Grob, Gerald, *Workers and Utopia, . . . 1865–1900* (New York: Quadrangle, 1969).

Gutman, Herbert G., "Work, Culture, and Society in Industrializing America, 1815–1919," *American Historical Review*, LXXVIII (1973).

Higgs, Robert, "Race, Skills, and Earnings: American Immigrants in 1909," *Journal of Economic History*, XXXI (1971).

Kirkland, Edward C., *Industry Comes of Age* (New York: Holt, Rinehart and Winston, 1961).

Lebergott, Stanley, *Manpower in Economic Growth: The American Record Since 1800* (New York: McGraw-Hill, 1964).

Long, Clarence D., *Wages and Earnings in the United States, 1860–1890* (Princeton, N.J.: Princeton University Press, 1960).

[17]See John Higham, *Strangers in the Land: Patterns of American Nativism, 1860–1925* (1955, reprinted New York: Atheneum, 1963).

[18]The test required adult immigrants (over 16 years of age) to read a short passage in a language of their choice. This particular method of restricting immigration had been recommended by a federal Immigration Commission in 1911, after a four-year study ending with a report highly prejudiced against the new immigration. In fact, the test proved ineffective in stemming the flow of the newcomers, as experience proved in 1919–1921. (Higham, *Strangers in the Land,* p. 308; Philip Taylor, *The Distant Magnet* [New York: Harper & Row, 1971], pp. 243–248.)

Rees, Albert, *Real Wages in Manufacturing, 1890–1914* (Princeton, N.J.: Princeton University Press, 1961).

*Spero, Sterling D., and Harris, Abram L., *The Black Worker* (1931, reprinted New York: Atheneum, 1968).

Taft, Philip, *Organized Labor in American History* (New York: Harper & Row, 1964).

Taueber, Conrad, and Irene B., *The Changing Population of the United States* (New York: Wiley, 1958).

*Taylor, Philip, *The Distant Magnet: European Emigration to the USA* (New York: Harper & Row, 1971).

Thomas, Brinley, *Migration and Economic Growth, 2nd ed.,* (New York: Cambridge University Press, 1971).

Ulman, Lloyd, *The Rise of the National Trade Union* (Cambridge, Mass.: Harvard University Press, 1955).

*Ware, Norman, *The Labor Movement in the United States, 1860–1895* (New York: Vintage Books, 1964).

Williamson, Jeffrey G., *Late Nineteenth Century American Development* (New York: Cambridge University Press, 1975).

Woytinsky, W. S., *Employment and Wages in the United States* (New York: Twentieth Century Fund, 1953).

Urbanization and minorities

*Chudacoff, Howard P., *The Evolution of American Urban Society* (Englewood Cliffs, N.J.: Prentice-Hall, 1975).

*Hauser, Philip M., and Schnore, Leo F., eds., *The Study of Urbanization* (New York: Wiley, 1965).

Hutchinson, E. P. *Immigrants and Their Children* (New York: Columbia University Press, 1956).

Lampard, Eric E., "The History of Cities in Economically Advanced Areas," *Economic Development and Cultural Change,* III (1954–1955).

*McKelvey, Blake, *American Urbanization: A Comparative History* (Glenview, Ill.: Scott, Foresman, 1973).

*Osofsky, Gilbert, *Harlem: The Making of a Ghetto* (New York: Harper & Row, 1966).

*Spear, Allan H., *Black Chicago, . . . 1890–1920* (Chicago: University of Chicago Press, 1967).

Thernstrom, Stephan, *The Other Bostonians: Poverty and Progress . . . 1880–1970* (Cambridge, Mass.: Harvard University Press, 1973).

*Warner, Sam Bass, Jr., *The Urban Wilderness: A History of the American City* (New York: Harper & Row, 1973).

The 1865–1914 era was marked by a continuation and broadening of the transportation revolution, which had already brought to the American economy improved wagon highways, steam navigation on inland and ocean waters, canals, and the steam railroad. The late nineteenth century belonged peculiarly to the railroad. Indeed, the construction of railroads absorbed an enormous portion of American resources and energies. The nation's rail network was built up from 53,000 miles in 1870 to more than 252,000 by 1914—more than all of Europe's railway mileage, and equal to a third of the world's. The new railroads, in turn, were of crucial importance in stimulating economic expansion. They were the commercial lifelines of an industrializing society.

By the end of the century there were other developments that were transforming communications: the electric-powered railway, the automobile, and electronic communications in telephony and telegraphy. But still, it was the steam railroads that carried the freight and most of the passengers. Moreover, their vast size and complexity had induced railway corporations to develop new concepts of management; they had spawned giantism and oligopoly structures, and they had required the society to reassess its legal norms in order to restore the balance between private power and the public interest. Their influence, in short, was pervasive in the American economy and in the society at large.

There were many paradoxes in the development of America's railways. They were liberating—expediting mobility and speed across space, and harnessing enormous power. But they could also be confining and menacing, as they held the power of economic life and death over countless communities; and they often abused that power. They carried a nation's rising production with efficiency admired throughout the world, and yet they were consistently the most troubled sector of corporate finance. The railroads were capitalism's most pampered children, recipients of lavish public subsidies in land and money; but they also became the first and most heavily regulated segment of the private sector.

RAILROAD EXPANSION

When the Civil War began, most of the nation's 30,000 miles of railroad were in the North. During the war there was continuing development of railroads in the North, with some new construction and a great increase in traffic and profits, which became the basis for massive new investments after the war. In the South there was widespread destruction of railways.

Figure 17–1 illustrates the pattern of railroad construction after 1865. By 1870 mileage had already reached 53,000. The spurt of construction continued until the Panic of 1873, an event itself partly attributable to overbuilding and overcapitalization of railroads. This postwar wave of building included the first of the transcontinental railroads to the Pacific coast. Another phenomenal period of railway growth began in the late 1870s; mileage was over 93,000 in 1880 and 167,000 by 1890. The

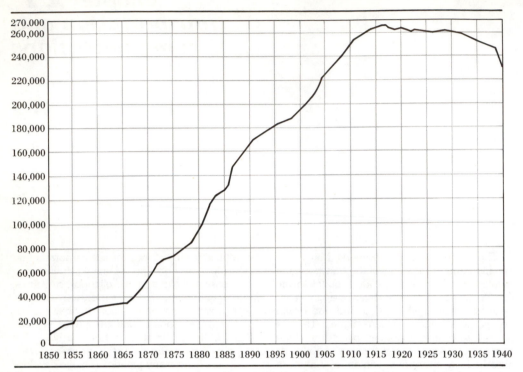

Figure 17–1. **Miles of Railroad in Operation, 1850–1940.** Source: *Statistical Abstract,* 1940, p. 424.

Panic of 1893 and the depression that followed hampered new construction, but it picked up again in the prosperous years after 1898. For twelve years thereafter, new mileage averaged 5000 per year. From 1910 to 1913, it was 3000 miles annually, and it declined rapidly thereafter. The point of saturation seems to have been reached. Indeed, by 1916 railroad mileage was being abandoned, a trend that has continued to the present day.

PRODUCTIVITY GAINS

Together with this extraordinary expansion of the railroad network from 1865 to 1914, there was a great increase in the *productivity* of the railroads. Recent scholarly estimates suggest that productivity doubled from 1870 to 1900; that is, all units of input (labor, capital, and fuel combined) in 1900 produced twice the ton-miles of freight and passengers carried as had been the case in 1870.[1] (See Tables 17–'1, 17–2.) What accounted for this rising productivity of the American railroad system?

[1]The estimates are by the economic historian Albert Fishlow, whose work is cited in Tables 17–1 and 17–2.

Physical integration

In the first place, the nation's rail facilities became truly integrated physically. Prior to 1860, as we have seen (Chapter 10), there had been many different gauges (that is, widths of track) in use. Hence there were few points at which "connecting" lines—lines that on a railway map seemed to touch—actually connected. The fragmentation of the system was aggravated by the fact that few cities served by two or more railways had a central or union station; connecting freight had to be hauled across town on the city streets. The actual physical integration of the network came in the mid-1880s,

TABLE 17–1. PHYSICAL OUTPUT ESTIMATES: U.S. RAILROADS, 1839–1910

FISCAL YEAR[1]	PASSENGER-MILES (BILLIONS)	TON-MILES OF FREIGHT (BILLIONS)	PASSENGER RATE (CENTS/MILE)	FREIGHT RATE (CENTS/MILE)	OUTPUT INDEX[2] (1910 = 100)
1839	0.1	0.03	5.0	7.5	0.04
1849	0.5	0.35	2.9	4.05	0.31
1859	1.9	2.6	2.44	2.58	1.74
1870	4.1	11.7	2.8	2.18	6.03
1880	5.7	32.3	2.51	1.29	13.78
1890	12.1	80.0	2.20	0.92	32.79
1900	16.2	144.0	2.00	0.73	54.79
1910	32.5	255.0	1.94	0.75	100.00

[1]Fiscal year for 1880–1910 ends June 30. For previous years the typical practice of individual roads was to report either on September 30 or at year's end, which would make the covered year correspond to a fiscal year ending in the autumn.

[2]The output index shown here is slightly different from that given in Table 17–2, which represents an adjustment of the estimates.

Source: Albert Fishlow, "Productivity and Technological Change in the Railroad Sector, 1840–1910," in National Bureau of Economic Research, *Output, Employment, and Productivity in the United States After 1800,* vol. 30 of *Studies in Income and Wealth* (New York: Columbia University Press, 1966), p. 585. Copyright 1966 by The National Bureau of Economic Research. Used by permission.

TABLE 17–2. INDICES OF U.S. RAILROAD OUTPUT, INPUT, AND PRODUCTIVITY (1910 = 100)

FISCAL YEARS	OUTPUT	PERSONS ENGAGED	CAPITAL	FUEL	TOTAL INPUT	TOTAL FACTOR PRODUCTIVITY
1839	0.04	.3	.8	.07	.5	8.7
1849	0.31	1.1	2.2	.2	1.4	22.1
1859	1.7	5.0	10.1	1.5	6.6	26.4
1870	6.0	13.5	16.6	5.4	13.9	43.4
1880	13.8	24.5	31.5	11.7	25.9	53.2
1890	32.8	44.1	61.9	28.7	49.3	66.5
1900	54.8	59.9	72.3	45.9	63.2	86.7
1910	100.0	100.0	100.0	100.0	100.0	100.0

Source: Albert Fishlow, "Productivity and Technological Change in the Railroad Sector, 1840–1910," in National Bureau of Economic Research, *Output, Employment, and Productivity in the United States After 1800,* vol. 30 of *Studies in Income and Wealth* (New York: Columbia University Press, 1966), p. 626. Copyright 1966 by The National Bureau of Economic Research. Used by permission.

when the four-foot–eight-inch gauge was adopted as standard. Also contributing to efficiency through integration was the development of "fast freight" and express companies, which in some cases built and operated their own cars.

From 1898 on, the railways engaged in construction of giant new central terminals in the major cities. Boston's South Station (1898) was the first; other monumental structures, many of them marvelous combinations of architectural innovation and utilitarian severity, were completed in New York, Washington, Chicago, Kansas City, and other railway centers. The continuing gains in efficiency were reflected in freight data: In 1898, each mile of railroad line carried an average of 618,000 tons of freight; by 1913 the average had risen to 1.19 million tons.

Improved technology

The second major source of productivity gains was the improved technology of railroad construction and equipment. Steel rails, which came into general use by the 1870s, outlasted the old iron rails by ten times and carried much heavier loads. The railroad companies also introduced heavier, more powerful steam engines, and rolling stock became heavier. The shift toward greater scale was expedited by development also of bulk loading and handling techniques. The greater power, size, and durability of trains and roadbed made the railroad more efficient and helped to bring freight rates down in the late nineteenth century.

Of crucial importance too was the Westinghouse air brake, first patented in 1868. Block signaling was introduced in 1865, and together with the continuous improvement of telegraphy to help control railroad movements, it further aided in development of efficient rail service.

Although new mileage added fell off after 1910, the railroad corporations continued to invest in their equipment and facilities, further increasing productivity. Much of the investment went into safety equipment, larger locomotives and cars, and construction of double tracks, sidings, and yard facilities.

GOVERNMENT AID AND PROMOTION

Private investors financed by far the major part of American railway expansion after 1865. But government aid and support did much to make the way easier.

Federal aid

The idea of a transcontinental railroad was an old one, dating back to the 1840s. In the 1850s Congress had authorized surveys of various routes between the Mississippi Valley and the Pacific coast, but not until the Civil War had begun was there action to assure that such a road would be built. In 1862 Congress chartered the Union Pacific Railroad to build a line from Nebraska west toward California; the Central Pacific was organized to build from the Pacific coast eastward to meet the Union Pacific. Congress awarded to each company large grants of land and loans as high as $48,000 a mile to aid in construction. In 1864 an even more generous grant was awarded to the Northern Pacific Railroad, incorporated by Congress to build from Lake Superior to Puget Sound in Washington State. The railroad received not only a right of way through federal lands, but also lands estimated at 45 million acres, to be chosen from within a strip of land along the route 80 miles wide in the states and 120 miles in the territories through which it passed. The road's promoters valued the grant at $165 million to $550 million. Additional large grants were awarded to the Southern Pacific (1866) and the Texas Pacific (1871), and smaller grants to smaller lines.

From 1850 to 1871 the federal government gave away more than 175 million acres. Of this amount, about 130 million acres were actually earned by the railroads; the remainder was forfeited and returned to the government because of failure to meet terms specified in the grant legislation. These grants became highly controversial. Potential settlers objected to the fact that all the lands in a wide grant zone along the line of each railroad were unavailable to purchasers for long periods of time. Often the railroad companies delayed in earning the lands and having them transferred formally, in order to avoid paying local taxes on them and in hopes that their value would rise. Bureaucratic inefficiency and confusion on the government's part made for further delays. The main complaint, however, was that much of the most desirable land in large portions of the West was thus placed outside the operation of liberal, settler-oriented land laws such as the Homestead Act. (See Figure 17–2.)

On the other hand, the grants did make a significant contribution to the timing and feasibility of western railroad construction. To the Central Pacific, for example, their value was 26 percent of investment expenditures; to the Union Pacific, 34 percent.[2] In addition, the railroad companies did have a stake in developing the country through which their lines passed. Most of them founded active land offices, and they advertised heavily and sent land agents to attract settlers from Europe and the East to colonize their grants. The railroads also offered credit terms to purchasers of their land. In most cases the land-grant roads were also required to carry government mail and military troops at reduced rates.

State and local aid

State and local governments also extended critical financial assistance to railroads, both in cash subscriptions to stock or cash subsidies and in land grants.[3] Most of the state-level aid was given in the southern states during Reconstruction. Texas alone granted 35 million acres

[2]Lloyd J. Mercer, "Land Grants to the American Railroads: Social Cost or Benefit?" *Business History Review,* (1969); Mercer, "Who Paid for the Land-Grant Railroads?" ibid., 46 (1972):286–293.

[3]Data on government aid are in Carter Goodrich, *Government Promotion of American Canals and Railroads, 1800–1890* (New York: Columbia University Press, 1960), and Edward Chase Kirkland, *Industry Comes of Age: Business, Labor, and Public Policy, 1860–1897* (New York: Holt, Rinehart and Winston, 1961). Detailed data on land grants are in David M. Ellis, "Comment on 'The Railroad Land Grant Legend,'" *Mississippi Valley Historical Review,* 32 (1946).

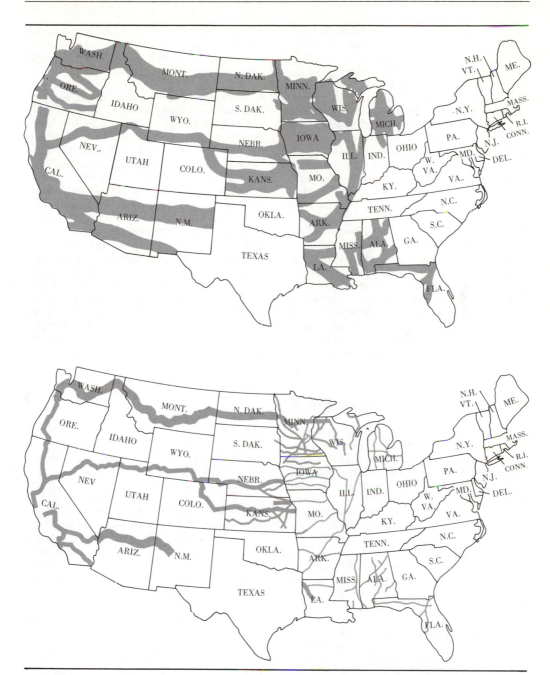

Figure 17–2. **Federal land grants to railroads.** The shaded portions in the top map show the outer limits of areas within which land grants were made to railroads. The railroad companies obtained only a portion of the lands within limits shown. Until formal transfer of the lands was actually granted, however, all of the land within the shaded areas were unavailable to settlers under federal laws for land disposal. After lands were granted formally, a substantial portion of remaining land within the limits was available only at $2.50 per acre or higher prices. The shaded areas in the lower map are of a size proportional to the amounts of land actually received by the railroads. Source: Robert S. Henry, "The Railroad Land Grant Legend in American History Texts," Mississippi Valley Historical Review, XXXII (Sept. 1945). Copyright 1945 by the Organization of American Historians. Reproduced by permission.

of land to its railroads, and total state grants amounted to over 51 million acres and $95 million in cash.

Aid by local governments—townships, cities, and counties—came to at least $175 million in the same period. This type of aid was common throughout the North and West. The railroad promoters did their best to stimulate this form of investment, commonly building their lines only through towns or counties that offered subsidies or took public subscriptions of stock. Extensive disillusionment and bitter political and legal fights often followed in the wake of local assistance, for some aided lines were never built, others went into bankruptcy and left local taxpayers with the burden of heavy interest charges on bonds issued to raise funds for railroad stock investments, and many other lines bogged down in construction because of frauds or operating losses. Incensed by these developments, several hundred communities challenged the legality of the bonds they had themselves issued only a few years previously. In the 1860s and 1870s, federal courts were clogged with such cases. The courts almost always sided with the bondholders and forced the local taxpayers to meet their debts, whether or not they had gained the benefits anticipated from the railroads they had aided.

Private investment and public aid

Total government aid from 1865 to 1890 probably amounted to $1.5 to $2 billion, including the value of granted lands. This was some 10 or 15 percent of the total investment in railroads during this period; the rest of the capital was raised privately. European investors proved important in American railroad finance, for they put up one-fourth or more of the total private capital, mainly in the form of railroad bond purchases. American investors—both the large investment banking houses of the East and smaller-scale individual investors, including many who lived along the new rail lines—provided the remainder of the capitalization. Widespread railroad bankruptcies in the 1870s and 1890s cost investors many millions of dollars. The flotsam and debris of wrecked fortunes were thus left in the wake of American railway financing in the late nineteenth century.

EXPANSION AND CONSOLIDATION

The most dramatic extensions of the railway network were in the vast region west of the Mississippi. Even by 1860 the Mississippi River was reached by ten different railroads building westward from the Great Lakes ports and the eastern seaboard; and nearly every one of these roads had ambitions to become part of a transcontinental line that would extend to the Pacific.

The transcontinentals

It was the big lines aided by Congress that first realized the transcontinental railroad dream. The design, surveying, and construction of the Union Pacific and Central Pacific lines involved a host of problems never encountered before in American railway building: the steep grades and the need for tunnels and bridges in the Rockies, the problems of dealing with mountain snow and debris, and the discipline and management of work crews in camps remote from settlements. By 1865 there were 7000 Chinese workers, brought from San Francisco and from their home country, and 2500 white laborers on the Central Pacific line. Equipment, materials, and supplies were hauled from the starting point to the limit of completed track. The joining of the Central Pacific with the Union Pacific line at Promontory Summit, Utah, in 1869 brought to its culmination the boldest transportation achievement in America since completion of the Erie Canal.

The second great transcontinental project was the Northern Pacific, also the child of a congressional land grant. Begun in 1867 and aided after 1869 through the financing of Jay Cooke & Company, the Northern Pacific floundered in 1873 when Cooke's firm failed after 500 miles had been built. A German-born promoter, Henry Villard, who made a fortune in railroad and steamship investments in Oregon, obtained control of the Northern Pacific with the backing of New York and foreign investors. The road was completed in 1883, by which time the Union Pacific was already extending its network northward into the Pacific Northwest to compete with the newly built road.

Still further competition on the northern route came from James J. Hill, who obtained control of a bankrupt 200-mile railroad in Minnesota, "a streak of rust running through a desert," as it was derisively termed. Although it lacked a federal land grant, Hill's line had a valuable grant from the state. With that fiscal base, Canadian investors' contributions, and his own driving entrepreneurship, Hill built his Great Northern Railway (parallel to the Northern Pacific) westward to Seattle in 1893. Not only did Hill's line weather the depression of 1893–1897 while the other transcontinentals all faced receiverships; he also obtained control of the Northern Pacific.

A land grant of 1866 established the initial fiscal base for the Southern Pacific line, which in 1883 completed a direct line between New Orleans and San Francisco and Los Angeles. The Southern Pacific was controlled by the "Big Four" who had controlled the Central Pacific: Leland Stanford, Collis Huntington, Mark Hopkins, and Charles Crocker. As they had done with the Central Pacific, they created a separate construction company to build their line, assuring themselves of a handsome profit by awarding the contract to themselves.

The Atchison, Topeka, and Santa Fe line, also generously aided by a congressional land grant, overcame determined opposition from the Southern Pacific interests and reached the Pacific coast with another transcontinental line in 1885. After this time, western railroad construction consisted mainly of efforts to broaden the reach of these main lines and increase their connections with Chicago, the Gulf ports, and other distribution centers in the East. Nearly all of the lines in the Far West, however, had initially built out ahead of demand and had paid high construction costs because of dummy companies and other questionable devices. They also had built up a legacy of public distrust and suspicion by their high-handed political tactics and the land monopoly they were charged with controlling because of the land grants.

Eastern and midwestern roads

Although railroad building west of the Mississippi went forward most intensively after 1865, carrying western mileage to half the nation's total of 253,000 miles in 1914, there was also considerable new construction elsewhere in the nation. From 1865 to 1900 in the midwestern region the "Granger lines" — the Chicago, Burlington, & Quincy; the Chicago, Milwaukee, & St. Paul; the Chicago & North Western; and the Rock Island — exploited federal and state land grants to finance the construction of systems that served the corn belt and wheat belt. About 40 percent of the railroad mileage built from 1865 to 1900 was located in the region lying between the Mississippi and the Rocky Mountains.

In the Northeast, the post-1865 period witnessed heavy construction for purposes of serving communities that had been bypassed by the main railroad lines. There was extensive local aid to railroad projects in both New England and New York State, and Massachusetts put some $18 million into state subsidies for railways and a massive tunnel project to permit completion of a new route through the Berkshire mountains to link the coast with Albany, New York.

But new mileage constructed in the northeastern region was only a small part of the national total. Railroad development in this area of the country centered around consolidation of existing lines and struggles for control of the routes to the West. Daniel Drew, Jay Gould, and Jim Fisk of the Erie Railroad, Cornelius Vanderbilt of the New York Central, and other free-wheeling financiers ruthlessly manipulated stock sales and bribed judges and legislatures in the competition for control of the main lines. Meanwhile, the Baltimore & Ohio, the Erie, the Pennsylvania, and other major systems extended the reach of their control over connecting lines to Chicago.

The southern lines

From 1865 to the mid-1880s the South continued to lag in construction of new lines. Most of the roads that were built in that period were designed to serve the needs of major southern port cities. During the national boom from 1887 to 1893, however, the South was the scene of intensive new construction of roads that were designed as parts of far-flung regional and national systems. There was extensive consolidation of small lines as well, and by 1890 more than half the regional mileage in the South was under the control of nine companies, the largest being the Louisville and Nashville. The southern roads were becoming so closely linked with larger systems that two-thirds of the directors in the bigger companies were northerners.[4]

These new railroad facilities in the South contributed importantly to the region's economic development in ensuing years.

Consolidation

The dominant national trend in railroad management and finance from the 1880s on was consolidation. By purchase, lease, or trust arrangements, the larger systems absorbed smaller lines. The giants of railroad strategy and

[4]John L. Stover, *The Railroads of the South, 1865–1900* (Chapel Hill: University of North Carolina Press, 1955), pp. 197, 207.

finance, such as the Big Four and New York's Vanderbilt group, reached out far beyond the regions where they had begun so as to control railroad interests to which they might tie their older holdings. Meanwhile the investment banking houses took advantage of railroad bankruptcies and crises to establish firm control over emergent rail groups, or "communities of interest," as they were commonly called.

By 1906 the division of ownership and territory had become fairly stabilized. Of the 228,000 miles of American railroad then in operation, about two-thirds had come under the control of seven groups. The New York–Chicago region was controlled by the Vanderbilt roads; the Pennsylvania system dominated roads to the west from Philadelphia and Baltimore; the Southeast was dominated by the Morgan interests; James J. Hill dominated the northwestern region of the nation; the Harriman interests controlled the central and southern transcontinental routes; and the Gould roads and the Rock Island system held sway in the Mississippi Valley. These seven groups controlled 85 percent of railroad earnings in 1906, and their ownership and management interlocked elaborately with overlapping directorships and numerous informal alliances.

RAILROAD ABUSES AND REGULATION

The emergence of giantism in the railroad corporate structure was only one of several major features of railroad development that created widespread concern and resentment in the nation at large. In fact, the railroads had long been the objects of popular distrust and demands for government action.

Construction companies

A leading abuse was the all-too-common practice by which promoters of a railroad set up a construction company to build the line, then (as managers of the railroad) concluded a dishonest contract with the construction company (that is, with themselves and their associates as owners of that company) to pay high prices for the construction work. The contract was used as a conduit to channel investors' funds to themselves and other insiders. Eliminating risk to themselves, they jeopardized the railroad corporation's fiscal integrity in the process; and many railroads, large and small, were set on the road to bankruptcy by such machinations. The most notorious example was the Crédit Mobilier, the company formed to build the Union Pacific's lines. The promoters sold stock at bargain-counter prices to selected congressmen, who in turn voted a generous land grant to the railroad.

Even where corruption was absent, railroad firms often paid contractors partly in common stock or bonds instead of cash—in which case the construction firm was bearing some of the risk, so that the securities were often rated at heavy discounts in the contract, resulting in a watering-down of other stockholders' equity. Such practices added further instability to railroad financing generally in the late nineteenth century.

Financial and political manipulation

No American industry has suffered more from stock watering than the railroads. Repeatedly corporations that might otherwise have weathered panics or depressions faced bankruptcy because of capitalization that had been run up far beyond increases in actual assets. In addition, the railroads attracted adverse attention for a wide range of corrupt practices that eroded the integrity of the political process. They commonly employed legislators as legal counsel; bribery of lawmakers and courts was endemic; and the companies liberally distributed free passes to judges, editors, and others whose influence might be useful to them. In an era when political corruption was widespread, the railroad interests were able to manipulate the lines of political power to their advantage nearly everywhere.

The arrogant uses and abuses of power intensified general popular concern about corporate bigness more generally. And when the railroads added the injury of discriminatory rates to the insults already meted out in other forms, it reinforced their image as the pampered brats of the corporate world, growing to maturity as monopolists and heedless of the communities that had supported and helped finance their early careers.

The Granger laws

The first effective popular agitation for railroad regulation came in the midwestern states of Illinois, Iowa, Minnesota, and Wisconsin, beginning in the late 1860s. Among those who most prominently pushed for regulation were the Grangers—members of the Patrons of Husbandry—who represented farm interests that were being hurt by discriminatory rate practices. But not all farmers were in favor of regulation; in fact, in areas not yet served by railroads, in the Granger states, farmers generally opposed it on grounds that it would discourage new railroad investment. And not all proponents of the regulatory laws were Grangers. In fact, urban merchant groups and shipping interests that were hurt by railroad rate practices were fully as active in the regulatory movement as were farmers.[5]

From 1869 to 1875 in the Granger states, a series of laws was enacted that established public regulation of railroad rates and operating practices. Warehouses also came under regulation. The Granger laws were important for an innovation later copied by the federal government, one that became the model as well for other states: the independent regulatory commission, with power to determine "the public interest" and impose regulations and rates on private corporations in the case of industries considered to be "natural monopolies."

The railroad interests, appalled by this development, immediately initiated lawsuits against enforcement of commission-mandated rates. Their main argument was that such regulation constituted, in effect, confiscation of their property in violation of the Fourteenth Amendment—which had been intended to protect black people against discriminatory treatment by providing that no state could "deprive any person of life, liberty, or property without due process of law; nor deny to any person within its jurisdiction the equal protection of the laws." The railroad lawyers also contended that state regulation violated the national government's exclusive power under the Constitution to regulate interstate commerce. Warehouse interests made similar arguments in contesting the constitutionality of the regulatory laws enacted in the Granger states.

The courts and state regulation

These legal issues came before the Supreme Court in 1876 and 1877, in the so-called *Granger Cases*.[6] In 1877 the Court ruled in favor of the states' regulatory power and against the corporations. Warehouses and railroads were no ordinary businesses, the Court said. Drawing from an English common-law doctrine that had long been employed in American law to justify giving railroads extraordinary privileges (especially the power to condemn privately owned land under eminent domain for their rights of way), the Court declared them to be businesses "affected with a public interest." As such, they "must submit to be controlled by the public for the common good." The Court held further that the fixing of rates was not a proper matter for judicial review, asserting that this function properly belonged only to the legislative branch.[7] As for the railroads' contention that only Congress could regulate interstate commerce, the Court ruled that in the absence of federal laws on the subject, the states could properly exercise regulation of "fares, etc., so far as they are of domestic [state] concern."

This federal constitutional doctrine stood for a decade. But changing personnel on the Court and a remorseless legal assault on the *Granger Cases* doctrine resulted in a surprising reversal of position in the *Wabash Case* in 1886. The Court then overturned an Illinois regulation governing railroad charges to the east coast, ruling that this was indeed a violation of the power over interstate commerce exclusively vested in Congress. Three years later the Court handed the railroads another major victory by ruling that the judiciary could, after all, exercise its power of judicial review over specific rates imposed by commissions. In this decision, the *Minnesota Rate Case*, the Court took the position that "reasonableness" of regulation was something federal judges must finally decide.

The movement for federal regulation

Those who wanted railroad regulation to be effective were thus forced by changing judicial doctrine to look to Congress for national legislation. Farm groups and business interests in cities that were dependent upon railroads for the very life of their commerce continued to join in pressing for regulation.

Meanwhile the railroad managers themselves were taking a fresh approach to the question. They found their lines under increasingly stringent regulation at the state level, as nearly 30 states adopted the principle of regulation by

[5]George H. Miller, *The Railroads and the Granger Laws* (Madison: University of Wisconsin Press, 1971).

[6]Munn v. Illinois, 94 U.S. 113 (1877), and other cases decided at the same time (known as the Granger Cases).

[7]Harry N. Scheiber, "The Road to *Munn*," in *Law in American History*, ed. Bernard Bailyn and Donald Fleming (Boston: Little, Brown, 1972), pp. 327–402, esp. 355–360.

commission; and so now the railroads looked to federal legislation as a means of obtaining more benevolent regulation. In addition, the intense pressures of competition had forced many railroads to give the larger shippers rebates (discounts, often costly ones for the railroads, on the published rates). A U.S. Senate committee thus found in January 1886 that railroad managers were showing "an increasing readiness to accept the aid of Congress in working out the solution of the railroad problem which has obstinately baffled all their efforts."[8]

When a railroad manager spoke of the "railroad problem," he meant rebates, declining profits, and ruthless competition. But when an irate Iowa or Alabama farmer, convinced that he was being overcharged by the railroads, spoke of *his* "railroad problem," he meant something else entirely. In the years that followed Congress's inauguration of federal railroad regulation in 1887, there was to be continuing tension on this score: Whose railroad problem was the government really going to solve?

THE INTERSTATE COMMERCE ACT

By 1886 the movement for a federal regulatory law had gained decisive momentum; farm groups, merchants, and some of the railroad managers had all put their weight behind the effort. Congress had debated the issue for more than a decade. Indeed, in 1872 a Minnesota senator, William Windom, had proposed that the federal government itself should operate some major canals and railroads, whose rates would be a yardstick by which to measure the fairness of private carriers' charges. In the late 1870s, many independent oil producers, stung by the rebates being paid to Standard Oil, had joined the ranks of those pushing for some form of strong federal presence in railroad affairs. But not until the *Wabash Case* in 1886, when the Supreme Court ruled that only the federal government could regulate interstate rates, did the gathering forces for regulation carry a bill through Congress.

The Interstate Commerce Act of 1887 was made law with the support of both major political parties and of pressure groups in all regions of the country. The chief provisions of the law, all of which applied only to railroads, were these:

1. Mandating of "just and reasonable" rate charges. This was the traditional language of the Anglo-American common law.
2. Prohibition of discrimination in the form of either special rates or rebates for individual shippers. This was a victory not only for the independent

oil interests and farmers, but also for the railroads themselves.
3. Prohibition of discrimination or unjustified "preference" in rates for any particular localities or shippers or products.
4. Forbidding of long-haul/short-haul discrimination. Unless an exception was allowed by the Interstate Commerce Commission, no company might charge more for a shorter than for a longer distance on the same route (and in the same direction).
5. Prohibition of pooling of traffic or markets.
6. Establishment of a five-member Interstate Commerce Commission.

The ICC was empowered to investigate railroad operations, to call witnesses, and to hand down decisions on all aspects of rates and other matters covered by the act. It thus became the first federal independent regulatory commission, a hybrid agency with elements of judicial, legislative, and executive powers.

In future years the ICC would become the model for numerous additional regulatory agencies, but in 1887 it was unique. Because of its uniqueness, but also because the act that created it was vague in many particulars, its precise powers and character remained to be defined. From the standpoint of pressure groups that wanted powerful federal controls, the Interstate Commerce Act was unduly restraining because it left enforcement to a judicial process: The ICC could not impose its regulations and rulings outright, but was required to bring suit in federal courts for compliance if a railroad company refused to accept its deci-

---

[8]Quoted in Gabriel Kolko, *Railroads and Regulation, 1877–1916* (Princeton, N.J.: Princeton University Press, 1965), p. 39.

sions. Moreover, the law left a potentially wide loophole open by authorizing the ICC to exempt railroads from the ban on long-haul/short-haul discrimination where the public interest (however that was to be defined) required it.

The ICC and the courts

In its first few years, the ICC bent to the railroads' interests in most important decisions. Many exemptions to the long-haul/short-haul discrimination ban were approved; the commission did not act vigorously to enforce discrimination prohibitions on types of freight; and the commissioners early decided against dictating detailed rate schedules, instead leaving the initiative entirely to the railroad companies.[9] And when the commission did become tough in its regulatory posture, typically the federal courts intervened to relieve the railroads. Thus in a series of sixteen Supreme Court cases on rate rulings by the ICC, railroad appeals were upheld in all but one. And when the ICC finally did propose to hand down detailed rate schedules for the roads to adopt in the 1890s, the Supreme Court ruled (in the *Maximum Rate Case*, 1897) that the commission did not have the power to do so.

In another ruling of 1897, in the *Alabama Midland Case*, the Court cut the heart out of the commission's power to eliminate long-haul/short-haul discrimination. This prompted the commissioners to declare in their annual report that they had been left impotent to establish meaningful regulation. "The people," they wrote, "should no longer look to this Commission for a protection which it is powerless to extend." The Court limited the commission's power to acting and ruling on the "reasonableness" of *existing* rates only, not *future* rates; and the judiciary also reserved to itself the final power to declare what rates would be deemed "reasonable" and what commission rulings violated the Fourteenth Amendment guarantee of due process because they were "unreasonable."[10]

For at least the first decade of the ICC, then, the railroad managers' strategy of having regulatory powers transferred from the states to a more amenable federal control was working out as they had hoped.

While the trend of federal judicial decisions was on the side of holding the ICC in check, the Supreme Court did deal one powerful blow to the railroads. In another decision of 1897 (the *Trans-Missouri Freight Association Case*), the Court held that railroads were subject to the terms of the Sherman Antitrust Act of 1890; hence pooling arrangements, even if they were effectively approved by the ICC, were illegal.

THE TIGHTENING OF REGULATION

The Supreme Court's successive rulings and the ICC's own occasional reluctance to take a strong stance on railroad regulation invited new action by Congress. The national legislature finally took up the challenge in 1903.

In 1903 the Elkins Act, a bill outlawing rebates, was passed. The law also restored ICC power to approve "joint rates" filed by companies acting in concert. Once such rates were approved, any deviation from them would be a violation of ICC rulings. In effect, then, the 1903 law made pools legal if they were validated by the ICC.

The Hepburn Act of 1906 established for the first time truly effective ICC control of inter-state rail traffic. Until then the ICC had been limited to reviewing rate changes ordered by the railroads. Now the Hepburn Act authorized the ICC to prescribe rates. Railroads were required to comply within 30 days of a rate order, leaving to the roads the burden of appealing to the courts. This key feature of the ICC's strengthened powers was upheld in 1914, when the Supreme Court acknowledged that the commission's judgment must be accepted as to the facts relevant to any such decision. No longer were "circumstances" a matter for judges alone to decide. Finally, the Hepburn Act enlarged the ICC's jurisdiction to include express and sleeping-car companies, pipelines, switches, spurs, tracks, and terminal facilities.

The Mann-Elkins Act, passed in 1910, strengthened the 1887 act's clause regarding

---

[9]Justifying its numerous grants of exemption from the long-haul/short-haul provision, the ICC claimed that "in some . . . parts of the country the immediate enforcement of an iron-clad rule would have worked changes so radical that many localities in their general interests, many great industries, as well as many railroads, would have found it impossible to conform without suffering very serious injury."

[10]Kirkland, *Industry Comes of Age*, p. 130; Sidney Fine, *Laissez Faire and the General-Welfare State* (Ann Arbor: University of Michigan Press, 1956), pp. 162–164.

long-haul discrimination and authorized the ICC to suspend for ten months the operation of a new scale of rates to allow time for investigation. It also set up a special Commerce Court to hear railroad cases, reviewable only by the Supreme Court itself. (Later, when the Commerce Court proved too favorable to the railroads, Congress abolished it.) And ICC jurisdiction was again enlarged, this time to include telegraph, telephone, and cable companies.

An additional commerce law was enacted in 1913 on the important subject of railroad valuation. The ICC was ordered to evaluate the investment in all railroads and to establish uniform accounting procedures. Progressives in Congress had long sought such a provision, as they believed only by independent ICC valuation could a strong rate policy in the public interest be instituted.

Other important legislation affecting railroads included the 1914 Clayton Antitrust Act, which embraced railway companies in its provisions barring interlocking directorates or purchase of stock in competing companies. Earlier legislation in 1898 and 1913 had encouraged arbitration of railway labor disputes.

In the Adamson Act of 1916, Congress further enlarged the government's interventionist role in the railroad sector by mandating a maximum eight-hour day for railway workers and forbidding the companies to cut wages commensurately.

The dilemma of defining "public interest"

By the end of Woodrow Wilson's first administration in 1917, therefore, the railroads had been brought under comprehensive regulation. The principle had been established, and accepted even by a conservative judiciary, that Congress could properly place in the hands of a regulatory agency the federal power to control a powerful private business interest. As of 1917, however, the ICC itself was still searching for an objective standard of the "public interest" that justified the exercise of wide discretionary powers of this sort by allegedly disinterested "experts." It was still caught, too, between pressure from the railroads and countervailing pressure for stronger regulation from various reform groups and special interests.

THE CHALLENGE OF CONSOLIDATION

While this new relationship between government and the railroad sector was being worked out over 30 years' time, the railroads themselves were engaged in a series of moves that would change many of their essential features. These moves, which affected the railroads' relationship both to the public and to the regulators, were mergers and consolidations that brought the railroad sector under the control of a few small groups. What good would it do the public to outlaw discrimination between shippers or locations on a particular railroad line if consolidation brought the much greater leverage of monopoly or oligopoly, and with it higher shipping rates?

Theodore Roosevelt and regulation

Although conservative in many of his policies regarding consolidation and private business power, Theodore Roosevelt was committed to seeing railroads brought under meaningful public control. Whether this was a matter of strong personal conviction or because Roose-

velt, as the historian George Mowry has written, was "never one to delay the inevitable, especially when it was supported by what looked like a majority of the country," is a matter of speculation.[11] His Justice Department moved against the Northern Securities Company, a holding company that brought three giant rail systems (the Burlington, Northern Pacific, and Great Northern lines) under unitary control, and in 1904 the Supreme Court agreed that this arrangement must be broken up.

The railroads on the eve of World War I

In 1912 the Court ordered the Union Pacific to divest itself of stock in the Southern Pacific, and in 1914 it dissolved the New Haven's holdings of steamer lines and urban transit lines. In the Panama Canal Act of 1913 Congress prohibited the major railroad systems from control-

[11]George Mowry, *The Era of Theodore Roosevelt and the Birth of Modern America, 1900–1912* (New York: Harper & Row, 1958), p. 200.

ling steamers that would haul freight between the Atlantic and Pacific coasts through the new waterway, in order to assure rail-water competition. And as we have seen, Congress included railroads in the terms of the Clayton Antitrust Act of 1914, a measure strongly supported by President Wilson.

All the while, the railroad corporations pressed Congress and successive Presidents to take a more benign view of consolidation. They had consistently sought to get the ICC to make lawful what they had failed to accomplish through voluntary arrangements that would "stabilize" their industry and end what they always described as "destructive" competition. Now the industry sought to have Congress legitimize the fruits of consolidation.

World War I and the Transportation Act of 1920

The advent of war in April 1917 crystallized these demands and gave the railroad problem a new configuration in public debates. To meet the war crisis, the federal government took over the railroads and operated them with a view toward integration, coordination, and cooperation on a national scale. This experience prepared the ground for a fundamental shift in public policy, embodied in the Transportation Act of 1920. This paid lip service to the older ideals, specifying that competition should be "preserved as fully as possible." (See p. 322.) But its main thrust was to cast the mantle of legality over the new status quo by encouraging consolidation.

STREET RAILWAYS AND ELECTRIC INTERURBAN LINES

During the 1865–1915 period, new forms of mass transport and rapid transit within the nation's large cities made it possible for these urban centers to spread in spatial area. Once large numbers of people could be moved cheaply and rapidly across lengthening distances, the development of specialized urban areas dedicated to residential, commercial, or industrial structures and uses was feasible. The modern-style city, with its people moving back and forth between home and work, and with enormous clusters of specialized businesses in spreading commercial or industrial areas, thus emerged in the late nineteenth century.

The horse-drawn streetcar, running on fixed tracks, was introduced prior to the Civil War. But this technology was not sufficient to meet the needs of the large urban centers. Congestion of the streets and the slow speed of horse cars prompted the cities' search for a different solution to the transit problem.

The first solution appeared after 1870 with the construction of elevated railway lines that accommodated steam-powered locomotives. Another variant of the same basic technology was the building of subway railroad lines beneath the streets. New York pioneered in ele-

vated ways in the 1870s; Boston was the first major city to complete a subway system, in 1898.

Still another innovation—one providing quieter rapid mass transit—was the electric-powered railroad. The so-called traction lines, using electric power, replaced horse-drawn streetcars in the 1880s and 1890s, and electric power was also introduced for subway and elevated lines. By the turn of the century many of the nation's cities were also linked with suburbs and other nearby urban centers with electric train lines. Reaching a peak of about 15,000 miles of line in 1916, the electric interurban railroads then met rising competition from automobiles. The interurban lines thus were abandoned as quickly as they had been built, it seemed, leaving a path of corporate bankruptcies in their wake. Ironically, by the 1960s many of the nation's major cities, strangling under the pressure of growing population and dense automobile traffic, began to seek new mass-transit policies to serve citizens in the very areas that once had been supplied so well with clean rapid-transit facilities in the era before World War I.

THE AUTOMOBILE, THE HIGHWAY MOVEMENT, AND AVIATION

By 1914 the number of automobiles registered in the United States was approaching 2

million. The popularity of the automobile, the advent of mass production (600,000 were built in 1914 alone), and the rapid development of automotive technology had made it clear that the next great wave of development in the transport sector would follow different lines from those of the railroad era.

Naturally, there was growing public demand for better roads. Government's response, like the technology itself, involved a series of important departures from earlier practices and precedents. In the first place, as state and local governments assumed the burden of building extensive networks of paved roads, they created new bureaucracies: highway departments and bureaus of engineering to oversee construction and maintenance. Second, automobile licensing and taxation of gasoline quickly emerged as major new sources of government finance, providing some 20 percent of all state-government receipts by the early 1920s. Finally, the federal government, after decades of playing a negligible role in road planning and development, bent to the new pressures. In 1916 Congress approved the first federal highways act, appropriating funds to be distributed as cash aid to states on the basis of a formula that took account of their areas, populations, and mileage of rural post roads.[12]

The 1916 Highways Act was important as a model for future grant-in-aid legislation as well. It required the states to engage in systematic planning to qualify for aid, to submit to federal audits and inspections, and to appropriate matching funds on a formula basis. In sum, the 1916 law introduced a new era in federal-state relations.

Early Aviation

The precursor of still another new era in transport came to fruition at Kitty Hawk in December 1903, when Orville and Wilbur Wright lifted a biplane off the ground in the first successful manned flight of heavier-than-air craft. A marveling and enthusiastic public soon became convinced of the airplane's practicability, and investment capital flowed into numerous competing firms that sought to develop commercially feasible aviation. Glenn Curtiss forwarded the technology in a major way in 1911, when he flew a seaplane of his own invention in San Diego. The use of pontoons made any lake or protected harbor a potential airport.

Meanwhile, scores of inventors experimented with lighter-than-air craft. The decade 1900–1910 was marked by colorful ventures of bizarre varieties of aircraft and endless tinkering with designs.

The first regular air service in America was instituted in Florida in 1914, but the science of airborne flight gained its greatest impetus from experience gained in World War I. Use of airplanes as a functional military weapon became a basis for rapid commercial development in the 1920s.

---

[12]F. L. Paxson, "The Highway Movement, 1916–1935," *American Historical Review,* 51 (1946); Merrill Roberts, "The Motor Transportation Revolution," *Business History Review,* 30 (1956):57–95.

INTERNAL WATER TRANSPORT

Although the United States is endowed with an excellent system of natural waterways, including 26,000 miles of navigable water on inland rivers and more in the Great Lakes, many of these facilities fell into disuse in the late nineteenth century. On the western rivers, for example, the peak year of traffic came in 1880, when just over 500,000 tons of shipping was registered. Tonnage had dropped to 139,000 by 1915, as the railroad gained dominance in the nation's heartland. There were some important exceptions, most notably the Great Lakes. There the traffic consisted largely of low-value bulk commodities, especially coal and iron ore, well suited to cheap water transportation and mechanized bulk-handling techniques. Hence Lakes tonnage rose from 671,000 in 1865 to 1 million in 1890 and nearly 3 million in 1915. Most of America's canal lines meanwhile fell into disrepair; only the Erie Canal in New York played a major role in interregional commerce in the last decades of the nineteenth century.

Although waterways became less and less important as carriers generally, there was persistent public interest in the possibility of revitalizing them as a way of providing competition for railroads. Merchants in the major commercial cities led the way in the 1890s, demanding federal construction and operation of canals and improvement of the intercoastal waterways network. Conservationists, attracted by the fact that water transport was relatively clean and efficient, also joined in the agitation. Two federal waterways commissions were appointed to hammer out a policy, one by Theodore Roosevelt and another by his successor, President William Howard Taft. Their main contribution was to sharpen public interest in development of the intercoastal system that linked the Atlantic and Gulf coast ports. Especially after the Panama Canal project opened up new possibilities for water transportation in competition with long-distance railway lines, Congress proved willing to appropriate funds to make coastwise waterborne commerce cheaper and safer. But the appropriations were tiny compared to the sums that government at all levels had poured into railroad subsidies. Moreover, Congress made no move to bring water transportation under federal regulation. And so until the 1930s, transport was a "regulated sector" only insofar as railroad operations were concerned.

TELEPHONES AND THE TELEGRAPH

The telegraph, introduced in 1836, was in wide use by the 1850s, and things were never quite the same afterward. Newspapers could obtain immediate information on events thousands of miles away; business firms could send orders across vast distances, and regional prices could be flashed instantly to other markets; railroad equipment operating across the continent was monitored closely; giant business firms were able to centralize decision making and at the same time decentralize many operations or diversify their activities greatly; and in the large cities, police and fire departments could be flashed to summon help in emergencies.

The telephone, introduced in the 1870s, complemented telegraphic communication and was immediately adaptable to common household use. By 1892 the nation's telephone network had stretched from the Atlantic coast to Chicago, and soon afterward it blanketed the whole continent.

Western Union

In most advanced industrial countries, telephony and telegraphy were early placed under government ownership and control, or at the least under close and detailed regulation. But in the United States these vital communications services were left to the private sector until the 1930s, without even the most rudimentary public regulation. Since the coordination and integration of the communications network were essential to its success, indeed to its very form as a "network," communications were almost perfectly suited to monopoly control by a giant firm. This sort of control came to the telegraph industry in 1866, when the Western Union Company swallowed up its competitors and emerged as the industry's giant. Soon it was a virtual monopoly operator of public telegraph facilities.

The Bell system

Western Union made a bid to control the telephone industry as well. Alexander Graham Bell, a Scottish-born teacher of the deaf, succeeded in designing and patenting a telephone in 1876. Many years of litigation and controversy over patent rights followed. Meanwhile, control of the Bell patent was given to the Bell Telephone Company, capitalized by a group of Boston investors.

Western Union's challenge failed in the face of aggressive Bell management, under the direction of Theodore Vail. He took Bell to a near-monopolistic position in the industry by the strategy of providing long-line service that connected small local companies with one another. Wherever possible, Vail bought out local or regional telephone franchises owned by independent companies. A holding company, the American Telephone and Telegraph Company (AT & T) was formed to control the Bell interests, and AT & T used its dominant position in long-distance service to force many independents to sell out.

Profitability was assured by AT & T's practice of neglecting rural areas, where settlement was thinly spread, in favor of urban centers, and by its aggressive development of wholly owned subsidiaries that built telephone equipment. The book value of the AT & T complex rose from $15 million in 1880 to over $180 million in 1900. By this time it was a choice plum for the giants of finance, and J. P. Morgan and Company soon moved in to obtain a large element of control.

The Bell System's facilities rose from 3 million miles of wire in 1880 to over 20 *billion* in 1916, when the independent firms controlled another 4 billion miles. From 1 telephone per 1000 of population in 1880, the number rose to 18 in 1900, then to 104 by 1915. By then Bell's invention had seemingly fulfilled Thomas Edison's assertion that it "annihilated time and space."

POSTAL SERVICE AND GOVERNMENT SUBSIDY

Although the newer forms of communication were left to private enterprise, the American postal service survived as a major government enterprise in the era of giantism. But, in common with the newer communications media, the Post Office greatly enlarged its capacity and its output (measured in volume of mail) during the 1865–1914 era.

One major factor in the Post Office's expansion was a series of reductions in postage rates. Common mail was carried at six cents for a single-sheet letter from 1816 to 1847; the rate was three cents in 1855; and in 1872 Congress approved the penny postcard. Congress also instituted new classifications of mail, carried at favored rates. These included newspapers and other printed material. The immediate effect was to make newspaper advertising the most important single method of carrying commercial messages to the public, and there was a fivefold increase in newspaper circulation between 1880 and 1900.

The Post Office also diversified its services. Beginning in 1863, urban residents received their mail by hand delivery instead of being required to visit the local post office to obtain their mail. In 1896 experiments with rural free delivery began, and rural carriers delivered mail in nearly all areas of the country by 1914.

Parcel post
An innovation with broad social and economic effects was the parcel post service, instituted in 1913. Until then the postal charges for large packages carried relatively short distances had been kept by Congress at prohibitive levels. This situation had left the railroad express companies—American Express, Wells-Fargo, and the Adams Express—with unchallenged control of that business. The rates charged by these private express firms were resented by consumers, especially in rural districts where mail-order houses (most notably Montgomery Ward and Sears, Roebuck of Chicago) had become important suppliers of goods at retail. Aligned with the express companies against the idea of inexpensive parcel service by the Post Office were legions of small-town merchants who felt keenly the competition of the mail-order firms. The political battle between these contending forces went on for many years, but the reform atmosphere of the Progressive period finally gave the decisive edge to the consumer interests.

Mail and the subsidizing of transport companies
Almost as controversial as parcel post was the matter of payments to railroad companies for their services in carrying the mails. Despite a general rate decrease in both railroad express and freight charges, the government continued to reimburse the railroads on the basis of rates agreed to in the 1870s. The progressive reformers in Congress denounced the government's payments, which rose from $5 million in 1870 to $49 million in 1910, as a subsidy to the railroad companies. Under reformers' pressure, Congress changed the basis of reimbursement in 1916 and the amounts paid annually for this purpose dipped briefly, only to be raised dramatically once again just after World War I.

The policy of subsidizing transport firms was even more explicit, and more controversial, in the case of steamship lines. Before the Civil War, Congress had followed a policy of subsidizing steamer lines that carried the mails, not only as a means of improving postal service but also as an instrument for building up the American merchant fleet. From 1864 to 1867 Congress voted new subsidy grants for steamer lines carrying mail to Hawaii, the Far East, and South America. The program lapsed in the mid-1870s, and its revival was a partisan issue for 15 years, the Democrats generally opposing ship subsidies and the Republicans in favor of them. From 1891 to 1910 the program of subsidy was given new life, only to be killed once again under pressure from the Grangers and other farm groups, who insisted that the funds be used instead to expand rural delivery routes, and from opponents of American expansionism and imperialism, who perceived the ship subsidies as a costly instrument for fulfilling imperialist designs.

SELECTED READINGS

General works

Barger, Harold, *The Transportation Industries, 1889–1946* (New York: National Bureau of Economic Research, 1951).

*Faulkner, Harold U., *The Decline of Laissez-Faire* (New York: Holt, Rinehart and Winston, 1951).

Goodrich, Carter, *Government Promotion of American Canals and Railroads, 1800–1890* (New York: Columbia University Press, 1960).

*Kirkland, Edward C., *Industry Comes of Age* (New York: Holt, Rinehart and Winston, 1961).

Railroads: special studies

Campbell, E. G., *The Reorganization of the American Railroad System, 1893–1900* (New York: Columbia University Press, 1938).

Cochran, Thomas C., *Railroad Leaders, 1845–1890* (Cambridge, Mass.: Harvard University Press, 1953).

Fogel, Robert W., *Railroads and American Economic Growth* (Baltimore: Johns Hopkins University Press, 1964).

————*The Union Pacific Railroad: A Case Study in Premature Enterprise* (Baltimore: Johns Hopkins Press, 1960).

Grodinsky, Julius, *Transcontinental Railway Strategy, 1869–1893* (Philadelphia: University of Pennsylvania Press, 1962).

Kirkland, Edward C., *Men, Cities, and Transportation: A Study in New England History, 1820–1900* (Cambridge, Mass.: Harvard University Press, 1948).

Klein, Maury, *The Great Richmond Terminal* (Charlottesville: University Press of Virginia, 1970).

Overton, Richard C., *Burlington Route: A History of the Burlington Lines* (New York: Knopf, 1965).

*Stover, John F., *American Railroads* (Chicago: University of Chicago Press, 1961).

————, *The Railroads of the South, 1865–1900: A Study in Finance and Control* (Chapel Hill: University of North Carolina Press, 1955).

*Winther, Oscar, *The Transportation Frontier: Trans-Mississippi West, 1865–1890* (New York: Holt, Rinehart and Winston, 1964).

Ulmer, M. J., *Capital in Transportation, Communications, and Public Utilities* (Princeton, N.J.: Princeton University Press, 1960).

Government aid and regulation

Benson, Lee, *Merchants, Farmers, and Railroads* (Cambridge, Mass.: Harvard University Press, 1955).

*Carstensen, Vernon, ed., *The Public Lands* (Madison: University of Wisconsin Press, 1962). (Articles by R. S. Henry, D. M. Ellis, and others on the land grants.)

Greever, William S., "A Comparison of Railroad Land-Grant Policies," *Agricultural History*, XXV (1951).

Harbeson, R. W., "Railroads and Regulation, 1877–1916," *Journal of Economic History*, XXXVII (1967).

*Kolko, Gabriel, *Railroads and Regulation, 1877–1916* (Princeton, N.J.: Princeton University Press, 1965).

MacAvoy, P. W., *The Economic Effects of Regulation* (Cambridge, Mass.: MIT Press, 1965).

Martin, Albro, *Enterprise Denied: Origins of the Decline of American Railroads, 1897–1917* (New York: Columbia University Press, 1971).

Mercer, Lloyd, "Land Grants to the American Railroads," *Business History Review*, XLIII (1969).

Miller, George, *Railroads and the Granger Laws* (Madison: University of Wisconsin Press, 1971).

Scheiber, Harry N., "Public Policy, Constitutional Principle, and the Granger Laws," *Stanford Law Review*, XXIII (1971).

———, "The Road to *Munn*," in D. Fleming and B. Bailyn, eds., *Law in American History* (Boston: Little, Brown, 1972).

Sharfman, I. L., *The Interstate Commerce Commission* (5 vols., New York: Commonwealth Fund, 1931–1937).

Other specialized studies

Bruce, Robert V., *Bell: Alexander Graham Bell and the Conquest of Solitude* (Boston: Little, Brown, 1973).

Danielian, N. R., *AT & T: The Story of Industrial Conquest* (New York: Vanguard Press, 1939).

Flink, James, *America Adopts the Automobile, 1895–1910* (Cambridge, Mass.: MIT Press, 1970).

Fuller, Wayne E., *The American Mail: Enlarger of the Common Life* (Chicago: University of Chicago Press, 1972).

Mazlish, Bruce, ed., *The Railroad and the Space Program: An Exploration in Historical Analogy* (Cambridge, Mass.: MIT Press, 1965).

*Rae, John B., *The American Automobile: A Brief History* (Chicago: University of Chicago Press, 1965).

Simonson, G. R., ed., *The History of the American Aircraft Industry: An Anthology* (Cambridge, Mass.: MIT Press, 1968).

internal commerce, foreign trade, and imperialism

The industrialization process that transformed other sectors of the economy after 1865 also brought sweeping changes in both domestic and foreign commerce. Some of these changes were quantitative: There was a vast increase in the volume of goods marketed, a rising proportion of national income was derived from distribution and commerce-related activity, and, not least important, a heavily urbanized mass market emerged, on a scale that sustained mass production of consumer goods. Other types of changes were qualitative or structural: New forms of organization appeared in marketing, and new types of business firms emerged. By the close of the century many of these changes had become prominent features of the American economic order, and they would remain so afterward. They became part of the organizational revolution that accompanied modern industrialization.

PATTERNS OF TRADE: INTERNAL COMMERCE

A major influence that shaped patterns of internal commerce was the "core" region of manufacturing in the northeastern quarter of the nation: New England, the middle Atlantic states, and the Great Lakes states.[1] Here, in what has also been termed the manufacturing belt, were found some 80 percent of the nation's manufacturing workers in 1880, and 70 percent in 1910. Nearly three-fourths of the urban population was also located in the industrial core region in 1910. Although the core region sustained mining, lumbering, and agriculture, in the larger pattern of internal commerce it purchased extensive quantities of raw materials and foodstuffs from the rest of the nation.

[1]See Eric Lampard, "Regional Economic Development, 1870–1950," in Harvey Perloff et al., *Regions, Resources, and Economic Growth* (Baltimore: Johns Hopkins University Press, 1960), pp. 109–191, and David Ward, *Cities and Immigrants: A Geography of Change in Nineteenth-Century America* (New York: Oxford University Press, 1971), for excellent analyses of regional development and interregional economic relationships.

The South remained heavily agricultural, though textile manufacturing developed in the Southeast and a major coal-and-iron complex emerged in the Birmingham region. Cotton remained foremost among the southern products that sought markets outside the region, and it was a major export product. Other major items of southern output included tobacco, lumber, and (after 1900) petroleum from the Southwest. The vast trans-Mississippi western region was dominated by agriculture, mining, and the extractive industries generally. Food processing was a major industry, especially flour milling in Minneapolis and meat packing in many of the western cities.

The framework for internal trade and distribution was provided by the major urban centers and smaller commercial cities that played an entrepôt role in the gathering and marketing of goods in trade. The cities were the nodes, or connecting points, in the distribution network; the production of their hinterlands was warehoused, wholesaled, financed, and shipped at these urban centers. The framework of com-

TABLE 18–1. DISTRIBUTION OF MANUFACTURING LABOR FORCE (LF) AND VALUE ADDED BY MANUFACTURE (VA), BY REGION, 1870–1910

REGION United States (LF, millions; VA, billions)	1870		1890		1910	
	LF	VA	LF	VA	LF	VA
	2.64	$1.58	5.53	$3.45	10.66	$8.19
Northeast	80%	84%	74%	82%	70%	77%
Southeast	10	6	10	7	13	10
West[1]	10	10	15	11	18	13

Source: Harvey Perloff et al., *Regions, Resources, and Economic Growth* (Baltimore: Published for Resources for the Future by the Johns Hopkins University Press, 1960), pp. 153, 154. Copyright 1960. Used by permission of the publisher.

[1]Includes Plains, Southwest, Mountain, and Far West states.

merce was superimposed, however, upon a political structure that permitted individual states to influence the costs—and even the very freedom—of commerce across state boundaries.

State laws as barriers to interstate commerce

Of course, the Constitution's provision that the power to regulate interstate commerce resides in the Congress had been designed to assure that the American common market should be relatively free of barriers or impediments created by the individual states. But in fact the state legislatures proved ingenious in finding ways to evade the spirit of that provision. In the farming states, for example, local interests were often given considerable protection against out-of-state competition. Thus Wisconsin and other dairying states prohibited outright the sale of margarine, banned commercial coloring of margarine to resemble butter, or imposed taxes so high on margarine that it could not compete with butter. Other states adopted plant or animal quarantines, which they claimed were necessary to prevent the spread of disease; but in fact the quarantines became instruments for reducing competition from out of state. Similarly, out-of-state interests were often disadvantaged by the imposition of grading, labeling, and inspection requirements.

A few states went so far as to impose blatantly discriminatory sales taxes on certain products, again to protect special local interests. A common form of protection for manufacturers and merchants in many states was "anti-drummer" laws, which placed a high license tax upon traveling salesmen who were trying to sell their products, manufactured by out-of-state firms, directly to wholesalers and retailers. In light of all these devices for directing and curbing the flow of commerce, it is not entirely correct to portray the internal market as free of barriers in full conformity with the constitutional requirement.

TRENDS IN WHOLESALE AND RETAIL SELLING

The typical retail merchant in the small town of the 1860s kept a general store. Although this quaint commercial artifact of an earlier time did not disappear entirely as industrialization went forward, the concentration of America's population in large cities and middle-sized urban areas gave far greater importance to the specialized store that concentrated on a few lines of merchandise (hardware, dry goods, food, and so on). There was, however, one trend that ran counter to specialized retailing: the rise of the department store, especially in the major cities.

This type of large-scale retail marketing, which retained the advantages of permitting the shopper to obtain many types of goods under one roof, was developed by Alexander T. Stewart in New York in the 1860s and in succeeding years by John Wanamaker in Philadelphia and Marshall Field in Chicago.

Mail-order houses and chain stores

In rural areas, retail selling was transformed by two new types of enterprise: the mail-order house and the chain store. The leading mail-order houses were Montgomery Ward and Company, founded in 1872, and Sears, Roebuck and Company, founded in 1895. Both grew rapidly, and they later took advantage of the major boost given mail-order sales by the introduction of the parcel-post system in 1913.

The chain stores were large-scale operations whose costs could be kept down by direct buying from manufacturers and processors, by bulk purchases, and by the additional savings to be gained through large-scale consolidated advertising and through cash (instead of credit) sales. The first and largest of the chain stores was the "A and P," the Great Atlantic and Pacific Tea Company, founded in 1858. The Woolworth chain was started in 1879, the United Cigar Stores in 1892, and the Kresge stores in 1897. In 1885 there were five chain-store firms, and in 1900 there were 58.

By 1920 chain operations numbered around 800, ranging in size from firms with only two or three stores to a few with several hundred stores. They specialized mainly in tobacco, notions, drugs, hardware, shoes, ready-to-wear clothing, and restaurants, but nearly 200 were grocery chains. These stores became leading fixtures on the Main Streets of towns and cities all over the nation. In smaller towns they controlled the bulk of retail trade, having driven thousands of general stores and small proprietary stores out of business. Aiding their growth was the effect of the automobile on farmers' buying habits. With a car the farm family could drive into the nearest town or small city every weekend to do its shopping. A survey of buying patterns in the 1920s revealed that rural people did their shopping in the towns and cities mainly for those goods in which variety, both of selection and of price, was important: rugs, furniture, guns and sporting goods, dress clothing, dry goods, and similar items. But for their work clothes, groceries, and other everyday items, America's rural families tended to shop at chain stores or independent proprietors' stores locally.[2] Otherwise, they relied on mail-order buying.

Advertising and brand names

Early in the nineteenth century, most consumer goods sold in retail shops were "generic" goods (not differentiated according to manufacturer — often not even identified as to source). Buttons, flour, molasses, candy, and other products were sold from barrels or jars, with no effort to inform the consumer as to manufacturer's name.

By midcentury, however, many food processing and consumer-goods manufacturing firms had begun to advertise their brand names, to package goods under their labels, and generally to induce consumers to look for their products on store shelves. Pianos, sewing machines, factory-made shoes, ready-made clothing, and other products relatively high in unit price led the way. By the 1870s brand-name selling and advertising had begun to spread throughout the retail trade. Estimated expenditures on advertising — mainly in newspapers and magazines, but also on billboards and barns alongside roads, and in streetcars and railroad stations — rose from only about $8 million in 1865, to $200 million in 1880 and over $800 million in 1904. By 1920, as professional agencies developed, total advertising expenditures had grown to about $3 billion.[3] In the tawdry tradition of the patent-medicine firms of that era, many advertisements were high-pressure in tone, blatantly fraudulent in content, and geared to exploiting people's anxieties. Legitimate advertising, however, did perform the important function of publicizing new products and conveying information on actual differences between brands.

Wholesale marketing

From the early days of the nineteenth century until about 1870, independent wholesale merchants of various kinds handled the distribution of most manufactured goods in the United States. The merchant typically took goods on consignment from manufacturing firms, warehoused them, found retail outlets for them, extended credit to the retailer, and generally played a commanding role in directing the flow of goods in commerce. Gradually the importance of such independent wholesalers declined. Even before 1860 firms such as McCormick in farm machinery and Singer in sewing machines began to build up their own wholesale marketing organizations. Supplying spare parts and servicing their goods maximized the manufacturing firms' advantages in dealing

---

[2] Surveys cited are reported in Lewis Atherton, *Main Street on the Middle Border* (Bloomington: Indiana University Press, 1954), pp. 364–368.

[3] Expenditures on commercial advertising in the media rose from about 0.7 percent of GNP in 1867 to 3.4 percent in 1904; then they remained at about that level, and it is interesting that the volume of advertising by 1904 proved to be characteristic of the prevailing percentage of GNP down to the present day. (Daniel Pope, "The Development of National Advertising, 1865–1920," *Journal of Economic History*, 34 [1974]:295–296.)

directly, or through specially franchised dealers, with retail consumers. Independent wholesale merchants were also bypassed by manufacturers of other expensive producers' durables — for instance, railroad equipment and factory machine tools — whose market consisted of a relatively small number of buyers. In such cases, there was little benefit in having middlemen stand between producer and final customer.

By the 1890s many of the giant corporations that had emerged in consumer-goods industries also had established their own marketing organizations, displacing the independent wholesaler. To do so became a leading strategy of vertical integration (see pp. 231–232).

The giant firms, ranging from biscuit manufacturers to oil companies, used their advertising as a way of building up consumer demand for their brand-name products. On the quaint maxim coined by the manufacturer of Pears' Soap, a leading product of that day — "Any fool can make soap. It takes a clever man to sell it" — manufacturers persuaded consumers to ask at the retail counter for particular brand names. "No substitute will do," read many an advertisment of the day. Once the consumer

echoed that refrain, a new era of commerce had dawned.

By the late 1920s that era was to be in full sunlight. A marketing survey conducted in 1929 revealed that only one-third of the flow of goods out of American manufacturing industries passed through independent wholesalers; the remaining two-thirds of manufactured goods were marketed directly to consumers or independent retail outlets through the manufacturing firms' own marketing organizations.[4]

Employment in wholesale and retail trade

One measure of distribution's importance in the national economy was the great rise in income originating in trade and the commensurate increase in the number of persons employed in wholesale and retail trade. There were more than 5 million people in this sector by 1919. They formed part of the larger service sector of the labor force, which included also workers in finance, transportation, government, and the professions. From 1870 to 1910 the number of workers in service occupations rose 337 percent, compared with a 205 percent increase in the work force as a whole.

TRENDS IN FOREIGN TRADE

As the national economy expanded, the foreign trade of the United States also underwent a vast increase in scale. By 1920 exports had increased 24-fold over the level of 1860 and imports had increased 16-fold. These great increases in absolute volume of American foreign trade, however, occurred at a time when the population of the world as a whole was rising — from 1.2 billion in 1850 to over 1.8 billion in 1920 — and when industrialization throughout western Europe and in North America was carrying the total volume of world trade from an estimated $2.8 billion in 1850 to a level in excess of $38 billion just before World War I. Hence the vast increase in U.S. foreign trade was enough only to bring its relative share of world commerce to a level of about 9 to 10 percent of all international trade.

The Civil War period

The Civil War had a profound effect on the course of American foreign trade. The high tariffs that were initiated then probably stimulated manufacturing. Also, the closing of trade with the South during the war forced northern pro-

ducers to seek other markets, with the result that between 1860 and 1865 there was an actual increase in exports other than cotton. The war temporarily ruined the cotton business of the South, and the amount of cotton exported did not reach the prewar level until 1875. This in turn cut down imports to the South. While the war ruined the merchant marine, it stimulated the building of railroads and further aided commerce by the concentration of capital and the better banking system introduced in 1863.

The patterns of foreign trade, 1865–1914

From 1865 to 1914, both imports and exports rose, but with important changes in the composition of trade. Up to 1890, the leading category of exports was agricultural, including

---

[4]Data from U. S. Bureau of the Census, *Fifteenth Census of the United States* (1930), cited in Glenn Porter and Harold C. Livesay, *Merchants and Manufacturers: Studies in the Changing Structure of Nineteenth-Century Marketing* (Baltimore: Johns Hopkins University Press, 1971), p. 228.

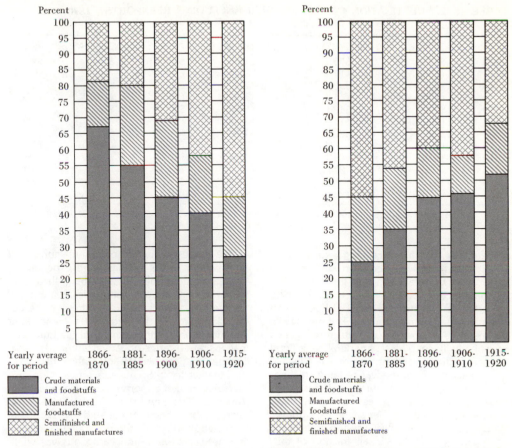

Figure 18–1. Composition of U.S. Exports by Commodity Classification. Adapted from *Historical Statistics of the U.S.*, p. 545.

Figure 18–2. Composition of U.S. Imports by Commodity Classification. Adapted from *Historical Statistics of the U.S.*, p. 545.

wheat, corn, and meat products, and such processed agricultural commodities as flour, cotton and vegetable oils, and butter and cheese. Of individual commodities, the largest by value included exported grains and flour, cotton, meat and meat products, iron and steel, and oil. In the import trade between the Civil War and 1890, the dominance of semi-manufactures and finished manufactures—comprising imports of iron and steel goods, textiles, and other products of industrial origin, mainly from Great Britain and continental European countries—began to give way in the 1880s to rising proportions of foodstuffs. By 1906, crude materials and foodstuffs comprised 58 percent of the total import composition, as compared to 42 percent for manufactures. (See Figure 18–1.)

By far the greatest market for U.S. exports up to 1890 was Great Britain, but there was growing demand for American foodstuffs and industrial products throughout Europe, especially in the northern countries. The volume and percentage of exports that went to each region of the world are shown in Table 18–2.

As the major source of imports into the United States, Europe held the dominant position, supplying 50 to 61 percent of all imports until 1910 and just under half thereafter. A wide variety of manufactured goods, foodstuffs, and raw materials was imported; but the group that increased in volume most rapidly was crude materials for use in manufacturing: rubber, hides and skins, raw silks, fibers.

TABLE 18–2.   DESTINATION OF U.S. EXPORTS (INCLUDING REEXPORTS), 1870–1914 (MILLIONS OF DOLLARS)

YEAR	TOTAL	THE AMERICAS	EUROPE	ASIA	OCEANIA	AFRICA
1870	$471	$79	$381	$4	$5	$2
	(100%)	(17%)	(81%)	(1%)	(1%)	(0.4%)
1880	$836	$93	$719	$12	$7	$5
	(100%)	(11%)	(86%)	(1%)	(1%)	(1%)
1890	$858	$133	$684	$20	$16	$5
	(100%)	(16%)	(80%)	(2%)	(2%)	(1%)
1900	$1394	$227	$1040	$68	$41	$19
	(100%)	(16%)	(75%)	(5%)	(3%)	(1%)
1910	$1745	$479	$1136	$78	$34	$19
	(100%)	(27%)	(65%)	(4%)	(2%)	(1%)
1914	$2365	$654	$1486	$141	$56	$28
	(100%)	(28%)	(63%)	(6%)	(2%)	(1%)

Source: Computed from U.S. Department of Commerce, Bureau of the Census, *Historical Statistics of the United States, Colonial Times to 1957* (Washington, D. C.: U.S. Government Printing Office, 1960), pp. 550–551.

The rise of manufacturing exports

A fundamental reorientation of American exports began to take shape in the mid-1890s, as manufactured goods became increasingly important. Between 1895 and 1914, American manufacturing output doubled. But meanwhile the nation's exports of manufactured goods rose nearly fivefold. Most remarkably, this flood of manufacturing exports was directed mainly at markets in the most advanced industrial nations of Europe; indeed, European industrialists began to express deep concern about what was commonly termed the "American export invasion."[5] However, manufactured exports in the aggregate were only a small fraction of total U.S. industrial output.

American manufacturers were delighted with this turn of affairs, for there was widespread concern that the U.S. industrial sector had reached an "overcapacity" state; and foreign markets were seen as the solution to gluts in the domestic market for manufactures. But Europe's industrial nations were experiencing the same difficulties in absorbing their own manufacturing output—difficulties that were, of course, the subject of most distress in the depression years of the mid-1890s. Hence after the turn of the century, many of the European nations raised tariffs on American goods, slowing the American penetration of their markets.

Meanwhile, U.S. manufacturers were also pursuing market opportunities in Canada, Latin America, Africa, and Asia. All the Third World markets had been dominated by European exporters, particularly the British, and penetrating these areas with American goods was a difficult task. But when World War I broke out, a magnificent opportunity was suddenly offered to American exporters, as the European manufacturers had to turn their energies to sustaining their war economies and their armies. (*See* p. 318.)

THE BALANCE OF TRADE AND INTERNATIONAL PAYMENTS

Prior to the Civil War, the United States had imported more merchandise than it had exported in foreign trade. To offset resultant trade deficits (the annual difference between export earnings and payments for imports), this country had relied upon earnings from shipping,

[5]David Novak and Matthew Simon, "Commercial Responses to the American Export Invasion, 1871–1914," *Explorations in Economic History,* 3 (1966):121–147; Burton Kaufman, "The Organizational Dimension of U. S. Economic Foreign Policy, 1900–1920," *Business History Review,* 46 (1972):17–44.

short-term credits, long-term investment capital borrowing, and lesser forms of cash transfers. Beginning in the mid-1870s, however, this historic situation was reversed: The United States became a net creditor in annual merchandise trade. The change was attributable to the massive increase achieved in the export of foodstuffs, as the western region of the country came into agricultural production. The high protective tariff of the 1870s also tended to hold down the volume of imports at a time when American prices were declining on many products more quickly than price declines abroad.

Figure 18–3. Merchandise Imported and Exported by the United States, 1850–1939. Source: *Statistical Abstract,* 1899, p. 92; 1921, p. 854; 1940, p. 487.

Beginning in the mid-1890s, annual surpluses in the balance of trade began to rise very steeply. Indeed, from 1895 to 1914 the nation's cumulative export earnings exceeded payments for imports by $10 billion.

The foreign debt

Despite the favorable balance of exports over imports, the United States continued to be a debtor nation, for there was a massive flow of investment capital (mainly from England and western Europe) in the late nineteenth century. This capital came in quest of relatively high yields on public and corporate bonds, as the general level of demand for capital in a vigorously growing economy kept interest rates above European levels. British, French, Dutch, and German investors put their money into American railroad securities and the stock of

land, mining, and cattle companies. Hence the cumulative debt owed to foreigners rose enormously, as the following data on that debt indicate:

1860	*$0.4 billion*
1885	*$1.9 billion*
1895	*$3.3 billion*
1908	*$6.4 billion*

Meanwhile some American capital had begun to flow in the other direction, but not so much to Europe as to Mexico and Canada. As soon as World War I broke out in 1914, foreign investors liquidated a large part of their holdings in the United States, and American bankers aggressively sought investment opportunities in the Third World.

THE MERCHANT MARINE

A merchant marine under the home country's flag is not essential to an extensive foreign commerce, and in the late nineteenth century the United States found it cheaper to hire the ships of other nations to carry American trade

than to maintain an extensive merchant fleet. The foreign shippers were heavily subsidized by their governments, whereas Congress supported American shipping in overseas commerce only through relatively small programs of mail subsidies from 1865 to 1875 and after 1891.

The British had taken a decisive lead in design and operation of steam-driven iron ships even before 1860. This development had quickly ended the Yankee clipper-ship era. The quality of shipyard engineering deteriorated in the United States relative to the European industry in the post–Civil War years, and the war itself dealt a hard blow because of loss of the cotton trade, causing many American ships to be sold to foreign operators.[6] Figure 18–4 shows that the 1861–1865 decline in the tonnage of American ships registered for foreign trade proved to be the precursor of long-term decline and stagnation.

The impact of this decline was reflected in the falling percentage of U.S. exports and imports that was carried in American-flag vessels:

1861	66%
1865	28
1870	36
1880	13
1890	9
1900	7

Meanwhile the American coastwise trade continued to be reserved to U.S. shipping by discriminatory legislation. The tonnage of vessels in the coastwise commerce rose gradually but steadily from 2.7 million in 1866 to 3.4 million in 1890, and then more rapidly, reaching nearly 7 million tons in 1914. In addition, some of the largest private fleets in foreign trade, controlled by American corporations such as United Fruit and Standard Oil, were operated under foreign flags.

As the merchant marine's problems became manifest, some powerful interests—naval planners, shipyards, steel manufacturers who supplied the shipbuilders, and organized labor—began to agitate for federal support of the fleet. Seeking to challenge the rising naval power of Germany, Italy, Japan, and Great Britain, the United States began to develop a new naval fleet in the 1880s; and in the 1890s four new major shipyards were built to handle private construction of naval vessels. This development provided the industrial nucleus for a massive effort at building of merchant ships during World War I.

THE PROTECTIVE TARIFF

The United States maintained high protective tariffs almost continuously from the initial ascendancy of the Republican party in 1861 until 1913. High tariffs served to protect industry, acting as a form of subsidy to the American producers of hundreds of extractive and manufactured goods. (See Table 18–3.) And as the total volume of imports rose, the tariff served as a major source of revenue for the federal government, indeed at levels high enough to account for frequent surpluses of revenues over federal expenditures.

The tariff as a political issue

The tariff was also a recurrent and hotly debated political issue. The Republican party generally was faithful to its ideological commitment to protectionism, and its congressional leadership was highly responsive to protectionist demands from manufacturers. The Democratic party—with a strong southern agrarian wing, a heritage of low-tariff ideology, and a

concern for consumer interests—generally championed freer trade. The Democrats frequently echoed the popular slogan that "the tariff is the mother of trusts." They contended that protectionism was "protecting" products made by highly developed American industries that no longer needed such help from the government, and that most tariffs supported high domestic prices. This helped feed the profits of industries that were already enjoying oligopoly profits in types of manufacturing whose technology made costs of entry high, discouraging domestic competition.

Yet in both major political parties there were sizable factions that stood for high or low tariffs on particular commodities. When it came to regional or industrial special interests, in other words, it was often a matter of whose ox was being gored.[7] Politicians did debate the tariff in ideological terms and along party lines. But no less a political reality was the candid admission of a senator from Indiana in 1883 that he was a

[6]John G. B. Hutchins, "The Declining American Maritime Industries," *Journal of Economic History*, 6 (1946):308.

[7]Stanley Coben, "Northeastern Business and Radical Reconstruction," *Mississippi Valley Historical Review*, 46 (1959):67–90.

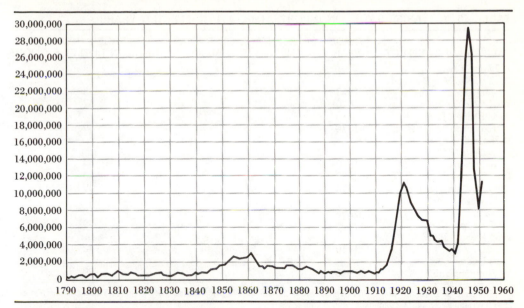

Figure 18–4. Tonnage of United States Merchant Marine Engaged in Foreign Trade, 1790–1960. Source: U.S. Dept. of Commerce, Bureau of the Census, *Historical Statistics of the U.S., Colonial Times to 1957* (Washington, 1960), pp. 444–445; *Statistical Abstract of the U.S., 1970.*

low-tariff man because as a Democrat he subscribed to the low-tariff creed, even though "I am a protectionist for every interest which I am sent here by my constituents to protect."[8]

The foundations of late-nineteenth-century protectionism were set during the Civil War, when the Republican-dominated Congress voted duties upon tea and coffee (previously admitted free), and also raised the formerly low tariff on sugar. All of these commodities were staples of every household, and the increases fell hard on the working class. In 1862 and 1864 tariffs were raised on a wide range of manufactured goods. (See Table 18–3.)

The Tariff Act of 1883

From 1875 to 1879, federal budgetary surpluses averaging over $20 million annually embarrassed the high-tariff advocates, and public pressure became intense when surpluses rose to five times that level during the expansionary period of the early 1880s. Even protectionist ideologues admitted that some "concession to public sentiment" was necessary, as even the secretary of the wool growers' lobby, appointed by President Chester Arthur to head a special

tariff-study commission, had to admit.[9] The result was the Tariff Act of 1883, which expanded slightly the list of duty-free goods. But under relentless pressure from protectionist forces in Congress, the act also *raised* tariff levels on most dutiable commodities, including textiles and iron and steel products.

Tariffs of the 1890s

In the late 1880s and early 1890s, the tariff became the chief policy issue dividing the national parties. President Cleveland threw his support to the low-tariff forces in 1887, then lost the presidency to Benjamin Harrison the next year as Republican majorities carried both houses of Congress. The result was the McKinley Tariff, enacted in 1890. It represented a determined expansion of the protectionist system, raising the duties on wool and textiles, cutlery and tin plate. It also retained protective rates on copper and on steel rails. Although the duty on raw sugar was repealed—in effect a concession to American investors in Cuban sugar plantations—a bounty of two cents a pound was voted for Louisiana's sugar producers to offset the bill's effects on them.

---

[8]Quoted in John A. Garraty, *The New Commonwealth, 1877–1890* (New York: Harper & Row, 1968), p. 246.

[9]Quoted in Paul Studenski and Herman E. Krooss, *Financial History of the United States,* 2nd ed. (New York: McGraw-Hill, 1963), p. 169.

TABLE 18–3. TARIFF RATES ON IMPORTS, 1861–1916 (SELECTED YEARS)

TARIFF LAW IN EFFECT	TRADE YEAR	PERCENTAGE OF TOTAL IMPORTS DUTIABLE[1]	AVERAGE AD VALOREM RATE ON DUTIABLE GOODS
1857 Tariff Act	1861	75%	19%
1861–1862 Morrill Act and Amendments	1863	87	33
1864 War Tariff Act	1870	95	47
1872 Blaine (Tariff-Reduction) Act	1874	73	39
1875 Tariff Act (repealing 1872 reductions)	1880	67	44
1883 Tariff Act	1888	66	46
1890 McKinley Tariff	1892	44	49
1894 Wilson-Gorman Tariff	1896	51	40
1897 Dingley Tariff	1900	56	49
1909 Payne-Aldrich Tariff	1910	51	42
1913 Underwood-Simmons Tariff	1916	32	29

Source: U.S. Department of Commerce, Bureau of the Census, *Historical Statistics of the United States, Colonial Times to 1957* (Washington, D.C.: Government Printing Office, 1960), p. 539.

[1]The percentage dutiable (subject to tariffs) is computed on the value of merchandise imports.

In 1892 the political pendulum swung the other way as both the presidency and Congress came under Democratic control and made tariff revision inevitable. Congress hammered out a compromise bill, the Wilson-Gorman Tariff Act (1894). Wool, copper, and lumber were placed on the free list, and average duties were reduced to about 40 percent. But the act made important concessions to protectionism, leading President Cleveland to denounce the bill as the fruit of "party perfidy and party dishonor." A duty was laid on sugar once again, and only slight revisions downward were made effective on iron and steel and other important articles. Cleveland allowed it become law without his signature.

The Wilson-Gorman Act was also important because it instituted a peacetime federal income tax for the first time in American history, a tax of 2 percent on those who earned $4000 or more. Its progressive feature, exempting low-income taxpayers, proved to be its undoing at the hands of the conservative judiciary: The Supreme Court declared the income tax unconstitutional in 1895.[10] (On the income tax's revival in later years, see p. 326, below.)

Returned to power in 1896, when William

McKinley defeated the Democratic-Populist candidate, William Jennings Bryan, the Republicans immediately reversed tariff policy once again. The Dingley Tariff Act of 1897 reinstituted higher protectionism, and it remained in effect for 12 years.

The Payne-Aldrich Tariff, 1909

The next major revision came in a compromise bill of 1909, the Payne-Aldrich Tariff, supported by Republican President William Howard Taft. It increased many duties while also decisively cutting tariffs on clothing, shoes, steel rails, pig iron, and iron ore.

In 1911 Taft initiated negotiations for reciprocal tariff reductions in a trade treaty with Canada, but his efforts were frustrated when western farmers mounted a strong protest, fearful that Canadian wheat and other farm products would flood the U.S. market, and finally Canada broke off negotiations.

The Underwood-Simmons Tariff, 1913

When Woodrow Wilson was elected as a reform Democratic candidate for president in 1912, he made tariff reform the centerpiece of his program and used his patronage powers ruthlessly to put pressure on Congress. The result was the Underwood-Simmons Tariff of 1913, the first element of Wilson's "New Freedom" program, which also included stronger antitrust laws and institution of the Federal Reserve System in American banking. It was a

[10]Pollack v. Farmers Loan & Trust Co., 158 U.S. 429 (1895). Ironically, President Cleveland's attorney general, Richard Olney, himself believed the income tax to be unconstitutional and so put up a feeble defense of it, at best, in arguments before the Court.

genuinely free-trade tariff in essential respects: Steel, raw wool, coal, and shoes and boots were all put on the free list, along with agricultural implements and other products. In other respects, however, protectionism continued, for the average rate on products that *were* subject to duties was 29 percent. But the net effect was to reduce consumer prices for many staple items.

World War I and foreign trade

Only a year after the Underwood-Simmons Tariff went into effect, American foreign trade was affected by the outbreak of war in Europe. Normal channels of trade were disrupted, and European manufactures that in peacetime might have entered in response to lower tariffs were unavailable for export, needed instead for war purposes in Europe. Nor did the lower tariff schedules undermine the hold of the trusts on American business, as Wilson had hoped. So great was the export boom induced by the war that American prices rose steadily and big-business firms could hardly fulfill the rising orders for their output.

Postwar tariffs

"Normalcy," defined in the context of 1913–1914, never returned, and the near-free-trade aspects of Wilson's tariff program had no chance to be tested. For as soon as the unusual conditions of war had receded, the Republicans were returned to power in the United States. They moved immediately to restore high protective tariffs. Fearful of renewed European competition, both farm and industrial interests pressed Congress to erect high tariff barriers, and the response came in the Emergency Tariff of 1921, which imposed high duties on many products.

Then, in September 1922, the Fordney-McCumber Tariff reinstituted the high levels that had been effective before the Underwood-Simmons Tariff of 1913. Especially high rates were placed on chemicals and dyestuffs—the "war baby" industries—and tariffs again protected iron and steel products. Textiles and agricultural products also gained protection at high levels. The only crack in the solid protectionist wall was a unique feature of the 1922 act that gave the president some flexibility in dealing with changes in market conditions. The president was permitted to order changes of up to 50 percent (upward or downward) on tariffs, on the recommendation of a federal tariff commission that would engage in continuous study of international prices and markets.

Presidential discretionary power

In subsequent years the presidents, both Democratic and Republican, down to the 1960s, consistently pushed Congress to enlarge still further the executive discretion they had thus won. By yielding tariff-setting powers to the executive branch, it was argued, Congress would place an important policy question above the petty partisan wrangling that characterized tariff debates in the legislative branch. Justified or not, this view found little favor with congressmen jealous of their own prerogatives; and so not until Franklin Roosevelt became president amidst a desperate economic crisis in 1933 did Congress yield further discretion in tariff matters. In the meantime, the United States in the 1920s was a staunchly protectionist nation—an anomaly in the world economy in which the United States would be running large annual trade surpluses, and in which American industry probably needed protection less than the manufacturers of any other nation.

ECONOMIC IMPERIALISM

The modern world has witnessed two distinct waves of imperialism. The first, often termed the Old Imperialism, was associated with the mercantilism of the European nation-states from the sixteenth to the eighteenth centuries. The American Revolution sounded the beginning of the end for the Old Imperialism; and when the long round of Anglo-French wars ended with Napoleon's defeat in 1815, there ensued a lull in the process of European imperial expansion.

The last three decades of the nineteenth century witnessed renewed interest and activity in expansion. This time the European countries that extended their dominion over foreign territory were industrialized nations or were undergoing rapid industrialization. Their objective was not to plant settlements of the sort that Spain, England, and other nations had established in the Western Hemisphere in the earlier era. The New Imperialism was a quest for political control of foreign territories whose own populations could provide markets for European export products and investment capital, and could also provide food and raw materials for European home markets and manufacturers.

Thus between 1870 and 1900 Great Britain added to its possessions about 5 million square miles with an estimated population of 88 million in Africa, Asia, and the southwestern Pacific region. France controlled 3.5 million square miles and governed a colonial population of 37 million; Germany, 1 million square miles with 14 million people. By the turn of the century Japan and Russia began to compete both with one another and with the European imperialist nations to extend their own power into Korea and northern China. Military and strategic factors played an increasingly important part in the diplomacy of big-power imperialism. Each enlargement of one big nation's power evoked counter-responses, and the need to defend distant possessions justified the buildup and modernization of naval forces on all sides.

The United States and the new imperialism

How did the United States fit into the emerging complex of imperial rivalries? In a sense, American expansion up to the 1890s had been a form of the Old Imperialism: It consisted largely of the migration of white population into territory that was relatively sparsely settled. The Indian inhabitants were ruthlessly brushed aside or destroyed, as the superior numbers and material resources of the invading white population were marshaled with aggressive fury. But the filling up of the continental United States had another dimension. Americans had always looked beyond the continent to some degree. For example, the aggressive war against Mexico was motivated partly by the desire of shipping and merchant interests for west-coast ports from which to develop their trade with the Pacific region. Similarly, the leaders of the plantation South had initiated several efforts before 1860 to establish American power in the Caribbean, especially in Cuba. Indeed, the Monroe Doctrine of 1823 had explicitly proclaimed the United States' special interest in the Western Hemisphere and warned the European powers that any effort to reestablish their political control in newly independent republics would be considered a threat to peace. This became the basis of a much more forward policy in the late nineteenth century, as the United States threatened military intervention in the 1890s and finally clashed with Spain over Cuba in what quickly escalated into full-scale war. At the end of the war in 1899 the United States gained possession of the Philippines, Guam, and Puerto Rico, and exercised virtual control over Cuba.

Meanwhile, American sailors had built up a brisk trade with East Asia, penetrated the long-closed Japanese sphere in 1854, and set the stage for American control of Hawaii (finally annexed in 1898). Against this background, as some scholars have argued, the outright New Imperialism of the United States can be interpreted as a logical extension of the earlier nineteenth-century American outlook and ambitions under new conditions.[11]

The turn of the century also found the United States plunging into big-power politics in Asia. In the aftermath of the Chinese-Japanese war of 1895, when Japan annexed Formosa (Taiwan) and made Korea a dependency, there were immediate demands by Britain, France, Germany, and Russia for long-term leases of important Chinese ports behind which they hoped to develop "spheres of influence": areas of China where each would control trade and capital investment opportunities.

The Open Door

At this time, with the Philippines already acquired, the American government issued the 1899 "Open Door Notes." Issued by Secretary of State John Hay, these notes were addressed to each of the great powers. They were partly political in content, in the sense that they expressed American concern for China's political integrity against foreign incursions. They declared: (1) that all existing treaty ports and established interests remain undisturbed; (2) that Chinese tariffs and no other trade levies be imposed on trade with China; (3) that they be collected by Chinese, not foreign, officials; and (4) that there be no discrimination in port charges or railroad rates between the citizens of any nation carrying on business in China. Ignoring the actual responses (mainly evasive) of the big powers, Hay unilaterally declared the Open Door policy as "final and definitive." After China's Boxer Rebellion of 1900, Hay reaffirmed the policy and demanded that no foreign nation use the rebellion as an excuse for acquisition of territory in China.

These bold declarations reflected not only American concern for Chinese integrity, but also the aspirations of American business interests for continued access to the China market. The purely economic motivations behind the U.S. policy, moreover, were reinforced by the determination of many State Department officials to persuade Americans that commercial

---

[11]This view is argued extensively in William Appleman Williams, *The Tragedy of American Diplomacy,* rev. ed. (New York: Delta Books, 1962). See also William Van Alstyne, *The Rising American Empire* (New York: Oxford University Press, 1960).

and strategic interests were inseparable. They were determined that the United States, too, should be a world power and defined its global interests accordingly. And in that ambition they were joined by people with whom they collaborated closely—some of the largest investment banking houses in the United States, which already were looking beyond the merely commercial opportunities in Asia to the day when their capital might find profitable outlets there, as China began to modernize its own economy.[12]

Expansionist aims

Both in the crisis that led to war with Spain in 1898 and in the debate of the new policy toward China, economic motivations were mixed with other factors. Not least important, in the case of Cuba, was the public sympathy in the United States for beleaguered Cuban nationalist rebels who were fighting their Spanish rulers on that troubled island. There was also an essentially racist view, supported by contemporary social science and popular prejudice, that nonwhite peoples were proper subjects of white dominance. But most critical in bringing the people who held the reins of power in the

United States—President McKinley, congressional leaders who favored imperialism, high-ranking naval officers—to take up the new policies and make the United States an imperialist power was a combination of two motives.

First there was the neo-mercantilist attitude of the advocates of imperialism, who viewed power and wealth as two sides of the same coin. Unless the United States behaved like a great power and defined its strategic and commercial interests in global terms, these people believed, the economic future of the country would become hostage to the power of other nations—European rivals, and also Japan—which would control the markets and resources of the Third World.

Second, there were the more purely economic motives of business interests, ranging from petty shoe manufacturers in New England who dreamed of a China market for their products to the nation's most powerful bankers and industrialists. These people looked to imperial expansion as an opportunity for immediate profits.[13] Hence they welcomed the readiness of Presidents Theodore Roosevelt, William Howard Taft, and Woodrow Wilson to use American power in more assertive ways.

THE CARIBBEAN

The practical results of the new American imperialism were most dramatic as they affected relations with Latin America. This was the one area of the world where the U.S. government was clearly prepared to use military force to back up national objectives.

Cuba

After the war with Spain, American troops were kept in Cuba until 1902. Although Americans' enthusiasm for war with Spain in 1898 had been founded upon sympathy for the nationalist Cuban rebels fighting the Spanish, all such idealism now seemingly disappeared. The objective of independence for Cuba was overwhelmed by the American determination to make Cuba a virtual protectorate of the United States. Hence President Roosevelt forced the Cubans to incorporate in their constitution the provisions of the Platt Amendment, first framed in the U.S. Congress when the 1901 treaty was considered. By its terms Cuba agreed to make

no foreign treaties that would impair its independence, or assume any public debt for which its ordinary revenues were inadequate; and Cuba would consent to the intervention of the United States for "the maintenance of a government adequate for protection of life, property and individual liberty." The Platt Amendment imposed effective protectorate status on Cuba. Further, it opened the way to massive penetration of the Cuban economy—especially investments in sugar plantations—by American capitalists.

The Panama Canal

Acquisition of the Philippines and Roosevelt's expressed desire to make the United States a major power in the Pacific meant that U.S. control of an interoceanic canal across Central America was a strategic necessity. The United States began a series of maneuvers that

---

[12]Charles Vevier, *The United States and China, 1906–1913: A Study of Finance and Diplomacy* (New Brunswick, N.J.: Rutgers University Press, 1955); Thomas J. McCormick, *China Market* (New York: Quadrangle, 1967).

[13]A full consideration of these factors and also the longer-term background of business expansionism is in Walter LaFeber, *The New Empire: An Interpretation of American Expansion, 1860–1898* (Ithaca, N.Y.: Cornell University Press, 1963).

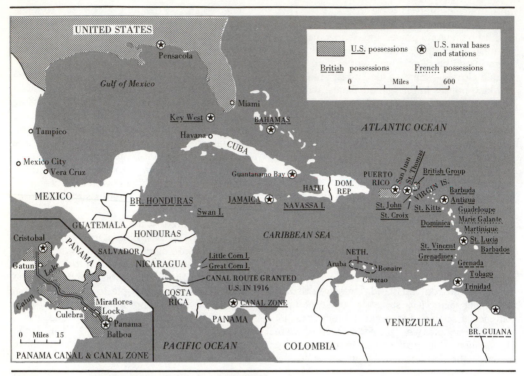

Figure 18–5.   The United States in the Caribbean. Source: Reprinted from *History of the American Way* by H. U. Faulkner, Tyler Kepner, and E. H. Merrill © 1950 with permission of Webster/McGraw-Hill.

involved a new treaty with Britain; instigation of a revolution in Panama, which until U.S. intervention was part of Colombia, to ensure installation of a government that would serve as a U.S. puppet regime; and purchase of the European interests in a canal linking the Atlantic and Pacific through the isthmus of Panama. The canal was built by the United States and completed in 1914.

The Roosevelt Corollary

Meanwhile, intervention in the Latin American nations' affairs became formal U.S. policy: In 1904 President Theodore Roosevelt declared that in cases of "chronic wrongdoing, or an impotence which results in a general loosening of the civilized society" (that is, rebellion against governments friendly to the United States), the United States would "exercise . . . an international police power."

Known as the Roosevelt Corollary to the Monroe Doctrine, this policy was first applied in the Dominican Republic. Chaotic conditions there brought the nation to bankruptcy in 1904, and it was unable to meet its foreign debt. In

1905 Roosevelt imposed an agreement (modeled on European interventions in Asia) whereby the United States took over the collection of customs. Then a major American banking house—Kuhn, Loeb and Company—funded the Dominican debt, so that U.S. military power was assuring collection of customs revenues that were then paid to support a debt held by a U.S. private investment syndicate.

Domestic disturbances provided an excuse for Wilson to send a force of marines to take over direct control of the country in 1916. American business interests, already dominating Dominican financial affairs, took over much of the sugar industry and other important resources. In 1915 the United States had landed troops in Haiti, on the western portion of the same island, ostensibly to maintain order. They were not withdrawn until 1934.

There were similar interventions in Nicaragua, where by 1912 the United States handled 35 percent of the imports and purchased 56 percent of the exports of the country; and American corporations, most notably the giant United Fruit Company, dominated the economies of Guatemala, Honduras, and Costa Rica. These manifold interventions and extensions of economic power made of the Caribbean basin an "American lake." By 1916, Puerto Rico had been annexed, part of the Virgin Islands had been purchased from Denmark, and other republics had been reduced to protectorate status. The Panama Canal was maintained under exclusive U.S. control, and a naval base had been built at Guantánamo, on the southern shore of Cuba.

Intervention in Mexico

Only Mexico, the largest and most heavily populated of the countries in Central America, survived as a truly autonomous nation. Encouraged by strong-man ruler Porfirio Díaz, who held sway in Mexico for thirty years, American mining companies, railroad builders, ranchers, and others had invested over 700 million dol-

lars in Mexico by 1910. Approximately 80 percent of investments in Mexican railroads was then controlled by the United States interests, and 70 percent of the country's oil was produced by American companies. The Revolution of 1910–1920 and ensuing domestic troubles menacing to U.S. economic interests induced President Wilson to order military action in 1914 and 1917. In response to a series of crises, State Department officials consulted closely with the officials of major corporations that had interests in Mexico, including the Southern Pacific Railroad; Phelps, Dodge and Company, the copper firm; and the Mexican Petroleum Company (Pemex). Although Wilson's policies contributed to the success of revolutionary forces in the Mexican struggle and served as a vital counterweight to possible European interventions, the legacy of American military force on Mexican territory was a bitter one.[14]

THE CHINA ADVENTURE

The Open Door policy of 1899 had been intended to assure continuing commercial equality for American merchants who traded in China. But this limited objective did not satisfy the ambitions of important American banking interests, nor did it please some of the career officers in the State Department who were seeking to push the United States into deeper involvement in the affairs of China. Indeed, it was typical of American diplomats serving in China to believe, as one of them wrote, that business and politics were "in reality but different expressions of interests which are fundamentally the same";[15] that these interests included pushing American investment capital into Third World markets; and that protection and nurturing of such interests required the United States to engage fully in big-power diplomacy. Under President Taft, diplomats of this persuasion were given numerous high State Department posts and appointments to major embassies abroad.

A new investment drive

By 1909 these members of the Foreign Service, winning considerable support from Secretary of State Elihu Root, had succeeded in re-

interpreting the Open Door policy. Instead of defining it narrowly by focusing on equality in commerce, they broadened its definition to include equality of access to China for purposes of capital investment in such projects as railroads, mines, and hydroelectric plants. At first the U.S. government thought in terms of a unilateral investment drive in Asia. Thus in 1908 the State Department assigned Willard Straight, one of the young diplomats closely associated with the expansive view of the Open Door, to collaborate with railway magnate Edward Harriman of the Southern Pacific in planning for U.S. investments in China. But in 1909 an international banking group composed of German, French, and British interests was formed to plan joint investment in Chinese railroads. The State Department then shifted its strategy, now urging Harriman, J. P. Morgan, the National City Bank of New York, and other banking interests to form an "American group" that could join the Europeans. This move succeeded, and a four-power consortium, including the American group, was formed with the understanding that the governments involved would stand behind their bankers—in effect, would

[15]"Address of Willard Straight . . . to the Associated Chambers of Commerce in China" (ms., Willard Straight Papers, Cornell University Library Regional History Collection); Harry N. Scheiber, "World War I as Entrepreneurial Opportunity," *Political Science Quarterly,* 84 (1969):488.

[14]See, on the spread of American investment generally, Harold U. Faulkner, *The Decline of Laissez Faire, 1897–1917* (New York: Holt, Rinehart and Winston, 1951), chap. 4; and Mira Wilkins, *The Emergence of Multinational Enterprise: American Business Abroad from the Colonial Era to 1914* (Cambridge, Mass.: Harvard University Press, 1970).

stand ready to use diplomacy and even force to assure the safety of the investments planned.[16] In 1911, however, revolution erupted in China; and meanwhile, Russia and Japan successfully demanded admission to the consortium, causing the American bankers to have second thoughts about their participation.

More significantly, in 1913, shortly after becoming president, Woodrow Wilson repudiated the whole adventure. Wilson sensed, correctly, that the proposed agreement committed the United States government to possible intervention in ways that posed a genuine threat to China's political integrity. Wilson also had little sympathy for the close alliance of imperialist-minded American government officials and giant banking firms in the consortium. And so ended, for the time being, a brief American adventure in Asia.

AMERICAN FOREIGN INVESTMENTS TO WORLD WAR I

A glance at Table 18–4 shows that American investments abroad increased fivefold between 1897 and 1914. It will also be noted that Mexico and Canada were the chief areas of American investment. Mexico had the largest total in 1897, and Canada in 1914. After that Canada maintained the lead until it was temporarily surpassed by Europe after World War I. Except for some "portfolio" investments (in stocks and bonds) in other industrial countries, most of the American foreign investment was "direct" (that is, used to build industrial plants, develop mines, establish marketing facilities, and the like.)

U.S. investments in Canada and Mexico

American economic penetration of Canada began well before 1900. The causes were chiefly three: the aims to exploit the Canadian market, to obtain raw materials needed in the United States, and to escape Canadian tariffs on commodities that could be manufactured there. The penetration concentrated in the manufacture of automotive goods, rubber, electrical equipment, machinery, metals, chemicals, pulp, paper, and lumber. By the 1920s American investments in Canada surpassed those of Great Britain, and by the 1930s U.S. firms controlled more than one-third of Canada's mining industry and electrical output, and at least one-fourth of its manufacturing. This penetration largely took the form of branches of American manufacturing concerns set up to take care of the Canadian market rather than private investments in Canadian firms.

Almost the equal of the investments in Canada in 1914 were those in Mexico. During the Díaz regime American money flowed into Mexico at the rate of $40 million a year. By 1914 the total amounted to about $850 million, almost three times the amount of British investments. The investments covered many fields, but the chief concentration was in the mining and smelting of metals, in railroads, and, in the later years, in oil. Despite the revolution and a decade of unrest, American investments continued to grow until the middle 1920s.

As late as 1914 American investments in Mexico were as large as those in the West Indies and the rest of Latin America combined. But the great era of economic penetration in Mexico was approaching its apex, and that of the rest of Latin America was on the verge of a great expansion. In 1897 investments in the West Indies were about one-fourth of those in Mexico; in 1919 they were two-thirds. South American investments, trivial in 1897, rose to $800 million in 1919.

U.S. investments in Cuba

Of all the fields for investment, it was Cuba that probably grew the most rapidly in the two decades after 1897, and particularly after the beginning of World War I. By the late 1920s American investments in that island amounted to over $1 billion in sugar, public utilities, railroads, mines, tobacco, and government securities, all fostered by branches of the National City Bank of New York and American brokerage houses. Over half the wealth of Puerto Rico was also soon concentrated in American hands. Despite protectorates and some artificial stimulations, American investments in other West Indian islands were relatively trivial in comparison to those in Cuba.

Central and South America

By 1914 investments in Central America, estimated at $90 million, were about one-third in railroads, one-third in tropical fruits, and the

---

[16]Ibid.; Vevier, *The United States and China;* and Raymond A. Esthus, "The Changing Concept of the Open Door, 1899–1910," *Mississippi Valley Historical Review,* 46 (1959):435–454.

TABLE 18–4. DIRECT AND PORTFOLIO INVESTMENTS BY GEOGRAPHIC AREAS (IN MILLIONS OF DOLLARS), 1897–1914

AREAS	1897	1908	1914
Europe	$151.0	$ 489.2	$ 691.8
Canada and Newfoundland	189.7	697.2	867.2
Cuba and West Indies	49.0	225.5	336.3
Mexico	200.2	672.0	853.5
Central America	21.2	41.0	93.2
South America	37.9	129.7	365.7
Africa	1.0	5.0	13.2
Asia	23.0	235.2	245.9
Oceania	1.5	10.0	17.0
International, including banking	10.0	20.0	30.0
Total: Long-term credits	$684.5	$2,524.8	$3,513.8

Source: Cleona Lewis, *America's Stake in International Investments* (Washington, D.C.: Brookings Institution, 1938), p. 606. © 1938 by the Brookings Institution, Washington, D.C. Reprinted by permission.

other third in the mining of precious stones, public utilities, and government loans. In South America, where United States investments had now started to expand rapidly, about two-thirds were in mining. Most of this was in copper, produced in Chile by the Anaconda Copper Company and the Braden Copper Company, controlled by Kennicott. A much smaller economic stake was concerned with the precious metals and stones. There was little interest in oil until after 1916. Compared with metals, American interest in railroads, public utilities, and manufacturing was small, but some $20 million in 1914 was tied up in selling organizations and a similar amount in oil.

Asia

Despite the exaggerated dreams and rosy predictions of American imperialists, the Far East failed to become either an important trading center for American industrialists or a profitable field for American investments. American exports to all Asia were valued in 1897 at about $39.27 million, or 3.7 percent of our total export trade. Twenty years later it was about $380.25 million, or 6.1 percent. Of this about $37.15 million went to China. The reasons for the relatively small amount are simple: the poverty of the mass of Asians and the severe competition of European countries and later Japan. In capital investments the story is much

the same. Total American investments (direct or portfolio) in Asia in 1897 have been estimated at $23 million, of which $20 million was in oil-distributing organizations and other trading and sales corporations. By 1914 total investments in Asia, including the Philippines, amounted to $245.9 million. About half of this was in portfolio investments, largely the result of loans to the Japanese government.

U.S. vs. European foreign investments

The $3.5 billion in U.S. foreign investments placed it alongside Germany and just behind France (with $8.7 billion) among the four leading investor countries in 1914. The leader, of course, was Great Britain, with over $18 billion in overseas holdings. In the Caribbean and Central America, however, U.S. investments exceeded those of Britain. The importance of the $3.5 billion of American holdings in foreign countries is indicated by the fact that the direct investments abroad by U.S. interests were equivalent to about 7 percent of 1914 American gross national product, exactly the same proportion as foreign investments were of GNP in the mid-1960s. Hence it is clear that in this element of the new economic order in the United States, as in so many other respects, a major structural feature of the advanced industrial economy had already taken form by 1914.

THE FRUITS OF IMPERIALISM

That the policy of economic imperialism had direct trade benefits for the United States business community is evident from the fact that exports to U.S. territories and possessions rose

from under $50 million in 1903 to $200 million in 1918. They peaked at $300 million just after World War I, and then were maintained between $200 and $300 million during the 1920s.

Imports of foodstuffs and raw materials from the American empire followed a similar pattern, although the dollar value consistently ran higher than exports.

Business expansion and extension of American power to nominally autonomous states in Latin America that in reality were under American control meant that the benefits of the New Imperialism went beyond trade and investment. The United Fruit Company in Central America, the major American oil interests in Mexico and Venezuela, the copper-mining firms in Chile, and the International Railways of Central America, all harvested a crop of profits in trade and enterprise that owed much to the U.S. government's uses of military and naval power.

For the countries and conquered peoples who lived in the American empire and its ancillary protectorates, the control of their railroads, banks, mines, plantations, and other economic institutions by American firms meant that their economic destinies were directed by foreign corporations. They lived, as it were, entirely in the shadow of American business enterprise and its needs. For many of these peoples, this meant as a practical matter that their economies would be geared increasingly to the work of providing raw materials and food for the American market; the interests (largely American) that controlled investment, shipping, and — through the influence born of economic power — even their national policies demanded it and demonstrated little concern for economic diversification or modernization.

Even where American economic hegemony was most successful in raising average living standards of the local people, as in Cuba, it proved most socially and politically explosive. On the one hand, the long-run effect of Americans' control of the Cuban economy was to raise average per capita incomes to nearly the highest level in Latin America. But, on the other hand, there were also increasing disparities between rich and poor, with a large mass of people — particularly those living in the rural areas — reduced to abject poverty and desperate political disaffection. Ironically, the group that improved its material status most dramatically during the period of American economic dominance — the "middle sector," including the lower-level managers, skilled workers, many professionals, and other white-collar labor — was totally excluded from the centers of political power and decision-making, where the influence of American investors prevailed. And so it became a major source of the cadre that Fidel Castro eventually led in raising mass support

and overthrowing the political status quo, initiating a radical revolution in Cuba in 1959.[17]

The multinationals

As big business reached its maturity in the United States at the turn of the century, this country's largest industrial interests became deeply intertwined with the largest banking firms: houses such as J. P. Morgan and the National City Bank, both of which were heavily involved not only in financing foreign commerce but in fashioning new "communities of interest" among giant domestic corporations. Thus there were many major manufacturing corporations that through direct investment in raw-materials production in developing areas, and also in manufacturing facilities in foreign industrial nations, became truly multinational in scale and operation. Indicative of their new structure was the response of the Western Electric Company's home office in 1907 to their Thailand marketing agent, who warned of local anti-American feeling:

> You speak of an anti-American attitude on the part of the [Government] Commission. We have offices and factories making our standard apparatus in Great Britain, Belgium, Germany, France, Russia, Austria, Italy, and Japan so that so far as this matter goes we are international rather than American. If there were time we could arrange to have the order go to any one of those countries that might be preferred.[18]

Western Electric and other corporate giants became associated through interlocking investments with bankers who controlled the bulk of American overseas capital flow. The close financial and management affiliations that linked such giant corporations with one another, and also with the investment bankers, lent a new dimension to business expansionism when World War I broke out. This new dimension was organizational: diverse large-scale corporate and financial interests joined together to compete more aggressively in the international

[17]Ramón E. Ruiz, Cuba: The Making of a Revolution (1968, reprinted New York: Norton, 1970), pp. 9–14; see also Irving Louis Horowitz et al., Latin American Radicalism (New York: Random House, 1969), pp. 249–291; and Gordon Lewis, Puerto Rico: Freedom and Power in the Caribbean (New York: Monthly Review Press, 1963).

[18]Wilkins, Emergence of Multinational Enterprise, quoting a 1907 letter of H. B. Thayer, Vice President of Western Electric.

economic struggle for foreign markets and investment opportunities. With the major European nations embroiled in war, and so withdrawing capital and trade with the Third World, a vacuum was left into which American business could move.

The American International Corporation

Hence new trade and investment organizations were formed. The most dramatic such move was formation of the American International Corporation. It was financed in 1915 by New York bankers and included among its officers and stockholders directors of Standard Oil, the Armour meat-packing firm, the McCormick farm-machinery company, General Electric, AT&T, and the Grace shipping complex. The AIC's officers announced that they were ready "to carry American capital into foreign fields, and to open the markets of the world to American mining and electrical machinery, harvesters, clothing, and foodstuffs"; to obtain concessions for building public utility facilities and other ventures in underdeveloped countries; to sell engineering services for large construction projects; and, in short "to put the

United States among the ranking nations in world commerce and finance."[19] By the end of the war, in late 1918, the AIC had extended its operations to include investments in Latin America and Russia. It held shipbuilding contracts in the United States, controlled several steel-making and machinery corporations, directed a major import-export trading firm, and was in the beginning stage of a major water project in China.

The AIC was only one of many new associations and business firms organized to build up an American investment and trade drive; and they became important forces in the renewed business expansionism of the 1920s, when the United States emerged as the world's leading banker in that era of dollar diplomacy.[20] Once again the call was heard in American business and diplomatic circles for "the securing of . . . an international open door for investments."[21] Only by the time the war was over, the open door was being aggressively sought everywhere in the world, and American business interests had emerged as the dominant force in the world economy—not as latecomers knocking at the door, the role they had played in the China market two decades earlier.

SELECTED READINGS

NOTE: The following works are on foreign and domestic commerce.

Ashworth, William, *A Short History of the International Economy, 1850–1950* (New York: Longmans, 1952).

Atherton, Lewis, *Main Street on the Middle Border* (Bloomington: Indiana University Press, 1954).

Barger, Harold, *Distribution's Place in the American Economy Since 1869* (Princeton, N.J.: Princeton University Press, 1950).

Emmet, Boris, and Jeuck, J. E., *Catalogues and Counters: A History of Sears Roebuck and Company* (Chicago: University of Chicago Press, 1950).

*Faulkner, H. U., *The Decline of Laissez-Faire* (New York: Holt, Rinehart and Winston, 1951).

Hower, Ralph M., *History of Macy's of New York, 1858–1919* (Cambridge, Mass.: Harvard University Press, 1943).

*Kirkland, Edward C., *Industry Comes of Age* (New York: Holt, Rinehart and Winston, 1961).

Novak, David, and Simon, Matthew, "Commercial Responses to the American Export Invasion, 1871–1914," *Explorations in Economic History*, III (1966).

[19]*New York Times*, Nov. 23, 24, 1915. See Scheiber, "World War I as Entrepreneurial Opportunity," p. 487 and passim.

[20]See Chapter 21.

[21]H. Overstreet, "Foreign Investment Relations." *Proceedings of the Academy of Political Science*, 7, Pt. 2 (1917): 644; Scheiber, "World War I as Entrepreneurial Opportunity," p. 509. See also George T. Mazuzan, "Our New Gold Goes Adventuring: The American International Corporation in China," *Pacific Historical Review*, 43 (1974):212–232; and Carl Parrini, *Heir to Empire* (Pittsburgh: University of Pittsburgh Press, 1969).

————, "Some Dimensions of the American Commercial Invasion of Europe, 1871–1914," *Journal of Economic History,* XXIV (1964).

Porter, Glenn, and Livesay, Harold, *Merchants and Manufacturers* (Baltimore: Johns Hopkins University Press, 1971).

*Scheiber, Harry N., "America and the World Economy," in *America: Purpose and Power,* Gene Lyons, ed. (New York: Quadrangle, 1965).

*Taussig, F. W., *Tariff History of the United States,* 7th ed. (New York: Putnam's, 1923).

Business expansionism and imperialism

Esthus, Raymond A., "The Changing Concept of the Open Door, 1899–1910," *Mississippi Valley Historical Review,* XLVI (1959).

*LaFeber, Walter, *The New Empire: An Interpretation of American Expansion, 1860–1898* (Ithaca: Cornell University Press, 1963).

Lewis, Cleona, *America's Stake in International Investments* (Washington, D.C.: Brookings Institution, 1938).

*McCormick, Thomas J., *China Market* (New York: Quadrangle, 1967).

*Nearing, Scott, and Freeman, Joseph, *Dollar Diplomacy* (New York: Viking, 1925).

Parrini, Carl, *Heir to Empire: U.S. Economic Diplomacy, 1916–1923* (Pittsburgh: University of Pittsburgh Press, 1969).

Scheiber, Harry N., "World War I as Entrepreneurial Opportunity," *Political Science Quarterly,* LXXXIV (1969).

Wilkins, Mira, *The Emergence of Multinational Enterprise: American Business Abroad from the Colonial Era to 1914* (Cambridge, Mass.: Harvard University Press, 1970).

*Williams, William A., *The Roots of Modern American Empire* (New York: Knopf, 1969).

Williams, Benjamin H., *Economic Foreign Policy of the United States* (New York: McGraw-Hill, 1929).

Other specialized studies

Hutchins, John G. B., *The American Maritime Industries* (Cambridge, Mass: Harvard University Press, 1941).

Nourse, Edwin G., *American Agriculture and the European Market* (New York: McGraw-Hill, 1924).

Noyes, A. D. *The War Period of American Finance, 1908–1925* (1926, reprinted New York: Johnson Reprint Corp., 1973).

Williamson, Jeffrey G., *American Growth and the Balance of Payments 1820–1913* (Chapel Hill: University of North Carolina Press, 1964).

Two important trends in the operation and structure of American government characterized the period 1861 – 1914. First, real power became more centralized as the federal government gradually took over functions that formerly had been left to the states. Hence there was a shift toward the central government in the locus of power, even though the states simultaneously increased the range of their own functions. And second, there was persistent tension between the dominant laissez-faire ideological doctrines and competing demands for government intervention. At the national level (less so at the state level), government did intervene from 1861 to the late 1880s to influence the course of economic change — but this intervention was mainly to *promote* various economic interests, not to *regulate* them for the presumed good of the larger community. This was certainly the effect of the protective tariff, railroad land grants, laws concerning the disposition of natural resources in the public domain, and other policies that we have considered. But by the 1880s the federal government was taking the first steps toward modifying (though to only a limited extent) the benign policies that it had pursued with respect to regulation of private business enterprise. And by 1914 the more general trend toward centralization of decision-making in the federal government included an important regulatory component.

THE CHANGING FEDERAL SYSTEM

The wartime congressional legislation of 1861 – 1865 and the policies of the Reconstruction period to 1877 — during all of which time the Republican party largely controlled federal policymaking — brought fundamental change in the nation's political economy. (See pp. 188 – 189.) So far as the West and its development were concerned, enactment of the 1862 Homestead Law and the lavish land grants to transcontinental railroads indicated Congress's intention to speed and nurture the region's settlement. In addition, Congress enacted a mining law in 1866 that ratified existing arrangements in California, Colorado, and other western mining states, encouraging private mining interests by making mineral resources available to them on the most liberal terms. The high protective tariffs instituted during the war years and continued thereafter were designed to foster manufacturing; so too was the Contract Labor Law of 1864, which authorized industrial firms' subsidizing of immigration in return for immigrants' agreement to work for them for specified periods. Also important were the Thirteenth, Fourteenth, and Fifteenth Amendments to the Constitution, which abolished slavery and extended voting rights, and sought to ensure that no "person" would be deprived of life, liberty, or property without "due process of law." This last guarantee, in the Fourteenth Amendment, was later to become a shield for business interests against regulation by government, in effect giving the federal judiciary a basis for striking down legislation by the states.[1]

[1] See pp. 299 – 300.

National banking policy

The tendency toward centralization was advanced significantly by wartime banking legislation. From 1840 until the Civil War, the federal government had withdrawn from any supervision of the nation's banking. Consequently banks that were chartered—or in some cases publicly owned—by the states had flourished. The paper currency used in the national economy consisted largely of bank notes circulated by these state banks. With some 1600 banks operating under state laws in 1862, the resultant complexity of the currency system was startling. It was therefore partly to eliminate the uncertainties of this decentralized system that Republican leaders formulated a new and controlling role for the central government.

Another consideration favoring a new national banking policy was the possibility that banks operating under federal laws would create a market for United States bonds and thereby aid in the financing of the Union's military effort in the Civil War. The idea of a national banking system also appealed to many reform-minded persons in the North because they believed that such a system would be consistent with the old Jeffersonian-Jacksonian ideal of making private financial interests more subservient to the popular government. The rapid increase of expenditures for the Union armies, together with extremely unsettled financial conditions from 1861 to 1862, made reform of some sort appear imperative.

Hence in 1863 the National Banking Act became law. With its 1864 amendments, this act granted charters for banking to groups of at least five stockholders, with the minimum amount of capital stock graduated according to the population of the places where they did business. Each was required to deposit with the federal government bonds equal in amount to one-third of the bank's capital. In turn, Congress authorized the banks to issue notes equal to up to 90 percent of the current market value (not exceeding par value) of the bonds. The notes would be legal tender; that is, collectible for payment of all debts owed the government.

The 1863 act also required national banks to maintain 25 percent cash reserves to back up note issues and liabilities represented by deposits—an important advance in bank regulation, since even the states with strong regulatory laws had seldom given any protection to deposits. At first, total note issues were not to exceed $300 million. Congress also voted a 10 percent tax on the note issues of state banks. Already de-

clining sharply in number and importance as more than 1600 national banks were started from 1863 to 1865, the state banks were temporarily driven from the field by this prohibitive tax. By 1865 only 350 state banks were still operating. They were not to become important again until the 1880s, when the growth of "deposit money" (funds in checking accounts) gave them a new opportunity to flourish.

Greenbacks

The consequent centralization of control over the nation's currency system is illustrated in Table 19–1. The note issues of the national banks replaced those of the state banks, supplemented by United States notes. These latter notes were to be issued by the government itself. Known as greenbacks, they were non-interest-bearing paper for common use as currency, their value resting on "the credit of the United States." In February 1862, in the face of rising war expenditures, Congress authorized issue of these notes to a maximum of $150 million; subsequent legislation raised the limit to $450 million. Nearly this full amount was actually issued, and the greenbacks became an important element in the inflationary situation during the war years. Not redeemable in specie, they fluctuated in value. The tendency was downward, however, and they fell as low as 39 cents on the gold dollar in 1864.

The national debt

Together with bond issues, which required payment of interest and redemption in specie, the federal debt rose at a dizzying pace during the Civil War years. On September 1, 1865, the total debt was over $2.8 billion. The drain upon the federal gold and specie reserves during the war led to the suspension of specie payments in 1861 and 1862, first by the state banks, later by the government itself. Two-fifths of this debt represented short-term obligations, redeemable in three years or less; and one-fifth represented greenbacks and "fractional currency," another form of paper issue authorized by Congress to meet war expenditures. The sheer magnitude of the federal debt in all its forms made national financial policy a factor of enormous importance to the economy. How the debt would be reduced, how specie payment could be resumed, and how tax policy would be adjusted (on what groups the burdens would fall), all were questions that focused public attention—and increasingly divisive, bitter debate—upon Congress. Bank-control and note-issue regu-

TABLE 19–1.   CURRENCY IN CIRCULATION AND PRIVATE BANK DEPOSITS, 1860–1914
($ MILLION, CURRENT)

YEAR	TYPES OF CURRENCY IN CIRCULATION					PRIVATE DEPOSITS IN BANKS
	GOLD COIN AND CERTIFICATES	SILVER COIN AND CERTIFICATES	STATE BANK NOTES	NATIONAL BANK NOTES	U.S. NOTES	
1860	$ 207	$ 21	$207	—	—	$ 149
1864	184	9	179	31	415	n.a.
1866	120	8	20	276	328	1,005
1875	82	15	1	340	371	2,022
1885	469	183	—	309	331	3,124
1896	497	442	—	215	256	5,059
1905	1,136	630	—	480	332	11,533
1914	1,638	709	—	715	338	18,432

Sources: U.S. Department of Commerce, Bureau of the Census, *Historical Statistics of the United States, Colonial Times to 1957* (Washington, D.C.: U.S. Government Printing Office, 1960), pp. 646–649, for all data except 1860 demand deposits, which are estimated from National Monetary Commission statistics.

lation by the states were relegated to an insignificant position.

Federal employment and spending

The new role of the central government was also reflected in its increased size and cost. Federal civil service employment had been only 37,000 in 1861. In the war period, because of the enormous need for supportive services behind the military effort, it rose temporarily to nearly 200,000. But in 1880, peacetime federal civilian employees numbered only 100,000. In 1891 there were nearly 160,000, and by 1910 the number rose to 388,000. Federal expenditures, on the other hand, did not rise markedly on a per capita basis; nor did they increase greatly even in absolute dollar terms until 1890, when they reached $318 million, which was below the 1867 level but $50 million higher than in the mid-1870s. Then federal spending rose to $605 million in 1899, and reached $735 million in 1914. Despite this absolute increase, federal expenditures were still only about 2 percent of GNP.

Centralization of power

The dual rise in civilian employment and in spending by the federal government after about 1890 was related to the new functions undertaken by the national government. These included the introduction of research activities, conservation and resource-management administration, new regulatory efforts, and the introduction of grant-in-aid programs by which federal funds were given to the states for sup-

port of reclamation projects, veterans' welfare, and agricultural research.

The Interstate Commerce Act of 1887 and the Sherman Antitrust Act of 1890 were both landmark laws that gave new impetus to the centralizing trend in government. Coming after nearly two decades of regulatory activity in the states, the 1887 law represented the first major step by Congress toward establishing federal business regulation. Similarly, at least two decades after the giant industrial corporation had become a distinct factor in the U.S. economy — and a well-recognized "problem," bringing forth various regulatory measures by the states — the Sherman Act marked Congress's first effort to provide continuing regulation of competitive practices in the business life of the nation.

Federal power
and the Supreme Court

The assertion of superior federal powers over the states also stemmed from the role of the national judiciary after 1865. In 1871 the Supreme Court legitimated one of the most striking centralizing policies, the declaration by Congress of greenbacks as legal tender, by affirming that the federal paper could be presented to satisfy any debt contracted before the legal-tender legislation had been enacted.[2] Later the Court dramatically redefined the meaning of "person" to include a business cor-

[2]Knox v. Lee, 12 Wall. 457 (1871), overruling Hepbum v. Griswold, 8 Wall. 603 (1870).

poration under the terms of the Fourteenth Amendment; and on that constitutional-legal basis, it passed on the validity of all kinds of regulatory legislation that sought to curb business practices or institute protection for workers.[3] Another doctrine of the Supreme Court late in the century was "liberty of contract," a phrase found nowhere in the Constitution but which the Court ruled was in the spirit of the fundamental law of the land. Under that doctrine, the Court, and also the state courts, found it possible to strike down other reform legislation. Superimposed upon these two doctrines was a third one, of "reasonableness," formulated in 1890 and applied to railroad regulation, under which the Court made itself the final arbiter as to whether a particular rate set by a railroad commission left a private railroad with a reasonable return on investment.[4]

Despite its conservatism, the Supreme Court was not an automaton reflexively striking down all regulatory legislation and approving all laws supportive of business. It was also motivated by the desire to achieve logical and doctrinal consistency in the law. Thus in the case of *Loan Association* v. *Topeka,* in 1874, the Court invalidated a Kansas statute that had authorized the use of public funds to aid a manufacturing firm. Although the Court in other cases had approved public aid to railroads, it now insisted that transportation firms had a distinct "public purpose" not present in the competitive business of manufacturing. To take tax money "to bestow it on favored individuals to aid private enterprises and build up private fortunes," the Court declared, was simply "a robbery." On the other hand, in 1877 the Court upheld state regulation of railroads in the famous *Granger Cases* (page 267, above). By the 1890s, however, the liberty-of-contract doctrine was regularly invoked by the Court to strike down other types of regulation in the states.

Another weapon of the Supreme Court in placing federal power between the state governments and their citizens was the labor injunction. The state courts themselves had pioneered in the use of this weapon against strikes, boycotts, and other labor tactics. (See Chapter 17.) But in 1894, in the *Debs Case,* the Supreme Court used its injunctive powers to imprison Eugene Debs, leader of the striking railroad unions, because he refused to follow court orders that would have ended strike action.

TRENDS IN STATE GOVERNMENT

Although power was shifting decisively to the federal government in vital areas of policy, the states were active, as they had always been, in legislating to promote and regulate the economy. Every state undertook promotional efforts and granted privileges and immunities that aided special local interests. As we have seen (page 262), the western states made liberal land grants to private railroad corporations. In addition, all states had some form of eminent-domain law that gave particular private firms the power to condemn and seize land or other property upon payment of compensation to private owners. In the western states, these laws typically went far beyond the limits that prevailed in the East, where they usually extended only to railroad and public utility companies. In the West, private business enterprises in mining, irrigation, drainage, lumbering, and various other activities were given the power of eminent domain. Moreover, in many states throughout the nation the actual judicial and statutory rules governing compensation were so favorable to the private interests that enjoyed powers of eminent domain that they paid little or nothing for the land and resources they obtained.[5]

Other major types of promotional legislation were tax exemptions and other special privileges extended to railroads, mining firms, and similar interests. In the western states, agencies were established to promote immigration from Europe and the East; they advertised, set up offices abroad, extended loans for travel fares, and aided in immigrants' settlement. Not least important were the generous incorporation laws adopted by numerous states. Nearly everywhere the incorporation privilege became general, and with it went limited liability for

---

[3]*See* Sidney Fine, *Laissez Faire and the General Welfare State* (Ann Arbor: University of Michigan Press, 1955), chap. 7.

[4]*See* Chapter 18.

[5]Harry N. Scheiber, "Property Law, Expropriation, and Resource Allocation by Government: The United States, 1789–1910," *Journal of Economic History,* 33 (1973): 232–251.

stockholders and other advantages. And in New Jersey, Delaware, and some other states, there were also few limitations upon trusts, holding companies, and other legal devices that bestowed special benefits upon corporations.

Localism and special privilege

Power remained decentralized in the area of property law, with the state legislatures and courts setting rules that varied widely from one state to another. This meant that particular local interests often received special privileges. For example, in California "hydraulic miners" (using high-pressure water flow to wash down hills and mountains, exposing gold ore) were permitted for many years to dump their debris and silt in the state's rivers. This practice did severe damage to farms and several cities in California's mining district, as the flood level of streams was raised severely by silt; but not until a federal court put a stop to hydraulic mining in 1884—more than a decade after the trouble had begun—was any sort of check put upon the mining interests. Similarly, coal-mining enterprises in Pennsylvania were allowed by the courts to pollute streams with their waste; and in the cattle-ranching states of the West, dirt farmers were long made to carry the whole burden of fencing costs. In the arid-land states, investors in irrigation projects were given comparable advantages as statutes and court decisions allocating water rights went in their favor. Generally, when such aspects of state law were challenged before the U.S. Supreme Court, the justices tended to validate local practice on the pragmatic grounds that "the Court must recognize the difference[s] of climate and soil which render necessary these different laws . . ." deemed to be "essential or material for the prosperity of the community."[6]

The regulatory state

As each state had its own policy mix, blending promotional and regulatory laws, it is difficult to say which element was generally dominant. Indeed, as we have seen, some regulatory laws, such as those in farming states that protected dairy interests by taxing or forbidding the sale of margarine, were actually designed to promote a particular interest group. But whatever the mix in any individual state, there is little doubt that the regulatory component of state law was of growing importance in the late nine-

teenth century. This was so despite laissez-faire ideas opposed to such regulation as contrary to the "natural" economic order, and despite the overturning of many laws by conservative state and federal judges.

The five most significant areas of state regulatory law were as follows:

1. Labor legislation, including laws regulating Sunday labor, hours of work on the railroads or in other dangerous fields of labor, wages and working conditions of women and children employed in industry, and accident-safety regulations. Also influential on wages and working conditions were compulsory schooling and rising minimum age for withdrawal from school, which became common outside the South.[7]

2. Railroad regulation (which dated from the Granger laws of the 1870s and scattered laws of the antebellum years), by which regulatory commissions established maximum rates of charge on specified intrastate routes.

2. Regulation of corporations, including laws against restraint of trade and prohibiting fraudulent or deceptive practices by the officers of corporations. (In addition, the courts in many states enforced common-law rules against conspiracy in price-fixing, pooling, and similar practices.)

4. Public-health laws, establishing standards for foods and other products, instituting various types of licensing and state inspection of goods offered for sale, and establishing boards of health to regulate sanitary practices or impose quarantines in local communities.

5. Employers' liability and workmen's compensation laws, a new type of labor legislation that began to appear in the 1890s, giving workers and their families legal protection in cases of loss of life or injury on the job.[8] These laws basically modified the harsh common-law rule known as the "fellow-servant rule" that throughout most of the nineteenth century had barred workers from holding employers liable for injury or death on the job.

Rising expenditures of state government

In their main thrust, such regulatory laws involved a shift to purposeful, coercive control

---

[6]Clark v. Nash, 198 U.S. 361 (1904). See also Scheiber, "Property Law, Expropriation, and Resource Allocation," 247–248.

[7]Fine, *Laissez Faire,* passim.

[8]Lawrence M. Friedman and Jack Ladinsky, "Social Change and the Law of Industrial Accidents," *Columbia Law Review,* 67 (1967), 50–79.

of private interests in the name of the public good. But they also carried with them the need for bureaucratization of state government, creating new functions for the states that required professional expertise and proliferating organization. As these new functions were assumed, the costs of state government rose. Thus in New York State, expenditures shifted as follows:[9]

	1860	*1880*	*1900*
Expenditures of regulatory agencies	$ *50,000*	$ *300,000*	$ *900,000*
Expenditures for social welfare and health:	*263,000*	*1,230,000*	*6,500,000*

By the turn of the century both state expenditures and state debts had begun to increase, gradually at first, then after 1910 quite rapidly. Spending by state governments thus rose from $188 million in 1902 to $388 million in 1913, growing to $1.4 billion by 1922. Meanwhile local government spending, swelled especially by highway and educational expenditures, rose from $959 million in 1902 to $2 billion in 1913, and to $4.6 billion in 1922. Spending by state and local governments combined was consistently about twice the amount of federal expenditures from 1870 to 1917.

The Wisconsin idea

Wisconsin was a leading state in the assault upon the limited-government principles of laissez-faire and the promotional policies epitomized by special-interest legislation. During the governorship of Robert La Follette (1900–1906) Wisconsin boasted that it had become a laboratory for new types of social legislation. The "Wisconsin idea," as La Follette's program was called, included strengthening railroad and insurance regulation, establishing a public utilities commission empowered to determine valuation independently and to set rates, and instituting an industrial commission to enforce labor legislation. The La Follette administration also began to explore new alternatives to the regressive property taxation upon which government finance had traditionally been based; and in 1911 the state adopted an income tax that became the model for both other states and the federal government.[10] Although

[9]Paul Studenski and Herman E. Krooss, *A Financial History of the United States* (New York: McGraw-Hill, 1952), chap. 17.

[10]Although an income tax had been imposed during the Civil War, in 1894 the Supreme Court declared a similar tax unconstitutional (Pollack v. Farmers Loan and Trust Company, 1895). Adoption of the Sixteenth Amendment in 1913 made possible the new federal income tax of that year.

Wisconsin, and also New York, New Jersey, Kansas, and Missouri, broke new ground in the United States with much of their social legislation, the spread of reform measures in this country in the first decade of the twentieth century represented movement along legislative paths already traveled by Germany, England, Australia, and other foreign countries.

Progressivism, the "interests," and reform

Much of the regulatory and social-welfare legislation enacted in the states from 1900 to 1914 was the result of the Progressive movement, exemplified and led by La Follette's Wisconsin idea. Unlike the populism of the 1890s, progressivism flourished in a period of economic expansion. The focus was now not on reversing economic distress but rather upon rooting out special privilege and achieving constitutional or legal reforms necessary to free government from "the interests." And unlike populism, progressivism had a solid urban political base, in addition having wide appeal among rural middle-class people.

Apart from their concern about special interests, the Progressives had two other objectives of great importance to redefining government's role in the economy. The first was a desire to make government more responsive to consumer concerns, including lower transportation rates, public health, clean and safe housing, and a price structure free of distortion by monopolistic business. The second was a faith in government by experts. With perhaps consummate naïveté, the Progressives believed that disinterested experts could be made immune from crass political and economic pressures. Hence, they worked to transfer policy and law-enforcement responsibilities to trained technical personnel in such fields as forestry, housing inspection, industrial safety, public health, and the like. Linked with broadly humanitarian objectives, these other concerns made progressivism, first, an initial step on the road to modern-day "consumerism;" and, second, a movement that helped build modern government on a foundation that was essential for effectual welfare and regulatory-state activity.

THE HERITAGE OF CIVIL WAR FINANCE

One of the legacies of Civil War finance was a 30-year battle waged by debtor groups, particularly farmers, to prevent contraction of the currency and to maintain prices at the levels they had reached during the Civil War, when farmers had contracted many debts. Three factors were primarily responsible for the decline of prices in postwar years: First of all was the cessation of the artificial demand for commodities produced by the war and accentuated by a disatrous panic in 1873. Second was the glut of foodstuffs, caused chiefly by the extreme rapidity which the trans-Mississippi West was brought under cultivation. The third factor was the currency policy of the bankers and the government, which looked toward the contraction of the paper currency and the resumption of specie payment.

Contractionist policy

The last of these was probably the most important. The government and banks were contracting their paper currency at a time when there was a growing need for more money in business.

The farmer fought bitterly and consistently against currency and credit contraction. Any revolution in prices is bound to injure certain groups, and in this case it was the debtor farmer, chiefly in the West and South, particularly the westerner who had pioneered during the war period of rising prices. Declining prices of foodstuffs and a contracting currency had brought real hardship, and debtor farmers put forth every effort to improve their terms of trade with the industrial sector and restore the former prices through currency inflation.

In its early stages the fight swung around the question of greenbacks. Three main problems pressed for settlement at the close of the war: (1) Had Congress the power under the Constitution to issue legal tender? (2) Should the existing issues be enlarged or contracted? and (3) Should specie payment be resumed? The first question was settled in 1871 by the Supreme Court in the case of *Knox* v. *Lee,* affirming the status of greenbacks as legal tender. The other questions reopened the conflict between those interests that favored inflation and those that sought to encourage contraction.

Before the constitutional questions were settled, the battle over inflation had begun. Under Presidents Andrew Johnson and Ulysses S. Grant, in the Reconstruction years, official Treasury policy was deflationist. From 1866 to 1868, Secretary of the Treasury Hugh McCulloch, an Indiana banker and politician, sought to withdraw greenbacks from circulation as they were returned to the government. This was welcomed by bankers, for the most part, and by mercantile and commercial groups that wanted specie payment resumed as soon as possible. "A legal-tender note [greenback] is a confession of weakness on the part of the government," one banking journal declared. "The substitution of a bank-note for legal tender is a conservative move, and in every way desirable and beneficial to the country."[11]

Many manufacturers, however, eager for cheap money with which to finance expansion and pay off previously incurred long-term debt, viewed the contractionist policy of the Treasury with alarm. Together with farm groups and other political elements that wanted to keep currency and credit buoyant, they succeeded in obtaining congressional action to stop the retirement of greenbacks. In 1874 and again in 1878, limits were placed on greenback retirements, so that over $346 million remained as part of the nation's permanent currency.

Still, however, paper currency held by the public remained under $600 million from 1867 until late 1879, despite the growing need for it. Indeed, as late as 1897 there would be less than $1 billion dollars of currency circulating.

The resumption of specie payments

Meanwhile the fight turned to the resumption of specie payments. The exchange of gold for paper by the government would bring the greenback to par, stabilize the currency, and raise the credit of the government. On the other hand, it was believed that this would further depress prices, and it was doubtful if gold in sufficient quantities could be obtained for the purpose. The defeat of the Republicans in the congressional election of 1874 caused the G.O.P. to hasten through a "resumption" bill in the following year, calling for the restoration of specie payments on January 1, 1879.

The Greenback party

This controversy over paper money, especially in its last phase, gave birth to a new political organization, the Independent National, or

[11]*Banker's Magazine,* quoted in Walter T. K. Nugent, *Money and American Society, 1865–1880* (New York: Free Press, 1968), p. 46.

Greenback, party. Formed in 1876, it presented national tickets in three presidential campaigns and called for a number of reforms radical for that day, particularly the redemption of war bonds in paper and the nonresumption of specie payments. Its greatest strength was

exhibited in the congressional elections of 1878, when it polled over a million votes. This, however, was no indication of the strength of the movement, for both major parties were shot through with sentiment for inflation.

THE PANIC OF 1873

In the meantime the distress of the debtors had been accentuated and the greenback movement stimulated by the Panic of 1873. The pace of industrial and agricultural activity in the North during the Civil War, aided by rising prices, had inaugurated a period of unprecedented prosperity. Immense regions in the West had been opened up to agriculture, and the easy profits of war prosperity had been invested freely in fixed forms of capital, notably transportation facilities. The prosperity had been too rapid, the expenditures too lavish, to be healthy; and the decade of the 1870s opened with underlying conditions far from encouraging.

Enormous amounts of capital had been sunk

in railroads to finance the 30,000 miles built between 1867 and 1873, from which small immediate returns could be expected. The opening of western lands had thrown older areas out of cultivation and decreased their value. Speculation and extravagance were rampant, and the morality of both politicians and capitalists, as witnessed by the Credit Mobilier scandal, left much to be desired. The failure in September 1873 of the country's leading brokerage firm, Jay Cooke and Company, precipitated the most severe financial panic in our history up to that time. This failure was followed by the partial suspension of specie payments. A period of severe retrenchment and depression ensued for several years.

THE SILVER ISSUE

The administration's determination in 1879 to return to specie payment drove the inflationists to another expedient. If the value of the currency could not be forced down to the level of inconvertible paper, perhaps enough silver could be injected into the monetary system at an inflated ratio to achieve the same end. In 1834 and 1837 the ratio of gold to silver, previously 15 to 1, had been changed to 16 to 1 (actually 15.98 to 1), the gold dollar thereafter containing 23.22 grains of pure gold and the silver dollar 371.25 grains of pure silver.[12] Since this overvalued gold slightly, silver disappeared and the gold came into circulation. In 1873 the silver dollar was worth $1.02 in gold and it was no longer profitable to coin it. So scarce was silver and so long had it been since any had been presented to the mints for coinage that Congress in 1873 dropped the further minting of the standard silver dollar.[13]

Far from a deep-dyed plot to demonetize silver, this act was merely legislative recognition

of the fact that silver dollars were not being coined. A congressional committee composed of a majority of silver men bitterly denounced this act three years later, pointing out that while silver possessed the function of money, it always stood guard against any considerable rise in gold.

> To divest either metal of the money function because temporarily out of use [was] reckless and unwise. . . . As well might the commander of an army while battle was raging disband and discharge his reserves because they were not engaged at the front. As well might the master of the ship cut loose and scuttle his lifeboats because the sky was clear and the sea calm.[14]

Well might the inflationists grow bitter when they contemplated the legislation of 1873, for the situation in regard to silver changed rapidly

[12]Standard weight was 25.8 grains of gold nine-tenths fine and 412.5 grains of silver nine-tenths fine.

[13]Coinage of subsidiary silver was maintained.

[14]Quoted in F. Flügel and H. U. Faulkner, *Readings in the Economic and Social History of the United States* (1929), pp. 695–697.

after that date. Germany in 1871, and Holland and the Scandinavian peninsula from 1873 to 1875, adopted the gold standard, and the Latin Monetary Union (France, Switzerland, Belgium, Italy, and Greece) in 1873 limited the coinage of silver. This threw a large supply of bullion on the market, which was augmented by the discovery of large deposits in Nevada. The price of silver dropped so sharply that in 1876 a silver dollar was worth only 90 cents in gold, with the prospect of further decline. As silver grew cheaper, it was evident that if enough could be coined at the old ratio of 16 to 1, the working of Gresham's law (that bad money drives out good) would displace gold and reduce the currency to the value of silver. The demonetization of silver was now called the "Crime of '73," and the debtor West and South, backed by the silver states, demanded that the government "do something for silver."

The Bland-Allison Act

Congressman Richard Bland of Missouri in 1877 offered a bill for the free and unlimited coinage of silver at the old ratio of 16 to 1. In the more conservative Senate the bill was toned down to limit the purchase of bullion to not less than $2 million and not more than $4 million a month, to be coined into silver dollars of 412.5 grains. That such a bill had wide backing there could be little doubt. Said the chairman of the resolutions committee at a mass meeting in Chicago:

> We would in this matter arouse the slumbering consciousness of the President and his advisers to some apprehension of the fact that there is a thunderstorm brewing in the West, and that unless they have a care, somebody is likely to be hit by the lightning of public indignation, unless they concede the just demands of the people.[15]

In spite of this sentiment, President Rutherford B. Hayes vetoed the bill, but it was quickly passed over his veto, and during the 12 years of its operation 378 million silver dollars were coined. The Bland-Allison Act of 1878 provided for the issuing of silver certificates in amounts of $10 and upward upon the deposit of silver dollars; but the metal money proved unpopular in business centers, and in 1886 the denomination of the certificates was reduced to include $1, $2, and $5 bills.

[15]Quoted by C. R. Williams, *Life of Rutherford B. Hayes* (1914, New York: DaCapo, 1971), vol. 2, p. 120.

To the great disappointment of both the silver interests and inflationists, the Bland-Allison Act failed to halt the decline in the value of silver or the downward trend of prices. Nor was there any indication that silver would drive out gold. For this situation a number of factors were responsible. The nation was going through a period of tremendous industrial expansion. A larger amount of currency was necessary and the silver dollars and certificates were absorbed without difficulty. Moreover, there were several years during the 1880s when the federal Treasury, fattened by rising customs revenues, enjoyed a surplus. Part of the surplus was stored in the Treasury and part was used to retire Civil War bonds. In either case the tendency was to reduce the circulating mediums and prevent inflation. Retirement of Civil War bonds reduced the bank-note circulation by $126 million between 1886 and 1890. While one type of money was pushed into circulation, another type was being withdrawn.

On the first of the year following the passing of the Bland-Allison Act the Treasury went back to specie payment. On January 2, 1879, Secretary John Sherman had a slender supply of $140 million in gold, which had been accumulated with great difficulty, to meet the expected rush of holders of paper. But the soundness of the government's credit was demonstrated by the fact that only $125,000 was presented for gold, while $400,000 in gold was turned in for paper.

Although the Bland-Allison Act was in force for 12 years, it was unsatisfactory to both the inflationists and their opponents. The inflationists looked upon it as simply an opening wedge to be pushed further if the purposes for which it had been passed failed to materialize. Prices of agricultural products continued to fall. By 1889 the silver in the dollar had declined to 72 cents, and hope persisted that if more silver were forced into the currency, inflation would take place. This was exactly what the gold advocates feared, and both President Chester A. Arthur and President Grover Cleveland urged the repeal of the act. Cleveland pointed out to Congress that the continued coining of silver dollars would eventually increase the currency beyond the needs of business, after which the unnecessary portion would be hoarded and thus the gold would be gradually eliminated.

The Sherman Silver Purchase Act

In spite of the opposition of the chief executive and the Treasury Department, the pressure for more silver became so great that the Republican party, as a matter of political expediency

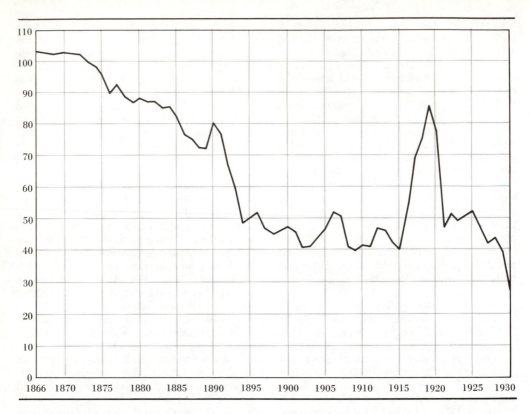

Figure 19–1.   Bullion Value of 371¼ Grains of Silver (Contents of One United States Silver Dollar) **in Terms of Gold at the Annual Average Price of Silver Each Year, 1866–1930.** Source: *Statistical Abstract,* 1930, p. 769.

and as a means of insuring the passage of the McKinley tariff, sponsored and passed the Sherman Silver Purchase Act in 1890. This bill required the secretary of the Treasury to purchase 4.5 million ounces of silver bullion a month and in payment for it to issue Treasury notes acceptable as full legal tender. These notes were to be redeemed in gold or silver at the discretion of the secretary, "it being the established policy of the United States to maintain the two metals on a parity with each other," a provision later interpreted by the executive as a promise to redeem all notes in gold.

The silver purchased under this act was practically the entire output of the American mines and was almost double that required by the Bland-Allison Act; it amounted to $156 million in the three years of its operation.

THE PANIC OF 1893 AND THE ELECTION OF 1896

The decade of the 1890s opened with the nation approaching the end of another business-cycle expansion. Railroad building during the 1880s had been accompanied by inordinate speculation that had undermined supposedly strong organizations. Corporations on the verge of bankruptcy declared stock dividends and paid regular dividends out of capital. The failure of the Philadelphia and Reading Railroad and the National Cordage Company early in 1893 aroused the nation to its unhealthy industrial situation, which had already been foretold by financial conditions in Europe.

Also there was the apprehension that the gold standard could not be maintained. Cleveland was elected in 1892 on a Democratic platform committed to a reduction of the tariff, a prospect that manufacturers contemplated with dark forebodings. Cleveland himself believed in the gold standard, but his party was shot through with inflationary sentiment.

From the point of view of those who would maintain the gold standard, the federal Treasury was in a precarious situation. This was due to a number of causes. The amount of silver purchased under the Sherman Act was too large to be readily absorbed, and gold, by the operation of Gresham's law, began to be crowded out of circulation. The financial crisis in England in 1890 brought about liquidation there, which resulted in a net loss of $68 million in gold exported from the United States. The bumper wheat crop of 1891, coincident with a failure of European crops, gave a temporary favorable balance of trade; but in 1893 the situation was reversed, with a net loss of $87 million in gold exported. To complicate the difficulties of the Treasury Department, by 1893 a Federal deficit was impending.

The ebb and flow of gold

An act of 1882 that authorized the secretary of the Treasury to suspend the issue of gold certificates whenever the amount of gold coin or bullion in the Treasury reserved for the redemption of United States notes fell below $100 million tacitly recognized the existence of a reserve and set a minimum safety point. Subsequent secretaries had not allowed the reserve to fall below this point, and so far it had been sufficient to maintain the gold standard, even after the added strain imposed by the Sherman Silver Purchase Act of 1890. Wiping out the gold reserve would mean the suspension of specie payments or the substitution of silver for gold in the payment of paper presented under the act of 1890. Either would mean the elimination of the gold standard and the cheapening of money. While this would have brought joy to the inflationists, the mere possibility paralyzed with fear the holders of fixed capital and business in general.

The crisis

When Cleveland was inaugurated the reserve was $100 million, and in November it reached $59 million. Failures of large corporations had already shaken public confidence in the business structure, and the decline of the reserve set in motion a period of the severest liquidation yet experienced. During 1893 over 600 banking institutions failed, and during the summer 74 railroad corporations passed into the hands of receivers. By June of 1894, at least

194 roads had failed, including the Philadelphia and Reading, the Erie, the Northern Pacific, and the Union Pacific. More than 15,000 commercial failures involving liabilities of $346 million were recorded for 1893. The production of iron and coal declined, and to add to the general distress there was a poor corn crop in 1894 and a decreased demand on the part of Europe for wheat. Unemployment, strikes, discontent, and much suffering characterized the winters of 1893 and 1894, a period that encompassed the Pullman strike in Chicago and the marching of "Coxey's army" to demand relief and public works for the unemployed.

Cleveland, a firm believer in the gold standard, was determined to maintain it at any cost. Absolutely convinced that the Treasury's distress and the panic itself were "principally chargeable to Congressional legislation touching the purchase and coinage of silver," he called a special session of Congress on August 1, 1893, and demanded repeal of the Sherman Silver Purchase Act. A bill to this effect passed the House with little delay, but the Senate held it up until October 30, when it was granted by a sectional vote, with the West and South aligned against the Northeast.

If President Cleveland's claim that to end the gold standard would bring a panic was true, then the repeal of the Sherman Act came too late to be of any value. In January 1894 the Treasury sold $50 million of 5 percent ten-year bonds to obtain gold and in November resorted to an additional loan of $50 million. The gold obtained in this way soon drained out, for there was nothing to prevent the man who lent gold one day from presenting paper and demanding it back the next day. Borrowing on these conditions seemed useless; and when in February 1895 the Treasury found itself with a reserve of only $41 million, and that declining at the rate of $2 million a day, Cleveland negotiated with J. P. Morgan and a group of bankers for a loan of 3.5 million ounces of gold, to be paid for in 4 percent United States bonds. It was agreed that half the gold should be obtained abroad and that the bankers would exert every influence to prevent its withdrawal until the contract had been fulfilled. Cleveland's action in borrowing privately from the bankers brought down upon him a storm of abuse, and when, a year later (January 1896), a fourth loan was resorted to, it was offered to the public. Liquidation by this time had run its course; the loan was several times oversubscribed, and during the year the gold reserve in the Treasury continued to mount.

The campaign of 1896

The efforts of the inflationists to expand the currency, continuously evident since the close of the Civil War, reached their climax in the campaign of 1896. Agricultural prices, which had been on the decline since the 1860s, touched bottom in the early 1890s. Wheat in 1894 sold at 49 cents, corn in 1896 at 21 cents; in Kansas and Nebraska it was cheaper to burn it for fuel than to sell it. Against this situation the People's party (Populists) made organized protest, and in 1896 joined with the Democratic farmers of the West and South. The Democrats, incensed by Cleveland's hard-money stand, drove the gold-standard easterners from control of their party, nominated William Jennings Bryan as their standard-bearer, and, with the Populists, engaged in one of the hardest-fought and most significant political campaigns in our history. The chief issue of the campaign of 1896 was the free and unlimited coinage of silver at a ratio of 16 to 1, but behind this demand was 30 years of agrarian unrest and a cumulative protest against the currency and credit system and against railroads and other monopolies that had borne hard upon them. Their failure in this crusade left the federal government at the opening of the new century in the control of the conservatives.

THE CURRENCY ACT OF 1900 AND THE REVERSAL OF THE PRICE TREND

Although the campaign of 1896 settled the long controversy over bimetalism, the silver advocates were still so strong in the Senate that the gold standard was not officially adopted until four years later. The Currency Act of 1900 finally provided that the gold dollar of 25.8 grains nine-tenths fine should be the unit of value and that all other forms of currency should be maintained at parity with this dollar. To maintain this parity, provisions were made to keep a gold reserve of $150 million in the Treasury. Other provisions of the act called for the retirement of the Treasury notes of 1890, their replacement by silver certificates based on coined silver dollars, and the liberalizing of the laws governing national banks.

At the time the act was passed it was doubtful if in a severe crisis the $150 million gold reserve could withstand the pressure of the existing redeemable money. But fortuitously, new discoveries of gold in South Africa, the Yukon, and Alaska, as well as the development of new processes for extracting the precious metal from the ore, flooded the world with gold during these critical years. The average annual coinage of gold, which had been $67.18 million in the years 1891–1900, increased during the following decade to $101 million. This, with additions to the supply of bank notes, increased the per capita circulation from $23.85 in 1893 to $33.86 in 1907 and $34.20 in 1911. Together with the rapid growth of deposit money, this helped enable the government to maintain the gold standard, and also to reverse the downward trend of prices. From the low point in 1896 to 1914 the general price level increased 40 percent. The demand for inflation subsided as a leading political and economic issue, and the debtor farmer enjoyed one of his few periods of economic prosperity. Gold, interestingly enough, thus had helped to provide an inflation that for years many believed could most easily be obtained through silver.

THE PANIC OF 1907 AND THE MOVEMENT FOR BANKING REFORM

In the campaign of 1896 William McKinley had been heralded as the "advance agent of prosperity." In truth, liquidation had about run its course, and he entered office on a returning wave of prosperity that continued with but few interruptions until it was temporarily halted in 1907. The discovery of fresh deposits of gold, a succession of good harvests, the greater activity of American exporters in foreign fields, coincident with the War of 1898 and imperialist expansion, all served to stimulate business. Rising prices and confidence in the McKinley administration helped to promote new investment.

This prosperity continued with but slight interruption until 1907, when a brief and severe "bankers' panic" ensued. This panic was due chiefly to overspeculation in the large money centers and was the culmination of a long struggle between the rapidly rising trust companies acting as commercial banks under inadequate reserve requirements and the more conservative and rigidly regulated commercial banks. It was precipitated by the action of the Knickerbocker Trust Company in closing its doors on October 22 to prevent a run on the firm. Many of the speculative ventures crashed, but efforts by the government and by leading capitalists did much to prevent the panic from becoming general. It was limited largely to the cities and its effects were not widespread, a fact that gave it the name of the "rich man's panic."

Defects of the banking system

The panic served one good purpose in bringing out clearly the defects of the national banking system. Although the national banks had marked a long step forward by providing relatively safe banking facilities and a standard bank note based on the credit of the national government, further improvements were necessary.

Probably the chief criticism brought against the system was its lack of elasticity. The Currency Act of 1900 had extended, under certain conditions, the issue of bank notes from 90 percent to the full face value of the bonds upon which they were issued, but in times of emergency this did not provide sufficient currency. Another great weakness of the national banking system was its inadequacy in providing credit facilities for the rural agricultural regions. The Currency Act of 1900 had reduced the minimum requirements for bank capital to $25,000 for towns of 3,000 or less, but even this reduction did not promote the establishment of adequate national banks in rural regions. Even when they did exist, their inability under the law to lend on real estate and their policy of extending commercial loans for 60 or 90 days did not fit the needs of the farmers. As a result, the rural communities were served, if banking facilities were available at all, largely by state banks whose interest rates were high and whose financial condition was often precarious.

Rural interests also complained that the whole banking system encouraged the flow of funds from communities where they had been accumulated to the large financial centers, where they were used for speculative purposes rather than for the legitimate needs of agriculture and industry. The efficiency of the system was hampered by the cumbersome and expensive exchange and transfer system and the decentralization of the gold supply. Many of these weaknesses had been evident for some time and agitation for improvement had been active for a decade before the 1907 panic.

The Aldrich-Vreeland Act

Profiting from the lessons of the panic, Congress in 1908 passed an emergency measure, known as the Aldrich-Vreeland Act, making temporary provision for the issue of bank notes upon approved securities of states, cities, towns, or municipalities and upon commercial paper, and providing for the formation of associations of national banks for the purpose of issuing notes. The act was in force until 1915.

The bill also called for the appointment of a national monetary commission to study banking conditions and report to Congress. Much popular interest was now aroused, and both major parties were pledged to some kind of reform. The report of the commission was submitted in January 1912, with specific recommendations known as the Aldrich plan. This plan did not suit either political group. President Wilson, having disposed of the tariff, next pressed for banking legislation that took form in the Federal Reserve Act of December 23, 1913.

THE FEDERAL RESERVE SYSTEM

The act of 1913 (as amended in 1916 and in later years) did much to eliminate certain defects of the national banking system. It divided the country into 12 districts, and provided that a Federal Reserve bank was to be located in the principal banking city of each district — tacit recognition that the nation was fundamentally a group of economic sections rather than an agglomeration of states. The Federal Reserve cities decided upon were Boston, New York, Philadelphia, Cleveland, Richmond, Atlanta, Chicago, St. Louis, Minneapolis, Kansas City, Dallas, and San Francisco. All national banks were required, and other banks were encouraged, to become members of the system by subscribing to the capital stock of the Federal Reserve bank in their district an amount equal to 6 percent of their capital stock and surplus.

Hence, each district Federal Reserve bank is owned by the various member banks scattered throughout the district. The district banks were to be directed by nine-member boards of governors, six named by the member banks and three by the Federal Reserve Board. This scheme of organization and management made the Federal Reserve System the first major agency of the national government to be created on a regional concept, embracing blocs of states and even cutting across state lines in order to make the jurisdictions of the administrative units consistent with the realities of the banking system and the economy generally. In addition, the mixed system of government's and privately owned banks' appointive powers in naming governors of the district banks represented a major departure in American government practice at the federal level.

The Board and
the district banks

The mixed public – private character of the system was evident in the organization of the Federal Reserve Board and its relationship to the banking community. The eight-member central board was all government-appointed, but it operated in consultation with a Federal Advisory Council (composed of one representative from each district bank), and it established overall policy in consultation with the district banks. Moreover, the system was decentralized, with some of the most significant powers exercised at the district level. Thus the power over rediscounting – the acceptance of member banks' commercial paper at a specified rate of charge as a means of permitting the member bank to expand the reserve basis on which it extended credit – was left with the district banks. In addition, beginning in 1916 the district banks were authorized to make outright loans to member banks, which similarly served as a means of providing member banks with reserves on which to extend credit to their customers.

By the manipulation of the rediscount rate (the rate of charge, or interest, on rediscounts to member banks), the district banks thus could have a major impact on the economy through the easing or tightening of credit available from banks. A low rediscount rate would enable member banks to make money available on easier terms. A high rate, on the other hand, would serve to discourage easy credit – unless, of course, the member banks did not need to rely upon rediscounts because their own reserves were adequate to sustain credit expansion.

The district banks were also designed to serve as clearing houses, to settle balances among member banks. The Reserve System served as well as the government's fiscal agent, and the system's banks issued Federal Reserve notes – a new form of paper money – on the security of short-term commercial paper. According to the language of the Federal Reserve Act, the system was designed "to furnish an elastic currency." By that means it sought to correct one of the persistently troubling features of the old national banking system, by which credit tended to grow tighter in periods of business contraction (that is, at the very time when looser credit was desired). The act also sought, however, to "establish a more effective supervision of banking in the United States"; and in this respect, its conservative intent was to assure the security and safety of member banks and of the money that they issued. Hence the act tied credit and money to the gold standard. The Federal Reserve banks were required to carry a 40 percent reserve of gold against their outstanding notes, and a 35 percent reserve against deposits.[16]

The original Federal Reserve Act gave no explicit recognition to the important potential effects of Federal Reserve open-market operations on the economy – that is, the buying and selling of government securities, with such operations having an immediate impact upon member-bank deposits and reserves, and thereby upon the easing or tightening of credit. Not until the early 1920s were the Federal Reserve System's open-market operations reorganized and closely integrated with the agency's other functions.[17]

A series of later policy reforms proved necessary to strengthen the power of the Federal Reserve System over credit and banking, especially its effectiveness in contracting credit. But even in its original form, it did correct some of the worst deficiencies of the old national bank system. It provided for the coordination of bank activities by a national body; regional organization consistent with patterns of regionalized trade, credit, and banking; improved facilities for clearing balances; and new mechanisms for elastic currency to meet the needs of business amidst short-term expansionary or contractionary trends.

---

[16]Milton Friedman and Anna J. Schwartz, *A Monetary History of the United States, 1867 – 1960* (Princeton, N.J.: Princeton University Press, 1963), pp. 189 – 196.
[17]Ibid., pp. 251 – 252.

CORPORATE CONCENTRATION AND CONTROL

While the reform of banking, money, and credit policies was being accomplished, there was also deep popular concern about the general tendency toward consolidation of American business. By the late 1880s, the opposition to giantism in business—popularly termed the "trust" problem—had come to a focus on the need for effective national legislation. Many state courts had applied common-law concepts of conspiracy and restraint of trade to curb anticompetitive practices, and some states had enacted legislation to deal with these abuses. But these proved generally ineffective, and by 1890 Congress could no longer resist the rising pressure from intellectual reformist elements, agrarian spokesmen, organized labor, small-business interests, and other sources.

The Sherman Antitrust Act, 1890

The result was the 1890 Sherman Antitrust Act, one of the great landmarks in the history of American political economy. In effect, the Sherman Act declared maintaining of competition to be a major national policy. It provided in very general terms that: (1) "every contract, combination in the form of trust or otherwise, or conspiracy, in restraint of trade or commerce among the several States, or with foreign nations," was illegal; (2) it was a misdemeanor to "monopolize or attempt to monopolize" in the course of interstate or foreign trade; and (3) either private parties or the Justice Department might sue under the act, which authorized court injunctions and also provided for fines and imprisonment of up to one year for violation. An injured party might, moreover, recover "treble damages": three times the value of damages sustained as the result of monopolizing or conspiratorial action.

The Sherman Act was probably something of a sham, designed to spike the guns of radical antibusiness reform. Its breadth of language left many openings for judicial interpretation—and the contemporary judiciary was known well for its solicitous, friendly attitude toward business interests. Moreover, a large bloc of conservative Republicans closely associated with giant business interests had lent their support to the measure—perhaps because they traded their votes in exchange for others' support of a higher tariff, but more likely because they doubted that the antitrust law would have any real clout.

The Sugar Trust Case

In any event, neither under Democratic President Cleveland nor under his Republican successor, McKinley, was there a serious determination to test and enforce the law. Only 18 federal suits were initiated down to 1901. The most important case to that time was the Sugar Trust Case (*United States* v. *E. C. Knight Company,* 1895), in which the Supreme Court refused to order that the giant American Sugar Refining Company, controlling 95 percent of the sugar market, be dissolved. Mere size and extent of market control were not evidence of Sherman Act violations, the Court ruled; and manufacturing was only "indirectly" related to "commerce or trade," which the act had specified was its subject. This almost incredible judicial doctrine, that manufacturing was not "commerce," seemed proof of what the contemporary humorist "Mr. Dooley" had prophesied when the Sherman Act was made law: "What looks like a stone wall to a layman is a triumphal arch to a corporation lawyer."[18]

The Sherman Act and organized labor

The Supreme Court's hard-line position softened, however, in 1899, when the Court unanimously ruled that a market pool that had been formed by six pipeline manufacturers was in violation of the act (*Addyston Pipe and Steel Company* v. *the United States,* 1899). In other decisions of 1897 and 1898, the Court also ruled that railroads came under the terms of the act.[19] Ironically, the Court also extended the reach of the act to include labor unions. In the crucial 1894 decision that enabled the federal government to break the Pullman strike, the Court declared that union actions in restraint of trade had been forbidden by the Sherman law (*In re Debs,* 1894). In a later decision, the famous *Danbury Hatters' Case,*[20] the Court went further, and held members of a labor union responsible financially, to the full amount of their personal property, for losses to business caused by an interstate union boycott. In vari-

---

[18]Peter Finley Dunne, quoted in *Liberty and Justice,* ed. James M. Smith and Paul L. Murphy (New York: Knopf, 1968), vol. 2, p. 285.
[19]United States v. Trans-Missouri Freight Association, 166 U.S. 341 (1897); United States v. Joint Traffic Association, 171 U.S. 505 (1898).
[20]Loewe v. Lawlor, 235 U.S. 522 (1915).

ous state and lower federal courts, moreover, some zealous antilabor judges even challenged the legality of labor unions as such. Because of their rules and restrictions on members, it was argued, unions could be prosecuted as conspiracies in restraint of trade.[21]

The muckrakers and the captains of finance

In view of this sort of judicial decision making, it is not surprising that the greatest wave of mergers and consolidations in American economic history should have occurred in the late 1890s and the first years of the twentieth century, after the Sherman Act had been on the books for nearly a decade. The sudden burgeoning of concentrated giant industrial enterprise occasioned wide comment in the press, and it coincided with several well-publicized state investigations of corporate activities and antilabor practices. More important still, the mid-1890s were a period of deep social unrest and spreading anxiety in the United States. The 1893–1897 depression, with its widespread unemployment, armed clashes between workers and company or public police in strike situations, and intense political attacks by the Populists and other radical groups upon the existing economic and political orders, gave new force to antibusiness sentiment.

Moreover, a group that won the name "muckrakers"—crusading investigative journalists—by the turn of the century was beginning to expose some of the most blatant and arrogant business practices of the large corporations in many industries. Writers such as Ida Tarbell, author of an expose on Standard Oil; Upton Sinclair, whose book *The Jungle* (1906) revealed the plight of workers in the packing plants and the filthy conditions in which meat was processed; and others, including Lincoln Steffens, Ray Stannard Baker, Charles Edward Russell, and Burton Hendrick, stirred the public consciousness, reinforcing the new antibusiness coalitions that had begun to emerge—joining labor interests, farmers, consumer splokesmen, and small businessmen—during the depression conditions of the 1890s.

Meanwhile, even some of the managers of large industrial firms and the captains of finance whose Wall Street firms were gaining a new voice in control of the giant corporations now expressed concern that the forces of industriali-

zation could not be left completely uncontrolled. For the most part, they abhorred the prospect of government intervention; their preference, of course, was for private control and "rationalization" of the competitive industrial order.

The intellectuals, the public, and big business

A powerful attack on the new business order meanwhile came from another quarter, the scholarly community. By the mid-1880s, Richard T. Ely, Edwin R. A. Seligman, and other influential economists had mounted an attack on *laissez-faire* ethics. They denounced the implicit approval of self-interest that underlay the sterile doctrines of classical economics, which for so long had served as the intellectual handmaiden of ruthless business behavior in the United States. They called instead for introducing altruistic ethical ideals into the "science" of economics. In reaction to this movement the neoclassical economists, led by John Bates Clark, reaffirmed the notion that social progress depended upon the maintenance of genuine competition in the business system. Ironically, however, even this neoclassical defense against the new altruistic style in economics lent weight to the movement to control big business more effectively. For as Clark himself insisted, it was government's responsibility to institute and enforce laws assuring the free working of a competitive order and thus stem any trend toward monopoly.

There had been other attacks, too, on *laissez-faire* ethics, from social critics with a vast reading audience. The book *Progress and Poverty*, by the journalist and radical reformer Henry George, had been published in 1879 and contained a sweeping indictment of the business system in general and the institution of private landownership in particular. It was one of the most widely read works of the nineteenth century. The socialist utopian Edward Bellamy had won wide attention, too, with his *Looking Backward* (1888) and other writings.

But the most trenchant theoretical critique of corporate capitalism came from Thorstein Veblen. In his famous work *Theory of the Leisure Class* (1899), and in later writings, this brilliant economist and maverick academic argued that the managerial bureaucracies, big bankers, and corporate manipulators had perverted the industrial order. His devastating logic and heavy-handed rhetoric came down equally hard on other institutions and values—small-town "monopolist" retailers, college and uni-

---

[21]Kealy v. Faulkner, 18 Ohio Sup. Comm. 498 (1908); Hitchman Coal and Coke Company v. Mitchell, 202 Fed. 512 (1912).

versity trustees, and the middle class all received his critical attention. Although later generations would read Veblen for the breadth of his radical social criticism, to contemporaries his writings were immediately important for the harsh light they cast on bigness and the exploitative practices of American business corporations.

Roosevelt as trustbuster

It was in this atmosphere that Theodore Roosevelt opened a campaign against the trusts shortly after he became President. In a 1902 speaking tour he condemned the trusts as citadels of special privilege; and the next year Congress, at his urging, passed the Expediting Act (which gave preference on court dockets to antitrust suits), the Elkins Act (for tighter railroad regulation), and an act creating the Department of Commerce and Labor (including the Bureau of Corporations, with power to investigate business practices). In 1902, Roosevelt ordered the suit against a giant railroad holding company, the Northern Securities Company, which culminated in a Supreme Court ruling in 1904 breaking up the corporation. (See p. 270.) Under Roosevelt, 19 civil suits and 25 criminal suits were instituted in federal courts. Under his successor, William Howard Taft, the effort to enforce the Sherman Act was carried on even more aggressively, nearly 80 cases being pressed.

Standard Oil and
the American Tobacco Company

Two notable antitrust decisions of the Supreme Court during Taft's presidential years illustrated anew the enormous power of the federal judiciary in giving practical content to the policy so vaguely mandated by the Sherman Act. The first of these was against the Standard Oil Company, which controlled 90 percent of the nation's petroleum market and had enlarged its corporate holdings by a variety of ruthless tactics that drove competitors to the wall or forced them to sell out. In four years of

litigation, the company's lawyers argued that there had been no conspiracy or monopolistic intent; rather, the corporation climaxed the "natural" growth of a highly successful business firm. But the Supreme Court upheld a lower court decision ordering dissolution of Standard Oil (*United States* v. *Standard Oil Company*, 1911). The firm was broken up, the holding company being dissolved and ownership of the constituent firms made individually distinct and separate. The second major case of the Taft years was against the American Tobacco Company—not a holding company like Standard Oil, but rather a single manufacturing concern engaged in producing chewing and smoking tobacco, snuff, cigars, cigarettes, and tinfoil. The Court ruled that the firm must be broken up into separate companies, each manufacturing one of the major products.

These decisions illustrated both the difficulties involved in restoring true competition in concentrated industries, on the one hand, and the enormous impact that the Court's doctrines had on the actual content of antitrust policy, on the other. In their basic purpose of restoring effective competition, the two judicially ordered dissolutions clearly failed. Equity stock in the new firms was distributed on a prorated basis to the stockholders in the dissolved corporations; hence the result was a community of interlocking interests, and the new companies often worked as harmoniously as they had done under single management. In addition, the Court revised the basic meaning of the Sherman Act by introducing in these decisions what was known as "the rule of reason." Years before (in the *Trans-Missouri Freight Case*, 1897) the Court had refused to recognize any difference between "reasonable" and "unreasonable" combinations in restraint of trade. But now, in the two 1911 decisions, the Court decided there was a difference after all. However, only efforts to establish thorough monopolies were "unreasonable," the Court declared, thus giving judges a large area of discretion in deciding future antitrust cases.

WILSONIAN REFORM AND THE CLAYTON ACT

The judicial "rule of reason" complicated further an already complex set of competing ideas in public debates of the nation's trust problem. For years the Democratic party had

assailed the Republicans as the defenders of big business—ironically so, since Cleveland, the only Democratic President since Lincoln's victory in 1861, had been as conservative a champion of corporate interests as any other major national politician, except that he had opposed high tariffs.

The 1912 confrontation: Roosevelt and Wilson

In 1912 the Democrats' Presidential candidate was Woodrow Wilson, progressive governor of New Jersey and a man with a burning faith that government could restore much of the older order of competition if only it was determined to do so. "American industry is not free, as it once was free," he said.

> American enterprise is not free; the man with only a little capital is finding it harder to get into the field, more and more impossible to compete with the big fellow. Why? Because the laws of this country do not prevent the strong from crushing the weak.[22]

Wilson's negative view of consolidated corporate power was challenged in 1912 both by Taft (running for reelection) and by Theodore Roosevelt, who as the third-party (Progressive) candidate was the real challenger. Roosevelt's view accepted the necessity of combinations and giantism: "This is an age of combination, and any effort to prevent combination will not only be useless, but in the end vicious," because it would destroy efficiency and cause purposeless government intervention. He denied the wisdom of any "sweeping prohibition of every arrangement, *good or bad,* which may tend to restrict competition" — a view paralleling the Supreme Court's distinction between good and bad trusts. But unlike the Court, Roosevelt believed that the President, as elected representative of all the people, should determine which large consolidated firms were good and which were not. Wilson's response was to charge Roosevelt with advocating paternalistic government. By leaving antitrust questions to the executive branch, Wilson charged, the Roosevelt Progressives would simply perpetuate the power of the very people who had corrupted government and destroyed competition with their enormous power.

Historians have differed in their interpretation of the Roosevelt–Wilson confrontation. Some scholars have stressed the difference between Roosevelt's essentially paternalistic

view and Wilson's insistence that uniform laws applicable to all were vital to attain restoration of competition. Other scholars argue that differences between the two candidates in 1912 were less important than the fact that neither one really challenged the dominant place of industrial and banking interests in American life. However that may be, certainly neither Roosevelt not Wilson adhered to the more radical alternatives that were presented to the public by foes of big business who represented the Populist strain in contemporary politics, or Eugene V. Debs, who polled nearly a million votes as the Socialist party candidate in 1912, committed to extensive government ownership of major industrial enterprises.[23]

The New Freedom

Wilson's victory in the 1912 elections, which also carried Democratic majorities in Congress, led to adoption of his "New Freedom" program. In 1913 Wilson successfully championed a sweeping tariff reform. Then he obtained from Congress enactment of the law establishing the Federal Reserve System in banking. The final element of his initial reform program was antitrust reform. In an intensive debate in Congress, the southern and western progressives and old Populist-style elements demanded stringent limits on the extent of markets that any single firm might control, while elements friendlier to business sought to push Roosevelt-style reform that would have left large discretion to the president. Out of this debate came legislation that took a middle position between the two camps.

The Federal Trade Commission and the Clayton Act

First, in 1914 Congress established the Federal Trade Commission, with power to issue orders requiring businesses to cease illegal practices, and also to bring such firms to court when they violated FTC orders. Second, in the same year Congress passed the Clayton Act, a full revision of the Sherman Act. The Clayton Act included the following major provisions:

---

[22]Woodrow Wilson, *The New Freedom* (New York: Doubleday, 1913), p. 15.

[23]See the various views presented in John Wells Davidson, "Wilson in the Campaign of 1912," in *The Philosophy and Policies of Woodrow Wilson,* ed. Earl Latham (Chicago: University of Chicago Press, 1958); Arthur S. Link, *Woodrow Wilson and the Progressive Era, 1910–1917* (New York: Harper & Row, 1954); James Weinstein, *The Corporate Ideal in the Liberal State, 1900–1918* (Boston: Beacon Press, 1968); Gabriel Kolko, *The Triumph of Conservatism* (New York: Free Press, 1963).

1. Prohibition of any discrimination in prices when the effect was "to substantially lessen competition or tend to create a monopoly" — an enlargement, in effect, of the Supreme Court's criterion, under the rule of reason, for naming "bad" trusts.
2. Prohibition of "tie-in" arrangements and "tying," by which a seller sold his goods to another under conditions requiring the buyer to purchase other products from the same seller or not to handle the products of competitors.
3. Prohibition of the purchasing of competitors' stock when the effect was to lessen competition.
4. A declaration that labor unions and farm organizations were not conspiracies in restraint of trade.

Long sought by organized labor, this last provision was hailed as labor's Magna Carta, and an end to court injunctions against unions was foreseen.

The high hopes for reform engendered by the Clayton Act were not to be realized. Antitrust prosecutions continued (there were 34 instituted in Wilson's first administration), but no fundamental change occurred in the competitive structure of American industry. Moreover, the FTC proved to be a business-oriented agency; and on the few occasions before 1920 when the FTC did take a tough stand against the corporations, the federal courts quickly disallowed such initiatives.

The Webb-Pomerene Act

American entry into World War I in 1917 terminated the new antitrust thrust in federal policy. Indeed, in 1918 the Webb-Pomerene Act amended the Clayton Act to permit combinations and inter-firm cooperation in the export trade.[24] And when the Republicans regained power after World War I had ended, they took a generally friendly position to business and refrained from vigorous enforcement of the antitrust laws.

In sum, the new business order that had become entrenched by the turn of the century — a high degree of concentration, giantism in industry, and significant control by banker-dominated communities of interest — survived the era of antitrust policy making without substantial alteration. Fundamental reform, or at least the establishment of an elaborate regulatory apparatus that significantly challenged the reach and strength of private corporate power, had to await the New Deal era of the 1930s.

SELECTED READINGS

General works

Fabricant, Solomon, and Lipsey, Robert, *The Trend of Government Activity in the U.S. Since 1900* (New York: National Bureau of Economic Research, 1952).

Fainsod, Merle et al., *Government and the American Economy,* 3rd ed. (New York: Norton, 1959).

*Fine, Sidney, *Laissez-Faire and the General-Welfare State* (Ann Arbor: University of Michigan Press, 1955).

*Garraty, John A., *The New Commonwealth, 1877–1890* (New York: Harper & Row, 1968).

* Kirkland, Edward C., *Industry Comes of Age: Business, Labor, and Public Policy, 1860–1897* (New York: Holt, Rinehart and Winston, 1961).

*Kolko, Gabriel, *The Triumph of Conservatism* (New York: Free Press, 1963).

McCraw, Thomas K., "Regulation in America: A Review Article," *Business History Review,* XLIX (1975).

Scheiber, Harry N., "Federalism and the American Economic Order, 1789–1910," *Law & Society Review,* X (1975).

[24]Pressure to authorize combined efforts by firms in marketing their goods abroad had begun in 1916, principally engineered by Edward Hurley, chairman of the FTC. Wilson himself lent his support to the Webb-Pomerene Act — indicating, as one historian has written, "how far Wilson had abandoned the ideological inflexibility of his 1912 program" (Melvin Urofsky, *Big Steel and the Wilson Administration* [Columbus: Ohio State University Press, 1969], p. 76).

Studies of money, banking, and fiscal policy

Dewey, Davis R., *Financial History of the United States* (New York: Longman, 1934).

*Friedman, Milton, and Schwartz, Anna J., *A Monetary History of the United States, 1867–1960* (Princeton, N.J.: Princeton University Press, 1963).

Klebaner, Benjamin J., *Commercial Banking in the United States: A History* (Hinsdale, Ill.: Dryden Press, 1974).

Mitchell, Wesley C., *A History of Greenbacks* (Chicago: University of Chicago Press, 1903).

Myers, Margaret, *A Financial History of the United States* (New York: Columbia University Press, 1971).

Nuget, Walter, *Money and American Society, 1865–1880* (New York: Free Press, 1968).

Ratner, Sidney, *American Taxation* (New York: Norton, 1942).

Studenski, Paul, and Krooss, Herman, *Financial History of the United States,* 2nd ed., (New York: McGraw-Hill, 1952).

Sylla, Richard, "Federal Policy, Banking Market Structure, and Capital Mobilization in the U.S. 1863–1913," *Journal of Economic History,* XXIX (1969).

———, "American Banking and Growth in the 19th Century," *Explorations in Economic History,* IX (1972).

Unger, Irwin, *The Greenback Era* (Princeton, N.J.: Princeton University Press, 1965).

Weinstein, Allen, *Prelude to Populism: Origins of the Silver Issue* (New Haven: Yale University Press, 1970).

Corporate concentration and antitrust

Burns, Arthur R., *The Decline of Competition* (New York: McGraw-Hill, 1936).

Jones, Eliot, *The Trust Problem in the U.S.* (New York: Macmillan, 1921).

Klebaner, Benjamin, "Potential Competition and the American Antitrust Legislation of 1914," *Business History Review,* XXXVIII (1964).

Letwin, William, *Law and Economic Policy in America* (New York: Random House, 1965).

*Mason, Edward, ed., *The Corporation in Modern Society* (Cambridge, Mass.: Harvard University Press, 1959).

Moody, John, *The Truth About the Trusts* (New York: Moody, 1904).

Thorelli, Hans B., *The Federal Antitrust Policy: Origination of an American Tradition* (Baltimore: Johns Hopkins Press, 1954).

Specialized works on reform

Faulkner, Harold U., *The Decline of Laissez-Faire* (New York: Holt, Rinehart and Winston, 1951).

Link, Arthur S., *Wilson: The New Freedom* (Princeton, N. J.: Princeton University Press, 1958).

*Mowry, George E., *Theodore Roosevelt and the Progressive Movement* (Madison: University of Wisconsin Press, 1946).

*Weinstein, James, *The Corporate Ideal in the Liberal State, 1900–1918* (Boston: Beacon Press, 1968).

Wiebe, Robert H., *Businessmen and Reform* (Cambridge, Mass.: Harvard University Press, 1962).

The Supreme Court, the law, and public policy

McCurdy, Charles W., "Justice Field and the Jurisprudence of Government-Business Relations," *Journal of American History,* LXI (1975).

Paul, Arnold M., *Conservative Crisis and the Rule of Law: Attitudes of Bar and Bench, 1887–1895* (Ithaca: Cornell University Press, 1960).

Roche, John P., "Entrepreneurial Liberty and the Fourteenth Amendment," *Labor History,* IV (1963).

When the guns of August sounded in Europe in 1914, the immediate effect on the American economy was disruptive. In 1913 and 1914, a persistent downward trend in the economy had been aggravated by the rumblings of the coming war in Europe. Probably the drastic revisions of American economic policy—the institution of the Federal Reserve System, the passage of the Clayton Act, and the sharp downward shift in protective tariffs legislated in 1913—had a dampening effect upon business investment. The outbreak of armed conflict in the Balkans in 1913 further unsettled world markets and domestic business conditions, especially as large exports of gold from the United States were stimulated by European hoarding and rising interest rates in England and on the Continent.

When the armies of Germany and the Allied powers clashed in August of the following year, a sudden wave of panic had just swept international money markets. The New York Stock Exchange closed on July 31, not to reopen until nearly the year's end; and commerce was paralyzed by the anticipation of European moratoriums on international debt payments, an event that in fact followed only a few days after hostilities began.

The outbreak of war caused a sudden, precipitous drop in American exports, intensifying the already perilous international monetary crisis. With the principal European customers for American cotton and food exports (Britain, France, and Germany) now involved in the fighting, the export trade was interrupted; food and cotton surpluses were stockpiled in America, and farm prices fell rapidly. German submarine attacks on British and other Allied shipping, and the British blockade of Germany, further disrupted foreign commerce. Steel exports dropped nearly 50 percent in 1914 from the previous year's level, and many other branches of manufacturing were nearly as hard hit. Prices of many industrial products fell to their lowest levels in ten years.

With European investors pulling out their capital, the pressure on U.S. gold reserves prompted the newly organized Federal Reserve Board to set up a special gold fund. Meanwhile the government also established a cotton loan fund to tide southern cotton interests through the crisis, the price of cotton having fallen by half between July and December 1914. By these extraordinary measures the government helped American banks and other financial institutions to avoid radical credit curtailment. At a time when all the European nations were placing a freeze on the payment of international debt obligations, therefore, the United States continued to support its banking system with pooled gold reserves and to meet current obligations. This successful stabilization prepared the way for American investment bankers and international banking firms to launch a successful challenge to Great Britain during the war years, in competition for the financing of world trade. [1]

[1]Alexander D. Noyes, *The War Period of American Finance, 1908–1925* (1926, reprinted New York: Johnson Reprint, 1973), chaps. 1–2.

AMERICA AND THE ALLIED WAR EFFORT

In the winter of 1914–1915 the economic crisis in the United States began to ease. European manpower was being mobilized for total war, and the belligerent nations turned to the United States for supplies of foodstuffs and raw materials. Moreover, the British and French placed large orders for armor plate, ordnance materials, explosives, and shells with American steel firms. Whereas more than half the nation's steel furnaces had stood idle in December 1914, by the end of the next year the industry was producing at virtually full capacity, the direct result of war orders from the Allies. (The Germans also attempted to procure war materials in the United States, but with little success.)

To ensure against vital supplies finding their way to Germany through American trade with neutral countries abroad, the British made covert arrangements with J. P. Morgan and other American banking firms to buy up the entire available supply of copper and other materials in early 1915, using dummy purchasers; and later that year they extended this tactic even to the cornering of the U.S. market in cotton, which once again was in short supply as prices rose.[2] Meanwhile there were massive increases in British and Allied purchases of American grain products and meats. As it had been a century earlier, during the Napoleonic Wars, the United States was a major source of food and raw material; but in addition it exported vast amounts of manufactures.

America's trade surplus

The effect on American trade balances soon became evident. For the ten years preceding the war, the United States had run an annual surplus, exports exceeding imports by $450 million to $500 million annually. By 1917, however, the surplus had grown under the impact of war purchasing to over $3.5 billion. Between 1914 and 1917 the value of explosives exported rose from $6 million to over $800 million; chemicals, dyes, drugs, and related products, from $22 million to $181 million; iron and steel, from $251 million to over $1.1 billion. The rise in value of agricultural exports was also enormous. Meat exports went

from $143 million in 1914 to over $353 million in 1917, and exports of wheat and flour increased from $88 million to nearly $300 million.

Once the United States entered the war in 1917, the flow of exports continued to go forward; and in the postwar years, even greater volumes of U.S. products were sold overseas. Throughout the entire period of hostilities, from 1914 to the war's end in November 1918, and afterward as well, American exports also rose dramatically in trade with Asia, Latin America, and the neutral European nations that formerly had purchased manufactures from the warring European powers. The war's overall impact on American foreign trade is shown in Table 20–1.

Rising production and employment

The expansion of foreign trade was only one element of the war's impact on American economic life. Rising exports led to expansion of production, both in farming and in industry, and rising employment levels also meant an upswing in domestic demand. Both incomes and prices rose; although real wages barely kept up with price increases, the drop in unemployment from 2.2 million workers in 1914 to only a tenth that number by 1916 still meant expanded opportunity for labor. Associated with this development was the great migration of blacks from the rural South to industrial urban centers in the North, a major demographic shift that gathered momentum as the war-induced boom progressed. (See pages 244, 323.) Corporate profits, especially in the war-related industries, reached historic high levels, and many industries producing goods formerly imported from overseas—especially dyes, potash, chemicals, scientific instruments, and optical goods—became spectacular growth industries (or "war babies," as they were called) during this period.

War loans

Not least important, the international position of the United States changed from that of a debtor nation to that of a creditor in international accounts. The shift began with Europeans' withdrawal of investment funds in the United States. (An estimated $500 million in specie had to be shipped to foreign creditors in Europe, in late 1914 and early 1915 alone.) In addition, the rising tide of war purchases by the Allies began to be financed by American bank-

[2]Harry N. Scheiber, "World War I as Entrepreneurial Opportunity," *Political Science Quarterly*, 84 (1969): 494–496; Arthur S. Link, "The Cotton Crisis, the South, and Anglo-American Diplomacy, 1914–1915," *Studies in Southern History* (Chapel Hill: University of North Carolina Press, 1957), pp. 122–138.

TABLE 20-1. FOREIGN TRADE OF THE UNITED STATES, 1914-1921 (IN MILLIONS OF DOLLARS)

YEAR[1]	EXPORTS OF DOMESTIC MERCHANDISE	IMPORTS OF MERCHANDISE	EXCESS OF EXPORTS OVER IMPORTS	SHARE OF AGRI-CULTURAL EXPORTS	SHARE OF MANU-FACTURED EXPORTS
1914	$2,329.7	$1,893.9	$ 435.8	48%	47%
1915	2,716.2	1,674.2	1,042.0	54	43
1916	4,272.2	2,197.9	2.074.3	36	62
1917	6,227.2	2,659.4	3,567.8	32	66
1918	5,838.7	2,945.7	2,893.0	39	58
1919	7,749.8	3,904.4	3,845.4	53	45
1920	8,080.5	5,278.5	2,802.0	43	52
1921	4,378.9	2,509.1	1,869.8	48	46

Source: *Statistical Abstract, 1921,* Table 482, pp. 840, 847, 849.
[1]Fiscal years ending June 30 to 1918; thereafter calendar years.

ing houses that extended credit to the belligerent governments and arranged for the sale of Allied war bonds (government securities) in the U.S. capital market. Initially the Wilson administration banned war loans as a violation of "neutrality in spirit." But as the war-goods purchases of the Allies became critically important to American economic expansion and recovery from the depressed conditions of 1912-1914, it became evident that either the loan ban had to be lifted or serious economic difficulties would follow. Hence Wilson reversed himself in October 1914. Immediately, both loans to the Allies by American banks and war-related exports began to expand.[3]

America moves toward war

By 1916 the economic expansion was also being affected by the possibility of America's entry into the war. A large-scale naval building plan was authorized by Congress to modernize the fighting navy, and in September 1916 Congress established the United States Shipping Board to promote the development of the merchant fleet. Meanwhile, Wilson organized the Council of National Defense, authorized by Congress in mid-1916, in response to pressures from industrialists who were looking toward close cooperation of government and the private sector in the development of a mobilization plan.

With Europe battling in a life-and-death struggle, it was unlikely that America could enjoy unmolested the profits of neutrality. As in the Napoleonic Wars, each side in the struggle was anxious to keep American products from reaching the other. To achieve this purpose both Great Britain and Germany violated neutral rights as they balanced their immediate needs against the displeasure and possible action of the United States. Great Britain, controlling the sea, blockaded German ports and arbitrarily extended the contraband list to include cotton, wool, leather, rubber, copper, and chemicals, which had formerly been free of seizure, and later foodstuffs. It also enforced the theory of "ultimate destination" and seized cargoes bound for the neutral nations of Europe on the grounds that they were destined eventually for the Central Powers. On its part, Germany proclaimed the waters around the British Isles a war zone and embarked on a policy of unrestricted submarine warfare that resulted in loss of American lives and property.

Economic causes of America's entry into World War I

The causes that made for war are extremely complex. Much emphasis was given after World War I to the economic causes of our entry. American economic life, it was pointed out, had become geared more and more to the task of supplying essential war commodities, and these commodities, owing to Britain's control of the seas, had gone to only one side. It was Germany's interference with this commerce that provided the technical cause for our declaration of war on April 17, 1917. Moreover, private loans to Allied borrowers amounted to over $2.5 billion before our entry into the war, compared with only $45 million to Germany.

That the United States had a strong eco-

[3]Joseph V. Fuller, "The Genesis of the Munitions Traffic," *Journal of Modern History,* 6 (1934); Richard W. Van Alstyne, "Private American Loans to the Allies, 1914-1916," *Pacific Historical Review,* 2 (1933): 180-183.

nomic interest in the success of the Allies is therefore indisputable. It probably oversimplifies the complexities of the neutrality period, however, to attribute American entry into the war solely to economic self-interest. There was a strong affinity to Great Britain in language and the predominant culture; and clearly, key members of the Wilson administration, as well as the President himself, from early in the course of hostilities regarded Germany as a serious threat to American interests. Moreover, both because of popular goodwill toward the Allies in America and because of effective anti-German propaganda efforts, many in this country viewed the

Allied cause as a fight for the survival of liberal democratic institutions. This was true despite fierce hostility to American involvement on the part of militant labor groups (especially the Socialists and the IWW), many of the 2 million German-Americans, and important liberal and pacifist elite groups.[4] But while all these factors were important in determining the direction of American foreign policy, it can also be said that the only viable option—an option that was defined, as the alternative to it was foreclosed, in large part by economic interests—became intervention on the Allied side. To that extent, at least, economic factors were determining.[5]

ECONOMIC MOBILIZATION

From mid-1916 forward there were serious efforts to prepare for mobilization, centering on the Council of National Defense's establishment of special boards of experts. Yet as late as six weeks before the United States declared war in April 1917, the U.S. Army had no concrete plans for the organization or equipment of a large force. Moreover, the council's decision-making processes were constantly hampered by powerful conflicts among competing interests. On the one hand, the sizable element in Congress opposed to American war preparation and to Wilson's policies used their influence to impede thoroughgoing planning for war. On the other hand, the principal personnel appointed to the council and its subordinate agencies and planning boards—chiefly businessmen—clashed with both professional military planners and the civilian authorities in the War and Navy departments as to who should be the dominant partner in the mobilization effort, private business interests or government officials.[6]

The War Industries Board
The near-chaos that prevailed in the economy when the nation suddenly found itself at war prompted efforts at reform of war planning and organization. Three months later, in July 1917, the Council of National Defense created the War Industries Board (WIB), with authority to develop plans for allocating priorities and increasing production systematically throughout

the industrial sector of the economy. For the first time in American history, a single centralized agency was given responsibility for integrating overall economic mobilization with military efforts in wartime.

At first the WIB relied upon the voluntary cooperation of private industry, with committees of volunteers drawn from business management circles authorized to oversee the war effort in specific sectors of industry. These committees tended to work closely with the national associations that had been formed earlier by business interests to forward cooperation and coordination in their industries. Their viewpoint was expressed by the automobile manufacturer Howard Coffin, who initially was the leading figure in the Council of National Defense, when he said that the nation must create a "closely knit structure, industrial, civil and military . . . in peace and in commerce, no less than in possible war."[7]

But soon, the government's reliance upon voluntary cooperation proved inadequate to meet the rising needs of the American armed forces and ensure an orderly flow of supplies to the Allies. Lacking coercive powers to compel cooperation from private firms, WIB officials soon came to favor stronger government direction of the war effort. But on the whole, these

---

[6]Paul A. C. Koistinen, "The 'Industrial-Military Complex' in Historical Perspective: World War I," *Business History Review*, 41 (1967):378–383.

[4]The substantial opposition to Wilson's war policy is given close analysis in H. C. Peterson and Gilbert C. Fite, *Opponents of War, 1917–1918* (Madison: University of Wisconsin Press, 1957).
[5]This argument is made brilliantly in a classic article by Paul Birdsall, "Neutrality and Economic Pressures, 1914–1917," *Science and Society*, 3 (1939): 217–228.
[7]Quoted in ibid., p. 385.

officials, being themselves leaders of the private industrial complex, sought to create a structure that would use coercive power in ways that were not dangerous to the system of private economic power.[8]

Bernard Baruch

Wilson responded to the pressures for more coercive authority by endorsing legislation in 1918 for sweeping executive authority in allocating priorities, fixing prices, and ordering controls over the use of manufacturing plant. He vested price-fixing authority in a special committee that worked in close association with the WIB but that made price-setting decisions outside the WIB structure. The WIB was now placed under the direction of Bernard Baruch, who won a reputation as an economic czar who exercised absolute control over industrial mobilization. In fact, Baruch served more as a broker than as a dictator, always seeking to balance the war effort's requirements against the realities of private power in the business community. Baruch established functional divisions in the WIB charged with control of conservation, priorities, prices, requirements of raw materials, labor, and coordination with Allied purchasing efforts.

Government partnership with industry

For a nation of immense size, conditioned to individualism and privatism in the management of its business, the task of mobilization was an enormous effort. Despite the appalling lack of preparedness in 1917, inefficiency, blunders, compromises with large-scale business interests, and failures in individual projects, still the war effort took on impressive strength and momentum. During the 19 months of American military participation, the U.S. government maintained a continuous flow of munitions and other goods to the Allies, raised and armed over 4 million men, and transported 2 million of its soldiers to Europe, where they tipped the military balance. To accomplish this, the Wilson administration increasingly accepted close partnership between government and the dominant corporate interests in American industry — a striking abandonment, ostensibly on a temporary-emergency basis, of the New Freedom ideals that Wilson had articulated in the 1912 presidential campaign.[9]

FOOD AND FUELS

As the stocks of foodstuffs and fuels declined in the warring nations, their production and conservation in the United States became matters of extreme importance. The situation led Congress to pass two acts in August 1917: the Food Production Act and the Food and Fuel Control Act. The first gave the Department of Agriculture power to stimulate the production and conservation of food products on the farm. The second gave the administration power to control "foods, feeds, fuel including fuel oil and natural gas, fertilizer and fertilizer ingredients, tools, utensils, implements, machinery, and equipment required for the actual production of foods, feeds, and fuel." It forbade hoarding, willful destruction, and discrimination or unfair practices in sale and distribution, and gave the President power under certain conditions to purchase, store, and sell wheat and other commodities. Even before this act was passed, Herbert Hoover was called back from the ad-ministration of relief for Belgium to tackle the food problem. He later headed the National Food Administration, set up to enforce the agricultural provisions of the act.

The National Food Administration

Hoover personally preferred voluntary cooperation, but as the war continued it became necessary to impose restrictions and to use the power granted by Congress. By licensing the manufacture, storage, and distribution of food products, effectual regulations limiting the use of sugar, wheat, meat, butter, and other foods were imposed. The people as a whole were stimulated to self-denial and to the use of substitutes, and meatless and wheatless days were imposed. While the consumer was urged to curtail consumption, every means was used to stimulate farmers to greater production.

Although the Food Administration had no legal authority to fix agricultural prices, it virtual-

---

[8]Robert D. Cuff, *The War Industries Board: Business-Government Relations During World War I* (Baltimore: Johns Hopkins University Press, 1973), pp. 81–85.

[9]Ibid., chap. 10; Melvin I. Urofsky, *Big Steel and the Wilson Administration: A Study in Government–Business Relations* (Columbus: Ohio State University Press, 1969).

ly did so, since its purchases for the army and navy, the Allies, Belgian relief, and the Red Cross comprised such a large proportion of the available supplies. It could and did guarantee minimum prices that it would pay, and it set them sufficiently high to stimulate production. Some of its purchasing operations were carried on through subsidiary nonprofit government corporations, which established policies that successfully set minimum prices — much to the delight of farmers and processors — as well as allocating supplies.

The Fuel Administration

The most acute shortage that developed during the war, both for civilian needs and for war industries, was in coal. Under the Fuel Administration, headed by Harry A. Garfield, almost every known means was used to overcome the difficulty. The problem was threefold: production, distribution, and rationing. To stimulate production, operators and miners were urged to eliminate waste and to introduce more efficient methods. The problem of distribution was met in part by introducing a zoning system that served consumers from the nearest mines and eliminated crosshauls. To make the coal go as far as possible, unnecessary illumination and heating were curtailed, and in April 1918 a system of general rationing for domestic users was established. Control over the distribution of fuel oil was instituted in January of that year and was later extended to natural gas and gasoline.

WARTIME CONTROL OF TRANSPORTATION

Preliminary efforts to enlarge the American merchant marine before we entered the war have already been noted. After our entrance the functions of the United States Shipping Board were enlarged to include supervision of the vast shipbuilding program, control of vessels under the jurisdiction of the government, and the training of men for service in the merchant marine. When the United States declared war, Germany was sinking shipping faster than it could be built. The problem now was to reverse this situation and to keep supplies moving on the high seas. In April 1917 the Shipping Board organized a subsidiary, the Emergency Fleet Corporation, with a capital of $50 million, to undertake the construction of merchant ships. Congress also authorized the President to take over 600,000 tons of German shipping interned in American ports. In August the government commandeered all steel vessels in process of construction; this added 3 million deadweight tons. Finally it took over all American ships of 2500 tons or over fit for use, but allowed their owners to operate them.

Shipping regulation

The Emergency Fleet Corporation commanded virtually unlimited funds from Congress. Its objective was to build a "bridge of ships" across the Atlantic, and its method was mass production from prefabricated parts and materials manufactured according to standardized designs. It expanded old shipyards already working to capacity and built new ones. The 61 shipyards of 1917 and their 235 ways had increased by November 1918 to 341 shipyards and 1,284 launching ways, and the number of workmen from 45,000 to 380,000. By September 1, 1918, the Shipping Board had control of 8.7 million tons of shipping. But, ironically, nearly all the new ships were completed *after* the armistice was signed.

Railroad regulation

Government regulation of the railroads had been the accepted policy since 1887, but it was only during the war that the experiment of government operation was tried. The inability of the railroads to cope successfully with the exigencies of war needs brought about this step. The position of the roads at the opening of the European conflict was far from strong. For 15 years the cost of railroad operation in maintenance, materials, and labor had been increasing. On the other hand, attempts to gain higher rates had been unsuccessful until 1914. The year 1914 was disastrous for the railroads, and 1915 found one-sixth (42,000 miles) of the railroad system of the United States in the hands of receivers. The war brought temporary prosperity with the enormous stimulation of the freight business in 1915 and 1916. But the rising cost of materials and higher wages absorbed much of the profits. The railroads for some time had been buying insufficient equipment and their rolling stock could not meet the pressure of war needs.

For several months a program of voluntary

cooperation was attempted. The War Industries Board created a five-man committee, the Railroads War Board, with the task of obtaining cooperation in sharing of equipment and other types of coordinated activity (supplanting competition among the roads) to aid the war effort. The private railroads joined willingly, but soon the voluntary program proved inadequate. Individual lines failed to live up to agreements, and shippers became enraged when the roads pushed for sizable rate increases. Also, pressure for higher wages from the unions became steadily stronger. Finally, Wilson ordered an outright government take-over of the railroads in December 1917. Congress legalized this move in March 1918, enacting a law that created a $500 million revolving fund to support railroad operations. Congress also provided the roads with a guarantee of federal payments that would match the average operating income of each company in the three-year period ending June 30, 1917 — a period of extraordinarily large business volume and profits for many lines — and mandated return of the roads to the companies not later than 21 months after hostilities had ended. Not least important, Congress rescinded the ICC's rate-making powers and transferred them to the Railroad Administration, the agency created to run the lines. In mid-1918 the federal government also took over control of the nation's telegraph and telephone systems, placing them under the direction of the Postmaster General.

The Railroad Administration did little to offend either railroad management or railroad labor. The industry's managers and lawyers dominated the government agency, while labor also made some gains. Increased wages were deemed necessary soon after the government took control, and then, in May 1918, rates on all classes of freight were raised 25 percent, and passenger fares were also increased. Contrary to standard peacetime ICC practice, this was done entirely without public hearings.

Viewed from one perspective, the government's operation of the railroads was a necessary rationalization of the industry to meet wartime needs. It brought joint use of terminals, equipment, and repair shops; new regulations for capacity loading of cars, which conserved resources but also assured the railroads a more highly integrated style of operation; and more efficient handling of troop and supply movements. From another perspective, however, the Railroad Administration can be interpreted as "a crippling blow to diversity and competition, on behalf of monopoly, in the name of 'efficiency' and standardization."[10]

The 1920 Transportation Act

When the war ended in November 1918, the major railroad interests of the country joined forces to head off a return to regulation on the prewar basis by the ICC and to the old competitive conditions. However, counterpressure by shippers and by reform-minded congressional factions frustrated the railroad managers' intentions in this regard. But out of the wartime experience came the 1920 Transportation Act, a compromise measure. In addition to authorizing moves toward consolidation of major lines, the 1920 act tempered the return of ICC control over railway rates by giving the roads a two-year guarantee of a "fair return" of 5.5 percent on investment and by granting the ICC power to establish *minimum* as well as maximum rates. (See p. 340.)

LABOR DURING WARTIME

The European war created a shortage of labor in the United States prior to actual military intervention in 1917. The normal flow of immigration declined from an annual average of 660,000 from 1912 to 1914 to 258,000 from 1915 to 1918. Then, the expanded operations of industry and agriculture were complicated by the conscription of civilians for military service after U.S. entry into the war.

The labor needs of industry attracted about a million female workers during the war. In addition, in occupations formerly the exclusive province of white labor, such as in the skilled craft jobs in railroading, blacks were recruited for the first time. Northward-migrating blacks from the rural South also found extensive employment in low-skill jobs in foundries, steel

[10]Murray N. Rothbard, "War Collectivism in World War I," in *A New History of Leviathan: Essays on the Rise of the American Corporate State,* ed. Rothbard and Ronald Radosh (New York: Dutton, 1972), p. 91. Cf. K. Austin Kerr, *American Railroad Politics, 1914–1920* (Pittsburgh: University of Pittsburgh Press, 1968), for a thorough analysis of the Railroad Administration and the policy debates.

TABLE 20–2.   ANNUAL EARNINGS, COST OF LIVING, AND INDEX OF REAL EARNINGS OF WORKERS, 1913–1920

YEAR	AVERAGE ANNUAL EARNINGS (NONFARM INDUSTRIES)[1]	COST-OF-LIVING INDEX (1913 = 100)	INDEX OF AVERAGE ANNUAL REAL EARNINGS (1913 = 100)
1913	$ 675	100.0	100.0
1914	682	101.4	99.6
1915	687	99.2	102.6
1916	765	108.8	104.2
1917	887	130.7	100.5
1918	1115	159.1	103.8
1919	1272	180.3	104.5
1920	1489	208.8	105.7

[1]Shown in current dollars.

Source: Computed from U.S. Department of Commerce, Bureau of the Census, *Historical Statistics of the United States, Colonial Times to 1957* (Washington, D.C.: U.S. Government Printing Office, 1960), pp. 91 (Series D-604), 127 (Series E-159).

mills, packing houses, construction, and other branches of industry.

Still, labor shortages persisted. Dollar wages therefore moved up rapidly during 1917 and 1918, and the eight-hour day became more common. For workers on all federal contracts, the eight-hour day was made mandatory.

Prices, too, advanced quickly during the war years and during 1919–1920. The average *real earnings* of American workers therefore increased only slightly, as shown in Table 20–2. Soon after the United States had become a belligerent in April 1917, President Wilson appointed special "adjustment boards" to mandate wages, hours, and conditions for workers in shipyards, construction firms under contract with the War Department, and other vital industries. Generally these adjustment boards (each of which included a labor representative appointed by the AFL) kept wage increases consistent with rises in the cost-of-living index. White-collar workers did not fare so well as those employed in factories and other wage workers.

Organized labor

Although the policy of government authorities in regard to unions was generally to give them recognition, in practice the AFL was fa-

vored. Meanwhile, the Wilson Administration embarked on a campaign to root out and destroy the radical unions, especially the IWW, which opposed American war policies. Militant antiradical employers took advantage of this to attack the IWW—and sometimes unions in general—on grounds of patriotism. Union membership increased, mainly in the AFL, from 2.7 million in 1916 to more than 4 million in 1919.

The War Labor Board and the War Labor Policies Board

Early in 1918 the War Labor Board and the War Labor Policies Board were established. The former was a quasi-judicial body to which disputes between employers and employees could be submitted. The board adjudicated some 1500 cases. The Policies Board sought to establish general policies and guidelines regarding hours, wages, and working conditions. Despite close cooperation with the AFL, these government efforts were insufficient to head off labor disputes or prevent strikes. Some 6000 strikes occurred during the 19 months of war; but most of them were of brief duration, and in general the AFL kept a restraining hand on its affiliates.

THE HERITAGE OF GOVERNMENT CONTROL

During the war period some 20 to 25 percent of production was geared to military needs. Government's efforts to rationalize, co-

ordinate, and generally shape the economy and manpower to meet the war crisis was without significant precedent in American history. Not the least of its effects was the new enthusiasm that the wartime experiment in market controls generated in the business community for similar measures in peacetime. Many leading industrialists who had been closely associated with the WIB and its coordinating industry committees thus endorsed the idea of continuing government involvement after the armistice, to ensure against a return to "destructive" competition, to set a floor on prices, and to perpetuate the involvement of government in maintaining stability in labor relations.

The wartime experiment, especially the experience with the WIB, persuaded many business leaders that "government control" did not necessarily mean control that would be hostile or damaging to their private interests. Indeed, many business spokesmen who a decade earlier had been in the forefront of the consolidation movement and champions of strictly private arrangements to reduce competition now sensed the enormous advantages they could derive from having government legitimize such arrangements. George Peek, an executive in the farm-equipment industry and later a major figure in New Deal farm programs of the 1930s, argued in 1918 and 1919 that the

country needed genuine "cooperation between Government, industry, and labor, so that we may eliminate . . . the possibility of the destructive forces" of competiton:

> *Proper legislation should be enacted to permit cooperation . . . in order that the lessons we have learned during the [war] may be capitalized in the interests of business and the public in peace times. Such questions as conservation to avoid wasteful use of materials, labor and capital; standardization of products and processes, price fixing under certain conditions, etc., should continue with Government cooperation.*[11]

But these ideas were resisted by the President. Whether because of Wilson's abiding New Freedom principles, despite their suspension and abridgment during the war, or because of his absorption with the postwar settlement and the League of Nations project, or because of his incapacitation by illness in 1919, the President permitted the abrupt dismantling of the wartime control apparatus immediately after the armistice.

FINANCING THE WAR

After the United States entered World War I it assumed the responsibility of financing not only its own participation but the expenses of its allies as well. The First Liberty Loan Act of April 1917 authorized the secretary of the Treasury, on the approval of the president, to make loans to Allied governments up to $10 billion. After that, private loans ceased. The problem of whether the war should be paid for immediately out of current taxes or shifted to later years by loans was resolved as usual by compromise. About one-third of the direct cost of the war was met by current taxation and about two-thirds by loans.

The expenses of the federal government had not greatly increased in the years before the war. The expenditures in 1916 ($674 million) were less than $35 million in excess of those of 1910. But succeeding years saw a tremendous increase. Within two years after the end of the war the federal government's interest charge alone had become greater than the entire cost of running the government before the war. The total direct cost of the war to the United States, including the $9.5 billion lent to

the Allies, was about $35.5 billion, an amount three times the total expenditures of the federal government during the first hundred years of its existence and more than $2 million an hour for the duration of the war. The national debt, which amounted to only $1 billion before the war, jumped to the unprecedented total of $26.6 billion by the end of August 1919.

War loans

To obtain these vast amounts spent at home and lent to the Allies, the government relied chiefly upon loans. Five bond issues were subscribed to by the people, in units of as low as $50 and with interest rates varying from 3.5 to 4.5 percent. The first four issues were known as Liberty Loans; the fifth, floated after the armistice, was called the Victory Liberty Loan. In the five loans the government asked for $18.5 billion, received subscriptions for $25 billion,

---

[11]Quoted in Rothbard, "War Collectivism," p. 106, and in Robert F. Himmelberg, "The War Industries Board and the Antitrust Question in November 1918," *Journal of American History*, 51 (1965): 72.

TABLE 20–3. AGGREGATE EXPENDITURES AND FOREIGN LOANS OF THE UNITED STATES GOVERNMENT, FISCAL YEARS 1917–1920

YEAR	NORMAL NET EXPENSE	NET WAR COST (EXCESS ABOVE ESTIMATED NORMAL EXPENSES)	
		EXCESS ARMY AND NAVY	EXCESS INTEREST, PENSIONS, ETC.
1917	$ 659,860,650	$ 393,852,949	$ 2,690,164
1918	682,458,285	6,770,295,897	120,952,611
1919	691,858,252	10,917,817,469	379,367,891
1920	826,550,410	1,073,892,747	1,073,392,874
	$2,860,727,597	$19,155,859,062	$1,576,403,540

YEAR	NET WAR COST (EXCESS ABOVE ESTIMATED NORMAL EXPENSES)		LOANS TO EUROPEAN GOVERNMENTS (LESS REPAYMENTS)
	SPECIAL WAR ACTIVITIES	TOTAL WAR COST	
1917	$ 33,060,510	$ 429,603,623	$ 885,000,000
1918	1,094,994,128	7,986,242,636	4,739,434,750
1919	2,487,710,885	13,784,896,245	3,470,280,265
1920	1,634,695,094	3,781,980,715	350,291,840
	$5,250,460,617	$25,982,723,219	$9,445,006,855

From E. B. Rosa, "Expenditures and Revenues of the Federal Government," *Annals of the American Academy of Political and Social Science*, 95, no. 184 (May 1921): 21, Table 3.

and allotted $21.4 billion. At the height of war enthusiasm almost $7 billion was subscribed in a single loan by over 22 million people. Of these war bonds, it is estimated that about $7 billion, or 30 percent, went to individuals with incomes of $2000 or less, about $10 billion to individuals with incomes of over $2000, and the remainder to corporations, including banks. In addition to the Victory and Liberty Loans, war saving certificates of $5 and war saving stamps of 25 cents were sold to a total of $1 billion. The grand total of the loans floated in these two ways was close to $22.5 billion.

Taxation

Not only was large-scale borrowing resorted to, but also new and heavier taxes were imposed. Contrary to the method pursued during the Civil War, the Democratic Congress, which had reduced the tariff in 1913, refused to consider import duties as an important source of revenue, and scarcely 5 percent of the taxes for 1918 were derived from this source. On the other hand, a comprehensive tax scheme was inaugurated. In 1913 the Sixteenth Amendment, authorizing an income tax, had been adopted. Income taxes on a sharply graduated progressive basis, ranging from 6 to 63 percent, were imposed. There also were war-profits taxes ranging from 15 to 60 percent,

new excise taxes on liquor and luxury goods, special war taxes on public utilities services, and an increase in estate taxes.

The total amount raised by federal taxation rose from below $800 million annually from 1914 to 1916 to $4.2 billion in 1918 and $4.6 billion in the year ending June 30, 1919. Together, the income and war-profits taxes yielded two-thirds of the total. Nevertheless, the American people were characteristically unwilling to finance the total war effort out of increased taxes. This had been true in the Civil War and would also be so in World War II and the Vietnam War. Much of the expenditures in World War I therefore was financed out of the inflationary increases in the money supply.

Inflation

So far as the monetary situation was concerned, the U. S. government and banks did not resort to freezes on settlements or suspension of specie payment, as occurred in other belligerent countries. There was, however, significant inflation, fed in part by the enormous amount of gold that was sent to the United States to purchase war materials or to escape the vicissitudes of war in the European counties; almost half the world's gold supply was in this country by 1919. Moreover, the Federal Reserve System adopted liberal credit policies.

And the vast issue of new government bonds was used as a reserve against bank-note issues and the expansion of deposit money. Commodity prices rose in response to increased demand as well as in response to money-supply expansion. Consequently price inflation proved nearly as great as it had been in the North during the Civil War.

THE EFFECTS OF U.S. PARTICIPATION IN WORLD WAR I

America's direct participation in the war was relatively brief, but it brought some major changes in the nation's own economy and in the economic relationship between the United States and other nations. The rapidity of productive expansion during the war left certain industries overly developed, in terms of what markets could absorb in the postwar period; among these industries were textiles, leather manufacturing, shipbuilding, and coal mining. A similar wartime expansion of agricultural production left farmers, once European production resumed after 1919, in a worse condition than after the Civil War. On the other hand, some industries, most notably chemicals, had been given a stimulus to expansion during the war that was sustained by continued postwar market growth.[12]

So far as costs were concerned, losses of life in combat were small compared to what the European nations suffered. There is no way, of course, to measure human suffering in dollar terms. But a comparison of economic costs of war is certainly possible. Total expenditures (in 1913 dollars) for all the belligerent nations were $82 billion, the United States accounting for $17 to $24 billion. The cost per capita in the United States was only one-third the cost in Britain and far less than in France, Germany, and other countries.[13]

In the war's aftermath, major readjustments in international markets occurred, not least of them the newly established role of the United States as the world's principal creditor nation. There was near-starvation to contend with in many parts of Europe in 1918 and 1919, and—over the longer run—the need to deal with the massive redistribution of wealth and economic power among nations that had occurred during the great conflict. The effects of both short-term and long-term readjustment upon the United States' own economy, and the way the new economic domestic order functioned, will be examined in the chapters following.

SELECTED READINGS

Birdsall, Paul, "Neutrality and Economic Pressures, 1914–1917," *Science and Society,* III (1939).

Clark, John Maurice, *The Costs of the World War to the American People* (New Haven: Yale University Press, 1931).

Cuff, Robert D., *The War Industries Board* (Baltimore: Johns Hopkins Press, 1973).

Douglas, Paul H., *Real Wages in the United States, 1890–1926* (Boston: Houghton Mifflin, 1930).

Himmelberg, Robert F., "The War Industries Board and the Antitrust Question in November, 1918," *Journal of American History,* LI (1965).

Kaufman, Burton I, *Efficiency and Expansion: Foreign Trade Organization in the Wilson Administration, 1913–1921* (Westport , Conn.: Greenwood, 1974)

Kerr, K. Austin, *American Railroad Politics, 1914–1920* (Pittsburgh: Pittsburgh University Press, 1968).

[12]In 1925 the index of manufacturing in the United States (1913 = 100) had reached 148; by contrast, Britain was at only 86 percent of 1913 output in manufacturing, France was at 114 percent, and Germany was at 95 percent (W. Arthur Lewis, *Economic Survey, 1919–1939* [London: Allen & Unwin, 1949], p. 35).

[13]War expenditures of the United States were equivalent to 8.7 percent of estimated national wealth. Comparable ratios for other countries were: Great Britain, 35 percent; France, 19 percent; and Germany, 32 percent (Margaret G. Myers, *A Financial History of the United States* [New York: Columbia University Press, 1970], p. 292).

Koistinen, Paul A. C., "The 'Industrial-Military Complex' in Perspective: World War I," *Business History Review,* XLI (1967).

Kuznets, Simon, *National Product in Wartime* (New York: National Bureau of Economic Research, 1945).

Parrini, Carl, *Heir to Empire* (Pittsburgh: University of Pittsburgh Press, 1969).

Paxson, Frederic L., *American Democracy and the World War* (Boston: Houghton Mifflin, 1939)

*Rothbard, Murray, and Radosh, Ronald, ed., *A New History of Leviathan: Essays on the Rise of the American Corporate State* (New York: Dutton, 1972).

Samuelson, Paul A., and Hagen, Everett, *After the War—1918–1920* (Washington, D. C.: National Resources Planning Board, 1943).

*Soule, George, *Prosperity Decade: From War to Depression, 1917–29* (New York: Holt, Rinehart and Winston, 1947). (Contains an annotated bibliography of primary and secondary sources).

Urofsky, Melvin, *Big Steel and the Wilson Administration* (Columbus: Ohio State University Press, 1969).

Watkins, Gordon S., *Labor Problems and Labor Administration in the United States During the World War* (Urbana: University of Illinois, Studies in the Social Sciences, 1919).

the modern economy

part 4

DEMOBILIZATION

To describe what happened after World War I as "reconstruction" would be a travesty of the term. Except for some decisions later made necessary in dealing with railroads and the merchant marine, neither the administration nor Congress gave much thought to postwar planning.[1] Few plans had been formulated to aid the 4 million veterans in search of jobs, to demobilize wartime industry, or to preserve some of the gains of wartime regulation of business. The one fundamental desire was to liquidate the war as quickly as possible and return to prewar policies, or to "normalcy," as Warren G. Harding called it in his presidential campaign of 1920. "Normalcy," of course, meant laissez-faire, and the time-honored tradition of minimum government was to dominate not only the period of reconversion but also the entire decade of the 1920s. Within a month after the armistice half of the uncompleted war contracts were canceled, and by the end of the year many of the government control boards had ceased to function. The War Industries Board began removing price controls two days after the armistice.

Despite lack of planning and military and economic demobilization so rapid as to seem chaotic, the nation not only survived the immediate strain but experienced a continuation of wartime prosperity. This is largely explained by the fact that the Treasury, in most unorthodox fashion, continued to spend during calender 1919 more than it received from the current income of the nation. This money went for loans to the Allies (largely spent in America), in shipbuilding and other industries not yet demobilized, in settlement of business contracts, and in current military expenditures and dismissal pay to soldiers. Although there was unemployment as a result of military demobilization and industrial reconversion, the latter was carried through with unusual speed and the income of the nation was not affected radically enough to curtail purchasing power. GNP was higher in 1919 than in 1918, and continued to rise through 1920. Moreover, two important industries, held back by the war, responded quickly to the coming of peace: the manufacture of automobiles and building construction. With all this went a generous expansion of bank loans to private individuals and a further rise in prices.

The depression of 1920–1922

This unusual postwar business activity lasted, with a brief setback, from late 1918 to January 1920. It ended in an acute but fortunately brief depression that troughed in July 1921. The reasons for the crash seem reasonably clear. First was the decline in government spending and the cessation of loans to the Allies. Combined with this was the situation in Europe, where the warring nations, impoverished by the struggle, staggering under crushing debts, and with exchange rates against them, no longer had either the funds or the credit to

[1]When Wilson was invited late in 1918 to address the Reconstruction Congress of American Industries, he could only reply, "You may be sure that I would send a message to the meeting in Atlantic City if I knew what message to send, but frankly I do not. It is a time when we must all thankfully take counsel and apply the wisest action to circumstances as they arise" (quoted in P. A. Samuelson and E. E. Hagen, *After the War—1918–1920* [Washington, D.C.: National Resources Planning Board, 1943], p. 6).

make extensive purchases abroad. This, of course, cut the market for American manufacturers and, as we shall see, brought disaster to American farmers. Exports and imports, which reached unheard-of figures in 1919 and 1920, declined radically in 1921.

Moreover, by 1920 the postwar boom had attained unhealthy proportions. Credit expansion had reached the legal limit and the banks were forced to retreat. The New York Federal Reserve Bank raised the rediscount rate to 6 percent in early 1920, the cyclical peak preceding the severe slump. Prices proved to be very sensitive to the slump, and dropped sharply. This price behavior was of course typical of the business cycle in the laissez-faire era.

Upon no group did the depression fall more heavily than upon the farmers. Encouraged by wartime prices and demand for foodstuffs, many farmers had borrowed heavily to purchase land and equipment in order to increase production, only to be caught in a glutted market in which values were declining to a point below the cost of production. Wheat, which sold for $2.15 a bushel in December 1919, dropped to $1.44 in December 1920, corn from $1.35 to 68 cents, oats from 72 cents to 47 cents, and cotton from 36 cents to 14 cents.

Labor, which had become accustomed to a higher standard of living, was loath to return to previous wage scales, and strongly organized labor succeeded in maintaining most of what it had gained during the war. Nevertheless, the number of those actively employed declined drastically during the depression, and the year 1921 saw an average of over 5 million, or almost 12 percent of the civilian labor force, unemployed. The average hourly wage as reported by the National Industrial Conference

Board was as follows: July 1914, 24.3 cents; peak, 1920, 62.1; December 1921, 48.2. Business as a whole probably suffered less than any other group, although, as in previous panics, the small businessman was hit hard. Mercantile and industrial insolvencies, which numbered 6451 in 1919, had more than tripled in 1921. Although bank suspensions reached a historic post–Civil War peak of 505 in 1921, with deposits of $172 million, the banks suspended were mainly rural banks with small capitalization, and the suspensions did not fundamentally endanger the general banking structure.

The effect of the economic collapse upon prices was to force them farther downward. According to the United States Department of Labor, the average index number of all wholesale prices of typical commodities (1926 = 100) was 154.4 in 1920, 97.6 in 1921, 96.7 in 1922, and 100.6 in 1923. With all the misery that the postwar depression undoubtedly caused, it had one fortunate effect. It pricked the bubble of inflation and substantially reduced prices. From 1922 to 1929 both retail food prices and the general cost of living remained relatively stationary—a remarkable phenomenon that sharply distinguished the prosperity of the 1920s from past prosperity periods.

By the end of 1922 deflation had run its course and industry had adjusted itself to a peacetime basis. Most of the principal industries were again working at close to capacity and unemployment fell to 3.2 percent of the civilian labor force by 1923. Certain industries, particularly agriculture, failed to respond to the renewed prosperity, however, and agricultural unrest remained a significant political and economic factor throughout the 1920s.

THE EXPANSIVE 1920s

In retrospect the postwar depression seems a typical phenomenon of the expansion of the war years. It is more difficult to explain the brevity of the depression and the intense business activity of the 1920s, a period in which the rest of the world was still suffering from economic postwar recession. Although there was much that was shaky about the economic life of the 1920s, the fact remains that during the six years from 1923 until the stock-market crash in the autumn of 1929, large groups of people and certain sections of the country enjoyed an era of

prosperity approaching that of wartime. A glance at Table 21–1 will show that the expansion of the 1920s, while not spectacular, was substantial. Real product, for example, rose at an annual rate of 4 percent.

Increased efficiency of production

One of the most valid explanations offered for the high level of economic activity and the prosperity of the 1920s was increased efficiency. This is suggested by the rise in product per capita in Table 21–1. It is further indicated by a

TABLE 21-1. ECONOMIC EXPANSION, 1920-1929

YEAR	INDUSTRIAL PRODUCTION (1913 = 100)	GROSS NATIONAL PRODUCT (BILLIONS, CURRENT DOLLARS)	REAL GROSS NATIONAL PRODUCT (1913 DOLLARS)	REAL GROSS NATIONAL PRODUCT, ANNUAL PER CAPITA (1913 DOLLARS)
1920	124.0	$85.3	$42.6	$400
1921	100.1	68.7	40.7	375
1922	125.9	69.5	43.7	397
1923	144.4	81.2	49.7	444
1924	137.7	81.8	50.7	444
1925	153.0	86.0	52.4	452
1926	163.1	92.0	55.8	475
1927	164.5	90.4	56.3	473
1928	171.8	92.2	57.1	474
1929	188.3	98.4	60.9	500

Sources: Industrial production: U.S. Department of Commerce, *Long-Term Economic Growth* (Washington, D.C.: U.S. Government Printing Office, October 1966), p. 169, Series A15. Gross national product: R. E. Lipsey, *Price and Quantity Trends in the Foreign Trade of the United States* (Princeton, N.J.: Princeton University Press, 1963), p. 424. Product per capita computed by the authors.

28 percent increase in real gross product per man-hour that took place between 1920 and 1929. Although the share of wage earners in the total national income increased only slightly, if at all, after 1920, real wages among certain groups showed a substantial advance.

Increased application of science to business helped to promote this efficiency. To many economists it is this last that furnishes the fundamental explanation. Wesley C. Mitchell, surveying the work of the Committee on Economic Changes, wrote in 1929:

Americans have applied intelligence to the day's work more effectively than ever before. . . . The whole process of putting science into industry has been followed more intensively than before; it has been supplemented by tentative efforts to put science into business management, trade-union policy and Government administration.[2]

New machinery introduced during reconversion, development of mass production and scientific management (advocated earlier by Frederick Winslow Taylor), a substantial reduction in average hours worked per week, and rapid expansion of research explain the greater productivity of labor. It is an acceleration of earlier tendencies rather than structural change that provides the key to an understanding of the economic lift of the 1920s.

[2]*Recent Economic Changes* (New York: McGraw-Hill, 1929), p. 862.

The automobile

Although industrial expansion in this decade was widespread, it rested fundamentally upon a sustained high level of investment in producers' durable goods,[3] the manufacture of automobiles and electrical equipment, and the boom in building construction. The great expansion in automobile production came in the decade and a half from 1914 to 1929. Indeed, the great era of growth of the automobile industry came to an end as the 1920s drew to a close. It is estimated that nearly 4 million jobs were created directly or indirectly by the automobile, a large figure in a total labor force of about 45 million in the mid-1920s. Although an appreciable part of the income that went into automobiles was income that would normally have been expended for other products, thereby injuring other industries, particularly transportation, the fact remains that enough new industry and wealth were created by the motor vehicle to speed up the whole economic machine. Of the many by-products of the automobile industry that created work and stimulated industry, the most important perhaps was better roads. By the mid-1920s outlays for federal-aid highway improvements were already over $200 million annually, to which must be added disbursements for state-administered highways in 1925 of over $600 million and county expenditures in excess of $100 million. Moreover, these aggregates seemed well insulated against serious declines in the ensuing depression years.

[3]Robert A. Gordon, *Business Fluctuations*, 2nd ed. (New York: Harper & Row, 1961), p. 408.

Electrical equipment
and consumers' durables

Next to the automobile, the most important industrial advance was in the manufacture of electric machinery and appliances. The penetration of these products was dramatic. Industry was turning to electric power and householders snapped up such appliances as electric irons, washing machines, vacuum cleaners, and refrigerators. The radio industry also had a phenomenal development in the 1920s, its product increasing in value from $10.6 million in 1921 to $411.6 million in 1929. It is little wonder that production of electric power more than doubled during the decade. The electrical industry produced machinery not only for factories and homes but also for the production of electric power itself. The value of its products almost tripled, from $809.6 million in 1921 to $2.334 billion in 1930.

Some historians have viewed the spread of consumers' durables of all sorts as a veritable revolution, but there was no revolution in a quantitative sense. Expenditures on automobiles did rise greatly as proportion of total consumer outlays. But with respect to household durables other than automobiles, the share of expenditures for the purchase of consumers' durable goods rose only moderately, as would be expected in a cyclical expansion. For the whole decade, outlays on durables averaged 11 percent of total consumption, only one percentage point above the average for the first decade of the twentieth century.[4]

The building boom

Outside of the spectacular development of the automobile and electrical equipment industries, the most striking aspect of the prosperous years of the mid-1920s was the extraordinary building boom, one of the greatest in our history. Normal construction demands, unmet during the war years, had to be met now, high rents stimulated building, a rapid increase of saving facilitated it, and modern improvements made even recent structures seem out of date. Building construction in 120 cities, which had reached the high point of $919 million in 1916, dropped to $373 million in 1918, rose to $1.2 billion in 1919, and finally to $3.4 billion in 1925, when the high point was reached.[5] Total

construction of all kinds for the country as a whole peaked in 1926 with total gross outlays of $12.8 billion (1929 prices).[6] Most of this was nonresidential, but $5.4 billion was housing.

Consumer finance

The vast consumer expenditures that supported this boom were undoubtedly stimulated by the development of high-pressure advertising and installment buying. Conservative estimates place the number of automobiles sold on installment in 1927 at around 60 percent, but other estimates for various years are much higher.[7] Seligman makes the conservative estimate of $4.9 billion as the total volume of retail installment sales for 1925. These figures were to increase in subsequent years until 15 percent of all goods were sold on the installment plan.

Despite the fact that most people were mortgaging their future income through installment buying and spending a large share of their wages in the purchase and maintenance of automobiles, the fact remains that during the speculative period from 1914 to 1925 the number of savings accounts increased nearly fourfold, from 11 million to 43 million and their amount from $8 billion to $23 billion. In addition it is notable that more than 25.5 million ordinary life insurance policies and over 76 million industrial policies were in force in the United States by the end of 1926, their total assets amounting to $12.5 billion. The number of building and loan policies increased from 3.1 million to 8.6 million in the ten years up to 1924, when over 11 million families owned their own homes.

Stagnation and
decline in an era of prosperity

Not all economists of the era were willing to grant unreservedly that this decade was a period of prosperity.[8] Prosperity, if such it was, was exceedingly uneven, for it did not include all sections or all groups. Coal mining, cotton manufacturing, shipbuilding, the shoe and leather business, the railroads, and particularly agriculture were stagnant or declining. The middle Atlantic, east-north-central, and Pacific states seemed prosperous; but New England, which suffered from the textile depression, and

---

[4]See H. G. Vatter and R. L. Thompson, "Consumer Asset Formation and Economic Growth: The United States Case," *Economic Journal*, 76 (June 1966):320. Data are from S. Kuznets, *Capital in the American Economy* (New York: National Bureau of Economic Research, 1966).

[5]*New International Yearbook, 1930*, p. 118.

[6]Gordon, *Business Fluctuations*, p. 407.

[7]E. R. A. Seligman, *The Economics of Installment Selling*, 2 vols. (New York: Harper & Row, 1927), vol. 1, pp. 111, 117; vol. 2, p. 426; and Presidential Committee on *Recent Economic Changes* (New York: McGraw-Hill, 1929), vol. 1, p. 390.

[8]Stuart Chase, *Prosperity: Fact or Myth?* (New York: Liveright, 1929), gives both sides of the picture.

the South, the agricultural areas of the Middle West, and the mountain sections, which suffered from the virtual failure of farm output to grow, did not participate greatly in the economic boom. Even in the most prosperous of these years there was considerable unemployment, due in part to technological improvements. Indeed, it is a striking fact that manufacturing employment was constant from 1919 to 1929, despite a strong rise in the index of manufacturing production.

These were not the only sour notes in the paean of self-congratulatory praise. Some students were quick to point out that, notwithstanding the increase in profits, in wages, and in the consumption of consumers' goods, practically no progress was being made in solving the problems of unemployment or of economic and old-age security. Moreover, the mania for gambling and speculation was a warning signal to the experienced economic navigator.

REVIVAL OF BUSINESS CONSOLIDATION

In spite of state and federal laws enacted in the hope of maintaining free competition and protecting the consumer, the consolidation of American business continued with little interruption. The decade following World War I witnessed a significant revival in business consolidation, comparable to that in the years 1897–1904. There was a steadily increasing number of mergers in manufacturing and mining, from 309 in 1922 to over 1200 in 1929. There was hardly an industry that did not show a notable development along this line. Important mergers took place in the automobile industry, in the manufacture of food, in the moving-picture industry, in banking, and most conspicuously, perhaps, in the field of public utilities. Over 3700 utility companies disappeared from 1919 to 1927, including many municipally operated concerns.[9]

Public utilities

While thousands of utility concerns were going out of existence, the larger ones that remained were being rapidly welded together into huge holding companies. "In 1915," asserted the Federal Trade Commission, "the 16 largest groups controlled about 22.8 per cent (generating capacity of the country), while in 1925 the 16 largest interests, consisting of 11 holding-company groups and five independent operating interests, controlled approximately 53 per cent of the country's total."[10] From 1925

until the Great Depression, this process of consolidation, chiefly through holding companies, went on rapidly. The speed with which the nation's electric power resources were consolidated brought the question of the effective control of this industry before the country as a problem of major importance, and the so-called power trust became a political issue after 1928.[11] Not only did the Depression end the period of utility consolidation, but under the Public Utility Holding Company Act of 1935 many of the fantastic structures erected during the 1920s were broken up.

New forms of consolidation

In the previous decades the consolidation of industry was closely identified with the development of the corporate form of ownership. By 1929, however, this form was so typical of American business, both large and small, that the process of consolidation was indicated in the census by a new classification of establishments according to type of management, whether independent or one of a number of plants under unified central control.

The heightened industrial activity of the decade 1919 to 1929 was not accompanied by any material alteration in the size of manufacturing establishments in general. The changes which occurred for the most part took other directions. Integration, for example, was accomplished not so much by the concentration of more wage earners in individual plants as by a common superstructure of ownership and control.[12]

[9]Ibid., p. 187.

[10]Federal Trade Commission, *Electric Power Industry: Supply of Electrical Equipment and Competitive Conditions,* 70th Cong., 1st sess., Senate Document 46, p. 176. The figures of the Federal Trade Commission are based on 1924 production. The Federal Power Commission, reporting as late as 1936, asserted that 90 percent of the electric generating capacity of the utility industry (book value $13 billion) was controlled by fifty-seven companies. Of these, twelve controlled 49.7 percent, and one of them, the Electric Bond and Share group, controlled 11.5 percent.

[11]See pp. 376–378.

[12]*Census of Manufactures, 1929* (Washington, D.C.: U.S. Government Printing Office, 1929), vol. 1, p. 61.

The postwar movement toward business consolidation differed also from consolidations of the past in several other respects. Not only did it include new industries that had appeared since the last era of consolidation, but it also embraced a much larger field than it did prior to 1917. For example, there was a rapid development of consolidation in retailing as well as in production. The growth of chain stores was particularly notable in the drug, tobacco, and grocery fields, and the small merchant came to feel the same competition from the large corporations that the small manufacturer had faced for decades.[13] The Great Atlantic and Pacific Tea Company, for example, which had 5,000 stores in 1922, had 17,500 by 1928, with an annual business of $750 million.

Bank consolidations

Space forbids a detailed treatment of consolidation in the various fields in which it operated, but special mention should be made of banking, where this trend was particularly evident. The lead was taken from 1928 to 1930 by the three titans in New York, when the National City Bank joined with the Farmers' Loan and Trust Company, the Guaranty Trust Company with the Bank of Commerce, and the Chase National Bank with the Equitable Trust Company, making the Chase the largest bank at that time in the world.

While large-scale mergers occurred among city banks, concentration of resources also took place through the development of chain banking. In California, where chain banking reached its greatest development, a huge holding company, the Transamerica Corporation, controlled the Bank of America of California and other large banks, which in turn had 500 chain banks spreading across the state. When the Pujo Committee insisted in 1919 that a "money trust" existed, financial consolidation was actually in its infancy.[14]

Reasons for revival of consolidation

What is the explanation for this extraordinary revival of consolidation during the 1920s? In the first place, the rather widespread industrial prosperity from 1923 to 1929 stimulated the movement. In spite of the fact that many mergers take place to soften bitter competition

and precarious prices, it is in times of prosperity that consolidations are more common.[15] The spirit of confidence and the ease of floating security issues may in part explain this. In the second place, wartime expansion had left American industry in an overbuilt and overexpanded condition, and salvation was sought by this method. In the third place, the changing attitude of the nation should be noted. The distrust of business consolidation that had been so evident up to 1910 appears to have been considerably lessened by the third decade of the century for a number of reasons: a tolerance for the tendency toward consolidation in a capitalist system, the futility of antitrust legislation to prevent it, the rising standard of living which made the masses less keen to scent evils in the movement, and finally, the incessant propaganda of big-business interests.

It must also be evident that the postwar movement toward concentration of control was greatly facilitated by the holding company, by the old methods of interlocking stockholding and directorates, and by the more recent devices of voting trusts and nonvoting stock. The result, as Laidler suggests, "has led to the development of combinations and trusts—vertical, horizontal and circular—with vaster ramifications, with greater resources than any combinations that have hitherto appeared."[16] In many cases concentration was carried to a point far beyond that justified by technological and organizational efficiency. By 1930 the 200 largest corporations controlled nearly half of all nonbanking corporate wealth (probably 38 percent of all business wealth), received 43.2 percent of the income of all nonbanking corporations, and were controlled by approximately 2000 individuals.[17]

Federal government and business consolidation

The changing attitude toward consolidation was, of course, reflected in the attitude and ac-

[13]F. Flügel and H. U. Faulkner, *Readings in the Economic and Social History of the United States* (New York: Harper & Row, 1929), pp. 600–607.

[14]Ibid., pp. 447–448.

[15]Willard Thorpe, in *Recent Economic Changes*, (New York: McGraw-Hill, 1929), vol. 1, pp. 183–184. See also Ralph L. Nelson, *Merger Movements in American Industry, 1895–1956* (Princeton, N.J.: Princeton University Press, 1959), Chap 5, App. C.

[16]H. W. Laidler, *Concentration of Control in American Industry* (New York: Crowell, 1931), p. 11. He defines a "circular merger" (p. 444) as a "merger of companies producing allied or complementary articles, usually, but not always, composed of those commodities which sell through the same channels or to the same market."

[17]A. A. Berle, Jr., and G. C. Means, *The Modern Corporation and Private Property*, rev. ed. (New York: Harcourt Brace Jovanovich, 1968), pp. 28, 29, 33.

tivities of the federal government, which were essentially conservative and business-oriented during the 1920s. In the first place, rather wide exemptions were made in the operation of the antitrust laws.[18] In the second place, the personnel of the Federal Trade Commission became more conservative, its rules of procedure were modified, and its work was rendered less effective. This situation was due in part to President Calvin Coolidge's very definite effort to pack the commission with members little interested in enforcing the law. Furthermore, Herbert Hoover, as secretary of commerce, contributed to the spread of monopolistic practices by vigorous promotion of industrial market control through trade associations. Finally, the decisions of the Supreme Court were of such a nature as to make public regulation of business increasingly difficult.

Figuratively speaking, the lid was taken off in 1920 when the Court refused to dissolve the United States Steel Company,[19] holding that neither mere size, short of actual monopoly, nor the possession of potential power to restrain trade was necessarily a violation of the Sherman Act. This decision was made despite common knowledge that United States Steel had virtually dictated prices in the industry for 15 years.

The earlier hope that regulation might be achieved by extending the principle of public interest over a larger number of activities was scotched when in three decisions in two years the Court held that gasoline dealers in Tennessee, employment agencies in New Jersey, and ticket brokers in New York did not fall into the category of "public interest" enterprises.[20] The Court also badly weakened effective regulation of public utilities, long recognized as vitally affecting the public interest, in a number of ways, but particularly by introducing into valuation cases the theory of "reproduction costs."[21] From a relatively simple and just method of determining rates, the Court made the problem extremely difficult and complex, with the consumer always at a disadvantage. The Court also appears to have put its stamp of approval upon trade associations, although the activities of such associations were often in contravention of the antitrust laws.[22] "It is highly significant," remarked one student in 1928, "that in recent years not a single adverse decision has been rendered requiring the dissolution of an actually functioning business merger."[23]

RAILROADS DURING THE POSTWAR PERIOD

One problem of reconstruction Congress could not evade: the future of the railroads. This was certainly a serious problem because, even without the deadly competitive threat of the motor vehicle, the growth curve of the railroad industry had reached maturation levels before World War I. Having taken over control and operation of the railroads during the war with the promise of return in substantially as good condition as when they were acquired, Congress could not delay action indefinitely. But the railroads were too important a part of the American economic structure for even a conservative Congress to restore to private owners without serious thought of the future.

In the active discussion of the future, Secretary of the Treasury William Gibbs McAdoo, director general of the Railroad Administration, advised continued government operation for five years. Labor, failing to anticipate the restrictions that would be placed upon unions in the government service in the future, strongly advocated government ownership and worked hard to popularize the "Plumb Plan." This proposal called for the government purchase of the roads and their operation by a board of direc-

[18]G. A. Fernby, "Special Privilege Under Our Federal Anti-Trust Laws," *Annals of the American Academy of Political and Social Science,* 147 (January 1930):38. Fernby noted 12 exempted groups: labor, farmers, planters, ranchmen, dairymen, nut and fruit growers, railroads, national banks, American steamship lines, those engaged in export business, producers of industrial alcohol, Philippine exporters. It should be noted, however, that the exemption extended to labor by the Clayton Act was weakened by Supreme Court decisions.
[19]251 U.S. 444.

[20]Williams v. Standard Oil Company of Louisiana, 278 U.S. 235 (1929); Rupert Ribnick v. Andrew F. McBride, 277 U.S. 350 (1928); Tyson v. Banton, 273 U.S. 418 (1927). See D. M. Keezer and Stacy May, *Public Control of Business* (New York: Harper & Row, 1930), pp. 108, 235; also H. S. Raushenbush, "Government Ownership and Control," *Annals of the American Academy of Political and Social Science,* 149 (May 1930):133.
[21]McCurdle v. Indianapolis Water Company, 272 U.S. 400 (1926).
[22]Maple Flooring Manufactures Association v. United States, 268 U.S. 563 (1925); Cement Manufacturers Protective Association v. United States, 268 U.S. 588 (1925).
[23]M. W. Watkins, "The Sherman Act," *Quarterly Journal of Economics,* (November 1928):37.

tors upon which the public, operating officers, and employees would be equally represented. The earnings, after operating expenses, maintenance, and liquidation of the purchase price had been taken care of, were to be divided between the government and the operating company. This ingenious scheme might have gone far toward solving many difficult aspects of the railroad problem, but it was too much of a social innovation to fit in with the conservative reaction following the war. Finally, Congress was spurred to action by President Wilson's threat to return the railroads to private hands on March 1, 1920, whether Congress acted or not.

The Transportation Act of 1920

The Transportation Act of February 28, 1920 (the Esch-Cummins Act), made up largely of amendments to the Interstate Commerce Act, increased the Interstate Commerce Commission to eleven members and gave it new responsibilities and powers. The commission was authorized to divide the country into rate districts, and in each of them to prescribe rates that "under honest, efficient, and economical management" would give a "fair return upon the aggregate value of the railroad property." In order that the weak roads might be preserved and the strong prevented from reaping too great profits, it was stipulated in a famous "recapture" clause that any carrier receiving in any year a net income in excess of 6 percent should turn over one-half of the excess to the Interstate Commerce Commission to be held as a revolving fund to be lent to the weak roads.

The commission was authorized to work out plans for the consolidation of the railroads into not less than 20 or more than 35 systems. At the same time it could permit pooling agreements subject to its supervision. It was given new power in regulating the capitalization of the roads, with the right to prescribe minimum as well as maximum rates. Additional powers were conferred upon it in the control of rolling stock and the use of terminal facilities and in respect to the control of new railroad construction. Severe strikes in 1919 brought home to the public the importance of uninterrupted transportation, and in the hope of preventing strikes the act created railroad boards of adjustment empowered to mediate between one road or group of roads and employees. It also established a railroad labor board of nine members, three representing the railroad employers, three representing the public, and three representing labor.

Up to this time the business of the commission had been essentially to protect the public from the railroads. By the act of 1920 it also became the commission's duty to see that the railroads received a fair return on the capital invested. The act showed a realization of the fact that efficiency would likely be promoted by further consolidation of many railroad systems.

Many of the innovations introduced by the Transportation Act of 1920 were undeniably desirable, but few of them were successfully applied. The labor board, unsatisfactory to management and labor alike, and powerless because its decisions were not binding, was abolished in 1926, and new experiments in labor mediation were tried.[24]

Efforts by the Interstate Commerce Commission to enforce the recapture clause of the 1920 act were fruitless, in spite of the fact that its constitutionality was upheld by the Supreme Court. The relentless opposition of the more prosperous railroads led the commission in 1930 to ask Congress to modify this part of the act. Great difficulties likewise were met in carrying out railroad consolidation. It was not until December 1929 that the commission finally offered a tentative scheme of consolidation into 21 systems. Even then little progress was made. No important consolidations were made under the act, and in 1940 Congress relieved the commission of any responsibility regarding consolidations.

Decline of the railroads

A survey of railroad statistics during the 1920s gives conclusive evidence of the weakened position of the railroads. While investment in rolling stock and other equipment substantially increased, and associated technological advances reduced total employment from 2 million in 1920 to 1.7 million in 1929, the burden of taxation grew heavier, freight revenue

---

[24]The Railroad Labor Act (Watson-Parker Act) of 1926 was amended by the Crosser-Dill Act of 1934. As a result of this legislation, disputes involving the interruption and application of existing agreements covering wages and working conditions might be referred by either party to a national railroad adjustment board created by the legislation. Disputes involving requested changes in wages or working agreements had first to be handled in conferences. If no settlement was reached, either party could take the dispute to a national mediation board. If the parties accepted arbitration, an arbitration board was created to decide the dispute. If either party refused to accept arbitration, the president could appoint an emergency board to investigate. The board was allowed 30 days to report, and no change in the conditions out of which the dispute arose could be made until 30 days after the report was submitted. This could delay a strike for 60 days in the hope that arbitration, investigation, and publicity might overcome the possibility of strikes. The important role played by unions under this act virtually ended the company unions in the railroads.

TABLE 21–2.   RAILROADS DURING THE 1920s

YEAR	INVESTMENT IN ROAD AND EQUIPMENT (IN MILLIONS)	FREIGHT REVENUE (IN MILLIONS)	PASSENGER REVENUE (IN MILLIONS)	PASSENGERS CARRIED (IN THOU-SANDS)	TAXES (IN MILLIONS)
1920	$19,849	$4,421	$1,305	1,269,913	$289
1925	23,217	4,648	1,065	901,963	366
1929	25,465	4,899	876	786,432	403

Source: Interstate Commerce Commission, *Statistics of Railways in the United States,* 1922, 1930, 1931. See also H. G. Moulton et al., *The American Transportation Problem* (Washington, D.C.: Brookings Institution, 1933), pp. 28, 29, 31, 77.

stagnated, and passenger traffic declined by one-third. The cause for this decline was obviously the rapid development of privately owned automobiles, motor buses, and trucks. Although domestic airplanes were carrying more than 400,000 passengers by 1930, competition from this source was not yet significant. It was obvious that motor transportation was enjoying temporary advantages during the 1920s because of the low burden of taxation under which it operated and the lack of efficient regulation, but these advantages to some extent disappeared in the 1930s.

In spite of this new competition, the low 4.3 percent average return on investment for Class I railroads[25] over the period 1921–1927, and the impending long-run stagnation of the industry, many were deceived by the large profits of the favored roads. Optimism was also fostered by a substantial investment performance. In the eight years 1920–1927, Class I railways and their subsidiaries spent over $5 billion for extensions, additions, and improvements. Until the depression that began in 1929 there was a steady increase in total track mileage, although "first-track" mileage just about held its own.

EXPANSION OF NONRAIL TRANSPORTATION FACILITIES

The revival of interest in the development of inland waterway transportation and in artificial waterways which occurred in the first decade of the century continued with little abatement, despite the tremendous development of motor vehicle traffic and the fact that railroads continued to improve their facilities and were adequately equipped to handle the normally slow-growing demand. A partial explanation is found in the fact that inland water transportation on the Great Lakes and the contributory canals had shown a notable increase, and in the recognition that water transportation is cheaper than rail for many kinds of bulk freight and should be encouraged.[26] A great impetus was undoubtedly also given by the agricultural distress of the Middle West during the 1920s and early 1930s and by the conviction that cheaper all-water routes to foreign markets would help to remedy the situation.

Two major projects had long been discussed: (1) the Lakes-to-the-Gulf Deep Waterway, which would follow the line of the Chicago Sanitary Drainage Canal, the Illinois and Michigan Canal, and the Mississippi River; and (2) the St. Lawrence Ship Canal. The first project, it was hoped, would restore the Mississippi traffic and provide a direct route from the Mississippi Valley to South American ports; the latter would connect the great agricultural regions of the Middle West with Europe by a direct all-water route.

The Lakes-to-Gulf Deep Waterway

The Lakes-to-the-Gulf Deep Waterway had the endorsement of successive administrations following Theodore Roosevelt's, and the project was furthered after 1917 by a succession of legislative acts and appropriations. The whole endeavor was entangled with the expensive

[26]In round numbers, the freight carried on the Sault Ste. Marie increased from 62.4 million tons in 1910 to 92.6 million in 1929, only to drop to 20.5 million in 1932. Tonnage on the Erie and other New York canals barely held its own. The freight carried in 1929 through the Sault Ste. Marie alone was more than three times that carried through the Panama Canal (*Statistical Abstract, 1930,* pp. 435, 436, 442).

[25]Class I railways prior to 1956 were those companies whose individual operating revenues amounted to $1 million or more annually. Beginning in that year the designation was applied to companies having operating revenues of $3 million or above. They represent about 95 percent of the mileage of the country.

problem of flood control, but the political strength of those desiring both flood control and inland water routes was great enough to achieve both objects. With the opening in 1933 of the Illinois River, which linked Lake Michigan, the Illinois River, and the Mississippi by canal, the through route from the Great Lakes to the Gulf was made available.

The St. Lawrence Seaway

The St. Lawrence Ship Canal project expressed an old dream of the Canadians dating back to their competitive response to the completion of the Erie Canal in 1825. The scheme met strong opposition in New York State, where over $200 million had been invested since 1903 in the Barge Canal (an enlargement and improvement of the Erie Canal) and which demanded an all-American route. It also encountered stiff opposition from the railroads and the various seaport cities of New England and the middle Atlantic states. But powerful interests in the Lakes states were strongly for it.

After various investigations had been made, Secretary Hoover recommended the St. Lawrence route as cheaper to construct, as a shorter route to northern Europe, and as providing greater savings to the shipper than the New York route. His advocacy of this project failed to accomplish much during his administration as president.

His successor, President Franklin D. Roosevelt, urged the Senate in 1934 to ratify the treaty that would make possible the construction of this project, but the Senate failed to act. On the ground that it was necessary for the long-range defense needs of both Canada and the United States, it was revived in 1941 in the form of an agreement (requiring only a majority approval of Congress) between the two nations. Congress, however, delayed action. Canada, in the meantime, announced its intention of developing this project whether the United States participated or not. However, in May 1954 Congress passed the Wiley-Dondero Act, providing for U.S. participation in the construction and administration of the St. Lawrence Seaway Channel, and the waterway was opened in 1959.

The Seaway diverted considerable tonnages of bulk freight from other means of transport. It helped Chicago to become one of the country's busiest seaports. In the year before the Seaway opened, Chicago handled 315,000 short tons of overseas cargo. This figure had risen to 4.5

million short tons by the late 1960s.[27] Ironically, imported iron ore could be brought by the Seaway to the blast furnaces of steel plants in the Midwest heartland, but so could competing finished steel from Europe be brought to steel consumers. The great threat to the Seaway in the 1970s appears to be "containerization" of products, which requires much larger ships than envisioned by the waterway's designers. The electric power developments connected with the Seaway appear to have a brighter future.

Pipelines

One fast-growing form of transport in the 1920s was originally, although no longer uniquely, connected with one product. The product is petroleum and the pipeline is the means of transport. Both date back into the nineteenth century; the first pipeline, running from the western Pennsylvania fields to the Atlantic coast, was built in 1878. On the eve of World War I there were already about 10,000 miles in the system, consisting of "gathering lines" from wells to collection points and permanent trunk lines linking major collection points with consuming or shipping centers. With the rise of the motor vehicle, petroleum production zoomed. Therefore, as we would expect, the prosperity of the 1920s was heavily underwritten by the triumvirate of motor vehicles, petroleum, and petroleum carriers (including railroad tank cars). Crude petroleum output—not all of which went into gasoline, of course—rose from 378 million barrels of 42 gallons in 1919 to slightly over 1 billion barrels in 1929.

The pipelines captured a large proportion of this expansion, and by 1929 there were almost 86,000 miles of gathering and trunk lines in operation. By the late 1960s they accounted for 20 percent by volume of all domestic intercity freight traffic, and by then had also become the main vehicle of natural gas transportation. The future looked even brighter for the industry, for the large-scale transport of solids by pipeline was by then a definite prospect. (See p. 451.)

The automobile

At the opening of World War I the automobile had scarcely completed the experimental stage. Its use was still largely confined to the wealthy and upper middle classes, the number of passenger cars produced in the United States in 1914 being 548,139, and the number of

[27]*Illinois Business Review*, Vol. 27, no. 1 (January 1970), p. 3.

motor trucks and buses only 24,900. During the next 15 years the industry had its greatest era of growth and the automobile became a pleasure and business vehicle for all classes of people.

The production of motor vehicles became the nation's leading manufacturing industry in 1929, just about the time its era of greatest relative growth permanently tapered off. This maturation process was accompanied by maturation in another sense. The industry that was a leading pioneer in mass-production continuous-assembly technology was fast becoming a small, tight-knit, exclusive group of large corporations dominated by a single giant. By the end of the 1920s the early structure of many small and medium-sized firms had disappeared, and for all practical purposes new, abiding entry into motor vehicle production was forever closed.[28] If the American dream had become ownership of a motor car, the American dream of free enterprise—many producers, vigorous price competition, and open entry for newcomers—was not to be realized in the country's leading manufacturing activity.

A study of transportation published in the early 1930s commented that the diffusion of the automobile within the population, vertically and horizontally had been without precedent.

> It has increased the mobility of people in all classes of society, and given them a control over their own movements that could not have been foreseen thirty years ago. It is bringing into existence new and integrated transportation systems, both within local communities, which it is helping to transform into larger and more closely knit regional urban areas, and between more distant points. It has multiplied enormously man's potential personal contacts in remote communities, and with his fellow townsmen as well. It is an innovation that has been reshaping many phases of contemporary life.[29]

When the saga of the motor car is finally written, it may well show that the coming of what John Kenneth Galbraith has harshly called "the insolent chariot" inaugurated a second industrial and social revolution. Yet not many in the boisterous 1920s envisioned the long-run implications of that revolution. Even fewer anticipated the later widespread hostility to the automobile represented by the comment of former Secretary of the Interior Stewart Udall on January 26, 1973, that "the automobile is the single most wasteful, destructive thing we've done in—and to—this generation."[30]

Road building

The agitation for better roads, essentially based on the desire to bring rural transportation to a level with urban transportation, had been stimulated in the late 1880s and early 1890s by the bicycle craze. It was given increased impetus by the automobile, but the work done prior to World War I was largely in local and state hands. Ignoring the constitutional limitations pointed out by Andrew Jackson in the Maysville Road veto, the federal government reverted in 1916 to the old policy that had built the National Road. By the Rural Post Roads Act of 1916, supplemented by subsequent legislation, it began aiding the states to build primary interstate roads and secondary connecting roads, the states contributing an amount equal to that given by the federal government.

But most of the burgeoning outlays for highway construction and maintenance in the 1920s were financed by the states, initially through bond issues and general taxes, later through the ultimately established method of highway user taxes. The gasoline tax, for example, was inaugurated in 1920, the year before Henry Ford produced his millionth car, and the same year in which he marketed the Model T at $440. Unlike the unstable pattern that had earlier characterized private investment in railroad construction, public highway building investment, which rose to over 8 percent of the total of all construction in the country in 1929, followed a fairly steady expansion path throughout the 1920s. Here was another activity related to the motor vehicle that underwrote the Great Illusion of unending prosperity.

Motor trucks

Motor truck production, like the stock of farm tractors, grew even more rapidly than production of passenger cars during the decade. Opposition from the railroads grew apace, and the attempt was made to stifle the growth of the industry through heavy user tax-

---

[28]See H. G. Vatter, "The Closure of Entry in the American Automobile Industry," *Oxford Economic Papers* (new series), 4, no. 3 (October 1952):213–234. The giant in the early twenties was, of course, Ford. General Motors became the dominant firm in 1927.

[29]M. M. Willey and S. A. Rice, *Communication Agencies and Social Life* (New York: McGraw-Hill, 1933) pp. 39–40.

[30]As reported in the Portland *Oregonian*, January 27, 1973.

TABLE 21–3.   AIRPLANE PASSENGER, FREIGHT, AND MAIL TRAFFIC, 1928–1940

YEAR	PASSENGERS	EXPRESS AND FREIGHT (POUNDS)	MAIL (POUNDS)	MILES FLOWN
1928	49,713	216,644	4,063,173	10,673,450
1929	173,405	257,443	7,772,014	25,141,499
1930	417,505	468,571	8,513,675	36,945,203
1931	522,345	1,151,348	9,643,211	47,385,987
1932	540,681	1,033,970	7,908,723	50,932,967
1933	493,141	1,510,215	7,362,180	48,771,533
1940	3,185,278	—	10,117,858	119,517,000

Source: *Statistical Abstract, 1933,* p. 371, for figures through 1932; ibid., *1940,* p. 457.

es, road use restrictions, and generally rigorous public utility regulation. But powerful shipper interests early saw the superior flexibility of shipment by truck, especially for goods of high value relative to weight and for comparatively short hauls. This gave the trucking industry, then organized mostly by small and middle-sized enterprises, a foothold that was later to devastate the rail freight business, yielding to the truckers well over a fifth of the volume of domestic intercity freight traffic by the early 1970s.

The airplane
Up to 1917 the story of aviation is largely a story of technical advance. Not until the early 1930s did the airplane become significant in the economic life of the nation; its importance up to that time had been chiefly military. By 1914 the airplane was sufficiently developed to be used in combat service in World War I, but its main value was in the field of reconnaissance and combat control. A glance at Table 21–3 will indicate the comparatively trivial commercial importance of aviation in the 1920s. Then came a sudden spurt from 1929 to 1931. Unlike most industries and other types of transportation, commercial aviation held its own during the depression. A second rapid advance came in the middle 1930s and a third boom at the end of World War II.

The U.S. government was the chief customer of the manufacturers of aviation supplies. In 1931, for example, 812 of the 2394 planes produced were military units. Actual transportation by air was even more dependent upon government aid than was manufacturing. The government became interested in aviation first in its military aspects and then in its commercial ones. In 1918 an experimental airmail service was established jointly by the Post Office Department and the army. This was soon aban-doned, but in the following year the Post Office Department, acting alone, inaugurated a mail service between Chicago and Cleveland, which in 1924 was extended to transcontinental proportions. When a government service was finally established on a satisfactory basis, Congress suddenly reversed itself and virtually ordered the Post Office Department to cease carrying airmail and to contract the business to private concerns. The result has been the subsidization of American aviation by means of airmail contracts.[31]

In the second period of rapid expansion during the middle 1930s, aviation began to free itself from its utter dependence upon government subsidy. After 1934 its chief source of revenue was its passenger traffic. Beginning in 1938, when thoroughgoing federal regulation was instituted under the Civil Aeronautics Act, the government received more from postal revenues than it paid to airmail carriers. In 1940 commercial passenger planes flew over 94 million miles and carried over 3 million passengers over a nation equipped with 2600 airports and landing fields. This was about 10 percent of the passengers carried on Pullman trains. Planes were carrying one-seventh of the first-class mail and one-fourth of the transcontinental mail. But few anticipated that the airlines would become the country's leading common carrier of intercity passenger traffic.

Stagnation of employment in transportation and communications
The general picture of expansion should not obscure the fact of slow growth in employment

---

[31]Estimates for 1932 put the various kinds of federal aid to air transportation at $26.3 million, and contributions from passenger and postal carriers at more than $15 million. In that year the government paid airmail carriers $19.9 million but received only $6 million in postal revenue.

in the transport and communications sector of the economy as a whole. Output did grow, but gains in productivity per worker generally offset the output growth, so that the number of persons engaged hardly increased. We have already noted the failure of total manufacturing employment to grow, and this was in spite of the increase in workers in the automobile industry. Similarly, the total number of em-ployees in transportation and other public utility industries, including the telephone industry, was 4 million in 1920 and 3.9 million in the peak year of 1929. It was therefore fortunate that employment in other activities, such as wholesale and retail trade, finance, insurance and real estate, and various private service activities was at least slowly growing during that peculiar prosperity decade.

THE STAGNATION OF AGRICULTURE

Just as the American farmers found themselves confronted with serious economic crises in the years following the Napoleonic and Civil wars, so also after World War I they were faced by a serious situation. While most economic interests recovered rapidly after the deflation of 1920 and 1921, agricultural employment and income failed to respond. Two basic factors help to explain this: (1) overproduction in the markets of the world brought on by the demands of the war and by improved agricultural machinery, particularly the gasoline tractor, and (2) the worldwide falling off in demand and the deflation of prices after the war. The first of these produced an agricultural revolution at a time when increased production was only temporarily necessary. The second, the worldwide deflation, was particularly hard upon agriculture, for in periods of deflation and falling prices, raw materials, and especially agricultural products, usually suffer first and worst. Whereas wages and retail prices declined more slowly, the bottom was knocked completely out of agricultural prices and the farmer found his income out of line with that of other groups.

Moreover, the European industrial countries suffered a serious decline in birth rate and population growth during the 1920s, largely because of the massive mortality among young men in World War I. This resulted in a slackening of their demand for food and fiber, a shift that hurt the terms of trade for all the primary producing countries and the U.S. farm sector.

Farmers were unable to adjust their production to market demands as quickly as manufacturers. Indeed, when prices fell they tended to work harder to produce more in order to maintain total income, and this only added to the oversupply. Manufacturers, on the other hand, cut output and employment and suffered only excess capacity. The war encouraged overexpansion and overemphasis upon the one-crop system, both of which proved ruinous in the postwar years. Finally, before any satisfactory adjustment was achieved, a second period of worldwide depression began in 1929.

The decline in farm prices and land values

The prices of most agricultural commodities recovered somewhat from 1923 to 1926, but then dropped again. With the decline in prices, the bankruptcy rate jumped from 6.4 percent of all farms in 1920 to an average for 1924–1926 of 17.7 percent, after which it drifted downwards to 8.7 in 1929. Total farm mortgage debt rose by almost $2 billion between 1920 and 1928, an increase of 19 percent from 1920 to 1925 and a rise of 1 percent from 1925 to 1928.[32] Under the circumstances, a decline in land values was to be expected, but the drop in the value of agricultural property from $67 billion in 1920 to $56 billion in 1927 was staggering.[33] At the same time, the population on farms declined from 31 million in 1920 to 30 million in 1930, with a net movement from farms during the decade of about 600,000 per year.[34] Expansion of the productive area, which had been rapid during the war, ceased immediately. Between 1919 and 1924, land in farms increased only 3 percent.[35] Total farm production was only 12 percent higher in 1929 than it was in 1919.

[32]The figures for the three years are $7.9 billion in 1920, $9.4 billion in 1925, and $9.5 billion in 1928. The bankruptcy rates are from U.S. Department of Agriculture, *Yearbook of Agricultural Statistics*, 1936, p. 354.

[33]*Historical Statistics of the United States*, series K-3, p. 278. During this period capital invested in corporations increased from $99 billion to $134 billion.

[34]*Yearbook of Agriculture, 1934*, p. 699. The figure 600,000 represents roughly the excess of those leaving the farms over those arriving at farms from the cities.

[35]*Historical Statistics of the United States*, series K-2, p. 278.

TABLE 21–4.   INDEX NUMBERS OF FARM PRICES, PRICES PAID BY FARMERS, FARM WAGES, TAXES, AND GROSS INCOME, 1910–1933 (1910–1914 = 100)

DATE	PRICES RECEIVED FOR FARM PRODUCTS	PRICES PAID BY FARMERS FOR COMMODITIES USED IN		FARM WAGES PAID TO HIRED LABOR	TAXES ON FARM PROPERTY (1914 = 100)	GROSS FARM INCOME
		LIVING	PRODUCTION			
1910	103	98	98	97	–	101
1911	95	100	103	97	–	88
1912	99	101	98	101	–	108
1913	100	100	102	104	–	97
1914	102	102	99	101	100	105
1915	100	107	104	102	102	108
1916	117	124	124	112	104	117
1917	176	147	151	140	106	188
1918	200	177	174	176	118	207
1919	209	210	192	206	130	218
1920	205	222	174	239	155	209
1921	116	161	141	150	217	120
1922	123	156	139	146	232	134
1923	134	160	141	166	246	148
1924	134	159	143	166	249	144
1925	147	164	147	168	250	174
1926	136	162	146	171	253	162
1927	131	159	145	170	258	157
1928	139	160	148	169	263	162
1929	138	158	147	170	267	168
1930	117	148	140	152	266	132
1931	80	126	122	116	–	106
1932	57	108	107	86	–	76
1933	63	109	108	80	–	79

Source: *Yearbook of Agriculture, 1932,* p. 900, and ibid., *1934,* p. 706. Farm gross income calculated from R. E. Lipsey, *Price and Quantity Trends in the Foreign Trade of the United States* (Princeton, N.J.: Princeton University Press, 1963), pp. 425–426, Appendix G, Table G-9.

Table 21–4 gives a reasonably accurate picture of the agricultural situation in the prewar and postwar years. The table shows how, after the slump of 1921, prices received by farmers fell behind the prices they paid and with one exception remained there throughout the remaining years of nonfarm prosperity. Farm prices were chronically below the 1910–1914 "par." The table also reveals the fact that gross farm income never again in the decade reached its 1920 level, even as the GNP fully recovered by 1923 and continued to rise thereafter. Agriculture was an ominous undercurrent in the mainstream of the great illusion, an undercurrent that should not have been ignored, for farm income was still about 10 percent of GNP in the 1920s.

The growth of farm tenancy

Since the savings of farmers customarily are invested in land and buildings, the decline of farm values and agricultural prices meant the wiping out of lifetime savings, and the increase in bankruptcy meant a growth in tenancy. For the nation as a whole, the growth in tenancy rose from 38 percent in 1920 to 42 percent in 1930. Moreover, this tenancy was of a discouraging type. Instead of a rung on the ladder upward to independent ownership, as had often been the case in the past, it was a descent toward the status of the agricultural laborer. There was no opportunity under these contracting conditions for the millions of southern blacks, whose migration from the South had become massive after 1910, to find a place in northern agriculture. Black migration in the 1920s, as before and after, was to northern and western cities.

The farm bloc

It was inevitable that the agricultural depression would have reverberations in politics and would result in legislation. In May 1921 senators and representatives of both parties from the agricultural states organized the farm bloc and led the movement for legislation to provide public subsidy to this "disadvantaged group." It is to be noted that this move considerably antedated the onset of the New Deal. Thoroughgoing legislation, the farm bloc asserted, was necessary not only to help remedy a very serious short-run situation, but also to put the farmers on an equal long-run status with other economic groups protected and favored by the federal government. The result of this agitation led to a considerable amount of legislation.[36]

The various tariff measures, including the Emergency Tariff of 1921, the Fordney-McCumber Tariff of 1922, and the Hawley-Smoot Tariff of 1930, all made an effort to protect agricultural commodities from foreign competition. The irony of "helping" an export industry, such as American agriculture, by a tariff was at last becoming evident even to Republican farm leaders, and this time-honored sop no longer satisfied them. The blind spot in the whole agricultural program of the 1920s was the failure of farm leaders to realize that in normal peacetime the private foreign market for agricultural products was permanently contracted. The future for U.S. agriculture lay mainly in public subsidy and in the frontier of higher productivity through improved technology and the application of more capital in production.

Credit and cooperative measures

A number of other acts were passed, designed to extend better credit to farmers and encourage them in cooperative efforts. These included revival in 1921 of the War Finance Corporation to finance the exportation of agricultural products and handle emergency agricultural credits, the Agricultural Credits Act of 1923,[37] and the Agricultural Marketing Act of 1929. These and other measures were de-

signed to extend the work inaugurated by the Federal Farm Loan Act of 1916.

The McNary-Haugen bills

Valuable as these acts might be, they did not effectively remedy the situation, and the more radical of the agricultural group pressed for a third type of legislation, which would actually raise prices. This hope was incorporated in the McNary-Haugen bills, twice passed by Congress in 1927 and 1928 and vetoed both times by President Coolidge.

While the details of the McNary-Haugen bills differed somewhat, the general method to be employed was the same. The bills provided that a government corporation should purchase certain agricultural products at a price that would yield a fair profit, and that the surplus should be sold abroad at the lower world price, the loss on the foreign sales to be assessed in the form of an equalization fee against every unit of the product sold by the producer. The net price to the producer would be the fixed price minus the equalization fee; the larger the surplus, the larger the fee and the smaller the return to the farmer. This kind of inducement to restrict output, a necessary part of any such monopolistic price-protection program, was utterly insufficient to contain the flood of surpluses. The chief significance of the agitation for the McNary-Haugen bills was that it accustomed both farmers and the urban population to the idea of price fixing, and thus prepared the way for the more comprehensive agricultural legislation of the New Deal.

The Agricultural Marketing Act of 1929

Both parties found it expedient to pledge themselves to agricultural relief in 1928, and after the veto of the second McNary-Haugen bill the Hoover administration sanctioned the Agricultural Marketing Act of 1929. By this act Congress appropriated $500 million to be loaned by a federal farm board to cooperative associations in the hope that this would promote "orderly" marketing and "sound" policies. But the inability of the board to restrict output and the downward trend of domestic and world prices brought disaster to its efforts. By mid-summer of 1932 the board—that is, American taxpayers—had lost $354 million. If agriculture was to be given a specially protected status, stronger techniques of monopoly control would have to be applied. And they were applied under the New Deal.

---

[36]A summary of this legislation from 1920 to 1928 is given in J. D. Black, *Agricultural Reform in the United States* (New York: McGraw-Hill, 1929), pp. 69–73, and in C. C. Davis, "The Development of Agricultural Policy Since the End of the World War," *Yearbook of Agriculture, 1940*, pp. 297–326. See also James H. Shideler, *Farm Crisis, 1919–1923* (Berkeley: University of California Press, 1957).

[37]This act set up a federal intermediate credit bank in each of the federal land bank districts, with a capitalization of $5 million and the power to issue debentures to ten times that amount. The purpose was to extend personal and collateral credit for periods intermediate between the usual short-term commercial loan and the long-term obligations secured by land.

THE DECLINE OF ORGANIZED LABOR

Although the international position of labor was stronger after World War I, the position of American labor was decidedly weaker. The American Federation of Labor, proudly conscious of its war record, laid down at its annual convention in 1919 a "reconstruction program" that called for the high-sounding objective of "democracy in industry," and the more bread-and-butter goals of abolition of unemployment, higher wages, shorter hours, equal pay to women for equal work, abolition of child labor, and the right of public employees to organize and bargain collectively. It also demanded curtailment of the power of the judiciary, government ownership of public and semipublic utilities, development and operation of waterpower, better federal and state regulation of corporations, absolute freedom of expression and association, extension of workmen's compensation, establishment of government employment agencies and the abolition of those conducted for private profit, the building of model homes by the government, aid in enabling workers to own their own homes, and a two-year cessation of immigration.

The failure of strike action

If labor had any idea that a grateful republic would be sympathetic to this program, it was doomed to speedy disillusionment. In the reaction against labor's wartime eminence which settled dismally upon the nation in the postwar years, labor found itself attacked from many quarters and its tenuous power badly impaired. In the economic depression that followed in the wake of war expansion, all but the most powerfully organized workers experienced wage decreases. Strikes to prevent wage deflation or to secure higher wages were generally unsuccessful. The federal government broke up a bituminous coal strike in 1919 by obtaining a sweeping injunction authorized, according to the attorney general, under the Lever Fuel and Food Control Act of 1917. A railroad shopmen's strike in 1919 collapsed through government opposition and the failure of labor to cooperate. The failure of the important steel strike in that same year would crush all effective unionization in that strategic industry for nearly two decades.

The speed with which the hard-earned gains of labor were disappearing and the ease with which they did so amazed Gompers, and he bitterly denounced the Bourbon policies of American industrialists. Conservative, craft-bound labor leadership, however, was an important cause.[38] The steel strike of 1919, for example, was a life-and-death struggle for industry-wide organization in which the demands of labor were eminently fair, the sympathy of a large element of the public was with them, and the chances for success were at least even. A united front on the part of American labor might have seen a different outcome. In 1919 there were nine major industrial disputes, in each of which more than 90,000 persons were involved, and in that year more than 4 million workers went on strike.[39] Most of the important conflicts terminated unsuccessfully for labor.

The courts and organized capital

Labor was also experiencing losses in other directions. The postwar depression and the absorption of 4 million soldiers increased the competition for jobs; corporations, as they saw their profits decline, curtailed their welfare operations; public interest in social legislation declined; and the hand of the judiciary grew heavier. The courts, which during the war had complacently watched constitutional and human rights repeatedly violated, continued to countenance extralegal proceedings, particularly those used to hinder the activities of labor radicals. At the same time, business, taking a leaf from war experience, increased the use of the labor spy and the *agent provocateur* and called repeatedly upon the state militia.

While organized labor grew weaker, organized capital became stronger. Manufacturers' associations devoted increased attention to combating labor and in many communities secured the close cooperation of chambers of

---

[38] Aroused to action in 1924, the AFL executive committee, for the first time in its history, officially supported a presidential candidate, Robert La Follette, whose consistent labor record could not be ignored. His defeat merely served to convince labor leaders of the correctness of their former policy, which, if possible, became more conservative than ever regarding political action. Not until 1952 did the AFL in annual session again endorse a presidential candidate, in this case Adlai E. Stevenson.

[39] The number of work stoppages reported for the year was 3630. See *Monthly Labor Review*, July 1929. The figures of workers on strike since World War I are interesting. The 4.2 million in 1919 dropped to 1.1 million in 1921, then rose in 1922 during the railroad strike, dropped to 428,000 in 1925 and again to 289,000 in 1929. See G. F. Bloom and H. R. Northrup, *Economics of Labor Relations*, 6th ed. (Homewood, Ill.: Irwin, 1969), p. 212, Table 7–2.

commerce. This effort to break the power of labor and promote the open shop was euphemistically called the American Plan and met with considerable success.

Particularly detrimental to labor were the reactionary decisions of the state and federal judiciary. Federal child-labor laws were declared unconstitutional in 1918 and 1922, and in 1923 a minimum-wage law for women in the District of Columbia fell under the ban of the Court. Not only was social legislation endangered, but the very existence of labor unions was jeopardized. In the Danbury Hatters' Case (1908) and other decisions, the Supreme Court had held that labor unions and their individual members were responsible without limit for actions of union officers which they had in any way sanctioned. In 1915 it declared unconstitutional a state statute aimed to prevent an employer from forcing an employee to agree not to join a union during the employee's term of service ("yellow-dog contract"),[40] and it even upheld a decision that it was illegal to organize employees who signed a yellow-dog contract.[41] It cut the heart out of the protection that Congress intended to give labor in the Clayton Act by declaring a secondary boycott illegal[42] and by permitting suit against an unincorporated union for violation of that act.[43] Particularly dangerous to labor was the continued and growing use of the injunction in labor disputes, a procedure that the AFL had long fought consistently and bitterly.

Company unions and employee stock ownership

Difficult as it was to counteract the decisions of a conservative judiciary, the activities of the *agent provocateur,* and the decline of middle-class sympathy, organized labor now found its influence undermined in much subtler ways. One of the chief weapons used to disrupt the organized labor movement in the 1920s was the company union, that is, a labor organization comprised of employees in only one company, not affiliated with any labor union, whose leaders are subservient to the management of that firm. Prior to 1917 not more than a dozen important plants had introduced this system,

but by 1927 there were hundreds, with a membership of over 1.4 million.

A more subtle weapon directed against organized labor was employee stock ownership. Although the promotion of this weapon could be ethically validated on the grounds that it improved morale, diminished labor discontent and turnover, and developed cooperative personnel, its chief effect was to weaken the organized labor movement. The leadership in the promotion of stock ownership in the utilities was taken by the American Telephone and Telegraph Company; in the industrial field by the Eastman Kodak Company, United States Steel, and Bethlehem Steel; in rails by the New York Central and the Pennsylvania; and in oil by the Standard Oil Company.[44] Encouraged chiefly through installment purchases, the number of employee stockholders grew to well over a million, and certain devotees of Pollyanna economics extravagantly and incorrectly hailed it as an indication of another economic revolution.[45]

Even the most casual examination quickly dispels the dream that any economic millennium was being achieved through this medium. A Federal Trade Commission investigation made in 1922, covering a cross-section of American business, found that employees comprised 7.5 percent of the common-stock owners and 1.9 of the preferred.[46] A later study made by the Industrial Relations Section of Princeton University found that only 4.26 percent of the stock of 20 important companies that had vigorously encouraged employee stock ownership was actually owned by employees.[47] When it is realized that a large proportion of this stock was held by the salaried office and executive force, the actual share owned by blue-collar wage earners appears even smaller. The democratization of capital and of business made little if any progress through employee stock ownership in the 1920s. Indeed, the wide dissemination of voting stock simply facilitated control of corporate policy by small management groups.

[40]Coppage v. Kansas, 236 U.S. 1 (1915).

[41]Hitchman Coal and Coke v. Mitchell et al., 254 U.S. 229 (1917).

[42]Duplex Printing Press Company v. Deering et al., 254 U.S. 443 (1921).

[43]United Mine Workers of America v. Coronado Coal and Coke Company, 259 U.S. 344 (1922).

[44]R. F. Foerster and E. N. Dietel, *Employee Stock Ownership in the United States* (Princeton, N.J.: Princeton University Press, 1927), p. 99.

[45]T. N. Carver, *The Present Economic Revolution in the United States* (Boston: Little, Brown, 1926).

[46]Federal Trade Commission, *Report on National Wealth and Income* (Washington, D.C.: U.S. Government Printing Office, 1926).

[47]Foerster and Dietel, *Employee Stock Ownership,* and R. W. Dunn, *The Americanization of Labor,* (New York: International Publishers, 1927), p. 153.

The diffusion of this kind of arrangement was a hallmark of the decade.

Welfare capitalism

Another antiunion device developed by business during the 1920s was a wide range of activities grouped under the term "welfare capitalism." The impetus for this policy was generally the desire to paralyze unionization or to develop a more loyal, stable, and efficient working force, even though it was sometimes also motivated by a sincere humanitarian concern for the health, safety, and general welfare of the worker. Welfare capitalism interested itself in innumerable projects: educational programs, encouragement of workers to own their own homes, low-cost cafeterias, free medical service, profit-sharing devices, vacations with pay, and subsidizing of recreational facilities.

Various forms of private group insurance (in addition to the compulsory workmen's compensation) were also widely established, covering disability and death. It was estimated in 1927 that group insurance had been taken out to the extent of $5.6 billion, covering 4.7 million employees. One insurance company alone, the Metropolitan, wrote policies for 2,500 firms and 815,000 workers.[48] Also worthy of attention was the development of employee pensions. A survey by the Pennsylvania Old Age Pension Commission in 1926 revealed that at least 400 firms employing 4 million workers had established pension plans, 88 percent of which had been started in the previous fifteen years.[49]

The decline of the AFL

Some types of welfare capitalism were helpful and of value to workers, but they indicated that the initiative in improving the condition of labor, aided by organized labor's own lack of initiative and hostility to social legislation, was shifting from the laborer to the employer. Moreover, the whole philosophy of craft unionism was being made increasingly obsolete by the spread of mass-production technology in blue-collar employment. Nor was labor's position strengthened by the union leaders' efforts to counter attacks upon it by trying to prove that unions were "industry's most able helpmeet."[50] The membership of the AFL dropped from the high point of 4 million in 1920 to 2.9 million in 1930.[51]

These figures tell but a part of the story of the decline of organized labor. The AFL failed miserably in organizing the workers in the automobile factories and in the southern textile mills, it watched strong unions like those of the bituminous coal workers rapidly disintegrate, and it failed badly in making the Amalgamated Association of Iron, Steel and Tin Workers a going concern. Gompers, who died in 1924, passed on his conservative policies to equally conservative but less able leaders, in whose hands they seemed for years to degenerate to even lower levels of do-nothingism. The more enlightened in the ranks of labor who questioned the policies (or, perhaps, lack of them) of the leaders were bitterly assailed by the spokesmen of the AFL and denounced as radicals. By the end of the decade, however, there were indications that the dissatisfied minority, who realized the stagnant position of the organized labor movement and sensed its impending crisis, were rapidly increasing and were eager to write a new chapter in American labor history.

IMMIGRATION IN THE 1920S

Closely related to the history of American labor after World War I was the drastic change in immigration policy. For decades organized labor had been agitating for greater immigration restrictions, and since the 1880s the laws had gradually tightened. Organized labor, fearful of a declining wage scale and unemployment, was now joined by groups of many types that thought that further large-scale immigration was fraught with danger to American institutions. Nor did employers vigorously oppose restriction, for there was practically no

[48]*Annals of the American Academy of Political and Social Science* (March 1927), p. 32.

[49]Abraham Epstein, *The Problem of Old Age Pensions in Industry* (New York: Vanguard Press, 1928), pp. 18–19.

[50]Joseph G. Rayback, *A History of American Labor* (New York: Free Press, 1966), p. 306.

[51]"Of the 105 international unions in the A.F. of L., 36 lost membership between 1924 and 1929, while 25 remained stationary. . . . These unions included some of the oldest organizations, which had in the past been the very backbone of the Federation" (L. L. Lorwin, *The American Federation of Labor* [Washington, D.C.: Brookings Institution, 1933]).

general labor shortage in the prosperous years of the mid-1920s. Unemployment as proportion of the civilian labor force, which had reached almost 12 percent in depressed 1921, averaged 4.2 percent for the other, prosperous years of the decade. Moreover, the black migration waves emanating from farm mechanization and disguised unemployment in southern agriculture continued to feed the unskilled labor supply in the cities of both North and South, providing a partial substitute for the foreign immigrant in the North.

The quota laws

Earlier immigration control acts, which had put every conceivable type of "undesirable" on the restricted list, had failed to prevent large-scale immigration, and the restrictionists now turned to the quota system. In 1921 the so-called quota law was passed, limiting immigration in any year to 3 percent of the number of each nationality in the United States according to the census of 1910.

This quota did not go far enough for ardent restrictionists, and in 1924 a new law was passed changing the quota to 2 percent of any nationality residing here in 1890. By pushing the date back another 20 years, the restriction-ists greatly extended discrimination against people from southern and eastern Europe. Canadians and Mexicans were exempt, as were travelers, merchants, seamen, and officials. Japanese were debarred under the 1924 act. This act cut the quota of the 1921 act in half.[52] The Immigration Act of 1924 also provided that the numerical quota scheme of 2 percent of 1890 residents should remain in force only until 1927, when a national-origins method should be applied. Government scientists were to attempt to find out the real origin of the American people as constituted in 1920 and then apportion the immigration among the nationalities, with the total quota immigration limited to 150,000 a year. So much opposition to this law developed that it did not go into effect until July 1929.[53]

Whatever may have been the weaknesses of the immigration legislation of the 1920s, it accomplished its objective: the radical curtailment of immigration. Thus the nation's historic policy of generally open immigration, which had contributed so much to economic growth in the past, was abruptly terminated. The specter of insufficient employment opportunities loomed up even as the Grand Illusion of permanent prosperity reigned supreme.

SELECTED READINGS

Berle, A. A., Jr., and Means, G. C., *The Modern Corporation and Private Property*, rev. ed. (New York: Harcourt Brace Jovanovich, 1968), chaps. 2–5.

*Bernstein, I., *The Lean Years: A History of the American Worker, 1920–1933* (Baltimore: Penguin Books, 1960).

Chambers, Clarke A., *Seedtime of Reform: American Social Service and Social Action, 1918–1933* (Minneapolis: University of Minnesota Press, 1963).

Chase, Stuart, *Prosperity: Fact or Myth?* (New York: Liveright, 1929).

Committee on Recent Economic Changes, President's Conference on Unemployment, *Recent Economic Changes*, 2 vols., (New York: McGraw-Hill, 1929).

Davis, C. C., "The Development of Agricultural Policy Since the End of the World War," *Yearbook of Agriculture, 1940*, pp. 297–326.

Davis, G. C., "The Transformation of the Federal Trade Commission, 1914–1929," *Mississippi Valley Historical Review*, v. 49 (1962), pp. 437–455.

Faulkner, H. U., *From Versailles to the New Deal* (New Haven: Yale University Press, 1950), chaps. 4, 8, 9.

Friedman, M., and Schwartz, A. J., *A Monetary History of the United States, 1867–1960*

[52]The quota for 1923 was placed at 357,803, and that for 1924–1925 at 164,667.

[53]July 1, 1929, the annual quota of any nationality for each fiscal year became a number bearing the same ratio to 150,000 as the number of inhabitants in 1920 having that origin bore to the total number of inhabitants in the continental United States in 1920. The 1929 law, which gave American consuls power to refuse visas to all applicants who might become public charges over here, helped to cut down immigration radically during the depression. Amendments to immigration legislation in 1965 and 1967 abolished the quota system based upon national origin, and an annual quota of only 153,261 in total was adopted.

(Princeton, N.J.: National Bureau of Economic Research, Princeton University Press, 1963), chaps. 6, 7.

*Galbraith, John Kenneth, *The Great Crash* (Boston: Houghton Mifflin, 1955).

Laidler, H. W., *Concentration in American Industries* (New York: Crowell, 1931), chap. 23.

*Leuchtenburg, W. E., *The Perils of Prosperity, 1914–1932* (Chicago: University of Chicago Press, 1958).

Nelson, Ralph L., *Merger Movements in American Industry, 1895–1956,* National Bureau of Economic Research (Princeton, N.J.: Princeton University Press, 1959), chap. 5, Appendix C.

Perlman, Selig, and Taft, Philip, *History of Labor in the United States, 1896–1932* (New York: Macmillan, 1935), chaps. 37–44.

*Potter, Jim, *The American Economy Between the World Wars* (New York: Macmillan, 1974).

Soule, George, *Prosperity Decade* (New York: Holt, Rinehart and Winston, 1947), chaps. 4–13.

Rae, John B., *The American Automobile: A Brief History* (Chicago: University of Chicago Press, 1965), chaps. 6, 7.

Schumpeter, J. A., "The Decade of the Twenties," *American Economic Review,* Supplement, May 1946, pp. 1–10.

*Vatter, Harold G., *Small Enterprise and Oligopoly* (Corvallis: Oregon State College Press, 1955).

——— "Has There Been a Twentieth-Century Consumer Durables Revolution?", *Journal of Economic History,* XXVII (March 1967), pp. 1–16.

—— "The Closure of Entry in the American Automobile Industry", *Oxford Economic Papers* (New Series), Vol. IV, No. 3 (October 1952), pp. 213–234.

*Wilson, J. H., ed., *The Twenties: The Critical Issues* (Boston: Little, Brown, 1972).

A CHANGING SOCIETY

An important crisis, economic or political, often speeds changes in a society that has never been static and forces the acceptance of new points of view and of reforms long needed. Such was the result of the economic depression that began in 1929. The remaining chapters should make clear the effects of this depression and of World War II upon the economy of the nation, and at the same time the new and enlarged role of government in the economy. Enough has already been said in this volume to emphasize the great economic achievements accomplished in the century previous to 1929. They had made the nation economically the most powerful in the world. But the economic structure had many inadequacies that the depression made only too evident. It was the effort to reform these inadequacies and the belief that reform could be accomplished that chiefly differentiates this period from that before the catastrophe of 1929.

These efforts, as we shall see, did little to weaken the capitalist economy. Indeed, in the long run they may have strengthened it. But they left small substance to the old theory and practice of laissez-faire. Under the circumstances, government, and particularly the federal government, had no other choice than to assume some guidance and control of the economy, a social decision by no means unique to the United States in the twentieth century. These efforts operated with varying degrees of effectiveness, but they apparently brought greater stability. They also brought higher levels of living. With these came for most of the people much greater protection from economic insecurity. Old conflicts as to the way the economy should perform and the way the fruits of economic growth should be shared continued under the new regime, but became to an increasing extent transferred to the political arena. And, of course, many partly noneconomic values, such as democracy, freedom of the individual, and popular education, have also played significant roles in these conflicts.

THE ECONOMIC CYCLE

The "new era" of the 1920s, which many believed had opened a never ending era of prosperity, closed in the most complete economic collapse in American history. Depressions, of course, were not new phenomena. As we have seen, they occurred intermittently in the United States, as in other parts of the capitalist world, from the time of its inception as a nation.

As a new school of practical or "institutional'' economics, as distinguished from the older neoclassical one, emerged in the early twentieth century, much study was devoted in the United States to the problem of the business cycle.[1] Some economists or pseudo economists went so far, in fact, as to organize commercial corporations purporting to forecast for businessmen, investors, and speculators the exact point reached in a cycle at a particular moment. The

fact that past cycles had shown certain common tendencies made this seem plausible.[2] As we glance back over the history of American cyclical fluctuations, we note that certain causes have been particularly characteristic of this country. In almost every case, depression in America in the nineteenth century followed an overexpansion of transportation facilities and land speculation.

FUNDAMENTAL CAUSES OF THE COLLAPSE OF 1929

The depression of the 1930s was also preceded by an overextension of transportation facilities, notably motor vehicles and road building. But by the 1920s other areas of private business investment had begun to supersede transport investment in carrying cyclical expansions to inordinate heights. One of these was residential construction, which had already begun to decline in early 1927. But all major categories of investment had been sustained at high levels for several years, creating new capacity at a rate apparently too fast for the growth of total expenditures to justify. After 1926, the year in which gross real capital formation peaked,[3] the continued high investment level began to generate excess capacity. The growing gap between ever larger capacity and expected business sales finally reached the breaking point. There was a wave of recognition within the business community, and unseeing optimism turned into self-reinforcing pessimism with amazing speed in late 1929 after the stock-market crash in October.

It is informative to note that the emergence of depression out of prosperity took place in the context of surface appearances that, aside from real estate and stock-market speculation, seemed generally very favorable for business activity. The banking system, underpinned by a conservative and moderate discount record on the part of the Federal Reserve Board under the leadership of Benjamin Strong of the New York bank, held down the increase in the money

stock to a rate approximating the growth rate of GNP. No one could blame subsequent events upon easy lending policies in the business loan markets (other than securities) by the commercial banking system. Hence the remarkable stability of prices in a cyclical expansion.

In other ways the world was good from the business standpoint. Taxes were light, federal government budgets were small and regularly in surplus as the debt declined, state and local government budgets were quietly drifting upward. Government regulation rested its case as antitrust activity came to a virtual standstill while a new wave of mergers added to business concentration. The tariff was highly protective. Labor unions were losing even their moderate wartime strength. The social reform movement, while not entirely quiescent, offered little threat to the almost unfettered functioning of the private market system. In short, the business community dwelled in a socially benign laissez-faire environment. It was the business system itself that produced the ensuing depression, and not external, hostile social forces.

Labor income
versus property income

Real wages failed to keep pace with the rapid productivity gains in industry. This may have been partly due to the growing weakness of the trade unions. The result was a relative shift away from labor incomes and toward property incomes. For example, the top 5 percent of income receivers increased their share of total income from 22 percent in 1920 to 26 percent in 1929. This shift acted as a drag upon the growth of total consumer spending.[4] In this re-

---

[1] One leading authority defines economic cycles as "recurring alternations of expansion and contraction in aggregate economic activity, the alternating movements in each direction being self-reinforcing, and pervading virtually all parts of the economy" (R.A. Gordon, *Business Fluctuations* [New York: Harper & Row, 1961] p. 249).

[3] See J. Swanson and S. Williamson, "Estimates of National Product and Income for the United States Economy, 1919–1941," *Explorations in Economic History,* 10, no. 1 (Fall 1972): 70, Table A2.

[2] See *Business Cycles and Unemployment: Report and Recommendations of a Committee of the President's Conference on Unemployment* (Washington, D.C.: U.S. Government Printing Office, 1921), pp. xii–xiii.

[4] In this connection see George Soule, *Prosperity Decade* (New York: Holt, Rinehart and Winston, 1947), p. 317.

spect the new era resembled other cyclical expansions: A shift to profits had been typical in the past, and indeed was a hallmark of boom conditions. The great rise in consumer installment buying of durable goods was insufficient to sustain the growth of total consumption after a point in the late 1920s.

Sick industries and sick agriculture

Moreover, the expanding industries had too heavy a burden of sick industries to offset. Certain industries, notably coal mining, cotton textiles, shipbuilding, rail transport, railroad equipment, and leather manufactures, failed to revive after the postwar depression. More important was the failure of agriculture to respond to the postwar economic recovery. Overexpansion during the war period, the slowing of population growth, dietary changes of the American people, increased competition from other parts of the world, and the development of economic nationalism in Europe explain in part the condition of the American farmer. What market the farmer still had in Europe was further curtailed by the exorbitantly high Fordney-McCumber Tariff (1922) and the Hawley-Smoot Tariff (1930), which reduced Europe's ability to exchange manufactured goods for agricultural commodities.

Stagnating employment

Another alarming fact was observable: There was little or no upward trend in employment in certain major sectors of the economy. In certain industries, such as mining, railroads, and agriculture, the number of persons employed actually declined. We have already noted the failure of employment in the important manufacturing sector to rise. The modest rise in total nonagricultural employment of only 1.5 percent a year between 1920 and 1929 relied heavily upon the service activities, and wholesale and retail trade. Construction, finance, real estate, and government also made some contribution.

The domestic economic picture, consequently, showed continued stagnation in certain lines, accompanied by maldistribution of the fruits of industry—conditions that tended to weaken the prospect for sustained expansion.

International contributions to economic collapse

While the domestic situation displayed these serious weaknesses, those latent in the international economy also contributed to the economic collapse. Europe's impoverishment and the high American tariffs made it impossible for Europe to pay its loans to us either in gold or in commodities. There was a tendency during the postwar years for the major portion of the world's gold to move to the United States, a phenomenon that tended to make more difficult the efforts of European governments to return to a gold basis. At the same time Europe recognized what the United States was loath to acknowledge: that it could not indefinitely continue to buy more from the United States than it sold to us. Even the large flow of U.S. foreign lending would not be sufficient to sustain the one-way traffic. The resulting economic distress of Europe reacted to create political instability there; this in turn created uncertainty in international finance, and the whole situation made for world economic insecurity. The excess of U.S. merchandise exports over imports failed to grow. It is small wonder that the Marxist movements gloated over the impending "general crisis of capitalism."

THE CLIMAX OF SPECULATION

Increase in speculation, particularly in securities, had been a characteristic of so-called boom eras. Many reasons account for the speculative extremes of this particular decade. Most segments of American industry and business were prosperous; the wealth of the nation and the real income of large numbers of people were increasing, a situation bound to be reflected in the values of securities, even if those values had received no additional speculative boost. Since the value of American business assets was increasing, and since this rise was inordinately reflected in the price of stocks, almost any purchase meant a profit. But the valuation of any asset is an estimate, and under the superoptimism then being generated, the expectation of rising values tended to justify itself, and the resulting inflated valuation became more and more self-reinforcing. Following the lead of the big investors and professional stock-market speculators, ever more people entered the market. By the time the frenzy ended, probably a million new customers were buying and selling on the various stock exchanges.

The sight of these lambs crowding to be shorn was too much for the captains of industry and finance to resist, and the business of producing and distributing securities became an important one.

> *The traditional theory is that business corporations issue stocks and bonds only when they need additional capital. . . . During this period, however, new securities were manufactured almost like cakes of soap, for little better reason than that there was gain to be made out of their manufacture and sale.* [5]

Meanwhile, the much larger volume of old securities outstanding continued to be traded at spiraling prices.

Industries, utilities, railroads, and banks hastened to print new securities to meet the insatiable demand, or split old stock to make it more easily purchasable. Between January 1, 1925, and October 1929, the number of shares of stock listed on the New York Stock Exchange increased from 443.4 million to over 1 billion. Upon the bona fide investor who had no desire to speculate but wanted chiefly to invest his savings, the bankers and bond houses palmed off foreign bonds and "guaranteed" real estate mortgages, some of which their own employee experts asserted were too risky to purchase. To catch what surplus funds still remained, banks and bond houses organized "investment trusts," which were often used to manipulate stocks owned by the sponsors of these trusts. A deterioration and degradation permeated the entire banking and investment business.

The traditional basis of judging the value of a stock was "ten times earnings." Some stocks in 1929 were selling at 50 times this, or more. The market, as one expert observed, was discounting not only the future, but the hereafter! The speculative frenzy was also accentuated by the retirement of the federal war debt at the rate of $800 million a year, which tended to increase the volume of free funds seeking reinvestment, and also by the disproportionately large amount of the national income that went to capital rather than to labor. In the end, speculation went to incredible lengths. Stocks were selling from three to 20 times their book value.

It might be supposed that experienced leaders of business and finance, to say nothing of economists, might have predicted the inevitable result. Most of them apparently did not. Optimism was widely prevalent that the country had entered a new era of never-ending prosperity and permanently high level of stock prices. [6] By the time the government began to worry, it was too late. The Federal Reserve Board issued a warning against the volume of margin trading early in 1929, and in February began to raise discount rates. Even the brokerage houses finally raised their margin requirements to 50 percent. But any control here was largely nullified by the huge amounts poured into the banks by large corporations and others eager to lend their money on call at interest rates that finally reached 20 percent. Until the final crash there was never lack of ample funds to finance the speculation.

The crash

There could be only one end. The period of stock-market panic— for panic in the old-fashioned sense it was—lasted five days. These five days inaugurated the massive collapse of business expectations. The first day was "Black Thursday," October 24. Said John Kenneth Galbraith in his brilliant work on the stock-market crash and its immediate origins and aftermath:

> *Of all the mysteries of the stock exchange there is none so impenetrable as why there should be a buyer for everyone who seeks to sell. October 24, 1929, showed that what is mysterious is not inevitable. Often there were no buyers, and only after wide vertical declines could anyone be induced to bid.* [7]

The climax came on October 29, 1929:

> *The big gong had hardly sounded in the great hall of the Exchange at ten o'clock Tuesday morning before the storm broke in full force. Huge blocks of stock were thrown upon the market for what they would bring. . . . Not only were innumerable small traders being sold out, but big ones, too. . . . Again and again the specialist in a stock would find himself surrounded by brokers fighting to sell— and nobody at all even thinking of buying. . . . The scene on the floor was chaotic. . . . Within half an hour of the opening the volume of trading passed*

[5]Soule, *Prosperity Decade,* p. 297.

[6]Typical statements from these sages are given in Edward Angly, *Oh, Yeah?* (New York: Viking Press, 1931).

[7]*The Great Crash* (Boston: Houghton Mifflin, 1955), p. 104.

three million shares, by twelve o'clock it had passed eight million, by half past one it had passed twelve million, and when the closing gong brought the day's madness to an end the gigantic record of 16,410,030 shares had been set; . . . the average prices of fifty leading stocks, as compiled by the New York Times, *had fallen nearly forty points.*[8]

Although all this produced a few suicides among well-known speculators, the popular notion of a great wave of suicides has been shown by Galbraith to be a myth. Embezzlement in high and low places was apparently a much more widespread reaction to the great losses suffered from the panic and its aftereffects.[9]

THE COURSE OF THE DEPRESSION

The stock-market crash of October 1929 was but the beginning of an economic decline that continued with little interruption until it bottomed in the spring of 1933. When the stock-market decline finally hit bottom in July 1933, some $74 billion, or five-sixths of the September 1929 value, had disappeared.

Prices of stocks were only an extreme reflection of the business situation as a whole. A general picture is given by the following index numbers compiled by the United States Bureau of Labor Statistics, using 1926 as a base year with an index number of 100:

payrolls given below show that the total paid in wages was more than halved during the first four years of the depression. In response to President Hoover's invocation to business not to cut wages too severely, the decline in wage rates was generally moderate until late 1931, after which it was more drastic. Meanwhile, however, weekly hours were shortened and layoffs were widespread. Wage-rate cuts and hours reduction together account for the greater drop in payrolls than in employment after 1930.

	Wholesale Prices	Employment	Payrolls
1929 average	95.3	97.5	100.5
1930 average	86.4	84.7	81.3
1931 average	73.0	72.2	61.5
1932 average	64.8	60.1	41.6
1933 average	65.9	64.6	44.0

These index numbers on employment, when expressed in terms of human beings, meant 4.34 million unemployed in 1930, 8.02 million in 1931, 12.06 million in 1932, and almost 13 million in 1933—about one-fourth of the entire civilian labor force of 51.59 million. It should also be remembered that a goodly proportion of these unemployed were heads of families upon whose wages others were dependent. Thus the number affected by unemployment ran into many millions more. A fair estimate of the number on public relief late in 1934 was 17 million.

The decline in wage rates and industrial activity

In addition to the millions thrown out of work, there were a larger number living on greatly reduced incomes. The index numbers of

As production under laissez-faire conditions rested primarily upon the purchasing power of the private market, it is not at all surprising to find industrial activity falling, and because of industry's greater sensitivity, falling more than proportionately. Thus total consumer expenditures, even when we ignore consumer price declines, fell 16 percent between 1929 and 1932, but the index of industrial production declined 47 percent. Human unemployment was matched by industrial excess capacity.

The decline in farm production and income

In agriculture the situation was somewhat different. The general level of production, as the following figures show, did not change so radically for certain of the principal crops:

[8]Frederick L. Allen, *Only Yesterday* (New York: Harper & Row, 1957), pp. 333–334.

[9]*The Great Crash,* pp. 105, 133–140.

	Corn	*Wheat*	*Cotton*
1929	2,622,189,000	806,508,000	14,919,000
1930	2,081,048,000	850,965,000	14,243,000
1931	2,567,306,000	900,219,000	17,097,000
1932	2,908,145,000	726,863,000	12,727,000

The income of the farmers, however, as we have already noted, declined sharply during these years. Between 1929 and 1932 farm values, already severely deflated, suffered a further decline of 33 percent. Remembering that agriculture had been stagnating throughout the 1920s, we see that these figures are extremely significant. The striking feature about agriculture, however, is the fact that while gross farm money income collapsed, the loss was almost all due to price declines, for farm production stayed close to 1929 levels. In fact, with minor fluctuations total farm output was about constant from 1929 through 1937. It actually increased by over $1 billion in 1931 over 1930. Millions of small, individually acting farmers reacted to falling prices by working harder to try to maintain their receipts. So excess output piled up in agriculture, in sharp contrast to excess capacity and human unemployment in concentrated industry. The later destruction of surplus farm products (for example, the killing of "poor little pigs") was widely and more vociferously lamented than the idle plants in the industrial cities.

The decline in foreign trade

More striking, perhaps, than any of the figures yet given to illustrate the devastation, national and international, wrought by the worldwide depression are those showing the decline in the current dollar value of foreign trade:

Year	Exports (Millions of Dollars)	Imports (Millions of Dollars)
1929	$5,241	$4,399
1930	3,843	3,061
1931	2,424	2,091
1932	1,611	1,323

For this it is possible to find an abundance of reasons. The most important would include: (1) the decline in purchasing power, not only in the United States but elsewhere in the markets of the world; (2) the cessation after 1929 of American foreign loans, which had provided funds for some of this international trade; (3) the premium on the American dollar in international exchange, which discouraged the purchase of American goods; and (4) the high tariff policy of the United States, which brought retaliatory tariffs and special discriminations by license or quota devices against American goods. There is no doubt that the collapse in America contributed to the depression in Europe, which in turn intensified and deepened the economic decline here. Curtailment of American loans forced a similar procedure in England with a freezing of bank credits, which ended in precipitating a banking collapse in Germany and Austria. Germany defaulted on its war debt in 1931, and President Hoover, to prevent a further world economic collapse, effected an agreement for the temporary suspension of intergovernmental debts and reparations payments. Shortly afterward Great Britain abandoned the gold standard in order to be freer to manage foreign exchange in the interests of domestic stability and high employment. England was followed by a number of other European countries; these nations thus sought to gain a temporary advantage in international commerce at the expense of the gold standard countries, including the United States.

U.S. tariffs

The uprising of the world against the American tariff system came after the Hawley-Smoot Act of 1930, which raised the already high duties of the Fordney-McCumber Tariff of 1922. In the new tariff the average of all the schedules went up; one-third of the dutiable items were changed, 890 being increased, including 50 transfers from the free list to the dutiable list; 235 were lowered, including 75 transfers from the dutiable list to the free list.[10] The general average of the increase may not have been tremendously high, but the effect appears to have been unfortunate in accelerating a trade decline and in arousing antagonism in other

[10] It is estimated that the average for the dutiable articles in the McKinley Tariff was 48.4 percent; in the Wilson-Gorman Tariff, 41.3; in the Dingley Bill, 46.5; in the Payne-Aldrich, 40.7; in the Fordney-McCumber, 38.5; and in the Hawley-Smoot Bill (based on imports for 1932), 53.2 percent (statement of U.S. Tariff Commission).

parts of the world. Over a thousand economists petitioned the president not to sign the bill, but Hoover insisted that the new tariff would improve the economic situation domestically and that any striking defects might be eliminated by the flexible provision allowing him to make changes upon recommendation of the Tariff Commission.[11]

Why did it happen?

Regarding the severity of the depression, statistics could be quoted almost without end. By 1934 students agreed with Colonel Ayres, who maintained that "this depression has been far more severe than any of the 20 major depressions that we have experienced in this country since 1790."[12] On the other hand, there was little unanimity as to the reasons for the unique severity and duration of this particular debacle. One business economist suggested two reasons: the uneven decline in prices and the long-drawn-out series of crises in credit.[13] For various reasons already discussed, agricultural prices slumped rapidly, but the prices of manufactured commodities, influenced by wage agreements and monopoly practices, revealed remarkable inflexibility. The series of credit crises was caused primarily by the weakness of the American banking system and the unsettlement of European finances, which culminated in 1931 when Great Britain went off the gold standard. The fact that 6987 banks in the United States failed in the decade ending in 1930, to which were added 2294 failures in 1931 and 1456 in 1932, explains much.

Another explanation offered for the severity of the depression was the large public and private debt that had been built up out of all proportion to the national income.[14] Still another was the large amount invested during the preceding years in such durable goods as automobiles, whose replacement could be delayed, thus retarding recovery.[15] Many attributed the severity to the coincidence of much technological unemployment with the coming of the depression. To these may be added certain factors

tending to accentuate the depression and delay recovery: world economic conditions; the increasing competition faced by the American farmer from other parts of the world; the collapse of the foreign market for industrial products, emphasized by the establishment of American factories in foreign countries to avoid their tariffs; the collapse of the foreign market as a place for safe investment; the growing rigidity of industrial prices (because of increased business consolidation) — that is, the failure of prices in certain concentrated industries to respond to deflation; and the difficulty of putting labor back to work because of the use of labor-saving machinery.

Actions of the Federal Reserve system

It seems clear that the Federal Reserve, except for one interlude in 1931–1932, generally pursued an easy credit policy, which, on the basis of the existing state of banking knowledge, was the right orientation for arresting the contraction. The New York bank led off with the purchase of $160 million of government securities in the last week of October 1929 and a reduction in the rediscount rate in November. There were further reductions in 1930 and in May 1931 to 1.5 percent. Although some authorities believe, perhaps rightly, that Federal Reserve policy was not by any means easy enough between late 1929 and 1933, especially with regard to open-market purchases, there was only one serious credit-tightening period (October 1931 to February 1932, following the gold drain subsequent to Britain's departure from the gold standard in September 1931). Indeed, between April and August 1932 the board's open-market committee purchased $1 billion of government securities, a strong credit-easing move for those times. It was in February of that same year that the historically important Glass-Steagall Act was passed, authorizing the use of government obligations, as well as commercial paper, for collateral against the issue of Federal Reserve notes. Unfortunately, other Federal Reserve banks failed to follow the lead of the New York bank when it lowered its rediscount rate in February and again in June 1932. Also, actual loan policy toward the public was tighter than the generally moderate levels of the discount rate might suggest. Furthermore, potential business borrowers were themselves pessimistic. Consequently the money stock quite steadily declined from October 1929 to April 1933: 38 percent in all. The general inepti-

[11]F. W. Taussig, "The Tariff Act of 1930," *Quarterly Journal of Economics,* 14 (November 1930):1–21.

[12]Leonard Ayres, *The Economics of Recovery* (New York: Macmillan, 1933), p. 5.

[13]Ibid., pp. 5–7.

[14]C. A. Beard and G. H. E. Smith, *The Future Comes* (New York: Macmillan, 1934), p. 9.

[15]J. M. Clark, *Strategic Factors in Business Cycles* (New York: National Bureau of Economic Research, 1935), pp. 108–109.

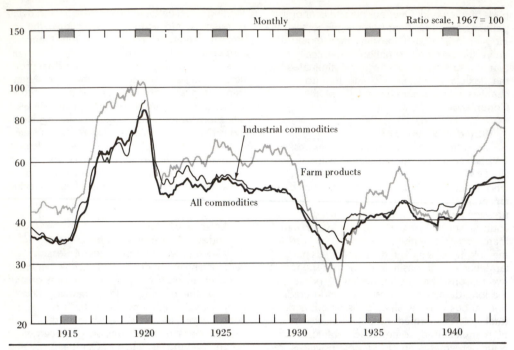

Figure 22–1.   **Wholesale Prices, 1914–1943.** Source: Federal Reserve Board, *Historical Chart Book,* 1971.

tude or ineffectiveness of monetary policy under the Hoover administration gave rise to the widespread conviction that it could do little to cure unemployment, and that fiscal policy was a more effective counterdepressant.

The new economics of John Maynard Keynes

During the depression years Harvard's Professor Alvin Hansen, leading spokesman for the "new economics" of England's John Maynard Keynes, advanced the hypothesis that capitalism was experiencing long-run stagnation. Hansen believed that the end of the frontier, the disappearance of great new private industries, the declining rate of population growth, and the spread of capital-saving innovations was bringing an end to new private investment opportunities, the heart of the capitalistic growth process.[16] He thus explained the severity and duration of the depression and emphasized that only large government expenditures could pull the economy back onto its long-run growth path. Unfortunately, Hansen's hypothesis was never put to an empirical test, for the

[16]See Hansen's testimony at the hearings before the Temporary National Economic Committee, 75th Cong., pub. res. no. 113, pt. 9, "Savings and Investment," May 16, 1939.

depression remained severe until large-scale military outlays connected with World War II took over, and thereafter big government spending continued to play a powerful role in maintaining total demand.

Overinvestment and fiscal drag

Other scholars argued that the depression was not interwoven with long-run stagnation. Probably most authorities today agree, rightly or wrongly, that the sustained high level of investment in the 1920s produced an overbuilt stock of plant, equipment, and housing that were bound to require years to work off.[17] There is now also general agreement that the federal government's budgets under the New Deal, for all their emotion-arousing current deficits, in most years would have been deflationary had full employment been secured. This fiscal drag meant that the government was not incurring sufficient deficits to do its part in overcoming the persistent mass unemployment.[18]

[17]See A. Smithies, "The American Economy in the Thirties," *American Economic Review,* 36, no. 26 (May 1946): 11–27.
[18]See E. C. Brown, "Fiscal Policy in the Thirties: A Reappraisal," *American Economic Review,* 46, no. 5 (December 1956):857–879.

Theorizing about the reasons for the ten-year duration of America's most severe depression will no doubt occupy scholars for a long time to come. It was increasingly evident to those involved as the years passed that the country·had entered a new era. But it was not the dazzling "new era" predicted in the inflated dreams of the 1920s.

HERBERT HOOVER AND THE GREAT CONTRACTION, 1929–1933

The depression following the stock-market crash of 1929 was not only the most severe in our history but also the first one in which the federal government entered aggressively into the situation to alleviate conditions. During earlier panics the government did little except to safeguard its own credit and sit by until the storms blew over. This was partly because earlier generations did not know what to do, or more likely because they were dominated by a laissez-faire philosophy, and did not consider it the function of government to interfere with the "freely working market system" to such extent. This does not mean that depressions did not eventually have an effect in speeding certain reform legislation, but it usually came after the event. By 1929 the days had already begun to pass when a government could sit by calmly and let its people suffer without some gesture of help. Too many revolutions had taken place in the world during the previous decade as a result of economic conditions, and too great a change had occurred in the philosophy of government functions, both in the United States and in western Europe, for any administration to adopt a do-nothing policy.

Public works and taxes

Despite the fact that the Hoover administration prided itself on its adherence to laissez-faire and glorified "rugged individualism," it had to make some effort to stay the continuing economic collapse. These mincing efforts gave certain Republicans sympathetic with the New Deal an opportunity to claim Hoover as its originator.

Be that as it may, President Hoover, after the stock-market crash of October 1929, called a series of White House conferences with railroad presidents, industrial and labor leaders, key men in construction and public utilities, and leaders in national agricultural associations. His objective was to stabilize business by securing declarations favoring the maintenance of normal business activity and prevailing wages. Through the time-honored method of incantation and moral suasion he earnestly urged private business as well as state and municipal governments to aid the situation by increasing, if possible, their normal programs of construction. He also urged this on a Congress whose Democratic majority made that body distinctly more activist and interventionist than the laissez-faire executive arm. Congress responded with alacrity by increasing appropriations for various types of public works. In the belief that tax reduction would counteract the depression, Hoover asked Congress in December 1929 for lower income-tax rates. Congress responded at once, but the only effect was to create a deficit and a new tax measure in 1932 increasing rates.

"Sound" finance

This sequence was most revealing, for it showed that the government was still more concerned about the presumed threat of bankruptcy of the public exchequer than it was about unemployment. Of course, the federal leadership at that time believed that the road to rising employment was by way of "sound" public (and private) finance. Public budget deficits, at the federal, state, and local levels, were considered "unsound" by the laissez-faire economic philosophy, and the actual federal deficit of $462 million in fiscal 1931 (the year ending June 1931) was threatening to be much larger in fiscal 1932. Tax receipts were falling and expenditures were not. To add to expenditures in such a situation in order to institute public works and relief not only violated Mr. Hoover's conviction that "we cannot squander ourselves into prosperity," but also violated the ancient shibboleth that public charity would destroy the moral fiber of the unemployed. The same philosophy dominated the budget policies of the state and local governments.

Farm programs

Because the conventional wisdom (to use Galbraith's revealing term) of the Hoover administration saw the road to recovery through the achievement of "soundness" in the country's financial and other business institutions, the thrust of policy was toward public charity for business enterprise. And the long-suffering,

vociferous farmers were among the first beneficiaries of this kind of largesse. Four months
before the crash the Agricultural Marketing Act
had been passed. Under its authority the Federal Farm Board created a grain stabilization corporation and a cotton stabilization corporation
whose purpose it was to raise the prices of those
commodities. Beginning in 1930, both corporations went into the market and by actual purchase of these commodities, or of "futures" in
them, succeeded for a brief period in maintaining their prices at levels slightly higher than the
world market averages. Almost $500 million
was spent to support the prices of farm commodities, but the net result, except for a cost of
some $148 million to the American taxpayer,
appears to have been nil.

The Bonus march of 1932

While the Federal Farm Board frantically
attempted to stay the decline of agricultural
prices, the government, after the Democratic
Congress in 1931 passed a veterans' bonus bill
over Hoover's veto, released almost $1 billion[19]
that offered temporary relief to needy veterans
but utterly failed to prime the pump of economic recovery. As the depression deepened
in the following year, the veterans demanded
the remainder of the bonus due them. A "Bonus Expeditionary Force" numbering about
20,000 moved into Washington to bring pressure upon Congress. The Senate refused to
comply, and on orders from Hoover federal
troops under General Douglas MacArthur
drove the Bonus Army from the city in one of
the most tragic incidents of the depression.

The Reconstruction
Finance Corporation

The deepening of the depression in conjunction with the coming presidential campaign
in 1932 led to a renewed effort on the part of
the Hoover administration to improve the economic situation. In January of that year Congress proceeded to extend further the principle
of recovery through the achievement of corporate financial soundness by creating the Reconstruction Finance Corporation (RFC), with a

[19]The Bonus Bill of 1924 provided for service certificates
that would mature in 20 years and against which a veteran
might borrow up to 22.5 percent of the matured value. The
act of 1931 raised this to 50 percent. In 1936 a new bonus act
was passed over Roosevelt's veto; it provided for the redemption of the adjusted service certificates held by the government life insurance fund by means of exchanging them for 3
percent bonds that in turn might be converted into cash.

capital of $500 million and power to incur debts
to three times that amount. Its purpose was to
make loans on security to banks, trust companies, building and loan associations, insurance
companies, mortgage and loan companies, agricultural and livestock credit associations, and,
with the approval of the Interstate Commerce
Commission, railroads. The RFC has been
uniquely identified as a Hoover innovation, yet
it is somewhat ironic that the institution was
adopted and nurtured by the Roosevelt New
Deal. In July the borrowing power of the RFC
was increased to $3.3 billion and its functions
were enlarged. It was now empowered to lend
to states and to public and private agencies
funds to promote self-liquidating projects of
public benefit. The RFC proved to be the most
valuable effort of the Hoover administration to
deal with the depression. During its first year
and a half it loaned about $3 billion. Many criti-
cized the RFC as a method of ladling out credit
to the rulers of banks and industries who had
already proved themselves incapable of directing the nation's economic life. About 80 percent
of all RFC loans under Hoover, went to railroads and financial institutions. (Under the New
Deal there was a reduction in this proportion,
with relatively much more going to state and
local government for relief and public works.)
The fact remains, however, that the RFC saved
many a tottering bank, railroad, and insurance
company from collapse and eased the strain on
the business community in one of the most
acute periods of the depression.

Two other acts of less importance but significant in rendering some immediate help and
establishing precedents for future action were
passed in 1932. One increased the capital stock
of the Federal Land Banks by $125 million to
augment their resources for lending to farmers.
The second was the Home Loan Act, authorized to create not less than eight or more than
12 home loan banks to extend emergency
credit to homeowners. Although the RFC and
the Home Loan Act were intended to supply
emergency credit, many hoped that they might
also contribute to a rise in prices.

Hoover the internationalist

Hoover was convinced that America's recovery was closely dependent upon that of
the rest of the world. He assumed the leadership in an effort to bolster the European economy, and also the initiative in bringing a one-
year moratorium on intergovernmental debts.
He supported the plan for a world economic

conference that met after he left office. In all this, and with the notable exception of his tariff stand, he took a more cosmopolitan view than did his somewhat provincial successor, who believed that American recovery was the central task and had to be achieved even, if necessary, at the expense of noncooperation with Europe.

The bankruptcy of moral suasion

It seems likely that the heavy reliance at almost all levels of officialdom upon moral suasion, incantation, and professions of confidence that prosperity was just around the corner, together with bankrupt private philanthropy and faith in the automatic power of the private market mechanism to initiate full recovery, were major reasons for the explosive nature of the policy reversal that was inaugurated under Franklin D. Roosevelt. The Hoover interlude stretched laissez-faire policy to the limit. The three dreary years of that interlude no doubt seemed unending to the millions of suffering Americans, and as the harsh winters rolled by their resentment and militancy mounted.

POLITICAL REACTIONS

That the economic depression would have its political reactions was obvious. Only one American president, James Monroe, ever politically survived a major economic depression, and he was probably saved only by the fact that there was no strong political party to oppose him. Hoover, as it turned out, was no exception to the rule. The congressional elections of 1930 wiped out the Republican majority in the House and cut its majority in the Senate to the slimmest margin. As the presidential election of 1932 approached, most voters were convinced that the Hoover administration had no policy beyond an effort to cushion the deepening depression, a policy that seemed utterly inadequate in the face of the by now almost complete loss of popular confidence in the capacity of the private market system, if left alone, to regenerate economic activity. The efforts of the administration were widely criticized as being too little and too late.

Although the platforms of the two parties in 1932, significantly enough, were much alike, and considerable attention was devoted during the campaign to the question of prohibition, there was only one real issue: the depression. Hoover and his spokesmen tried to convince the voters that the Republicans had accomplished all that could be done safely and that a Democratic victory would precipitate an even greater economic collapse. The Democratic candidate, Franklin D. Roosevelt, presented his views on economic problems in a series of speeches. He spoke in general terms, including, however, specific reference to the great virtues of a balanced budget, but he implied that a change in policies would improve conditions. In brief, he promised a "New Deal."

This was enough. The Democrats were overwhelmingly victorious not only in the national but also in state and local elections. For the first time since 1919 the Democratic party had control of both legislative and executive branches. What the New Deal would mean in practice no one knew, but if the new administration had any real program with which to meet the existing economic catastrophe, its opportunity had come.

SELECTED READINGS

*"Essentials for Prosperity," *The Annals,* American Academy of Political and Social Science, January 1933.

Faulkner, H. J., *From Versailles to the New Deal* (New Haven: Yale University Press, 1950), chaps. 10, 11.

Fisher, Irving. *Booms and Depressions* (New York: Adelphi, 1932).

*Friedman, M., and Schwartz, A. J., *The Great Contraction, 1929–1933* (Princeton, N.J.: Princeton University Press, 1965).

*Galbraith, J. K., *The Great Crash* (Boston: Houghton Mifflin, 1955), chaps. VIII–XI.

Hansen, Alvin H., *Economic Stabilization in an Unbalanced World* (New York: Harcourt Brace Jovanovich, 1932).

Hoover, H. C., *Memoirs, vol. 3: The Great Depression, 1929 – 1941* (New York: Macmillan, 1952).

Mitchell, Broadus, *Depression Decade* (New York: Holt, Rinehart and Winston, 1947), chaps. 1 – 3.

Nash, Gerald D., "Herbert Hoover and the Origins of the Reconstruction Finance Corporation," *Mississippi Valley Historical Review,* XLVI (December, 1959), pp. 455 – 468.

*Romasco, A. V., *The Poverty of Abundance: Hoover, the Nation, the Depression* (New York: Oxford University Press, 1965).

Schlesinger, A. M., Jr., *The Age of Roosevelt: The Crisis of the Old Order* (Boston: Houghton Mifflin, 1957), chaps. 19 – 27.

Schwarz, J. A., *The Interregnum of Despair: Hoover, Congress and the Depression* (Urbana: University of Illinois Press, 1970).

*Sobel, Robert, *The Big Board, A History of the New York Stock Market* (New York: The Free Press, 1965), chap. 13.

Soule, George, *Prosperity Decade* (New York: Holt, Rinehart and Winston, 1947), chaps. 13, 14.

Warren, Harris G., *Herbert Hoover and the Great Depression* (New York: Oxford University Press, 1959).

It would be difficult to exaggerate the utter economic collapse and the dark pessimism of the nation when Franklin D. Roosevelt became president on March 4, 1933. General business had sunk to less than 60 percent of normal; more than one-fourth of the civilian labor force was unemployed; exports had sunk to close to the lowest point in thirty years; commodity prices had reached the lowest point since the beginning of the depression.

Equally serious at the moment, perhaps, was the disintegration of the credit and banking structure. More than 1400 banks had failed during 1932 and the situation became worse in the early months of 1933. It reached a climax on February 14 when leading banks in Detroit closed and the state of Michigan declared an eight-day moratorium. This action was quickly followed elsewhere, until by March 2 there were 21 states, besides the District of Columbia, where either moratoriums had been declared or the banks were operating under special regulation. On the day of Roosevelt's inauguration, New York and Illinois declared bank holidays, which closed the stock and commodity markets in the country's greatest financial centers.

BEGINNINGS OF THE NEW DEAL

Roosevelt, whose ideas and plans for meeting the depression had been expressed during the presidential campaign in only the most general and largely conservative terms, now acted with unexpected speed. He immediately called Congress into special session and on March 6 declared a nationwide bank moratorium and placed an embargo on the withdrawal or transportation of gold. Thus began the famous "Hundred Days" (March 9 – June 16) of intense presidential and legislative activity that launched a whole new epoch of growth in the power of the presidency.

The Emergency Banking Act of 1933

When Congress met on March 9 it passed an emergency banking act that confirmed the proclamation of the president and gave him emergency powers to regulate transactions in credit, currency, gold and silver, and foreign exchange. It empowered the secretary of the Treasury to require deposit of all gold and gold certificates and authorized the comptroller to appoint a conservator for any national bank in difficulty and for the reorganization of such banks. It also provided that national and state banks that were members of the Federal Reserve System might open under license, and it sought to strengthen the position of the weaker banks by empowering the Hoover-founded Reconstruction Finance Corporation to purchase their preferred stock or take it as collateral for loans. To help break the credit impasse, the note-issuing power of the Federal Reserve banks was enlarged. On March 13 the bank moratorium officially came to an end when banks that had obtained licenses reopened.

There were now 14,771 banks in the United States compared with 1929's 25,568.

Altogether, during the special session of the 73rd Congress, that body passed almost a score of major acts dealing with various aspects of the economic situation, which inaugurated what the nation came to term the New Deal.

Relief, recovery, and reform

Before we proceed with an intensive description of the New Deal, certain general statements may be offered to aid in threading the maze of numerous legislative acts. Three main objectives dominated the entire program: relief, recovery, and reform. Sometimes these were interwoven in a single piece of legislation, sometimes separated. The primary objective was to pull the nation out of the disastrous depression. The second was to remedy economic defects of the private market system, which rising public clamor over the decades had now, finally, made all too evident and which had reached the boiling point in the present catastrophe. A time-honored reform argument, employed now by the President with all the vigor at his command, was to assert that the economy was out of "balance." Reform proposals allegedly looked toward a better balance of the economic system: strengthening the weaker segments, such as labor and agriculture, and bringing others, such as finance and industry, under stronger federal control. Said Roosevelt:

> *What we seek is balance in our economic system — balance between agriculture and industry and balance between the wage earner, the employer and the consumer. We seek also balance that our internal markets be kept rich and large, and that our trade with other nations be increased on both sides of the ledger.*

The imbalance argument actually expressed in an elliptical way the conviction that certain socioeconomic groups needed government help in order that they might exert more countervailing power. Of course, either side in a power struggle could freely employ the imbalance argument, as was later easily seen when the New Deal labor legislation came under attack from the business side.

Since these objectives necessitated a certain amount of overall planning, they inevitably meant extended government supervision, control, and activity. The result was a rapid expan-

sion of the power of the presidency and of the federal bureaucracy, but not, as many contended, a movement toward socialism. What was involved was the inauguration in the United States of the "mixed economy" — a private capitalistic system with a large admixture of public intervention designed to assure improved performance and continued economic growth. The New Deal contemplated no fundamental change in the economic system. The essential elements of capitalism remained: private ownership of the means of production and distribution and the profit system. In fact, the main business of the New Deal appeared to be to save capitalism. In this respect the new administration was adhering, without knowledge or acknowledgment of it at the time, to the economic philosophy of the eminent Englishman John Maynard Keynes. It was Keynes's advocacy of public expenditures, financed through budget deficits when necessary, in his *General Theory of Employment, Interest, and Money* (1936), that made him the theoretical sire of the mixed economy everywhere in the western world.

The First New Deal
and the Second New Deal

As the Roosevelt programs unfolded, a shift of emphasis was discerned which has led students to differentiate between a "First New Deal" and a "Second New Deal." During the first period the administration sought recovery by close cooperation with private enterprise. The effort was to encourage "price rises which would increase profits and seep down in the form of higher wages, to groups which would use their increased purchasing power to stimulate recovery."[1]

In the Second New Deal, which began in 1935, the administration shifted to permanent intervention and reform by pouring purchasing power into the hands of the less privileged groups and minimally underwriting their economic future through social security.

Although this distinction between early and later New Deal programs has merit, it should not obscure two major lines of continuity that ran from 1933 to 1940. First, both before and after 1935 the Roosevelt administration placed great stress on the need to afford relief to the destitute and the unemployed. And second, although there was close cooperation with

[1]Basil Rauch, *The History of the New Deal, 1933–1938* (New York: Capricorn Books, 1963), p. 157.

private enterprise in the First New Deal period, still the programs of 1933 and 1934 involved far-reaching, often radical, departures from long-accepted constitutional and ideological norms—above all, because they gave the central government, and particularly the executive branch, unprecedented power to control economic life. The market forces of supply and demand had never before been purposefully manipulated by government to such an extent. Nor had "social-reform" (or simply, humanitarian) concerns ever been so important a consideration in the shaping of the federal government's policies.

Improvisation and morale

Among other aspects that should be emphasized is the fact that the New Deal began without any overall or detailed plan. It was experimental, improvised as the months went on, and with few precedents in the laissez-faire background of the country's history to base it on. Nevertheless, it can be said that the central theme and direction was in that broad and loose heritage known as American progressivism. Although the President sought counsel from the leaders of industry and finance, he came to rely mainly on the so-called brain trust, a group of experts drawn from university circles. And another factor in the situation should be noted: It was not the legislation and the policies alone that improved the economic situation beginning in the second quarter of 1933; it was in part the improvement of morale and the restoration of confidence inspired by the President's quick and able handling of the bank crisis and his activity in attacking the depression on many fronts.

CURRENCY AND CREDIT

The financial program of the New Deal, as far as it concerned currency and credit, had three objectives: inflation, banking reform, and better supervision of the securities and commodity exchanges. In every major depression experienced by the United States there had been a strong demand for inflation. By 1933 the clamor became so insistent that it could not be denied. The arguments for inflation rested partly on the simple fact that rising prices and recovery had always been positively associated, but primarily upon the facts that the increased value of the dollar bore heavily upon the debtor class, which included in one way or another the great majority of the population, and that restoration of currency values to the level at which the debts were contracted was necessary to restore "balance" between debtor and creditor and thus halt the economic collapse. As Roosevelt said later:

> We had determined definitely to seek an increase in all values. Two courses were open: to cut down the debts through bankruptcies and foreclosures to such a point that they would be below property values; or else to increase property values until they were greater than the debts. Obviously the latter course was the only legitimate method of putting the country back on its feet without destroying human values.

The Farm Relief and Inflation Act, 1933

Mention has already been made of efforts to expand credit facilities in the Emergency Banking Act of March 9, 1933. A broader legal basis was established in May by the Farm Relief and Inflation Act (First Agricultural Adjustment Act), one of the major enactments of the Hundred Days. It gave the President power, if he desired to exercise it: (1) to require the Federal Reserve banks to expand their credit up to $3 billion; (2) to issue United State notes secured solely on the credit of the United States up to $3 billion, these notes to be used only to retire outstanding federal obligations but to be legal tender for all debts, public and private; (3) to devalue the gold dollar by as much as 50 percent; (4) to accept silver for six months up to $200 million at a price not exceeding 50 cents an ounce, in payment of war debts due from foreign governments; and (5) to coin silver without limit at any ratio to gold he might decide.

This act gave the President power to inflate the currency in almost any way he pleased. He could print more paper money, the old demand of the greenbackers, or he could buy more silver, the old aim of the silver group in the 1880s and 1890s.

Executive orders on gold

Under the authority of these two acts, inflation may be said to have begun with executive orders of March 10,1933, halting the export of gold except when licensed by the Treasury; of April 5, forbidding the hoarding of gold and gold certificates; and of April 19, forbidding the export of any gold. The last is generally regarded as taking the nation off the gold standard. This was technically true, but as the gold was impounded in the Treasury, it remained, in the words of pro-gold-standard economists, a "psychological reserve." This was made more definite by the Gold Repeal Joint Resolution of June 5, which canceled the gold clauses in public and private obligations, making debts payable in legal tender. A rise in prices in the spring and early summer of 1933 halted for the moment further tinkering with the currency, but their decline in the early autumn simultaneously with the marketing of summer crops revived agitation for "reflation."

Up to this point the President had used only one of the five powers of inflation given him in the Farm Act by putting $600 million in circulation by Federal Reserve bank purchases of federal securities. In October the administration decided to stimulate inflation further by reducing the gold content of the dollar. On October 22 the President announced that the Treasury would buy gold at a price determined by the RFC. Instead of the long-established legal price of $20.67 an ounce, the price was initially set at $31.26 and eventually raised to $35 (January 31, 1934). This operation was carried out in practice by giving sellers of gold more paper dollars for the same amount of gold than they had previously received.

As long as the government could peg the price of gold in the open market, it could theoretically devalue the dollar and, it was thought, raise domestic prices. To the surprise of those who believed in the illusion that prices were determined by the gold content of the dollar, prices did not rise proportionately to the depreciation of the dollar; so on December 21 the President took what was believed to be another inflationary step and ordered the Treasury to purchase at 64.5 cents an ounce all of the silver mined in the United States; this price was 21.5 cents higher than that at which silver was then selling on the open market.

The Gold Reserve Act of 1934

When the President started the gold purchase plan in October 1933, he stated that he was "moving toward a managed currency." Indeed, his manipulation of the dollar and killing of the gold standard was condemned as "the end of civilization" by many anti-New Deal people. That he might have even more

clear-cut authorization, he asked Congress in January 1934 for legislation containing specific power to devalue the dollar to between 50 and 60 cents in terms of its former gold content, to manage the dollar within these limits, to impound in the Treasury the gold held in the Federal Reserve banks, to assure to the government the profits that might accrue from devaluing the dollar, and, finally, to use part of this profit to create a $2 billion fund to stabilize the dollar. Under the authority of the Gold Reserve Act (January 1934) the value of the dollar was officially fixed in February at 59.06 percent of its former (1900) value in terms of gold. In the particular method it pursued to raise prices, the administration appeared to have been influenced by the school of economists that held that the domestic price level of commodities is closely influenced by the gold content of the monetary medium. That such a relationship exists is debatable, to say the least, and it proved in this case no short cut to inflation, or rather "reflation," as the administration preferred to call it.

Three months later it was discovered that while the gold content of the dollar had been reduced by law 40.94 percent, wholesale commodity prices had risen only 22 percent. At the insistent clamor of the silver advocates, the administration consented to further legislation, and in June 1934 the Silver Purchase Act was passed, the "ultimate objective" of which was to increase the use of silver in the nation's currency stock until the proportions were one-quarter in silver to three-quarters in gold. This was viewed as an additional inflationary move.

Legislation on credit and housing

At this point the administration shifted its emphasis to the field of credit, a much more traditional approach. This orientation had been anticipated during the Hoover administration with the establishment of the Reconstruction Finance Corporation. The powers of the RFC, as we have seen, were extended under the Emergency Banking Act and again in June 1934, when the Loans-to-Industry Act authorized direct loans to industrial businesses of up to $580 million. The latter act aroused considerable criticism on the ground that it was poor economy to attempt to save the weaker units in an already overbuilt industrial system, but the great need of keeping people at work was the important argument for the loans.

Another effort to stabilize the credit situation, and at the same time save the small homeowner, began under Hoover in 1932 with the Home Loan Bank Act, which established federal banks to lend to private banks and building and loan associations on real estate mortgages. This was supplemented in 1933 by the Home Owner's Loan Act, setting up a corporation that could issue bonds up to $2 billion to refinance first mortgages on homes whose value did not exceed $20,000. Interest on the bonds was guaranteed and an amendment of 1934 extended this guarantee to the principal. The HOLA in its three-year life refinanced over a million home loans, and extended more than $3 billion at low interest rates to try to stabilize residential real estate values. The lending activities of this corporation were taken over by the Federal Housing Administration, which also insured against losses from loans on real estate. Underwriting the housing construction industry was to become typical of all advanced capitalistic economies that faced a similar predicament. This was made necessary again by public pressure when it was recognized that the private market, if left alone, could not produce housing at a price low enough to provide shelter for the low-income groups.

The Banking Acts of 1933 and 1935

The tragic shortcomings of the American banking system had been amply demonstrated, during both the boom years of the 1920s and the early depression years. Reform of some sort would have been probable under any administration. That adopted by the Democrats was incorporated in the Banking Acts of 1933 and 1935. The most widely discussed and perhaps the most important parts of the Banking Act of 1933 were those that separated security affiliates from the parent banks in the Federal Reserve System and those that set up the Federal Deposit Insurance Corporation to provide insurance on deposits.[2] The FDIC not only improved bank supervision, but it ended the time-honored custom of runs on banks and fundamentally softened the public's attitude toward banks and bankers in general.

The provision requiring banks to relinquish their security affiliates was designed to confine them again to a strictly commercial banking business, and the insurance scheme was devised to safeguard the almost defenseless depositor. Under the latter, all Federal Reserve banks were required to insure deposits, and state banks approved as solvent by the state banking authorities might participate. Other clauses in the act restricted the use of Federal

Reserve bank credit for stock-market speculation,[3] broadened the power of national banks to establish branch banks in those states that permitted branch banking, and restrained national banks from dealing in the securities of foreign countries and other foreign securities. It forbade private banks that underwrote and promoted the sale of securities from acting as banks of deposit, and established a quick liquidating procedure for the benefit of depositors in banks that had failed. The act also allowed industrial and savings banks to join the system. Many wished that the act had gone further on the road of banking reform; nevertheless, it was a major effort to rectify some of the worst abuses that had developed since the establishment of the Federal Reserve System in 1913.

In the Banking Act of 1935 an important effort was made to extend federal power over money and credit. First, although the amount insurable under the Federal Deposit Insurance Corporation was reduced, the supervisory powers of that corporation were considerably extended. Second, the Federal Reserve Board was reorganized into a seven-member board by eliminating the secretary of the Treasury and the comptroller from ex officio membership, in the hope of lessening political influence and making it more impartial and disinterested. It was not yet understood that the new, forthcoming managed economy would demand a strategic role for the Treasury in the determination of monetary policy. Third, the credit policy of the separate banks was transferred to the vitally important Federal Open Market Committee (already created by the act of 1933), made up of the seven members of the Federal Reserve Board and five regional representatives of the Reserve banks. The FOMC was in the long run destined to become the major instrument for monetary control through its power to buy and sell government securities. Fourth, the board could now vary within certain limits the reserve requirements of the member banks and review periodically the rates charged by the Reserve banks. Furthermore, it was required to give its approval to appointments for president and vice-president of each Reserve bank. Finally, certain technical changes enlarged the credit facilities of the system. The Federal Reserve banks, for example, were authorized to make advances to their members on any satisfactory security, and member banks might make a larg-

---

[2]The amount that could be insured for each account was fixed in 1935 at $5,000. This was increased to $10,000 in 1950 and again in the late 1960s to $20,000.

[3]For example, Federal Reserve member banks could no longer lend on the stock market "for others"; that is, they could not receive idle funds from corporations or individuals placed in the banks for the purpose of lending for stock market speculation.

er volume of real estate loans. The latter provision allowed loans for ten years up to 60 percent of the value of the property submitted as loan collateral, and up to a certain proportion of the bank's assets.

Securities and commodities regulation

The widespread popular resentment against the banks and security houses that had foisted securities of questionable value upon a gullible public in the 1920s also brought in 1933 the passage of the Sale of Securities Act, which sought to protect prospective investors by affording them certain information regarding new securities sold in interstate commerce. Under this act a concern offering securities was required to file detailed information with the Federal Trade Commission (later with a newly created body, the Securities and Exchange Commission), and even after approval was granted by the commission, sellers might be held liable in civil or criminal suits for untrue statements.

This was a preliminary to another act, the Securities Exchange Act of June 1934 (amended in 1936 to include unlisted securities), which provided for the regulation of securities exchanges and established the Securities and Exchange Commission to supervise them.

Both acts were bitterly opposed by the financial interests, and in the second act they succeeded in reducing the liability of underwriters, officers, and directors of the concerns issuing securities as originally provided in the Sale of Securities Act.

Regulation of a somewhat similar type was extended to certain agricultural commodities in 1936 by the Commodity Exchange Act, which set up the Commodity Exchange Commission to regulate transactions on commodity futures exchanges, to limit short selling, and to curb manipulation.

These acts did not guarantee the safety of an investment, but they attempted to protect the investor by securing honest information from corporations regarding new securities and those listed on the exchanges. Moreover, it was the business of the commissions to eliminate manipulation and dishonest practices. The result brought a marked improvement in the ethics of these exchanges.

Investment trusts

One notable contribution of the SEC was the preparation of an act passed by Congress in 1940 for the registration and regulation of investment trusts. Such companies were organized to sell their own stock, the funds from which were invested in a variety of stocks and bonds, the income (after management expenses were deducted) being then distributed to their own stockholders. Such companies were designed for small investors who did not have the time or the knowledge to look after their own financial interests. The opportunities for the misuse of such funds were many, and strict regulations were necessary. Although a number of investment trusts were organized in the 1930s, the great development came in the 1940s and later, when they came to be called mutual funds. By the late 1960s their total assets had expanded from the $2 billion of 1946 to some $48 billion, with over 4 million individual and institutional investors.[4]

A NEW DEAL FOR AGRICULTURE

No group, it was believed, would benefit more from higher prices than the "disadvantaged," rebellious farmers who had been treated so harshly by the operation of the private market. As the agricultural legislation of the New Deal developed, its major objective was to restore the farmer's purchasing power and his general economic position to that which he had enjoyed during the prewar "golden age"; that is, from August 1909 to July 1914, a time when the prices the farmer received for his products were sufficiently in "balance" with those he paid for commodities to maintain what was then thought to be a decent standard

of living.[5] This was to be done in part by in-

[4]R. P. Black and D. E. Harless, "Nonbank Financial Institutions," Federal Reserve Bank of Richmond, *Monthly Review*, December 1969, p. 29.

[5]As stated specifically in the Farm Relief and Inflation Act, the purpose was: "To establish and maintain such balance between the production and consumption of agricultural commodities, and such marketing conditions therefor, as will reestablish prices to farmers at a level that will give agricultural commodities a purchasing power with respect to articles that farmers buy, equivalent to the purchasing power of agricultural commodities in the base period. The base period in the case of all agricultural commodities except tobacco shall be the pre-war period, August, 1909–July, 1914. In the case of tobacco, the base period shall be the post-war period, August, 1919–July, 1929."

flation of farm prices and in part by adjusting farm production to market requirements, both of which methods would prepare the way for establishing parity prices and therefore, it was thought, parity income. In addition there was a definite policy to aid in debt reduction. Also included in the program was general rural relief and the rehabilitation of submarginal farmers. Important for the future was a growing interest in soil conservation and land improvement. This broad program the government followed with an enthusiasm that hardly envisaged either the complexities of the agricultural situation or the long-run commitment that was being undertaken. It is nevertheless significant that the administration was adopting a policy that was typical of the cartel: a monopoly agreement to maintain prices and restrict output. Such a monopolistic policy was to provide the cornerstones for the codes of fair competiton under the National Industrial Recovery Act, as we shall soon see.

The First Agricultural Adjustment Act

In response to widespread farm militancy, the program began in earnest in May 1933 with the Farm Relief and Inflation Act, more commonly known as the First Agricultural Adjustment Act. It moved to cut the surplus and raise the income of the farmers by three methods: (1) by cotton options under which cotton growers were to reduce their cotton acreage at least 30 percent and for which they were given options to purchase an amount of cotton corresponding to the amount they agreed not to raise (cotton that was still held by the former Federal Farm Board, renamed the Agricultural Adjustment Administration), and which the option holders might sell if prices went up; (2) by "rental" or benefit payments under which the government gave bonuses for acreage temporarily taken out of cultivation; and (3) by marketing agreements that might eliminate waste and provide for more scientific marketing. The cost was to be paid by processing taxes levied on products manufactured from the "basic" commodities concerned.

The expanding farm programs

During the first year the Agricultural Adjustment Administration concentrated on cotton, wheat, corn, hog, and tobacco reduction. The results seemed sufficiently successful for it to enlarge its operation in 1934 to include beef and dairy cattle, peanuts, rye, barley, flax, grain sorghums, sugar beets, and sugar cane.

The tobacco and cotton curtailment programs were strengthened by special acts. At the same time the government encouraged submarginal farmers to retire from commercial agriculture and attempted through trade agreements (reciprocal tariffs) to stimulate foreign trade in agricultural commodities.

No part of the New Deal program inspired more widespread criticism than that pertaining to agriculture. The whole idea of curtailing the production of foodstuffs while millions were on the point of starvation seemed to humanitarians little short of insanity. Because farmers produced food instead of steel, this form of insanity seemed to the popular mind more severe than that represented in idle steelmaking capacity. An effort to promote a scarcity economy at a time when the opposite was needed seemed incredible. Furthermore, it largely shifted the burden to the hard-pressed consumer. Even from the point of view of monopolistic scarcity economics, however, there was no clear-cut evidence in the early months that the program was going to be successful. Despite government efforts, the violation of acreage reduction contracts, favorable climatic conditions (some thought unfavorable, since it raised production!), and more intensive farming produced crops of cotton, corn, and hogs in 1933 not much below those of 1932. While the controlled crops were somewhat reduced, farmers turned to other crops.

The sudden increase in the cost of foodstuffs brought consumer resistance, and the general rise in nonfarm prices kept the puchasing power of the farmer's dollar about where it had been. American curtailment also stimulated foreign agricultural production in order to expand shares of world markets. Nor were the prospects of increased foreign trade through reciprocal tariffs particularly bright for the farmers because in some cases such tariffs were bound to bring foreign agricultural products in greater competition with domestic products.

Despite these retarding influences, however, there was no question that the economic conditions of the farmers after 1933 improved rapidly. The Agricultural Adjustment Administration noted early in 1935 that the purchasing power of farm products in 1934 averaged 73 percent of the prewar level, as compared with 55 percent at the low point in March 1933. Some of this improvement was doubtless the result of the faster rise of farm prices than of nonfarm prices typically characterizing a general economic improvement, but it was also due in part to the New Deal program. Whatever may have been the immediate economic contributions of the Agricultural Adjustment Act, they were suddenly arrested when in January 1936 in *U.S. v. Butler* the Supreme Court declared parts of the act unconstitutional on the grounds that it invaded the reserved rights of the states and was an improper use of the taxing power.

Soil conservation

The probability that the Court might do this had led the government to canvass the possibilities of continuing agricultural controls in some other way, and the method decided upon was soil conservation. The drought of 1934 and the dust storms in the spring of 1935 were fixed upon to call attention to the tragic results of soil destruction, and Congress recognized the problem by creating in 1933 the Soil Erosion Service and by enacting in 1935 the Soil Erosion Act. This legislation created the Soil Conservation Service, under the secretary of agriculture, to conduct soil-erosion surveys and carry out preventive measures. The scope of this work was greatly enlarged after the AAA decision by the Soil Conservation and Domestic Allotment Act (1936), the effective transitional substitute for the defunct AAA. This law provided $500 million for the preservation and improvement of soil fertility, the promotion of the economic use and conservation of land, and the protection of rivers and harbors against soil erosion. For two years direct aid might be given to cooperating farmers, after which it was to be extended only to states that had adopted authorizing legislation and a conservation plan acceptable to the secretary of agriculture.

This last requirement was emblematic of the rising concern among New Deal policy makers for more formal planning, not only to meet the short run crisis but also to establish the basis for a more systematically ordered national economy.

The Second Agricultural Adjustment Act

The Soil Conservation and Domestic Allotment Act was a makeshift. With the reelection of Roosevelt in 1936 and a more sympathetic Supreme Court, Congress in 1938 passed a new Agricultural Adjustment Act (the second AAA). This measure retained certain features of the old acts and added new ones. As in earlier legislation, its primary aim was to maintain parity prices; that is, to keep the prices of certain agricultural products (wheat, cotton, corn, tobacco, and rice) at the same level in relation to the cost of commodities typically bought by farmers as that which obtained, on the average, during the years 1909–1914.[6] This was to be achieved by the government's setting a parity price and a quota each year for the commodity to be raised. If the price fell below this, the government would in part recompense the farmer for the difference between the actual price received and the parity price. If production in any year was far beyond the amount set by the government, marketing quotas might be established if two-thirds of the farmers producing that commodity agreed. Such agreements would be enforced by penalty taxes for selling beyond the quotas. In determining the amount of a commodity to be raised in a year, the Department of Agriculture was to include a surplus so that in case of drought or other emergency a sufficient quantity would always be on hand. This policy, a new feature of the act, was expected to maintain an "ever normal granary." Another new feature was the establishment of crop insurance (on wheat). The maintenance of soil resources as provided in the Soil Conservation and Allotment Act was retained as a permanent rationale.

The dust bowl

The Great Plains region suffered special problems in the 1930s and offered a particularly challenging set of conservation needs: needs that captured Roosevelt's own attention and became a subject of concentrated effort by his Secretary of Agriculture, Henry A. Wallace. Here was the source of the great "Okie" and "Arkie" outmigration made famous in John Steinbeck's *Grapes of Wrath*. In this semiarid territory a series of major windstorms in the thirties laid waste to vast farming sections that drove tens of thousands of people from the parched land. The New Deal's agricultural and conservation experts, and especially Wallace, advocated contour plowing and the building of "shelterbelts" of trees across the plains as a way of protecting the land against such devastating wind-induced erosion. A grandiose plan to build windbreaks of this sort on a north-south axis across the entire Plains region fell far short of accomplishment, despite the almost evangelical zeal of federal officials. But more than 200 million seedling trees were planted under the auspices of several federal agencies, from 1935 to 1942, in the region stretching from North Dakota to Texas. They proved remarkably successful. Ironically, in 1975, forty years after the program was initiated, a government

---

[6]For tobacco the years 1919–1926 were to be used.

study found that farmers were removing the shelterbelt trees to put more land into crops, or to make room for irrigation facilities. And predictably enough, some of the old problems of devastating erosion were coming back to bedevil farmers in the counties where tree removal was most advanced. Indeed, the 1975 study expressed urgent concern that dust storms like those of the 1930s could once again produce widespread farm losses in the Great Plains, should tree removal continue.

Debt reduction

The second great objective of the New Deal agricultural program, debt reduction and security against foreclosure, was also pushed aggressively. The First Agricultural Adjustment Act aimed to aid the farmers' credit situation by authorizing the federal land banks to issue $2 billion in 4 percent bonds—the interest but not the principal to be guaranteed by the government—to refinance farm mortgages at an interest rate not to exceed 4.5 percent. To increase administrative efficiency the President in 1933 consolidated the government's various agricultural credit agencies in the Farm Credit Administration. This consolidation, authorized under the Farm Credit Act (June 1933), grouped the credit facilities into four divisions dealing with land banks, production credit, intermediate credit, and cooperative credit, and considerably enlarged existing facilities.

Farm mortgages

From providing easier credit facilities the program moved on to the mortgage problem. Congress passed three acts in 1934: (1) the Farm Mortgage Refinancing Act, creating the Federal Farm Mortgage Corporation to aid further in refinancing farm debts; (2) the Farm Mortgage Foreclosure Act, extending the authority of the land bank commissioner to enable him to make loans to farmers for the purpose of enabling them to redeem farm properties owned by them prior to foreclosure; and (3) the Frazier-Lemke Bankruptcy Act, providing that in cases of bankruptcy the farmer might demand a "fair and reasonable" appraisal and might repurchase his property over a period of six years with interest at 1 percent. If creditor or mortgagee objected to the settlement, the farmer might retain the property for a period of five years at a reasonable rental, bankruptcy proceedings being halted. The Frazier-Lemke Act was declared unconstitutional in 1935 as a violation of the Fifth Amendment, but a similar substitute act shortening the retention period to

three years was upheld in 1936. Within a year and a quarter after the acts had been passed, the Farm Credit Administration had made 1.4 million loans totaling $2 billion. The result was a virtual stoppage of farm foreclosures.

Other farm legislation

The legislation so far mentioned by no means encompassed the entire program of agricultural aid. The program included the much-criticized Resettlement Administration, established in 1935 to financially rehabilitate and to relocate on decent agricultural lands destitute marginal farmers, croppers, tenants, and unemployed farm migrants. Some relocation involved settlement on better individual farm units, some took the form of newly founded rural communities enjoying, for the first time for many, good roads, schools, and sanitation facilities. Small as the operation was, it aroused the usual invectives against New Deal paternalism and coddling of the presumably inept. The RA was absorbed two years later into the Farm Security Administration, which established the famous migrant labor camps, helped set up cooperative homestead communities, and made loans to indigent tenants and submarginal producers with a view toward transforming them into the American ideal of self-supporting family farmers. From its inception to World War II the FSA spread thinly over 656,000 recipients about $131 million—woefully inadequate but still another one among the many New Deal social and economic betterment efforts.

The Federal Surplus Relief (later Commodities) Corporation undertook, in order to bolster prices and aid the hungry, to purchase and distribute surplus products among state relief organizations, one of the more directly humane measures of the administration, and the one that inaugurated the famous food-stamp plan, very much operative today. It rendered great aid to agriculture through flood-control projects (the TVA and others), by larger appropriations for interstate highways, and by substantial allotments for rural electrification. The Rural Electrification Administration supervised an enormous and badly needed expansion of the use of electricity on American farms.[7] Moreover, the reciprocal tariffs sought to aid farmers as well as other groups. In fact, it would be difficult to

---

[7]Rural electrification loans became a bitter bone of contention between President Nixon and congressional opponents in 1973, after 37 years of efficient administration and successful aid to farmers by the REA.

think of any method, unless it be complete socialization, neglected by the federal government to rehabilitate American agriculture. It is of great significance that every advanced industrial country has pursued similar programs of subsidy for its farm sector.

Farm legislation, 1933–1938

A survey of the farm legislation passed during the five years 1933–1938 makes clear certain facts. First of all, economic planning was carried further with respect to agriculture than to any other economic interest. The government took upon itself the responsibility of attempting to determine both production and prices as well as maintaining soil resources and handling most of the credit resources of the farmers. The new regime in agriculture — making it a managed sector — caused old-style individualists to raise the spectre of Bolshevik "collectivization," comparing Roosevelt to Stalin, Hitler, and Mussolini. In the second place, this program was carried out at the expense of the consumer. Agriculture was to be a favored industry, with the taxpayer and consumer paying the bill. This, of course, did not disturb the farmers who insisted that agriculture was now merely receiving protection as industry had long received it through the protective tariff. Finally, it should be noted that the government entered so definitely into the program of financing agriculture that by 1937 its agencies held about half of the long-term agricultural debt paper of the country.

At the same time, private agencies largely abandoned the business of financing agriculture, a business that had never had a strong appeal to the financial community. All this made serious inroads on the so-called free-enterprise system and was indeed a big step from the laissez-faire policies of earlier decades. It is perhaps ironic that these inroads were made at the insistence of people who had always thought of themselves, and been thought of, as rugged individualists. The irony is understood, however, when it is realized that farming at that time was a small business sector in a world of big business. The farmers had a long tradition of organized resentment against market failures due to monopolistic elements in the nonfarm economy. A better "balance" was again the watchword.

INDUSTRY AND THE NEW DEAL

The New Deal's policy toward industry, as preeminently represented in the National Industrial Recovery Act (1933), was both akin to and more comprehensive than its policy toward agriculture. It aimed, said Roosevelt in signing the act, to assure "a reasonable profit to industry and living wages to labor with the elimination of piratical methods and practices which have not only harassed honest business but also contributed to the ills of labor." More simply stated, the NIRA aimed to promote recovery by introducing self-regulation of business, curtailing overproduction, increasing wages, shortening hours of labor, and raising prices. Along with this the act authorized the federal financing of public works to the impressive extent of $3 billion.

The act's highly important section 7(a) gave workers the right to organize in all industries covered by its "codes of fair competition," a stunning new departure in national labor policy. Important groundwork for this new direction in labor legislation had been laid the year previously, due to persistent labor pressure, by passage of the Norris-La Guardia act, which asserted labor's right to organize, restrained the courts' use of the injunction against labor in industrial disputes, and made the "yellow-dog" contract legally unenforceable.

The President was authorized to establish codes of fair competition that industry was to accept voluntarily but which could be enforced through a system of licensing. Theoretically these codes were to be worked out through the cooperation of government, industry, labor, and the consumer. In actual practice they were largely the work of representatives of the larger firms in industry, with some participation from labor where unions were strong. As in the case of the agricultural legislation, the interest of the consumers was largely ignored. Behind the NIRA was the theory that the efforts of the older antitrust acts to maintain unlimited competition failed, and that in their place, at least temporarily, should be substituted an attempt to establish "industrial cooperation" under government control. Technically the antitrust acts were still in force; actually they were pushed into the background.

The background of the NIRA

The background of the NIRA was wider than the depression. Throughout the 1920s the nation had taken a lenient attitude toward monopolies, and this was reflected in the attitude of the Supreme Court and the failure of the enforcement agencies to prosecute infringements of the antitrust acts. The government had cooperated closely with big business during World War I and later with the trade associations. The trade associations in turn had developed a precedent of industrial cooperation and had modified unbridled competition within the separate industries. And there was, of course, the propaganda of industry that self-regulation with the force of law would bring better results than government regulation.

The NRA

To carry out the NIRA, the National Recovery Administration (NRA) was set up under the direction of General Hugh S. Johnson as administrator and Donald Richberg as general counsel. These men, with a staff of expert assistants in cooperation with representatives of the leading concerns in industry and labor, where possible, drew up what were believed to be fair codes, held public hearings, and finally promulgated the codes over the President's signature.

As several thousand industries were eligible for codification and the duration of the act was only two years, the first problem was to decide whether it would be better to hammer out a few perfect codes for the basic industries or to formulate as many as possible as quickly as possible in the hope that defects could be eventually ironed out. The latter course was followed. But as a stopgap until separate codes could be drawn up, a blanket agreement on hours and wages, known as the President's Reemployment Agreement, was promulgated in July. This blanket code banned child labor, established a working week of 35 hours for industrial workers and 40 for white-collar workers, and set minimum wages of 40 cents per hour for industry and from $12 to $15 per week for others, depending on the size of the community. Employers who would adhere to this temporary agreement (to last six months but later extended to May 1, 1934) would receive the symbol of the Blue Eagle.

Unlike the industry codes, the blanket code was not enforceable at law. The pressure of public approval, however, gave it strength and hastened the process of code making in the individual industries. In the meantime, Washington took on a hectic atmosphere reminiscent of war days as representatives of industrial trade associations and labor unions flocked to the capital to participate in code making. Eventually over 576 basic codes were approved, along with 189 supplementary codes, and the majority of industrial workers operated under the Blue Eagle.

Criticism of the NIRA

No effort to codify and integrate industry on such a scale had ever before been made in America, and the difficulties were great. The desperate condition in which the nation found itself, however, created, at least in the early months, a willingness to cooperate in carrying the NIRA into effect. Nevertheless, there was criticism from the start. There were frequent charges that the codes were evaded ("chiseling") and that the interests of the consumer and the small businessman were ignored in making the codes. Unorganized and inadequately represented as these critics were, their complaint had a strong basis in fact. But as the months went by, criticism also developed rapidly on the part of labor, which insisted that there had been widespread evasion of those parts of the codes applying to labor, especially of the spirit and intention of the crucial Section 7(a) of the NIRA, which guaranteed the right of labor to organize and to be represented by persons of their own choosing. In the end there was considerable opposition also from some sections of industry, particularly from small enterprise, which often felt that the codes favored the larger firms and which in many cases submitted its own codes in opposition to those drawn up by the leading concerns.

The barrage of criticism brought the appointment of the National Recovery Review Board, headed by the famed lawyer Clarence Darrow, to investigate the operation and effect of the NIRA. Dissatisfaction by labor finally culminated in the textile strike of September 1934, the resignation of Johnson, and the reorganization of the National Recovery Administration. In the face of the criticism, the administration claimed that the NIRA had lifted the nation out of its economic slough and put it on the road to recovery. Many opponents, on the other hand, asserted that it had delayed recovery. This is one of those controversial problems the truth of which can never be ascertained. Certainly, as we shall see, labor gained important initial benefits, industry escaped temporarily from the antitrust laws, and there was, fortunately for the administration, an accompanying improvement in the general economic situation. But the consumer as usual seemed lost in the shuffle. By 1935, some historians assert, Roosevelt himself had become so skeptical of the NIRA approach to industrial problems that he personally was prepared to abandon the experiment.

The Court acts against the NIRA

Whatever may have been the gains or losses through the organization of industry under the NIRA, the whole question became largely irrelevant when the Supreme Court, in the Schechter Case (May 1935), held that the code-making provisions in the NIRA were an invalid transfer of the legislative power from Congress to the President and that the attempt to regulate industry in the manner prescribed was an improper use of the interstate commerce power. The result of the decision, which was unanimous, was quickly to liquidate the NRA.

Despite the Court's decision, Congress tried to maintain its monopolistic principles in another of the nation's demoralized industries. In the Bituminous Coal Conservation Act (1935) the mining of bituminous coal was declared "affected with a national public interest" and a commission was set up to formulate a bituminous coal code. The Supreme Court also cracked down on this legislation.

Modification of the antitrust laws

It is clear from a study of all this legislation that during the early years of the New Deal the government was in a mood to soften the antitrust acts in order to help big business by restraining unbridled competition. The limitation of unbridled competition was turned more in the direction of trying to help small business in later legislation, however. The Robinson-Patman Act of 1936, for example, aimed to sharpen and clarify certain prohibitions of the Clayton Act to make illegal the sale of goods where there was discrimination between individuals and localities or where the price was so low as to destroy competition or eliminate a competitor. This new act, which was principally directed against chain stores, was expected to give relief to the local storekeeper. The New Deal was thus forging its political alliance with little business.

In the meantime, various states had attempt-ed to aid business of all sizes by monopolistic, anticonsumer legislation allowing agreements between manufacturers and their distributors or retailers which fixed minimum prices for trade-marked commodities. This was legalized in interstate commerce by the Miller-Tydings Act of 1937, which amended the Sherman Antitrust Act. The Antitrust Division of the Justice Department was strongly opposed to these state "fair trade" laws and to the Miller-Tydings enabling act in particular.

The monopoly investigation

Interestingly enough, the attitude of the administration toward monopoly appeared to have changed by 1938. Believing that the recession of 1937 and 1938 was in part caused by high and cyclically unresponsive monopoly prices, President Roosevelt asked Congress for funds for a full investigation by a special committee. The Temporary National Economic Committee's "Investigation of the Concentration of Economic Power" exhaustively probed the methods used and the extent reached in the concentration of economic power. It was the most thorough examination ever made of the problem of monopoly in this country by any agency, public or private.

From the committee's report it was evident that, contrary to their generally progressive orientation, New Deal business policies had strengthened and encouraged monopoly development rather than hindered it. The war soon to come had the same effect. It is true that the antitrust division of the attorney general's office under the liberal Thurman Arnold became increasingly active after 1938 in opposing monopoly practices, but the results were slight in a period of close cooperation between government and industry during World War II. But it had now become harder for the Department of Agriculture to try to make restriction of production look like conservation of resources rather than monopolistic price raising and output control.[8]

REGULATION OF THE POWER INDUSTRY

No American industry was more subject to criticism in the 1920s and 1930s than the private electric power industry. Inflated financial structures that bore little actual relation to the money invested or to the value of the property, and a complicated structure of holding companies imposed one upon the other, so confused the investing and consuming publics as to make it difficult for them to determine the financial position of the corporations or the fairness of rates. State utility comissions, except in two or three states, seemed utterly incapable of controlling the situation, partly from bias on the

[8]B. Mitchell, *Depression Decade*, (New York: Holt, Rinehart and Winston, 1947), p. 199.

part of some commission members, partly from lack of adequate consumer representation on these regulatory commissions, and partly because the business had long ago outgrown state boundaries. In 1936 the 12 largest utility holding companies controlled almost half the power produced in the nation, their lines crossing state boundaries in all directions. In brief, by the early 1930s the business of producing and distributing electric power had reached a stage similar to that of the railroads a half century earlier. The conditions and abuses of the railroads in their early days were being duplicated and were leading again to the same sort of demand for federal control.

Federal regulation had begun in a tentative manner with the Federal Water Power Act of 1920, which set up the Federal Power Commission to exercise administrative control over all power sites erected on public lands of the United States and on navigable rivers. The commission had the power to license for 50 years concerns desiring to erect such plants, and to require uniform accounting systems; and it was given power over their security issues and over rates for power sold across state boundaries.[9] Perhaps the most important aspect of the utility problem that confronted the nation was whether the authority of this commission should be extended to cover all companies operating in more than one state and all concerns transporting power across state lines. There was also the question as to whether the federal government itself should enter the field of power production. It was the latter question, as it turned out that was taken up first.

Muscle Shoals

The implications of government operations could hardly be dodged because the federal government had authorized during World War I the building of two plants at Muscle Shoals on the Tennessee River to produce nitrates for the manufacture of explosives. To provide electric energy for these plants, the Wilson Dam was also authorized; it was completed in 1925, making the total government investment about $145 million. Whether the government should operate these plants or turn them over at nominal cost to private companies was the question before the nation. Urged on by conservationist Senator George W. Norris, Congress twice passed bills authorizing enlargement of the plants and government operation. Coolidge pocket-vetoed the first, and

---

[9]As in the case of railroads, this power had been denied by the courts to state commissions.

Hoover vetoed the second with the words that such a project was not "liberalism" but "degeneration." Before his inauguration Roosevelt visited Muscle Shoals and announced that he would support a bill for government operation.

The TVA

One of the most far-reaching, famous, and significant acts of the Roosevelt administration, and one that affected agriculture, industry, and other economic interests as well as public utilities, was the Muscle Shoals–Tennessee Valley Development Act (May 1933). It created a board of three members, known as the Tennessee Valley Authority, to maintain and operate properties owned by the government at Muscle Shoals, Alabama, in the interest of national defense and the development of agriculture and industry in the Tennessee Valley, to improve navigation on the Tennessee, and to control the floodwaters of that river and the Mississippi. The TVA was given wide authority to acquire real estate, build dams and powerhouses, install hydroelectric plants, develop a program of flood control, prevent soil erosion, and aid reforestation, besides manufacturing nitrogen products for fertilizers and explosives. Within a decade the TVA had accomplished all these objectives. It was one of the most enduring achievements of the New Deal. The whole project was both a masterpiece of economic planning and a monumental experiment in the regeneration and development of a geographic region that is also essentially an economic unit.

Although the act affected many interests, the chief opposition in the courts came, significantly enough, from the public utilities. Despite numerous legal attacks, the act was upheld by the Supreme Court. So certain was the administration of the success of the TVA experiment that in 1937 Roosevelt, in a special message to Congress, advocated that six similar regional planning agencies be set up which would cover most of the nation. He did not get even one.

Putting the government into direct competition with private power companies was denounced with special virulence as a prime example of New Deal socialism. The private utilities claimed that the region was already as fully provided with services as "the market" would absorb. It turned out, however, that TVA's cheap power brought the percentage of farm homes with electricity in the region up from 10 percent in 1933 to 90 percent by the early 1940s. In post-New Deal years, ironically, the TVA came under increasing attack for being too heavily bureaucratic, too little reform-minded (especially on environmental

protection issues), and devoted in too ortho-
dox a "business-minded" way to balancing
the books by producing revenues at the expense of nonself-financing projects in the areas
of recreational facilities investment and conservation.

The Public Utilities Holding Company Act, 1935

Two years after the Tennessee Valley development was launched, Congress attacked
the problem of more effective federal control of
power projects and greater protection to the
investing and consuming public. The Public
Utilities Holding Company Act (1935) was one
of the most bitterly fought pieces of New Deal
legislation. Among other things it granted to the
Federal Power Commission authority to regulate rates and business practices of utilities
doing interstate business, prohibited holding
companies beyond the second degree, and
required federal sanction through the Securities
and Exchange Commission for the issuance of
securities, the acquisition of properties, and the
handling of other kinds of business. After three
years holding companies had to limit their operations to single integrated systems and to business directly connected with the supply of
power service to consumers.

At the time of its passage, the act was loosely
discussed as one that inflicted the death penalty
upon holding companies. Whatever it did, it
apparently did not injure the private electric utility business, for it was one of the first to push
out of the depression and by 1937 enjoyed the
greatest gross revenues of its history. No company died that seemed to have the slightest
excuse for living. Opposition by utility companies and the difficulties of reorganization slowed
up enforcement, but by 1950 the objects of the
act were virtually accomplished.

TRANSPORTATION

No branch of American industrial life felt the
depression more than transportation, especially
railroad transportation. Like agriculture and
bituminous coal, this "disadvantaged" industry
was destined for an era of government protection and subsidy, the American alternative to
European nationalization. Much aid had already been extended through the RFC, but
Congress in 1933 took a further step by passing
the Railroad Emergency Act, which set up a
federal railroad coordinator whose orders, unless revoked by the Interstate Commerce
Commission, to whom appeal could be taken,
would have the force and effect of the commission's. With the aid of coordinating committees
of railroad representatives, he was to devise
means to avoid waste, promote financial organization, reduce fixed charges to the extent
required by the public interest, and improve the
credit of the railroads. In the accomplishment of
these purposes, the antitrust laws, if necessary,
might as usual be set aside. The act repealed
the famous but unsuccessful recapture clause of
the Transportation Act of 1920,[10] but, on the
other hand, it sought to remedy one great
weakness of the earlier legislation by placing
railroad holding corporations under the supervision of the Interstate Commerce Commission.
Although Coordinator Joseph B. Eastman and

his aides made surveys of the railroad situation
and recommendations for improvement — some
of which were followed by the railroads — the
most permanent effect of the Emergency Act of
1933, as far as railroads were concerned, appears to have been the modifications of the act
of 1920. The office of federal railroad coordinator, created as an emergency measure, was discontinued in 1936.

More important than the emergency legislation of 1933 was the Wheeler-Lea Transportation Act of 1940, which enlarged the powers
of the ICC to include supervision over water
carriers operating in coastwise, inland, and
intercoastal trade. The act also relieved the
commission of the necessity of proposing railroad consolidation, but no consolidation could
be effected without the commission's approval.

Trucking and aviation legislation

It was not in railroads, however, that the
Roosevelt administration made its greatest contribution to the problem of American transportation. One of the recommendations of Coordinator Eastman and his staff was for a federal act
governing motor vehicles engaged in interstate
commerce. By the Motor Carrier Act (1935)
such transportation was put under the regulation of the Interstate Commerce Commission
and its activities were coordinated with those of
other carriers. The commission was empowered
to establish just and reasonable rates and pre-

---

[10]One-half of net earnings above the fair rate of return to
revert to the commission.

scribe uniform systems of accounting, and the carriers were forbidden to grant rebates or to discriminate as to rates, localities, and persons. The commission also had the power to establish standards for hours of work, safety, and equipment. In brief, a real beginning was made in extending federal control to the growing trucking industry engaged in interstate commerce. By 1940 the trucking industry had already come to account for 10 percent of all intercity freight traffic, to say nothing of intracity and farm haulage.

Although the development of commercial aviation, which was at that time overwhelmingly a passenger traffic industry, was temporarily halted by the depression, the industry did not by any means collapse. On the contrary, it advanced rapidly during the 1930s. The government's problem was therefore not one of saving aviation, but rather one of improving federal control. Charges of fraud and favoritism in awarding mail contracts led President Roosevelt in 1934 to cancel all these contracts, and for a brief period the army carried the mail. By the Air Mail Act of 1934 the transportation of mail was returned under new contracts to private carriers. Congress in 1938 consolidated much of the control under the new Civil Aeronautics Authority, with the semi-independent Air Safety Board to investigate accidents and study safety measures. The work of these two bodies helped to inspire greater efficiency and safety in civil aviation and was popular with private air companies. It was believed to be nonpolitical. Consequently, there was criticism when the President in 1940, under the powers given him to reorganize the government service, consolidated these boards and placed them within the Department of Commerce.

Maritime legislation

By 1936 a number of factors contributed to direct the nation's attention again to the question of the merchant marine. A succession of maritime disasters called for more thoroughgoing regulation and supervision, acute labor-management conflicts pointed to the need for better working conditions, and the general decline of the merchant marine called for new subsidies if it was to be saved. This situation was made particularly clear by a report from the Maritime Commission in 1937, which showed that of the 9 million gross tonnage built during the previous decade, only 5 percent had been registered in the United States. Although this country still ranked second in tonnage volume, it ranked fourth in speed and last in age of vessels. At least one-quarter of the tonnage was obsolete and seven-eighths would be in that condition by 1942.

To deal with this problem in an industry always thought to be affected with a national public interest, the Merchant Marine Act of 1936 was passed. It ended the construction loans under the old Merchant Marine Act of 1920, dissolved the former United States Shipping Board Merchant Fleet Corporation, and established a new agency known as the United States Maritime Commission. It directed the commission to survey the American merchant marine to determine what additions and replacements were necessary, to investigate employment and wage conditions, and to consider applications for construction subsidies, at the same time laying down conditions under which they might be granted.

The old system of subsidization through mail contracts was to be replaced by direct subsidies. These subsidies were chiefly of two kinds. First, ships might be built on government contract and sold to the shipper (on long-term easy payments) at cost minus the difference between the cost of building here and abroad. Second, operating subsidies might be granted to vessels engaged on essential trade routes, these subsidies to be sufficient to offset the difference in cost between operating American and foreign ships. The commission was also given power to determine wages, minimum crews, and working conditions, and the Maritime Labor Board was established to mediate labor disputes.

The emergence of all these new control agencies, along with others to be discussed below, shows clearly that there was a dramatic increase in federal regulatory administration under the New Deal.

RELIEF AND SECURITY

We now come to one vital category of New Deal policy that contributed enormously to launching the mixed economy in the United States: the economy with a large and growing government budget and with the assumed responsibility of the federal government for high employment, stability, and growth. The detrimental effect of the depression on labor with respect to unemployment and decline in income has already been noted. Income decreased more rapidly than the cost of living. There was conclusive evidence of an increase in industrial accidents reflecting a letup in safety and accident-prevention activities; there was a general increase in sweatshop conditions and in the overworking of women and children. Until the tide was turned by the codes of the NIRA, there was a weakening of the position of union labor. On the other hand, the long-drawn-out depression and the militancy of the workers, as we shall see, stimulated interest in new forms of protective labor legislation.

In response to labor unrest the Roosevelt administration developed a threefold policy. The first and most pressing need was to relieve the unemployment situation. The second was to improve the economic security of the wage earner or salary earner through unemployment insurance, old-age insurance, and other methods. The third was to strengthen the disadvantaged position of organized labor in the American economic system. It will be noted that all three of these phenomena expressed, in one form or another, defects in the operation of the private market system—or defects, at least in the view of those adversely affected.

The CCC

The attack on unemployment began almost immediately after Roosevelt's inauguration with an act empowering the President to employ young men in a Civilian Conservation Corps to construct public works in connection with reforestation, flood control, and similar projects, in an effort to relieve unemployment among the younger men. During the first year more than 300,000 men enrolled in the CCC camps. A pet project of the administration, the all-male CCC was maintained as a permanent feature of the New Deal policy until Congress finally ended its appropriations in 1942.

Work relief and public works

In May came the Emergency Relief Act, creating the Federal Emergency Relief Administration and directing the RFC to make available $500 million for emergency relief to the states. The period of significant expenditures of FERA ended in 1936, during which time it had dispensed about $3 billion, mostly for direct relief. Then came the NIRA, which set up the Public Works Administration with initial funds of $3.3 billion to promote construction in the public interest. The PWA spent over $4 billion during its eight-year career, but despite all efforts failed to absorb the millions of unemployed. Next, the Civil Works Administration was established in November 1933 as a winter job program. By January 1934 it had over 4 million on its payrolls, and had dispensed $1 billion by the time it was absorbed into FERA in mid-1934. To speed reemployment, Congress in 1935 again made large appropriations for a second public works program and the President by executive order established the Works Progress Administration (later called Works Projects Administration) to coordinate the entire works program.

The WPA initiated many projects outside the limited category of public works. These programs represented a massive and historical shift to the federal government of the social responsibility for relief, poverty, employment, and security. The long age of private and local charity was approaching its demise. All this was then thought to be a temporary response to an emergency, but of course we now know it was to become a regular feature of a whole era in modern American economic history.

The WPA continued until the increased economic activity produced by World War II solved, at least for the time being, the problem of mass unemployment. During the seven years from 1935 to 1942, when Congress ordered it liquidated, the WPA spent about $10.5 billion plus $2.7 billion contributed by sponsors, chiefly local governments. It is noteworthy that the state and local governments also thus became caught up in the process of inaugurating the mixed economy. They subsequently remained involved.

The WPA alone never solved the unemployment problem, but at the height of its activity in 1938 it provided jobs for 3.8 million, about one-third of the unemployed. At one time or another it employed 8.5 million persons. Counting dependents of workers, it benefited directly more than 25 million persons. Among the many things accomplished by the WPA were the construction of 122,000 public buildings, 664,000 miles of new roads, 77,000 new bridges, 285 new airports, and 24,000 miles of storm and water sewers, and the repair of thousands of existing facilities. In addition it built parks, playgrounds, reservoirs, and innumerable other things that were greatly needed. Not only did the WPA provide jobs for skilled and unskilled workers in the various building projects, but it helped white-collar workers, including teachers, actors, artists, and writers. It also reached out through the National Youth Administration to aid high school and college students to obtain an education. It represented an almost incredible transformation in thought and policy pyramided into a span of less than a decade.

It was clear from the start that the policy of unemployment relief went beyond make-work jobs and priming the economic pump. It was based on a fundamental belief, vigorously stated by a depression-laden laboring population, that human beings had a right to work, that most were unemployed through no fault of their own, and that it was better for all to live by work rather than by charity. Nevertheless, this program was bitterly criticized. It was charged with waste and inefficiency, with coddling the shiftless, with the expenditure of millions for political purposes, and with failure to accomplish its major objective, the elimination of unemployment. In reply, the administration insisted that the self-respect of millions had been saved by jobs rather than the dole, that much needed work had been done, and that the whole program had helped materially to ease the depression.

The United States Housing Authority

A start was likewise made under the PWA on the problem of low-cost housing and slum clearance. To speed this program the Wagner-Steagall Housing Act of 1937 established the United States Housing Authority, with power to make loans and contributions for slum clearance and the building of low-rent houses. The Housing Authority was allowed to lend up to $500 million (tripled in later years) for housing projects. The loans were to be made and the construction done by private contractors in cooperation with local public housing agencies.

By the middle of 1940 the USHA had made contracts for the construction of over 400 housing projects containing almost 150,000 homes. When it is remembered that the President had stated that one-third of the nation was poorly housed, the work of the PWA and later of the USHA was but a tiny beginning. Nevertheless, it was a start in the right direction. Moreover, it indirectly stimulated private interests to build some new housing projects in slum areas. It also established a precedent for federal aid in veterans' housing after World War II. It will be noted that the New Deal was again pursuing a program similar to those of European governments in recognizing the need for government intervention in the housing market. But again the American solution was subsidy of the relevant private sector rather than, as in many European countries, direct public construction and ownership.

Economic security

The second great labor objective of the Roosevelt administration, improvement of the security of the wage earner, was provided by many types of legislation. The National Employment Service Act (1933) created a national system of exchanges to cooperate with state employment offices, subsidized in part by the federal government. By the Railroad Retirement Act (1935) the federal government took over the machinery of handling pensions of railroad workers. This was to be done by a payroll tax split half and half between worker and employer. In 1936 Congress passed the Walsh-Healey Government Contracts Act, providing that public contracts (except for certain specified articles) in excess of $10,000 made by any department or agency of the federal government must include stipulations requiring that the contractor be a manufacturer or regular dealer in the materials for which he was contracting, that he pay not less than the prevailing wages for persons employed in the industry, that he permit no one to work more than 8 hours in one day or 40 hours in any week, and that he employ no male under 16 years of age and no female under 18. The work, furthermore, had to be done under conditions that were not unduly hazardous.

The Wages and Hours Act, 1938

This type of legislation was climaxed in 1938 by the Fair Labor Standards Act (Wages and Hours Act). This was one of the major steps in long-run social reform that has elicited from historians the interpretation that there was a Second New Deal beginning in 1935. Some regard this phase the true or only real New Deal. The Wages and Hours Act proposed to put a floor under wages and a ceiling on hours. Maximum working hours were set at 44 a week for the first year, 42 for the second, and 40 thereafter. Minimum wages were to start at 25 cents an hour for the first year and be increased to 40 cents over a period of seven years. The act applied to all labor engaged in interstate commerce or the production of goods entering that commerce, and was expected at the time to cover from 12 million to 13 million workers. Agriculture was not covered, nor were numerous other categories. Although the minimum wages under this act bore little relation to a decent American standard of living, the provisions were generally accepted as a step in the right direction. Nevertheless, it was not until 1949 that Congress raised the minimum wage to 75 cents an hour, and subsequently raised it again to try to keep pace with a rising price trend. As of January 1976 the minimum was $2.30 an hour in manufacturing and other lines engaged in interstate commerce, $2.20 for smaller retailing and service firms, and $2.00 in agriculture. This was a fivefold increase over 1938, but meanwhile comparable hourly wage increases, for example in retail trade, were sixfold.

One important part of the act, significant because it compensated somewhat for the failure of the ratification of the child-labor amendment, is that concerning child labor. It prohibited the shipment in interstate commerce of goods produced in establishments engaging in "oppressive" child-labor practices. The latter was defined as the employment of minors under 16 in any occupation covered by the act and the employment of minors between 16 and 18 in occupations declared to be hazardous by the chief of the Children's Bureau. Children between 14 and 16 might be employed in nonmanufacturing and nonmining occupations under regulations issued by the Children's Bureau when such employment did not interfere with their schooling or their health and well-being. The act was upheld by the Supreme Court.[11]

Social Security

A more important element of the new "welfare state" than the legislation just discussed was the promotion of unemployment insurance, old-age pensions, and other benefits provided for by the Social Security Act of 1935, as amended in 1939 and later. This was a landmark in the U.S. social legislation and more than any other single enactment infused the new interventionist regime with a welfare component. It also substantiates very much the Second New Deal interpretation by historians of federal policy in the Great Depression.

Unemployment insurance had made little progress in the 1920s; only one state, Wisconsin, had introduced such a system up to 1934. More rapid progress had been made with old-age pension schemes; by 1929 at least 29 states had some kind of old-age pension law. It was the federal Social Security Act that made their application nationwide, a measure that represented a delayed response to organized agita-

[11]United States v. Darby (1941), which overruled Hammer v. Dagenhart (1918).

tion by, among others, the elderly — for example, the "old people's crusade" under Dr. Francis E. Townsend (the Townsend Plan) and the "End Poverty in California" (EPIC) movement of novelist Upton Sinclair. The law provided for a system of old-age pensions to aged needy persons over 65 years of age through federal grants on a 50–50 matching basis with the states, except that the federal government's share in no case would exceed $20 a month. To take care of the future, the law provided for a contributory old-age insurance scheme to be paid for by an income tax on employees and a payroll tax on employers beginning with 1 percent in 1937 and rising each three years until 1949, when the contribution from both would be 3 percent. The payroll tax followed conservative tradition in two senses: (1) it established a link, however loose as it turned out, between contributions and benefits, and (2) it represented a regressive form of taxation. This latter feature endeared the idea of extending coverage and raising benefits to later conservative federal administrations.

Under this new law the monthly retirement payment was expected to range between $10 and $85, depending on wages earned between January 1937 and the retirable age. Major amendments to this act have been enacted many times since 1935 to improve and expand the program. Among these changes were increased payments to more than meet the inflation since the war and to widen the eligibility for insurance. The original act covered chiefly wage and salary workers in commerce and industry. By subsequent amendment farm workers, self-employed farmers, regularly employed domestic workers, employees of nonprofit organizations, and certain other groups were added. Today almost everyone in the nation who works for another, or even for himself, is covered by old-age, survivors', and disability insurance.

Unemployment insurance

In addition to old-age insurance, the Social Security Act also sought to encourage the development of state systems of unemployment insurance that would meet certain minimum requirements. This was accomplished by a special federal tax on payrolls levied against employers. If the state cooperated by adopting an approved unemployment insurance system, the employer was allowed to deduct up to 90 percent of his federal tax from the tax imposed by the state.[12] Fear of federal encroachment and a traditional emphasis on states' rights prompted this peculiar state-federal administrative arrangement. Other features of the Social Security Act carried appropriations, usually based proportionately on similar appropriations made by the states (1) to take care of needy dependent children; (2) to promote the health of mothers and children in areas suffering severe economic distress; (3) to provide medical, surgical, and corrective services for crippled children; (4) to aid homeless and neglected children; (5) to rebuild vocationally the physically disabled; (6) to aid the needy blind; (7) and finally, to promote adequate public health service.

This legislation was a notable step forward in the search for social security. However, strong criticism has found fundamental weaknesses in the structure. One weakness, the limitation of coverage, was largely eliminated after World War II, as we have seen. But since the insurance is based on the income of the worker, those who need it most are likely to get the least. This feature, together with the regressive payroll tax for the old-age retirement system, exposes some of the more serious inequities in the welfare structure of the new interventionist arrangements. In the absence of supplemental grants out of the general revenues, such as was resorted to in the mid-1970s, unemployment insurance is not adequate to cope with either inflation or a long period of unemployment. The scheme has been criticized further because it fails to deal with the problem of unemployment caused by illness.

THE REVIVAL OF ORGANIZED LABOR

The third labor policy of the New Deal was to strengthen the power of organized workers. The 1920s had seen a serious decline in the membership, prestige, and morale of unions, and it was the belief of many that something should be done to restore a better balance in the employer—labor relationship. This effort started with Section 7(a) of the NIRA, and to labor the principles embodied in this section formed the crux of the New Deal. Briefly, it provided that employees should have the "right to organize and bargain collectively through representatives of their own choosing, and shall be free from interference, restraint, or coercion of employers of labor, or their agents, in the designation of such representatives or in self-organization." No employee as a condition of employment might be required to join a company union or to refrain from joining a labor organization of his own choosing, and employers had to comply with the code regulations of their industry respecting labor. Indeed, this seemed like a new charter of liberty to labor.

Under the circumstances it is hardly surprising that independent union membership, along with company-dominated unions, increased rapidly. It is also noteworthy that many unions formed under 7(a) were structured along industrial rather than craft lines, and in a number of cases there was a direct line of descent from these NRA industrial unions to the later CIO unions[13] in the mass-production industries. Also, some of the company-dominated unions later revolted and provided an organized center for independent unions.

In addition to advantages under Section 7(a) of the NIRA, labor was expected to benefit under the codes established for the various industries. The first of the codes, somewhat typical of their general character, was that for the cotton textile industry; it forbade the employment of children under 16, prohibited the speeding up of work, and established minimum wages of $13 a week in the North and $12 a week in the South. Contrary to the intention of the administration, the minimum wages in the codes tended to become the maximum, and as prices of commodities began to swing upward the benefit to labor was doubtful. The banning of child labor, however, was an unquestioned blessing.

The high hopes raised in the minds of labor by the NIRA were not realized under the act. Opposition by many employers, widespread evasion of the codes, and the government's failure through the various labor boards vigorously to enforce the act greatly weakened its operation long before the Supreme Court declared it unconstitutional in 1935. As the fact dawned upon labor that the NIRA was no short

---

[12]The unemployment insurance systems adopted by the states differed, but in general they provided at the beginning for about half the weekly salary, with a maximum of $15 for a maximum period of 16 weeks. The benefits followed a waiting period to prove the validty of the unemployment.

[13]See pp. 384–385.

cut to the millennium, and that in the end enforcement was primarily labor's own task, the number of strikes increased rapidly. The number of workers directly involved in work stoppages, which had sunk to 183,000 in 1930, increased to 1.17 million in 1933 and to considerably more in 1934. The inability of the National Recovery Administration to enforce Section 7(a) or the code provisions regarding labor was due not to reluctance but chiefly to inability to cope with the enormity of the task. Congress tried to help by establishing a nonpartisan National Labor Relations Board; and the President, in the face of actual or threatened strikes, appointed special boards of arbitration to handle industrial disputes affecting longshoremen and automobile, steel, and textile workers.

The National Labor Relations Act, 1935

The Supreme Court decision that ended the NIRA did not involve its labor provisions, and Congress continued them in the National Labor Relations Act (1935), a landmark in the history of labor legislation. The new act was strongly pro-labor, and sought to promote equality of bargaining power between employers and employees and to diminish the causes of industrial disputes. Specifically, it forbade employers: (1) to interfere with, restrain, or coerce employees in the exercise of their rights to collective bargaining; (2) to refuse to bargain collectively; and (3) to dominate or interfere with membership in a labor organization by discrimination with regard to hire or tenure. To enforce the act, a permanent National Labor Relations Board was established.

If adequately enforced, the National Labor Relations Act was bound to be extremely significant. It not only encouraged labor organization, but it made collective bargaining compulsory on the employer, and by its working seemed to doom the company union, the yellow-dog contract, and the labor spy. Enforcement, of course, was handicapped until the Supreme Court passed judgment, but the act was eventually affirmed when the Court in a single day (April 12, 1937) upheld its constitutionality in five decisions. These cases in general involved the question as to whether certain industries, including steel and men's clothing, were sufficiently concerned with interstate commerce to be covered by the act. With the exception of the Fansteel decision in 1939, which virtually banned sit-down strikes, the Court during succeeding months not only approved the constitutionality of the act by impli-

cation but time and again upheld the procedure and decisions of the National Labor Relations Board.

The Senate Committee on Education and Labor

Important as was the National Labor Relations Act and its approval by the Supreme Court, the growth of organized labor depended on other factors as well. First of all was the need of regaining middle-class sympathy, which had been lost in part during the 1920s. The depression helped in this because many were convinced that labor had suffered severely and needed greater protection. Help came also from the activities of the Senate Committee on Education and Labor, headed by Robert La Follette, which received special instructions to investigate "violations of the rights of free speech and assembly and undue interference with the right of labor to organize and bargain collectively." As this committee spread on the record the facts pertaining to the use of labor spies, strikebreakers, tear gas, and deadly weapons by supposedly reputable employers and the abridgment of civil liberties in company-controlled towns and regions, the middle-class public increasingly came to recognize the historic and immediate difficulties faced by labor in its efforts toward organization.

The growth of organized labor

More important than government aid and encouragement was the ability of labor to help itself. The government might protect and encourage, but labor must do its own organizing. Spurred on by the NIRA and the National Labor Relations Act, legislation itself prompted in considerable part by labor activity across the country, organized labor rose to the occasion. Organizing machinery that had grown rusty with bureaucracy and the defects of craft unionism was put in commission, older leaders were shunted aside or forced into the field, and younger men who had demonstrated stronger motivation were called on. During the first three years of the New Deal organized labor added more than 1.5 million to its membership, and in the following years the growth was more rapid.[14] As previously noted, in the drive for labor membership after 1933 it was often found more practical to organize shops on the basis of industry rather than craft, and the AFL granted many charters to these "federal unions." The

[14]Average membership of U.S. labor unions was 2.69 million in 1933, 3.99 million in 1936, and 8.76 million in 1939.

new recruits included a large number of workers as yet unacquainted with the conservative traditions of AFL craft unionism. They gave a more militant tone to organized labor, a tone that was reflected in an overwhelming vote at the annual convention in 1934 to promote industrial unionism in certain mass industries, particularly steel, automobiles, rubber, radio, and aluminum. Failure of the Executive Committee of the AFL to pursue this mandate aggressively led certain unions under the leadership of John L. Lewis and the United Mine Workers of America to organize the Committee for Industrial Organization (CIO) in 1935.[15]

The CIO

Although suspended from membership by the AFL, the CIO unions swung into action. The initial objective of the CIO was the steel industry, but the movement for industrial organization spread so rapidly that, contrary to plan, the first battle was fought in the automobile industry. Following spectacular strikes early in 1937 in the General Motors and Chrysler corporations, the CIO succeeded in effecting compromise settlements that recognized the CIO automobile union as the bargaining agency for its own members. In actual practice this meant the recognition of organized labor in practically all of the major units in the hitherto unorganized automobile industry, except the Ford Motor Company. This concern finally gave up its intransigent and often violent opposition in 1941.

As the battle front shifted to steel, the United States Steel Corporation, instead of opposing labor, reversed a historic policy to the surprise of all and signed contracts with the CIO. Although other steel corporations immediately followed in granting recognition, a few of the more important independents did not, and a strike against "little steel" in the late spring of 1937 resulted in the first important reverse for the CIO. But, under the stress of war preparations, even little steel agreed later to recognition.

In the meantime the CIO spread rapidly. By 1942 it claimed over 40 national unions and a membership of 5 million, not far behind that of the AFL. Despite efforts both within and outside organized labor, the two factions were as yet unable to reconcile their differences. In 1938 the Committee for Industrial Organization changed its name to the Congress of Industrial Organizations, adopted a constitution, and took on a more permanent form. Its early leader, John L. Lewis, resigned the presidency in 1940 and was succeeded by Philip Murray, who had led the drive for organization in the steel industry.

The wave of strikes that accompanied efforts in 1937 to organize the automobile industry was watched with particular interest because for the first time in this country labor used the sit-down technique on a wide scale. This refusal by the worker to leave the plant during a strike, on the theory that he had a vested interest in his job, proved a powerful weapon because it forced the employer to commit the first violence in a strike. Employers, of course, denounced sit-down strikes as illegal trespassing on property rights, and certain states passed legislation to ban them. The practice ended after the Fansteel decision of 1939. Many of the strikes in the 1930s were also characterized by mass picketing, which sometimes resulted in violence and gave opportunity for agitation for new laws to make labor "more responsible." On the whole, labor was able to resist this agitation, at least in the federal legislature, until the war and postwar years.

GOVERNMENT SPENDING AND THE NEW DEAL

The New Deal inaugurated an era of government responsibility for the successful performance of the economy. This was the chief distinguishing feature of the new era of the mixed economy that had its counterpart in all the advanced industrial capitalist economies of western Europe. Britain had initiated large social security and unemployment compensation programs in the 1920s, a decade of heavy unemployment. Social expenditures alone by government at all levels in that country had risen from 5.5 percent of national income in 1913

---

[15]The unions composing the original committee suspended from the AFL in August 1936 were as follows: United Mine Workers of America; Amalgamated Clothing Workers of America; International Ladies' Garment Workers' Union; United Textile Workers of America; Oil Field, Gas Well and Refinery Workers of America; International Union of Mine, Mill and Smelter Workers; Federation of Flat Glass Workers of America; Amalgamated Association of Iron, Steel and Tin Workers; International Union, United Automobile Workers of America; United Rubber Workers of America. The ILGWU later withdrew from the CIO and eventually rejoined the AFL.

TABLE 23-1. FEDERAL FISCAL OPERATIONS,[1] 1932-1941 (IN BILLIONS OF DOLLARS)

FISCAL YEAR	RECEIPTS	EXPENDITURES	DEFICIT	TOTAL PUBLIC DEBT SECURITIES[2]
1932	$1.924	$ 4.659	$2.735	$20.8
1933	1.997	4.598	2.602	23.6
1934	3.015	6.645	3.630	28.5
1935	3.706	6.497	2.791	30.6
1936	3.997	8.422	4.425	34.4
1937	4.956	7.733	2.777	37.3
1938	5.588	6.765	1.177	39.4
1939	4.979	8.841	3.862	41.9
1940	6.879	9.589	2.710	45.0
1941	9.202	13.980	4.778	57.9

Source: *Economic Report of the President,* January 1969.

[1]Administrative budget, 1932–1939; consolidated cash statement, 1940–1941.
[2]Calendar year.

to 10.3 percent in 1924 and 13 percent in 1938.[16] "Keynesian" doctrines of public spending for high employment had been developed before Keynes by a number of prominent Swedish economists. And Sweden, as well as Australia and New Zealand, developed interventionist policies to guide their economies' performance simultaneously with and independently of what was happening in the United States.

It is important to recognize the international character and the common timing of this experience, lest interpreters be misled into thinking the New Deal in its economic aspects was historically unique. Furthermore, awareness of the basic similarities, modified by national peculiarities to be sure, of major government interventionism in all developed capitalistic systems dispels the notion that the broad changes introduced in the United States would not have occurred had it not been for Roosevelt or the Democratic party. This was widely believed at the time, but now we know that, when seen in world perspective and with the benefit of historical hindsight, there were many things profoundly unsatisfactory to most people both in the United States and elsewhere about the way in which the private market system had for a long time been functioning.

To assume government responsibility for more satisfactory economic performance in the depression conditions of the 1930s meant large federal spending and borrowing. Such a program violated all the traditional values. According to these views public budgets were be-

[16]Sidney Pollard, *The Development of the British Economy, 1914–1967,* 2nd ed. (London: Edward Arnold, 1969), p. 204.

lieved analogous to private business and household budgets, government spending and taxing were a burden and should be minimized, popular decisions made collectively through government distorted the allocation of resources ordinarily made individually through the private market, government debt was an evil, and the federal government could go bankrupt. All of these ancient precepts were brought under attack by John Maynard Keynes and overthrown by New Deal fiscal measures. It is small wonder, then, that the new regime was referred to as revolutionary. A fiscal revolution it was. Or more broadly, as New Deal economist Gardiner Means stated, it was a revolution in point of view. A social, economic, and political revolution it was not.

The Hoover deficits

A brief overview of the fiscal upheaval wrought between March 1933 and the eve of World War II can be gleaned from Table 23-1. It must first be noted that President Hoover's administration had been unable to stem the fiscal tide of mounting deficit and debt after 1930. Declining receipts and slightly rising federal expenditures in fiscal 1931 (the year ending June 30, 1931) produced a deficit of $462 million in that year, a shocking outcome in view of the prevailing conviction that the financial guidelines in a slump demanded retrenchment. But in fiscal 1932 the deficit increased to $2.74 billion, which was large even compared to subsequent New Deal experience. Roosevelt, himself a nominal believer in traditional fiscal philosophy when he assumed office and for some time thereafter, inherited a $21 billion federal debt, as the table shows. Conservatives in Congress were warning of bankruptcy.

TABLE 23-2. ECONOMIC TRENDS UNDER THE NEW DEAL 1933-1941
(DOLLAR FIGURES IN BILLIONS)

YEAR	GROSS NATIONAL PRODUCT	GROSS PRIVATE DOMESTIC INVESTMENT	GOVERNMENT PURCHASES OF GOODS AND SERVICES		CONSUMER PRICES (1957-1959= 100)	UNEMPLOYMENT RATE[1]
			FEDERAL	STATE & LOCAL		
1933	$ 55.6	$ 1.4	$ 2.0	$6.0	45.1	24.9%
1934	65.1	3.3	3.0	6.8	46.6	21.7
1935	72.2	6.4	2.9	7.1	47.8	20.1
1936	82.5	8.5	4.9	7.0	48.3	16.9
1937	90.4	11.8	4.7	7.2	50.0	14.3
1938	84.7	6.5	5.4	7.6	49.1	19.0
1939	90.5	9.3	5.1	8.2	48.4	17.2
1940	99.7	13.1	6.0	8.0	48.8	14.6
1941	124.5	17.9	16.9	7.9	51.3	9.9

Source: *Economic Report of the President,* January 1969.

[1]Percent of civilian labor force.

The Roosevelt deficits

There was an uneven pattern of deficits recorded for every subsequent year of the depression, even as most New Dealers and members of Congress gave sincere lip service to the conventional doctrine of balanced budgets. Only a minority (such as the pre-Keynesian Marriner Eccles, governor of the Federal Reserve Board) came to embrace the Keynesian argument that deficits were a social and private boon when they put income into the hands of the unemployed. This minority struck back at the conservative attack, pointing out alternatively during various phases of the battle that the public debt was held almost exclusively by Americans and that it could be adjusted to rise in depression and to be retired in prosperity. It also emphasized that there was no problem if the debt rose more slowly than GNP, that bankruptcy was impossible since the federal government could always pay it off if necessary since it had the power to create money, whereas private debtors did not. Furthermore, the real burden of the debt was represented only in the annual transfer of interest payments from average (lower-income) taxpayers to average (higher-income) bondholders. Even this last was minimized by the government's policy of maintaining low interest rates on its bonds and notes and by the mildly progressive federal income tax.

It will be seen that the New Deal was increasing its outlays each fiscal year through 1936. It was in that year, in November, that Roosevelt, in a bitter campaign against the "economic royalists," won one of the greatest landslide election victories in history. Yet fear, guilt, and uncertainty about the unorthodox budget policy being pursued was welling up in administration circles and the Congress, despite the extremely modest gains made on the unemployment front, as seen in Table 23-2. It is noteworthy that the Democratic platform promised a balanced budget "at the earliest possible moment." The administration had never been committed to sufficient expenditures to completely wipe out unemployment, and it considered large deficits a necessary evil.[17] Already in January 1935 the President had declared that "the Federal Government must and shall quit this business of relief." With attitudes such as this, it was easier to be lulled by the upward trend in prices and the rise in GNP from $55.6 billion in 1933 to $82.5 billion in 1936.

The recession of 1937-1938

Most authorities now agree that the sharp recession, interwoven with the continuing depression, from May 1937 to June 1938, closely overlapping the 1938 fiscal year, was largely attributable to the failure of the administration to pursue what was now well known as a Keynesian policy of vigorous deficit spending.

Federal Reserve actions drastically arrested the growth of the money supply.[18] For fiscal 1937 total receipts rose, total expenditures fell, and the income-stimulating deficit dropped

---

[17]Lewis H. Kimmel, *Federal Budget and Fiscal Policy, 1789-1958* (Washington, D.C.: Brookings Institution, 1959), pp. 213-228 (reprinted in H. N. Scheiber, ed., *United States Economic History* [New York: Knopf, 1964], pp. 511-523).

[18]M. Friedman and A. J. Schwartz, *A Monetary History of the United States, 1867-1960* (Princeton, N. J.: National Bureau of Economic Research, Princeton University Press, 1963), p. 544.

sharply from $4.425 billion to $2.777 billion. For one thing, in that fiscal year the federal government collected over $225 billion in employment taxes under the new social security law, but paid out in benefits practically nothing.

The result was a further drastic drop in the deficit in fiscal 1938 and a sharp climb in the annual unemployment rate for calendar 1938. GNP also declined and sensitive private investment plummeted. It was fortunate that state and local government purchases of goods and services were at least maintained.

The administration finally realized in early 1938 that it had a serious recession on its hands, and that its own budgetary policy had had something to do with it. This new shock brought a change in fiscal approach. The President sent to the Congress in April his path-breaking "Recommendations Designed to Stimulate Further Recovery." This was a definitely pro-Keynesian document containing "the first outright recommendations by the President designed to achieve recovery through fiscal policy . . . noteworthy for the omission of any recommendation for increased taxation."[19] But this first mincing step toward adoption of the kind of fiscal machinery necessary for running a managed economy was still at that point breaking a new path. It was to be many, many years before the University of Chicago's eminent conservative economist Milton Friedman was to declare, "We are all Keynesians now."

Deficit fluctuations

In fiscal 1939 the deficit jumped back up to one of the three largest for the entire period shown in Table 23-1. This was attended by a new buoyancy in the economy in calender 1939 as investment and GNP rose and the unemployment rate declined. The New Deal had primed the pump with conscious fiscal policy It was fortunate that private spending responded, for the federal deficit dropped sharply in fiscal 1940 to $2.7 billion from $3.9 billion in 1939. Nor did state and local finances help. These levels of government combined ran surpluses on income and product transactions in all years after 1933, and their joint surplus jumped from $94 million in calendar 1939 to $722 million in calendar 1940. This was clearly a depressant. However, the great question with which 1940 has left economic historians is: Would this private spending response have been sufficient to

bring the economy to a full employment level in the absence of war? We will never know, for as early as the fiscal year ending June 30, 1941, federal expenditures jumped from $9.6 billion to almost $14 billion, with an appropriate jump in the federal deficit. Only the wartime deficits, which by fiscal 1942 had already reached over $19 billion, represented applications of Keynesian medicine in sufficient quantitites to accomplish the elimination of mass unemployment. But at the least those deficits demonstrated what the New Deal had not: that adequate doses could cure the ailment.

Tax policy

New Deal tax policy did little to alter the distribution of income, despite strong attacks upon the alleged extreme progressivity of the federal income tax and the soak-the-rich Revenue Act of August 1935. The latter was in part a response to agitation by such radical groups as Senator Huey Long's "Share Our Wealth" movement, the Townsend old-age pension movement, and Father Charles E. Coughlin's League of Social Justice. This New Deal high point in liberal income-tax legislation raised surtax rates on personal incomes and on estates, and made the corporation income-tax rates progressive. However, as Sidney Ratner has pointed out, the mildly progressive effects of this law were reduced by the payroll tax in the Social Security Act of August 1935:

> *The quarter of a billion dollars a year raised through the income, estate and gift taxes checked the concentration of wealth to the extent of one half of 1 per cent of the estimated annual national income. . . . But the social security payroll taxes, although they were allocated for the benefit of the contributing workers, were borne by low income groups which could not afford the loss of purchasing power entailed by this regressive type of taxation.[20]*

E. Cary Brown has gone to the root of the matter by pointing out that the last federal revenue measure under the Hoover administration (1932), which lowered personal exemptions and raised all rates, especially those on lower- and middle-income strata, determined the basic income-tax structure for the entire New Deal period up to World War II.[21]

[19]A. Smithies, "The American Economy in the Thirties," *American Economic Review,* 36, no. 26 (May 1946):11–27 (reprinted in *Issues in American Economic History,* ed. G. D. Nash [Lexington, Mass.: Heath, 1964], p. 450).

[20]*Taxation and Democracy in America* (New York: Wiley, 1967), p. 472.

[21]"Fiscal Policy in the Thirties: A Reappraisal," *American Economic Review,* 46, no. 5 (December 1956): 868.

Meanwhile, although the states were introducing and spreading the income tax, they were even more active on the sales-tax front. The repeal of the Eighteenth (Prohibition) Amendment in 1933 added another federal excise tax on mass consumption. The general result was a shift of state and local taxes in the direction of greater regressivity. The total tax system—federal, state, and local revenues combined—was estimated by Alvin Hansen[22] to have looked as follows, in percentage terms, in 1938:

	Percent of Total Taxes	
	1930	*1938*
Property taxes	48	32
Income, inheritance, gift, and corporation taxes	28	28
Consumption taxes (motor vehicle, liquor and tobacco, sales, excises, customs)	24	30
Payroll taxes	—	10

Since payroll taxes were regressive and fell largely on consumption, it seems clear that progressive taxes occupied no more important place in the total tax structure than in 1930, and indeed, consumption taxes had probably increased some in importance. Hansen's further estimates reveal that consumption and payroll taxes as proportion of total federal revenues were the same in 1940 as they were in 1933.[23] Certainly the New Deal wrought no revolution in the redistribution of tax incidence as between people of high and low incomes. Roosevelt's tax proposals, as presented and then enacted beginning in 1935, were widely regarded as "soak-the-rich" schemes, and his imposition of inheritance taxes on a graduated basis were seen as a particularly radical and threatening blow to the sanctity of property and to vaunted individualism. On the other hand, the New Deal's supporters viewed heavy taxation of inherited wealth as perfectly consistent with true individualism and the principle that each generation should prove its own worth in the marketplace.

ECONOMIC IMPLICATIONS OF THE NEW DEAL

This summary of New Deal legislation and policies should clear the ground for certain additional general comments. The New Deal is significant, it is obvious, as the first real effort made in this country to attack a depression by bringing to bear upon it the new economic policy weapons being developed and employed in all the advanced business societies of the North Atlantic world at the time. In earlier depressions in the United States, laissez-faire administrations had contented themselves largely with protecting the credit of the federal government and allowing the private market to work itself out of the depression as best it might. However, the economic catastrophe following World War I had already developed throughout the European world various controls over economic life. The New Deal was America's way of attacking its own depression, but the majority attitude in the United States gradually yielded economic programs remarkably similar to those being developed in western Europe, including Great Britain.

Efforts to pull the country out of the depression were made in various ways. One was "re-

flation" and a weak easy-money policy[24] to help debtors and stimulate production. Another was the continuation of the Hoover program designed to restore business confidence by pouring funds into banks, insurance companies, railroads, and industries to prevent bankruptcy and reestablish them on a sounder basis. Still another was the finding of jobs for labor by speeding public works and by a large program of make-work projects. This program of saving the economic structure and finding jobs meant, of course, deficit spending. Moreover, the enlarged policy of government spending would act to prime the pump of economic recovery.

Recovery and reform

The depression stimulated reform, much of it, as it inadvertently turned out, essential to the management of a mixed economy. Recovery and reform were closely interwoven in the New Deal, a fact that illustrates in a striking way the admixture of intended short-run and unintended long-run effects. The banking structure was

---

[22]*Fiscal Policy and Business Cycles* (New York: Norton, 1941), p. 129. Proportions calculated from Table 14.

[23]Ibid., p. 128. Calculated from Table 13.

[24]For a cogent argument that New Deal monetary policy was basically restrictive, see Friedman and Schwartz, *Monetary History*, pp. 511–545.

not only saved but reformed. The same was true of the electric power industry. Some control of stock exchanges and dealing in securities was established. The situation gave an opportunity for the TVA and for a wide program of soil and forest conservation as well as the construction, through the WPA and other agencies, of innumerable facilities for the welfare of the people. The New Deal's extension of the progressive income tax, the adoption of an unemployment compensation system, and the price parity program of farm aid provided built-in partial stabilizers to cushion short-run fluctuations in the economy.

The conservation of human resources

The New Deal moved toward the conservation of human resources. This included the effort not alone to strengthen organized labor but to find jobs for the unemployed through the CCC, WPA, and National Youth Administration. It was part of this program to establish minimum rates of pay and maximum hours of work and to prohibit child labor. It brought old-age and unemployment insurance, and the other objectives in the Social Security Act. The New Deal was impregnated with the desire for conservation and the ideal of humanitarianism. Said Roosevelt in 1937 in a special message urging the Fair Labor Standards Act:

> The time has arrived for us to take further action to extend the frontiers of social progress. . . . One-third of our population, the overwhelming majority of which is in agriculture or industry, is ill-nourished, ill-clad and ill-housed. . . . A self-supporting and self-respecting democracy can plead no justification for the existence of child labor, no economic reason for chiseling workers' wages or stretching workers' hours.

It was this aspect of the New Deal that won it the permanent approbation of most of the people, no matter what their political affiliations might be.

The expanded role of government

Quite as obvious as anything yet said about the New Deal is the fact that the program necessitated an expansion of government activities and a more active participation by government in the economic and social life of the nation. More definitely and rapidly than ever before, the state was deserting the policy of laissez-faire

and replacing it with publicly managed capitalism. Louis Hacker wrote in 1938, in the very midst of this transition to the mixed economy:

> Today the state is operating to defend the underprivileged, to increase the national income, and to effect a more equitable distribution of that income among the various categories of producers. To achieve these ends not only has the American state taken on the whole job of assuring social security, but it has also become a participant in and an initiator of business enterprise. Our state, in short, has become the capitalist state, where only yesterday it was the laissez-faire, or passive, state; it constructs and operates plants; it buys and sells goods and services, lends money, warehouses commodities, moves ships and operates railroads. In one sense, the state is seeking to erect safeguards for the underprivileged against exploitation; in another it is competing with and replacing private enterprise — without, however, parting company with capitalist relations.[25]

While Hacker somewhat exaggerates the extent of public ownership and operation and the degree of direct government competition with private enterprise, he did see clearly the mixture of low-income welfarism and subsidy to business that was to become characteristic of the new interventionist capitalism. Furthermore, he did recognize that basic "capitalist relations" were destined to abide in the new mixed economy era. Hacker's appraisal is consistent with a much more recent judgment by historian Otis Graham, Jr.:

> The outlines of the New Deal achievement are now reasonably clear. There was no sweeping success in income redistribution, elimination of poverty, organization of the unorganized, restraint of corporate power; there were barely measurable advances toward economic recovery and racial justice; there were modest steps in organizing industrial labor in the northern cities, in underwriting the economic security of land owning farmers and the unemployed, in liberalizing the Democratic Party, in restoring "faith" in ailing political and economic institutions. . . .

[25]Louis Hacker, *American Problems of Today* (Englewood Cliffs, N.J.: Prentice-Hall, 1938), p. vii.

The New Deal attempted and failed to ensure economic security for all, cradle to grave; to sufficiently control the activities of enterprisers so as to eliminate monopoly and the exploitation of men and environment; to shape political institutions so that majorities could effectively focus their power; to foster a cooperative ethic. It never intended to equalize wealth and income, to achieve racial equality, to abolish or fundamentally alter capitalism.[26]

Graham thus correctly emphasizes that the assertion of many that the New Deal marked a revolution in the American economy is a gross exaggeration. Indeed, the whole controversy among historians as to whether it was a revolution turned out to have been a quite sterile one.

While much of the change in relationship between the government and the economy was far-reaching and did specifically initiate the mixed economy era, there was much that was extension and continuation of older methods and older philosophies.[27] This was particularly true in the field of government regulation and government subsidy of business. There is both discontinuity and continuity in the historical process, just as there is in the physical world. Roosevelt, like the English Tory Keynes, asserted that he was trying to save the capitalist system rather than destroy it, and the legislation affecting finance, industry, and agriculture is indisputable proof of that. The new element in the New Deal was the acceleration of the decline of laissez-faire and its replacement with the foundations of a publicly managed capitalism.

Selected Readings

Bernstein, Irving, *The Turbulent Years: A History of the American Worker, 1933–1941* (Boston: Houghton Mifflin, 1970).

Brown, E. C., "Fiscal Policy in the 'Thirties: A Reappraisal", *American Economic Review,* XLVI, No. 6 (December, 1956), pp. 857–879.

*Chandler, Lester V., *America's Greatest Depression, 1929–1941* (New York: Harper & Row, 1970).

Crawford, A. W., *Monetary Management Under the New Deal* (New York: Da Capo Press, 1972).

Cushman, Robert E., *The Independent Regulatory Commission* (New York: Oxford University Press, 1941).

Derber, M., and Young, E., eds., *Labor and the New Deal* (Madison: University of Wisconsin Press, 1957).

Fine, Sidney, *The Automobile under the Blue Eagle* (Ann Arbor: University of Michigan Press, 1963).

*Freidel, Frank, *The New Deal in Historical Perspective* (Washington, D.C.: Service Center for Teachers of History, 1965).

Friedman, Milton, and Schwartz, Anna J., *A Monetary History of the United States, 1867–1960* (Princeton, N.J.: Princeton University Press, for the National Bureau of Economic Research, 1963), Chaps. 8,9.

Fusfeld, Daniel R., *The Economic Thought of F.D.R. and the Origins of the New Deal* (New York: Columbia University Press, 1956).

*Graham, Otis L., Jr., ed., *The New Deal: The Critical Issues* (Boston: Little, Brown, 1971).

Hansen, A., *Fiscal Policy and Business Cycles* (New York: Norton, 1941), pts. 1–3.

Hawley, Ellis, *The New Deal and the Problem of Monopoly* (Princeton, N.J.: Princeton University Press, 1966).

*Himmelberg, Robert F., ed., *The Great Depression and American Capitalism* (Boston: Heath, 1968).

*Hoover, Calvin B., *The Economy, Liberty and the State* (New York: Twentieth Century Fund, 1959).

[26]Ottis Graham, Jr., ed., *The New Deal: The Critical Issues* (Boston: Little, Brown, 1971). p. xv.

[27]This point of view is developed more fully in H. U. Faulkner, "Antecedents of New Deal Liberalism," *Social Education,* 3 (March 1939): 153–160.

*Kindleberger, Charles P., *The World Depression, 1929–1939* (Berkeley: University of California Press, 1973).

Leuchtenberg, William E., *Franklin D. Roosevelt and the New Deal: 1932–1940* (New York: Harper & Row, 1963).

Lubove, Roy, *The Struggle for Social Security, 1900–1935* (Cambridge, Mass: Harvard Univerity Press, 1968).

Mitchell, Broadus, *Depression Decade* (New York: Holt, Rinehart and Winston, 1947).

Parrish, Michael, *Securities Regulation Under the New Deal* (New Haven: Yale University Press, 1970).

*Potter, Jim, *The American Economy Between the World Wars* (New York: Macmillan, 1974), Chaps. 4, 5, and 6.

Rauch, Basil, *The History of the New Deal, 1933–1938* (New York: Capricorn Books, 1963).

Rothbard, M., *America's Great Depression* (New York: Von Nostrand, Reinhold, 1963).

Schlesinger, Arthur M., Jr., *The Age of Roosevelt: The Politics of Upheaval* (Boston: Houghton Mifflin, 1960).

*Shannon, Fred A., ed., *The Great Depression* (Englewood Cliffs, N.J.: Prentice-Hall, 1960).

Shonfield, Andrew, *Modern Capitalism: The Changing Balance of Public and Private Power* (New York: Oxford University Press, 1965).

Smithies, Arthur, "The American Economy in the 'Thirties," *American Economic Review,* Supplement, XXXVI (May, 1946), pp. 11–27.

*Sobel, Robert, *The Age of Giant Corporations* (Westport, Conn.: Greenwood Press, 1974), Chaps. 5, 6.

Stein, Herbert, *The Fiscal Revolution in America* (Chicago: University of Chicago Press, 1969).

Studenski, Paul, and Krooss, Herman E., *Financial History of the United States,* 2nd ed. (New York: McGraw-Hill, 1963), chaps. 27–29.

Wessel, Thomas R., "Roosevelt and the Great Plains Shelterbelt," *Great Plains Journal,* VIII (1969), pp. 55–74.

*Wolters, Raymond, *Negroes and the Great Depression* (Westport, Conn.: Greenwood Press, 1970).

The network of relatively stable international economic relationships under the old gold standard entered a protracted period of crisis in the two decades between the end of World War I and the beginning of World War II. All the major trading nations of the North Atlantic world contributed, in varying degrees, to the persistent disequilibrium of those years. When the Great Depression came, it put the finishing touches upon the international system that the British pound had built before 1914 and the dollar had tried to build thereafter. The time-honored gold standard collapsed forever after over a decade of fruitless effort to rehabilitate it. The foreign economic policies of the leading countries hardened after the depression's onset into aggressive, nationalistic, beggar-my-neighbor strategies. International cooperation, feebly introduced in the 1920s, was roundly rejected as mass unemployment, beginning in some European countries in the "prosperity decade," directed national policy toward domestic recovery regardless of the cost to the foreigner.

And so, amid depression conditions, there was a spread of economic autarchy: the raising of tariffs and other barriers to trade, the manipulation of exchange rates without regard to the effects upon international commerce, and generally the pursuit of narrowly self-interested economic goals by each country. By the mid-1930s this increasingly chaotic situation was complicated further by the emergence of Japan's new imperialistic inroads into Asia and the rise to power of Hitler in Germany and Franco in Spain. The clouds of war were gathering over Europe at a time when international cooperation had already broken down in the economic field. The already existent tensions founded upon ideological and other differences between the western countries and the Soviet Union were now overlain with a new set of conflicts arising from the threat of expansionist Nazi designs on Europe and the Japanese expansion by war in East Asia that had begun in 1931.

EXPORT OF AMERICAN CAPITAL, 1914–1940

In no sphere within the international arena between the wars was the pattern of normality–crisis–collapse more evident than in the U.S. private foreign investment record. Following a period of massive lending in the 1920s, the boldly built network rapidly disintegrated in the first flush of the contraction. In the years between the Spanish-American War and the opening of World War I, American investments, direct and portfolio, in foreign nations had increased over five times, from $684.5 million (1897) to $3.5 billion (1914). American capital had moved during this period chiefly into Canada, Mexico, Europe, South America, and Cuba.

As against American investments abroad of $3.5 billion in 1914, foreign investments in the United States amounted to $7.2 billion, leaving the United States a debtor to the extent of approximately $3.7 billion.[1] These investments had come chiefly from Europe, over half from Great Britain, with Germany and the Netherlands as the next largest investors. European investments had found their way into almost every type of American enterprise, but over half were in railroads.[2] (See pp. 283).

U.S. foreign investment and World War I

World War I not only revealed the large amount of capital in the United States that could be called upon for foreign loans, but quickly ended the debtor position of this country. Between the opening of the war in 1914 and the entrance of the United States in 1917, over $2 billion in American securities owned in Europe was returned to this country. Much of this was done through the British and French governments, which induced their citizens to lend their American securities or exchange them for domestic loans. Of equal significance in reversing the debtor position of the United States were the dollar loans advanced to foreign governments, mainly the Allied nations of Europe, which reached approximately $2.6 billion. With American entry into the war, private loan transactions ended.[3] The federal government then took over the problem of financing the last year of the war and aiding in European reconstruction. Under the Liberty Loan Act of 1917 the United States advanced $9.58 billion to European governments.[4]

These figures do not tell the whole story or even the most important part. The war left Europe so exhausted economically that during the following years the United States continued to be the great source of capital. The world's financial center shifted from London to New York. With the end of the war, restrictions on the international lending operations of private agencies were lifted and the expansion of American investments in the 1920s reached fantastic proportions. Omitting government loans, American long and short term foreign investments grew from $3.5 billion in 1914 to $7 billion in 1919 and $17 billion in 1929.

After that, as we shall see, they declined rapidly.[5] By 1940 the total was down to $12.2 billion.

Direct investments abroad in the 1920s

In a study of the debts owed to private American citizens, the Department of Commerce in 1930 estimated that one-half of the money lent abroad was in the form of "portfolio investments" — that is, in ownership of foreign securities, public and private, by individuals or institutions in this country — and one-half in "direct investments" made by American corporations in agricultural, industrial, commercial, mining, public utility, and other enterprises abroad. The chief investment areas at that time in order of importance were Europe, Canada, and South America.

The migration of billions of American dollars to other parts of the world did not come simply because the prosperity of the 1920s created surplus wealth that high interest rates lured into foreign investment. It came in part because American economic interests were stretching far and wide to extend business. Most of the big American concerns, such as the Ford Motor Company, General Motors, General Electric, Standard Oil, International Telephone and Telegraph, and International Harvester, set up their own plants or bought control of foreign companies. Many economic factors led to this movement of capital into foreign industries, and of these the high tariffs that developed rapidly in the 1920s were one of the most important. When American manufacturers found it impossible to break through the foreign tariff barriers, they simply set up branch factories abroad to serve foreign markets. Every observer in Canada, for example, finds there numerous branches of American concerns, which represented in 1948 over $6 billion of American long-term direct investments. Thereafter they continuously increased until by 1972 they totaled $26 billion, over a quarter of all U.S. long-term direct foreign investments.

Portfolio investments abroad in the 1920s

While many of the direct investments, notably those in Canada, were perfectly sound and of benefit both to the American investor and to world economic development, the same cannot be said of a large portion of the portfolio invest-

---

[1]Cleona Lewis, *America's Stake in International Investments* (Washington, D.C.: Brookings Institution, 1938), p. 445.

[2]Ibid., p. 546.

[3]Ibid., p. 355.

[4]Reduced to $9.39 billion by 1922, when negotiations for debt payments were started. Ibid., p. 362.

[5]Ibid., p. 606.

ments. Many of them were for nonproductive purposes and were sold by governments or private corporations whose ability to pay was extremely uncertain, to say the least. American investment houses that floated these loans, says George Soule, "were often more concerned with their underwriting profits than with the probable safety of the capital."[6] Such institutions searched the world for opportunities to lend money; they literally forced it upon borrowers even when the Department of Commerce and their own experts warned them of the danger. Said one of the more conservative bankers:

> I have in mind reports . . . of American bankers and firms competing on almost a violent scale for the purpose of obtaining loans in various foreign money markets overseas. Naturally it is a tempting thing for certain of the European governments to find a horde of American bankers sitting on their doorsteps offering them money. It is rather demoralizing for municipalities and corporations in the same countries to have money pressed upon them. This sort of competition tends to insecurity and unsound practices.[7]

This policy, so typical of the 1920s, was too fantastic to last even if world economic relations had been on a sound and stable basis. The Latin American countries were borrowing more than they could pay even under normal conditions. Europe, impoverished by the war, had to meet its obligations with American dollars that could be obtained only by rendering services and exporting commodities. One type of service, the transportation of American commodities on the ocean, was curtailed by the development of a new American merchant marine. Export of foreign commodities to this country was hindered by the high American tariffs. The untenable situation was maintained chiefly by continued American loans and intense economic activity. With the cessation of loans and the coming of the depression at the end of the decade the structure collapsed.

The United States government during the 1920s showed little comprehension of the international economic problem, nor did it offer

much leadership. It simply permitted private enterprise to go its own way, assuming that entrepreneurs and bankers were the best judges of what was "sound" (that is, profitable) investment. The return of the United States to higher tariffs when the opposite was indicated for a creditor nation was a mistaken policy. From a conventional point of view the scaling down of the war debts by the United States seemed liberal enough, but the conflicting interests of the various nations prevented a cooperative approach and the whole war-debt problem clogged the machinery of economic recovery. The Department of Commerce under Secretary Hoover not only promoted foreign exports despite the handicap of domestic tariffs, but in general encouraged rather than warned against unwise foreign investments.

U.S. foreign investment in the 1930s

The large flow of American capital declined in 1928. With the crash in the following year it dwindled to a tiny trickle. The depression of the 1930s wiped out almost $11 billion from the equity of American foreign investments. Until the situation was altered by World War II, the income from direct investments in Latin America was relatively low. United States holdings in Latin American dollar bonds (most of them government securities) amounted in 1940 to almost $1 billion, but approximately two-thirds of these bonds were in partial or complete default.

In continental Europe the situation was even worse. Direct investments there amounted to $1.37 billion in 1940, a large amount of which was in Germany and Italy. For years exchange controls had prevented heavy remittances of income from these countries, and the withdrawal of capital had been largely halted. The greater proportion of assets were frozen, and when liquidation was permitted it was accompanied by heavy losses. Indirect (portfolio) investments there amounted to $636 million at the end of 1940, but 59 percent was in default. Moreover, the Debt Default Act of 1934 (Johnson Act), which prohibited loans to any government in default in its payments of obligations to the United States, automatically ended the possibility of loans to most European governments. The war between China and Japan and the increasing tension throughout East Asia boded ill for the future of American investments

---

[6]George Soule, *Prosperity Decade* (New York: Holt, Rinehart and Winston, 1947), p. 269.

[7]Thomas W. Lamont of J. P. Morgan and Company, in an address before the International Chamber of Commerce, 1927. Quoted in Lewis, *America's Stake*, p. 380.

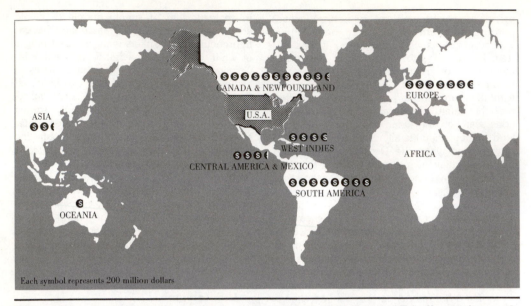

Figure 24–1. **United States Foreign Trade, 1940.** Source: H. U. Faulkner and Tyler Kepner, *America, Its History and People* (New York: Harper & Row, 1934), p. 692.

in that area. As a ratio to GNP, U.S. foreign investments, direct and portfolio, had thus fluctuated as follows:

> 1914:   **9.7 per cent**
> 1929:   **16.3 per cent**
> 1940:   **10.8 per cent**

The return in 1940 to a proportion close to that obtaining a quarter century earlier attests to the severe impact of the world depression upon international lending.

In the meantime, foreign investors looking for an outlet turned to the United States. By the end of 1940 long- and short-term foreign investments in the United States totaled $13.5 billion. This exceeded by over $1 billion the total of American investments abroad, and represented a far different picture from that of a decade earlier. It should be noted, however, that $5.4 billion of this was short-term money, much of it having fled from the intense uncertainty resulting from Hitler's threat to the peace of Europe.

THE WAR-DEBT PROBLEM AND THE NEUTRALITY ACTS

Although the problem of the debts of World War I seems remote today, it was closely interwoven with U.S. international policy for two decades. When the United States entered that war, the credit of the Allied nations was exhausted and these loans were necessary to win the war. They were, however, supposedly made in good faith, under the illusion that they would and could be repaid. They had reached such staggering proportions that in 1922 the United States established the World War Foreign Debt Commission to take up with each nation the question of refunding the debt.

Long before this the debtor nations had

begun a vigorous campaign for cancellation of the debts. They argued that these loans should be considered as part of America's contribution to the common cause, that this money had enabled the Allies to hold off the enemy until the United States had time to prepare for war, and that the money was largely spent in the United States and so had aided this country as well as the Allies. Moreover, the debtor nations insisted that they could not pay in gold since there was not enough gold in Europe and what existed was needed to support their currencies. As for paying their debts in goods, ultimately the only way in which payment could be made,

TABLE 24–1. UNITED STATES LONG-TERM INVESTMENTS IN FOREIGN COUNTRIES, BY TYPES OF INVESTMENT AND BY GEOGRAPHIC AREAS, DECEMBER 31, 1940 (IN MILLIONS OF DOLLARS)

AREA	DIRECT INVESTMENTS	PORTFOLIO INVESTMENTS			GRAND TOTAL
		FOREIGN DOLLAR BONDS	MISCELLANEOUS FOREIGN SECURITIES	TOTAL	
Canada and Newfoundland	$2,065	$1,390	$285	$1,675	$ 3,740
West Indies	755	74	5	79	834
Central America and Mexico	650	26	–	26	676
South America	1,615	893	5	898	2,513
Europe	1,370	506	130	636	2,006
Asia	460	155	5	160	620
Oceania	135	95	3	98	233
Africa	105	2	17	19	124
International	25	–	–	–	25
Total	$7,180	$3,141[1]	$450	$3,591	$10,771

Source: U.S. Department of Commerce, *Balance of International Payments of the United States in 1940* (Washington, D.C.: U.S. Government Printing Office, 1940), p. 51.

[1] The estimated market value of these holdings was $1.79 billion.

that was impossible because of the high tariff policy of the United States and the fact that the United States would be unwilling to accept such a large flow of imports because of the devastating effect it would have on U.S. employment.

In this country the official attitude was to make large reductions in the amounts owed but to insist upon some payment. Gradually over a period of seven years arrangements were made with 15 European nations by which the total principal was fixed at $11.5 billion to be paid during a period of 62 years, since the interest amounted to $10.6 billion and the grand total to $22.1 billion. The annual payments were to vary from an average of $204 million during the first decades to $414 million during the last ten years. The former figure would have amounted to almost 40 percent of the U.S. export surplus on its merchandise account during the middle 1920s. These arrangements involved a 23 percent reduction of the British debt, a 46 percent reduction of the Belgian debt, 52 percent of the French, and 75 percent of the Italian. While these reductions appear extremely liberal, it must be remembered that the debts were contracted during the high-price period of wartime, that most of the money was used to purchase American commodities, and that the reductions merely tended to cancel wholly or in part the postwar deflation, on the basis of which the debts were to be paid.

Whether the terms were liberal or not, agitation in Europe for complete cancellation continued. This was in part due to the fact that a large part of the reparations obtained from Germany

came to the United States for the payment of Allied debts. The Treaty of Versailles originally fixed German reparations at $33 billion, but it quickly became evident that Germany could not meet its payments. Not only that, but the draining of gold from Germany threatened its very ability to survive internationally under the gold standard, and attempts to collect reparations in goods of course upset the economy of the creditor nations.

The Dawes Plan

A committee headed by Charles G. Dawes adopted a plan in 1924 by which Germany's annual payments were scaled down and an effort was made to balance the German budget. This effort lasted as long as American loans in gold poured into Germany. The gold went immediately to France and England in reparations and then completed the circle by being returned to the United States in debt payments. This curious situation existed until American loans to Germany began to dry up.

The Young Plan

The collapse of the Dawes Plan led to another attempt to revamp the reparations program by a committee under the chairmanship of Owen D. Young. The Young Plan further radically reduced the German debt and provided that the size of certain yearly payments would be conditional upon a reduction of the Allied debts by the United States. This joining of reparation payments and Allied debts the United States would not officially recognize; but, practically speaking, such a connection existed, since four-fifths of the German payments eventually found their way to the United States. How close the connection was became evident in 1931 when the economic situation forced Germany to default and, to avoid a world economic collapse.

President Hoover in June 1931, after consultation with Allied governments, declared a moratorium for one year on all government debts and reparations payments. By June 1933 only Finland made full payment of its interest; Britain, Italy, Latvia, Czechoslovakia, Romania, and Lithuania paid a small part in silver as token, and Belgium, France, Hungary, Poland, and Estonia defaulted. After 1934 only Finland paid interest.

Reconsideration
of the war-debt problem

It was evident by 1932 that the whole war-debt problem would have to be reconsidered. The obvious possibilities were three: further postponement of payment, further reduction, or outright cancellation. There was considerable sentiment in this country for each of these plans, because many now felt with Secretary of the Treasury Andrew Mellon that "the entire foreign debt is not worth as much to the United States in dollars and cents as a prosperous Europe as a customer." Others believed that the money was not worth the harvest of hatred and suffering being reaped, and still others (who proved to be right) felt that the United States would never collect anyway and might as well let it go on the best terms possible. At the other extreme was the sentiment, expressed by Coolidge, that the Allied nations had "hired it" (the money) and should pay it back. The least that can be said about the whole business of reparations and war debts is that it provided an experience that proved of some value in later years.

The Debt Default
Act and neutrality

Resentment over the European attitude regarding war debts, along with other factors, led in 1934 to the Debt Default Act. It was also one of the many things that produced a program to maintain America's neutrality in future wars. A Senate investigation of the munitions industry greatly strengthened the belief (although it did not prove it) that the United States had been drawn into World War I because of the close economic relations that had bound it to one group of belligerent nations. Determined if possible to prevent the recurrence of certain influences tending to break down neutrality, Congress passed three neutrality acts culminating in that of May 1937. In addition to requiring all persons engaged in the manufacture of munitions to register with the Secretary of State and to export only under license, the act provided for mandatory embargoes on loans, munitions, and implements of war to foreign belligerents or to factions in a civil strife of such proportions as to threaten the peace of the United States. It prohibited American citizens from traveling on belligerent vessels except under conditions prescribed by the president; it forbade the transportation of munitions by American merchantmen; established the National Munitions Control Board, with which all manufacturers and exporters of munitions must register; restricted the use of American ports as bases of supply in wartime; allowed the president to exclude belligerent submarines and armed merchantmen from American ports; and prohibited the arming of American merchantmen.

The act of 1937 also gave the president optional power for two years to require payment and transfer of ownership before export to belligerents of any commodities. When an embargo was proclaimed, all trade in these commodities must be in accordance with the cash-and-carry principle. In other words, America's ownership in such commodities must end before they left our shores and they must be transported by foreign ships. The neutrality acts represented the climax of a sentiment toward isolationism that had been growing since World War I. For the sake of peace the country had abandoned a policy as old as the nation itself, that of freedom of the seas. Whether even this could keep America out of an impending European war was soon to be determined.

THE PROBLEM OF INTERNATIONAL TRADE

The competitive position
of the United States in world markets

Three aspects of the American position in international trade between the two world wars should be emphasized. The first was its changing character. As already noted, although farm exports continued to be important, the long-run trend was for the proportion of exports of raw

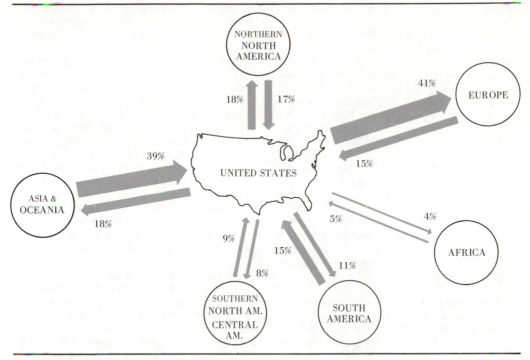

Figure 24–2. **American Direct Investments, 1940.** Source: H. U. Faulkner and Tyler Kepner, *America, Its History and People* (New York: Harper & Row, 1934), p. 687.

materials and foodstuffs to decline while that of semimanufactured and finished manufactured commodities increased. At the same time the proportion of the imports of raw materials increased and that of manufactured commodities declined. This reflected the industrial maturation of the United States and its growing capacity to compete in world markets for fabricated products, a capacity already evident early in the twentieth century. It also reflected the changing structure of demand and terms of trade in the world economy. For during the 1920s and 1930s the prices of primary products (food and raw materials) declined in relation to the prices of manufactured goods (ignoring relative quality changes). At the same time the industrial countries were increasing the volume of their trade with one another at a far higher rate than the increase in their purchases of primary products from the less developed countries.

The relative insignificance of foreign trade to the U.S. economy

Secondly, foreign trade did not attain the significance in the overall economic life of this country that it did in that of most other nations.

The possession of many essential raw materials, the high industrial development, and the diversity of the domestic national product made the nation less dependent upon foreign trade for its economic prosperity. At no time during these years did the value of either imports or exports represent more than 8 percent of the national income. This does not mean that a rise or decline in the exports of certain commodities or the prices paid for them did not affect in an important way specific groups of American producers. On the one hand, the decline of the European market for certain American foodstuffs hurt our agriculture. The cotton growers, for example, depended heavily upon exports. On the other hand, many industries profited from an active foreign market. The chief exports during the two decades were machinery, petroleum, automobiles, iron and steel products, cotton, and wheat and flour.

The fact that international trade did not play such an important part in American economic life as in that of certain other nations likewise does not mean that American imports were not significant. Despite its large resources of raw materials, there were commodities—notably raw silk, tin, and crude rubber—which the

United States did not have. There were others, such as sugar, copper, paper and pulp, and hides and skins, of which this country did not produce sufficient for its needs. And there were coffee, tropical fruits, and other luxuries that it was eager to buy. These represent the chief imports. About 66 percent of the imports consisted of raw materials and semimanufactured commodities for use in industry. Most of the rest consisted of raw or processed food; only 6 percent of the total value of imports comprised finished manufactured goods (other than food) ready for direct consumption. Next to Great Britain, the United States at the end of the 1920s was the chief importing nation of the world. The large purchases made by the United States in Canada, Cuba, Brazil, Japan, and the East Indies were extremely important to them and enabled those areas to buy in Europe and elsewhere and so helped to bolster the whole structure of international trade.

The excess of exports over imports

A third aspect of the American position was the continued excess of exports over imports. This was not a new phenomenon; it had been almost continuous since 1876. What was new and in the long run fraught with trouble was the fact that this so-called "favorable" balance of trade was now combined with America's position as a creditor nation. In brief, the United States was developing a creditor position by both foreign loans and an excess of exports. The resulting situation was by no means a healthy one, at least from the long-term point of view. In an extended period of an unequal balance of trade, creditor service charges or balances can be paid only in gold or in goods or in additional loans. Gold was largely disappearing from the debtor nations, accumulating in American banks to a large extent; and the free flow of goods was obstructed by high tariffs. In such a situation the annual service charges due the creditor had to be financed by new foreign loans or investments abroad. This was what was happening in the 1920s, when American trade was to no small extent supported by such loans. This disequilibrium could not go on indefinitely, for the continued export of capital by the creditor nation merely accentuated an already unhealthy situation. Conditions were in the making which led to the almost complete debacle of international trade and of the international gold standard at the end of the decade.

Impediments to foreign trade

Many statesmen and economists were by no means blind to the dangers lurking in the area of international commerce. These dangers were not alone the results of the unusual position of the United States; they were the heritages of World War I. Embargoes, quotas, and other impediments to trade, natural during wartime, had been revived after the war by various nations in an effort to maintain domestic employment or to protect their supply of hard currency reserves: gold or pounds sterling or dollars. The League of Nations sponsored numerous conferences aimed at ending such restrictions and at reversing the developing high-tariff policies, but with few tangible results. The United States was persuaded to participate in at least two of these conferences, including the International Economic Conference of 1927. Here it joined in signing the conference report that "the time has come to put an end to the increase in tariffs and move in the opposite direction."

Economic nationalism

The worldwide depression finally destroyed the uneasy equilibrium that had existed in the North Atlantic trading world under the gold standard from the 1870s to World War I. During that era of peace between the major powers, their foreign exchange rates were tied to a specific amount of gold; the leading world trader, Great Britain, followed a free-trade policy; and the important foreign-trade countries developed more or less in step. The volume of trade grew almost as fast as the growth in volume of world production.

But the war in 1914 began the conversion of the gold standard into a major weapon of international warfare, a conversion of which the participants were but dimly aware for some time thereafter. The nations "went off gold," temporarily it was believed at the time. But more important, Britain, the leading trader until the United States took its place after the war, abandoned permanently its free-trade policy. Since all the other leading industrial powers had been pursuing protectionist policies beforehand, this meant, as it turned out, the inauguration of a half century of what Robert Triffin has called "international monetary anarchy."[8] In the given historical context, economic nationalism meant for foreign financial and product markets that concern with domestic employment superseded the attempt to guarantee stability of

---

[8]*The Evolution of the International Monetary System: Historical Appraisal and Future Perspectives,* Princeton Studies in International Finance no. 12 (Princeton, N. J.: Princeton University Press, 1964). Since Triffin was writing in 1964, the terminal date should no doubt *not* be interpreted to indicate that the era of "anarchy" ended at that time.

the foreign exchanges that had dominated policy goals under the gold standard.

The United States was one of the worst offenders in building the new international mercantilist order. It insisted upon exporting more than it imported, and it reinforced that policy by tariffs in 1921 and 1922 that reversed the mildly liberalizing trend obtaining since the Underwood Act of 1913. That act had reduced average rates to pre–Civil War levels. The U.S. response to the urging of the 1927 World Economic Conference that countries lower tariffs and take multilateral action to expand the volume of world trade was in part, as we have seen, the all-time high Hawley-Smoot Tariff of 1930.

This was the beginning of a depression-aggravated retreat to further economic nationalism, and there followed a wave of retaliations by European countries. Retaliations took the form of competitive, beggar-my-neighbor currency devaluations starting with Britain's suspension of the gold standard in 1931, followed by 15 other nations within three months, and additional tariffs and import quotas.

The gold standard abandoned

The United States, in the hope of raising domestic prices, abandoned gold in April 1933. This was on the eve of a world economic conference scheduled for June in London with the object of temporarily stabilizing international foreign exchange rates. But this threatening move was only a precursor. When the conference was assembled, the United States was represented, but Roosevelt turned it into a fiasco with a message indicating that recovery and "reflation" were more vital to his administration than stable foreign exchange ratios. This perhaps justified position was further driven home when Roosevelt, under the authority of the Gold Reserve Act of January 30, 1934, competitively devalued the dollar to $35 an ounce of gold on the next day. This put the country back on an international gold bullion standard with a cheapened dollar that made U.S. exports cheaper for foreigners and U.S. import prices higher for American consumers. One result was an accentuation of the long-continued "gold rush" from abroad into the United States which had resulted from chronic U.S. balance-of-payments surpluses. By the end of the decade the United States had garnered an inordinate portion of the world's monetary gold stocks, a drain that eventually wrecked the gold standard.[9]

Meanwhile other countries lashed back at the United States, and world trade languished. France suspended gold payments in September 1936 and drastically devalued the next month. As a result of all this and similar moves toward nationalism and the chronic use of bilateral trade agreements, the volume of world trade in industrial products between 1920 and 1938 rose by only 20 percent, whereas the volume of world industrial production doubled. World trade in raw materials and foodstuffs increased by only 35 percent over the same period.[10] This was not merely a depression phenomenon. The demand for these primary products of the less developed countries came chiefly from industrial countries. But both the decline in the rate of population growth and the tendency in the manufacturing countries to conserve and find synthetic substitutes for natural raw materials restricted their long-run increase in demand for primary products.[11]

Liberalization of trade policy

During the decades between World War I and World War II the United States had raised its productivity at such a rapid rate that it was increasingly able to outcompete the other leading industrial nations. Hence it had ever more and more to gain from a policy of freer trade, and this condition, as it turned out, persisted until after World War II. Ironically, therefore, in the midst of the international rivalry so aggravated by the depression, the United States suddenly turned about and Congress in 1934 passed the Reciprocal Trade Agreements Act.

Under this act Secretary of State Cordell Hull attempted quite successfully over an extended period to negotiate country-by-country trade agreements that bargained down tariff barriers. These specific agreements were independent of congressional logrolling. Although the agreements were bilateral in form, their object was to rebuild multilateral free trade by attaching to the agreements an unconditional most-favored-nation clause. According to this policy, if there were no reservations, the concessions granted by the United States would be equivalent to the best treatment enjoyed by any competitor country of the other signatory. The reduction of customs barriers in bilateral reciprocal trade agreements was automatically extended—that is, made multilateral—vis-á-vis other supplying countries. However, the exten-

[9]See J. P. Day, *An Introduction to World Economic History Since the Great War* (London: Macmillan, 1939), p. 125.

[10]International Monetary Fund, *International Financial News Survey,* Supplement, 15, no. 4 (April 12, 1963):125.

[11]See W. Arthur Lewis, *Economic Survey, 1919–1939* (New York: Harper & Row, 1969).

sion of most-favored-nation treatment by the United States was soon limited to minor suppliers.[12] Still, this represented a loosening up of the historically tight trade policy of the United States. But it was to be a long time before significant and general tariff reductions were to become effective. Meanwhile the agreements did stimulate U.S. trade, and stimulated exports more than imports.[13]

Implicit in the trade agreements program was the hope of improving international relations. The program was pushed with particular vigor in Latin America, where it became an integral part of the Good Neighbor Policy. In addition to the trade agreements, the Roosevelt administration attempted to improve interna-

tional relations and the domestic economic situation by resuming diplomatic relations with the Soviet Union (1933). This move came after 16 years of nonrecognition and was accompanied by a special commercial agreement.

The next significant step toward tariff reduction was to come only after World War II in the General Agreement on Tariffs and Trade (GATT), signed in 1947 by 23 countries. But much more than negotiated tariff reductions was to be necessary after the war if both industrialized countries and less developed nations were to achieve high employment, reasonably stable domestic prices, foreign exchange stability, and a rising volume of world trade.

SELECTED READINGS

Brown, Wm. A., Jr., *The International Gold Standard Reinterpreted, 1914–1934,* 2 vols. (New York: National Bureau of Economic Research, 1940).

Condliffe, John B., *The Commerce of Nations* (New York: Norton, 1950).

Dowd, Douglas F., ed., *America's Role in the World Economy* (Boston: Heath, 1966).

Feis, Herbert, *The Diplomacy of the Dollar 1919–1939* (New York: Norton, 1950).

Gardner, Lloyd C., *Economic Aspects of New Deal Diplomacy* (Madison: University of Wisconsin Press, 1964).

Haberler, Gottfried, "Integration and Growth of the World Economy in Historical Perspective," *American Economic Review,* March, 1964, pp. 1–21.

Lary, Hal B. et al., *The United States in the World Economy* (U.S. Department of Commerce, Bureau of Foreign and Domestic Commerce, Economic Series No. 23; Washington, D.C.: U.S. Government Printing Office, 1943).

Lewis, Cleona, *America's Stake in International Investments* (Washington, D.C.: Brookings Institution, 1938).

Madden, J. T., Nadler, Marcus, and Savain, H. C., *America's Experience as a Creditor Nation* (Englewood Cliffs, N.J.: Prentice-Hall, 1937).

Maizels, A., *Industrial Growth and World Trade* (New York: Cambridge University Press, 1965).

Mintz, Ilse, *Deterioration in the Quality of Foreign Bonds Issued in the United States, 1920– 1930* (New York: National Bureau of Economic Research, 1951).

Mitchell, Broadus, *Depression Decade* (New York: Holt, Rinehart and Winston, 1947).

Moulton, Harold G., and Pasvolsky, Leo, *War Debts and World Prosperity,* A Brookings Institution Study (New York: Century, 1932).

National Industrial Conference Board, *Trends in the Foreign Trade of the United States* (New York: NICB, 1930).

Nurkse, Ragnar, *International Currency Experience: Lessons of the Inter-War Period* (Princeton, N.J.: League of Nations, 1944).

Ohlin, Bertil, "The Reparations Problem: A Discussion," *Economic Journal,* XXXIX (June, 1929), pp. 172–178.

*Potter, Jim, *The American Economy Between the World Wars* (New York: Macmillan, 1974).

---

[12]John B. Condliffe, *International Trade and Economic Nationalism,* Carnegie Endowment for International Peace, International Conciliation pamphlet no. 476 (December 1951), p. 568.
[13]Ibid., p. 569.

Stocking, George W., and Watkins, Myron W., *Cartels in Action* (New York: Twentieth Century Fund, 1947).

Svennilson, Ingvar, *Growth and Stagnation in the European Economy* (Geneva: United Nations, 1954).

Tasca, Henry J., *The Reciprocal Trade Policy of the United States* (Philadelphia: University of Pennsylvania Press, 1938).

Taylor, Alonzo E., *The New Deal and Foreign Trade* (New York: Macmillan, 1935).

The outbreak of World War II in September 1939 had two immediate effects upon the United States. First, it quickly ended any hope of maintaining the political isolation marking the period since World War I and drew the nation back again into a world orbit. In the second place, it pulled the country out of the economic doldrums into which it had sunk with the recession of 1937. It is true that most Americans had hoped, until Pearl Harbor (December 7, 1941), that the country might avoid war, but the strong belief of the great majority in the justice of the Allied cause soon ended all pretense of neutrality. Indeed, it ended American isolationism for decades to come.

PREPARATION FOR WAR

Convinced that Britain and its allies were fighting the cause of this country as well as their own, the United States adopted an official policy of helping them in every way short of war. This policy, combined with Axis victories during the first years of the war, made it necessary to embark on a large-scale defense program. Aid to the nations fighting Germany and military preparedness at home changed the whole economic picture in America.

Revision of the neutrality acts

Within three weeks after the outbreak of war in 1939 Roosevelt called a special session of Congress to revise the neutrality acts to allow the belligerents to purchase arms and munitions in this country. The president's request was granted, but, as we have seen, all sales to combatants had to be made on a cash basis with deliveries in their own ships (the cash-and-carry plan), except sales to their territories far distant from the war zones. Because of Britain's supremacy on the seas, this meant that war goods would go only to the Allies, except for Japan, not yet in the war. As Germany invaded one European nation after another, the American government froze the assets of these nations in the United States in order to protect the property of American nationals abroad. This was also done with German assets after our entry into the war. In the meantime, with private loans abroad declining because of unwillingness to take risks or prevented by the Debt Default Act and the neutrality acts, aid to other nations devolved upon the government. After the war began, virtually all loans to foreign governments were made by the RFC through the Export-Import Bank or by other means. "Eximbank" had been created in 1934 to underwrite with federal funds, at interest, both private foreign loans and U.S. exports.

Lend-lease

A second step in breaking down the neutrality acts was taken in January 1941 when the president called for all-out aid to the embattled democracies and asked for power to sell, exchange, lend, or lease any war equipment to any nation whose defense he might think vital to the defense of the United States. Bitterly opposed by those who believed that this was a definite step toward war, the legislation requested was finally granted after two months' debate. So also was the president's request for large grants to implement the Lend-Lease Act. This act virtually nullified both the cash-and-carry principle and the Debt Default Act of 1934.

Between March, when lend-lease began, and the end of the year, almost $750 million worth of materials were sent to the Allies. As a result of the Lend-Lease Act and other legislation and executive orders, the United States actively engaged in large-scale economic warfare before it entered the fighting war. It was also clear that the administration was determined to reassert the old American principle of freedom of the seas, which had been relinquished in the neutrality acts. At the famous Atlantic Conference in August 1941, President Roosevelt and Prime Minister Winston Churchill made freedom of the seas part of the Atlantic Charter.

The defense program

The demands of lend-lease added new impetus to the development of a war economy already stimulated by a defense program that had begun seriously in 1938. This program was stepped up after the European war began and particularly after the evacuation of Dunkirk and the fall of France. In 1940 Congress voted $17.7 billion for various types of defense, and appropriations (not actual expenditures, which lagged greatly) in 1941 reached the staggering figure of approximately $50 billion. Total expenditures jumped from $9.6 billion in fiscal 1940 to almost $14 billion in the year ending June 30, 1941. Massive federal outlays were finally ending the Great Depression by a thorough application of Keynesian medicine. The required size of the dose had apparently been too large for the American people to prescribe under peacetime conditions.

The regressive income tax

In 1940 Congress committed itself to a two-ocean navy and for the first time in American history to a system of compulsory peacetime conscription. The heavy appropriations of 1941 were accompanied by the heaviest tax bill in our history up to that time, a bill that it was hoped would raise the total federal tax income to $13 billion. Actual total federal receipts in calendar 1941 were $15.4 billion, well toward twice those for the preceding year. One reason was a tremendous shift toward regressivity: Many millions were bracketed into the individual income-tax category for the first time when personal exemptions for a single person, de-

spite rising prices, were lowered from $1000 in the income-tax year 1939 to $800 in 1940, $750 in 1941, and $500 in 1942–1943. National defense thus wrought a major long-term change that brought new millions of low-income people into the tax system. Yet Americans were still not willing to pay for war on a pay-as-you-go basis. Deficits zoomed and the public debt rose from a "modest" $45 billion in 1940 to its wartime peak of $278 billion in 1945. War has been the major contributor by far to the long-run rise in the federal debt since 1929.

Coordination of the defense program

The execution and coordination of the vast defense program was a tremendous task and the setting up of the administrative organization brought confusion and many false starts. It began in 1939 with the War Resources Board, set up to make an overall survey of the problem. Then the president established in 1940 the Council of National Defense, composed of six cabinet members, with the National Defense Advisory Commission to aid it. After the invasion of the Netherlands, the president created the Office of Emergency Management, which was superior to the National Defense Advisory Commission and soon absorbed its functions. The OEM had two principal agencies. One was the Office of Production Management, which was concerned with production, priorities, purchases, materials, labor, contract distribution, and civilian supply—in brief, the production of commodities for war and civilian use. The other main agency was the Office of Price Administration, whose duties were chiefly to control prices. Among the other agencies under OEM were the Office of Civilian Defense, the Office of Defense Transportation, the Office of Lend-Lease Administration, the Office of Scientific Research and Development, The National War Labor Board, the Board of Economic Warfare, and the War Shipping Administration. This array of agencies, and many others that appeared and disappeared during the war, was often confusing, but the agencies show much similarity to those created during World War I.

The president raised the Office of Production Management in January 1941 to the top position in handling war production, with William S. Knudsen, president of General Motors, as director, and Sidney Hillman, president of the Amalgamated Clothing Workers (CIO), as associate director. But progress under the OPM was still too slow, and in September the presi-

TABLE 25–1.   ECONOMIC TRENDS IN THE WAR DECADE (DOLLAR FIGURES IN BILLIONS)

CALENDAR YEARS	GROSS NATIONAL PRODUCT	PERSONAL CONSUMPTION EXPENDITURES	GROSS PRIVATE DOMESTIC INVESTMENT
1940	$ 99.7	$ 70.8	$13.1
1941	124.5	80.6	17.9
1942	157.9	88.5	9.8
1943	191.6	99.3	5.7
1944	210.1	108.3	7.1
1945	211.9	119.7	10.6
1946	208.5	143.4	30.6
1947	231.3	160.7	34.0
1948	257.6	173.6	46.0
1949	256.5	176.8	35.7

CALENDAR YEARS	FEDERAL GOVERNMENT PURCHASES OF GOODS AND SERVICES		CONSUMER PRICE INDEX (1957–1959 = 100)	UNEMPLOYMENT AS PERCENT OF CIVILIAN LABOR FORCE
	MILITARY	OTHER		
1940	$ 2.2	$3.8	48.8	14.6%
1941	13.8	3.1	51.3	9.9
1942	49.4	2.5	56.8	4.7
1943	79.7	1.4	60.3	1.9
1944	87.4	1.6	61.3	1.2
1945	73.5	.7	62.7	1.9
1946	14.7	2.5	68.0	3.9
1947	9.1	3.5	77.8	3.9
1948	10.7	5.8	83.8	3.8
1949	13.3	6.8	83.0	5.9

Source: *Economic Report of the President*, 1969.

dent created a new defense organization known as the Supply, Priorities, and Allocations Board (SPAB). Its executive director was Donald Nelson.[1] Except for the president, this board had the final direction of defense production when Pearl Harbor at last took the nation into the war.

The wartime economy

The impact of the European war in 1939 affected the American economy almost overnight. Said Price Administrator Leon Henderson in reviewing the early weeks:

> Memories of the First World War— memories of insatiable demand, of shortages, of inflation — were rekindled and there was an immediate and sharp

increase in buying. The business man who customarily bought one carload put in orders for three. . . . The rise in prices itself evoked widespread accumulation of inventories and further fed the stream of buying. A speculative boom was on.[2]

But the American economy was soon influenced by much more than fear of shortages and hopes of profits. Revision of the neutrality acts to allow the cash-and-carry plan, the Lend-Lease Act, and the large-scale defense program gave a more substantial basis.

Industrial production approximately doubled between August 1939 and December 1941.[3] Since a substantial portion of this production was sold to the Allied nations, the situation was reflected in an increase of exports from approximately $3.1 billion in 1939 to $5.15 billion in 1941. But the European war and the domestic defense program were by no means

[1]Other members during the early years of the war were the secretaries of war, navy, and agriculture, the federal loan administrator (Jesse Jones), the officer in charge of War Department production (Lt. Gen. William S. Knudsen), the administrator of the Office of Price Administration (Leon Henderson), the chairman of the Board of Economic Welfare (Vice-President Henry A. Wallace), and the defense aid administrator (Harry Hopkins).

[2]Office of Price Administration, *First Quarterly Report, for Period Ended April 30, 1942*, p. 1.

[3]Using the average of 1935–1939 as 100, the Federal Reserve Board puts the index figure of industrial production in 1938 at 88 and that of December 1941 at 167.

the only cause of the skyrocketing of industrial production to heights hardly dreamed of in 1929. The increase in consumers' goods (25 percent between August 1939 and August 1941) was also large. This is explained by increased employment, zooming payrolls, and the desire of wage earners to acquire commodities denied them during the bleak depression days of the 1930s. The early years of the war had not yet solved the unemployment problem, as Table 25–1 shows, but the number of non-agricultural workers had increased from 35.3 million in April 1940 to 41 million in December 1941. At the same time the index figures of payrolls showed an increase approximately equal to that of industrial production.

What made the economic picture brighter, particularly for wage earners in the durable goods industries, was that income moved ahead more rapidly than prices. Average hourly earnings for production workers in manufacturing increased from 66 cents in 1940 to 73 in 1941, and average weekly earnings, resulting in part from the increased number of hours, went up even more, from $25.20 to $29.58, a 17 percent rise. At the same time the consumer price index for goods purchased by wage earners increased only about 5 percent (see Table 25–1). As was typical in a generally rising price level, the farmers profited by a far greater differential between the rise in the prices they received for their products and the increase in the cost of commodities they purchased. The failure of retail prices to move upward immediately after the European war broke out was probably due to the rapid increase of production to serve consumer demands. The wholesale price index did not advance perceptibly until August 1940, or seriously until February 1941, when it began to spread out to include retail prices.

PRODUCTION FOR WAR

When war came to Pearl Harbor in December 1941, the nation was still by no means adequately prepared. Defense production was in the formative stage and the administrative organizations had not yet been established on a basis of reasonable efficiency. However, the preliminary work had been done and the pattern of defense production laid out. With war the machinery of production slipped into high gear more speedily than had been expected by even the most optimistic. Preparedness during the years 1940 to 1941 paid off in 1942 in what to many seemed a miracle of production, a miracle that was much facilitated by the existence of large excess capacity in industry and large unemployed reserves of labor power.

The chief sinews of war are people, materials, technical knowledge, and administrative expertise. The United States found an adequate supply of all these. Military personnel were obtained mainly through the Selective Service Act of 1940, as amended and broadened after Pearl Harbor. Sufficient labor was provided by employing the formerly unemployed together with additions to the civilian labor force itself, including millions of women ordinarily not in the labor force. The main problem was that of materials. This involved not only the production of raw materials of every kind, including food, but the conversion of civilian manufacturing to wartime production, the building of new facilities for manufacturing arms and munitions, and the administrative task of establishing systems of priorities, allocations, and rationing.

Implicit in any adequate handling of production and distribution of war materials is efficient administration. Reorganization and realignment of administrative agencies continued during the war, but relative stabilization was secured by 1942.

Except for the purely military aspects, defense efforts as a whole were largely grouped under the Office of Emergency Management, a framework within the Executive Office of the President.

Facilities for war production

The first and most important problem of the WPB and its predecessors was the conversion of existing facilities to war production and the increase of those facilities. The latter was brought about largely by the federal government, which spent about $16 billion in the construction of war plants through the Defense Plants Corporation. At least five-sixths of the new plant construction during the war was done by government financing, and this comprised the newest and best of the manufacturing facilities. At the end of the war the federal government owned over 90 percent of the facilities for producing synthetic rubber, aircraft, magnesium, and ships; 70 percent of the aluminum capacity; and 50 percent of the facilities for building machine tools. It had also constructed plants for steel, high-octane gasoline, and chemicals, to say nothing of 3800 miles of oil pipelines (the Big Inch and Little Inch) to carry petroleum to the east coast.

Conversion to war production necessitated the shifting of tools, equipment, facilities, labor, and floor space and to a large extent the retooling of industry. Two years of preparation and of selling equipment to the Allies had its advantageous effect. With America's entry into the war the whole program proceeded with unexpected speed. The United States, said Donald Nelson toward the end of May 1942, "is actually doing things today which were unthinkable a year ago. It is executing programs which sounded utterly fantastic no more than six months ago."

Thousands of factories hitherto engaged in manufacturing peacetime products turned to war production. The automobile industry, for example, converted itself almost entirely to the manufacture of airplanes, tanks, trucks, jeeps, and other war needs. Industrial production (1935 – 1939 = 100) rose to 239 in 1943, and durable manufactured goods to 360. Production of machinery quadrupled, and transportation equipment (automobiles, aircraft, railroad equipment, and ships) increased seven times. As J. A. Krug, later chairman of the WPB, summarized the situation:

> In 1939 . . . this country devoted less than 2% of its total national output to war, and about 70% to satisfying immediate civilian needs, the remaining 28% going to civilian government expenditures, capital formation, and exports. By 1944, war outlay had mounted to 40%, and the civilian share — though just as large in physical quantity — represented only half of our total output.[4]

The slow growth in personal consumption expenditures during the war years may be observed in Table 25 – 1. Unlike World War I, this war truly converted the nation to a military economy. Nevertheless, consumption per capita was maintained between 1940 and 1945.

The production miracle

During the five years of defense preparation and war (July 1, 1940, to July 31, 1945) the

nation spent $186 billion for munitions production. The result was equally amazing. At the time of Pearl Harbor the armed forces possessed only 1,157 planes suitable for combat and about the same number of usable tanks. During the five years of production the nation produced 86,338 tanks, 297,000 airplanes, 17.4 million rifles, carbines, and side arms, vast quantities of artillery equipment and munitions, 64,500 landing vessels, and thousands of navy ships, cargo ships, and transports. During these five years the United States merchant fleet quadrupled, and navy firepower increased tenfold. By mid-1944 it was estimated that the combined war production of Great Britain, Canada, and the United States was four times as high as that of the Axis powers. This ratio dramatizes the fantastic miscalculations of the latter, who had hoped at the outset that they could prevent the realization of the great Allied production potential. So well was production going that by late summer of 1944 the WPB felt safe in ordering cutbacks in war production and allowing some resumption of the manufacture of civilian goods. It should be remembered that not all of this tremendous production was used in this country. From March 11, 1941, to December 1, 1945, goods transferred and services rendered under lend-lease amounted to approximately $49.1 billion. Of this, about 60 percent went to the United Kingdom and 22 percent to the Soviet Union.

The spectacular munitions production depended to no small extent upon the increased production of raw materials and the administrative ability to distribute them. The index for mineral production (1935 – 1939 = 100) rose to 148 in 1942 — "particularly noteworthy," said Secretary of the Interior Harold Ickes, "because the nation skimmed much of the 'cream' from its mineral resources during the First World War." The production of fuels (coal and oil) also reached new levels with the index figure at 145 in 1944. The history of agricultural production is quite as remarkable. Production here increased each year from 1938 to 1944 with the index reaching 136 in the latter year.[5]

The transportation miracle

No area of the American economy met the challenge of war more successfully than transportation. The inability of the railroads to cope with the situation in World War I had forced the

[4]J. A. Krug, *Production: Wartime Achievements and the Reconversion Outlook,* WPB document no. 334 (Washington, D.C.: U.S. Government Printing Office, October 9, 1954), p. 4.

[5]The index figures in this section are from the *Statistical Abstract, 1947,* pp. 629, 816.

government to take over and operate a large part of the system. In World War II the railroads did such a superb job under the direction of the Office of Defense Transportation that the government found it unnecessary to extend further controls. Railroads reported that they had moved two and a half times the number of ton-miles of freight in 1944 that they had in 1929, and four and a half times the passenger traffic. This enormous increase was handled with practically the same number of locomotives as in 1939 and but a slight increase in freight and passenger cars. The Office of Defense Transportation under Joseph B. Eastman (until 1944) not only supervised the railroads but had jurisdiction over air transport, inland and coastwise shipping, pipeline facilities, and rubber-borne transportation.

Shortages

Despite the notable records of manufacturers, miners, farmers, and transportation workers, serious shortages of military as well as civilian commodities existed at one time or another. The early difficulties had to do chiefly with manufacturing facilities, but this problem was largely solved by mid-1943. By that time the needs for most classes of military goods were being fully satisfied and the peak of the munitions program was reached in the last two months of that year. Shortages of raw materials, however, were more acute and persistent, although the bottlenecks shifted as time went on. The first great shortage, that of aluminum, brought the government into action with a program of government-built but privately operated expansion that quadrupled production over that in prewar years, and introduced new enterprises into that highly concentrated industry.

Aluminum shortage for war needs vanished by the end of 1942, but shortages appeared in iron, ships, rubber, gasoline, fuel oil, and other commodities. Although the United States at that time had an ample supply of iron resources and a productive capacity greater than that of any other nation in the world, the fantastic demand for steel products outdistanced the supply. The shortage was explained in part by failure to obtain scrap metal, and this in turn was ascribed to the low ceiling on scrap prices. There was also strong evidence that the steel industry in the early years of the war was reluctant to add to its capacity for fear of excess at the war's termination.

Fortunately for the war effort, as time went on the situation improved through increased capacity, better utilization of scrap metal, and

the channeling of steel into war production rather than civilian commodities. Steel was in acute demand not only for munitions but for the building of ships for both the navy and the merchant marine. The shortage of merchant ships was caused chiefly by the successful German submarine campaign in the Atlantic, which destroyed over 600 Allied cargo ships by the end of 1942. A shipbuilding program that launched 3 million tons of merchant shipping in 1942 and 9 million in 1943, combined with a successful Allied attack on submarines, overcame this problem in 1943. No sooner was the submarine menace under control than the increased needs of 4 million soldiers overseas again strained shipping facilities to the limit.

Oil transport and synthetic rubber

One of the most disastrous aspects of the German submarine activities was the interference with the transportation of gasoline and fuel oil, most of which was normally moved from the Gulf ports to the eastern seaboard by tankers. Reduction of civilian use by strict rationing, the construction by the government of huge pipelines from the oil fields to the east coast, and increased production made available a sufficient supply for military needs.

Quite different from the aggressive efficiency with which the government handled the aluminum, shipping, and oil situations was its muddling slowness in meeting the rubber shortage. After Japan's conquest of the East Indies had closed the source of virtually all the natural rubber used by the United States and its allies, it was clear that immediate and decisive steps were overdue. The solution was the production of synthetic rubber by methods already known to chemists. Existing rubber stocks were frozen and tires rationed, but it was six months after Pearl Harbor before the government organized a synthetic rubber program. Confusion, divided responsibility, and politics all slowed up the program. The delay seems to have been caused largely by the insistence of the farm bloc that rubber be manufactured from agricultural products as well as from oil. Action finally came after the president named a national rubber conservation director to put a program into action. With the aid of government-built synthetic plants, production by mid-1944 had reached the rate of 836,000 tons a year compared with pre-war imports of natural rubber ranging from 550,000 to 650,000 tons a year. This took care of the expanding military needs but left little for civilians.

RATIONING AND PRICE CONTROL

Perhaps the greatest economic failure in World War I had been lack of adequate rationing or price control. During the 19 months of that conflict the price index (1914 = 100) rose to 162. During World War II, in which American participation lasted twice as long, the wholesale price index (1939 = 100) rose only to 133. Failure adequately to control prices in the earlier conflict substantially increased the cost of the war and reduced the standard of living of millions of people. As America began to feel the impact of World War II, the government realized the importance of price pressures but was slow to move toward the necessary price-control measures. Some efforts to protect and acquire strategic raw materials had been made even before the Division of Price Stabilization, under the National Defense Advisory Commission, was established in May 1940. The Division of Price Stabilization became increasingly important and was made an executive agency known as the Office of Price Administration in August 1941. However, very little had been done to control prices even at this date.

The OPA and pressure for inflation

The OPA had little power in the prewar days. It could set up price schedules and through publicity, informal agreements, requests, and warnings sometimes bring compliance. It could not impose penalties. Nevertheless, its influence was felt to some extent, for it supplied government purchasing agencies with fair-price schedules that they could follow. After the coming of war, Congress, by the Emergency Price Control Act of January 1942, gave the OPA statutory power to control prices and rents and set forth specific penalties for violations.

That the pressure for inflation was great there can be no doubt. Both the government and consumers were buying intensively and there was not sufficient of most commodities to go around. Although industry was actually producing more consumers' goods than before the war, the income of consumers had grown tremendously and thus increased the demand. Yet it was not until the end of April 1942 that the general maximum price regulation was instituted. With farm prices exempt until they reached 110 percent of parity and with the substantial enforcement lags and administrative weaknesses, prices continued upward. But beginning in 1943, as shown in Table 25–1, there ensued a most remarkable three-year period of essential

stability. This was a most notable record of wartime price control.

The OPA estimated in 1942 that income payments for that year would approximate $117 billion, of which $31 billion would be returned to the government either in taxes or in individual savings in the form of war bonds or stamps, leaving a balance of $86 billion available for spending on civilian goods and services. At the same time it estimated that goods and services produced during the year would total approximately $69 billion, leaving $17 billion of purchasing power as an inflationary gap to threaten the price structure. Government policies to close this gap and thus hold back inflation included increased taxes, wide efforts to promote bond sales, curtailment of installment buying, rationing, and price control. The last two methods were the responsibility of the OPA.

Among the many complications involved in the battle against inflation was the control of wages and the special protection that farmers had received on prices. President Roosevelt, who took the lead in the fight against inflation, asked Congress in the autumn of 1942 for full power to regulate farm prices. This was granted, along with the power to stabilize wages and salaries. The president followed with an order directing (1) the National Labor Board to limit wages and salaries, (2) the OPA to fix ceilings on retail and wholesale prices and on rents not yet curbed, and (3) the Department of Agriculture and the OPA to cooperate to hold down farm prices. To supervise all this control he created the Office of Economic Stabilization and as its head appointed James F. Byrnes, who resigned from the Supreme Court to accept the position.

Rationing

Within a month after the war started, the OPA began the rationing program with tires (January 5, 1942). In May it began to ration gasoline on the east coast and in December extended gas rationing to the entire nation. In similar manner rationing was imposed on fuel oil in the East in the fall of 1942 and made nationwide in the late winter of 1943.

Shortages in food first occurred in sugar and coffee. During normal prewar years Americans consumed close to 8 million tons of sugar, two-thirds of which was imported from the Philippines, Hawaii, and Cuba. With Japan's entry into the war the Philippine supply was cut off, that of Hawaii seriously reduced, and that from Cuba curtailed by lack of shipping and submarine activities. At the same time, the demand was enlarged by lend-lease shipments and the increased use of sugar in manufacturing alcohol for explosives. Coffee, most of which is imported from Brazil, also became temporarily scarce because of large shipments to the Allies and interference with shipping. Rationing of sugar began in May 1942 with the issuing of stamp books to consumers, and coffee was rationed in November, although the latter restriction was discontinued eight months later.

By the end of 1942 the armed forces and lend-lease were absorbing 25 percent of the foodstuffs produced in this country, particularly canned, bottled, frozen, and dried vegetables, fruits, juices, and soups. As these commodities began to disappear from grocers' shelves, the country was not surprised when Food Administrator Claude Wickard on December 27 ordered Price Administrator Henderson to ration them. Consumers registered in February for Ration Book 2, and March 1, 1943, the rationing of various kinds of canned and packaged goods went into operation under a point system. Four weeks later rationing under the same system was extended to include meats and fats. Under the point system coupons were valued for a certain number of points and the amount of goods that could be purchased was determined by the point value assigned to each commodity by the OPA. By mid-1943 rationing covered 95 percent of the food supply and ensured a fairer distribution, but it by no means solved the problem of shortages.

The OPA was also assigned the task of controlling rents in defense areas and establishing price ceilings on all commodities affecting the cost of living. Both jobs were difficult and complicated. Nevertheless, by mid 1943 the OPA had designated 456 defense-rental areas and had established control over most of them by freezing rents at the March 1942 level.

The achievement of the OPA

Probably no government agency ever affected more intimately the lives of so many people as the OPA, and it received more than its share of criticism. The fundamental necessity of its work was understood, however, and the great mass of American consumers loyally supported it. Unfortunately, a small minority attempted to evade these regulations and a black market, particularly in gasoline and meats, existed at various times and places, which the OPA found itself inadequately equipped to prevent. Despite the difficulties, the OPA did a remarkable job. It not only saved the taxpayers billions of dollars in the cost of the war, but it prevented widespread chaos and suffering that would inevitably have followed failure to ration commodities and impose price control.[6]

LABOR IN THE WAR

In regard to labor the federal government faced three major problems. The first was to obtain an adequate supply of trained workers for the war industries. The second was to develop a successful policy for handling labor disputes. The third was the difficult job of determining a wage policy that would dovetail with government efforts to control prices.

The labor supply

The first and primary task, that of developing an adequate supply of labor, seemed at the beginning an insuperable job. It was necessary not only to replace approximately 11.5 million men and women drawn into the armed forces, but to take care of the need for greater war production while still providing for minimum civilian requirements. Nevertheless, this task was eventually accomplished. Between 1940 and 1944 the civilian labor force declined about 2 percent, from 55.6 million to 54.6 million. Gross civilian output (GNP minus national defense expenditures) decreased only about 5 percent, so the smaller civilian labor force accounted for enormous increases in military hardware and other supplies.

The gaps made by workers drawn into the armed forces were filled from many sources. First of all, the new demand largely absorbed the 9.5 million unemployed in 1939. It also drew from youth of school age, from aged workers who had retired, and above all from the ranks of women. The number of civilian women working outside the home increased by 5 million during the war, a 37 percent rise. The

[6]Leon Henderson resigned as administrator of the OPA in January 1943. He was succeeded by Prentiss M. Brown, formerly senator from Michigan, who in turn was followed in October by Chester A. Bowles.

number of women factory workers doubled between 1939 and 1944.

Even with this additional force, the job of war production plus the maintenance of civilian production at prewar levels could never have been done without a willingness to work longer and harder. In the years from 1939 to 1944 the average work week increased from 37.7 to 45.2 hours (20 percent) in manufacturing, from 32.4 to 39.5 hours in construction, and from 32.3 to 43.9 hours in mining. At the same time, said the WPB, "productivity— output per man hour—climbed sharply, as volume increased, manufacturing methods improved, and workers responded to appeals to move the munitions to the fighting fronts faster and faster."[7]

The addition of millions of new wage earners and the shift of millions of others from their regular jobs to new ones in war industries created many problems. One of the most difficult was the training for new jobs. This involved refresher courses for adults, vocational training for youth, and enlargement of apprentice training in virtually every factory in the land. Another problem was the movement of workers into defense areas, which resulted in a housing shortage, crowded conditions, increased sickness, and high rates of absenteeism. Long hours exhausted all but the hardiest. Many women were doing factory work in addition to their home duties; men also tried to add war work to their regular jobs. The government constructed temporary housing in many areas of concentrated war production, and subsidized child-care and other social services to make it possible for women to work. Almost the entire structure of child-care centers was dismantled after the war.

Labor policy

As in World War I, the federal government understood the need of close cooperation with labor and set up machinery to maintain it at all stages. One method was to put labor representatives in all important war agencies. Even before America's entry into the war, labor had a place on the Advisory Commission of the Council of National Defense. As already noted, Sidney Hillman, president of the Amalgamated Clothing Workers, was appointed associate director of the Office of Production Management when that body was set up to prepare for defense and possible war. The war policies of the federal government with relation to labor

[7]Krug, *Production,* p. 2.

were carried out chiefly through two bodies: the War Manpower Commission and the War Labor Board.

The War Manpower Commission

The War Manpower Commission was "to establish basic national policies to assure the most effective mobilization and maximum utilization of the nation's manpower in the prosecution of the war." It had supervision of job recruiting and job training in war industries and the placement of workers where they were most needed. It performed a useful function in deciding overall policies and in the end had virtual control over the Selective Service System in determining draft deferments.

Quite as important and much better known was the national War Labor Board. Established to function as a sort of supreme court for labor disputes, it had the final power over labor conflicts. Refusal to obey its decisions left government seizure and operation as the only alternative. It was a 12-member body with equal representation from the public, employers, and labor. With its 12 regional offices and its subsidiary boards, it ironed out thousands of difficult disputes and did a valuable service. It was recognized as a body of strategic importance in the war effort and had the confidence of the public. It became increasingly unpopular with labor, however, after it was given the responsibility of stabilizing wages.

Work stoppages

As a whole, labor gave excellent support to the war effort. Leaders of organized labor pledged a no-strike policy and urged their membership to the fullest cooperation. There were numerous strikes, however, most of them unauthorized, but on the whole the pledge was kept as far as responsible labor leaders were concerned. There were some exceptions, notably John L. Lewis and his United Mine Workers, whose interruptions of coal production will be noted below. From January 1, 1942, to August 14, 1945, the Department of Labor records 14,647 work stoppages involving 6.7 million workers and 36 million man-days lost. The average length of the stoppages in 1943 was 5 days and in 1944 it was 5.6 days. The time lost, however, was but one-tenth of 1 percent of the total working time (1943–1944). Considering rising prices, the strain of speed-up, and longer hours, the total record was unusually good. Meanwhile, active participation in the war effort and its administration, together with the tight labor markets, resulted in a very large growth in union membership. By the last year of the war union membership had burgeoned to over 14 million, and as a percentage of total nonagricultural employment it stood at 35.8, an all-time high.

Wage control

The chief friction arose over wages. On the theory that wage control should follow price control, the administration ordered the War Labor Board in 1942 to stabilize wages at a level equal to the rise in the cost of living up to that time. When 180,000 workers of the Bethlehem, Youngstown, Inland, and Republic Steel companies sought a dollar-a-day raise, the WLB granted them 15 percent on the theory that this represented the rise in the cost of living between January 1, 1941, and May 1942. This was known as the Little Steel formula and was followed thereafter by the WLB. Labor economists presented data to prove that prices had gone up more than 15 percent, that they were continuing to rise, and that the profits of farmers and industries were increasing. The WLB, however, refused to abandon its figure, insisting that the actual take-home pay equaled the rise in the cost of living. Nevertheless, it softened its policy by allowing vacation pay, higher wages for overtime, and other indirect ways of increasing income. This experience was a stimulus to the postwar rise in the importance of fringe benefits in all major labor contracts.

The War Labor Disputes Act, 1943

Friction between the policies of the WLB and the unions demanding higher wages became acute in 1943 and 1944 and many efforts were made to break through the Little Steel formula. The most successful were those of the United Mine Workers, led by John L. Lewis, who suspended work four times in 1943 and forced the government to take over the mines and to grant miners substantial increases. Threat of a railway strike in December of that year also brought government seizure of the railroads and government operation for three weeks until the wage disputes were adjusted. Strikes and threats of strikes during wartime aroused resentment. The reaction of Congress was the War Labor Disputes (Smith-Connally) Act of 1943, passed over the president's veto. It extended for the duration of the war plus six months.

The War Labor Disputes Act aimed primarily to prevent interruption of war production. It strengthened the power of the WLB, authorized the president to take possession of any industry producing materials needed in the war effort, and forbade any person to promote strikes, lockouts, or other interruption in production after the government had taken possession. Workers contemplating a strike in private industries were required to notify the government, and the WLB was to hold a ballot within 30 days to determine whether the workers would strike. The act also forbade corporations, banks, and labor organizations to contribute to any election involving federal officials. Since there were more strikes and more workers involved in strikes in 1944 than in 1943, it appeared that this legislation had little immediate effect. It was significant, however, in showing the strong antiunion feeling in Congress and the growing strength of the antiunion group. It marked a definite shift in congressional attitudes toward labor and was a portent of more such legislation in the postwar years.

FINANCING THE WAR

The problem of financing World War II was greater than that of World War I; the struggle was longer and the amounts involved relative to the capacity of the country were very much greater. But as a whole, the job was better done. Experience in the earlier conflict may have helped. Closer government connection with various segments of the economic life, including banking, made it easier. Better control of inflation kept expenses down and left the consumer with a larger surplus to invest in the rapidly growing volume of government securities, and these the government was able to sell at lower interest rates. Taxation was more far-reaching and yielded relatively larger returns. While GNP increased by over 100 percent between 1940 and 1945 (see Table 25–1), internal revenue receipts of the federal government rose over eightfold. Nevertheless, deficits were also enormous, peaking at almost $55 billion in 1944. The great wartime rise in public debt has been noted earlier.

It was fortunate that all this was so, for the cost of the war was stupendous. The budgetary expenses for the fiscal years 1941–1945 amounted to approximately $317.6 billion, of which $281.5 billion (88.6 percent) was spent directly for war. Federal budget expenditures including the social security and other trust fund accounts climbed from $13.3 billion in fiscal 1941 to almost $100 billion in 1945. The public debt in 1941 was $56.3 billion; in 1945 it was $252.5 billion. Of the $281.5 billion direct cost of the war, $159.6 went to the army and $88.4 billion to the navy, the remainder being spent by the United States Maritime Commission, the War Shipping Administration, and various other government departments and administrative units. Of these vast expenditures for war and other government needs, only about 43 percent was obtained from taxes and other nonborrowing sources during the period July 1, 1940, through December 31, 1945. This was a better record than that of World War I, when less than one-third of total expenditures came from such sources. Of course in real terms wars are always paid for while they are being fought (through foregone civilian consumption), but Americans in wartime have never been willing to tax themselves to this extent, choosing rather to indulge in major fiscal delusions.

Tax legislation

War financing may be said to have begun with the Revenue Act of 1940, designed to produce larger funds for the defense program. No new forms of taxation were introduced, but the law increased the rates and, as previously pointed out, broadened the base of existing sources of revenue. In general this was true of later finance measures.

One innovation came in the Public Debt Act of 1941, which made interest on future issues of securities of the government subject to all federal income taxes. A more important innovation came in the Tax Payment Act of 1943, which provided for withholding income taxes at the source on wages and salaries, thus permanently introducing a new pay-as-you-go plan for non-property incomes. Tax receipts for the fiscal years 1941–1945 were approximately $138.5 billion, of which income and excess profits taxes from individuals approximated 36.2 percent, from corporations 34.2 percent, and the remaining 29.6 percent from other sources, such as excise taxes, employment taxes, and tariffs. It is important to note that the number of individuals, estates, and trusts paying taxes increased from 7.6 million in 1939 to 43 million in

1943. In the latter year about 284,000 corporations also paid taxes.

Treasury securities

Between May 1, 1941, the day that President Roosevelt bought the first savings bond of Series E, until the last dollar from savings bonds sold during the Victory Loan drive was deposited with the treasurer of the United States on January 3, 1946, the Treasury sold $185.7 billion of securities to finance the war. Of this amount the seven war loans and the final Victory Loan took care of approximately $156.9 billion. About two-thirds of this amount ($102.2 billion) was purchased by corporations, one-third by individuals ($43.3 billion), and the remainder by commercial banks and treasury investment accounts.

Government planning and administration: an overview

The administration in World War II drew heavily on the experience of the earlier conflict. The president himself had been assistant secretary of the navy in World War I and was acquainted with the problems faced by his colleagues and the administrative bodies set up to carry on the effort. In administrative expertise Roosevelt's war cabinet eventually surpassed that of Wilson. Moreover, with peacetime conscription and the decision to build a two-ocean navy, defense preparations had begun earlier and more intensely in the period before World War II.

Where the second struggle surpassed the first, however, was chiefly in relative economic magnitude, in financing, and in the extent of administrative controls. As noted previously a larger percentage of the war's financing was handled by taxes rather than by passing on the fiscal burden to future generations. More important, perhaps, was the superior handling of rationing on the consumer level and the comparatively successful efforts after 1942 to control wages and prices. Wage and price control prevented a runaway inflation and saved billions for the taxpayer, to say nothing of distributing the burdens of war more evenly upon the nation as a whole. World War II was carried on more efficiently than any other war in our history. And it carried economic planning to a point and with a degree of efficiency totally unprecedented in American historical experience.

RECONVERSION AND DECONTROL

Except in international relations, where the United States repudiated its earlier policy of isolation, the years after World War II resembled in many respects those after the earlier conflict. After VJ Day (Victory in Japan) in August 1945, the nation had the same desire to liquidate the war as quickly as possible and the same overwhelming urge to return to "normalcy" as it had in 1918. Reconversion, which began in earnest during the several months between VE day (Victory in Europe, May 8, 1945) and VJ Day was pushed quickly and successfully. Decontrol was also pushed quickly, all too quickly, with the inevitable unfortunate inflation. Among the immediate results of that inflation were serious labor unrest and a wave of strikes, as after World War I. They were soon followed by antilabor legislation. All this was accompanied not alone by economic uncertainty but by a revival of intolerance and reaction.

The GI Bill

During the war the government made many promises to veterans of educational subsidies and business loans in the Serviceman's Readjustment Act of 1944 ("GI Bill of Rights"), which it fulfilled with considerable success. Except for this, any overall program of social or economic reconstruction was as lacking as after World War I.

The GI Bill did much to ease the unemployment problem as well as to extend aid to veterans in other ways. The act provided hospitalization, unemployment benefits, aid in obtaining jobs, and loans for homes, farms and business. It also took hundreds of thousands of veterans out of the labor market by helping them to continue their education for a period of up to four years. The employment situation was, of course, aided by the maintenance of a large peacetime army without precedent in American history.

Truman's "do-nothing" Congress

The congressional elections of 1946 brought an antiadministration Congress for the first time in 14 years and thus ended any possibility of close cooperation on the part of all branches of government in dealing with domestic problems or developing a wise policy of reconstruction. The program of the new Congress, as far as it had one, was primarily to reduce taxation and pass antilabor legislation. Congress not only was little concerned with a wise program of reconstruction, but on the contrary seemed interested rather in weakening some of the more intelligent New Deal legislation and reviving the past.

President Harry Truman, who had found little Democratic interest in maintaining price control, found less in the Republican-dominated legislature. Inflation had followed the end of the war, and with it severe labor disputes aimed at raising wages. At a special session of Congress called in November 1947, Truman asked for wide powers to control inflation as well as for aid to Europe. Congress replied by granting some minor powers that the president accurately described as "pitifully inadequate."

As the president predicted, these minor powers were of little use. The inflation continued throughout the larger part of 1948, and the 80th Congress adjourned without further legislation to check it. When the president found that the platform of both major parties favored action on a number of problems left unsolved, including housing and inflation, he recalled Congress in special session in July to deal with them. To his request for wide powers to control inflation Congress again responded only with authority to curb consumer installment buying and to increase the amount of cash that Federal Reserve banks must keep on hand, thus curbing their ability to grant business loans.

Reconversion

Reconversion in a sense began as early as late 1943 and early 1944, when the War Production Board began to cut back orders on certain war goods that were ahead of schedule and to allow resumption of production of civilian commodities. Dissension over the problem of cutbacks between military and civilian personnel in the government was, in fact, one of the causes for the resignation of Donald Nelson, head of the War Production Board (January 1942 to September 1944), and the appointment of his successor, Julius A. Krug. It also brought, in October 1944, the establishment of the Office of War Mobilization and Reconversion. This organization was to unify the programs and establish the policies regarding the use of natural resources and manpower until the end of the war and in the meantime to take over the responsibility and planning for demobilization and reconversion.

There can be no doubt as to the efficiency and speed of reconversion. The productive machinery of the nation, of which at the peak

50 percent had been devoted to the war effort, shifted over to civilian production with amazing success. By mid-1947 the job of conversion was practically finished. The impetus came from a market eager to overcome shortages that had accumulated for three and one-half years. With equal speed the administrative war agencies were disbanded. Exclusive of army and navy units, approximately 165 emergency war agencies had been established between late 1939 and the middle of 1946. Some of these were absorbed in existing departments or agencies; others were eliminated. By the latter date not more than a dozen of the main agencies remained. As to the wisdom of this speed, some reservations can be made. The rapid elimination of price controls, as we shall see, proved disastrous. Even on the strictly military level, the armed forces were cut from 11.4 million in 1945 to 3.5 million in 1946 and 1.6 million in 1947. In less than three years, however, the nation instituted a massive military buildup.

The employment picture

The most satisfying and perhaps surprising aspect of reconversion was that it was accomplished with relatively little unemployment. The rise in unemployment, unlike 1920 and 1921, was very moderate. The labor force decreased by 3.5 million between 1945 and 1947 as wartime participants, including the armed forces, left the labor market. There was a temporary absolute drop in women's labor force participation (much greater than that for men), from 19.3 million in 1945 to 16.9 million in 1947.

Total civilian employment increased between 1945 and 1947 from 52.8 million to 57.8 million. Many factors help to explain this fortunate situation. First was the continuation of prosperity. Three main temporary props for this prosperity were: business expenditure for reconversion and for new construction and equipment; heavy consumer spending, much of it for commodities unobtainable during the war; and heavy export of goods and services in 1947, which yielded the largest excess over imports in history: $11 billion. Since at least half of this export trade was financed by the federal government, some of this prosperity was made possible by the taxpayers. Also fundamental in the whole picture was the enlarged productivity of the nation. It might be noted in this connection that the railroads spent an average of a billion dollars a year in rehabilitation during the eight years following the war.

Shortages in consumer goods

The two most important remaining economic problems facing the nation in the immediate postwar years were shortages of consumer and capital goods, and inflation. United States participation in the war had lasted over three and a half years, twice as long as in World War I, and shortages were more acute. Although production of civilian goods was large during wartime, few commodities were produced in quantities adequate to meet the demand. Fortunately the rapid reconversion of industrial plants largely solved this problem. Within two years after VJ Day most shortages had been overcome. Volume purchases of consumer durable goods almost doubled between 1945 and 1946. This was the main reason why an immediate postwar recession was avoided.

Among the shortages in consumer items that persisted into 1948 were automobiles and houses. By the end of 1948, automobile production had actually reached a rate of 4 million a year, but it could not meet the demand.

By 1950 only a moderate proportion of our economic activity could be attributed to shortages created by the war. Not only were shortages of necessary commodities overcome, but certain vital needs such as the expansion of rural electrification were being met. And new commodities, notably television, were introduced.

The housing shortage

More acute was the housing shortage, which had been chronic before the war. Except for the army and defense workers, the construction of housing had practically ceased for four years. The Office of Mobilization and Reconversion estimated that more than 3 million people would be seeking new homes in the two postwar years 1946 and 1947. Government agencies set their sights for the yearly construction of from 1 to 1.5 million housing units a year, but actual production fell far below that. Retarding factors were shortages of raw materials and labor and the perennial problem of the high cost of construction. It is also possible that continuance of rent controls may have been a factor in keeping new capital from housing construction.

Congress in 1946 provided $400 million for subsidies to speed production of bottleneck materials and authorized large loans to promote home building. Veterans were given preference and might receive direct aid under the GI Bill of Rights. Housing subsidies had begun during the depression, and this was to prove, as in all industrialized countries, a lasting government commitment, for the private contractor could not supply housing at prices that low-income groups could pay without public help. Federal Housing Administrator Julian Zimmerman declared in 1959 that "the lethargic state of the housing industry was the most serious unsolved problem of the depression."[8] The Housing Act of 1949 established as a national goal "the realization as soon as feasible . . . [of] a decent home and suitable living environment for every American family." It is a sad commentary that the goal had not proved "feasible" over a quarter century later.

During the 1940s the birth rate was high and the population increased by 19 million. Although permanent nonfarm dwellings increased from the end of the war through 1950 by over 4.87 million, acute shortages remained, particularly in certain large urban areas.

Inflation

Of greater significance than shortages for the future welfare of the nation was the problem of inflation, for shortages were eventually overcome. But the disastrous results of inflation were far more permanent. For the policy makers of 1945 and 1946, history had no lessons. With virtually no price control on the retail level, many prices during and after World War I had almost doubled. About half of this rise had occurred after the war. Inflation had lasted until mid-1920, when high prices combined with the end of heavy government spending had brought a collapse, a shakedown of prices, and a new start. The consumers' price index for moderate-income families in large cities as prepared by the Bureau of Labor Statistics of the Department of Labor (1935–1939 = 100) had risen from 70.7 in 1913 to 107.7 in 1918, then had continued upward to 143.3 in 1920, only to drop to 127.7 in 1921.

As already noted, the price history during World War II was different from that of the earlier struggle because of more extensive rationing and price control. As seen in Table 25–1, the consumer price index rose from 48.8 in 1940 to 62.7 in 1945. This was inflation, but not to the extent of that of World War I, particularly when the greater length of the last war is remembered. After World War II ended and controls were lifted in July 1946, the experience was much the same at first. But there was no

price shakedown after World War II. As Table 25–1 shows, prices continued to rise, and the halt in the recession of 1949 was hardly noticeable (it was slightly more noticeable in wholesale prices, always the more sensitive series). In 1950 they headed back up again.

The extent of this inflationary movement was by no means the result solely of the too-rapid ending of priorities and price control, although that may have been the predominating influence. Shortages of badly needed commodities and pent-up buying power were also fundamental. Some responsibility may undoubtedly be attributed to the financial wartime policies of the federal government, which left too much excess buying power in the hands of civilians. Undoubtedly one additional important cause of the inflation was the fact that the government continued to loan heavily abroad to provide the chief support of the United Nations Relief and Rehabilitation activities, and later to implement the European Relief Program (Marshall Plan). It will also be noted in Table 25–1 that federal government purchases began to mount again in 1948, thus beginning their long upward trend that was to leave behind for the indefinite future the small government budgets of the laissez-faire era. The era of the mixed economy was well under way, for it was begun during the Great Depression. And it was not to be reversed.

The buoyancy of postwar prices, and particularly of consumer expenditures, to which private investment responded strongly through 1948, confounded the gloomy Keynesian forecasters, who had predicted a severe slump in response to the drastic drop in federal spending. But their downward-working multipliers for federal spending were so strongly offset by the activation of accumulated money balances that there was hardly a ripple in total GNP from 1944 through 1946, which thereafter rose rapidly for two years. (See Table 25–1.)

The end of controls

In any event, these wartime accumulations of money and near-money balances pointed to the need for a continuation of controls. Nevertheless, even before VJ Day the War Production Board began to lift priorities on hundreds of materials, and this process continued until the WPB went out of existence in November 1945. The day after Japan surrendered, the OPA removed gasoline, fuel oil, and certain canned goods from the ration list. During the rest of the year the OPA struggled to control prices, but widespread opposition and the

[8] Federal Housing Administration, *The FHA Story in Summary* (Washington, D.C.: U.S. Government Printing Office, May 1, 1959), p. 2.

growth of the black market led the administration to end the rationing of other commodities before the end of the year: butter, meats, shoes, automobiles, tires. By the time the life of the OPA under the Emergency Price Control Act of 1942 was to run out in June 1946, President Harry Truman had become sufficiently worried over the extent of inflation to urge Congress to extend its life. Congress responded with a bill so useless, in the opinion of the president, that he vetoed it as a "choice between inflation with a statute and inflation without one." Congress then passed the new watered-down act continuing a greatly weakened OPA for a year, but the main business of the new office was to decontrol all prices except those on rents and agricultural commodities, now shifted to the Department of Agriculture.

All price controls had been lifted by the end of 1946 except those on sugar, rice, and rents; a year later only rents remained, and on these a 15 percent increase had been allowed, if the tenant agreed.

The Defense Production Act, 1950

Thus the situation remained until mounting inflation and the Korean War brought the Defense Production Act of September 1950. This act again granted almost complete control over prices, wages, credit, and rationing. The president appointed Charles E. Wilson, president of General Motors, as defense mobilization director, and under him established the Economic Stabilization Agency with two divisions, one for prices and one for wages. It was not until 1952 that prices began to show some stabilization. However, at least 76 percent of the wholesale market transactions were still under active price control in late 1952. With the advent of the Eisenhower administration early in the next year, all federal price controls including rents were ended. The result was continued high prices.

LABOR

Although widespread discontent existed over rising prices and bitter criticism was directed against Congress for failure to act, the unorganized consumers as usual had little influence. Farmers in general were basking under a favorable parity ratio. Prices received, adjusted for government payments, had risen from 88 percent of prices paid (parity index) in 1940 to a peak of 116 in 1947. They slid in 1948, but still stood at 111 in that year. The only powerful group that exerted pressure for counterinflationary action was organized labor. When it failed, it turned its energies to obtaining higher wages. Labor, moreover, was the one group able to defend itself. Membership, as in World War I, grew in strength, as previously noted, and continued to mount after the war was over. Membership increased to 14.8 million in 1947, which was over a third of total nonagricultural employment.

Strikes

In a demand for wage increases adequate to meet the rising prices and to collect labor's share of accumulated productivity increases, thousands of strikes were called in the last half of 1945 and in 1946. The latter year turned out to be one of the stormiest in American labor history, with almost 5000 work stoppages involving 4.6 million workers. This wave of strikes was led by some of the larger CIO unions in such mass-production industries as automobile manufacturing, electric equipment, meat packing, and steel, and were generally successful in achieving wage increases approximately equal to the inflation.

Continued rising prices quickly threw the 1946 wage scales out of line, and new strikes or threats of strikes brought a second round of increases in 1947. With prices still high in 1948, a third round followed. Although in obtaining wage increases leadership was often in the hands of the automobile and steel workers and the miners, the results quickly extended to workers in other industries. Union success in obtaining higher wages was not alone the result of strong organizations. These were years of prosperity, high industrial profits, and near to full employment. Many factors thus worked for the benefit of labor.

Wages and inflation

However, criticism of labor that had resulted during the war in the War Labor Disputes Act (1943) grew in the postwar years as the result of numerous strikes and repeated efforts to raise wages. As had happened before, labor was now blamed for the high prices and inflation. Labor disclaimed the responsibility, pointed to the essential causes of inflation: shortages of commodities, a backlog of buying power, continued heavy purchases by the government, and failure of the government to maintain brakes of various kinds. Organized labor also pointed out that it had been the chief group to oppose ending controls after the war. Wage earners maintained further (and with much truth) that the profits of industry were so large that wages could be increased without raising the retail price of the product. In any event, workers insisted that they could protect themselves against inflation only by higher wages and, if necessary, strikes to obtain them.

The decline of labor power

Although unions had grown in numerical strength during the war and in their ability to obtain higher wages, their position in other ways had declined. While they had lost much of the goodwill of the middle-class public that had been conspicuous in the 1930s, their opponents within the business community had grown in economic and political strength. As after World War I, the years after World War II were characterized by reaction and conservatism. The crusade for reform had largely ended. Many felt that the strikes during wartime were unpatriotic and the postwar strikes inflationary. The persistent propaganda of antilabor groups, that the National Labor Relations Act had given the workers too much strength and that a better balance should be established, was finally having its effect. On its part labor had failed to maintain good public relations or to explain its position as successfully as had its opponents.

While labor lost prestige with the general middle-class public, its strength relative to management also declined. The reputation of business leaders, which had been badly deflated during the depression, had revived as a result of their affirmed contribution to the war effort. Their confidence had also increased with profits and prosperity. The same was true of the strength of the Republican party, which as we have seen, had won control of Congress in the midterm elections of 1946. Neither the AFL nor the CIO had officially backed either party, but the Political Action Committee of the CIO had supported the Roosevelt candidacy since 1936, as had the American Labor party and the Liberal party, whose backing came largely from labor. It seemed evident that the majority of organized workers had thrown in their lot with the Democrats. (This was even more evident in the Eisenhower–Stevenson presidential campaign of 1952, when both the AFL and the CIO officially backed the Democratic candidate.)

Labor legislation

The changing attitude toward labor evident in the War Labor Disputes Act continued after the war. The Lea Act (1946) forbade featherbedding practices in the Musicians Union, and in the same year the Hobbs Anti-Racketeering Act curbed certain activities in the Teamsters Union. Congress also passed the Case Bill, which contained many restrictions later incorporated in the Taft-Hartley Act, but failed to pass it over the president's veto. Although Congress passed legislation to restrict unions, it ignored until 1949 the repeated suggestion of the president to increase the minimum wages of the Fair Labor Standards Act. This was the record of Democratic Congresses, and it was not likely to be reversed after the Republicans took over early in 1947. Legislation to curb and weaken unions became, in fact, a major item in the 80th Congress and an outstanding feature of the reconversion period.

The Taft-Hartley Act

The theory behind the Labor–Management Relations Act of 1947 (Taft-Hartley Act) was that labor had become so powerful under the National Labor Relations Act that the employer was no longer able to bargain on equal terms and that the "balance" must be restored. In addition there was the belief that certain labor practices were injurious and should be banned. Many argued that accomplishment of these objectives would promote industrial peace. The National Labor Relations Act of 1935 stated that certain acts of employers that interfered with workers' rights to join unions and bargain collectively were unfair and that workers might appeal to the National Labor Relations Board against employers violating such acts. The new Taft-Hartley Act retained these provisions, and also forbade certain "unfair" labor practices, against which employers, workers, or even other unions might appeal to a new NLRB set up by the act.

The bans on unfair labor practices under the act included: (1) No one may interfere with the right of a person to join a union. (2) A union may not discriminate against a worker or influence an employer to discharge him because he is not a union member. (3) A union may not refuse to bargain collectively. (4) Certain strikes and secondary boycotts were declared unfair labor practices. For example, workers were forbidden to strike to force an employer to join an employers' association or to force one employer to cease dealing with another (secondary boycott).[9] (5) The act also forbade jurisdictional strikes. (6) Unions having union-shop contracts with employers were forbidden to charge "excessive or discriminatory" initiation fees. (7) Featherbedding, that is the attempt to compel an employer to pay for services not actually performed, was made an unfair labor practice. (8) It was also an unfair labor practice under the act for a union having a contract to strike without giving notice, sixty days before its expiration, of a desire to change the agreement and bargain with the employer. If no agreement was reached within 30 days after the notice was sent, the union must notify the Federal Mediation and Conciliation Service and the state mediation board, if such a board exists.

Enforcement

Responsibility for enforcement of the new law was placed with the National Labor Relations Board, now increased from three to five members. The board might issue "cease and desist" orders or its general council might ask for injunctions from federal courts forbidding violations of the law. Refusal to obey could be punished by fine, imprisonment, or both. The services of the NLRB were open only to unions that fulfilled two primary conditions. First, each local, national, or international union had to file certain information regarding itself, such as its constitution, bylaws, annual financial statements, and names and salaries of all officers. Second, each officer of a local or national union was required to file annually a sworn statement that he was not a member of the Communist party or affiliated with it and that he did not believe in the overthrow of the government by force or unconstitutional means.

One blow at labor that was warded off was a strong demand to ban any contract providing that all workers hired by a concern be union members. A compromise was written into the law forbidding a *closed* shop but allowing a *union* shop. In other words, the law allowed an employer to hire anyone, union member or not, as he pleased. However, if the majority of all the workers in a shop voted in favor of a union shop, the nonunion worker must join the union 30 days after he was hired. While the union shop was saved, labor lost severely when

the act revived (if it did not encourage) the use of the injunction. Labor had fought against the injunction for half a century; the Clayton Antitrust Act had tried to limit its use, and the Norris-La Guardia Act (1932) had forbidden it in labor disputes except under unusual circumstances. In one blow the act swept away the gains achieved by decades of struggle. Not only was the use of the injunction revived, but employers might sue unions for violation of contract or for damages resulting from a secondary boycott. In such suits unions were bound by the acts of their agents, but the courts could not fine individual members, only the union as a body.

As for money earned by workers, the employer was forbidden to deduct dues from workers' pay (the checkoff system) unless each individual gave written permission. The employer might, however, deduct payments to union welfare funds, but on condition that new contracts provided for equal representation of labor and management in administration of the fund. The act forbade the use of union funds in any election for federal office.

Strikes

The act also provided a method of delaying strikes that might "imperil the national health and safety." In the event of such a "national emergency dispute" or threat of strike, the president was empowered to appoint a board of inquiry to investigate the dispute and make its findings public. Upon receipt of the report the president might seek an injunction in a federal court to restrain the union from striking for 80 days. The act also forbade strikes by employees of the federal government.

Such were the main provisions of the most important legislation aimed definitely to curtail the power of labor. Truman, in a decision exhibiting profound insight into the future, vetoed the bill as an act discriminating against labor in a "consistent pattern of inequality" which would surround collective bargaining with "bureaucratic procedures" and "time-consuming legislation." Congress passed it over his veto.

The Taft-Hartley Act established the basic legislative framework for labor–management relations in the mixed economy for the next quarter century. Labor asserted that the act nullified essential rights won by a century of struggle and reduced labor to a status of slavery. Labor's opponents insisted that it merely restored bargaining equality and ended abuses recognized as harmful to both labor and the public. In the heat of conflict, both sides undoubtedly exaggerated, but it does seem clear

---

[9]As interpreted by this act, a secondary boycott generally concerned a situation in which workers refused to handle materials produced by nonunion workers or made in a shop where a labor dispute was in progress. Secondary boycotts involving picketing, but not strikes, appeared to be legal.

that the act went further than eliminating abuses and restoring equality; it took away hard-won gains and reduced labor to an inferior position. In addition, it imparted to labor–management negotiations a far-reaching public aspect that was to characterize for the indefinite future these and many other formerly private decisions of most large organizations and institutions.[10] The unexpected victory of the Democratic party in 1948, pledged to a repeal of the act, presaged at least drastic revisions. But Congress was little interested and only one minor revision was secured.

SELECTED READINGS

Blyth, C. A., *American Business Cycles, 1945–50* (London: Allen and Unwin, 1968).

*Brady, Robert A., *The Citizens' Stake in Price Control* (Paterson, N.J.: Littlefield, Adams, 1952).

Buchanan, A. Russell, *The United States and World War II,* 2 vols. (New York: Harper & Row, 1964).

Catton, Bruce, *The War Lords of Washington* (New York: Harcourt Brace Jovanovich, 1948).

Chandler, Lester V., and Wallace, Donald H., *Economic Mobilization and Stabilization: Selected Materials on the Economics of War and Defense* (New York: Holt, Rinehart and Winston, 1951).

Craf, John R., *A Survey of the American Economy, 1940–1946* (New York: North River Press, 1947).

Friedman, Milton and Schwartz, Anna J., *A Monetary History of the United States, 1867–1960* (Princeton, N.J.: Princeton University Press, 1963), Chapter 10.

Galbraith, J. K., "The Disequilibrium System," *American Economic Review,* 37 (June, 1947), pp. 287–302.

Hamberg, D., "The Recession of 1948–49 in the United States," *Economic Journal,* 62 (March, 1952), pp. 1–14.

Harris, Seymour, ed., *Foreign Economic Policy for the United States* (Cambridge, Mass.: Harvard University Press, 1948).

Janeway, Eliot, *The Struggle for Survival* (New Haven: Yale University Press, 1951).

Johnson, Sherman E., *Changes in American Farming* (Washington: U.S. Dept. of Agriculture, Misc. Pub. #707, December 1949).

Mansfield, Harvey, *A Short History of OPA* (Washington: Office of Temporary Controls, Office of Price Administration, 1948).

Murphy, H. C., *The National Debt in War and Transition* (New York: McGraw-Hill, 1950).

Nelson, Donald, *Arsenal of Democracy: The Story of War Production* (New York: Harcourt Brace Jovanovich 1946).

Novick, David, et al., *Wartime Production Controls* (New York: Columbia University Press, 1949).

Seidman, Joel, *American Labor from Defense to Reconversion* (Chicago: University of Chicago Press, 1953).

U.S. War Production Board, *Industrial Mobilization for War* (Washington: U.S. Government Printing Office, 1947).

[10]See Harold G. Vatter, *The U.S. Economy in the 1950's* (New York: Norton, 1963), p. 237.

chapter 26

the postwar mixed economy: government guidance, foreign policy, and business

Laissez-faire had passed from the scene in every industrialized capitalistic economy by the end of World War II, and the United States was no exception. The mixed economy — that is, the economy of large government budgets and extensive public intervention into private decision making — had originated as a response to the Great Depression in the United States and in a number of other leading countries.

Only a minority recognized at first the permanence and pervasiveness of the new regime. Both the general public and the nation's politi-

cal leadership little understood that long-run economic growth with high employment under the existing conditions of advanced capitalism required continued government underwriting of total demand. Even a quarter century after the war's end, each new policy step toward further implementation of the inevitable trend toward economic planning was resisted. Often the resistance was not by rock-ribbed believers in laissez-faire, or even by moderate conservatives, but rather by liberals, who feared, perhaps rightly, bureaucracy or the rise of a police state.

FOUNDING THE NEW REGIME

The Employment Act of 1946

In any case, the broad shape of the interventionist regime that was in the offing was clearly suggested by the bipartisan passage, early in 1946, of the Employment Act. Perhaps the most historically important piece of economic legislation in the twentieth century, this law committed the federal government in principle to the maintenance of "maximum employment, production, and purchasing power." The act also established the President's Council of Economic Advisers and the Joint Congressional Committee on the Annual Economic Report. While abjuring the term "full employment" and any policy of making the federal government the employer of last resort, the act did express the new national consensus that mass unemployment would never again be permitted. Subsequent events, for reasons to be examined later, were consistent with the act's stated objectives, because the first period of over a

quarter century in U.S. economic history since the Civil War passed without a protracted depression. The same experience obtained in other mixed economies of the North Atlantic world. By the 1970s there seemed little doubt that popular demand would soon operate under the legal aegis of the Employment Act at any time in the foreseeable future to avert the approach of mass unemployment such as existed in the 1930s.

In later years it was seen that persistently high employment and capacity utilization were associated with inflationary pressures. Yet the application of anti-inflationary monetary and fiscal measures that generated unemployment were not permitted to carry unemployment to an extreme. There was nothing automatic about this, however, as illustrated by the fact that unemployment rates in the neighborhood of 9 percent were tolerated in 1975. It was only public determination to sustain the goals of the

Employment Act that assured its lasting strength, for no law is any stronger than the will and the power to enforce it.

Other goals related to the Employment Act

Other national goals put forward by various interest groups were closely related to maximum employment, but were not specifically envisioned and included in the Employment Act. For example, achievement of a given total employment level would do little to direct resources into any particular desired channels; the questions of the *composition* of total output and the *occupational mixture* within the total of employed persons were thus not specified. Also, short-run concern with cyclical unemployment caused framers and supporters of the act to overlook the fact that they were implying a commitment to long-run economic growth, a goal that became extremely prominent because of rivalry with the Soviet Union and a new concern for the less developed countries after the war. The growth commitment was a corollary because the labor force grows every year and also because some persons are technologically disemployed every year. Hence a maximum employment goal includes jobs for both these groups.

There were also other evolving policy concerns, related less directly to the act's employment target, but nonetheless related and requiring policy integration with the act's implementation. Such concerns eventually included education, environmental quality, discrimination against blacks and women, poverty, military objectives, urban improvement, health, research, price stability, regional development, and more stability for the world economy. All these and more were thrown into a grab-bag phrase in the act: "consistent with . . . needs and obligations and other essential considerations of national policy." Yet the act still stands as the most prominent hallmark of the emerging mixed economy and as a tribute to the humanistic concern of the American people for economic justice in the case of involuntary unemployment.

The Cold War

The last years of the 1940s were rich with such vital social, political, and economic decisions as the Employment Act and the Taft-Hartley Act, decisions that shaped future policy in their respective spheres for many years to come. Another such decision was to embark on the Cold War. Arthur Schlesinger has dated the Cold War from the World War II years themselves, when suspicion and distrust already took hold within the Allied coalition.[1] Surely the Cold War itself evolved, and had roots going as far back as the Bolshevik Revolution of 1917. But if one were to select a specific date, it should probably be during the Truman administration. Perhaps the clearest indicator of forthcoming events was the adoption of the containment policy toward the Soviet Union in 1947, and first applied in the Greek crisis of that year. The Truman Doctrine declared in words delivered personally before Congress on March 12, 1947, that "it must be the policy of the United States to support free peoples who are resisting attempted subjugation by armed minorities or by outside pressures." The president asked for $400 million for military and other support, in effect to keep the right-wing Greek government in power and to keep Greece and Turkey out of the Soviet sphere of control. Congress responded affirmatively within two months.

The next year military spending began to rise from its 1947 low of $9.1 billion, and by 1949 was already up to $13.3 billion, almost twice the volume of federal civilian purchases of goods and services. The entire postwar pattern of the federal budget was now firmly established. In the American mixed economy, central government discretionary spending was to be overwhelmingly dominated by military outlays for at least a quarter century.

THE PANORAMA OF CHANGE, 1948–1975

An outline of economic evolution from the end of the 1940s to the mid-1970s will clarify the distinguishing features of the new epoch and provide a setting for the more detailed esperience of the American people to be examined below. Some of the broad major trends may be seen at a glance in Table 26–1.

[1] "Origins of the Cold War," *Foreign Affairs,* 46 (1967): 22–52, reprinted in *The Record of American History: Interpretive Readings,* ed. Irwin Unger, David Brody, and Paul Goodman (Waltham, Mass.: Xerox, 1971), esp. pp. 384–389.

TABLE 26–1. TRENDS IN THE MIXED ECONOMY, 1949–1975
(DOLLAR FIGURES IN BILLIONS)

YEAR	GROSS NATIONAL PRODUCT	HOUSEHOLD CONSUMPTION OUTLAYS	GROSS PRIVATE DOMESTIC INVESTMENT[1]
1949	257	177	36
1950	285	191	54
1951	328	206	59
1952	346	217	52
1953	365	230	53
1954	365	237	52
1955	398	254	67
1956	419	267	70
1957	441	281	68
1958	447	290	61
1959	484	311	75
1960	504	325	75
1961	520	335	72
1962	560	355	83
1963	591	375	87
1964	632	401	94
1965	685	433	108
1966	750	466	121
1967	794	492	117
1968	864	536	126
1969	930	580	139
1970	977	618	136
1971	1055	667	154
1972	1158	729	179
1973	1295	805	209
1974	1397	877	209
1975	1499	963	183

| | GOVERNMENT PURCHASES OF GOODS AND SERVICES | | | |
| | FEDERAL | | | |
YEAR	DEFENSE	OTHER	STATE AND LOCAL	CONSUMER PRICES[2] (1967 = 100)	UNEMPLOYMENT RATE[3]
1949	13	7	18	71	5.9
1950	14	4	20	72	5.3
1951	34	4	22	78	3.3
1952	46	6	23	80	3.0
1953	49	8	25	80	2.9
1954	41	6	27	81	5.5
1955	39	6	30	80	4.4
1956	40	5	33	81	4.1
1957	44	5	37	84	4.3
1958	46	8	41	87	6.8
1959	46	8	43	87	5.5
1960	45	9	46	89	5.5
1961	48	10	50	90	6.7
1962	52	12	54	91	5.5
1963	51	14	58	92	5.7
1964	50	15	64	93	5.2
1965	50	17	70	95	4.5
1966	61	17	79	97	3.8
1967	72	18	89	100	3.8
1968	78	21	101	104	3.6
1969	78	20	111	110	3.5
1970	75	22	123	116	4.9
1971	71	27	137	121	5.9
1972	75	30	151	125	5.6
1973	74	32	170	133	4.9
1974	79	38	192	148	5.6
1975	84	39	208	161	8.5

Source: *Economic Report of the President,* January 1976. Federal Reserve Bulletin, December 1975.
[1]Including new business construction, residential construction, business equipment, and inventory changes.
[2]For urban wage earners and clerical workers.
[3]Percent of civilian labor force.

Growth rates

The record of growth for the whole period was moderate but almost steadily upward. Some of the long-run GNP rise was of course due to inflation, but total physical output—that is, GNP adjusted for price change—increased at an annual rate of about 3.75 percent for the whole period 1950–1973. Between 1955 and 1968 or 1969 U.S. gross product rose at an annual rate of about 4 percent, whereas, according to estimates of the Organization for Economic Cooperation and Development, French gross product grew at 5.7 percent, West German at 5.1 percent, Italian at 5.6 percent. The average growth rate for all the smaller countries was 4.4 percent over the same period. Only the United Kingdom had a slower growth rate of gross domestic product: 2.8 percent. The Japanese rate was an incredible 10.2 percent.

Thus in the world of North Atlantic economies the United States was one of the slow growers, and it also had an above-average unemployment rate. At the same time, the United States held in check its inflation rate as compared with most European countries, and this was helpful in keeping the nation competitive in international markets as well as in protecting the domestic market to some degree from import competition.

Recessions

A remarkable feature of the economy's performance was the absence, as mentioned previously, of depressions. There were only "recessions," or mild downswings. Table 26–1 makes clear how mild they were. The unemployment column shows that the highest rate during the whole 27 years was below 7 percent, in the recession of 1958. One major reason was the insensitivity of consumer spending in all six recessions of the postwar period. Indeed, in all cases, beginning with the first postwar recession of 1948–1949, total household consumption in current dollar terms actually rose. Not until 1975–76 did unemployment rates of over 8 percent reappear—this time, paradoxically it seemed to most, simultaneously with serious inflation.

Government spending

This was a new historical phenomenon. In past cyclical slumps, total consumption typically declined. There were good reasons for its not doing so after World War II. For one thing, gov-

ernment spending, which was cyclically insensitive, was now a far larger component of total spending than under laissez-faire. In 1929, for example, all levels of government combined spent a total equal to 8.2 percent of GNP; but already by 1950 the proportion had risen to 13.3 percent, and in 1975 it was 22.1 percent. Government purchases were both high and rising, a development that did much to underpin private spending. Total government outlays rose every year throughout the period, except for a brief three-year period in the mid-1950s after the end of the Korean war. State and local government expenditures, heavily influenced by outlays for education, were a particularly buoyant influence because they were ever larger and steadily growing. It will be observed from Table 26–1 that these expenditures much exceeded federal nondefense spending, and grew faster until the 1960s.

Transfer payments

Another growing stream of payments that supported spending, part of which was even specifically counterslump in its behavior, was the whole collection of social security payments such as retirement benefits and unemployment compensation. The latter came to be called a "built-in stabilizer." These so-called transfer payments to persons from all levels of government were already $11.6 billion, or 4.5 percent of GNP, by 1949. By 1960 they amounted to 5.3 percent, and in 1975 had further risen to 11.3 percent. The public transfer payment not only supported spending against cyclical declines, however. As a major form of underwriting income security, the public transfer in all advanced countries was another hallmark of the new mixed economy and, insofar as that regime could be viewed as a welfare state, it was one of its outstanding features. In 1929 such payments had been minuscule, and were almost entirely composed of veterans' benefits.

Private investment

It should furthermore be noted that even gross private investment, which had been notoriously unstable in the past, seemed to respond to the absence of serious slumps by exhibiting considerably dampened fluctuations in magnitude. Nevertheless, it was a still somewhat unstable spending stream, and therefore from the standpoint of dampening cyclical fluctuations it was probably fortunate that investment was of slightly declining importance in total economic activity as the years passed.

Military spending

The large military budget was primarily a destabilizing factor. Table 26–1 shows, for example, a large jump in 1951 when the United States became seriously involved in the Korean war. This upsurge in national defense outlays peaked in 1953, and after the war settlement such spending dropped for three years, only to climb again through 1962. Then followed another plateau of roughly constant outlays until involvement in the Vietnam war induced a substantial increase again, beginning in 1966. This peaked in 1968–1969, and another absolute decline occurred. The decline bottomed out in 1971, followed by a rise.

Such a pattern of behavior, in the context of a large military budget, clearly makes it very difficult to speak of a federal fiscal policy designed to induce stability and growth at high employment. Ordinarily the term refers to some roughly planned economic performance target, but in the United States it was difficult to apply the notion when the overwhelming bulk of federal expenditures was presumed to be (some contended otherwise) determined by international military-strategic criteria.

Inflation

Table 26–1 also reveals a further characteristic of the new interventionist regime: chronic inflation. The consumer price index rose from 72 percent of its 1967 average in 1948 to 161 percent in 1975. On the annual basis portrayed in the table, prices never fell, whether the economy was in a recession or in an expansion period. In the days of laissez-faire, cyclical downswings brought downward adjustment of the general consumer price level, even though the long-run trend of prices was upward, as in the present instance. Such downward adjustment had apparently disappeared in the mixed economy, a phenomenon also found in the interventionist economies of western Europe. It was a world of chronic inflation, and the chief remaining question became: how fast would prices rise?

It is noteworthy that the inflationary trend in the United States occurred despite a very conservative rise in the money supply (only about 3 percent a year for the whole period, slower than the annual rise in total output), more conservative under Eisenhower, less conservative under Kennedy and Johnson. It could not be said, therefore, that the absence of a domestic gold standard released the forces of wildcat banking to run the printing presses, inflate the currency, and flood the country with unsound loans. As prices rose about 2.5 percent a year, some of the pressure must have come from cost-push increases by business, labor, farmers, and such professions as medicine; and that cost push was accommodated on the monetary side by the willingness of the American people to turn over their money more rapidly each year. But whatever the relative weights of the causal factors, the impressive result remained: inflation, however mild, was apparently the order of the day under the new economic arrangements.

Bipartisan character of interventionism

It was significant that the new arrangements proceeded to unfold despite the political complexion of the administration in Washington at any particular time. In some respects the rate at which they unfolded varied during shorter periods of time, but there was apparently no question of a sweeping return to laissez-faire. During twelve of the years from 1948 to 1975 there was a Republican president (although the majority party in the Congress was Republican for only two years: 1953 and 1954). The eight Eisenhower years, from the end of the Korean war in 1953 through 1960, did produce a cessation of growth in nonmilitary federal spending, but military outlays continued throughout to be close to Korean war levels despite the absence of major military engagements abroad (see Table 26–1). Total federal government purchases of goods and services, by remaining high but failing to grow, fell slightly as proportion of GNP. But then, perhaps nothing about overall trends is more significant than the fact that federal government purchases as proportion of GNP hardly grew during the Democratic Kennedy-Johnson years (1961–1968) either. The big increase in the proportion was between 1950 and 1955; thereafter, changes in political complexions wrought no significant changes in the importance of federal purchases in the total economy. There was only the slight change in federal civilian expenditures from a bit less than 2 percent of GNP under Eisenhower to a bit over 2 percent under Kennedy and Johnson. It was the relative importance of state and local expenditures that rose between 1948 and 1975, not federal civilian purchases, although the public probably believed the opposite was the case. The old call for debt reduction and budget surpluses was reiterated by every administration throughout the period.

Social welfare payments

But there is more to the federal budget than purchase of goods and services. There are federal grants to the state and local governments. There are also social security transfer payments, perhaps the most prominent feature of federal welfarism. Here the Republican Eisenhower administrations scored. In 1954 Congress responded to Eisenhower's request for expanded coverage of the social security and unemployment compensation systems, in 1956 coverage was again enlarged, and in 1957 the president requested (in vain) extended minimum wage coverage. Average monthly benefits for a retired couple were raised from $78.90 in 1951 to $121.60 in 1959. This was a much greater increase than had occurred in consumer prices, a most fortunate comparative change in view of the low level of benefits. Meanwhile, tax rates and the maximum taxable earnings under the Old Age and Survivors program (OASDI) were raised also.

As mentioned previously, the strongly regressive nature of the payroll tax tended to make social security extension more palatable to conservative opponents than a progressive method of tax financing, such as a graduated income tax, would have been. The number of beneficiaries of OASDI monthly cash benefits increased, partly because of Eisenhower administration extensions, from 3.5 million in 1950 to 14.8 million in 1960, and total benefits paid under OASDI increased from about $1 billion to $10.7 billion over the same space of years. This enormous rise compared favorably with extensions and benefit increases in the 1960s. Indeed, most of the ultimate enlargement in social security coverage had taken place by the end of the Eisenhower administration.

If a distinction were to be drawn between the Eisenhower 1950s and the Kennedy-Johnson 1960s, it would appear to be largely one of degree. In the former period economic growth was a bit slower, federal budget policy was more conservative, the money supply was slower to grow, prices rose more slowly than in the 1960s, and federal transfers to persons only doubled, whereas they almost tripled in the 1960s. In general, the Kennedy-Johnson policies were more actively Keynesian regarding the use of the federal budget to underwrite economic stability and growth. Monetary policy in the 1960s was easier, as attested to by the more rapid growth in the money stock. The Democrats built the interventionist regime slightly more vigorously than their immediate presidential predecessor.

FISCAL AND MONETARY MANAGEMENT

The prime weapons of government control in the mixed economy everywhere were fiscal and monetary policy. The former was generally deemed, in the spirit of Keynes, the more active and influential agent. Much controversy raged down the years, however, over which variety of policy was the more appropriate for the given situation at the time, and over the problems of coordinating the two. The National Commission on Money and Credit of the Committee for Economic Development concluded in its report in 1961 that fiscal and monetary policies were in a sense substitutes for each other, at least in situations in which the required economic adjustments were moderate.

The Federal Reserve System

It became abundantly clear after a decade or so that monetary policy had to be executed in step with the federal government's views of what was fiscally correct. Yet there were a few who nurtured the hope for a semi-independent Federal Reserve. Such hopes were excited especially during the early years, when the inflationary trend prompted the Federal Reserve Board to insist upon release from its prewar and wartime subservience to the Treasury's low-interest-rate policy. This release it got in the famous March 1951 accord with the Treasury. However, the struggle that preceded the accord and the victory for the Federal Reserve merely lent vitality for a while to the unfortunate illusion that a central bank could somehow go its own way as it did in the regime of laissez-faire.

Responsibilities of the Federal Reserve Board

While the Federal Reserve could not act independently of national economic objectives, it did replace in the early 1950s some of the Treasury's monetary policy influence. As such, it assumed major responsibilities for counteracting balance-of-payments disequilibrium, for stabilizing total income, employment, and the price level, for assuring a market for government securities, and for protecting financial markets against wide deviations from what were thought to be normal interest rates. With respect to the fourth responsibility, it was originally deemed important for interest rates to be relatively low so that the state and local governments and the residential construction industry could borrow inexpensively. Unfortunately, when the inflation threat appeared to be severe, as it did after the mid-1960s, the goal of stable prices was thought to require high interest rates so as to dampen the rise in the money stock with its associated increase in money demand for goods and services. The same was true when there was pressure on the balance of payments, as in the 1960s, for high interest rates attracted short-term funds from abroad. Similarly, the Federal Reserve authorities at times had trouble trying to apply the interest-rate tool to the two tasks of arresting inflation, which demanded high rates, and reducing unemployment, which required low rates. But of course that same dilemma confronted fiscal policy.

The Federal Reserve's weapons of monetary control

The Federal Reserve Board's weapons of monetary control included the discount rate it charged member banks for loans to get more reserves; the reserve ratio, dictating how much reserves commercial banks needed to hold on deposit at the "Fed" against their holdings of the public's deposits; and open-market purchases or sales of government securities. For practical purposes the last named was the most important, and the Federal Open Market Committee was by far the most strategic policy-making body within the Federal Reserve System.

The main elements in commercial bank reserves throughout the period were the Fed's holdings of government securities and the gold stock. For reasons that will be elaborated later, the United States was in general losing gold to the rest of the world during the postwar decades. The Fed's gold stock was $24.6 billion in September 1949 and $11.6 billion in November 1975. Hence it fell upon federal government securities to provide overwhelmingly the bulk of the expanding monetary base needed to accommodate the increasing money supply for a growing economy. This provided a direct connection between the Treasury's budget and debt operations on the one hand and the Federal Reserve's monetary responsibilities on the other hand.

Growth in the 1950s

From the early 1950s to 1961, the Fed's government security acquisitions only moderately offset the outward drain of gold, so that the monetary base grew slowly. This, together with the demand for money, produced an accordingly moderate growth in member bank reserves from $17.4 billion in 1950 to $19.3 billion ten years later. The stock of money in the economy also expanded moderately, from $116 billion to $142 billion, a modest annual rate of 3.5 percent. It was a decade of mild price rise, 2.25 percent a year. The federal debt reflected in part the fact that during the 1950s the social security and other trust-fund accounts increased slowly, the annual deficits (except for the slump year 1958) were comparatively small, and there were budget surpluses in five of the ten years. Thus while the gross debt rose from $257 billion in 1950 to $290 billion in 1960, Federal Reserve holdings expanded by only $6.6 billion. The rate of economic growth was quite slow.

Growth in the 1960s

But the 1960s were a different story. The first half of the decade saw the continuation of the sluggish price rise that had marked the late 1950s. There was only one recession, a mild one, occurring in 1960–1961. Total federal expenditures in the first half of the decade increased moderately, but the total concealed a mixture of very slight increases in the military outlays required to install the strategic missile establishment, coupled with almost a doubling of civilian expenditures (current dollars). Real GNP growth was substantial, however. This growth was to a great extent the result of the application of deliberate Keynesian fiscal policies designed to stimulate growth and close the large gap that had existed in early 1961 between actual and potential (full employment) GNP. Expanded civilian outlay was one of those policies. In addition there were tax cuts in 1962, 1964, and 1965—measures that, along with accelerated depreciation and other tax concessions to business, lowered the proportion of total federal revenues coming from income taxes.

The inevitable concomitant of these stimulative policies was a slow growth in tax receipts and the related stimulus of budget deficits.

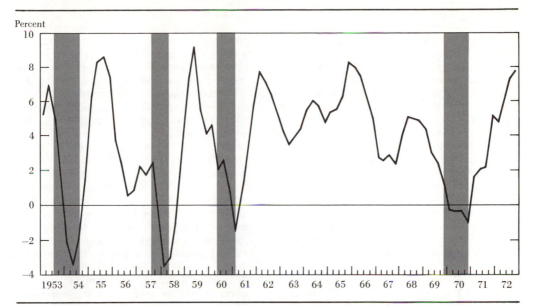

Figure 26–1. **Percentage Changes in Real Gross National Product (Seasonally Adjusted).** (Shaded areas represent recession periods, according to the National Bureau of Economic Research chronology.) Source: U.S. Department of Commerce, Bureau of Economic Analysis.

These and the continued growth of trust and other government account holdings produced another $30 billion rise in the federal debt over the first half of the decade. This accelerated the expansion of member bank reserves and the money stock, but the growth of total production was able to embrace it so that prices were but little affected.

In the last half of the 1960s the situation changed drastically. From an initial position of high unemployment, the private economy entered a period of rapid expansion as federal military and civilian expenditures burgeoned. These expenditure increases did not elicit tax increases from the government until the fiscal year 1969. Consequently, substantial deficits were incurred in calendar 1967, 1968, and

1970. The federal debt was pushed upward by these budget deficits, and by the growth in trust-fund and other government agency accounts. The latter added over $37 billion to their holdings between 1965 and 1970, accounting for over half the increase in total debt of $68 billion. The Federal Reserve's holdings rose $21 billion, thus pushing up its share of the federal debt to 21 percent in late 1970 and accommodating an accelerated expansion of the money supply, despite attempted policies of restraint. While the growth of the economy and the moderate unemployment rates (lasting until late 1974) were welcomed, one result was definitely not intended, and that was the most rapid inflation since the Korean war.

INTERNATIONAL RELATIONS

The domestic regime of government interventionism had its counterpart in the international arena. With World War II the United States joined the United Nations and cast off isolationism for the indefinite future. The ensuing era of foreign interventionism on the part of the United States reflected the challenge of So-

viet expansionism, the alleged global socialist threat to the institution of private property, wherever found, the extreme disorganization of international economic relations in the noncommunist world, and the rising demands for material betterment by the people in the less developed countries.

It had been a principle of U.S. foreign policy to advance American trade and to protect American persons and property situated abroad. But now a new dimension was added. In the context of communist political gains abroad, a threat to any of the wide variety of existing private property institutions in different countries now was viewed as an encroachment upon cherished American principles, whether or not substantial U.S. assets were actually or even potentially involved in the particular area. In consequence, the government committed itself first to the Cold War and then to military involvement with the United Nations in Korea (1950–1953) and without the United Nations in Vietnam (mid-1960s to 1975). These commitments, together with sustained military preparedness, were the chief single source of deficits in the nation's foreign balance of payments and in the large federal budgets of the new atomic and space age. It was not the welfare state that created such large federal budgets, although there was a growing welfare component, as has been pointed out. Much of the responsibility for social welfare, and for education particularly, was shouldered by the state and local governments.

There was no single area of public policy during the last years of the 1940s and early 1950s that could exceed in importance the collection of major new programs in the international sphere. Cold War policies, based in the United States on the supposition that the communist world was politically monolithic, lasted well into the 1960s. During that grim confrontation of the two major powers, it was inevitable that both countries would initiate, to the extent of their abilities and preferences, programs of economic and military aid to other countries, to say nothing of expensive counterintelligence activity, in order to retain the latter in friendly orbit.

The Marshall Plan

Thus after a brief pre-Cold War period during which Washington first ended its lend-lease program (September 1945), and then provided several billions of economic aid through the United Nations Relief and Rehabilitation Administration (UNRRA) to eastern European and other countries, the United States embarked upon an extensive foreign aid and military assistance program. The first major step coincided with the declaration of the Cold War, when Secretary of State George C. Marshall proposed the European Recovery Plan (ERP) in June 1947. This "Marshall Plan" was initially humanitarian in intent, but its early predominantly political character could not be escaped in view of its denouncement by the Soviet Union, the absence of the Soviet bloc from the ensuing planning conference that summer in Paris, the Soviet blockade of Berlin in 1948 and 1949, and the supportive role of $12 billion of economic aid to established anti-communist governments in western Europe. Hence it was not accidental that this first administratively independent aid agency, from its very inception in April 1948 to its termination in December 1951, was caught up in the struggle to "save Europe from communism." Of retroactive significance also was the fact that the ERP task in Europe was militarily supplemented in 1950 by the formation of the costly North Atlantic Treaty Organization (NATO), and then taken over in 1952 by the Mutual Security Administration, whose explicit objectives were to consolidate economic and military aid in order to "strengthen the economies and the defenses of non-Communist countries in Europe and Asia against the spread of Russian and Chinese Communism."[2] This agency was abolished in 1955 and its operations were transferred to the departments of state and defense.

AID FOR UNDERDEVELOPED COUNTRIES

Meanwhile, humanitarian concerns, the desirability of expanded world trade, and popular demands for development emanating from the less developed countries, all raised the issue of foreign aid for the Third World. But political unrest in that world, and the drive of the two power centers to win the allegiance of its billion people, largely predetermined the character and global distribution of foreign aid. The Soviets lagged behind the United States in this area-

na, being almost forced by resource scarcity and high political priorities to concentrate until the mid-1950s upon eastern Europe. But the United States officially called for such a program in January 1949, when President Tru-

[2]Hugh B. Killough and Lucy W. Killough, *International Economics* (New York: Van Nostrand, 1960), p. 261. See also Agency for International Development, *Foreign Aid in Perspective* (n.d.), pp. 1, 10.

man, in Point Four of his inaugural address, urged a "bold new program for making the benefits of our scientific advances and industrial progress available for the improvement and growth of undeveloped areas." Gradually the notion spread through Congress, and 17 months later the Act for International Development was passed. Said the eminent economist Jacob Viner of the new venture:

> *The only factor which could persuade us to undertake a really large program of economic aid to the underdeveloped countries would be the decision that the friendship and alliance of those countries are strategically, politically and psychologically valuable to us in the cold war . . . and that the cost to us of a greatly enlarged program of economic aid would not be an excessive price to pay for these strategic gains.*[3]

There was no question that motivation behind foreign aid was more complex than this. The same was true of other countries. Mixed in were humanitarian and guilt feelings; the desire for export markets, attested to by tying aid directly with U.S. products and the unloading of farm surpluses upon beneficiary countries under Public Law 480; the wish to assure the flow of various imported raw materials; the hope that U.S. aided development would improve the American world image; and the endeavor to create a favorable environment for U.S. firms operating in other countries.[4] Nevertheless, Harvard's Lamont Professor of Economics Edward S. Mason has emphasized the facts that over 80 percent of U.S. total aid went to countries around the periphery of the communist world, that the program was typically sold to Congress as a means of preventing communist penetration, and that there was a marked coincidence between fluctuations in the size of the total aid package and the intensity of the East–West confrontation.[5]

The Alliance for Progress

A case in point was the Alliance for Progress, the chief Latin American aid program. This program was launched by President Kennedy in March 1961, primarily as a response to the threat of Castro's Cuba to export its revolution throughout Latin America.

The response from Latin America (except Cuba) was almost immediate. The *Alianza* was inaugurated at Punta del Este, Uruguay, in August 1961, a ten-year, $100 billion economic and social betterment program, of which the United States was to contribute $20 billion in the form of public funds and private foreign investments. In the eight years 1961–1968 the United States provided $9.2 billion of assistance as follows: Agency for International Development, $4.1 billion; Public Law 480 (farm surpluses), $1.3 billion; Export-Import Bank (a U.S. government agency dating from the depression and devoted to stimulating exports), $1.8 billion; and $2 billion contribution to the Inter-American Development Bank, chartered by the Organization of American States. The House Committee on Government Operations found in 1968 that among the original goals of the Alliance, Latin American performance recorded general failure in meeting growth targets, agrarian reform "moving only glacially," a housing shortage "growing at an alarming pace," and underemployment increasing rather than decreasing. On the other hand, some progress was reported in education, and there was significant improvement in tax systems in terms of total revenues collected and in tax administration.[6] However, the Latin American aid program was also under sharp scrutiny by the Congress as the 1960s waned, and appropriations were tapered off.

Expenditures for foreign economic and military aid

The total of foreign economic and military aid to all countries from 1946 through 1973 was about $164 billion, of which some 62 percent was classified as economic aid, the remainder military. Much of the former no doubt contributed to the reconstruction and development of the recipient countries. The flow totaled over $5 billion a year in the 1950s, but in the 1960s it was around $6.6 billion a year. In the Kenne-

[3]Cited in Edward S. Mason, "United States Interests in Foreign Economic Assistance," in *The United States and the Developing Economies*, ed. Gustav Ranis (New York: Norton, 1964), p. 16.

[4]See Benjamin I. Cohen, "U.S.–U.S.S.R. in Developing Countries," Yale University Economic Growth Center paper no. 179 (New Haven, Conn., 1972), pp. 22–23. The full title of "PL 480" was the Agricultural Trade Development and Assistance Act, passed by Congress in 1954.

[5]Paraphrased by Gustav Ranis in the Introduction to ibid., p. xi.

[6]U.S. Congress, House Committee on Government Operations, *U.S. Aid Operations in Latin America Under the Alliance for Progress*, 36th report, 90th Cong., 2d sess., House report no. 1849, August 5, 1968 (Washington, D.C.: U.S. Government Printing Office, 1968).

dy-Johnson years the officially recorded military component of the aid programs was smaller than the economic component; in the Eisenhower years it was about equal; but in the early 1970s the military somewhat outranked the economic. Also, in the 1960s proportionately more aid went to less developed countries, and there was an accompanying shift toward grants rather than loans. The linkage of aid with farm surplus disposal began with the Agricultural Trade Development and Assistance Act of 1954.

The decline of outlays relative to GNP in the 1960s was consistent with several possible explanations, such as a growing belief that economic aid was being wasted, was the object of corruption, should not be combined in a single package with military aid, was ill adapted to the developmental needs of recipients, could not close the gap between rich and poor nations, and was in any case much too expensive. It was also consistent with the hypothesis that the split in the so-called monolithic communist world, particularly between the Soviet Union and

China, with its attendant cooling off of the East–West conflict and the diplomatic rapprochement instituted by President Richard M. Nixon, permitted a drastic reduction in the foreign aid effort. As of 1969 the net flow of resources from the United States to developing countries alone amounted to only about 0.5 percent of its GNP.[7] The corresponding proportion for the United Kingdom was 1 percent, for France 1.24 percent, for Germany 1.33 percent, Italy 1 percent, and Japan 0.75 percent. The 0.5 percent of GNP contributed by the United States, which included outlays to South Vietnam of $446 million, could hardly be considered a substantial global antipoverty program. As the 1960s closed it was increasingly uncertain to what extent the leading industrial nations would continue to provide loans and grants to the poverty-stricken Third World. But it did seem clear that in the late 1970s the content of whatever nonmilitary aid was advanced would shift from capital goods to human resource development.

INTERNATIONAL MONETARY CRISES

The other major problem confronting the United States and the rest of the noncommunist world at the end of World War II was the disorganization of international economic and financial relations. It has been pointed out that this disorganization had set in as far back as World War I, and was reflected in the enduring crisis of the gold standard during the interwar years.

The United States and a few other leading noncommunist countries had a vision of a postwar economic world characterized by the growth of nondiscriminatory, multilateral trade and capital movements, stable foreign exchange ratios (fixed parities among currencies), and convertibility of one country's money into another's without foreign exchange restrictions, all to be linked to a high-employment policy within each nation. Essentially, they wanted planned laissez-faire in the international sphere, something on the order of the conception of the old international gold standard, and interventionism in their respective national economies.

The Bretton Woods conference

A conference of 28 nations convened at Bretton Woods, New Hampshire, in July 1944 and laid the foundations of a system designed

to implement these goals. Acutely conscious of the disarray in which the interwar years had left the pre-1914 gold standard arrangements, the government representatives assembled there were able to agree upon a new set of institutions. Ratified by the war's end or soon thereafter were three institutions: the International Bank for Reconstruction and Development, or World Bank (1945), to aid, in affiliation with the United Nations, the flow of long-term capital funds, particularly to less developed countries; the strategic International Monetary Fund (formally instituted in March 1946), to "supplement the world's inadequate gold supply by credit facilities and in various ways to promote orderly adjustment of balance-of-payments disequilibria";[8] and the General Agreement on Tariffs and Trade (GATT, 1947), to "provide an agency for the gradual elimination of non-tariff barriers to trade and of discriminatory trading practices, and the

[7]This and the following estimates are from the Organization for Economic Cooperation and Development, Economic Survey, France, April 1971, Statistical Annex Q, p. 92.

[8]Harry G. Johnson, The World Economy at the Crossroads (New York: Oxford University Press, 1965), p. 18.

gradual reduction of tariffs through international negotiation.''[9] This institutional complex came to be known as the Bretton Woods system, and provided the foundation for international economic relations within the Third World and the advanced countries.

The World Bank and its affiliates

The World Bank was slow to get under way, and its explicit loan restrictions, together with its conservative loan policy, turned out to be most inadequate to meet the capital-importing needs, to say nothing of technical-assistance needs, of the less developed countries. In consequence, it began to spin off affiliates (for example, the International Finance Corporation, 1956, and the International Development Association, 1960) that would make long-term loans employing easier criteria and for more diversified purposes. In any case, United Nations technical assistance, financed in part by U.S. funds, came to be centered in a number of economic commissions and such other U.N. agencies as the Food and Agricultural Organization and the World Health Organization. It slowly came to be realized that technical progress was at least as important for economic development as was capital-goods investment. In the Latin American area the United States, along with 19 other countries, instituted in 1960 the Inter-American Development Bank to make loans, part of the foreign aid program, to member countries, governments, and private enterprise.

The General Agreement on Tariffs and Trade

GATT transferred tariff negotiation from a formally bilateral approach to a formally international basis. However, from the U.S. standpoint negotiation was conducted under the reciprocal trade agreements acts, and was largely in the service of aid to American exports. Professor Harry Johnson commented in 1965 that GATT

> is not basically a free trade organization, but instead a device by which rich protectionist countries can negotiate with each other for more efficient means of achieving protectionist objectives. The emphasis of GATT was on receiving better markets for a country's efficient industries

from other countries, at the "cost" of allowing other countries' efficient industries better access to the country's markets at the expense of its inefficient protected industries.[10]

Nevertheless, with the notable exception of agricultural products, very substantial tariff reductions were effected under GATT, and particularly as a result of the round of multilateral negotiations in Geneva from 1963 to 1967, known as the Kennedy Round. Unfortunately, aside from widespread, justified dissatisfaction on the part of the less developed countries with the impact of the Kennedy Round upon their disadvantaged status in world markets,[11] the tariff reductions left largely untouched the onward march of nontariff barriers, such as quotas, licensing, and other quantitative controls and discriminations, and antidumping regulations, border-tax adjustments, and health regulations, which in the 1960s were becoming more important than ever.[12] Also, as the 1970s opened, the threat of restrictionist policies emanating from a possible power struggle between the United States and such giant trading blocs as the European Common Market[13] had begun to loom large on the international competitive horizon. It was hoped that the big steps toward liberalization of trade marking the historic Kennedy Round would carry over into the future relations of the great regional economic blocs.

The International Monetary Fund

The chief element in the Bretton Woods system was the International Monetary Fund (IMF),[14] another United Nations affiliate. It

[9]Ibid., p. 68.

[10]In a paper presented to the Conference on Measures for Trade Expansion for Developing Countries, held at the Japan Economic Research Center, Tokyo, November 9–12, 1965, pp. 12–13 (mimeo).

[11]See the statement of Eric Wyndham White, director general of GATT, at the meeting of the Trade Negotiations Committee, Geneva, June 30, 1967.

[12]See, for example, the statement of William Diebold, Jr., Council on Foreign Relations, Subcommittee on Foreign Economic Policy, Joint Economic Committee, *Hearings* 90th Cong., 1st sess., July 19, 1967 (Washington, D.C.: U.S. Government Printing Office, 1967), pp. 219–223.

[13]A powerful, united free trade union of all the leading European countries, founded January 1, 1959. Great Britain joined in the early 1970s.

[14]The following discussion of the fund, its evolution, and its changing historical context relies heavily upon the splendid review by Christopher L. Bach, "Problems of the International Monetary System and Proposals for Reform, 1944–70," Federal Reserve Bank of St. Louis, *Review*, 54, no. 5 (May 1972):24–32.

must be recalled in this connection that at the end of World War II the United States held about 70 percent of the world's monetary gold stock, the traditional reserve money held by most nations. Each nation kept itself liquid through its holdings of gold or some other hard currency of a leading country, such as dollars or pounds sterling. Since the United States had run a persistent trade surplus in its international goods and services account, and during the depression had practically stopped providing foreign countries with dollars through its capital account (mostly private loans), the rest of the world was very short of both gold and dollars. Reserves and liquidity of the rest of the world were dangerously low. Everyone seemed to recognize that such disequilibrium could not be allowed to persist. Moreover, other nations felt they needed some institution to provide them with international means of payment and adequate reserves in the event that they might experience a drain of cash due to either a continued excess of imports over exports or a related sudden attempt by speculators to unload their currency in favor of gold or some harder, preferred currency.

The attempted solution found in the IMF for providing reserves and affording liquidity was the privilege granted each member (there were 54 by 1953) to draw (borrow), under certain constraints, from the fund's pool of gold, U.S. dollars and other members' currencies placed there by each participant according to the subscribed quota of such monies. Voting power in the administration of the IMF was proportional to quota, and therefore was dominated by the big nations, which committed the largest amount of monetary resources. Continued borrowing by any country experiencing chronic pressure on its balance of payments (that is, its imports exceeded its exports) would likely elicit an agreed-upon depreciation or devaluation of its money in the foreign exchange markets, since only by cheapening its money could it hope to make its exports more attractive and its imports more expensive. By such downward adjustment of its parity rates the country could presumably correct the fundamental disequilibrium in its balance of payments. Each country's parity rates with the money units of other countries was defined in terms of a stipulated amount of gold, and therefore all the different national money units were tied to gold and indirectly to one another. The ability to draw from the fund expanded world monetary reserves considerably beyond existing gold stocks plus newly mined gold.

The dollar shortage

But there was still the shortage of dollars, which for many years was to be the world's leading reserve asset and international money. This expanded use of dollars by other countries as working balances to provide liquidity and to finance payments imbalances had not been nearly so widespread before World War II. For some years after the war, U.S. policy was deliberately contributing to the expanded use of dollars as the dominant international currency. The United States wanted to relieve the dollar shortage in order to help make the new IMF arrangements reestablish a stable world economy and to assure sufficient dollar holdings abroad for the purchase of U.S. products.

Since the United States was not willing to relinquish its historic excess of exports over imports, the rest of the world continued to lose dollars. Hence other means had to be found to provide the rest of the world with dollars. The large U.S. quota subscription of gold and dollars in the IMF was one minor way in which this was accomplished. This amount grew with U.S. national income over time.

Another, much more important source of dollars was U.S. government military expenditures abroad and grants and loans to other countries. These averaged almost $5 billion annually in the 1950s. In addition, private U.S. business firms initiated an enormous outflow of long-term funds that was vastly to augment America's foreign asset holdings all over the world. By 1960, U.S. private long-term investments abroad totaled over $49 billion, and ten years later were approximating $100 billion. Even though the income on these investments was large and growing, the sum of the government payments and the private capital outflow was so large that it exceeded the current account surplus on products and investment income, so that already in the 1950s the country had begun to incur deficits on its total international balance of payments. The subsequent growing payments deficits, the demand for dollars as an international currency, and the removal of exchange controls in Europe in the early 1960s induced foreigners to hold increasingly large sums of "Eurodollars" on deposit in European banks for financing overseas investment and other general purposes.

The dollar glut

In view of the U.S. policy to eliminate the dollar shortage, these deficits in the 1950s did not yet appear as a threat. But as the decade waned the shortage began its transition to a world dollar glut. Professor Emile Despres stated on July 1, 1959, that so far as western Europe was concerned, the persistent problem of a dollar shortage was at an end.[15] Consequently, continued deficits in the 1960s gave an entirely different complexion to the entire U.S. international position and to its foreign policy. The value of the dollar began to fall as continued deficits meant that the supply of dollars came to exceed the demand for them. The threat that there might be a sudden decline in the desire of foreigners to hold dollars began to appear increasingly imminent.

There were several reasons for the aggravation of the famous U.S. balance-of-payments deficits in the 1960s. Among the more important was the fact that while world trade outside the Soviet bloc reversed its interwar pattern, growing more rapidly than world industrial production, the U.S. share of that trade, particularly in the industrial products category, declined. U.S. exports in 1950 were 16.6 percent of world exports, but by 1960 the percentage had slipped to 15.9, and by 1973 it had sharply fallen to only 12.2 percent. The reasons for that decline were complex, but may be summed up in the statement that competition from leading European countries and Japan, whose payment balances were persistently in surplus, was paramount. That competition was located in both world markets and the U.S. home market. Thus the U.S. merchandise trade surplus, which averaged $5.4 billion a year from 1960 to 1964, had fallen to only $2.8 billion during the years 1965–1969.[16] Hence, with negative items such as military outlays abroad averaging almost $3 billion from 1965 to 1969, an equal negative figure for the balance on direct private investment, and a substantial negative total on other long-term capital flows, the reduced positive totals on the merchandise account were unable any longer to hold deficits down. The foreign exchange costs of NATO alone amounted to two-thirds of the total deficit in the 1960s. Those deficits averaged $2.8 billion yearly from 1960 to 1964, and rose to $3.4 billion from 1965 to 1969. The world became overloaded with dollars, and after the mid-1960s dollar

holdings (claims) by foreigners exceeded the available U.S. stock of gold. In May 1971

> . . . *official foreigners indicated their unwillingness to accumulate more dollars. On August 15 the United States indicated it was no longer willing to tolerate the projected balance-of-payments deficits. It suspended convertibility of dollars into gold, imposed an import surcharge (of 10%), and announced its intention to seek a realignment of parity rates and multinational cooperation on reform of the international monetary system.*[17]

"Fundamental disequilibrium" had toppled the IMF system of (sluggishly) adjustable fixed rates among the currencies of a number of countries several times within the 1950s and 1960s. Now, with President Nixon's termination of dollar convertibility into gold on August 15, 1971, it had toppled the parity rate of the country whose money unit had long been the world's leading international reserve currency.

Devaluation

The United States, like other nations, had been reluctant to devalue its money unit despite accumulating pressure on its balance of payments. It had a unique responsibility as the country whose money unit was the de facto international reserve asset. It also probably had more reason to delay than a country whose foreign balance is, unlike that of the United States, large relative to its GNP. Such a country faces severe unemployment when its imports get larger and its exports smaller. But devaluation is an aggressive international weapon, even when it is done in reluctant consultation with the IMF membership. It can lead to retaliation. Throughout the entire years of international monetary crisis following the British devaluation of the pound in 1967, the United States, as the key currency country, could not change dollar exchange rates with other currencies without fear of retaliatory rate changes or disruption of international monetary arrangements. Now the United States itself could no longer delay. The dollar was plummeting in the international money markets. But the U.S. move precipitated a crisis that had long been brewing for the

---

[15]See U.S. Congress, Joint Economic Committee, *Hearings,* 86th Cong., 1st sess., June 29–July 2, 1959, pt. 5: "International Influences on the American Economy" (Washington, D.C.: U.S. Government Printing Office, 1959), p. 1034.

[16]These estimates and those immediately following are from Christopher L. Bach, "U.S. Balance-of-Payments Problems and Policies in 1971," *Federal Reserve Bank of St. Louis, Review,* 54, no. 4 (April 1972):13.

[17]Ibid., p. 8.

Bretton Woods system.[18] A new set of international monetary arrangements was in the offing for the 1970s. And it seemed quite possible that the improved prospects for trade with the communist countries would result in the inclusion of those countries in the new arrangements.

BUSINESS STRUCTURE

The evolution of the business structure in the quarter century following World War II was marked by a radical extension of past trends and patterns, with the appearance here and there of some novel features. In many ways it might be said that earlier historical developments reached maturation, implying that the next phases of business history would bring significantly new trends and patterns.

Corporate versus noncorporate enterprises

For generations the corporate form of business in the private nonfarm economy had been increasing in importance while at the same time the number of noncorporate enterprises in that sector had continued to increase in numbers. Because corporate enterprise was on the average relatively large and noncorporate enterprise relatively small, economic and business historians, along with many economists, were inclined to distinguish analytically the corporate and noncorporate sectors and to deal broadly with the former as big business, the latter as small business. This "dual economy" approach recognized an overlap, but nevertheless presumed significant differences in behavior and problems in the two sectors.

After World War II business continued to favor the corporate form. The number of corporations rose 188 percent between 1950 and 1972, whereas the number of proprietorships rose only 48 percent. These increases may be compared with the rise in the population of the United States from 152 million to 209 million, or 38 percent, over the same period. The greater rise in the business population is all the more striking in view of the very large decline in the total number of farm proprietorships during that time. Apparently the mixed economy was an environment that generated about as much optimism among potential entrepreneurs as did laissez-faire. The total number of proprietorships and partnerships vastly outnumbered the corporations in 1972: over 11 million as compared with 1.8 million corporations. Astonishingly enough, over 11 million enterprises could account for as little as 15 percent of all the private business sales in the country.

But of course not all the corporations could be considered big business by any means: 94 percent had year-end assets of less than $1 million in 1971, and this group of about 1.6 million small corporations accounted for only about 7.5 percent of the assets of all active corporations filing income-tax returns. Hence "small business" would include about 11 million proprietorships and partnerships and 1.6 million corporations, the sum of the two accounting for approximately 98 percent of all business firms. In terms of numbers, American economic activity revealed a world of small enterprise; but in terms of sales and control of productive wealth, it revealed a world of large enterprise. There was a middle-sized group, of course, and we can get a broad glimpse of it from the corporate sector. The middle group in 1971 (cutting off the "large" at the asset level of $50 million or more and using the same criterion for "small") accounted for about 6 percent of all active corporations and for approximately 19 percent of total corporate assets. Hence the middle-sized businesses were numerically minor but carried notable weight in terms of corporate wealth.

Nevertheless, the U.S. economy clearly revealed a high degree of concentration with respect to control of productive wealth and total economic activity. Ordinarily, historians presume that along with economic weight there is economic power, and that with economic power there is associated social and political power.

Market concentration versus aggregate concentration

With the possible exception of major industry groups having high levels of merger activity, the extent of economic concentration between

[18]See, for example, "Bretton Woods, Twenty-Five Years After," address by Mr. Pierre-Paul Schweitzer, managing director, IMF, at Queens University, Kingston, Ontario, Canada, June 2, 1969. Published as a supplement to the IMF *International Financial News Survey*, 21, no. 22 (June 6, 1969).

1945 and 1975 apparently did not increase if one employs the criterion of the percentage of total sales accounted for by, let us say, the top four companies within each industry. Industry is here defined as a group of companies producing some given product or close substitute products. This is called the degree of "market concentration." But on the criterion of the position that the largest enterprises occupy in the total assets or economic activity of a given sector, concentration did increase in the period under review. This is called "aggregate concentration."[19] An example may be found in the important manufacturing sector of the economy, wherein the largest 200 corporations held 48.2 percent of all assets in 1948 and 60 percent in 1972.

It is also noteworthy that in the manufacturing sector, at least, profit shares were typically even more concentrated than asset shares. For example, the 422 largest (out of over 200,000) manufacturing corporations in 1974 held 68 percent of the assets but received 71 percent of the profits. Clearly the profit system, in the economic as distinguished from the ideological sense, was largely confined to the big-business sector.[20]

Diversification and conglomeration

Such a contrast between the asset-profit ratios of small and large enterprise is but one of the many criteria suggesting a different market status for small and big business in the American economy.[21] Another criterion suggesting differential status was the fact that the large firm was much more diversified, geographically or in terms of numbers of commodities produced, than small enterprise.[22] This insulated the large firm better against fluctuating fortunes in the markets for particular products or areas. Diversification positively associated with size also

explains in large part why aggregate concentration in the economy could be greater than market concentration and why market power could exceed market share. Conglomerate enterprises—that is, firms producing either a variety of items unrelated in buyers' commodity concepts or items in more than one geographic market, especially when achieved through mergers—occupied the center of the stage in the great wave of merger activity in the 1960s.

Commercial banking mergers

Not all merger activity was linked with product diversification. The more "old-fashioned," horizontal type of merger was prominent in the commercial banking field, especially in the 1950s, and accounted for the major structural changes in banking in the United States between 1950 and 1975. Unlike the business population in the small-enterprise activities, the numbers of commercial banks declined slightly over the period, with the absolute decline in the 1950s being less than fully compensated for by the very small increase in the 1960s.[23] With a roughly constant commercial banking population of between 13,000 and 14,000, and with entry into banking made complicated by an intricate network of state and federal regulations, the moderately strong advantages of large size, especially in metropolitan areas, led to long-run increasing concentration. This concentrating tendency was more in evidence in the 1950s than in the 1960s. But by the mid-1970s, despite the constraints offered by such legislation as the Bank Holding Company Act of 1956 and the Bank Merger Act of 1960, and by a number of Supreme Court decisions applying the Sherman and Clayton antitrust laws, concentration was considerable. For example, the 50 largest commercial banking organizations in 1974 represented less than 1 percent of all such banks, but they held over one-third of the total deposits.

---

[19]See U.S. Congress, House Committee on the Judiciary, *Investigation of Conglomerate Corporations,* staff report of the Antitrust Subcommittee, 92d Cong., 1st sess. (Washington, D.C.: U.S. Government Printing Office, June 1, 1971), pp. 19–21.

[20]Data from *Statistical Abstract, 1975,* p. 503.

[21]For a more detailed analysis than can be presented here, see Robert T. Averitt, *The Dual Economy* (New York: Norton, 1968); and Harold G. Vatter, *Small Enterprise and Oligopoly* (Corvallis, Oregon: Oregon State College Press, 1955).

[22]It should be noted, however, that this is a relative matter. An examination of product diversification only by *Fortune* magazine (June 15, 1967) revealed a "surprisingly low degree of diversification among the 500 largest industrials" (cited in *Investigation of Conglomerate Corporations,* p. 4).

[23]In various ways the mixed economy was kind to commercial banks viewed exclusively as business firms. For example, the insurance of deposits, begun under the New Deal's Federal Deposit Insurance Corporation, ended runs on banks, apparently forever. This, together with the long-run decline in the importance of banking's agrarian critics, seemed to have removed the notion of banking as an evil money monopoly. Also, deposit insurance, together with more rigorous regulation and surveillance by government, cut down insolvency. It was truly a historic record when from 1961 through 1973 there were only 47 commercial banks closed, either permanently or temporarily, on account of financial difficulties, by order of supervisory authorities or directors of banks themselves.

Spatial diversification

Conglomeration included *spatial* diversification, and the large firm exhibited great flexibility in both initiating and adapting to the great regional shifts of economic activity toward the South and the West that characterized the postwar decades. Small business was mobile, too, but it typically located in one particular metropolitan market as an adaptation to such regional shifts. The great bulk of small businesses were concentrated, like employment for blacks and women, in more or less segregated activities such as the retail and service trades, and operated in local but not in regional markets.

The multinational firms

The corporate conglomerate was further differentiated from small enterprise in that it assumed, as the large corporation had done in the past, the unique role of expansion into foreign lands. One of the important and dramatic extensions of past corporate policy that stood out in the postwar period was the spread of the large multinational firm. Such a firm has a U.S. headquarters, direct investment in at least one foreign country, and a global management perspective. The number of U.S. parent firms controlling foreign affiliates rose from 2,800 to 3,500 between 1957 and 1970, and the number of affiliates from 10,000 to 25,000.[24] Multinational corporations at the end of the 1960s contributed about 15 percent of the gross product of the noncommunist world outside of the United States, or an estimated $180 billion a year.[25] U.S. multicorps accounted for over half of all merchandise exports and over one-third of all merchandise imports in 1970.

THE LARGE CORPORATION

For these and other reasons pertaining to the differential status of small and large corporate enterprise, and the overwhelming economic domination of the latter, it seems highly suggestive to employ the notion of a dual economy within the U.S. private nonfarm sector, and to concentrate upon the large corporation in order best to understand the nature and role of American business in the postwar world. This large corporate sector was what John Kenneth Galbraith used as his model of the economic power center in the contemporary American economy.[26] In his presidential address to the thirty-second annual meeting of the Economic History Association, Alfred D. Chandler, Jr., declared that the central office managers in this sector were

> surely the most important set of economic decision makers in the United States today. . . . They manage more funds, supervise more workers, make larger investments than did the governments of nation-states in the eighteenth and even the twentieth century. In 1965 General Motors' revenues of $20 billion were just under those of Great Britain and France. . . . This economic class has more to say than farmers, small businessmen, labor leaders and

> government officials about pricing, investment, employment, output and technological innovation. . . .[27]

Management of the large corporation

The giant corporation, thus viewed, had by the onset of the 1970s carried the historic separation of ownership and management to a new high level of development. Small stockholders in particular were essentially separated from traditional ownership powers of decision making and reduced to the status of corporate creditors. The older form of family enterprise had all but disappeared in these corporations.

The manager was professionalized and converted into the "organization man." Within the hierarchy of management, managers higher up managed other managers. The knowledge revolution in technology, embodied in electronics, automation, and the computer, had brought the highly skilled technician and even

[24]Chase Manhattan Bank, *Business in Brief,* no. 99 (August 1971).

[25]See the statement of N. R. Danielian, president, International Economic Policy Association, U.S. Congress, Joint Economic Committee, Subcommittee on Foreign Economic Policy, *Hearings,* 91st Cong., 2d sess., pt. 4, "The Multinational Corporation and International Investment," July 29, 1970(Washington, D.C.: U.S. Government Printing Office, 1970), p. 848.

[27]Alfred D. Chandler, Jr., "Decision Making and Modern Institutional Change," *Journal of Economic History,* 33, no. 1 (March 1973): 13.

[26]See John Kenneth Galbraith, *The New Industrial State,* rev. ed. (Boston: Houghton Mifflin, 1972).

the scientist onto the top rungs of the corporate organizational ladder. These technical specialists augmented the managerial staff positions, complicating administrative problems in many cases by their policy conflicts with the old-line managers, who were closer to both the actual production process and the firm's employees.[28]

Administration was further complicated by the problems of coordination. While intraorganizational information and communication technology had made enormous strides, the problems of coordination between boards of directors, top management, middle management, and the strong individual executive were by no means solved.[29] Further coordinational problems due to the decentralized, multiplant, multiproduct, and multinational nature of enterprise were being attacked chiefly by an administrative trend toward decentralization of decisions; that is, toward heavier reliance upon local management initiative. Another clearly discernible trend in the 1960s was the heavier use of management teams, and quantitative managerial science began to adapt the economic theory of games to a new theory of teams.

Administration
versus supply and demand

The role of large corporate management came in for increasing public scrutiny, greatly changing the environmental setting of managerial decision making. To a certain extent, administration had come to replace market demand and supply, although perhaps less so than Professor Galbraith argued. It was contended by management spokesmen that its administrative role was to mediate between the often clashing interests of suppliers, stockholders, creditors, employees, and buyers—all in the interests of "the firm," or, as Galbraith and others would have it, "the organization." A. A. Berle, Jr., viewed this situation as constituting the possession of power without property (ownership). Be that as it may, questions arose regarding why corporate managers dared assume such power of adjudication between the various interests surrounding the corporation. Perhaps more important, there was the question, in the absence of fully operative demand and supply forces, including the "sovereign consumer," of what kind of criteria management was to employ in exercising its great

command over the allocation of human and material resources. It seemed most unsatisfactory for management to retort that it "balanced" the claims of all the various interest groups. Besides, in addition to the groups dealing directly with the corporation, there was the indirect matter of the impact of management decisions on the interests of society at large; for example, society's interest in technological progress and in environmental quality.

The question of maximizing

The "balance" retort led to another central question: What was the corporation maximizing? The older economic theory argued that the business firm strove to maximize short-run profits. But the balancing act appeared to imply a serious conflict with short-run, or even long-run, profit maximizing at times. Thomas C. Cochran seemed to answer the question as well as any when he declared:

> The primary problem of management . . . was not so much the division of returns as the deployment of assets in such a way as to strengthen the company's position in its markets, which generally meant to maintain profits and sales volumes at least equal to those of major competitors.[30]

And since GNP was growing, most large firms had to grow, in assets and sales and investment in plant, equipment, and inventories. Growth was still, as always, a goal of business operation.

To grow, firms with heavy investments in plant and equipment had to plan far in advance. Such planning demanded that market uncertainties needed to be minimized, and one important way to accomplish this was to acquire the funds for investment expansion to the greatest possible extent from internal sources rather than to expose fund raising to the judgment of the outside capital market. Hence large firm managers typically retained for expansion purposes the bulk of the firm's gross income. They maximized depreciation allowances and withheld from stockholder dividends as much of net income as they could without incurring active stockholder resistance. Dividends came to be looked upon by management as a cost of doing business, just like interest charges paid to bondholders and other creditors. Hence undistributed profits after taxes were usually as large as dividends, or larger. Management maximized

[28]See Thomas C. Cochran, *American Business in the Twentieth Century* (Cambridge, Mass.: Harvard University Press, 1972), p. 213.
[29]Ibid., pp. 208, 209, 215.
[30]Ibid., p. 207.

internal "cash flow" — the sum of undistributed profits and depreciation allowances. In 1974 this cash flow equaled 104 percent of all non-farm nonfinancial corporation investment in plant and equipment.

Financial managers versus industrial managers

Management reticence about exposure to uncertainties, and even about possible threats to its autonomy, from external financing can be better understood when it is realized that it was not individual investors but rather large institutional investors like pension-fund holders, insurance companies, building and loan associations, and big commercial banks that increasingly acquired the bulk of the securities issued. Hence, "coalitions of these financial interests could buy the stock necessary to overthrow the management, or gain control over companies by 'over-head' tenders made directly to the institutional and individual stockholders."[31] But of course, a powerful role for management in the financial community vis-à-vis management in the industrial community was not a historically novel phenomenon in this period. It merely augmented its position. The *Wall Street Journal* reported on March 2, 1973, that banks, institutional pension-fund holders, insurance companies, mutual funds, and other large financial intermediaries held collectively more than 50 percent of the outstanding stock of the most favored, highest caliber growth companies in the nation.

Even with the strong emphasis upon internal financing, large volumes of stocks and, much more importantly, bonds were floated annually. The market value of corporate and foreign bonds outstanding rose 386 percent, from $37.4 billion in 1950 to $181.8 billion in 1970. Meanwhile, the number of shares of stock listed on the New York Stock Exchange increased 582 percent and the market value of all corporate stockholdings rose sixfold. This great upsweep was accompanied by the greatest stock-market boom since the 1920s, producing enormous capital gains that, being subject to preferential tax treatment in both federal and state income-tax laws, made many thousands of operators rich from mere speculative activity. Some observers called the period the capital-gains prosperity era. Here was another respect in which the government-managed economy had created a benign environment for the business community. The financial community was somewhat surprised to experience the great rise in the Dow-Jones stock price index from 78 in 1950 to 319 in 1965, when the wholesale price index was rising rather moderately, followed by a downward stock price trend from 1965 to 1970, when the wholesale price index began to rise much more rapidly. This was a reminder that general inflation was not favorable for stock price increases, a phenomenon quite consistent with the stock-market boom of the 1920s, a period in which general prices were quite stable.

CHANGES IN THE BUSINESS ENVIRONMENT

If the evolution of business structure was characterized by essential continuity from 1945 to the mid-1970s, the relationship of business, and particularly large corporate business, to its general social and political environment changed markedly. The most far-reaching change was the government commitment to high employment without depressions. Although this meant at times an unemployment rate that was serious enough in human terms, business had never before functioned in an environment in which total money income was always rising. Even total physical output was highly unresponsive to recession. In the four recessions after the end of the Korean war,

gross physical output never fell as much as 4 percent.

Total income equals total business sales, and government underwriting of total sales under existing property institutions meant underwriting the profit system. For 20 years after the 1948–1949 recession, total corporate profits before taxes never fell more than 12 percent in any year of decline — a historically unprecedented performance. This experience added greatly to the already bewildering dilemma of profit theory, for if the interventionist economy could so drastically reduce the major source of sales uncertainty — cyclical depression — then the argument that profits were a reward to enterprise for assuming uncertainty (risk) became very tenuous. It was also significant that under the interventionist system, once bitterly op-

[31]Thomas C. Cochran, *Business in American Life* (New York: McGraw-Hill, 1972), pp. 258–259.

posed by big business, there was a remarkable stability—in the corporate manufacturing sector, for example—in profits (after federal income taxes) per sales dollar.

Price policies and inflation

Because of the public commitment to high employment and economic growth, a new environment for business price policies had also been created. As in the case of wage increases, so it was with business's ability to pass on cost increases or administered price rises in general. For with serious unemployment and excess capacity ruled out insofar as public policy was concerned, the government through fiscal and monetary policy dared not do other than validate wage and price increases administered on the industry-wide level.

This kind of cost-push validation, together with government support for rising total demand, created a new, chronically inflationary environment. Industrial enterprise, except for exporters, was likely to favor this development, provided inflation were restrained; but the burgeoning financial community, with its creditor interest in a more or less stable purchasing power of money, was articulately anti-inflationary. A public policy of inflation control through creating more unemployment, however, brought industrial and financial business into alliance, for they believed that the more unemployment there was, the greater would be the downward pressures on wage costs.

The tendency to validate monopolistic cost-push inflation through additional money, or through the community's faster rate of use of its money, increasingly called for more direct measures to restrain wages and prices. Such measures had already been resorted to in several European countries, and were known as "incomes policies," because with given quantities of labor and capital employed, the setting of wages and prices determined the incomes of labor and property.

With the onset of a more rapid upward price trend in the mid-1960s, it became difficult to get compliance with either presidential exhortation or the voluntary wage-price guideposts inaugurated by President Kennedy's Council of Economic Advisers in 1962. These guideposts had urged, with the usual exceptions, that labor unions and large corporations hold hourly money-wage rises to the trend of increase in productivity in the entire economy, and that they hold prices constant in all industries whose productivity record conformed to the trend. But by 1966, when the council for the first time

specifically recommended a guidepost of 3.2 percent annual increase in wages, the rise in consumer prices and corporate profits induced labor to break out of the constraints.

Stagflation

Despite continued inflation during the Nixon administration, the president prominently resisted for some time the pressure of a Democratic Congress to institute comprehensive direct wage and price controls. This he could readily have done by implementing its 1970 Economic Stabilization Act, giving him authority to freeze wages, rents, and other prices at levels not lower than those prevailing on May 25, 1970. But 1971 saw the continuation of a substantial inflation rate coupled with high unemployment (known as "stagflation"), to say nothing of the persistent balance-of-payments deficit. Hence the Nixon administration, under the influence particularly of Treasury Secretary John B. Connally, conservative Federal Reserve Board Chairman Arthur F. Burns, and later a petition by 14 Republican senators, quietly prepared and then instituted its famous 90-day wage-price freeze on August 15, 1971. The subsequent stop-go phases of decontrol followed by reinstitution of a 60-day freeze on June 14, 1973, suggested that the long run future might well witness an ever more extensive use of incomes policy as a necessary adjunct to monetary and fiscal policies in the management of the mixed economy.

The union of private and public sectors

The new era of what Professor Cochran has called "business and government in partnership" infused all the major decisions of large "private" enterprise with a public aspect. Government incomes policies, taxes and direct subsidies, the depreciation rules of the Internal Revenue Service, investment credits for business expansion, the growing intervention of government in management's relations with labor under Taft-Hartley, the formation of what President Eisenhower called the "military-industrial complex" linking less than 200 giant prime defense contractors with the Pentagon's enormous expenditures, the administration of public regulatory commissions by "officials who are merely the pale reflections of the very interests they are supposed to regulate,"[32] the basically common viewpoints of top-level govern-

---

[32]Cochran, *American Business in the Twentieth Century,* quoting E. Pendleton Herring, p. 173.

ment administrators and big-business leaders in the sphere of foreign policy[33]—all these and other points of contact fed the "blending of the private and public sectors."[34] Clearly, the former dichotomy of private-public in the sphere of government-business relationships was fast disappearing. The fusion developed even though there was by no means full agreement in all policy areas. Other socioeconomic groups exerted at times a countervailing influence, and rough compromises were often reached, after the manner of the American political system.

Adaptation to the mixed economy

The business power elite came to accept the mixed economy and to adapt the behavior of that new system to its own objectives. The adaptation entailed less reliance upon the trade association than had been the case in the historical past. It rather involved working within numerous mild regulatory restraints in areas such as antitrust under the Federal Trade Commission and the Justice Department; interstate commerce under the old ICC and the newer Federal Power and Communications Commissions; civil aviation under the Civil Aeronautics Board; protection of the investing public under the Securities and Exchange Commission; and the deterrence of industrial conflict under the more powerful National Labor Relations Board. Indeed, so benign were the policies of federal regulatory agencies that when President Ford proposed discontinuing most of their powers in 1976, spokesmen for some leading regulated industries—especially trucking, airlines, and broadcasting—were opposed to such deregulation.

It was largely among the small- and middle-business elements, for example in the local chambers of commerce, that the older hostility toward government, and the belief that "that government is best which governs least," retained much strength. This was remarkable in view of the far-reaching benefits to small business that resulted from the new, governmentally underwritten economy. These might be seen in the fact that the business failure rate was, on the average, approximately half that for the so-called prosperous 1920s and in the fact that total business and professional income exhibited scarcely a ripple in response to all postwar recessions.

New criteria used in antitrust cases

Postwar enforcement of antitrust laws was fairly vigorous when viewed historically. In several important antitrust cases decided after 1945, the older and partially obsolete criteria of industrial structure and efficiency were put into the background, and the more relevant criteria of size (market control) and the constraint of economic power were highlighted by the courts. These criteria were rather more useful in the context of the conglomerate corporation. Yet even here the regulatory constraint was mild. As summed up by business historians Herman E. Krooss and Charles Gilbert, "the growth of big business, whether fed internally or externally, seemed to proceed along a trend line regardless of the lax or rigid attitudes of antitrust enforcers."[35] Passage of the Celler-Kefauver ("antimerger") Act in 1950 failed to alter the trend.

Consumerism

All business, but particularly large corporate management, had to confront important new socioenvironmental challenges as the postwar era unfolded. For example, for the first time in the twentieth century the voice of the consumer began seriously to be heard. The enormous effort of business to create and direct consumer preferences continued after World War II. Total advertising expenditures, for example, which had been about $6 billion in 1950, rose to over $25 billion in 1973, with television the most rapidly growing medium.

In response to this kind of push to create a "consumerist" public, together with the baffling technical complexity of many household products, various representatives of the consumer interest demanded improved quality control of products, more complete and accurate information, and greater responsibility in advertising. Private organizations like Consumers' Union, serving mainly the large middle-income stratum; government agencies like the older Food and Drug Administration and the newer federal Office of Consumer Affairs (later transferred to the Department of Health, Education, and Welfare), and consumer protection agencies on the state level; and private consumer protection leagues under leaders like the consumer militant Ralph Nader (head of the Public Interest Research Group and the Center for the Study

---

[33]Cochran, *Business in American Life*, p. 321.
[34]Morton S. Baratz, *The American Business System in Transition* (New York: Crowell, 1970), p. 78.

[35]*American Business History* (Englewood Cliffs, N.J.: Prentice-Hall, 1972), p. 262.

of Responsive Law) had made a small beginning in the 1960s toward greater consideration of the consumer interest in business calculations than had been the case in the past.

Labor-management relations

In the sphere of labor-management relations the new features were two. The first was the belated public acceptance of the permanence of labor organization, and the final recognition of that condition by corporate management. There were considerable areas that were relatively new to labor organization, as well as older lines of economic activity (such as agriculture), in which business still resisted the right to organize. The numerous state "right to work" laws, abetted by Taft-Hartley, tended to encourage this resistance. But by and large in the major mining, fabrication, construction, transportation, power production, and communications sectors, negotiation between big management and big labor became thoroughly institutionalized, as it had become earlier in most western European countries.

The second environmental change affecting industrial relations, previously referred to in connection with the Taft-Hartley law, was government monitoring or direct participation in the decisive periods of negotiation. The big labor-management contracts were "affected with a public interest" and the government was at the least a silent partner in the formulation of such contracts. The whole atmosphere surrounding the major settlements was highly charged politically, and it was impossible for either party to ignore the economic ramifications of breakdowns. And always in the background was the almost ultimate government weapon: the "national emergency," a legal instrument for assuring industrial peace that was made all the more potent by the practically chronic international crises attending the Cold War, the Korean war, and later the war in Indochina. The strike was not outlawed, however; it was instead ever more securely bound by a web of constraints.

Business was similarly bound by the increasingly imperative necessity to take into consideration the larger economic impact of its demands upon labor. These included such things as the spread effects of wage settlements on other wages and workers, the impact of wage agreements on inflation, the consequences of hiring policies upon minorities, and the repercussions of possible prolonged work stoppages. All such matters impinged upon public policy at many points and elicited high-level government concern, with which management had to reckon.

Public responsibilities of big business

Also new in the setting of the management decision-making process was a host of public concerns with the "external" effects of business decisions upon the welfare of great masses of the urban population. Since "the market" was judged by more and more people to be less responsible for production and related decisions than was deliberate corporate (as well as consumer and government) behavior, social evaluation of that behavior extended, particularly in the 1960s, into such areas of fresh popular concern as the quality of the physical environment, the character of urban life, the nature of technological advance and of output growth, and the human value of work. With power went responsibility, critics asserted. If corporate management was, as it claimed, a great public trust, then the narrow pursuit of self-interest was utterly inadequate. The public responsibilities of the large corporation included, as in the position taken by business leader David Rockefeller, "an absolute obligation for which corporate ownership and leadership should be held strictly accountable" to work energetically "to prevent urban decay, to train and place hardcore jobless, and to minimize pollution."[36] It was certain that the future would bring the prescription of ever more numerous and more encompassing social rules of behavior for business management to abide by and to incorporate into its ordinary profit calculations.

Yet so far the great upsurge in popular demand for corporate social accountability, while significantly altering the business climate, had not challenged the fundamental legitimacy of the profit system or of profit as a property income share. It was only expected that profit, like other incomes, would be "fair" and would pay its "fair share" of income taxes, which meant for corporations on the average rather less than half of before-tax profits. By 1976, with unemployment continuing at high levels, inflation also persisting, and industry fearing severe shortages of new capital for investment, many prominent business leaders—especially

[36]Rockefeller's position is paraphrased in Carl H. Madden, *Clash of Culture: Management in an Age of Changing Values* (Washington, D.C.: National Planning Association, October 1972), p. 74.

those associated with major banking houses—had begun to speak out strongly in favor of more comprehensive national economic planning, although of course with business interests to play the major role in policy decisions.

TECHNOLOGICAL PROGRESS AND ITS EFFECTS

It must be noted that the spread of public apprehension with regard to both technological advance and the attendant growth in production was directed at the consumer and government as well as at business. The material sources of technological advance, which resided in education and in basic and applied research, emanated chiefly from government. The education explosion, which more than doubled high school and higher education enrollments between 1950 and the late 1960s, was largely a state and local function, one that explained in great part the huge growth in expenditures at those levels of government after World War II. The funds for, and the performance of, basic and applied research came mostly from the federal government. (This is readily understandable when one notes that in the mid-1960s about half of all research and development outlays in the United States were military- or space-related—a costly concentration for which the nation paid in weakened international market competitive power and other ways domestically.) Nevertheless, it was recognized that the private business sector accounted for over 90 percent of total output and output growth. Furthermore, the application of technological and educational advances was made overwhelmingly in the business sector.

Insofar as technological advance was linked with research and development, it is worth noting that, according to data gathered by the National Science Foundation, research and development activity in general increased with size of firm. However, there was no strong evidence that the *relative* amount of R & D increased with firm size. Rather, it appeared that the R & D efforts of larger firms were devoted to improvement and refinement of basic innovations originating elsewhere.

Externalities and environmentalism

Public apprehension over technological progress was spreading primarily because of social recognition that it was not all progress. An area of activity that had historically been delegated largely to individual businesses and households, it was almost suddenly discovered, was producing unanticipated, damaging external effects upon people at large. Since technology was embodied in products, the desirability of the production of ever more goods and services, once unquestioningly accepted, was called into question now. The resulting environmentalist movement thus contained several wings, including an antitechnology wing and an antigrowth wing. The former was given added support by the spreading conviction that technology was a *deus ex machina* that moved irrevocably onward with the assistance of an elite corps of scientists and engineers, removed from all meaningful contact with ordinary people. The antigrowth wing was aided by the comparative material affluence of the United States, its high level of per capita consumption, and "the pile-up of trivialized products, the advertising messages that push and huckster the psychedelic bazaar or corrupt grand human ideas such as love into the equivalent of a soft drink."[37]

American technical virtuosity

In traditional terms the technical virtuosity of the American economy seemed impressive enough. Putting men on the moon was only the most spectacular example of this virtuosity. Massive research and development expenditures rose as proportion of GNP. Advances in pure science, especially biochemistry and physical chemistry, were dramatic. The 1950s saw the beginning of automation (automatic feedback) with the first commercial electronic computer in 1951.[38] Diffusion of the computer was rapid thereafter, spreading particularly to banking, aerospace, insurance, electrical machinery, motor vehicles, airlines, oil exploration, the construction industry, and the federal government. The use of instruments for sensing, measuring, acquiring data, and controlling flows in the continuous production systems of mass production was another rapidly growing area of technology. There were also many

[37]Ibid., p. 75.

[38]This paragraph draws heavily upon Edgar Weinberg and Robert L. Ball, "The Many Faces of Technology," U.S. Department of Labor, Bureau of Labor Statistics, *Occupational Outlook Quarterly*, 2, no. 2 (Washington, D.C.: U.S. Government Printing Office, May 1967).

more conventional improvements in equipment, such as in railroad track maintenance machinery and pneumatic conveyors for moving granular materials. In communications technology, copying machines, videotape recorders, closed-circuit TV, and long-distance telephone dialing were prominent. In 1953 about one-fifth of all homes had television sets, but by 1973 almost all homes in the country had black-and-white sets, at least, and 67 percent had color TV.

Household technology was thought by some to have outpaced industrial technology with respect to equipment innovations and their diffusion. In the important field of metalworking technology, automatic operation, known as "numerical control," was introduced, and its diffusion, sometimes with the aid of computers, was begun. Electronic control systems in classification yards, the complete dieselization of locomotives, and piggy-back freight were notable changes in railroading. The conversion to jet aircraft and electronic controls in the airlines, heavier trucks, and containerization in ocean shipping stood out in the other transportation industries.

New products, processes, and materials were developed in many industries; prominent examples were synthetics in textiles and construction, and freeze drying in food manufacturing. Many new kinds of construction materials were also introduced and adopted by the building industry. One of them was plywood. Yet the lumber industry as a whole failed to enjoy total output growth between 1950 and the mid-1970s. Finally, new management techniques, such as operations research, systems analysis, and mathematical programming became widely adopted. These techniques speeded the making and the transmission of managerial decisions; whether they contributed to the quality of those decisions was a matter for further examination.

Private versus public expenditures

The productivity results of these and other changes, as indicated by output per labor-hour in the private economy, rose at an annual rate of 2 percent, which was quite good on a basis of historical comparison for the United States, although not comparable to the postwar record of a number of western European countries and Japan. But the *composition* of total output, including government output, became the subject of critical scrutiny. Critics maintained that the individual household consumer was spending too much on private goods and not enough on

publicly provided goods and services. In a seminal work on the affluent society, John Kenneth Galbraith spoke for many when he contended that the American consumer, unduly influenced by the unremitting sales barrage of business, was devoting a large portion of expenditures to frills while starving the public sector.

The automobile

The devotion to the automobile came under particularly heavy attack, not only for the emphasis on stylistic matters, but also for its role as a noise and air polluter, creator of solid wastes, traffic congester, and despoiler of the urban and rural landscapes. It was the automobile, these critics claimed, that was also primarily responsible for the creation of suburban sprawl and the physical and social decline of the central city; the alarming deterioration of urban mass transit; the attendant immobility of the elderly, the young, the poor, and the handicapped; the inordinate rise in urban commuter costs; the heavy commitment of tax funds to automobile transport investment and law enforcement; and the staggering loss of life and property from motor vehicle accidents.[39] All these were adverse external effects of business' and the consumer's emphasis on growth in total output, including the motor vehicle.

Negative output

Such adverse externalities, given the dubious designation of "discommodities" in the jargon of economics, represented an apparently enormous negative output that by rights should be subtracted from GNP growth in order to estimate actual growth. It may readily be seen that this line of reasoning led to questioning the very facts of output growth, the composition of growing output, and, as seen from the demand side, the desirability of continued population growth.

Waste and pollution

But this was not all. Similarly placed under review was the technology that in the service of such output growth absorbed energy at a rate almost twice that of the other most materially advanced countries. With only 6 percent of the world's population, the United States was consuming in the early 1970s more than one-third of the world's annual consumption of exhaust-

[39]See U.S. Congress, Joint Economic Committee, *The Economics of Federal Subsidy Programs*, pt. 6: "Transportation Subsidies," 93rd Cong. 1st sess., February 26, 1973 (Washington, D.C.: U.S. Government Printing Office, 1973), pp. 798–799.

ible natural resources. Furthermore, wider and deeper recognition of air, land, water, and noise pollution, together with the burgeoning tasks of waste disposal, led to a new awareness—but hardly yet a policy—that the nonhuman energy and other natural resources absorbed in production is not merely dissipated or made to vanish in the economist's "final consumption." Energy that is consumed in production becomes degraded into bound energy no longer available to do work. Indeed, it came to be acknowledged in more informed scientific circles that ever more resources and applied technology would have to be devoted to arresting the tendency of waste and material pollution to accumulate at a faster rate than so-called useful output. This tendency was a central problem for all attempts to generate electricity from nuclear power plants, and accounted in large part for the slow development of such power units despite the emerging energy crisis in the early 1970s.

The energy crisis

The energy problem was focused in a growing public fear that the nation might be running out of mineral fuel reserves. Increasing reliance upon imported fuels raised the specter of long-run exhaustion of domestic reserves, to say nothing of the short-run problems of price inflation in fuels, added pressure on the nation's balance of trade, and the political uncertainty connected with such reliance. All the advanced countries had shifted away from coal toward petroleum and natural gas for fuel, and this meant, in the case of petroleum, tapping the reserves of the Middle East and North Africa.

In the United States, coal reserves were large (778 billion tons as of 1970), but future utilization costs promised to be inordinate compared to those of other fuels. In iron ore, petroleum, and natural gas the nation was already in deficit (at normal long-run relative prices). The long-run adequacy of uranium was dependent upon the future development of a breeder reactor. Furthermore, the older economic problem of providing adequate energy at the lowest cost had now been additionally complicated by the simultaneous problems of minimizing environmental damage.

The latter challenge was particularly acute with respect to the spreading of nuclear energy plants for the production of electricity. Controversy raged among experts and the concerned lay public over possible safety defects in both the installations themselves and, perhaps more threatening, the prevalent method of long-lasting radioactive waste disposal in vats sunk deep into the ground. Leakage from the disposal vats of lethal material into the surrounding terrain and atmosphere was an ever present portent of disaster that could kill millions. These and related issues were dramatized in early 1976 by such incidents as the California nuclear safeguards initiative designed to place the future of the state's nuclear development before the voters, and the sudden resignation in January of three experienced General Electric engineers with many years of intimate contact with that corporation's nuclear safety operations.

The conservation movement

Controversy over production and use was only one of the matters that infused new life into the natural-resource conservation movement. That movement was now further strengthened by an easy alliance with the environmentalists and the population alarmists. Their joint attack, revitalizing the resource-scarcity doctrine, was represented in somewhat extreme form by the so-called Club of Rome's apocalyptic forecasts of doom for the human race within about a century if the exponential growth in population, resource use, and pollution continued at current rates.

Faith in technological advance

On the other side of the doomsday debate was a good part of the economics profession. The economists relied chiefly, as they traditionally had done ever since they slew the dragon of Malthusian population theory, upon technological advance. For example, at a symposium on the limits to growth at Lehigh University in 1973 Professor Robert M. Solow of MIT argued that the price system would most likely assure a long-run exponential increase in the *productivity of natural resources*. He and many others also contended that technological advance would no doubt continue to find cheaper substitutes for dwindling natural resources; that is, it would create essentially new resources to replace exhausted natural ones. Since technological progress was not subject to diminishing returns (indeed might be self-reinforcing), its onward march could even accelerate the creation of new possibilities for natural-resource substitution. While economists granted that the status of future generations should be considered in calculating the costs of present natural-resource utilization, they accused the conservationists and their allies of having a fixation on

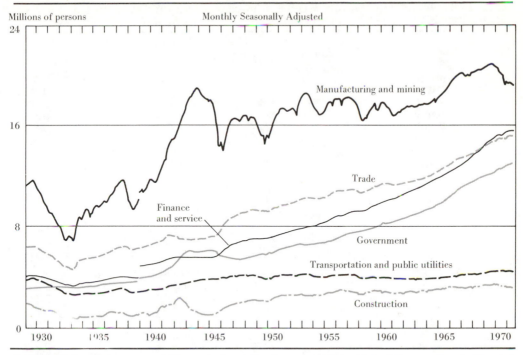

Figure 26–2. **Components of Nonagricultural Employment.** Source: Federal Reserve Board, *Historical Chart Book.*

husbanding the existing physical stock of every natural resource.

As for pollution connected with resource use, the economists recommended such things as the formulation of a national energy policy, support for research by such competent institutions as Resources for the Future, greater investment in technological research and development, and strengthening the work of the Federal Water Pollution Control Administration, the National Air Pollution Control Administration, the Bureau of Solid Wastes Management, and the Environmental Protection Agency. Through such means and agencies the true social costs of economic growth could be internalized into the private cost calculations of business firms and households. Lastly, it was emphasized that the United States, at least, was already close to a zero population growth rate.

Neither side in the doomsday debate was likely to "win" in the foreseeable future. But that was not the important thing. What was important was the public airing of the issues and the likely fruitful effects of the debate on the advance of ideas and the furtherance of policy measures. Not the least among the side effects was making the optimum family size a public issue.

THE MAJOR INDUSTRIAL SECTORS

Technological advance and production growth were interwoven with significant changes in the industrial structure of the economy after World War II. One way of viewing the economy's production structure is from the employment standpoint.

Manufacturing employment

The largest single nonfarm sector was manufacturing (mining employment was less than one million, and declining). Manufacturing employment was extremely sensitive to cyclical changes in the depression, and enjoyed an

TABLE 26–2. WAGE AND SALARY WORKERS IN NONAGRICULTURAL
ESTABLISHMENTS, 1929–1975 (ALL EMPLOYEES; THOUSANDS OF PERSONS)

| | | MANUFACTURING | | | | |
YEAR	TOTAL WAGE AND SALARY WORKERS	TOTAL	DURA-BLE GOODS	NON-DURA-BLE GOODS	MIN-ING	CON-TRACT CON-STRUC-TION
1929	31,339	10,702	—	—	1,087	1,497
1933	23,711	7,397	—	—	744	809
1939	30,618	10,278	4,715	5,564	854	1,150
1940	32,376	10,985	5,363	5,622	925	1,294
1941	36,554	13,192	6,968	6,225	957	1,790
1942	40,125	15,280	8,823	6,458	992	2,170
1943	42,452	17,602	11,084	6,518	925	1,567
1944	41,883	17,328	10,856	6,472	892	1,094
1945	40,394	15,524	9,074	6,450	836	1,132
1946	41,674	14,703	7,742	6,962	862	1,661
1947	43,881	15,545	8,385	7,159	955	1,982
1948	44,891	15,582	8,326	7,256	994	2,169
1949	43,778	14,441	7,489	6,953	930	2,165
1950	45,222	15,241	8,094	7,147	901	2,333
1951	47,849	16,393	9,089	7,304	929	2,603
1952	48,825	16,632	9,349	7,284	898	2,634
1953	50,232	17,549	10,110	7,438	866	2,623
1954	49,022	16,314	9,129	7,185	791	2,612
1955	50,675	16,882	9,541	7,340	792	2,802
1956	52,408	17,243	9,834	7,409	822	2,999
1957	52,894	17,174	9,856	7,319	828	2,923
1958	51,363	15,945	8,830	7,116	751	2,778
1959	53,313	16,675	9,373	7,303	732	2,960
1960	54,234	16,796	9,459	7,336	712	2,885
1961	54,042	16,326	9,070	7,256	672	2,816
1962	55,596	16,853	9,480	7,373	650	2,902
1963	56,702	16,995	9,616	7,380	635	2,963
1964	58,331	17,274	9,816	7,458	634	3,050
1965	60,815	18,062	10,406	7,656	632	3,186
1966	63,955	19,214	11,284	7,930	627	3,275
1967	65,857	19,447	11,439	8,008	613	3,208
1968	67,951	19,781	11,626	8,155	606	3,306
1969	70,442	20,167	11,895	8,272	619	3,525
1970	70,920	19,349	11,195	8,154	623	3,536
1971	71,216	18,572	10,597	7,975	603	3,639
1972	73,711	19,090	11,006	8,084	622	3,831
1973	76,833	20,054	11,814	8,240	638	4,028
1974	78,337	20,017	11,838	8,179	672	3,984
1975	77,668	18,344	10,676	7,668	745	3,455

Source: U.S. *Economic Report of the President,* January, 1976, p. 282

upsurge after the start of World War II. But after the war the growth of manufacturing employment was sluggish. If supervisory, professional, technical, and managerial employees in manufacturing are segregated from blue-collar production workers, the record shows very little rise in blue-collar employment between 1947 and 1974. The same overall sluggishness was found in the important transportation, public utilities, and construction sectors. These were all industries that had featured prominently in the economic development of the country in the latter part of the nineteenth century, when industrialization was the keynote.

The rise in service employment

The most striking aspect of nonfarm employment change after 1945, as seen in Table 26–2, was the great absolute and relative rise in so-called service employment: wholesale and retail trade, finance and services narrowly defined, and government. When combined, these

TABLE 26–2. *Continued*

TRANS-PORTA-TION AND PUBLIC UTILI-TIES	WHOLE-SALE AND RETAIL TRADE	FI-NANCE, INSUR-ANCE, AND REAL ESTATE	SERV-ICES	GOVERNMENT	
				FED-ERAL	STATE AND LOCAL
3,916	6,123	1,509	3,440	533	2,532
2,672	4,755	1,295	2,873	565	2,601
2,936	6,426	1,462	3,517	905	3,090
3,038	6,750	1,502	3,681	996	3,206
3,274	7,210	1,549	3,921	1,340	3,320
3,460	7,118	1,538	4,084	2,213	3,270
3,647	6,982	1,502	4,148	2,905	3,174
3,829	7,058	1,476	4,163	2,928	3,116
3,906	7,314	1,497	4,241	2,808	3,137
4,061	8,376	1,697	4,719	2,254	3,341
4,166	8,955	1,754	5,050	1,892	3,582
4,189	9,272	1,829	5,206	1,863	3,787
4,001	9,264	1,857	5,264	1,908	3,948
4,034	9,386	1,919	5,382	1,928	4,098
4,226	9,742	1,991	5,576	2,302	4,087
4,248	10,004	2,069	5,730	2,420	4,188
4,290	10,247	2,146	5,867	2,305	4,340
4,084	10,235	2,234	6,002	2,188	4,563
4,141	10,535	2,335	6,274	2,187	4,727
4,244	10,858	2,429	6,536	2,209	5,069
4,241	10,886	2,477	6,749	2,217	5,399
3,976	10,750	2,519	6,806	2,191	5,648
4,011	11,127	2,594	7,130	2,233	5,850
4,004	11,391	2,669	7,423	2,270	6,083
3,903	11,337	2,731	7,664	2,279	6,315
3,906	11,566	2,800	8,028	2,340	6,550
3,903	11,778	2,877	8,325	2,358	6,868
3,951	12,160	2,957	8,709	2,348	7,248
4,036	12,716	3,023	9,087	2,378	7,696
4,151	13,245	3,100	9,551	2,564	8,227
4,261	13,606	3.225	10,099	2,719	8,679
4,311	14,099	3,381	10,622	2,737	9,109
4,435	14,704	3,562	11,228	2,758	9,444
4,504	15,040	3,687	11,621	2,731	9,830
4,457	15,352	3,802	11,903	2,696	10,192
4,517	15,975	3,943	12,392	2,684	10,656
4,646	16,665	4,075	12,986	2,663	11,079
4,699	17,010	4,161	13,508	2,725	11,561
4,499	16,950	4,222	13,997	2,748	12,023

service activities employed 22.7 million wage and salary workers in 1950 and 50 million in 1975, a rise of 120 percent compared with a 72 percent rise in total nonfarm wage and salary workers. The fastest growing category was government employment, with state and local government leading federal civilian employment by a wide margin. Most of this increase is attributable to employment in education. While federal civilian workers increased, the increase was only 41 percent between 1950 and 1974, so the federal civilian *share* of total nonfarm employment declined from 4.3 percent to 3.5 percent—a trend no doubt surprising to many. "Big government" on the federal level meant largely military employment (including the Department of Defense).

Growth patterns in manufacturing production

Analysis of the growth pattern in the nonfarm economy according to production shows broadly similar trends. However, productivity trends differed among the sectors, so that manufacturing, for example, grew relatively more in output terms than in terms of employment. The service sectors (excluding transport and communications) had poor productivity performances, so their employment growth roughly coincided with their output growth.

The manufacturing sector as a whole, with a net output of over $291 billion in 1972, accounted for about 30 percent of the national income throughout the quarter century after the end of World War II. While this was easily the largest activity on the basis of any of the usual structural classifications of the economy, it probably understates the importance of manufacturing. It was in this sector that almost all the reproducible capital goods, outside of construction, were produced; and those capital goods embodied a substantial portion of the strategic advances in knowledge that came to account for the bulk of the productivity rise in the system. Producers' durable equipment, fabricated entirely within the manufacturing sector, accounted for 60 percent of all gross private investment other than housing construction in 1974. The previous review of major technological innovations, most of them involving manufactured products, further highlights the critical role of this activity in economic development as usually conceived. Moreover, American manufactures accounted for between two-thirds and three-fourths of the country's total exports and over one-fifth of world exports of manufactured products in the late 1960s. The home-appliance segment of the industry had transformed the character of home life and household work. And the motor-vehicle group, the largest of all, shaped the pace and quality of American life, for good and evil, to an extent probably unapproached by any other commodity-producing activity. Thus, although many social observers, prompted by the great expansion of public and private service functions, and the obvious termination of the historical industrialization process, spoke of our postindustrial society, manufacturing was still crucial to both the economy and the standard of living.

Trends in trade and services

Wholesale and retail trade and services, those heterogeneous havens of both insecure small enterprise and multi-outlet corporations, including the chain supermarket, just held their own in the national economy for a quarter century. As represented by share of national income, the combined group accounted for ex-

actly 26 percent in both 1950 and 1973. But there were many internal shifts within trade; for example, the exodus of retail trade out of central cities and into the suburbs (along with population). A surprising change within trade as a whole reversed longer run trends and recorded a relative gain in wholesale as compared with retail trade. The gain was paced by manufacturers' sales branches and offices.

The multifarious service lines expanded sales much faster than wholesale and retail trade. At the end of the 1960s the big service activities, in terms of income originating (which is determined by price as well as output), were medical and other health services, and miscellaneous business and professional services, including advertising. But advertising did not grow as rapidly as the other components of business and professional services. The very rapid price increases in medical care accounted for much of the rise in income in that sector. The finance, insurance, and real estate sector grew rapidly in the 1950s but in the 1960s seemed to have lost some of its dynamism.[40]

Trends in transportation

Transportation, taken as a business activity (that is, excluding personal automobile transportation), was a laggard sector. Its gross output in physical terms rose only 32 percent between 1947 and 1965.[41] So far as land transport is concerned, the totals are deceptive, however, because of the failure of the railroads to grow, together with the great weight their declining relative share still represented in total freight traffic. Inland waterway traffic saw a moderate absolute increase and no relative increase. The fast growers were both regulated and unregulated intercity trucking, oil pipelines, and, of course, airlines, where the great bulk of the traffic was passenger rather than freight. Airline freight traffic in 1950 was still less than 1 percent of the volume of intercity freight traffic. But domestic revenue passenger-miles flown had grown almost astronomically, from 10 billion in 1950 to 133 billion in 1972. Oil pipeline transport grew substantially.

Railroad employment suffered an almost catastrophic decline from slightly under 1.25

[40]Sheldon W. Stahl, ''The Service Sector: Where the Action Is,'' Federal Reserve Bank of Kansas City, *Monthly Review,* March 1970, p. 7.

[41]Victor R. Fuchs, *The Service Economy* (New York: National Bureau of Economic Research, Columbia University Press, 1968), p. 209, Table C-3. The increase was 83 percent between 1950 and 1972.

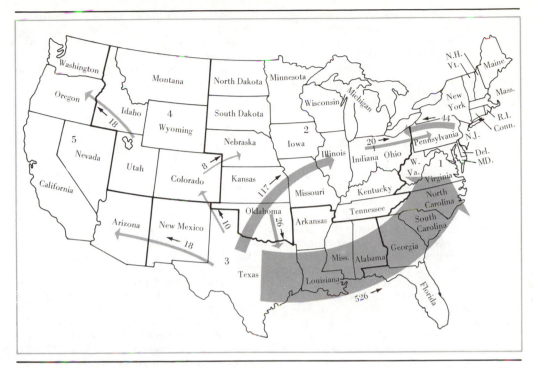

Figure 26–3. Products Flow by Pipeline in 1971 Between PAD Districts (millions of barrels). Source: The Oil and Gas Journal, August 14th, 1972.

million in 1950 to only 555,000 in 1971. The consolidation of rail systems and abandonment of many lines, together with loan guarantees under the Transportation Act of 1958 and enormous federal subsidies, still left most roads in virtual bankruptcy. With the formation of Amtrak in the mid-1970s, maintenance of railway passenger traffic had clearly become a government responsibility, and could not be treated as profit-making private enterprise in any traditional sense. Yet nationalization, the route taken long ago by many European countries, did not appear near as a socially acceptable solution in the American political climate.

The merchant marine

The story of the U.S. merchant marine is, like that of the railroads, one of decline, albeit much less drastic, after World War II. The deadweight tonnage of active U.S. flag merchant vessels in all trade areas fell from 13.8 million in 1950 to 12.8 million in 1973, with the drop in the foreign trade more drastic than that in the domestic. Despite vast construction and operation subsidies based on various alleged commercial advantages, national security demands, and balance-of-payments arguments, the gross

tonnage of merchant ships completed in U.S. shipyards after the war was insufficient for replacement. Employment on U.S. flag merchant vessels was 56,629 in 1950 and only 37,580 in 1970. Most of the operating subsidies went into wages, and in 1969 subsidies covered nearly a quarter of the total operating expenses of U.S. cargo vessels.[42] Yet foreign ships and shipping services continued to increase relative to American. This decline induced the Nixon administration in 1970 to launch a fresh subsidy program to rebuild and revitalize the country's merchant marine, starting with 300 additional vessels including several 250,000-ton supertankers. But as the program got under way it was already clear that scarce shipyard capacity and spiraling construction costs would offer serious impediments to fulfillment.

Transportation employment is much greater than employment in public utilities, and trans-

[42]See Gerald R. Jantscher, "Federal Aids to the Maritime Industry," in Joint Economic Committee, *Economics of Federal Subsidy Programs,* pt. 6: "Transportation Subsidies," 93d Cong., 1st sess., February 26, 1973 (Washington, D.C.: U.S. Government Printing Office, 1973), p. 763.

portation output is greater still. Hence transportation's declining employment record almost engulfs the moderately rising trend in communications and other public utilities. In terms of production, between 1947 and 1965, as Victor R. Fuchs has estimated, while the transportation industries grew by only 32 percent, com-munications and public utilities increased a whopping 258 percent. Thus, with moderately growing employment, communications and public utilities activities exhibited a tremendous advance in productivity (production per worker).

HOUSING AND HOUSING POLICY

While the construction industry is relatively small in terms of employment—3.6 million, or about 5 percent of all nonfarm wage and salary workers in 1973—the industry much increased the total of jobs it provided between 1950 and 1973. This was a strong employment growth record, but contract construction was important for other reasons. In the first place, it accounted for almost half of all investment in the economy in 1974. In the second place, it served two very vital categories of demand. One was the demand for commercial, industrial, and public buildings and for other, heavier construction such as highways and bridges. The other demand category was dwellings.

The pattern of
residential construction

The pattern of the large residential construction segment provides a third reason for the economic importance of the construction industry. The pattern was strongly cyclical, but because of the peculiar linkage between lower interest rates in general recessions and the accompanying flow of deposits into mortgage loan institutions, the housing construction cycle ran counter to the general business cycle, thus acting as a rough stabilizer for the economy.[43] On the other hand, performance of that countercyclical role meant depriving society of a steadily enlarged supply of dwellings, as in the housing crises of 1966 and 1969–1970, when housing starts dropped off because deposit thrift institutions were unable to pay sufficiently competitive interest rates to attract new funds.

Trends in housing

Private nonfarm dwelling construction averaged about one-half of all private construction, some 30 percent of gross private domestic investment, and between 4 and 5 percent of GNP. Housing is a major item in consumer budgets and is a basic component of the level of living and the quality of life. Following the low levels of construction during the depression and World War II, pent-up demand and government assistance induced a rapid rise in the 1950s. As in the construction boom of the 1920s, the number of housing starts each year exceeded the average annual number of new households formed, the latter being one of the main ways in which population growth influences the demand for housing. The excess continued to pile up the supply of housing units faster than demand for almost all years between 1950 and 1970. The square footage of the single-family house component of the total also rose until 1971. However, in the late 1960s the numbers of this component declined relatively from 57 percent in 1964 to 45 percent in 1970,[44] and apartments and mobile homes—both shorter on floor space—increased in importance. Mobile homes, produced in the manufacturing sector rather than the construction industry, experienced a phenomenal growth over this six-year period, from 11 percent of the total number of new dwellings to 22 percent (401,000 units in 1970).

Of the total stock of dwellings of all types, and ignoring quality, one-fourth had been built in the 1960s and nearly one-half after 1950. The heaviest new construction took place in the suburbs, where one-third of the housing stock was post-1960. By way of sharp contrast, the densely populated central cities reported only 18 percent of the dwellings (with few sites for mobile homes) newly constructed in the same period.[45]

Public housing and
mortgage underwriting

The inability of the private residential construction industry to build housing for the lower-income strata induced major federal intervention into the housing market during the Great Depression. This intervention has contin-

[43]Chase Manhattan Bank, *Business in Brief,* June 1972.

[44]Robert O. Harvey, "The New Crack in the Picture Window," *Illinois Business Review,* 29, no. 4 (April 1972): 6.

[45]*Illinois Business Review,* 29, no. 9 (September 1972) p. 9.

ued up to the present time. In many European countries such intervention took the form of the construction of publicly owned apartments and other types of dwellings. The United States did embark upon a small federally supported public housing program yielding about 35,000 units annually. Under this program there were 1.15 million units in management as of December 31, 1974. The program was carried out under the Housing Act of 1949 and administered by the Public Housing Administration. It was fraught with inconsistent goals and enormously costly administrative failures.[46] The government did also provide some funds for community development and rent subsidies. But these were minor efforts, and the chief federal interventionist measures were the underwriting, through the provision of a secondary mortgage market, of home mortgage loans.

Housing agencies

The chief agencies designed to stimulate housing supply or demand and to promote homeownership were administered through five constituent bodies by the Housing and Home Finance Agency, established in 1946. One of the most important of the five was the older (1938) Federal National Mortgage Association ("Fannie Mae"). Others were the Federal Housing Administration and the Veterans Administration. In 1968 Fannie Mae was converted into a government-sponsored private organization and replaced by the Government National Mortgage Association ("Ginnie Mae"), an agency armed with new underwriting powers and a new type of loan paper. The common characteristic and avowed purpose of all such agencies is well summarized by Philip H. Davidson:

> . . . they have provided a more effective channel between the typical mortgage loan and the highly competitive capital markets than existed in the past, especially during tight money periods. For years, the traditional mortgage loan, with all of its unstandardized features, has had great difficulty competing for funds whenever credit conditions tightened. . . . The development of an effective secondary market has helped to channel more funds into residential mortgages than ever before.[47]

In other words, federal underwriting has tried to compensate for the fact that housing has had to depend upon whatever loan money was left over after most other loan demands were met. The magnitude of this underwriting may be gauged to some extent by the fact that in the mid-1960s, 38 percent of the total nonfarm residential mortgage debt carried federal insurance or guarantees.[48] In 1970, of 793,000 new privately owned one-family houses, 44 percent were either insured by the Federal Housing Administration or guaranteed by the Veterans Administration. This no doubt helped solve the new-home financing problem for many people, but not for the poor, for whom only 33,000 new publicly owned housing units were intended, or for the low-income nonpoor. The median price of a new home in 1970 was about $27,000, but it was authoritatively estimated that nearly half of all American families could not pay more than $15,000 for a new home.[49] In his *Second Annual Report on National Housing Goals* to Congress on April 2, 1970, Nixon clearly indicated, as had been declared explicitly in the 1968 Housing Act, that the 1949 Housing Act goal of a decent home for every American family had by no means been realized. It devolved upon the construction industry in the 1970s to cope with this long-standing, enormous task.

AGRICULTURE AND FARM POLICY

The phenomenal transformation of American agriculture in the quarter century following World War II was unparalleled in any previous period of equal length. Two closely connected events were the most dramatic of all: the massive reduction in the farm population by 1 million between 1950 and 1973, and the incredible rise in farm output per man-hour of 6 percent per year. No other major sector, with

[46]Eugene Smolensky and J. Douglas Gomery, "Efficiency and Equity Effects in the Benefits from the Federal Housing *Program* in 1965," in U. S. Congress, Joint Economic Committee, *Benefit-Cost Analyses of Federal Programs*, 92d Cong., 2d sess., January 2, 1973 (Washington, D.C.: U.S. Government Printing Office, 1973), pp. 144–177.

[47]Federal Reserve Bank of Richmond, *Monthly Review*, September 1972, p. 6.

[48]Federal Reserve Bank of Richmond, *Monthly Review*, August 1966, p. 7.

[49]Federal Reserve Bank of Cleveland, *Economic Commentary*, October 26, 1970, p. 3.

the possible exception of communications and public utilities, could vie with this labor productivity performance of the agricultural sector.

Farm population trends

The propulsion of the farm population into the already crowded cities of the country greatly aggravated the fiscal problems of metropolitan government and considerably augmented urban welfare and relief loads. At the same time, the associated drop of almost 4 million in farm employment added substantially to the rate of increase of the nonfarm labor force. By 1974 the farm population was down to less than 10 million, or only 4.4 percent of the total population; and agricultural employment was only 4 percent of the total labor force. Of 3.46 million persons in the farm labor force, 1.15 million were wage and salary workers and only 1.81 million "self-employed" workers (presumably farmers). This was a very different kind of society from that of only 35 years previously, when one person in every four lived on a farm. Now there were less than 3 million farms, with almost all of the decline, except for some important changes in the census definition of a farm, accounted for by the elimination of small farms.

The decline in the number of farms, farmers, and farm workers was by far the most striking in the South. These years in agriculture wrought the greatest rate of farm tenancy reduction in history, and witnessed all but the elimination of the black sharecropper as the South experienced an industrial renaissance and blacks migrated by the tens of thousands to southern, northern, and western cities.

Farm production

So enormously efficient were the remaining 3 million farms in the nation as a whole that they produced all the agricultural products for domestic consumption and net farm exports; and one farm worker, who supplied 15.5 persons with such products in 1950, supplied 52 people in 1972. Certainly in terms of standard concepts of production, the world had never known such a productive commercial agriculture.

Actually, 3 million very much overstates the number of productively significant farms. Elimination and acquisition of small farms by larger commercial enterprises went far toward raising concentration in agriculture and transforming it into a semi-industrial type of activity. In agriculture as in industry there has long existed a dichotomy between large and small enterprise.

This may be appreciated from the 1974 data on farm sizes, which show that the largest 17 percent of all farms, rather less than 500,000, received 60 percent of the total realized net income of agriculture, while at the other extreme, the smallest classes of farms, making up 63 percent of all farms by value of sales, accounted for only 15.8 percent of aggregate realized net income.[50] There were 1.77 million "farms" in 1974 with annual value of sales below $20,000. Clearly the other 1.03 million farms could have absorbed the total market of these tiny units without much adjustment required.

The riddle of the rise in productivity

How was the almost revolutionary productivity performance in output per man-hour accomplished in American agriculture in only 25 years? The general answer is both simpler and perhaps less glamorous than might be expected. Total gross farm production was growing slowly, at around 1.3 percent a year, between 1950 and 1973 — about what could be expected in view of the close link between population growth (1.4 percent a year) and the roughly equivalent demand growth for food products. Exports of farm products were a slightly buoyant influence on the growth of demand in the 1950s, reaching 13.6 percent of the total in 1960, and by 1973 exports were 20.5 percent of total utilization. Production for exports commanded about one crop-acre in every four. Since labor input was reduced more than half, and total crop and other land used for production declined slightly, the riddle of productivity rise is solved through recognition of two factors: increased capital use and technological advances.

Capital and technology

There were substantial increases in the use of mechanical power and machinery, feed, seed, and — the most rapidly growing — fertilizer and liming materials. Inputs of government services, such as research, technical assistance, and subsidies, also rose notably. These shifts greatly raised the ratio of farm production inputs purchased to on-the-farm inputs, making nonfarm agricultural business activities — activities serving agriculture — ever more important in farm productivity. They also made farming

[50]Bickel, "Revolutions in American Agriculture," Fed. Res. Bank Kansas City, *Monthly Review*, June 1973, p. 9, Table 4; and Statistical Abstract, 1975.

much more capital-intensive. Thus agricultural production was becoming more and more like industrial production.

The shift toward more capital use reduces the meaningfulness of our earlier output-per-man-hour measure of productivity rise. If one were to calculate the productivity rise inclusive of all inputs — labor, farm real estate, and all varieties of capital — the rise would of course be much more moderate, only 1.4 percent a year, contrasted with the earlier 6 percent rise in labor productivity. But such a figure is still good compared to the performance in other, nonfarm sectors. This 1.4 percent annual rise in production per unit of all farm inputs is a rough measure of the output-raising effects of all kinds of technical and qualitative improvements in the agricultural arts. For example, already between 1920 and 1950 about 65 million acres of farmland were released from the production of feed for draft animals by virtue of the increased use of tractors, trucks, and other farm machinery. The elimination of much burdensome hand labor, the greater use of skilled labor, continuous production of hybrid corn in narrower rows, extensive application of herbicides and pesticides (whose adverse social effects, especially in the case of DDT, increasingly became a cause for alarm), conversion to hybrid grain sorghum, irrigation, the spread of contour and strip farming, the growth of the specialized feed lot for livestock and poultry (in contrast to industry's more product-diversified firm), and the rise in level of farm-management training — all these and many more technological developments[51] contributed to both the rise in total farm productivity and the vast changes in structure and function in American agriculture.

The unprosperous farmers

Some 470,000 relatively prosperous farm firms as of 1974 did not represent all of American agriculture. A million and a half small farms and 5 million people living on farms represented a different kind of rural world. The incidence of poverty was twice as great in agriculture as outside it. Large numbers, as elsewhere in the economy, lived in substandard housing and received a substandard education. Returns to farm labor and the small-farm entrepreneur were much lower than comparably skilled workers received in the nonfarm economy. While official farm unemployment rates were comparatively low, disguised unemployment,

like underutilized land and capital, was high. A greatly inflated trend of farmland prices relative to other prices made it ever more unlikely that young people could enter farming as a career. Rural towns were in dire fiscal straits and their social services were deteriorating.

Federal farm policy

Some of this dichotomy in the welfare levels of farming and farm people could be attributed to a federal farm policy based on what Marion Clawson has called the "production-control, price-support, storage trinity," with its greater emphasis on property values than on the value of people.[52] It will be recalled that the extensive farm program was inaugurated by the New Deal, which unlike the earlier Republican price-support efforts, used output restriction under the 1933 Agricultural Adjustment Act to bolster selected basic farm-product prices. Through such price supports, implemented by government acquisition and storage of surpluses and the subsidized disposal of some of the surplus abroad under Public Law 480 (1954), it was hoped that farm incomes would approach parity (1910–1914 levels as compared with nonfarm incomes). But the fundamental approach was restriction through control of acreage cultivated. As Clawson points out, this meant that the government was concerned with land as a factor of production, and for all practical purposes ignored labor, fixed capital, and current capital inputs such as fertilizers. The long-run effects were, as we might expect, to stimulate the ordinary business tendencies to substitute capital for labor, raise productivity, and increase output.

This added stimulus was further bolstered by many contradictory, technology-furthering activities of the Department of Agriculture itself, such as Experiment Station research, marketing research, other agricultural extension services, subsidies for irrigation and flood control, plant and animal disease control, and pesticides regulation. Furthermore, the distribution of price-support payments and loans was distinctly partial to the larger firms, thus again quickening the pace at which differentiation by size within the sector proceeded, with consequent acceleration of the process of poverty creation and eventual expulsion of marginal firms at the low-income end of the size array. Before the mid-1970s no limit was placed upon the amount of

---

[51]See ibid., pp. 4–6.

[52]Marion Clawson, "Contrasts and Choices in American Agriculture," *Resources for the Future, Annual Report,* 1967, p. 18.

price-support payments that could be made to any one farmer in any one year.

Monopolistic pricing in agriculture

The philosophy of the farm program was and remains based upon the premise that "agriculture should not be expected to operate with a free market in an economic environment that is characterized by inflexibility and administered prices."[53] In other words, monopolistic pricing is acknowledged as pervasive in the nonfarm economy, and such acknowledgment requires that the government assist the multifirm farm industry to practice monopolistic price administration in self-defense. Monopolistic planning is thus spread throughout the economy, and many other cases of this kind could be cited, such as minimum resale price laws (finally, after over 40 years, made unenforceable in 1976), public utility pricing, and the legalization of cartels in the export market under the 1918 Webb-Pomerene Act.

Price supports

There was general agreement during the postwar years that the acreage allotments and marketing quotas provided for in the 1938 Agricultural Adjustment Act were adequate to achieve quantitative supply-demand balance. Attention was focused rather upon the appropriate mandatory price-support levels for the relevant products, usually cotton, corn, wheat, rice, tobacco, peanuts, dairy products, wool, and feed grains.[54] The total of market sales under some kind of price support amounted to from 40 to 44 percent of total farm marketings between 1950 and 1973. The object was to stabilize farm prices and income in a "fair" relation to other sectors of the economy. But, as may be seen in Figure 26–4, the indexes of adjusted prices received by farmers were typically lower than the indexes of prices of nonfarm products typically bought by farmers. The usual rebuttal to the apparent implications of such an evolving discrepancy in price indexes is that the prices-paid index is not adjusted for

presumed quality improvement, whereas there was little quality change in farm commodities.

In any case, a sharp controversy began in the Congress in 1954 over the issue of whether farm parity could best be attained by high, fixed price levels or by "flexible" price supports— flexible meaning farm prices that were somewhere below 100 percent of parity.[55] The farm legislation of 1954 and the several enactments in later years represented a compromise; that is, varying degrees of flexibility on different products were introduced. In 1956 farm legislation inaugurated the "soil bank" method of controlling acreage cultivated. This program paid farmers for renting a part of their allotted productive acreage to the government, or for retiring acreage or even whole farms from production. Clearly, potential supply was thought to exceed demand, and this continued to harass the farm economy, despite the ever higher costs of the government's restrictionist program.

A definite welfare element was insinuated into the surplus control and disposal policy by the Kennedy administration's food-stamp plan of 1961. This became a solid and important part of the nation's antipoverty effort. Persons participating increased enormously, from 633,000 in 1965 to 13.59 million in 1974, and the cost to the federal government rose from $33 million to $2.71 billion over the same period.

The Food and Agriculture Act of 1965

Some noteworthy modifications in policy were made in the Food and Agriculture Act of 1965. While most price-support and production programs were extended for a four-year period with little change (except for cotton), government price-support "loans" were set at or near world price levels rather than at the higher percentage-of-parity levels stipulated earlier. This reduced the cost of export subsidies. Also, there was heavier reliance upon voluntary rather than mandatory acreage diversion. The act explicitly recognized the existence of chronic excess capacity in agriculture. But planned restriction could backfire. Policies in the United States and elsewhere to avoid surpluses by acreage restriction, in the case of wheat for example, led to the 1972–1973 world wheat fiasco, when huge sales to the

[53]Gene L. Swackhamer, "Agricultural Outlook: Approach of the 1970's," *Federal Reserve Bank of Kansas City, Monthly Review,* January 1969, p. 4.

[54]The following brief review of policy alterations relies strongly upon U.S. Congress, House Committee on Agriculture, *Government Subsidy Historical Review,* 91st Cong. 2d sess. (Washington, D.C.: U.S. Government Printing Office, 1970) chap. 6, "Agricultural Subsidy and Related Programs," prepared by Walter W. Wilcox.

[55]Parity meant the ratio of prices received to prices paid by farmers that obtained in the so-called golden age of the farmer, August 1909 through July 1914.

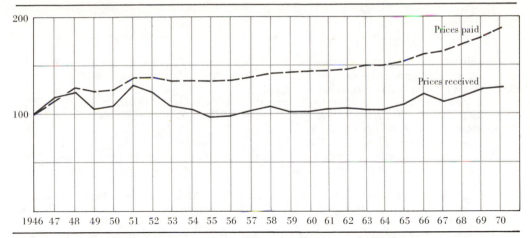

Figure 26–4. Indexes of Prices Received and Prices Paid by Farmers, 1946–1970 (1946 = 100). Source: U.S. Congress, House Committee on Agriculture, *Government Subsidy Historical Review*, 91st Cong., 2d sess., December 1970, (Washington, D.C.: U.S. Government Printing Office, 1970).

USSR suddenly transformed the U.S. and world supply situation from planned surplus reduction to crisis-level shortages.

The decline of farming as proportion of GNP

By 1973 government payments to farmers totaled $2.6 billion, or some 19 percent of the value of all farm marketings that were subject to some kind of price support. In the late 1960s all federal agricultural expenditure far exceeded the totals of federal aid for urban housing, or for education, or for health.[56] Yet farming as a part of the economy was becoming ever smaller. Farm gross product as a proportion of GNP, which amounted to about 7 percent in 1950, had slid to only 4 percent in 1973. Four percent! Probably few persons in the general public were aware of the extent of the decline. Of course, that 4 percent was mostly food, and food is vital. Yet it was not vital enough to arrest the waning political influence of the farm bloc in both the Congress and the state legislatures. It was urban problems that were ever more the center of attention as the economy moved through the 1970s.

SELECTED READINGS

*Belassa, Bela, ed., *Changing Patterns of Foreign Trade and Payments,* revised ed. (New York: Norton, 1970).

*Clayton, James L., ed., *The Economic Impact of the Cold War* (New York: Harcourt Brace Jovanovich, 1970).

Cochran, Thomas C., *American Business in the Twentieth Century* (Cambridge, Mass.: Harvard University Press, 1972).

Fuchs, Victor R., *The Service Economy* (New York: National Bureau of Economic Research, 1968).

*Galbraith, John Kenneth, *The New Industrial State,* 2nd ed., revised (Boston: Houghton Mifflin, 1972).

*Johnson, Arthur M., ed., *The American Economy: An Historical Introduction to the Problems of the 1970's* (New York: The Free Press, 1974).

Kendrick, John W., *Postwar Productivity Trends in the United States, 1948–1969* (New York: National Bureau of Economic Research, 1973).

[56]Clawson, "Contrasts and Choices," p. 19.

Machlup, Fritz, *The Production and Distribution of Knowledge in the United States* (Princeton, N. J.: Princeton University Press, 1962).

Mancke, Richard B., *The Failure of U.S. Energy Policy* (New York: Columbia University Press, 1974).

Peach, W. N., *The Energy Outlook for the 1980's,* a Study Prepared for the use of the Subcommittee on Economic Progress, Joint Economic Committee, U.S. Congress (Washington, D.C.: Government Printing Office, December 17, 1973).

*Reagan, Michael D., *The Managed Economy* (New York: Oxford University Press, 1963).

*Ruttan, Vernon W., Arley D. Waldo, and James P. Houck, eds., *Agricultural Policy in an Affluent Society* (New York: Norton, 1969).

*Ulmer, Melville J., *The Welfare State* (Boston: Houghton Mifflin, 1969).

U.S. Senate Committee on Banking and Currency, Subcommittee on Housing and Urban Affairs, *Congress and American Housing, 1892–1967,* 90th Cong., 2d Sess. (Washington, D.C.: Government Printing Office, February 1968).

U.S. House Committee on Banking and Currency, *Third Annual Report on National Housing Goals,* 92d Cong., 1st Sess., House Doc. No. 92–136 (Washington, D.C.: Government Printing Office, June 1971).

U.S. House Committee on Banking, Currency and Housing, Subcommittee on Housing and Community Development, *Evolution of Role of the Federal Government in Housing and Community Development,* 94th Cong., 1st Sess., Committee Print (Washington, D.C.: Government Printing Office, October 1975).

Vatter, Harold G., *The U.S. Economy in the 1950's* (New York: Norton, 1963).

*Wolozin, Harold, ed., *American Fiscal and Monetary Policy* (New York: Quadrangle, 1970).

We shall be concerned here with the public policies affecting the general conditions of life, and also with the actual material conditions, of the great majority. This necessarily means the low- and middle-income groups. The upper-income groups are usually presumed to enjoy material conditions sufficiently favorable to exempt them from most policy concerns regarding social welfare.

LABOR AND WELFARE

"Labor," in the broad sense of the term, may be linked with social welfare in general. Labor excludes the self-employed, proprietors, the higher ranks of the professions, and corporate managers. Of about 84 million persons in the civilian labor force in 1973, about 26 million were professional and technical workers, managers, officials and nonfarm proprietors, nonretail sales workers, and self-employed persons in farming. On this broad classification, the rest of the labor force and the laborers' families, accounting for between two-thirds and three-fourths of the total population, could be thought of as "labor" in the ordinary sense. At the minimum, the labor group in 1970 may be thought of as the following (in millions):

Clerical workers	*14.5*
Blue-collar workers	*29.2*
Service workers	*11.1*
Farm wage and salary workers	*.7*
Retail sales workers	*2.4*
Unemployed	*4.3*
	62.2

These figures exclude other family members. In addition, several million low-income retirees should be considered part of the group. It is the history of the material welfare of this group that has been the main concern of social welfare policy in the mixed economy.

The affluent society

While the segregation of certain socio-economic strata from the total population or labor force is essential in dealing with human welfare problems, much can be discovered by an initial review of what happened to certain aggregates over the quarter century of economic history following the end of World War II. While the *distribution* of the benefits of economic growth touches the heart of the welfare question, there can be no doubt that any advances in the aggregate will trickle down to some extent to almost everyone, even to those at the bottom. For example, it is of enormous welfare significance that real private household consumption per person (in 1958 dollars) rose from $1,520 in 1950 to $2,548 in 1974, a 68 percent increase. In 1974 prices, the consumption per capita was $4,139. With an average family size of 3.48, this meant total consumption per family of $14,404 for the year.

Such an average was widely acknowledged to be "affluent," a value-laden term justified by both history and contemporary international comparison. Within this average 99 percent of all homes were wired for electricity, one or more cars were owned by 80 percent of all households, all wired households had at least one television set, 98 percent of all households had washing machines, and all wired homes had refrigerators. Ninety-nine percent of all dwellings had some kind of heating system in 1973, and 96 percent of the occupied housing units had all the customary plumbing facilities, an increase from 84 percent in 1960. There was telephone service in 92 percent of all households, a rise from 62 percent in 1950.

Vital statistics

The crucial area of vital statistics told a similar story of material progress. Deaths of infants under one year old fell from 47 per 1000 live births in 1940 to 29 ten years later, and 18 in 1973. Maternal deaths per 100,000 live births from deliveries and complications of pregnancy, childbirth, and the puerperium, which had been a disgraceful 376 in 1940, plummeted to 83.3 in 1950 and 15 in 1973. While no progress was made with respect to the death rate between 1950 and the late 1960s, the crucial welfare index, expectation of life at birth, was raised from 62.9 years in 1940 to 68.2 in 1950 and 71.3 in 1973. Average life expectation for a white woman 20 years old was increased from 54.6 years in 1949 to 57.7 years in 1973, while for a man it rose notably less, from 49.5 to 50.5 years. Life expectancy for nonwhites was distinctly lower than for whites.

Education

In the sphere of education it was common during the period to refer to the education explosion. School expenditures at all levels, both public and private, more than doubled in ratio to GNP, from 3.4 percent in 1950 to 7.4 percent in 1974. Government expenditure on education expanded from 16 percent of general outlays in 1950 to over one-fifth in 1975. State and local governments, as we have seen, bore the great bulk of the responsibility for this vast educational effort. In higher education there

was a big shift from private to public, so that by 1972 about 75 percent of all undergraduate college students were in public institutions. Education was the chief reason for the very rapid growth in state and local expenditures, taxes, and employment. A million classroom teachers in elementary and secondary schools were added between 1955 and 1970.

Appraisal of the quality of the learning that came out of the education explosion is too complicated for treatment here, but in brute quantitative terms it is clear that Americans were much better educated at the end of the period than they were in 1940 or 1950. For example, the average (median) number of school years completed by all persons 25 years old and over was 8.6 in 1940, 9.3 in 1950, and 12.3 in 1973. In that same age group, 7.7 percent had completed four years or more of college in 1960, and 12.6 percent had achieved that level by 1973. While this represented a definite advance, there was clearly much room for further improvement.

Other indicators, other trends

These aggregate socioeconomic indicators provide a cursory impression of some of the more important conventionally defined overall benefits of economic growth. There were, of course, other overall indicators in which progress was minimal or absent. Cases in point were the increase in the incidence of mental illness, the decline in the number of hospital beds and active dentists per 1000 population, and the very slow growth in the number of physicians per 1000. The last trend was associated with a rise in physicians' fees of 120 percent between 1950 and 1970, compared with a rise of 61 percent in the overall consumer price index.[1] Nor do the rising indicators take account of the many adverse externalities connected with economic growth: land, air, water, and noise pollution, the loss of nature's amenities, the costs of natural-resource diminution shifted to unborn generations, and many other costs adversely affecting the quality of life.

DISTRIBUTION OF THE BENEFITS OF GROWTH

Aside from the failure of the country's impressive growth record in total output, in consumption, and in other respects to encompass all the material conditions of people's lives, and aside from the adverse ecological and other effects of economic development, there remained the question of how the benefits of growth were

distributed. In an incisive discussion of perspectives on growth in the less developed countries,

[1] If one goes back to 1950, however, the respective increases are 228 percent (all medical care) and 177 percent, the reduction in the gap being attributable to the lag in the rise of medical-care prices behind other prices during the World War II decade.

Mahbub ul Haq, a senior adviser to the World Bank, unfolds a critique of conventional development policies that has a direct bearing on the American experience in the postwar decades. He declares that those policies went astray in two important respects. Noting the extent of poverty in the Third World, Haq asserts that policy makers conceived of their task not as the eradication of poverty but as "the pursuit of certain high levels of income." That pursuit in the United States had still left one-eighth of its 210 million civilians in poverty in 1974. Second, these same policy makers assumed that "income distribution policies could be divorced from growth policies and could be added later to obtain whatever distribution" was desired.[2]

Social welfare expenditures

Such time-hallowed policies were without doubt predominant also in the United States. Not that a concern with distribution and poverty was completely absent. Social security and other income security programs became more pervasive as time passed. Social welfare expenditures under public programs, veterans' programs, education, housing, model cities, manpower training, food stamps, legal aid, and miscellaneous social welfare outlays expanded from 8.9 percent of GNP in 1950 to 18 percent in 1974. The two largest components were social insurance, largely a federal budget item, and education, mainly state and local. Social insurance outlays doubled between 1969 and 1974, mainly because of benefit increases that more than offset price inflation. Federal grants to state and local governments for social welfare purposes rose over 16-fold from 1950 to 1974, and as a proportion of the total receipts of such governments from their own sources they increased from 8.2 percent to 15 percent.

These were all parts of what came to be called the large and growing "grants economy," interwoven with the "exchange economy," an interpenetration distinguishing the new interventionist system and making obsolete all analyses of income distribution and welfare that confined themselves to the private economy alone. There was a definite welfare component in the government policies of the mixed economy, a component that to some extent placed a floor, as did the federal minimum wage, under the incomes of the low-income strata. This was true even though regressive taxes were widely used to finance welfare expenditures, and the floors were distressingly low; for example, $165

a month in medium-range Oregon in 1971 for an ADC family of four. Nevertheless, the number of families living below the official poverty line was gradually reduced.

The war on poverty

The so-called war on poverty, launched officially on March 16, 1964, by President Lyndon Johnson, also revealed a concern with the failure of economic growth to solve the distributive problem. Some claimed the program was a response to the frightening ferment in the black ghettos, the black upsurge in the South, and the generally spreading civil rights movement. Be that as it may, the heterogeneous antipoverty war, encompassing the community action programs, the Job Corps, VISTA, the Neighborhood Youth Corps, and various youth work-training programs, under the 1962 Manpower Development and Training Act, obligated over $9 billion of federal funds between 1964 and 1970. Aid to the poor in federal programs of all types totaled over $26 billion in 1974. The federal government also belatedly inaugurated a national health program for the elderly under the social security system in 1965.

In his January 1967 economic report, President Johnson, in the spirit of his Great Society perspective, responded to the widespread criticism of the existing welfare programs and to the growing interest in the proposal for a government-guaranteed minimum annual income for all Americans by proposing a study of the matter. Yet, aside from a few pilot projects designed to test the effect of income maintenance on work incentives, it remained for President Richard Nixon to officially propose a (most austere) income-maintenance system, a proposal that was later shelved as politically infeasible.

Despite all these antipoverty efforts, together with other, more minor measures, President Johnson could still most accurately declare in his message to Congress on the fiscal 1968 budget that "poverty remains an ugly scar on the nation's conscience." Economic growth there had been, but the distribution of income had scarcely changed, although the mixed economy's growing system of taxes and grants did transfer on balance some income from the nonpoor to the poor.[3] One student of income distribution concluded that "we have not taxed the rich to give to the poor; we have taxed both

[2] Agricultural Development Council, "Employment in the 1970's: A New Perspective," Reprint, October 1972, p. 3.

[3] See, e.g., Robert J. Lampman, "How Much Does the American System of Transfers Benefit the Poor?" reprinted in part in *Poverty in Affluence*, ed. Robert E. Will and Harold G. Vatter, 2nd ed. (New York: Harcourt Brace Jovanovich, 1970), pp. 56–58.

TABLE 27–1. PERCENT OF AGGREGATE INCOME RECEIVED BY EACH FIFTH OF FAMILIES, SELECTED YEARS, 1947–1974

INCOME RANK	1947	1960	1965	1969	1974
Lowest fifth	5.1	4.8	5.2		5.4
Second fifth	11.8	12.2	12.2	12.3	12.0
Middle fifth	16.7	17.8	17.8	17.7	17.6
Fourth fifth	23.2	24.0	23.9	23.7	24.1
Highest fifth	43.3	41.3	40.9	40.6	41.0
Total	100.0	100.0	100.0	100.0	100.0

Source: *Statistical Abstract*, 1975, p. 392, Table 636.

Note: The basis of computation here differs slightly from that in Table 1–4 (page 15), which computes money income only for 1947–1968.

the rich and the poor, and at least since 1940, contributed only a small fraction of the proceeds to the welfare of the poor."[4] Government programs had only a moderate impact on the overall distribution of income.[5] The distributive pattern remained highly skewed throughout the postwar period, and shifted in the lower ranks hardly at all. For example, the lowest 60 percent of all families, all of whom may readily enough be classified as "labor," received 33.8 percent of total family income in 1947 and 34.8 in 1972. The lowest 80 percent received 57 percent in 1947 and 59 percent in 1974. (See Table 27–1 on aggregate income distribution.)

Regional shifts in income distribution

Regional shifts in the distribution of income per person within the economy after World War II followed a broad pattern that had begun to emerge decades earlier. Regional incomes per capita converged more and more. Income growth was fastest in the southern and western regions. The fastest growing region in the 1960s was the Southeast, whose per capita income rose from 68 percent of the national average in 1950 to 84 percent in 1971. This represented a massive improvement in the average level of income. The extent to which this might have been attributed to the regional distribution of federal expenditures was difficult to determine, but it was noteworthy, by way of example, that the Southeast's share of the nation's personal income in fiscal 1970 was exceeded by its shares of National Aeronautics and Space Administration contracts, federal civilian and military wages, federal grants-in-aid, farm price

supports, veterans' payments, and social security transfers. A somewhat similar although less pervasive pattern existed in the Far West. Yet the regions did not experience any significant shifts in their personal income per capita positions relative to one another: High per capita income regions remained high, low ones remained low, including the fast-growing Southeast, which continued to be the lowest in the nation in 1971.

Incomes below the national average

Perhaps the most meaningful test of the distribution of the benefits of growth in a materially advanced society (and at the same time a measure of the possible reduction of poverty) is the percentage of income receivers that falls significantly below the average (median) income each year. One analyst found that between 1947 and 1965, one-fifth of all family income receivers had incomes that were consistently less than half the average family income.[6] A society or a public policy that was interested in transferring some of the fruits of economic growth to the large disadvantaged strata at the bottom of the income ladder would reduce the percentage falling below half (or some other arbitrary percentage) of the average. In other words, it would raise the floor under the incomes of the lowest strata.

Discrimination against nonwhites

Black Americans, with the possible exception of the Mexican Americans, remained the most materially disadvantaged major group. In an urban world, they became the most urban of all. In almost all respects, the 22 million

[4]Gabriel Kolko, quoted in Letitia Upton and Nancy Lyons, *Basic Facts: Distribution of Personal Income and Wealth in the United States* (Cambridge, Mass.: Cambridge Institute, May 1972), p. 2.

[5]Ibid., pp. 2–5.

[6]Victor R. Fuchs, "Redefining Poverty and Redistributing Income," reprinted in part in *Poverty in Affluence*, ed. Will and Vatter, pp. 14–18.

TABLE 27–2. MEDIAN INCOME OF FAMILIES, BY COLOR OF FAMILY HEAD, SELECTED YEARS, 1947–1974

YEAR	ALL FAMILIES	WHITE	NONWHITE	RATIO OF NONWHITES TO WHITE
1947	$ 3,031	$ 3,157	$1,614	51%
1950	3,319	3,445	1,869	54
1955	4,421	4,605	2,549	55
1960	5,620	5,635	3,233	55
1965	6,957	7,251	3,994	55
1969	9,433	9,794	6,191	63
1972	11,116	11,549	7,106	62
1974	12,836	13,356	8,265	62

Source: *Statistical Abstract, 1966* and *1975,* Tables 480 and 631 respectively.

blacks had lower economic status and poorer educational opportunities than whites. Of all American families living in standard metropolitan areas in 1972, about 61 percent of whites lived outside central cities but only 21 percent of the blacks lived outside those metropolitan areas. The famed problems of the central cities largely overlapped the problems of black Americans: pollution, slums, decaying neighborhoods, crime, inferior schools.

The median number of school years completed was 12.4 for whites and 10.7 for blacks in 1974. Nevertheless, this represented a relative gain for blacks over 1950. A similarly slight relative gain was recorded in median incomes: That for blacks was 54 percent of the white median in 1950, but had risen to 62 percent in 1974, as shown in Table 27–2. In the North, black heads of families under 24 years of age finally achieved parity with their white counterparts in money income in 1968. Black people, however, were inclined to emphasize the continuing discrepancy rather than its reduction. They felt much the same about the relative improvement in other respects, such as expectation of life, which at birth was still in 1973 only 65.9 years for blacks and 72.2 years for whites. In that same year the maternal mortality rate for nonwhites was still over 3.5 times the white rate, and infant mortality was 75 percent higher. Another of the more glaring differentials was the black unemployment rate, persistently twice that for whites.

The Mexican-Americans were another important minority experiencing extensive material and cultural deprivation. Approximately 5 million of these people were spread over the nation, the majority of the 9 million persons with Spanish surnames. Mexican-Americans were heavily concentrated in the Southwest and California. Their median family income in 1971 was only 70 percent of that for the rest of the population. In the southwestern states in that year, about 28 percent were below the poverty level. Unemployment rates ranged from one-fourth to three-fourths higher than the average in various states. Educational levels were distinctly below average. Of persons with Spanish surnames in the Southwest and California taken as a whole, between 43 and 62 percent, according to the states, had completed less than one year of high school. The range among states for those who had completed less than five years of elementary school was from 13 to 34 percent.

Market discrimination: women

The January 1973 *Annual Report of the Council of Economic Advisers to the President* contained a chapter surveying the changing role of women in the economy. This review was one response to the women's liberation movement and the larger effects of that movement among women generally. The report points to the well-known fact that there has long been a rising proportion of women in the total labor force and of "working" women (that is, working for compensation in the market) among all women of working age. The two proportions were about one-fourth in 1940. During the war years the proportions jumped to 30 and 36 percent respectively, then dropped slightly, only to rise again by the mid-1950s to their wartime levels. Jobs held by women accounted for two-thirds of the increase in total employment in the 1960s. By 1973, women made up 38 percent of the labor force, and over 44 percent of all women of working age were in the labor force.

These participation rates were far below those of men, but the long-run trend was unmistakable. The relative growth of public and private employment in the service activities was one reason for increased female participation. Another was the rise in real wages of workers over the years, a trend that made housework ever more costly in terms of the income forgone by not working in the market. One of the more striking facts about the postwar trend was that the increasing participation was almost entirely due to the addition of married women.

This trend sharpened the now public issue of subsidy for child-care centers, for despite women's spreading rejection of the exclusive homemaker role, and despite the long-term decline in the average number of children per family, child rearing remained the major barrier to young married women's participation in the market economy. Child rearing also contributed importantly to the curtailment and interruption of some women's work records outside the home. Rumors (but not statistics) of high job turnover rates among women employees, particularly those with children, furnished some employers with excuses for discrimination that reinforced women's culturally disadvantaged work backgrounds. Such encumbrances, plus powerful traditional images regarding women's proper role, still relegated them overwhelmingly to clerical jobs, factory jobs, and service occupations, and to earnings rates far below the rates for men performing similar tasks.

Female heads of households

Little progress was made regarding the occupational aspect, and there was some regression in the earnings aspect between the late 1950s and early 1970s.[7] The cultural and deliberate prejudice was particularly strong in the case of earnings of black women. For example, the median full-time, year-round personal income of black women who were heads of households was $4226 in 1973, compared with $6560 for similarly situated white women. But white or black, the problems of the 6 million woman-headed households in the early 1970s were especially acute and were often compounded by perverse regulation and administration of public assistance under the program of Aid to Families with Dependent Children.

Government action and female workers

Government was beginning to respond to some extent to women's agitation in the 1960s. The Equal Pay Act of 1963 required employers to pay the same wage for equally skilled work and responsibility (but typically they still did not). Title VII of the Civil Rights Act of 1964 prohibited discrimination in hiring, firing, and compensation (but despite some gains, such discrimination still continued). The federal Revenue Act of 1971 provided a much more liberal deduction for child-care expenses for working mothers than prevailed previously (but the deduction still did not even approach the cost of child care for most working mothers). And the Equal Rights Amendment to the Constitution, which passed the Senate on March 22, 1973, had still not been ratified by the requisite two-thirds of the states in the mid-1970s.

NUTRITION AND HEALTH

President Franklin Roosevelt, in his second inaugural address in January 1937, referred to "one-third of a nation . . . ill nourished." The validity of his reference during the worst depression years may not be doubted. But World War II with its full employment had improved matters greatly. Continued high employment and the diffusion of rising real income per capita after the war further reduced the extent of undernourishment in the country. Yet again, a penetrating look into the distributive picture reveals the usual extremes as late as the mid-1960s. For example, the Citizens' Board of Inquiry into Hunger and Malnutrition in the United States found extensive hunger and malnutrition, particularly among blacks and in rural areas of the South. The board found that "hunger and malnutrition exist in this country affecting millions of our fellow Americans and increasing in severity and extent from year to year, 'and taking their toll' in the form of infant death, organic brain damage, retarded growth and learning rates, increased vulnerability to disease, withdrawal, apathy, alienation, frustration and violence."[8] It was difficult to determine what the picture was in the mid 1970s, but there was no doubt that malnourishment due to repetitive periods of prolonged hunger, if not acute malnutrition, afflicted millions among the poor. As we saw in Chapter 26, participants in the federal food-stamp plan rose very strongly,

[7]Chase Manhattan Bank, "Sex Discrimination in the Labor Force," *Business in Brief*, no. 108 (February 1973).

[8]See the board's report, *Hunger, U.S.A.*, (Washington, D.C.: New Community Press, 1968), pp. 8–9. See also, U. S. Senate, Select Committee on Human Needs, 93d Cong., 2d Sess., *National Nutrition Policy Study, Report and Recommendation—VIII* (Washington, D.C.: Government Printing Office, June 1974).

yet other federal programs languished in terms of quantity of food disbursed.[9] The essential point, however, is that undernourishment could have been eliminated at comparatively small cost to the affluent society, but, like poverty, it was not.

Medicare and medicaid

In the sphere of health, passage by Congress of a hospitalization insurance program together with a voluntary supplementary medical insurance plan (SMI) in 1965 — for the aged only — fulfilled after 30 years an endorsement of such a program by President Franklin Roosevelt's Committee on Economic Security. Soon after that program went into effect on July 1, 1966, its hospitalization benefits under the Social Security Act ("medicare"), financed by the regular social security tax, covered almost all of the nation's 19 million people aged 65 and over. Over 90 percent of the persons in the hospital insurance program enrolled voluntarily in SMI. In addition, a companion piece of legislation in 1965, known as "medicaid," provided federal matching funds for states that set up programs to furnish medical services for the poor and medically indigent through public assistance channels. Federal, state, and local expenditures under medicaid rose from $1.7 billion in the fiscal year 1966 to $13 billion in 1975, and federal outlays under medicare increased from $4.6 billion in fiscal 1967 to $14.8 billion in 1975.

Much of this rise in government expenditures for health care was due to the inordinate rise in hospital costs and doctors' fees, but there could be no doubt that there was some improvement in the comprehensiveness of health care for the elderly and the poor. Meanwhile, private expenditures for health also continued to rise, and the total of private and public health-care expenditures as proportion of GNP increased from 4.6 percent in 1950 to 5.2 percent in 1960 and 7.7 percent in 1974.

The shortage of health-care personnel

The supply of physicians, dentists, and paramedical personnel had for decades not been keeping pace with need. Private provision of a service on the private market meant that at best the rising equilibrium price trend would always at any given time price many people out of the market. In addition, monopolistic factors were at work to restrict medical school capacity and

medical training. An emphasis on quality restricted the growth of training programs in the nursing and paramedical fields. Acute shortages beset hospital staffs and extended-care facilities in the late 1960s.[10] The ratio of 1 physician for every 562 persons in the resident population in 1972 compares favorably with the 1 to 767 in 1923, but the comparison fails to take into account the number of physicians in research, military service, and administration, and to allow for the substantial growth in specialization within the profession.[11] The Comprehensive Health Manpower Training Act and the Nurse Training Act, both passed in 1971, authorized institutional grants on a per student basis, designed to relieve the shortage of medical and hospital personnel by providing incentives to medical schools and other health-care training institutions to undertake enlarged educational programs.

Limitations of health care in the United States

These increases reflected the spreading public consensus that adequate health care is a matter of right, and should not be a function of income. The conviction stemmed partly from increased awareness of comprehensive national health programs in European and other countries, shockingly absent in the United States, an awareness whose significance was sharpened by the recognition that while the United States had the highest per capita income in the world, it did not have the lowest mortality rates or the best health levels in certain other respects. It also stemmed from the fact that health care is to a certain extent unique among all things consumed by the public: frequently it is literally a matter of life and death; its cost often looms so suddenly large that it becomes a financial catastrophe; and it varies enormously in quality and availability.

The distributive pattern of health care

The distributive pattern of health care left much to be desired. On the supply side, despite gains over time, public health programs discriminated against youth, the poor, migratory farm labor, blacks, and persons not in the labor market. Medical services were maldistributed

---

[9]*Statistical Abstract, 1972*, p. 83, Table 124.

[10]William F. Berry and James C. Daugherty, "A Closer Look at Rising Medical Costs," *Monthly Labor Review,* reprint no. 2590 (1968), p. 1.

[11]Ibid., p. 2.

geographically.[12] The shortage of physicians was particularly acute in rural areas. Residents of counties with 5 million or more population in the early 1970s had five times as many patient-care physicians per capita as did persons in counties with fewer than 50,000 inhabitants; and they had 15 times as many specialists per capita.

Many of the poor could not pay for the transportation necessary to secure health care, although during the late 1960s low-income groups made some progress relative to high-income receivers regarding the number of physician visits per capita. The poor were neverthe-

less still much less likely than the well-to-do to receive medical care in physicians' offices, generally tending to go to outpatient clinics of large hospitals, where they waited for hours before a harried physician could give them a few minutes of attention.

The state medicaid plans and services differed enormously, partly because of differences in eligibility requirements. In the early 1970s only half the states provided any coverage for the medically indigent under medicaid. Near-poor families might have most medical expenses covered in some states but be completely unprotected in others.

PRIVATE AND PUBLIC PENSIONS

Distribution was also a vital matter in the important pension field. There can be no doubt that the growth in the comprehensiveness of pensions and retirement benefits, from the noteworthy beginnings in the private and government pension movements in the 1920s through the New Deal's Social Security Act, was the most striking welfare achievement, next to the Employment Act, of the American economy in the twentieth century. Labor unions pioneered in retirement pensions. After World War II the labor unions demanded and got ever higher proportions of employee compensation per labor-hour in the form of fringe benefits, of which pensions were one of the most important. Legal sanction of pensions as an issue in collective bargaining was provided by the Supreme Court decision in the *Inland Steel Case* in 1949.

The extension of old-age retirement coverage under the Social Security Act to 77 million persons in 1973 nevertheless left protection sufficiently inadequate to encourage the spread of these private pension plans. With the usual variation from industry to industry and from firm to firm, the number of persons covered by such plans, including union pension systems, increased from 9.8 million in 1950 to 21.2 million in 1960 and 29 million in 1973. The greatest growth therefore came in the 1950s. State and local government retirement plans covered another 9 million in 1972.

Patterns of private pension fund investment

The vast pools of savings channeled through the great financial corporations holding these funds endowed them with great economic power in the nation's capital markets. Private insured (operated by insurance companies) and noninsured (operated by trustees, usually banks) pension reserves amounted to $180 billion in 1973 compared to $52 billion in 1960. The growth rate of the assets of private pension funds was much faster than those of public funds between 1950 and 1970. In the early 1970s Congress was becoming increasingly critical of the fact that private pension-fund investment policy favored corporate stocks in excessive amounts and neglected investment in socially desirable programs that were financially starved.

Vested rights in pension funds

Labor strove to achieve a vested right in its pension funds, so that a worker who left the job before he was eligible for a pension might still collect one when he did retire. Success in this area was varied. By 1967 about 70 percent of private pension plans had provisions for some kind of vesting, but only one-third had full vesting with ten years or less of service.

Private retirement plans not only lacked full vesting rights, but by the end of the 1960s still covered only half of all nongovernment employees. Furthermore, they discriminated against low-paid and temporary employees and restricted workers' mobility. Most plans gave inadequate protection against inflation. Congressional committees collected "reams of testimony about workers who were denied pen-

[12]The immediately following distributive points are taken from Charles L. Schultze, Edward R. Fried, Alice M. Rivlin, and Nancy H. Teeters (with Karen Davis), *Setting National Priorities: The 1973 Budget* (Washington, D.C.: Brookings Institution, 1972), pp. 219–226.

sions they thought they had earned, bankrupt and merged companies that had to renege on their pension pledges, and assorted knaveries by pension-fund managers."[13] A preliminary Senate study in 1971 disclosed, against employer criticism, that on the basis of a sample of 87 pension plans, some 6.7 million, or over two-thirds of the 9.8 million workers covered, had left their jobs before retirement. Of the 6.7 million, 5.9 million, or 60 percent of all covered workers, forfeited all claim to a pension. The Senate report averred that the ratio of entitlement to forfeitures had risen in the last half of the 1960s, but that the number of people leaving jobs without a vested interest still much exceeded those leaving with some claim to future benefits.[14]

Not only was there little if any federal protective surveillance over the operation of pension funds, especially the noninsured type, but the Internal Revenue Service steadfastly refused to allow personal income-tax deductions for workers' contributions to such funds. President Nixon in late 1971 proposed in a special message to Congress that all workers be allowed to claim tax deductions for pension contributions. But as late as the end of 1975 no such deduction was allowed.

After years of political pressure and congressional study of this most complex, chaotic and inequitable state of affairs, Congress in August 1974 passed the Employment Retirement Income Security Act. This act attested to the utter inadequacy of the simple availability-of-records approach contained in the 1958 Welfare and Pension Plans Disclosure Act, and belatedly inaugurated federal regulation of pension plans initiated at employer discretion. The law provided employers with three alternative methods of guaranteeing the right to a pension (vesting). All plans would have to make annual reports to the federal government and summary statements to employees. Also, fiduciary standards were stipulated to minimize the risk of investment loss. Of particularly vital importance to employees, a Pension Benefit Guaranty Corporation in the Department of Labor was created to collect premiums from each private pension plan with which to finance the difference, if any, between a terminating plan's assets and the amount necessary to pay all vested benefits up to a maximum of $750 per month for any individual beneficiary.

Social Security pension benefits

In most of the advanced European countries in the mid-1970s, the great bulk of pensioners received as retirement payments from 50 to 70 percent of their final or maximum pay. In the United States the average retiree got less than 25 percent of his terminal or maximum wage.[15] Average monthly benefits under the old-age provisions of the Social Security Act, despite substantial increases over the years, were $196.92 for men and $163.44 for women (who lived longer) in 1973. As in other public arrangements, the size of benefits was linked to prior earnings levels, reflecting the income distribution pattern rather than need. Even more dubious, a retiree could receive any amount of property income without penalty, but there were specific ceilings on the amount of wages or salary one could earn without reduction in benefit payments. Clearly, in the retirement area the economic security of the American people was extended in the quarter century following World War II. But the effort was rather less than might have been expected in a nation so rich in material goods.

WORK AND LEISURE

A further welfare indicator is leisure time and its utilization. Labor economists are wont to equate leisure with nonworking hours. As a first approximation, this might be done. When this criterion is employed, it is evident that average standard or scheduled hours worked per week in the private nonfarm economy changed but little after passage of the Fair Labor Standards Act in 1938. Under that legislation the minimum wage was gradually raised until it had reached $2.30 per hour by January 1976, exactly a decade after historic amendments to the act that extended minimum wage coverage to 10 million workers not previously included. But the work week of 40 hours then established, with time-and-a-half pay for over-

[13]Gilbert Burck, "That Ever Expanding Pension Balloon," *Fortune,* October 1971, p. 100.

[14]Merv Knoblock, "Labor and the Economy in 1971," *Monthly Labor Review,* January 1972, reprint no. 2783, p. 26.

[15]Ibid., p. 100.

time, became and generally remained the maximum standard for interstate and many local industries.

Upward and downward trends in hours worked

However, standard hours are not necessarily actual hours, and there was some downward drift in actual hours in the total private nonfarm sector from 40 in 1948 to about 37 in the early 1970s. Furthermore, there was considerable dispersion surrounding this average. In the mid-1960s it was reported that between 1948 and 1965 the number of nonfarm employees working more than 48 hours a week almost doubled, rising from 4.8 million to 9.4 million; that is, to almost 20 percent of the full-time nonfarm labor force.[16] There were apparently three types of persons working long hours: professional and technical employees who enjoyed their work, managerial salaried employees expected to devote extra energy to show devotion to the enterprise, and low-income workers needing additional income. This latter group included many "moonlighters" holding more than one job. These multiple jobholders in the nonfarm sector numbered about 4 million in 1974, or 5 percent of all employed persons.

On the other hand, some groups of workers were moving toward shorter work weeks. Between 1950 and 1973 the proportion of full-time nonfarm employees working between 35 and 40 hours decreased from 83.6 percent to 72.5 percent of the full-time nonfarm labor force. Retail trade was one sector in which the average work week declined markedly, from 40.3 hours in 1947 to 32.4 in 1975.

Despite these wide variations, there was a notable rise in the average of nonwork ("leisure") hours between 1945 and the early 1970s. But most of the increased leisure was taken in the form of fringe benefits: longer paid vacations, more paid holiday time, and more paid sick leave. There was also a reversal in the 1950s of the long-term rise in the length of working life for male workers. Work life expectancy declined six months over that decade.[17] Earlier retirement was stimulated by social security and private pensions, adding to the pool of average leisure time.

The work week and organized labor

Meanwhile there was increasing pressure from organized labor for a shorter work week with no cut in pay. Unlike the older movement for shorter hours, which was based upon arguments of health, safety, and the deprivation of leisure, the contemporary argument proceeded in terms of spreading work to avoid unemployment. The Executive Council of the AFL-CIO, the policy-making body of 13.5 million union members, declared in February 1964 that there was no alternative to the shorter work week to spread employment.[18] The union's position reflected a deep concern over the possible impact of automation on employment.[19]

The basic point regarding the work week was that it was no longer sharply juxtaposed against leisure time, and labor's striving for more leisure was largely confined to fringe benefits. Labor did not even seem to be aroused about the considerable nonleisure hours devoted each week to commuting to and from the job.

The use of leisure time

The more significant aspect of leisure time from the welfare standpoint was not its modest increase, but rather the way it was utilized and the external conditions for its utilization. On this score, most Americans apparently spent their leisure time in easily accessible activities such as rest, relaxation, watching television (one survey concluded that the average adult would spend from 10 to 15 years of his or her life watching TV),[20] visiting with friends or relatives, driving or walking for pleasure, bicycling, reading, studying, watching sports events (often on TV), outdoor recreation, cultural activities, travel, and participating in clubs and organizations.[21] The effects of some leisure activities on the individual and on society, such as drug intake, gambling, and TV watching in particular, were considered highly controversial. On the other hand, the enormous increase in the number of visits to national parks, from 33 million in 1950 to 276 million in 1973, would be almost universally acclaimed, if one ignored pollution, overcrowding, and the immobile poor.

[16]Peter Henle, "Leisure and the Long Work Week," *Monthly Labor Review*, July 1966, reprint no. 2500, p. 721. The immediately following points are from the same study.

[17]U.S. Department of Labor, Office of Manpower, Automation and Training, "The Length of Working Life for Males, 1900–60," Manpower Report no. 8, July 1963.

[18]Reported in the *Minneapolis Morning Tribune*, February 22, 1964, p. 2.

[19]Federal Reserve Bank of Philadelphia, "The 40-Hour Workweek After 25 Years," *Monthly Review*, January 1964.

[20]*New York Times Magazine*, July 14, 1968, p. 26, cited in Richard Kraus, *Recreation and Leisure in Modern Society* (Englewood Cliffs, N.J.: Prentice-Hall, 1971), p. 328.

[21]Ibid., p. 319.

Total personal consumption expenditures for recreation provide a very rough aggregate index of one major category of leisure activity. These rose from $11.1 billion in 1950 to $52.3 billion in 1973. But as a percentage of personal income such outlays were rising only slightly.

Despite visits to national parks and other

forms of country outdoor recreation, most leisure time, like most work time, was spent in an urban environment. That environment was an essential factor in material welfare. Most general indicators of social well-being in America's cities during the 1960s and 1970s pointed toward progress.

WELFARE IN THE CENTRAL CITY

The nation had long been urbanized by the end of World War II. But the next 20 years brought a number of remarkable changes. The rise in the urban population from two-thirds to three-fourths of the total population of 212 million in 1974 was one of the more moderate changes. But the rise in the percentage of people living on the urban fringe, which encompassed suburbia, was certainly one of the more dramatic shifts, almost a doubling, from 14 percent to 27 percent. Here lived the middle class and the well-to-do. The central cities housed, after a fashion, the blue-collar workers and what has been called "the other America". It was a large group, but as a proportion it did not grow: 32 percent of the country's population in 1950 and the same in 1970.

Income and population in the central city

The median annual metropolitan white income outside central cities in 1969 was $11,217; for whites in central cities it was $9,798, a metropolitan differential that was *increasing* in the 20 years following the end of World War II.[22] The median for blacks was $6,799. The discrepancy in white–black median family incomes in central cities was less than it was for white–black family median incomes in the country as a whole. This reinforces the notion that the central city did concentrate the low-income groups in the population, although there were well-to-do and even rich in parts of many central cities. While the proportion of people below the poverty level (nonfarm families with income below $3410) was highest, surprisingly enough, outside metropolitan areas, the incidence of poverty in the central cities in 1973 was over twice that in the suburbs.

However, the number of families living in the so-called poverty areas of the major cities declined between 1960 and 1969. In the latter year there were 30 percent fewer white families and 9 percent fewer black families in such areas than there had been in 1960.[23]

While central city population was a constant percentage of the total population of the nation, the racial and social composition changed greatly in 20 years. In many big cities the black ghetto came to dominate much of the residential central city. Meanwhile the commercial, administrative, and managerial parts became the increasingly polluted areas of work for white commuters, who swelled the daytime population by 30 to 50 percent. Well over half of the black population lived in central cities in 1970, and the black proportion of central city population increased from about 13 to about 20 percent between 1950 and 1970. One in every four among the black population received an income below the poverty level in 1969, in contrast to one in ten among whites.

Social welfare expenditures and fiscal problems

Because of the historic role of central cities as reception centers or zones of passage for low-income immigrants,[24] the needs of an already low-income population for heavy municipal expenditures for social services and housing were accentuated. This was as would be expected in a society that rejected the more efficient cash transfer from the well-to-do to the poor in favor of a gerrymandered system of service benefits. For example, while almost three-fourths of the families with dependent children

[22]See James Heilbrun, "Poverty and Public Finance in the Older Central Cities," in U.S. Joint Economic Committee, *Urban America: Goals and Problems,* 90th Cong., 1st sess., August 1967 (Washington, D.C.: U.S. Government Printing Office, 1967), pp. 141–143.

[23]Conrad Taeuber, testimony, in U.S. Congress, House Committee on Banking and Currency, Ad Hoc Subcommittee on Urban Growth, *Hearings on the Quality of Urban Life,* 91st Cong., 1st and 2nd sess., pt. 2 (Washington, D.C.: U.S. Government Printing Office, 1970), p. 222.

[24]Committee for Economic Development, *Guiding Metropolitan Growth* (August 1960), p. 19.

receiving public aid in 1969 lived in metropolitan areas, 56 percent were in central cities. Central-city housing dilapidation dictated a high concentration of local and national urban-renewal efforts. Again, while the unemployment rate for the country as a whole was 4.9 percent in 1970, it was 7.6 percent in the urban poverty neighborhoods of metropolitan areas having over 225,000 population — 6.3 percent for whites and a doubtless undercounted 9.5 percent for blacks.

Yet the growth of the pressing need for additional social welfare services was accompanied by enlarged income disparity between central city dwellers and others, and declines in the tax base of property and income of residents in the central cities. This fiscal disparity was scarcely alleviated by discriminatory property-tax assessment procedures that extracted taxes at substantially higher rates from inferior housing in blighted inner-city neighborhoods occupied by low-income people, especially blacks, than from materially better neighborhoods. It therefore became ever clearer to policy framers that the attendant fiscal problems were metropolitan, and even state and federal, in scope, a condition dramatically highlighted by the fiscal crisis of New York City in the winter of 1975–1976. From this it appeared to follow that the deepening social and political antagonisms between people dwelling in central cities and those dwelling in the suburbs would have to be overcome in order to formulate appropriate policies for the megalopolis of the future. It was estimated in 1969 that only 12 leading urban areas would absorb 85 percent of the nation's entire population growth by the year 2000.

CITIES AND THE ENVIRONMENT

Of all the problems pertaining to the quality of the American environment, probably none were more numerous and concentrated than those of the inner city. Hence a brief examination of environmental trends as they impinged upon the largely low-income heartlands of urban society will bring into focus not only the evolving interconnections between environment and welfare in urban society as a whole, but also the larger ecological changes, other than those already discussed in connection with natural-resource exhaustion and the doomsday debate, that occurred after World War II.[25]

The White House Conference on Youth in April 1971 commented that

> *although environmental degradation has become recognized in recent years as a major social crisis, the public focus on this issue has usually been directed towards problems that are important to middle-class Americans. The issues of urban transportation, slum housing, inadequate health care, recreation and education, and unemployment are vital to urban poor people; but have not been properly understood in an environmental context or dealt with from an ecological perspective.*

Thus the conference urged a broadening of the traditional ecological concerns with clean air and water and wilderness preservation to include not only specifically urban environmental matters such as noise pollution, the psychological impact of density and space shortages, sanitation, rat infestation, and litter and solid-waste accumulation, but also related socioeconomic phenomena such as high crime rates and drug addiction.

Air and noise pollution

In 1972 President Joseph L. Fisher of Resources for the Future called attention to the fact that of all segments of society, the poor are the least responsible for pollution, since their material consumption is the smallest of all social strata. Conversely, the concentration of polluted air, whose annual toll on health, vegetation, materials, and property values was conservatively estimated by the federal Environmental Protection Agency (established in 1970) at $16 billion, was found to be much greater in the inner city than in the surrounding urban area. The bulk of the air pollution and smog in most cities is attributable to auto and truck emissions. Since cities are the areas of greatest density of traffic and of industrial and residential fuel burning, concentrations of particulate matter, carbon monoxide, and sulfur oxides thin out as one moves into suburbia, and as one moves even farther on to rural points the lowered concentrations range from 10 to 50

---

[25]The following review relies heavily upon *Environmental Quality,* second annual report of the Council on Environmental Quality (Washington, D.C.: U.S. Government Printing Office, August 1971).

percent of urban averages. This is likewise the case with noise pollution and dust fall. Lead levels in the blood, commonly linked with proximity to heavily traveled streets and freeways, have been found to be particularly high among urban dwellers. Under the 1970 amendments to the Clean Air Act, stringent national emission standards for new automobiles were to go into effect by 1975, but the industry steadfastly claimed it could not meet the standards without prohibitive costs by that date. In April 1973 Environmental Protection Agency Administrator William O. Ruckelshaus gave the industry a delay until 1976, and set reduced but moderately high standards for the interim period.

Water pollution

A quip that gained currency in the 1960s was that Cleveland's Cuyahoga River was the only stream in the United States that was a fire hazard. This only pointed up the severity of urban water pollution (but not drinking water, whose general purity was an achievement of which the country could justly be proud). The river courses and harbors within or near large cities often contained dangerously high levels of bacteria, petroleum, and other pollutants. The accessibility of clean recreational water is to an important degree a function of income via informational and transport costs. Of 491 million acres of public recreation area in the country, less than 3 percent is within one hour's driving time from the large metropolitan centers containing 90 million people.

Urban blight

Large areas of all major cities were afflicted with the relentless spread of urban blight despite substantial outlays for the improvement of civic facilities. The property tax penalized homeowners for making improvements. Owners' neglect of residential and commercial property in one place tended to spread, often creating dilapidation for block after block on commercial streets backed up by deteriorating residences. The abandonment rate appeared to accelerate after it reached 5 percent. Substantial blocks of land became underutilized or fell into disuse. Vacant lots and abandoned structures, concentrated in the inner city, were typically strewn with refuse. Blight was exacerbated by the accumulation of litter and other solid wastes, not the least of which were abandoned automobiles that had been stripped of all usable parts. Residents of 9 out of 20 cities surveyed by the National Advisory Commission on Civil

Disorders, a commission set up to study the ghetto riots during the summer of 1965, gave inadequate sanitation and garbage removal as major grievances.

Freeway networks

The years since the end of World War II can readily be called the freeway era (or the expressway era, depending on where one lives).Freeways and expressways no doubt relieved urban traffic congestion even as they simultaneously strengthened the coercive power of the individual as driver over the individual as creative human being. Nevertheless, congestion continued to be a critical problem that generated large adverse side effects. One such was lost time, the economic value of which was estimated in 1968 to have approximated $20 billion.

A prominent aspect of the freeway explosion, rivaled by the resulting drastic decline in urban public transit, was the penetration of almost all central cities by the freeway network, popularly known as spaghetti. Although the city-center freeway network, with its attendant expanse of feeder streets, parking lots, and garages, at times encountered stiff public resistance, it had substantially changed the physical, and therefore the aesthetic and psychological, countenance of the metropolis. It had frequently diminished or destroyed neighborhood cohesion in the affected land strips. Public concern finally elicited aid to displaced persons under the Uniform Relocation Assistance Act; and transportation planners as well as highway commissions became persuaded, in accordance with the Urban Mass Transportation Act of 1964, to make environmental impact studies before embarking on construction. The results varied with the strength of public organization and action.

The crisis in urban mass transit

Freeways and expressways raised the use of private automobiles until they accounted for over 90 percent of all means of commuting to work, but at the same time those in the inner city who had to rely upon public transportation were faced with a rising cost barrier between place of residence and place of work. This barrier was erected not only by increased fares, but also by the spreading tendency of fabricating and marketing firms to locate their plants in outlying areas. As a partial consequence of the ensuing crisis in public mass urban transit, a movement toward government subsidy of such transit began to develop, and by the mid-1970s rapid-transit rail systems were being considered or were under construction in 16 large cities. Perhaps the most impressive of these are the San Francisco Bay Area system and the Washington, D.C. underground.

Federal outlays for urban welfare

Even a cursory review, such as this, of the experience of inner-city people and their environment since World War II shows that the social welfare of people in urban America encompassed most of the welfare achievements and problems of the country as a whole. The several major federal grant programs specifically addressed to metropolitan problems did not begin to indicate the total urban welfare outlays even of the federal government. For example, the sum total of funds allocated to such city-oriented grant-in-aid programs in the fiscal year 1971, including Model Cities, Urban Renewal, Community Action, urban mass transit, public housing, open-space land, and neighborhood facilities, was only a bit over $3 billion.[26] Estimated outlays by the mammoth federal Department of Health, Education, and Welfare that year were almost $62 billion (including the whole social security program). As the seventies waned, it became ever more clear that the tax base of the inner cities was utterly inadequate to cope with their welfare and other needs; and their deepening fiscal crisis could only be attacked through greater reliance upon outside revenue sources.

The future of inner-city society

It was abundantly clear in the mid-1970s that in the future the inner-city society would tend to spread out to what David Burch has called the "inner suburb," and from there to the "outer suburb." Indeed, it had already started to do so. The continuation of the past income-distribution pattern could not but have some kind of impact upon the spatial distribution of the population. How that spatial distribution would shape itself in the absence of social planning was not at all clear.

Secretary of Housing and Urban Development George Romney seemed to show great prescience when he declared in testifying before the Ad Hoc Committee on Urban Growth on October 27, 1969, that

> *building a better urban environment is far more complex than sending three men, or a hundred men, to the moon. Yet, our space program succeeded only because vast expenditures of human energy, money and materials were harnessed to serve a single goal under the guidance of scientific, technical, and managerial know-how.*[27]

Yet it was pointed out that the annual cost of meeting decent pollution-abatement standards, while large, would not be prohibitive. One estimate of the cost in 1970 was about $8.5 billion (in 1967 dollars). Robert M. Solow guessed that an active abatement program might reach $50 billion a year by A.D. 2000, which would amount to only 2 percent of the projected GNP for that year.[28]

SELECTED READINGS

*Boulding, Kenneth E., and Pfaff, Martin, eds. *Redistribution to the Rich and the Poor: The Grants Economics of Income Distribution* (Belmont, California: Wadsworth, 1972).

*Council on Environmental Quality, *Environmental Quality,* Second Annual Report (Washington, D.C.: Government Printing Office, August 1971).

*"The Conscience of the City," *Daedulus,* Fall 1968. Issued as vol. 97, No. 4 of the Proceedings of the American Academy of Arts and Sciences.

*Frakes, G. E., and Solberg, C. B., eds., *Pollution Papers* (Englewood Cliffs, N.J.: Prentice-Hall, 1971).

[26]Schultze et al., *Setting National Priorities,* p. 311.

[27]*Hearings on the Quality of Urban Life,* p. 270. The Department of Housing and Urban Development was established in 1965 to coordinate federal housing policies with a view to providing "a decent home and a suitable living environment for every American family."

[28]"Is the End of the World at Hand?" *Challenge,* March–April 1973, p. 39.

*Henle, Paul, and Schmitt, Raymond, "Pension reform: the long hard road to enactment." *Monthly Labor Review,* November 1974, Reprint 3008.

*Jarrett, Henry, ed., *Environmental Quality in a Growing Economy* (Baltimore: Johns Hopkins University Press, 1970).

*Miller, Herman P., *Rich Man, Poor Man* (New York: Crowell, 1971).

*Pechman, Joseph A., and Okner, Benjamin A., *Who Bears the Tax Burden* (Washington, D.C.: Brookings Institution, 1974).

*Revelle, Roger, and Landsberg, Hans H., eds., *America's Changing Environment* (Boston: Beacon Press, 1970).

*Vatter, Harold G., and Palm, Thomas, eds., *The Economics of Black America* (New York: Jarcourt Brace Jovanovich, 1972).

*Will, Robert E., and Vatter, Harold G., eds., *Poverty in Affluence,* 2nd ed., (New York: Harcourt Brace Jovanovich, 1970).

The organized labor movement was little better prepared than business for the era of public capitalism. In many ways this was not a serious lack, for, as we have seen, there was sufficient historical continuity with laissez-faire capitalism to permit much to be done in the old ways.

There was still a great deal of both overt and subtle business resistance to union organization and collective bargaining, particularly in the unorganized sectors and in the South. The long struggle for union organization was far from being ended. The historic dichotomy between wages and profits remained a primary source of conflict. A focus on the money wage rate continued to characterize trade-union activity despite the new importance of the fringe benefit and the growing awareness of persistent inflation. The strike as a bargaining instrument and private "unfettered" collective bargaining with management appeared to labor as up-to-date as ever. And the old fear of mass unemployment lingered on.

LABOR AND THE PUBLIC SECTOR

The persistence of moderate unemployment until 1974–1975 made it hard for organized labor to realize it had almost won the battle for sustained high employment. Apparently even more difficult for it to grasp were some of the implications of the new large role for the public sector that accompanied the commitment to high employment. With all government expenditures plus public transfer and similar payments growing from a bit over one-fifth to almost one-third of gross production between 1950 and the mid-1970s, it was small wonder that labor and labor management matters, formerly viewed as a private affair, became increasingly affected with a public interest. Labor, like management, was slow and reluctant to accept this change.

Essentially the change involved a three-party formulation and administration of many policies formerly approached on a usually private, two-party basis. Now the government was ever more frequently the silent or active partner, along with labor and management, in a policy triad.

Union wages, employment, and inflation

This last development may be seen in the presumed impact of wage negotiations and wage settlements. Money wage rates affect the distribution of income and the level of general prices.[1] Through both these channels they affect the performance of the mixed economy. Union wage rates were widely believed to influence the level and structure of the wages of unorganized workers as well as wages in the unorganized sectors of the economy. Hence, in the context of an economy having a persistent inflationary bias and a national policy objective of more or less stable prices, labor's traditional wage-increasing program was rightly or wrong-

[1]See, e.g., Sidney Weintraub, *Employment, Growth, and Income Distribution* (Radnor, Pa.: Chilton Books, 1966).

ly thought directly to affect the ability of the public authorities to restrain inflation. Wage settlements were public issues, whether one believed with Professor Kenneth Boulding that unionism tended to hold down wages to prevent them from rising faster than they otherwise would, or with Professor Charles E. Lindblom and the late Professor Edward H. Chamberlin that union pressure on wages led to inflation.[2] The incorporation of escalator clauses automatically adjusting money wages to price changes in many labor–management agreements beginning in the 1950s further added to the conviction of sections of the public and government authorities that wage agreements had a potential impact on prices.

It was also a widely accepted belief that union wage policy was connected with the level of employment. An Australian economist named Phillips constructed what became an enormously influential "curve" showing that lower unemployment rates elicited, via wage increases, higher price rises. On this line of reasoning, the national goals of keeping people employed and constraining inflation required holding wage increases in check. Hence what labor and management did about wages affected high-priority national objectives.

Full employment
equals unemployment

Nor was the presumed connection severed for policy makers in the late 1950s and in 1969–1971, when wage rates, prices, and unemployment all rose together, even though such "stagflation" was inconsistent with the theory behind the Phillips curve. Hence, the first Nixon administration employed Phillips-curve assumptions when it tried to control the inflation at the end of the 1960s by deliberately increasing unemployment, a policy that subsequently led to the most severe recession in the history of the mixed economy. The political authorities steadfastly refused to acknowledge the widespread and deeply-penetrating substitution of administered pricing for competitive supply and demand forces. The only cause of inflation in their view was classical demand-pull—"too much money chasing too few goods." So intense was the fear of inflation in high places that "full employment" came to be defined as at least 4 percent unemployment,

and the eminent economist Paul Samuelson at one point went so far as to say:

> Our mixed economy—like that of Germany, Japan, England, France, Sweden and Belgium—reveals a tendency for prices to creep upward even when there is substantial unemployment. To keep wholesale prices stable and the implicit-GNP-deflator index growing at a moderate 1.5 percent might well require that U.S. unemployment be, in the short run, 5 percent or more.[3]

It is most significant that by the mid-1970s this notion of a meaningful economic and public policy trade-off between unemployment and inflation was widely rejected, even by eminent conservatives such as Arthur F. Burns, Chairman of the Federal Reserve Board.

The union stake in public policy

The currents of causation linking union wages, the unemployment rate, and price change flowed in both directions. Hence, not only was union wage determination affected with a public interest; unions also had a stake in public policy pertaining to employment and prices. Union traditions, inherited from laissez-faire and consequently hostile to direct government intervention in industrial relations, endowed the labor movement with a poor preparation for the new, broad social and political responsibilities of labor accompanying the enlargement of the interventionist regime.

The same applied to collective bargaining between labor and management and the enforcement of bargaining agreements. Adherence to or disruption of agreements often affected the continuity of production. After all, it was through this institutionalized process that wages, hours, fringe benefits, and job conditions were determined. Clearly, big government as trustee for the execution of national economic policy goals had a vital interest in the functioning of the collective bargaining system and in the maintenance of industrial peace within the context of that system. Labor was ill prepared to accept the implications of this fact.

The framework of labor policy

All these changing relationships that were making formerly private issues into public issues

---

[2] These and other views are cited in William H. Miernyk, *The Economics of Labor and Collective Bargaining,* 2nd ed. (Lexington, Mass: Heath, 1973) pp. 495–498.

[3] Paul Samuelson, *Full Employment, Guideposts, and Economic Stability* (Washington, D.C.: American Enterprise Institute for Public Policy Research, 1967), p. 54.

underlay the tortuously evolving legal frame-work of a national (as well as state and local) labor policy. As Archibald Cox had suggested, that policy focused upon four main aspects of the union movement: organization, negotiation of collective bargaining agreements, administration of such agreements, and internal union affairs.[4] Accordingly, the major legislative cornerstones were

1. The Norris–La Guardia Act of 1932, which imposed severe restraints upon the power of the courts to issue injunctions restricting labor's actions.
2. The National Labor Relations Act of 1935, which asserted employees' right to "bargain collectively through representatives of their own choosing," and established the National Labor Relations Board (NLRB) to determine union representation through elections.
3. The Labor–Management Relations (Taft-Hartley) Act of 1947, which made certain substantive pro-management changes in existing law, including:
   (a) Prohibition of the closed shop.[5]
   (b) Stipulation of a long list of unfair practices on the part of unions.[6]
   (c) Assurance of free speech for employers.
   (d) Regulation of the procedures for renegotiation of existing contracts.
   (e) Prohibition of union-shop agreements in states that forbade such agreements.[7]
   (f) Establishment of delaying procedures, under the initiative and direction of the president of the United States, that would guarantee a cooling-off period in the case of "emergency" disputes.[8]
4. The Labor–Management Reporting

and disclosure (Landrum-Griffin) Act of 1959, which set down detailed procedures under the supervision of the secretary of labor, the federal courts, and the NLRB, designed to assure internal union democracy and prevent bureaucracy, corruption, and racketeering.[9]

In addition, the 1960s saw the passage, following state leadership after 20 years, of the country's first federal fair employment practices statute, Title VII of the Civil Rights Act of 1964. Though it was designed primarily to protect the rights of black workers against discrimination by either employers or unions, as the 1960s closed the women's liberation movement amply demonstrated to the Equal Employment Opportunities Commission, which administered the law, that the "sex amendment" to Title VII would entail a full-scale campaign to eliminate discrimination against women. Also in the 1960s the courts appeared to reaffirm in a few cases the general inapplicability of the antitrust laws to collective bargaining and other union activities.

This summary of the main body of labor law and its major stipulations will indicate the enormous enlargement of government's role in the spheres of unionism and what used to be simplistically called "industrial relations." Clearly, the trend toward a planned public capitalism had moved forward at a rapid pace after the Great Depression, a pace whose longer-term promise was still but dimly appreciated by both management and labor.

Political activity of organized labor

One consequence of the enlarged role of government in labor–management relations, and in labor's economic status generally, was the increased political activity of the labor movement. It is true that the AFL-CIO merger convention in 1955 reiterated the old philosophy of Samuel Gompers and the early AFL that the house of labor should avoid entangling alliances with any political party and should support labor's friends in elections regardless of party affiliation. But through the years, beginning with vigorous support for FDR in 1936, labor's loose identification with the Democratic party appeared stronger as election followed election. The AFL and the CIO also identified with the Cold War and the anticommunist struggle within the World Federation of Trade Unions in the late 1940s, which led to the

---

[4] Cox's classification was presented in lectures in late 1959 and published in *Law and the National Labor Policy* (Los Angeles: UCLA Institute of Industrial Relations, 1960). This reference as used here is cited in Benjamin Aaron and Paul Seth Meyer, "Public Policy and Labor-Management Relations," University of Wisconsin (Madison), Industrial Relations Research Association, *A Review of Industrial Relations Research* (1971), 2:1–61. The immediately following list relies strongly upon this latter source.

[5] An arrangement under which only union members can be hired.

[6] See pp. 419–420.

[7] States having "right to work" laws.

[8] Disputes that might threaten national health or safety.

[9] See Harold G. Vatter, *The U.S. Economy in the 1950s* (New York: Norton, 1963), pp. 239–240.

breakup of the WFTU and the establishment of the International Confederation of Free Trade Unions in 1949. Later on the labor movement avidly supported the Korean war and, until close to the end, the Vietnam war. (As a corollary, military-related employment was prized equally with other civilian jobs.) In 1969 the AFL-CIO withdrew from the ICFTU in disapproval of the latter's insufficiently hostile attitude toward Soviet bloc nations and also because of ICFTU failure to comply with AFL-CIO demands that it reject admission of the United Auto Workers.

Rewarding friends and punishing enemies of labor in elections became important goals of the CIO's Political Action Committee and other union political-action agencies. The top echelons of organized labor were active, pro or con, on most vital pieces of legislation affecting labor's economic and legal interests. Passage of the Taft-Hartley Act prompted the AFL to set up Labor's League for Political Education, and after the merger the PAC and LLPE were joined in the AFL-CIO's Committee on Political Education. Affiliate unions and independents such as the Teamsters, long on autonomy, set up their own political-action agencies. Beginning in the mid-1950s the AFL-CIO inaugurated the new election strategy of preparing and submitting labor programs to both major parties. There was no movement for a labor party.

The role of arbitration

One already clear implication of the enlarged postwar role of government was that the strike (or lockout) in the big industries was, if not already a historically obsolete form of conflict, very much under attack. The chief role of the NLRB was to insist upon the duty to bargain collectively. But to an ever growing extent this duty was transformed into a pattern of conflict resolution without production stoppages of major dimensions. Furthermore, arbitration was given an ever more crucial role in the settlement of industrial disputes in the 1960s.[10] In a symposium on compulsory arbitration published in the *Virginia Law Review* in 1965, one leading authority pointed out that industry and labor "cannot expect to impose their bargaining stalemates upon the economy, and at the same time oppose compulsory arbitration of their disputes."[11] Still, nothing pertaining to these great issues was resolved during the years under examination. In the highly charged sphere of emergency disputes in the transport and ubiquitous military production industries, the president stepped in from time to time on an ad hoc basis, which only served to emphasize that no general solution had been discovered.

THE STRIKE AND THE PUBLIC INTEREST

As for the general record of work stoppages, there was no discernible trend between 1950 and the early 1970s with respect to duration, proportion of total employed persons involved, or worker days idle as percent of total working time.

The strike record suggested that traditional "more and more" attitudes remained strong where organization was strong, and that collective bargaining rights were featured where organization was weak and/or employer resistance to unionization was particularly firm. The biggest and last great strike wave occurred during the years immediately following the war's end, and especially in 1946. In that period the removal of wartime price controls and the ensuing inflation was accompanied by stagnation in the average real spendable earnings (deflated gross earnings less social security and income taxes) of workers in the private sector. During these years of ferment and work stoppages, labor and management constructed the main contours of the format and the content of industrial agreements for the postwar era. This format included tying money wage increases with productivity rise plus price rise in order to retain labor's share of total income; the extension of fringe benefits, which relied heavily upon privately provided rather than more generous governmentally financed security supplements, as was typical of Europe; the long-term contract with reopening and renegotiation arrangements; and the practice of "pattern settlements," according to which agreements in major industries were copied in other industries.

The major contested issues between labor and management from 1947 to 1950 were also in general typical of the entire postwar period. These were dominated by wages and supplementary benefits, accounting for the main point at issue in almost half of all work stoppages.

[10]Aaron and Meyer, "Public Policy," p. 33.
[11]Ibid., p. 43.

Next came general working conditions, such as plant administration (22 percent), and third in importance were union organization rights and union security (14 percent). It was and remained noteworthy that only a small percentage of stoppages was caused by interunion jurisdictional fights or intraunion matters.

After the 1946–1950 upheavals, the frequency of big strikes and the incidence of violence definitely subsided in American labor–management conflicts. Some labor experts referred to the "withering away of the strike." Nevertheless, some important work stoppages that lasted so long that idleness accounted for noteworthy percentages of estimated total working time occurred in 1952, 1959, and during the closing years of the 1960s.

Major disputes in steel and bituminous coal dominated the 1952 strike scene. When 600,-000 steelworkers struck in April 1952, months after the Korean war's Wage Stabilization Board recommendations had been rejected by the companies, President Truman, illegally as it turned out, seized the steel mills. The Supreme Court denied Truman's power to make the seizure, and steel production was finally resumed on August 2.

The strike scene in 1959

The 1959 strike scene, with its backdrop of consumer price rises, featured another steel strike, lasting 116 days — the longest in the history of the industry. While the initial breakdown in the protracted negotiations regarding new contract terms was over proposed wage and fringe-benefit increases, the central issue changed when management demanded that the union, in exchange for concessions in these areas, virtually surrender any participation in the determination of employee placement and work rules, particularly stipulation of the number of workers assigned to the performance of various tasks. The lengthy negotiations, from January through June, gave buyers plenty of time to build up their inventories. It was in this strike that President Eisenhower secured an 80-day injunction under the Taft-Hartley national emergency provisions. The Supreme Court upheld the constitutionality of the act's provisions, its applicability to the steel strike, and the allegation that the stike imperiled the national "safety" (but not necessarily the national "health"). One new trend established as a result of the strike was the setting up of permanent labor–management committees to main-

tain industrial peace between periods of contract renegotiation.

Strikes in the 1960s

An upsurge of strike actions in the late 1960s was primarily a response to rising demand for labor and the price inflation that followed the remarkably stable price record of the decade's first half. Consumer prices (1967= 100) rose from 93 to 116 between 1964 and 1970 (see Table 26–1), average spendable weekly earnings in the private nonfarm sector stagnated, and man-days idle from work stoppages mushroomed from 0.15 percent of total working time to 0.44 percent over the same period. Labor decisively rejected the presidential Council of Economic Advisers' wage-price guidelines (3.2 percent maximum wage rise per year) in 1966, concluding that they were no longer meaningful in the light of rising prices and attendant burgeoning profits. These guidelines were the U.S. "voluntary cooperation" substitute for Europe's stricter, governmentally directed, inflation-limiting "incomes policies."

The guideline approach held sway until President Nixon's first wage-price freeze of August 15, 1971, implementing his authority under the Economic Stabilization Act of 1970. To many this seemed to be the beginning of an incomes-policy move appropriate to the management of a mixed economy perpetually living with inflationary pressure. But if so, it was not yet to materialize, for the stricter controls of the Economic Stabilization Program's Phase II were deliberately dismantled beginning with the "progressive decontrol" policy of Phase III in January 1973. Decontrol was accelerated following a two-month freeze (June 13 to August 12, 1973), when Phase IV was inaugurated. The "return to a free market economy" proceeded apace in late 1973 and 1974, despite the hyperinflation beginning in July 1973 and lasting throughout 1974. Controls were terminated on April 30, 1974, and President Ford's opposition to further incomes policies received, at least for the time being, widespread support.

Strikes of government employees

Employee organizations in the public sector became more active in the use of the strike as their ranks expanded. In addition to inflation and a lag in public-sector wages behind those of private skilled labor, public workers, especially in local government, displayed growing strike and related evidences of militancy over union

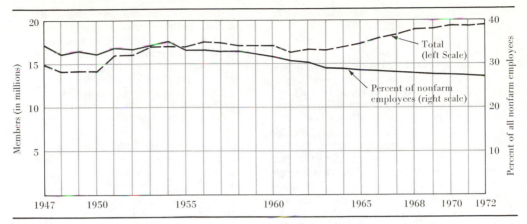

Figure 28-1. Labor Union Membership, 1947–1972. Source: *Statistical Abstract,* 1975, pp. 343, 371.

organization rights and union security. Union recognition and security were the major issues in about one-fifth of all public-service stoppages in the 1960s. In consequence, all measures of government-worker strike activity rose substantially between 1960 and 1970, the number of worker days idle peaking in 1968, the year of the long New York teachers' strike.

THE CRISIS IN UNION ORGANIZATION

Organized labor was apparently not well prepared for the special problems connected with organization and collective bargaining in the burgeoning public sector. One reason labor had historically been chary of nationalization was that many public employees were especially restricted in what they could do as a group. Hence, retention of the right to strike, if the Wobblies' old dream of "one big union" were realized, was doubtful. The increase in civilian public employment from 10.1 percent of total civilian employment in 1946 to 16.6 percent in 1974 indicated the magnitude of this growing organizational challenge to the trade unions' traditional constituency. It indicated only one of the many great structural changes in the labor force itself that confronted union labor with awesome new organizational tasks.

The decline in union membership

These structural changes have been described earlier and somewhat differently in connection with the shifts in the major industrial sectors. Here certain other, related aspects need to be noted. The AFL and CIO merged, after lengthy preliminary negotiations, in December 1955. In that year trade-union membership was 16.8 million, or 32.5 percent of all civilian wage and salary workers. Thereafter the membership of the AFL-CIO failed to grow, partly because in 1957 the Teamsters Union was accused by the organization's executive council of corrupt practices and expelled.

This was a loss of almost 1.5 million members—the largest union in the country. The AFL-CIO had 16.1 million members in 1955 and 15.6 million in 1968, the year the United Auto Workers, the second largest union, broke with it because of abiding differences over union structure and because Walter Reuther and the leadership of the UAW wished to protest what they believed to be the AFL-CIO's complacency about the broad social, political, and economic issues facing the labor movement. The merger in 1955 of the AFL and CIO did not produce numerical growth. Nor did the new Alliance for Labor Action, formed by the UAW and the Teamsters, who held their first national convention in 1969.

American trade-union membership as a whole, after expanding in the early 1950s, showed slow long-run growth from its 1956 peak of 17.5 million to its 19.4 million in 1972. With civilian wage and salary workers meanwhile increasing, this meant a relative decline to 26.7 percent of that total in 1972.

The unions and white-collar workers

It was persuasively argued that most of this relative decline could be explained by the large comparative increases in occupations traditionally reluctant to organize. Trade-union strength had historically been concentrated in the blue-collar stratum of the manufacturing, mining, construction, transportation, and public utilities industries. Over 70 percent of all union members were in these industries in 1972. Employment in these five sectors rose only 13 percent between 1955 and 1970, a trend remarkable in itself since output rose by about two-thirds. Blue-collar employment rose notably less than 13 percent, so in the aggregate blue-collar union membership merely held its own in these five sectors. In the strategic manufacturing sector, union membership was 49 percent in 1956, but had dropped to 43 percent in 1972. Regional shifts did not help, for there was a sharp relative rise in manufacturing in the South, a region in which union organization was weakest. In the manufacturing sector, the ratio of production workers to total wage and salary workers had significantly experienced an accompanying drop from 77 to 71 percent. Nevertheless, the big United Auto Workers made very substantial membership gains over the same period.

It was hypothesized that trade unionism had but a weak appeal to wage earners outside the blue-collar categories. If that were so, the 58 percent growth between 1955 and 1970 of wage and salary employment in all the sectors other than the previously mentioned five would certainly have been inimical to union growth, and could explain a large part of the observed membership stagnation. On the other hand, there was substantial unionization in the other sectors, and it was possible that the unions needed time to acquire a proper approach to organizing white-collar and service workers. One labor authority concluded in 1969 that

in many respects the large and rapid growth of these [white collar] unions is the most striking development in trade union membership trends in recent years. Since 1956 the three unions which show the highest relative gain are those representing public service workers — the American Federation of State, County and Municipal Employees, the American

Federation of Government Employees, and the American Federation of Teachers. Each of these unions has more than doubled its membership during this 12 year period, predominantly accounting for the jump in the proportion of union members in government from five per cent of the total union membership in 1956 to 11 percent in 1968.[12]

The same writer noted that government union organization was encouraged on the state and local levels by legislation that extended or strengthened the bargaining privileges of employees, and on the federal level by Executive Order 10988 early in 1962, reinforcing collective bargaining rights.[13]

But the gains were not merely in government employment. They were spread generally although unevenly through the white-collar occupations, where membership had risen over a million, from 2.2 million in 1960 to 3.4 million in 1972. There were over a million labor-union members in the elite professional, technical, and kindred categories of workers in 1970.[14] Still, only about 10 percent of all white-collar workers were in labor unions, although that category of workers by then constituted almost 54 percent of the employed civilian wage and salary workers. This left the future of white-collar unionization uncertain. It was entirely conceivable, however, that the experience of other countries might be relevant. In the United Kingdom in the early 1970s, for example, only 30 percent of all industrial employees were organized, but 75 percent of the white-collar and professional employees were in unions.[15] It was significant that in 1967 the AFL-CIO established a Scientific, Professional, and Cultural Employees Council, made up of 17 unions in the white-collar and professional areas, whose object was to find new approaches to organizing that group of workers.[16]

[12]Woodrow Ginsburg, "Review of Literature on Union Growth, Government, and Structure: 1955–1969," University of Wisconsin (Madison), Industrial Relations Research Association, *Review of Industrial Relations Research* (1970), 1:212–213.

[13]Ibid., p. 213.

[14]Data for 1970 here cited are from U.S. Department of Labor, Bureau of Labor Statistics, *Selected Earnings and Demographic Characteristics of Union Members, 1970,* report no. 417 (October 1972).

[15]Joseph P. Goldberg, "Public Employee Labor Relations in Other Democracies: A Review Essay," U.S. Department of Labor, *Monthly Labor Review,* October 1972, reprint no. 2838, p. 37.

[16]Ibid., p. 231.

The unions and black workers

Blacks and other ethnic minorities were about as well represented in union ranks as they were in the civilian labor force—12 percent of all union membership compared with 11 percent in the civilian labor force in 1970. But blacks were more heavily concentrated in blue-collar occupations than whites, and this was not reflected in any higher proportion of unionized blacks in the total of blue-collar unionists—a condition consistent with the allegations of many black leaders that Title VII of the Civil Rights Act needed more rigorous enforcement in the many cases of union discrimination. The construction industry in particular was singled out. By contrast, while only 9 percent of all clerical workers were black, almost 14 percent of all unionists in clerical jobs were black in 1970. A similar, less discriminatory set of ratios obtained in the field of public administration.

The unions and women workers

Women workers probably suffered more discrimination from employers than from unions. It was significant that the post-World War II era saw the virtual disappearance of the "ladies' auxiliaries." Still, the low rate of unionization of women reflected mainly the concentration of women in lightly unionized occupations, and probably some male chauvinism among the trade-union leadership. As late as 1973, women employees constituted about 40 percent of all civilian wage and salary workers (excluding 760,000 female unpaid workers in family enterprises), but accounted for only 21 percent of total union membership. The reasonableness of the emphasis upon an occupational distribution hypothesis for this situation is underscored by the fact that in that year 82 percent of all employed women were in white-collar and service activities. Still, contrary facts could always be cited. For example, one of the fastest growing unions in the 1960s was the Retail Clerks.

External factors inhibiting union growth

The main explanations for the stagnation in trade-union membership after the mid-1950s, despite the generally favorable levels of total employment,[17] were both external and internal

to the labor organizations. The external inhibiting factors emphasized here were restrictive legislation (especially Taft-Hartley and state "right to work" laws), employer hostility, the shift of industry to the South, and the changing structure of employment, including especially the relative decline of jobs in traditionally unionized blue-collar industries and the rise of private and public white-collar employment. Connected with this last was the rapidly increasing number and proportion of women in the labor force.

Internal factors inhibiting union growth

Theorists of union organization have advanced a number of hypotheses concerning the internal factors that inhibit union growth.[18] Among these were the alleged unadaptability of an essentially blue-collar labor movement in the face of a growing service economy. This factor is both internal and external, and its explanatory validity still appeared questionable in the mid-1970s. Most of the other internal explanations for union stagnation could be subsumed under the general rubric of bureaucracy. These included the loss of the earlier missionary spirit, the failure to educate the rank and file regarding the unions' goals, the reluctance of the leadership to encourage initiative from below, the lack of adequate procedures for transmitting members' grievances, the insensitivity of leadership to such grievances, and the absence of appropriate appeals machinery for members subjected to disciplinary action. A Louis Harris survey in 1968 revealed that 40 percent of all union members felt their organization represented the wishes of a few leaders rather than the rank and file.

Still other organizational practices could also be loosely classified as involving bureaucracy. Among them were the domination of conventions by the leadership and the long tenure of office of the top leadership in many cases. One explanation seemed particularly challenging, inasmuch as it pointed to a way out. That was the adherence of the AFL-CIO to the old arrangement whereby the affiliate unions had almost complete autonomy to do organizing work. This autonomy was readily abrogated in the case of internal corruption by the establishment of the Ethical Practices Code. The question then raised was: Why could not the federation cut across hallowed affiliate lines and merge them for organizing purposes, or, on a

---

[17]Some labor theorists have suggested that unions thrive on economic crisis. Yet history also reveals a strong positive correlation between high employment and increasing union membership.

[18]The immediately following summary draws upon Ginsburg, "Review of Literature," pp. 215–250.

lower level of unity, form multiunion and in smaller cities community-wide organizing councils to conduct unionization drives? This was the model for the Scientific, Professional, and Cultural Employees Council, and it was also the basic idea behind the step taken by the United Auto Workers and the Teamsters Union when they created the Alliance for Labor

Action in 1968. On a higher level, the merger in 1969 of four railroad unions into one union with some 448,000 members, set a striking example. Organizational innovations such as these were apparently frustrated by the bureaucratic propensity to preserve timehonored jurisdictions and national union autonomy.

THE EARNINGS RECORD

In appraising the achievements of the trade unions, and these were considerable despite the long-run stagnation in membership, it is fruitful to glance at the earnings record.

The median earnings of year-round, full-time union workers were $8609 in 1970. The average for nonunion workers was $1157 less, at $7452. The union average for blue-collar workers was almost $2000 larger than that for nonunion blue-collar workers. Union construction craftsmen and carpenters had average annual earnings over 40 percent larger than their nonunion counterparts.[19]

Similar disparities applied to the averages for union and nonunion service workers. These annual averages for union workers may be

compared with the median annual income of $9867 for all families in the United States in 1970. The discrepancy between that figure and the $8609 may be explained in part by the added income of working spouses, by moonlighting, and by the upward bias to family incomes inserted by nonunion professional, technical, and managerial income receivers. Whereas one-third of the wives of white operatives and craftsmen worked in 1960, 44 percent worked in 1969. But it was still clearly an income advantage to be a union member in a union-organized occupation. However, such a generalization reflected occupational wage differentials that might well have persisted even if all occupations were equally well organized.

THE BLUE-COLLAR BLUES

A final development of significance to labor and society, whether or not that labor was unionized, was the emergence in the late 1960s of a new attitudinal complex among wage earners. Observers noted what came to be called the blues among apparently significant numbers of blue-collar workers, alongside a trend toward reexamination of the role, significance, and meaning of work in American and similar materially advanced societies.[20] It was hypothesized that continuous and massive business sales-pro-

motion campaigns had raised aspirations far beyond workers' financial ability to realize them, that workers' feelings rankled under their inferior educational status, and that mechanization and automation had degraded, routinized, and dehumanized work. One study of 11 major industries concluded that out of 7 million workers employed, 4.4 million had dead-end repetitive jobs or only moderate prospects for escape.[21] Another study found that only about one-third of the jobs surveyed were "ego-involving," with most of these concentrated in the upper echelons of white-collar workers.[22] It was pointed out that the proliferation of on-the-job training courses reflected a growing concern with the need to offset a deteriorating sense of employee commitment to the job by humanizing the work process and elevating work roles toward aspiration levels.[23] The goal of equal

[19]These data are from Bureau of Labor Statistics, *Selected Earnings*, p. 2.

[20]See, e.g., Harold L. Sheppard, "Discontented Blue-Collar Workers: A Case Study," *Monthly Labor Review*, 94, no. 4 (April 1971): 25–32; Sar A. Levitan and Robert Taggart III, "Has the Blue-Collar Worker's Position Worsened?" *Monthly Labor Review*, 94, no. 9 (*September 1971*): 23–29; Denis F. Johnston, "The Future of Work: Three Possible Alternatives," *Monthly Labor Review, May 1972*, reprint no. 2806; Richard Parker, "Those Blue-Collar Workers Blues," *New Republic*, September 23, 1972, pp. 16–21; and Murray Kempton, "Blue Collar Blues," *New York Review of Books*, February 8, 1973.

[21]Levitan and Taggart, "Has the Blue-Collar Worker's Position Worsened?" p. 28.

[22]Johnston, "Future of Work," p. 4.

[23]Ibid., p. 6.

opportunity pursued by the disadvantaged, women, and elderly people who were the objects of discrimination was another source of tension on the job. Discontent among male workers, according to another study, was positively connected with jobholding by their wives.[24] Another major survey emphasized, among other things, the prevalence of archaic authority patterns and the widespread lack of work autonomy—that is, worker participation in job-related decisions—as major sources of apathy and dissatisfaction.[25] However, it was difficult to determine from available data such as labor turnover, industrial sabotage, and absenteeism whether there was any trend toward increasing discontent that had behavioral results.

Low-paying occupations

An earthy comment on discontent, perhaps of the traditional labor-leader type, was made by William W. Winpisinger, general vice-president of the International Association of Machinists: "If you want to enrich the job, enrich the pay check. The better the wage, the greater the job satisfaction. There is no better cure for the blue-collar blues."[26]

Without denying the possibility of a trend toward increased discontent among workers, and in apparent support of Winpisinger's bread-and-butter approach, one labor expert noted that undesirable work and low pay—for example, in most domestic service, farm labor, and the 20 million nonfarm jobs paying less than $2.50 per hour in April 1970—were undoubtedly strongly correlated. Nevertheless, such things as the persistent adverse reports of job dissatisfaction emanating from the relatively high-paying automobile assembly lines[27] and the slow 1 percent annual rise in the real weekly spendable earnings of private production workers from 1949 to 1974 seemed to provide some basis for continued concern. Furthermore, it appeared most likely that attitudes toward work were closely connected with labor's larger social environment. Assistant Secretary of Labor Jerome Rosow presented to President Nixon in April 1970 a report on "Problems of the Blue-Collar Worker," asserting that employees in the middle family income range, $5,000–$10,000, were exhibiting a growing sense of dissatisfaction. This resulted from three sets of squeezes: economic (inflation and limited improvement) social (environmental deterioration and intergroup conflicts), and workplace.[28] In considerable part the problem stemmed from the education explosion of the postwar era. That explosion had brought millions of young workers with broadened perspectives into daily boring work routines in clerical and other occupations, occupations in which enrichment of either the job or the paycheck seemed all too remote.

SELECTED READINGS

Bernstein, Irving, "The Growth of American Unions, 1945–60," *Labor History,* v. 2, No. 2 (Spring 1961), pp. 131–157.

Blackman, John L. Jr., *Presidential Seizure in Labor Disputes* (Cambridge: Harvard University Press, 1967).

Blum, Albert A., "Why Unions Grow," *Labor History,* v. 9, No. 1 (Winter 1968), pp. 39–72.

*Dubofsky, Melvyn, ed., *American Labor Since the New Deal* (New York: Quadrangle, 1971).

Fishman, Betty G., and Fishman, Leo, *Employment, Unemployment and Economic Growth* (New York: Crowell, 1969).

Godson, Roy, "The AFL Foreign Policy Making Process from the End of World War II to the Merger," *Labor History,* v. 16, No. 3 (Summer 1975), pp. 325–337.

*Jackson, Julius, ed., *The Negro and the American Labor Movement* (New York: Doubleday, 1968).

[24]Sheppard, "Discontented Blue-Collar Workers," p. 29.

[25]U.S. Department of Health, Education, and Welfare, *Work in America,* December 1972, cited and reviewed in Harold Wool, "What's Wrong with Work in America? A Review Essay," *Monthly Labor Review,* 96, no. 3 (March 1973): 38–44.

[26]Cited in Wool, "What's Wrong with Work?" p. 43.

[27]See "The Dirty Work: Millions of U.S. Laborers Still Toil at Jobs That Are Filthy, Hot, Backbreaking, and Dull," *Wall Street Journal,* July 16, 1971, p. 13.

[28]Cited in ibid., pp. 38–39, and reviewed critically in Richard Parker, loc. cit.

*Kennedy, Robert, *The Enemy Within* (New York: Harper & Row, 1960).

Krislov, Joseph, "Organizing, Union Growth, and the Cycle, 1949–1966," *Labor History*, v. 11, No. 2 (Spring 1970), pp. 212–222.

*Mangum, Garth L., *The Emergence of Manpower Policy* (New York: Holt, Rinehart and Winston, 1969).

Marshall, F. Ray, *The Negro and Organized Labor* (New York: Wiley, 1965).

*Miernyk, William H., *Trade Unions in an Age of Affluence* (New York: Random House, 1962).

O'Brien, F. S., "The 'Communist-Dominated' Unions in the United States Since 1950," *Labor History*, v. 9, No. 2 (Spring 1968), pp. 184–209.

*Pierson, Frank C., *Unions in Postwar America* (New York: Random House, 1967).

Sultan, Paul, *The Disenchanted Unionist* (New York: Harper & Row, 1963).

Tyler, Gus, *The Labor Revolution: Trade Unions in a New America* (New York: Viking, 1967).

A glance at Table 29–1, taken from a National Planning Association study of national priorities, will show the broad outlines of the American experience concerning the things considered important and unimportant in the last decade of the quarter century under review. It does not show what ought to have been the high and low priorities in terms of expenditures devoted to each category of goods and services. It shows the actual priorities.

Business investment

It was abundantly clear that private business investment in plant and equipment, although influenced by government-induced cyclical expansion factors, was nonetheless assigned a high place in the hierarchy of resource allocation. For a longer period, 1950–1969, investment only slightly exceeded the GNP rise. Nothing could have been more time-hallowed, more in keeping with the institutional and intellectual heritage of a private capitalist economy. Yet the great magnitude of those expenditure flows should not be allowed to conceal the fact that they were by no means private in the old-fashioned sense. This has been made clear earlier in the discussion of government underwriting of aggregate business sales. The economic expansion period shown in Table 29–1 was one of greatly stepped-up war effort in Vietnam, of a 52 percent real rise in state and local government expenditures, and of a 69 percent increase in the real value of government transfer payments to individuals. Clearly business and the community at large responded in historic fashion to the government-supported economic upswing.

Private consumption

For private consumption to keep in approximate pace with the rise in total output was equally in keeping with the longer historical record. Indeed, during the years shown in Table 29–1 the growth in real personal private consumption did a bit better than that, for in the very long run from 1929, private consumption, along with gross business fixed investment, drifted downward as proportion of real GNP.

That downward drift was matched by an upward drift in government expenditures relative to GNP. For the period 1950–1974, however, real household consumption exactly kept pace with the real GNP rise of 131 percent, while all government purchases of goods and services rose 176 percent. Thus the mixture of public and private was getting richer.

Military expenditures

The greater admixture of public with private was due in considerable part to military expenditures. Those rose in real value for the whole period from the postwar "peace" year 1950 to 1969 by about 200 percent, much faster than real GNP. But Table 29–1 does not reveal how that rise had leveled off in the early years of the 1960s, only to jump up moderately in the Vietnam war step-up of the late 1960s. The years 1968 through 1972 were notable for a constant military budget in current dollars and a sharp absolute real drop in constant dollars. This seemed to indicate some shift in the social consensus toward such expenditures, perhaps an expression of public hostility toward the Vietnam war.

**TABLE 29–1. EXPENDITURES FOR NATIONAL GOALS, 1962 AND 1959
(IN BILLIONS OF 1969 DOLLARS)**

GOAL AREA	EXPENDITURES IN 1962[1]	EXPENDITURES IN 1969	PERCENT CHANGE 1962 TO 1969
Private consumption	$418.5	$579.6	38.5
Private plant and equipment	62.0	98.6	59.0
Urban development	84.0	94.7	11.0
Housing	37.5	35.4	−5.5
Other urban facilities	46.5	59.3	13.0
National defense	66.5	78.8	18.5
Social welfare	46.4	71.1	53.0
Health	43.5	63.8	46.5
Education	41.8	64.3	54.0
Transportation	39.3	61.5	56.5
Research and development	21.1	26.9	27.5
Natural resources	7.1	10.1[2]	42.0
Agriculture	8.2	7.8	−5.0
Environmental quality	3	6.3	[3]
International aid	6.1	5.3	−13.0
Job training	0.1	2.0	[4]
GNP	678.0	931.4	37.5

Source: Leonard A. Lecht, *Changes in National Priorities During the 1960s: Their Implications for 1980* (Washington, D.C.: National Planning Association, September 1972).

[1]Derived from Leonard A. Lecht, *Goals, Priorities, and Dollars: The Next Decade* (New York: Free Press, 1966), Table 1–2, p. 36. The estimates in Table 1–2 have been converted from 1962 to 1969 dollars.

[2]The estimate for natural resources for 1969 is a preliminary figure that is in the process of revision.

[3]Not available.

[4]1962 outlays are a poor basis for estimating rates of change in spending, since the present program was started in 1962.

Social welfare

One major allocation that clearly did raise the public-private ratio may be seen in Table 29–1. That was the allocation to social welfare. The 53 percent rise between 1962 and 1969 compared with the GNP rise of 37.5 percent fairly well represents the excess of the social welfare outlay growth for the longer period. Real expenditures for health and medical programs under public auspices, a subcategory under social welfare, fell from about 12 percent of the welfare total in 1950 to about 7 percent in 1969. Hence the table's representation of the slower relative rise in health outlays as compared with all social welfare is accurate for the longer period. It seemed likely that health would receive relatively increasing attention as the 1970s unfolded.

Federal versus state and local outlays for social welfare

It should be noted that while the federal outlays for social welfare were larger than the state and local outlays for this purpose (and had been since 1966), the state and local social welfare expenditures in 1970 were still 86 percent as large as the federal. However, a significant part of the state and local expenditures was federally financed through grants ("revenue sharing"). Also, real federal civilian outlays rose faster per year than state and local government expenditures between 1965 and 1970. Hence there was fairly clear evidence that Americans were turning away from their historic tendency to place the financing, if not the administration, of welfare in the hands of public agencies closer to home. But the old issue of federal versus local was still very much present.

Universal versus categorical welfare measures

An even larger reform issue was that regarding the appropriate kind of social and economic reform. Americans proceeded in two directions on the matter: across-the-board measures for all income groups, as in the case of social security pensions, and categorical measures usually addressed to specific low-income groups, as in the case of medicaid and job training for the unskilled poor.

It was contended that liberal reformers, being acutely conscious of distributional inequities, were biased in favor of the latter. Being in the forefront of the effort to institute reform legislation, the liberal reformers put their stamp on the pattern of social welfare programs in the quarter century after World War II. That pattern exhibited an extremely complex and often administratively unwieldy structure that, it was alleged, often locked in the poor, leaving them with a lack of incentive to enter the labor market. Such was not the case with social and economic reform measures that encompassed all levels of the population. Furthermore, it was contended that the bias of liberal reformers toward the elimination of poverty by hundreds of specific programs acted to prevent adoption of more universal and therefore more politically feasible measures, such as a national system of health insurance or a negative income tax (income maintenance for all).[1]

Whatever validity may have existed in that criticism, the social welfare legislative record after World War II suggested a public preference for the liberal reformers' bias. At the same time, on the two major reform issues that had been raised but not resolved—national health insurance and income maintenance—the evidence of liberal support was very strong. In the case of income maintenance, it was not the diversionary activities of liberal reformers that appeared to block adoption, but rather its enormous expense and its redistributive effects.

Housing

It was housing and the cities that suffered truly serious neglect in the hierarchy of national priorities. In real terms (1958 dollars), and ignoring mobile homes, investment in residential structures was $23.5 billion in the peak year 1950 and $22.3 billion 20 years later. Few could accept the belief that such stagnation and relative decline represented realization of the often legislatively stated consensus to provide all Americans with decent housing. As the period closed the intent was restated, but the jump in new housing starts to over 2 million in 1971 and 1972 was followed by a drop in 1973 and a drastic fall in 1974 to 1.35 million. In 1975 national housing starts were only 1,161,500, the fewest in 30 years.

Urban development

Almost enough has been said earlier regarding the national effort on the urban front to underscore the expenditure data on urban development in Table 29–1. The point should be recalled, however, that while social welfare expenditures might not fit easily into a strict construction of urban *development*, a good

[1] This general line of criticism of the liberal reformers is well represented by Irving Kristol, Henry Luce Professor of Urban Values at New York University. See his discussion in the *Wall Street Journal,* April 16, 1973.

part of them could be construed as addressed to urban social *problems*. This follows from the predominantly urban character of the nation's population and the concentration of the poverty groups in cities.

Transportation

An urban view of the substantial real growth in expenditures for transportation shown in Table 29–1 is enlightening. Of course, the largest single component with respect to intercity freight was the relatively declining railroads (to 38 percent of total traffic volume in 1972). Trucks and oil pipelines, both relatively increasing their shares, accounted for over one-fifth each of the remainder, with inland waterway about constant. But when one turns to intercity passenger traffic, the airlines were the great growth industry of the post–World War II period, rising from 2 percent by volume in 1950 to 10 percent in 1972. Intercity railroad passenger traffic was threatening to disappear almost completely. This left almost 87 percent to the private automobile.

The overwhelming dominance of the private car in urban passenger traffic has already been pointed out, but it needs to be added that in the period from 1950 to 1972 the passenger-car driver was reducing the less environmentally destructive urban mass transit system to a crisis level of operations. While urban automobile-miles were rising 211 percent, urban bus-miles rose only 50 percent. And over the period 1950 to 1969 the revenue vehicle-miles operated by electric surface railways (largely urban) plus subways and elevated lines fell absolutely by over one-half, the trolley coach from 206 million to 36 million and the motorbus from 1.9 billion to 1.5 billion vehicle-miles. This underscored the evolving crisis in urban mass transit. The phrase clearly suggested that in the 1970s Americans were beginning to suspect their individual behavior as car drivers had aggregated to a result producing such large adverse side effects that perhaps a giant mistake had been committed. Dawning recognition of the mistake again involved turning to government, and the Urban Mass Transit Act of 1970 authorized $10 billion to aid the development of mass transit in the coming decade. Also, strong moves were afoot to divert some of the earmarked tax monies from the federal Highway Trust Fund for the same purpose.

R & D and education

The economics profession conclusively demonstrated that material growth in the twentieth century was ever more attributable to technological advance rather than to increases in the quantity of capital, except insofar as capital embodied technology. "Investment in human capital" was given more and more stress in explaining both economic growth and the moderate increase in the employee share of the national income. The 54 percent rise in educational expenditures shown in Table 29–1, when viewed in the light of the education explosion during the 1950s, seems to indicate strong public sympathy, however unaware the public may have been of the technicalities, for the economists' emphasis. It is therefore somewhat surprising that research and development, a closely related field, should have lagged. Still, the two fields might well be joined into one so far as their relation to economic development is concerned. As the 1970s commenced, however, the high priority on education, including the urge to democratize higher education, seemed to have lost ground. On the other hand, research and development, including space research and technology, gained somewhat, in part by virtue of the concern with the nation's deteriorating international competitive position. Still, the picture was blurred. The defeat of the appropriation for a supersonic transport plane in the early 1970s seemed to represent a turning away from technology when research and development goals clashed with anticipated environmental havoc.[2]

Low-priority goals

The remaining goals in Table 29–1 have been referred to sufficiently in the earlier discussion. Of the low-priority goals shown for the 1960s, there were persuasive reasons for expecting a greater emphasis by government in the late 1970s on at least two: research and development, and urban development. The latter in particular seemed destined for larger allocations. The fate of international aid no doubt depended largely upon external pressures from the less developed countries and upon international political rivalry.

Publicly versus privately provided products

In the 1960s there was a discernible upward shift in Americans' preferences for government goods over privately provided products. Americans apparently came to believe to an increasing extent that government, and particularly the federal government, was the chief instrumentality for solving their problems. Within the public sector, the federal government seemed to have the edge in growth rate. In the first half of the 1960s, real federal civilian outlays grew at an annual rate of 5.8 percent, but in the last half they grew at 9.1 percent.[3] Both rates were substantially higher than the GNP rate. Truly the mixed economy was on the march, and no longer, at least for a time, because of the federal military budget.

The management of demand

The mixed economy was also on the march with regard to the accumulation of experience in the management of total demand. As Arthur Okun emphasized, the sluggish post-Korean war performance of the economy led to much more sophisticated policy measures in the 1960s. Notable in that advance was the shift in policy from a focus upon short-run expansion and contraction to prime concern for steady growth at a rate approaching the economy's potential.[4] Innovative fiscal and monetary policies, including the famous tax cut in February 1964, were effectively applied so that the economy moved up close to its potential by 1965. Whether it could have been held at that precarious level for long without the emergence of serious inflation cannot be known at the present state of knowledge, because political resistance to fiscal restraint and the sudden escalation of the Vietnam war took matters out of the hands of government economic managers. Meanwhile, the private sector had responded with what Okun called a "stubborn boom"[5] in 1968, paced by increases in housing, consumption, and fixed investment. Even by the mid-1970s public policy had still much to learn about the responses of private demand to its growth prescriptions, and particularly how to constrain a boom without tolerating continued substantial inflation or precipitating a recession. Nevertheless, much had been learned about demand management, to which had been added a dawning recognition that perhaps supply management would in the future be its necessary concomitant.

[2]Leonard A. Lecht, *Changes in National Priorities During the 1960's: Their Implications for 1980* (Washington, D.C.: National Planning Association, September 1972), p. 8.

[3]Schultze et al., *Setting National Priorities*, p. 399.
[4]Arthur M. Okun, *The Political Economy of Prosperity* (New York: Norton and Brookings Institution, 1970), pp. 41–43.
[5]Ibid., pp. 91–96.

A BACKWARD GLANCE

For three and a half centuries the drama of American history has been unfolding for us. We have seen one generation of frontiersmen after another push their way westward until they conquered a continent and left for their children a splendid material heritage. We have seen a simple agricultural economy broaden its base under the stimulus of limitless raw materials to become a nation whose economic life has widened into almost every activity. And we have seen an economically dependent people achieve first political, then economic independence, until finally the nation assumed a strong economic and political role that made it the decisive factor in two world wars. It has been a history of the opening and exploitation of a region enormously rich in raw materials and overflowing with possibilities. The United States became the only nation with resources and wealth sufficiently great to give important aid in the reconstruction of many nations after these two great wars.

Americans met the task of developing a continent with confidence, buoyancy, and optimism. But their methods were often crude and wasteful. Much of value was needlessly squandered and lost forever. Irreparable inroads were made in the most valuable raw materials. Much of this took place in a period of laissez-faire. But complete laissez-faire in the economic realm is impossible; only relative laissez-faire ever existed. It was quite absent in the colonial period, when legislation governed almost all aspects of economic life. It grew during the nineteenth century, but even in those years high tariffs and state and federal aid to transportation cut deeply into such a philosophy, as did the control of banking by state and federal governments. By the mid-twentieth century laissez-faire had ended. By this time the main economic problems could not be solved "automatically" by such a policy.

Many obvious causes contributed to the decline of laissez-faire. One was continued demand of economic groups for government aid and protection. Another was the disregard of the public interests and the monopoly practices of big business, which finally forced government regulation. Business itself first cracked the existing structure of laissez-faire when it combined to save itself from the ruin of unrestricted competition. The crack was widened by the continued growth of public regulation. But it was unemployment that finally dismantled the structure and introduced its successor, the mixed economy. When recurrent mass unemployment became intolerable, the people invoked the power of the federal government to assure steady high levels of production and economic growth. And, of course, as the overall economic and social life became more intricate, public controls became increasingly necessary and inevitable if the delicate structure of society was to be held together.

As the nation grew older it experienced many of the economic and social problems of the older industrial nations of Europe. As it grew rapidly and almost chaotically into a mighty manufacturing nation, population increased and concentrated in cities. There economic groups became more differentiated and class feeling became strong. Fortunately, as the nation grew to maturity many early faults were rectified. The overall income of the people had risen, and with it the level of the lower-income groups. Although poverty still persisted people dressed better, ate better, worked fewer hours, and lived more comfortably.

As to the future, predictions are of dubious value. If international tensions were to subside and the nation drastically cut its military expenditures, if atomic energy could be shifted from destructive purposes to the needs of a peaceful world, if the environment could be protected, the country could look forward to continued economic development, the reduction of poverty, and improvement in the overall level of living. But this could be accomplished only in a world functioning through leadership dedicated both to the encouragement of individual initiative and to the wise control of the mixed economic system.

SELECTED READINGS

*Blechman, Barry M., Gramlich, Edward M., and Hartman, Robert W., *Setting National Priorities, The 1975 Budget* (Washington, D.C.: Brookings Institution, 1974).
*Galbraith, John Kenneth, *The Affluent Society* (Boston: Houghton Mifflin, 1958).
*Haveman, Robert H., *The Economics of the Public Sector* (New York: Wiley, 1976).

Heller, Walter W., ed., *Perspectives on Economic Growth* (New York: Random House, 1968).

*Lecht, Leonard A., *Changes in National Priorities During the 1960's: Their Implications for 1980*, Report No. 132 (Washington, D.C. National Planning Association, September 1972).

Myrdal, Gunnar, *Beyond the Welfare State* (New Haven: Yale University Press, 1960).

*Okun, Arthur M., *The Political Economy of Prosperity* (New York: Norton, 1970).

*Titmuss, Richard M., *Commitment to Welfare* (New York: Pantheon Books, 1968).

*Ulmer, Melville J., *The Welfare State* (Boston: Houghton Mifflin, 1969).

U.S. Joint Economic Committee, *Hearings before the Subcommittee on Priorities and Economy in Government*, Congress of the United States, 92nd Cong. 2nd Session, May 30 and 31, June 1, 16, and 27, 1972. *National Priorities—the Next Five Years* (Washington, D.C.: U.S. Government Printing Office, 1972).

Weidenbaum, Murray, *The Modern Public Sector* (New York: Basic Books, 1969).

index

76 77 78 7 6 5 4 3 2 1